HUSTLING IS NOT STEALING

Hustling Is Not Stealing

STORIES OF AN AFRICAN BAR GIRL

John M. Chernoff

THE UNIVERSITY OF CHICAGO PRESS : *Chicago and London*

JOHN M. CHERNOFF is the author of *African Rhythm and African Sensibility: Aesthetics and Social Action in African Musical Idioms* (1979), also published by the University of Chicago Press. Chernoff spent more than seven years in West Africa, based in Accra and Tamale, Ghana, where he also researched popular music and the music and culture of the Dagbamba people. His recordings of Dagbamba music include *Master Fiddlers of Dagbon* and *Master Drummers of Dagbon,* volumes 1 and 2.

The University of Chicago Press, Chicago 60637
The University of Chicago Press, Ltd., London

Printed in the United States of America
12 11 10 09 08 07 06 05 04 03 1 2 3 4 5

ISBN: 0-226-10350-1 (cloth)
ISBN: 0-226-10352-8 (paper)

Library of Congress Cataloging-in-Publication Data

Chernoff, John Miller.
Hustling is not stealing : stories of an African bar girl / John M. Chernoff.
p. cm.
ISBN 0-226-10350-1 (cloth : alk. paper)—ISBN 0-226-10352-8 (pbk. : alk. paper)
1. Women—Ghana—Social conditions. 2. Women—Togo—Social conditions. 3. Women—Burkina Faso—Social conditions. I. Title.

HQ1816 .C48 2003
305.42′09667—dc21

2003010647

⊗ The paper used in this publication meets the minimum requirements of the American National Standard for Information Sciences—Permanence of Paper for Printed Library Materials, ANSI Z39.48-1992.

For my wife Donna, my daughters Eunice and Eva, and my sons Harlan and Avram

CONTENTS

PART FIVE *The Life in Togo*

ACKNOWLEDGMENTS

I would like to thank the Joint Committee on African Studies of the Social Science Research Council and the American Council of Learned Societies for a Postdoctoral Fellowship for African Area Research that helped me to develop some of the data for this book. I would also like to thank the following people for reading and commenting on drafts or for helping with various aspects of this book: Abraham Adzenyah, Emmanuel Akyeampong, Marianne Alverson, Kelly Askew, Deborah Benkovitz, John Berthelette, Willem Bijlefeld, Kenneth Bilby, David Brent, Alan Brody, David Byrne, Amina Jefferson Bruce, Donna Chernoff, Harold Chernoff, Michael Chernoff, Richard Closs, Ben DeMott, Peter Edidin, Mark Ehrman, Kai Erikson, Steven W. Evans, Alan Fiske, Steven Friedson, Arnold Gefsky, Dawn Hall, Maxine Heller, Kissmal Ibrahim Hussein, Angeliki Keil, Charles Keil, Bruce King, Sarah LeVine, David Light, Rene Lysloff, Yao Hlomabu Malm, Michael Mattil, Leighton McCutchen, Will Milberg, David Mooney, Mustapha Muhammed, Steven Mullen, Judy Naumburg, Deborah Neff, Samuel Nyanyo Nmai, Timmy W. Ogude, James Peters III, Charles Piot, Carl Rollyson, Marina Roseman, Eric Rucker, Nadine Saada, Philip Schuyler, Paul Stoller, Deborah Tannen, Robert F. Thompson, Richard Underwood, Christopher Waterman, Andrew Weintraub, David Wise. Betsy Morgan DeGory assisted with the research and contributed many ideas to the work. The following people provided technical assistance on writing the various languages in the text: Eric O. Beeko, J. H. Kwabena Nketia, Lilly Nketia, and Joseph Adjaye for Asante Twi; Kathryn Geurts, Kojo Amegashie, and Felix K. Ameka for Ewe and Mina/Gen; Beverly Mack and John Hutchison for Hausa; Philip Schuyler for Arabic; Paul Stoller and Jean-Paul Dumont for Verlan and French argot. Also, of course, I would like to thank the woman who is called Hawa in this book and also all the people in Ghana, Togo, Burkina Faso, Nigeria, and other West African countries who helped me understand their world as they know it.

To understand just one life, you have to swallow the world.

SALMAN RUSHDIE, *MIDNIGHT'S CHILDREN*

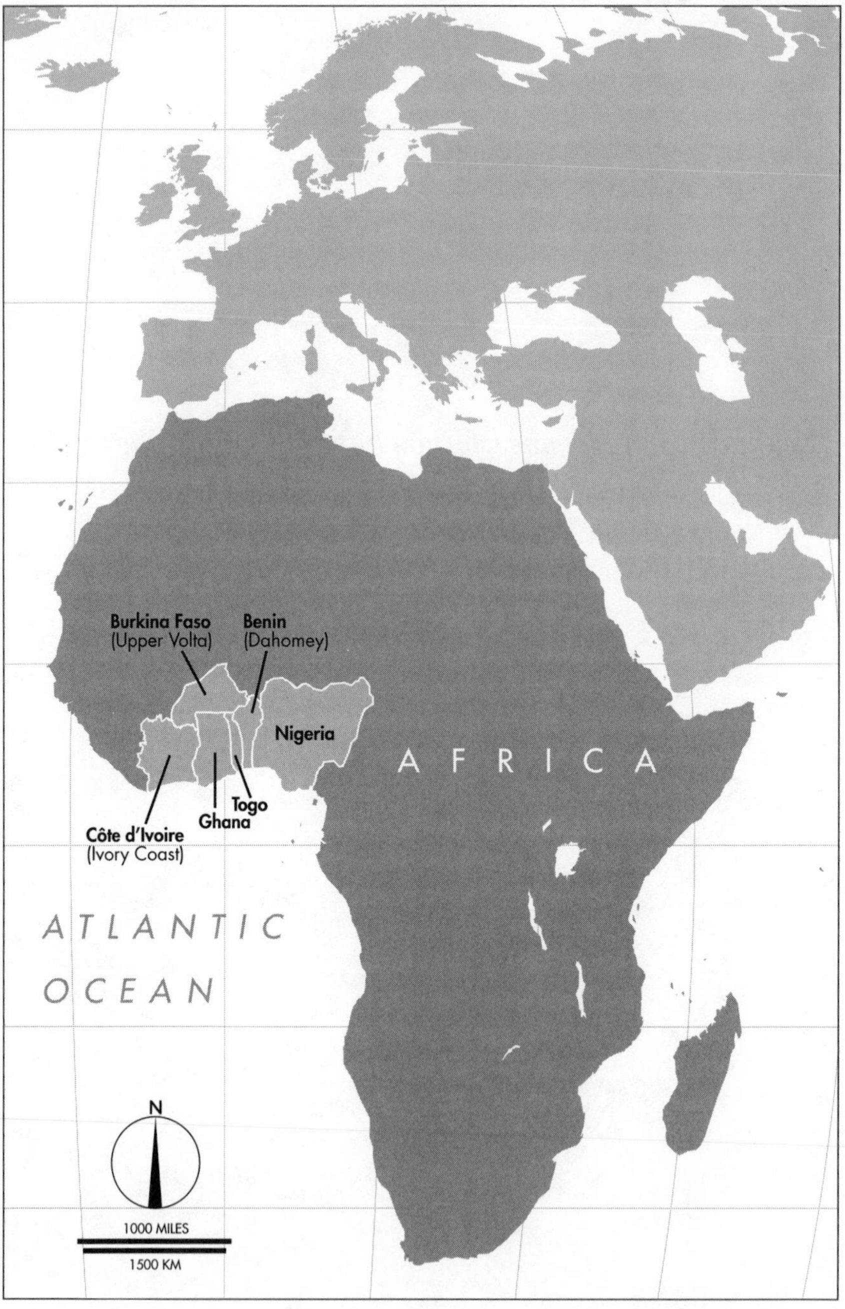
Burkina Faso
(Upper Volta)
Benin
(Dahomey)
Nigeria
A F R I C A
Togo
Ghana
Côte d'Ivoire
(Ivory Coast)
ATLANTIC
OCEAN
N
1000 MILES
1500 KM

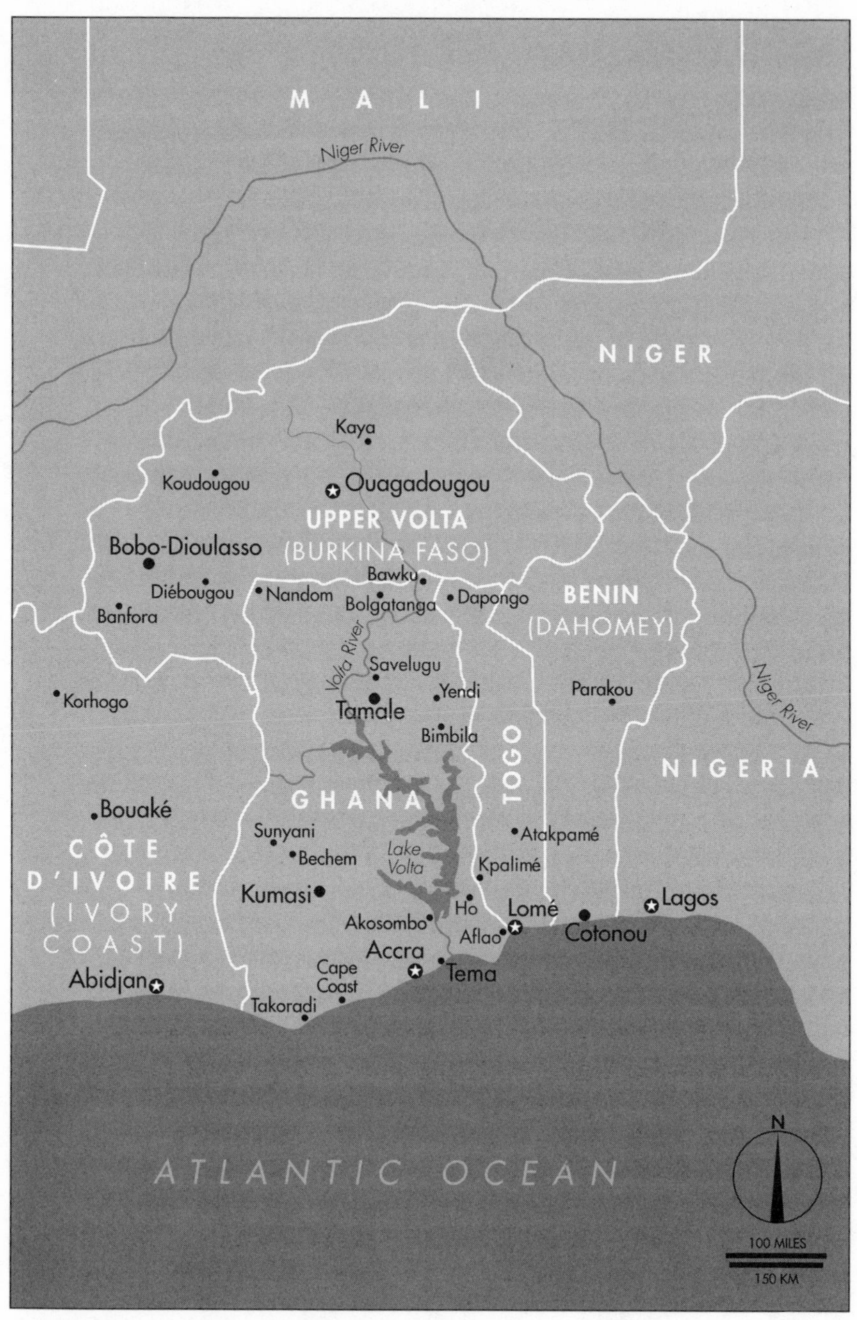

West African locations mentioned in Hawa's stories

INTRODUCTION

Excerpt from "Junior Wife"

Then they said I must marry. So I had to go back to my father's place to make this *amariya,* this Muslim marriage. The Hausas[1] call it *amariya,* and you the new wife, you are the *Amariya.*[2] That is their marriage. . . .

So they brought a man. They were going to make me Amariya with him. He was a young man, but he was a bit grown. Maybe he was about twenty-eight, or something. He was not too old, and he was not young,

1. The Hausa are the major cultural group in northern Nigeria; Hausa traders travel and live widely in West Africa, and the Hausa language is a lingua franca well beyond the Hausa traditional area.

2. The Amariya is the most recently married, or newest, wife in a polygamous household. The word can also refer to a woman without cowives who was married in a Muslim ceremony, since she is still the new wife, or to the ceremony itself.

either. I was sixteen. Then my aunt talked to me a lot. She said, "This boy is rich." He's that and this, so if my father tells me to marry him, I shouldn't refuse. If I refuse, what my father will tell me, it will be bad for me after, and so I must agree with my father, and all this.

So I said, "OK."

They made me Amariya to this man, and this man had two other wives, and I was tired. I had thought that if you marry, you are free. I didn't know that in the Muslim way, if you marry somebody who has a wife, you are a slave. *Yeah!!* It's *true.* Because: everything! You are the young one: you have to do it. I am the one who is cooking. I am the one who washes this man's clothes. The first wife: I am the one who washes her dresses. As for the second wife, I didn't do anything for her, but the first wife of my husband, I had to do everything for her.[1]

Then I thought, "Ah! I thought if you grow up and marry —" One day I thought of this. That day I did a lot of work: I washed many things, then I started cooking, then I went into the room. As for me, my groove:[2] even if I was married, I smoked. I went inside and smoked some groove, and then I started thinking, "Ah! Look at the way I suffered when I was young! I thought if I grow up and marry, I will be free. And now I'm a prisoner. Or a slave. To some people. What I don't even do in my family, I am doing for some people. No. I don't think I can stay."

When this man came home, I told him, "Did you marry me, or did you buy me to be a slave for you? I want to know."

Then he said, "What question are you asking?"

"No. I want to know. Because I think this way is not the way to marry. My big sisters have married, and I go to them all the time. And I didn't see that they are suffering like me."

Then he said, "No-o-o, you are young. You are the last woman, and you are the Amariya. You have to do this, do that and that."

"*Ah-hah!* Is that the way? Then what time am I going to leave doing this?"

He said, "Yes, if I marry another woman."

"*Ah-hah!* So I have to wait until you marry another woman? Maybe it will take you ten years to marry another one before I will come and shift, too. I cannot stay with you."

Then he said, "OK. If you like, I will get one room for you. You can

1. It is customary for the Amariya in a polygamous Muslim household to be in a position of subservience to the other or "senior" wives.

2. marijuana

cook by yourself. And then you can cook for me and you, and the other women will cook their food."[1]

Then I said, "If that, then it will be better. If it's that, I will accept. But: to wash your first wife's dresses, I cannot do it. OK?"

So then he took a room for me and him, and he gave the first room to the two other women.

Then I thought I wouldn't be washing things, you know, because I already told him that I could not wash the first wife's things. Then one day I was doing washing, then the first wife brought her things out. She said, "Sister Hawa?"

"I'm not your sister. You know? I'm not your younger sister to do this business for you."

Then she said, "What?!! *What?!!* What are you saying?! I didn't hear it. Repeat it again!"

Then I repeated it. I said, "Yes. I'm not your younger sister to do this fucking work for you every day. I have been here two months. Every day I have to wash your things. Why? Are your hands cut off? Can't you wash? Or do you think my family brought me here to be a slave for you, or to be a washboy for you. If you want a boy, you have to tell your husband to get you a boy. I can't do it."

Then she said, "*Oh-Kay!* We are going to see who is going to live with this man. We will see."

"Hey! You can live with your man. I met you people together. And I can fuck off even today, if I like."

Then she said, "OK. I think that will be better for you, because you cannot live here to control people."

And I said, "You can't control me, too! We married the same man, no? The way he fucks you, it's the same way he fucks me. So you can't tell me this."

Ba-ba-ba-ba-ba! Ba-ba-ba-ba!! "You don't respect." And that and this. "If you play with me, I'll beat you." And that and this. But she didn't beat me. There were many women in the house, and they separated us.

1. In a compound house, the man has a room and each wife has a room. A new wife may originally be placed in a room with one of the senior wives. Wives generally cook in rotation for the whole household, and a wife sleeps with the husband on the day she cooks. By separating the wives' cooking, the husband is releasing Hawa from cooking for the household, but he is mainly preventing the wives from quarreling by suspecting or accusing their cowives of putting something in their food. Nonetheless, this kind of preferential treatment for the Amariya would be likely to provoke jealousy from the senior wives.

So I went inside. I had many things; I could not carry them. These our people, they are fools. If you marry, they bring you big, big pots like drums, with mirrors, packed all full of clothes, and many cooking pans, and this and that. So I went inside. Which one can I take? I took a small bag, and I put three cloths inside, and I closed it. Then I went to my father's house.

I said, "Hey, Papa, where you gave me, I cannot stay. I'm coming to tell you the truth. And whatever you do, I won't go back. So if you people like, you can go and take your things."

Then my father said, "No. It's not possible. In Muslim marriage, you cannot leave like that. Two months: you cannot leave the husband. Even if you don't like him, you have to be patient for three months."

"*Heh?!* To be a prisoner for three months? Or a slave? I cannot do it. If God will punish me, let Him punish me. Or if you want to punish me by yourself, you can punish me. But I'm not going back."

So: we were in the house in the evening time when this man came. I think the wives told him what happened, and they saw me take my bag and go out, and since morning I didn't come. So he came to my father's place. He came and met me. Then he started: he's coming to beg — and that and this — his wife — he talked to the wife — and she wouldn't do that and this again. And so he told my father.

Then I said, "Hey, father. I talked to this man about this palaver first, and he said, 'No.' That's why he took one room to give me to live together with him. Then any time, when he means to sleep with the other woman, he can go with the other woman and sleep with her. But the room where he and I live, all his things and my things are there.[1] And I talked all this. This is the palaver: I told him I cannot wash the first wife's things. And he said, OK, I wouldn't have to do that again. But the first wife brought the things again today, and then she told me I have to wash them or we can see. *We can see!* We Africans, if somebody tells you that you can see, it's very hard, because that person can make some juju to kill you or make you crazy.[2] She is the first wife for him. I cannot challenge her. When she tells me I will see, I don't think I should step in that house again. If I go there again, then I will see! What am I going to see?" So I asked my father

1. Normally, the husband would have his own room, and the wife who cooked in her rotation would go to his room to sleep with him. For the husband to be keeping his things and staying in the Amariya's room would also provoke the senior wives.

2. Hawa is saying that the senior wife threatened her with juju. The words "We will see" mean "We will see the result," that is, no one will see the juju at work, but once it has finished, the people involved will look at what happened but may only suspect that there was something behind it.

this question: "This woman says I will see. If I go there again, and something happens to me, what are you going to do?"

My father said, "No, she cannot do anything to you."

Then I said, "No. Whether she can do something or she cannot do something, I am fed up. I cannot go there again."

Then my father said, "*He-ey!* If you can't go there, then you can find where to live. You cannot live with me."

Then: now it's between me and my father, you know. Yeah! Then I said, "OK. If you don't want me, I can go away. I don't care. The people who don't have a father: did you hear that somebody hasn't got a father, and some animal ate his meat?"

He said, "No." Then he asked me, too, "Have you heard someone who hasn't got a daughter, the animals ate his meat?"

Then I said, "No-o. It's finished. You looked after me; you tried. I thank you very much. Because you took me when I was three years old, you suffered with me. And now I have grown up. I can feed myself; I can look after myself. So this is it. Bye-bye."

Preamble: Stories and Their Critics

This book is the true story of a young woman in West Africa, but some colleagues who read early drafts advised me to write it as a novel. They said the book seems more a novel than a work of nonfiction. It's a collection of stories. It has a colorful main character, striking situations, and amusing dialogue. They said that more people might read the book if it were a novel, that I shouldn't waste the material on a scholarly publication. The advice sounded flattering, but the implications were demeaning, on one hand as if writing scholarly work resembles dropping things into deep wells, and on another hand, as if the book's dramatic format were a perversion of scholarly purpose. Turning my research into a novel would classify it as fiction, an announcement of sorts that my research is not true. The word "fiction" is synonymous with invention and creation but also insinuates myth and fantasy, fabrications of the imagination—vehicles of enlightenment, perhaps, but not of knowledge.

In contrast, at the Hartford Seminary Foundation, where I did graduate studies, my professors took pride in the fact that they never forgot the importance of storytelling. They placed their faith in the intellectual style of poets and artists. My philosophy of religion professor, Richard Underwood, told me that storytelling is the only thing he knew of that links the activities of teaching philosophy and taking care of babies. Most of what people claim to know, including their ideas of who they are, has been passed down to them in stories. Many people see their own lives as a story. For most people in the world, a religious heritage of stories informs their values, thoughts, plans, and actions. Throughout history, people have chosen stories to be the preferred vehicle of knowledge. Even scientific knowledge is generally represented as a story, such as evolution and natural selection in biology or the big bang and the expanding universe in cosmology.

My teachers were concerned about what they viewed as an increasingly limited capacity to comprehend the significance of stories. There are probably too many stories, too many points of view. In our contemporary world, people understand that all knowledge is bounded, relative to perspective and position, and thus is somewhat like fiction, for one person's truth can be another's lie. People who embrace stories less skeptically are considered less modern, even ignorant. But many people need extra help with stories: media moguls deliver extravagant melodramas with special effects to grab people's attention and with twists and turns to trick people into awareness. Either way, stories appear shallow. Their logic can be easily circumscribed or their probability easily impugned. It is no wonder many people associate knowledge with critical distance and believe that a story has more trustworthy value only after it is interpreted or put into context. To an extent, this introduction supports that premise by providing some background on our storyteller and her world.

It is possible to select several perspectives and build a limited framework for understanding our heroine, but I hope the full text of this book will do its part to dismantle any particular perspective's claim to definitive validity in assessing the meaning of her life. Readers may then share with her an important part of her storytelling work, a gradual and cumulative process, to assess her own integrity in relation to the customs and mores of the society into which she was born and found herself. The storyteller in this book lacks noisy devices, but she does lead us into unfamiliar territory where wild and surprising things happen. Her stories resonate with unmistakable realities. They have concreteness and immediacy. They are full of recognizable people. In her own context, for herself and for those who listened, her stories were a chosen vehicle of knowledge and truth. She may simply have been telling her own story, but in another sense she was more interested in describing a world she herself found fascinating. Thus are her stories a deliberately assembled portrait of a world rather than merely a self-reflection.

To my mind, therefore, this book could easily be considered an ethnography, a description of the lifestyles and cultural ways of several contemporary societies in West Africa. Our storyteller lacked formal education, but she was driven by her intellectual curiosity. Her experience was broad because she sought always to broaden it, like any seeker who would comprehend the world. In that attitude perhaps lies one thread that can catch a reader in a web of credibility. She treats fragments of her experience as artifacts, and her stories do their ethnographic work in bits and pieces. To those who can hear stories, this portrait might seem more revealing than what can be learned from discussions built on abstract and critical concepts. Certainly, one will search through vast storehouses of knowledge to learn what the stories tell about modern Africa, and one will not find much to compare.

Her attitude also sets an ironically convincing tone. It would be difficult to think up the outrageous circumstances in the heroine's destiny. Her story is a pitiful chronicle of hypocrisy and exploitation, and to some people, telling it is probably just as bad as making it up. Yet her story is mainly a giddy celebration of her will to dignity. Indeed, she was giggling all the while she talked to me. Either she herself saw her story as a comedy or else she is the kind of person who laughs in the face of tragedy. Perhaps it is not unusual to disregard suffering when one is getting good data, but it is always difficult to present the results. Is it possible that she found it easy? Can an amazingly detailed ethnography issue merely from the kinetic energy in the running mouth of a laughing girl? No: the role of her intelligence is deceptively transparent. She controlled that energy with discipline, and she observed and remembered and testified. And like so many other instructors in human history, she found it suitable to bequeath her knowledge through the vehicle of storytelling.

What connects the apparent genres that this book suggests—novel, ethnography, life history, or autobiography—is a simple justification by the goal of sympathetic understanding of other people in other times and places, in this book, in contemporary Africa. The standard complement to that justification is that coming to terms with other people makes us aware of ourselves. When we move across space or time to encounter other lives and other realities, however, we must always be wary of ourselves. Things that look alike are not always the same. The very words we use might have different meanings in other contexts. Our terms of reference as readers may reflect our concerns, but by the same token, those terms can be confusing. For scholarly writers, one technique employed to handle the situation is to refine their terms in order to separate the confusing connotations of African life. The problem with that method is that minutely precise terms can become so vaporous that they have no earthly distillate: they cannot be subsequently condensed and used except in specially fabricated ivory towers. The more one reads such work, the more one is inescapably drawn to at least one sure conclusion, which is that on the entire African continent, no one is having fun.

The contrasting technique employed in this introduction is to attempt to eliminate or invalidate certain terms and their complexes of associated ideas. The problem is that one can hardly be said to have defined something by saying what it is not. Nonetheless, the technique does have the advantage of clearing a space for what literary critics call "the governing claims of the text," that is, to assist readers to enter the world the text represents without being burdened by too many preconceptions. This introduction is a parallel text that takes readers on a leisurely stroll through some of the perspectives on problematic issues that influence what many people think they need to know about Africa in order to have at least the illusion of knowledge regarding what is happening there. Foremost in the array are Africa's image itself, poverty, the processes of modernization, and the commodification of sex. Sometimes knowledge is not what one knows or can say; rather, it is what one cannot say and can no longer think.

This book's characters and the social world they inhabit are real. While we are thinking about their lives, they are dealing with them. Readers will only meet the heroine on the pages of this book; I knew her. Those who are impatient to meet her and those who think they know about modern Africa may skip this introduction. Its justification is simply: what would many other readers make of the heroine if they had not read the introduction? Some of the stories will support the ideas I discuss, but in the end, the stories speak for themselves. Perhaps the types of engagement the stories engender would not differ significantly were this book a novel. Whatever genre guides a reader's approach, it is important to know that this book is not fiction, the better to appreciate the challenges that its reality presents.

Africa: The End of the Earth Where the World Began

As an ethnography, this book is as much about modern Africa as it is about the heroine. Formerly the Dark Continent, Darkest Africa has never shed its bad name: now it is Modern Africa, land of dark statistics. Statistics: we want them, we need them, we love them. It's hard to know what's going on over there, but we have lots of dismal statistics. For those of us who are blessed to live in the Western world, our lives seem threatened by what we think is coming out of Africa, and we've got to get more facts. Looking at the news, one might assume that the worst part of the African AIDS epidemic, or the occasional outbreaks of Ebola or Lassa or whatever, must be the fact that African governments won't tell the World Health Organization how many cases have been discovered. On Western television, evangelists solicit help for starving children, newsmen show two-minute filmed scoops on the latest South African or Rwandan or Congolese or Liberian developments, telejournalists give us twelve-minute TV-magazine overviews of drought and corruption and civil strife. Facts and statistics. We can't even enjoy a peaceful moment contemplating an elephant lolling about in a cool mud hole, or an annoyed rhinoceros running into the jeep, because the nature shows must report the body counts in the competition between game wardens and poachers, those local hunters who in their poverty serve the whims of some sophisticated but superstitious Hong Kong businessmen in need of aphrodisiacs and macho ashtrays for their Sobranie cigarettes. Everything seems to be a problem: government, food, transportation, health, modern society, traditional culture, life, death, it's all a problem. Modern Africa is a nightmare supported by statistics.

We Westerners have been awakened from our old dreams, our dreams of natural innocence and the purity of atavistic savagery, dreams of happy Pygmies dancing in the moonlight, of clever Bushmen surviving in the desert, of graceful women carrying babies on their backs and water pots on their heads, of jovial market traders, of handsome warriors fighting lions with spears, of initiations into adulthood that are more meaningful because they hurt, of grisly rituals and missionary stews, of our bearers running away in the night, of snakes and bugs and swamps and heat and sweat. For the Western world, Africa was always and still remains a dream and a fantasy, a reality so distant and indistinct that human beings were traded as commodities for centuries, and abolitionists had to shout long and loudly just to wake people up to what was going on. Now we keep statistics to remind us how far away Africa is from our technological paradise. There's no jungle here: here, though, there are lots of anthills, shiny ones with elevators, and some very fancy raceways for rats. But the jungle is still over there. Our Hollywood fantasies now give us a land without Tarzan, who has been replaced: in lighter fare, Hollywood teenagers protect endangered creatures from gun-happy soldiers, and a tiny Bushman protects school children from mercenaries. And when our filmmakers get serious, they tell us about the romantic and decadent last days of colonialism, days that are somehow sad because the film stars share our bittersweet awareness that having a gin and tonic and watching an antelope from the veranda is a privileged moment of moral corruption that must pass.

Africa: Mother Africa, mother of depressing statistics and bad news. Formerly mother to some, Africa is now mother to all. Africa: where humankind was born. In our search for our ancestry, our imagination was most captivated by a special find the Western world took to heart for several generations as our earliest human ancestor, in Africa, as mother of all the different strains of humanity. The home of Mother Africa was not the Garden of Eden. When our eminent paleontologists found her, she was a fossil in a rugged gorge. They gave her a name—Lucy—because that was a name in a popular Beatles song they were all singing while they dug. They might as well have thought to name her after another famous Lucy, Lucy Gray, muse of the poet William Wordsworth. There are some similarities between the fossil and the poet's sentimental vision:

> She dwelt among the untrodden ways
> Beside the springs of Dove
> A maid whom there were none to praise
> And very few to Love . . .
> She lived unknown, and few could know
> When Lucy ceased to be;
> But she is in her grave, and, oh,
> The difference to me!

Our fossil mother Lucy was in her grave for a few million years, and we have found her. Oh, the difference! There she is in a public television documentary, on the table, the residues of her life only a tooth and a piece of bone, pushed around by a metal instrument for better camera angles. Every book needs a poet: let Wordsworth be ours for this book. We call on him as he himself called Milton: he should be living at this hour; we have need of him. The famous lines he penned two centuries ago are still memorized by schoolchildren: "The world is too much with us; late and soon,/Getting and spending, we lay waste our powers . . . " The words are good for schoolchildren; after graduation, they give their hearts away and put his vision on a shelf. Thus, out of tune, traveling between life and death, we replace the poet's sentimental image with fossil evidence. Our new Mother Africa, Lucy, is too much with us. She stood up from all fours and gave birth to Genus Homo. We need a poet's lens in our microscope: "I saw her upon nearer view,/A Spirit, yet a Woman too!"[1] But why did they give the fossil a name, if not from sentiment?

1. Quotes and allusions in the preceding passages are from "She Dwelt among the Untrodden Ways," "The World is Too Much with Us; Late and Soon," "London, 1802," "She Was a Phantom of Delight," in *Poetical Works* of William Wordsworth, with Memoir and Notes (New York: American News Company, 188?).

Yes, Wordsworth is appropriate here in this introduction to a book dictated by a woman. We should be concerned with her spirit. In her modern habitat, there are none to sing her praise and no poet to celebrate her. In this book, she must sing her own praise in a record of her times. She lives unknown among untrodden ways, hidden in a tangled jungle of statistics. She has not ceased to be; she is neither a fossil nor a muse of poetry. Yet she can indeed evoke a muse of a type, for the mother of the ancient muses was *Mnemosyne,* Remembrance. We will catch a glimpse of her life as she sat in remembrance, and the book issued from her as a musing. She speaks no poetry but she does a poet's work, providing glimpses to make us less forlorn and extending an ironic apology to the spirit. The poet's words, once spoken, still remain with us in our hearts, to be retrieved by sympathy.

In this book we will try to see through the statistics by looking at one person's dilemma and resolution. In the text that follows this introduction, her testimony is presented in her own words as a series of dramatic encounters. As she sat within her memories, her eyes would open wide as if she were watching a movie. When she talked, she spoke the parts of her fellow actors and actresses as if she were dictating a screenplay, recreating events in dramatic narrative. Therefore, this introduction is something like a stage setting. Because I shall not be telling her tale myself, I shall describe her in this introduction, so that we can have a look at the heroine first before we look at the African landscape she roams. Our example of African womanhood in this book, our "Lucy," is called Hawa (Eve), though Hawa is not her real name. A diamond in the rough, she has in common with a fossil only that she is a carbon-based entity under pressure. I will tell you about some of that pressure shortly, but let's imagine her physically first.

As she sits to tell us her stories, she is a tiny woman, under five feet tall, and very cute. Her coloring is copper, tinged with tan. She has a round face, nice teeth, well-formed lips, and a pretty smile. She has a compact and youthful body with good skin and muscle tone. Her movements are pleasantly confident and self-contained; when she sits, she maintains good posture, and she often folds her hands in her lap. Her voice is light and tinkling, somewhat musical. She was born in Ghana and spoke English before she learned French, but since living in French-speaking Togo and Burkina Faso, she speaks English with a slight French accent, for example, pronouncing "pussycat" as "pooshycat." *Très charmante!* Today when we meet her, as years ago when she spoke, her hair is braided with cowrie shells and colored beads. Her beauty is enhanced by a thin, graceful, tribal scar that runs from her upper cheeks across the bridge of her nose. The scar emphasizes her almond eyes and her cheekbones and adds a note of definition and angularity to the roundness of her face. She dresses well, often in A-line dresses that speak of modesty. She keeps herself very clean but does not spend an inordinate amount of time on vain grooming. Where she lives is also well swept and orderly: her bed is made; her cooking utensils are organized; her clothes and shoes are stored neatly. In summary, she is not remarkable or stunning, but she is doll-like and totally presentable. That said, let's move on to social and political matters.

The Politico-economic Techno-philosophical Socio-historical Global-developmental Backdrop

Who is to say what is happening in Africa? The setting of this book is a world about which even professional students of Africa have very little knowledge. It is also a world where generalizations are as treacherous as qualifying adjectives would be tiresome. Tourists still travel to "Africa" and are not asked further about where they're going, but the Africa Westerners discuss with a single word is a continent of diversity. Even if we exclude North African and Mediterranean countries and exclude the technically developed anomaly of South Africa, we still face problems in discussing Africa as a single place. There are many large cities, each with its own ambience, and the rural areas where traditional cultures flourish are even more diverse. In this introduction I hope to highlight some more or less common themes about modern societies in sub-Saharan Africa. The action in this book takes place in several countries of West Africa, in specific towns and cities, but in this section of the introduction, we will first hang a broad backdrop to the action. The props that occupy the stage will be shifted around and changed from scene to scene, but behind them is a tapestry that we may tend to forget when we become caught up in the personal motives and intimate daily lives of the players; it will fade like a social-realist mural on the walls of a public building, until we will hardly notice it.

This backdrop features what we think we know about the world of the players, based on the statistics and the research of the stage designers and their critics, all of whom have done a great deal of serious work to learn more about the grand scale of what is happening in Africa — the transition from traditional to modern social life. This transition is a story that encloses within itself the broad sweep of precolonial, colonial, and postcolonial history. If we listen to the dominant voices of our day, it is clear that the metaphoric image of Africa — the emblem of the main storyline — has been refashioned from the chaotic natural processes of the jungle to the chaotic social processes of modernization. In the story, the word "traditional" refers to societies that used to be called "tribal" but currently would be considered "ethnic": they have their own languages, indigenous institutions, community sentiments, customary practices, and cultural patterns; but they are also distinguished by not being Western or, by extension, modern. "Modernization," to students of society, is characterized by a three-fold path involving urbanization, bureaucratization, and industrialization. The transition necessitates, coincidentally, the abandonment or replacement of many aspects of traditional community life.

As we well know, the change is toward a better life and is inevitable anyway, and the associated discombobulation is definitely worth it. The authoritative work promotes a material view: Africa is a place that one may claim to know based on ideas of what is there or what isn't there. Do not be confused by the notion that, fundamentally, what is there is poverty, which is a word for what isn't there. Journalists and politicians seem always to be talking about a benevolent process of globalization that will bring poor and underdeveloped countries into the world economy and make them democracies as well. This process will create enough wealth to give enough people enough of a stake in the process that there will be enough economic stimulation and enough political momentum to motivate enough parochial traditional groups to reorganize their societies to participate in the institutions of the modern states. That has been the dominant story since colonial days, and the best part of the contemporary update is that the richer the West gets, the better it is for the poor people of the world. The story may have happened somewhere else, but actually, people in Africa have participated in the global economy for centuries, where they have been and still are exploited for commodities such as minerals, animal products, agricultural products, and human labor.

Many informed observers of Africa have abandoned the colonial notion that modern African history could reflect a straightforward if somewhat awkward process of replacing indigenous traditions with Western ones. It is clear that no such straight line exists. And of course, there are no current borders where the gerrymandered conglomeration of traditional African societies inside can be easily integrated into a modern nation state. Fortunately there are experts, and the great Nigerian musician Fela Anikulapo Kuti eulogized them in his song, "Mr. Grammatologylisationalism is the Boss." Demographic, socioeconomic, political, and ecological changes have been identified and described in voluminous theoretical overviews and reports and in many community and institutional case studies. In the far view, there are discussions of how the situation is an extension of history and what is called the world system. In the near view, there are discussions of networks of association and conflicting loyalties, of separations and interminglings, and of processes of working out multiple syntheses of available options. A modern society is being decreed from the top down, but no matter how much those at the top and their international colleagues of whatever political stripe would like to see it be otherwise, what is coming into being is not Western; it is something else. Even when one acknowledges that point, it is difficult for most people, including even social scientists, to get to the nitty-gritty of how ordinary people are experiencing their options and working through the changes of their encounter with the modern world.

Some social planners don't care because the common people seem to have so little say in these monumental processes: move the people to the right position and it doesn't matter what they think. A high-level Ghanaian bureaucrat once told me point blank that the people in traditional societies don't know what is happening. He was right in the sense that they think about things differently from the bureaucrats. Whether the common people know it or not, though, in most decent and respectable views, they are supposed to be the whole point of any development effort. Their lot in life must be improved. Nonetheless, within the plans, the people are usually dead weight, the obstacles to progress who have to be educated or made more efficient or brought up-to-date in their attitudes or taught how to do this or that. Something always has to be done with them or to them or about them. We know this to be true because sophisticated administrators and social engineers spend so much money on projects that look great on paper yet somehow achieve nothing or make things worse. It must be the people.

Employees of the governments and the international agencies with whom I occasionally carouse have told me that their development initiatives have a 10 to 20 percent success rate. "Development in Africa," one United Nations officer said, "is a litany of disasters." The experts are sincere, dedicated, bright, learned, and ever more experienced. But they also have a fantastic vocabulary and can make even total failure seem like an operational concept. I quote from a recent essay by a U.S. Agency for International Development (USAID) employee on directions in development anthropology: "Voiced from a variety of quarters, but particularly from several developing country governments, is an interest in simplifying development assistance to the Third World by 'de-projectizing' financial aid and offering direct budget support in the form of cash transfers or some other mechanisms of debt relief."[1] Personally, I look forward to the day when the National Science Foundation and the National Endowment for the Hu-

1. Willian H. Jansen II, "Future Directions of Development Anthropology," *Anthropology Newsletter* 30, no. 7 (October 1989): 31.

manities will adopt a similar system so that we intellectuals will not have to bother with lengthy applications but rather can receive grants for de-projectized work with a simple registration form that we can pick up when we play the lottery.

Development workers are unlike intellectuals, though. Intellectuals have made their peace with the cold shoulder that they receive from the powers-that-be. Development workers have a place in budgets. Development workers are supposed to be there to do something about people's problems, about suffering and poverty. Development workers are symbols. Even if they do not actually achieve their goals, then their visible presence at least testifies to a social will to do something. Political rhetoric justifies their efforts and guarantees continued if declining funding. But the situation is beyond them. They get paid because they are experts, so it's not their fault that they cannot everywhere duplicate the successful model projects they sometimes have. When they fail, it is because the situation is too bad. It must be the people.

The people: they are the unknown factor. These days no one approaches the task of bringing African societies up-to-date with the hypocritical posture of moral superiority attributed to caricatured colonial administrators. The terminology of the postcolonial burden reflects continuing concern with such well-established notions as capital formation, labor and production relations, the distribution of wealth, levels of integration, evolutionary stages of growth, class structure, and elites. Some new buzzwords rely on concepts such as information dissemination, indigenous perceptions, behavior modification, population management, and infrastructure development. There is a bewildering quantity of discussions and points of view regarding what people are doing and should be doing about the situation. Send for Mr. Grammatologylisationalism, quick! The more one reads of these discussions, the more one must believe that we really know a lot and that we could do a lot if we had the will. The will: the fact is that the concern and commitment of the international community are marginal, and the resources and capabilities of the local governments are minimal. The engineers come in on major contracts for a few years handing out smaller local contracts and start-up resources, and then the projects are turned over to communications experts whose concern is to get the people to use whatever has been built or put into place. We get a lot of reports. The underlying idea is still to move the common people into a dream society that resembles a technocratic state. In this book we will be thinking about the level on which many of those people are dealing with that dream society in the making.

What is it about the basic nature of society that makes it so difficult to manipulate? Sometimes it seems that everybody knows what society is, except for social scientists: the people who are supposed to know the most about society cannot agree on even a basic metaphor to describe it. Before we paint a social backdrop, let us think for a moment about a couple of sociology's seminal terms about society in order to mix up some of our colors. One of the founders of the science of sociology, Émile Durkheim, long ago made a distinction between traditional and modern societies by characterizing the integrity of the former as "mechanical" and the latter as "organic."[1] By that metaphoric dichotomy he meant to suggest that in traditional societies the individuals or segments or parts are more or less self-sufficient and therefore somewhat interchangeable; they can replace one another within a coherent whole. Simply put, if half of a population of farmers or hunters gets wiped out, the remaining half will still be able to farm or hunt, and their decreased productivity will feed a correspondingly decreased number of mouths. Modern societies, Durkheim said, are characterized by a differentiation of various elements that have to work together to ensure the cohesive functioning of the whole: if one organ in an organism fails, the whole thing collapses or breaks down. Modern sociology, to Durkheim, was the study of how those differing elements cohere and function as an entity, according to its own logic, as something that is more than the sum of its parts.

In the century since Durkheim, a major school of social science developed the organic metaphor of societies as systems that are continually readjusting to maintain a complexly balanced integrity. But this view has its limitations because of the inherent difficulties in putting an observational boundary around anything we wish to understand: societies are like unstable science-fiction organisms that transmute and transmogrify into totally new kinds of species. Also, there are organisms that are hard to classify, and there are other organisms within organisms and around organisms; organisms develop cancers and warts for inexplicable reasons; little organisms invade and vanquish larger organisms; large organisms step on or dominate smaller organisms; different types of organisms need to work together to solve a basic problem, as if they were really parts of one organism. There is always some sophisticated point at which the apparent clarity of words breaks down, along with the sense of a system, where knowledge seems a pathetically bounded thing. Nonetheless, we still get a lot of mileage from the notion of an organism, whether looking at a protozoan or at the planet. An organism seems to be a unit, its wholeness a vital system with acknowledged boundaries, and as such do we often picture society.

1. Émile Durkheim, *The Division of Labor in Society,* trans. George Simpson (1895; reprint, Glencoe, Ill.: Free Press, 1958).

As it turns out, though, the language with which we respond to the social organism tends to be mechanical, for machines are also systems. A mechanical orientation to the world permeates our modern mentality to our very souls, and another of sociology's founders, Max Weber, developed this particular mechanical metaphor in a different direction. Weber pointed out an odd connection between, of all things, Protestant theology and the scientific approach to the world.[1] According to Weber's well-known and ironic characterization of the modern spirit, the medieval idea that an infallible God had created everything in a week, pushed a starter button to set the wheels in motion, and then relaxed, fit rather well with the notion that the world is a kind of sophisticated machine, orderly and reliable, and that studying its preordained movements was both a proper and a blessed calling for secular science. For most of us who have inherited the modern spirit, just using the technocratic terminology of social science is about as far as we have to go in order to claim an authoritative handle on the whole works. Formerly people prayed, wept, or offered sacrifices, but technical talk is our way of dealing with a crisis: we learn and talk on and on about weapons systems when we wage war, design redundancies when engineered objects collapse or explode, biochemistry when we face failing health, macroeconomic trends when we lose money. But ironically, with social issues as with other areas, it seems to happen that when we try to apply the insights of social science to the problems of modernization, we never seem to have the kind of categorical control we would like our terminology to deliver. It is no wonder. What are we dealing with, for example, an organism or a machine, that allows us to talk about something like planned growth or to discuss in the same breath the machinery of state and the branches of government?

If we know so much, why is our knowledge of society so pliable that it can fashion its logic within these metaphors on an as-needed basis, so changeable that it can animate uncountable learned discussions of protean terminology? What is all this talk about? A skeptic would say it's about money. Somebody is trying to make some money, and knowledge — even merely the illusion of knowledge — is like good credit in business. Some anthropologists who work in Africa cherish an image of the ancient Herodotus as a peripatetic soul who seemed motivated merely to satisfy his senses of curiosity and wonder. Yet by colonial times, even anthropologists and missionaries who in their hearts served other masters were extensions of colonial organization. Somebody supported them, and when things got hot in the jungle, most of them sought protection with their compatriots. Their work, from studying kinship to cultivating literacy to deciphering

1. Max Weber, *The Protestant Ethic and the Spirit of Capitalism,* trans. Talcott Parsons (New York: Charles Scribner's Sons, 1958).

chieftaincy succession to ministering to the faithful, was almost always an adjunct to administration and development. They helped Europeans to understand the indigenous cultures and to prepare the ground for interaction. Now, academic concern about aspects of "traditional" culture is marginalized. There must not be much money in it. Where is the profit in understanding or appreciating outmoded and marginal realms of life that are being bypassed by development?

Sometimes it seems that everybody wants to modernize, and everybody is studying development. Education is the key: literacy is the road away from the life of a peasant and into the life of a clerk. The African governments are paying people to be bureaucrats, and the governments pay for them to study what they need to know to become extensions of the Western world. Many of these bureaucrats study overseas. The Western universities get money and students. Sometimes the universities get new buildings. There is a need for teachers and staff, and suddenly a lot of people are experts on development. There is also a need for Westerners and other international types to interface with the local experts. There are a lot of papers read at conferences on development. International agencies and multinational corporations are involved. There are contracts to be won. The corporate set and their government cronies know that those foreign bureaucrats are going to buy machines and spare parts and fertilizer and pesticides and so on and so on. There are still some natural resources that can be developed, that is, sold and resold. Africa is getting hooked and wired in to the world market system. Why is this process happening? What feeds it? Who is getting fed? Who is to say what is happening? The experts who are supposed to know about development are part of the industry that provides development services. What they know about and what they do for a living and what they say is happening are all the same thing. Modernization: that is what's happening, at least for those who talk about it and those who are at its leading edge.

Are there alternatives? Those poor, suffering, traditional people who don't know what is happening: there is no reason to expect them to master the sociology of knowledge. When the people are perceived as potential consumers, their problems usually have to do with what isn't there and how to get it there. Learned people who are solving the people's problems through development are more likely to worry about the connotative reverberations of organic and mechanical metaphors than to worry about exploring any possible affinity with the assorted reactionaries, conservatives, fundamentalists, and troglodytes who raise questions against the whole process and want little or nothing to do with it. Such critics can be characterized as extreme, as antidemocratic, or as irrelevant to the dynamics of history. Most of them may like electricity and running water and antibiotics. But some of them are looking at the children who no longer adhere to them; some are not interested in being consumers of our goods and media wares; some object to the disproportionate distribution of wealth and power that characterizes development. Obviously, none of them has a justifiable case, we say: if they had their way, they would oppress people and throw away the benefits of years of work. But we may be deceiving ourselves: did the ancient African past ever see genocide and destruction to compare to what has happened since Africa came into really profound contact with the West?

There is a troublesome issue regarding the role of "knowledge" in our own image of modern African societies. What do we think we need to know in order to think we know about Africa? The answer seems to be that we need to know about problems. Those who understand the problems of the situation contend among themselves for the opportunity to respond. They work against one another to jockey for position. Their arguments resemble proposals for funding. Their successes and their failures are all presented as evidence that they need more money. Their mandate for compliance is their claim to have an overview of the system and a plan to manage the details of giving the people what they need. Social scientists and politicians resemble each other in that regard: both project confidence and ask us to put our faith in them, and not somebody else. Some social scientists assert an affinity with harder sciences based on faith in accumulating knowledge, the hope that we will eventually comprehend what we now see dimly. But in social science, we survey the complexities and depth of a social universe as if with modest binoculars teetering on wobbly bipods. There is a huge gap between the presumptions of our knowledge and our ability to apply what we claim to know.

The failures aside, the process of development seems as much a cause of disorder as a solution. A project may successfully develop some resources or products yet also create social stratification or family disruption or ecological disturbance; those who do the assessment may use a narrow lens on what has been put in place in order to measure success while they construe these ancillary results as temporary aspects of adjustment that will sort themselves out or will be dealt with later. It is as rare to see a bureaucratic organization disavow or rescind a development initiative as it is to see a corporate contractor abandon a funded bid. But it is even more rare to see social scientists admit the irrelevance of their research projects. Their product is the representation of order: showing order is how their work makes sense. No matter what, a social scientist will never investigate a situation and tell you, "My research is insignificant, and I'm confused." That is not how they get their advanced degrees or publish their research or fulfill their contracts. They dance with the randomness or chaos or disorganization that is outside the configurations and structures of their models, but they return to their chairs after the music stops. A bit flush from the dance, they confess no complete understanding at the moment, just a choice of points of view that all reflect a belief that if a degree of order can be discerned somewhere, it should be valued. They buttress their work with defensive acknowledgments of its limitations at the same time as they assert confidence that their knowledge can be applied in ways that affect people's lives. Confidence is desperately needed in a chaotic social situation, in a world of problems. Nonetheless, if there is a way for social science to deal with disorder in social life, perhaps the first step is to recognize that disorder occasionally is a manifestation of the limitations of our instruments and motives.

For social scientists in Africa, the chaos represented in imagery of social disorganization is more than a sign of our inability to understand the situation, more than an invidious evaluation of our presumed ability to control or affect social action, more than a potential justification when things don't work out. The chaos cannot be comprehended because it is the very thing we struggle against, just as our colonial predecessors struggled against the jungle. The imagery of social problems favored by bureaucrats and academics, and the imagery of the chaotic disintegration of the social world, so favored by our news media, present an updated return of the jungle metaphor of Darkest Africa. Transformed into a modern jungle, Africa is a place to be approached with a sense of the perils of unbalance, a place where you are unprotected by society, a jungle without lions but where there are things that will eat you and swallow you up into something nasty: potholes, shanty towns, open gutters, mud puddles, smelly toilet holes, epidemics, bugs, mosquitoes, parasites, police roadblocks, drunken soldiers with automatic weapons, child soldiers brainwashed into compassionless zombies, fraternal strife, internecine conflict, and a host of other jungle clichés such as territoriality, rampaging tribalism, warlords, bureaucratic labyrinths, breeding grounds of despair, and superstition.

The jungle metaphor lies underneath the surface of the story of modernization. Corruption, brutish authority, primordial sentiments, the substratum of sex and violence, and the savage struggle for survival: these are the elements that spoil the story; they are external to the incorporation of the state and the economy; they make African countries remain something other than Western. But the youngsters with their automatic weapons are wearing T-shirts, shorts, and flip-flops, and they are listening to hip-hop music on headphones. The despots and their bureaucratic lackeys are dressed in suits and speak better English or French than many native British or French. Sierra Leone, Rwanda, Congo, Sudan, Somalia, Ethiopia, Nigeria, Chad, Zimbabwe, Mali, Liberia, Angola, Mozambique: were these places always like that? What one sees in Africa (or in many parts of the Third World) are not the societies or cultures that existed there previously and are breaking through to the surface, like a resurgent jungle, in spite of the processes of modernization. These places are the rough edges of those processes, an aspect of Western contact and influence, writ large and made visible. The purpose of the jungle imagery has always been to put distance between Africa and the West. At one time, social scientists worked to separate ideas about indigenous African societies from the image of the primordial jungle, to use reason and empathy to promote a sense of common humanity. Now the jungle has extended its metaphoric scope and absorbed the precolonial societies. When they are not in the way of modernization, their relevance is that of romantic nostalgia, like the pastoral and agrarian fantasies of the Western world, and their traditions are not to be taken too seriously as a rallying point. Modern historians and social scientists have reinterpreted the ancient traditional cultures to show that they were never isolated and they were always in flux, that there were no pure traditions, and those people who believe otherwise are deluded, clinging to primordial myths of things that were never really there like that. The indigenous societies have changed and changed, and what is happening is the same as ever, with the same solution. It's the people. The people need to get out of their jungle life and get with the program.

There is a territorial metaphysics of morals at work in the dichotomies of order and chaos, of civilization and the jungle, of modernization and underdevelopment. The systematic advancement of learning is also a gradual encroachment on the realm of chaos, just as development domesticates the natural and the social jungles. Organic or mechanical, the modern social order is a system that defends us against the threat of chaos percolating from outside, from uneducated people, from foreigners, from the past, from bounded primitivism breaking loose, from something other than it. Why? Maybe in some situations, the purpose of knowing about something is not to understand it. Maybe in some times and places, the purpose of building and sustaining our knowledge is merely like that of a sermon, or even an incantation, in which Western social thought and social science function theologically as a bulwark against chaos, drawing boundaries to keep chaos away or to project it outward.[1] If one assumes that there are things we will never understand, then chaos is another word for the limitations of our

1. Leszek Kolakowski, "The Priest and the Jester: Reflections on the Theological Heritage in Contemporary Thought," in *The Modern Polish Mind: An Anthology*, ed. Maria Kuncewicz (New York: Grosset and Dunlap and Little, Brown, 1962), 301–26.

knowledge and capability, a word like nature or uncertainty or irony or fate or mess. Perhaps disorganization is a part of the system, a regressive part that is beyond what we know and work with everyday, yet nonetheless is a part that is serving the system or helps in a mysterious way, something like the imagination of the system. At least, for some philosophers and most fools, chaos represents the capacity to make fun of self-evident knowledge and of people who claim to know what is happening. Faced with a mess, the narrator of this book and her acquaintances do not need a teleology grounded in social policy or social theory. They need a theodicy grounded in a comic vision, a pathway to redemption, or at least an assertion of hope.

And with regard to modern African nations, hope is everything. Call the situation one of overwhelming complexity or call it beyond us, instead of humming along and following the sure and steady growth and progress that a devotee of the ordered view might wish to see, social development proceeds in an uneven and discontinuous way, as in organisms. As might be expected, though, the organic metaphor breaks down because the modern nations are still organisms in the making. In this context, social development implies the increasing organization of all the various activities in the nation, linking things together and plugging everybody in. What of the people? Everybody inside the boundaries of the social order is undoubtedly a part of it or is supposed to fit somewhere. The new elites are certainly part of the new countries, so the process is not bad for them. Tenured economists assure us that teeny-tiny, itsy-bitsy droplets of what the emerging elites accumulate will undoubtedly trickle down to the people, some day. What is really happening, though, is that the social order is still more dream than reality, and the situation is actually still quite disorganized.

It is important to free ourselves of inflated ideas about the social systems portrayed in geography books and in the reports of the international players. In general, the times when such systems can be seen as the dominating reality of a situation are times when the reality is one of domination. It is not only in modern Africa, of course, that history is frequently the story of some people trying to get other people into their organizational program, with many of those other people resisting or resenting or ignoring them. For many people, wealth and power energize a persuasive legitimacy, but wealth and power do not energize what they do not reach. In a developing country particularly, there is always a question of resources. From every direction and every point of view, there are issues about whether and what resources are available and who is involved and doing what. For the people in this book, the issues are remarkably alive because much of what happens occurs at the boundaries of order and organization, wealth and power.

The names of the new nations roll off our tongues easily, suggesting entities, but if organic metaphors are too garbled to apply, mechanical metaphors are even more dubious. Distant observers have the luxury of being philosophical about disorder or pointing a finger and saying, "What a mess." Those responsible for overseeing progress have a job to do and tend toward the mechanical view. They call themselves social planners, architects, or engineers. Politicians and bureaucrats and capitalists and socialists are inheritors of the Western spirit and exhibit little doubt that the boundaries of the nation constitute a social order that has somehow or other emerged as part of God's handiwork from which there is no turning back. The social order has been given to them, complete with a number of paying positions in an ordained hierarchy. It is not wagging a finger at them to point out that engineers naturally tend to think in terms of mechanical models.

To exercise leadership and control development, social engineers must challenge the organic nature of problems that Martin Luther or John Calvin would have shrugged off as signs of preordained destiny or the fate of the damned. An African elder once advised me, "One shouldn't blame the present generation; one should pray for them." Indeed, those in authority seem to have been damned, like Sisyphus pushing his rock up a hill and watching it roll down again, to the task of treating the whole social entity as really something like a big machine that one can stand over and watch or tinker with. It is their fate to see "problems" standing in the way of "progress," problems that must be "operationalized" in order to be addressed or solved. Only when things are beyond control do they revert to organic metaphors, and stubborn problems are described and treated like cancers that the state can excise with tools made of metal. But normally, they adopt the mechanical terminology: they are building society, adjusting the economic engine, mobilizing resources, fueling the system, firing up the will of the people.

It is frustrating work: they cannot put all the pieces into place so that things can function according to the designed plan. Bearings get stuck. Valves get clogged. Rivets pop out. Gaskets leak. Gears get stripped. Crankshafts break. The mechanics and those at their bidding speed around to targeted areas of the comprehensive plan. One thing gets developed while its necessary complements do not. The unbalances thus created mean that very few things function as they were intended. In a developing country, these unbalances rule even the rulers. If we were prepared to accept that even in our Western mechanical paradise, disorder is a part of the system, then we might be prepared to believe that in the Third World disorder is in the nature of the system.

What do these unbalances look like in ever-expanding circles? Nations have been created. In many developing countries, the national system is charged with promoting and maintaining new unities. The system is a mechanism of stability and exchange, the official channel of communication with the outside world, the conduit through which the movement of resources and goods is ministered, generally resources out and goods in. On the inside, the boundaries of the system are not the same as the borders of the nation, but there is little or nothing to counterbalance the rule of the system, however weak its institutions may seem. Elites emerge and consolidate their interests. In many developing countries in Africa, for example, a few people in the government have control over the allocation of import licenses or imported goods to a few distributors, and the natural opportunities deflect even the best intentions. Eventually, some people become very rich and the majority of people remain very poor. The distribution of wealth is shockingly inequitable, even mind-boggling. Police and soldiers and bureaucrats who don't become rich become powerful, though quite a few manage to become both. Fela Anikulapo Kuti wrote a song about them: "V.I.P.: Vagabonds in Power."

But it's all relative. The powerful and the wealthy are only local extensions of the world system they represent, and West Africa is a very small portion of the big picture. In a West African country, those at the top have next to no power in the world. In the outside world they are only slightly better than the poor people of their own countryside, perhaps only because they have a voice, albeit a voice that the world hears or ignores at will. Within the world community, the more they consolidate their nation, the more closely they are tied to places where they are the instruments of others. They are dependent on people on other continents, people in boardrooms of multinational corporations and people in drawing rooms and assembly rooms where affairs of state are decided. They are big people in their countries, but the world doesn't mind them. They are supposed to lead their countries into the modern age, but they have never been able to get all they need to do the job.

The law of entropy seems a relevant scientific analogy: unless energy is added to a system, the disorder in the system increases. Nonetheless, we in the West devote inadequate money and resources to sustain the developing nations, or just enough to sustain the parts of the system we do business with and damn the rest. We loan them money, our governments at low interest and our banks at high interest, and we send a few social engineers to advise them how to spend it. Mechanics without tools, fabricators without materials, corporate bodies without assets: the word for the problem is "poverty," of course, but as noted, the word is a relative one that refers the eye of the beholder to whatever is not there. The word "poverty" is applied to the developing countries, but it is also implied in decisions about how much the developed countries can afford to do without impoverishing themselves in their own view. After all, cheap commodities from the Third World help to support our standard of living. Does anyone believe that all the pleas and protestations of the Third World leaders can convince us to alter the balance? We're crying ourselves about how expensive everything is these days. We're poor ourselves and we're in debt, we say in conversations, and the Third World owes us money; we even get annoyed at the Third World for its poverty. We have cut spending on our own human services to a trickle. Our own problems are so threatening to us that we only manage token assistance to the Third World, and we even argue about that. As Hawa says, did you ever see a rich person who didn't want to become richer?

Of course, the developing countries have a stronger case for claiming rights to the word "poverty," based on all that they lack. As the 1990s began, business folk and politicians in the Western world gloated about the failure of centrally planned economies, but it is not that market-capitalist economies have succeeded in eliminating the exploitative ruthlessness that made planned economies seem at least worth the effort. It has been argued that development has only brought the Third World more inequality, exploitation, and suffering. But development is not entirely a way for the elites of the world to recirculate their money. Advocates of globalization claim that it would be good for us if Third World countries were better organized. Why would we want them to become more developed? First, we want them to become better markets, able to buy more things from us, and second, we want them to be able to produce their exports more efficiently and reliably. But if the developing countries produce more, what they produce becomes cheaper. If they spend their money to buy our goods, where will they get the money to invest in their own development? If they borrow it, they'll use too much of their profits servicing their debts. The leaders of the Third World walk a thin line. If they squander their resources, they jeopardize their future. If they squeeze the current generation, and maybe the next, and maybe the next, then who benefits? The bottom line is that, based on comparative growth rates, we've known for a very long time that they'll probably never catch up. For the moment, looking at the panoramic backdrop, we should remember that African countries in particular are very poor in comparison with their international counterplayers. They were poor to begin with, lacking in so many things, and on the bottom line, they don't even have credit. The developed nations want to buy cheap and still sell them everything, but the road is long and risky, and we measure out our commitment to their journey in coffee spoons.

In the unpredictable shadows of the future, the African countries only get some things, a little at a time, and then what is missing shows itself. Entropy increases: even in the best-laid plans, payment and timely delivery are the elements of problems that affect the cohesive functioning of the social organism from top to bottom. There are shortages of spare parts and supplies to maintain cars, trucks, buildings, agricultural efforts, health services, any type of business. Things that break cannot be repaired. Things that grow on special foods cannot be fed. The people are desperate. The government imports food and controls prices. The government subsidizes certain commodities that the people have come to need. Somebody corners a particular market. The shortages extend to what are now called "essential" commodities. Ever-patient people line up to buy a few tins of milk, a kilo of sugar, or a liter of kerosene. As one can imagine, it is damn annoying to stand in a long line in the sun to buy some stupid little thing, maybe because your kids are begging for it or you have a guest coming to visit. The government would like to respond to the extent of its limited means, but it is also inside the mess, and its efficiency is also crippled. The phones don't work, and just to ask someone a question requires a trip to another office building, where the person one must see has gone out to stand in a line somewhere or find a spare part or see someone else.

How does this situation come about? As an example, let us consider a synopsis of the historical background of Ghana, one of the settings of this book. Ghana was formerly the Gold Coast Colony. The European presence — Portuguese, Dutch, and British — was conspicuously established by the seventeenth century in a series of forts along the coast. These forts were there for the purpose of trading in slaves and gold and other commodities of use to a more advanced and enlightened civilization. Everything proceeded through coastal intermediaries like the Fanti and Ga peoples. The great Ashanti Confederacy was the main inland supplier, and the payoff was in the usual manner still practiced today: they gave us what we wanted, and we gave them guns. Eventually the British locked up the rights to the coast. Economic historians tell us that by the middle of the nineteenth century, however, when the British were no longer buying slaves, they needed to extend their control over the inland territories in order to get the Gold Coast to produce different kinds of useful items but particularly to enable the colony to become a consumer of British goods. That latter goal was a vain hope, because the Gold Coast Colony obviously had little of the market potential of a place like India; nonetheless, once decreed in London, the policy was applied everywhere. It was only at the end of the nineteenth century, only a hundred years ago, that the British finally pushed inland in a serious way to declare their stewardship over the Ashantis, who fought a war with the British before accepting the fact that the people who had given them the guns for their own mercantile-imperialist fantasy had even more and better guns. The Ashantis were defeated and their paramount chief exiled. The political problem thus settled, the administrators began to preach, and much to everyone's surprise, the farmers of the Gold Coast Colony, whom most people had thought of as a rather conservative and lowly group, bought into the whole British fantasy with gusto. Forsaking their food crops and slash-and-burn agriculture, they became venture capitalists and planted cocoa trees, patiently tended the trees to maturity, and became the major suppliers of cocoa to the world.[1] The Gold Coast became a rich place, for a colony.

After the Second World War, in which many Ghanaians had served and seen the world, their eyes were open when leaders like Kwame Nkrumah emerged to lead the Gold Coast to independence in 1957 as the Republic of Ghana. The Ghanaian leadership was of the natural opinion that Britain had been profiting to an undue extent from her colonies; Ghana needed its rightful share of the pie, and the leaders wanted the job of cutting and sharing the portions. Cynics maintain that Britain saw a turnaround in the balance of payments and a lot of expenses down the line, and just bailed out. Building roads and schools and hospitals and dams and ports, or putting in systems for water and sewerage and telephones and telegraphs and electricity: it all costs money. It also requires the importation of machines and materials from the Western countries, whose leaders would rather accept payment or extend credit in pounds and marks and francs and dollars and other types of foreign exchange than pay for these improvements from their own budgets. In that sense, granting independence was the final colonial trick. The unfortunate problem was that the British had not really concerned themselves too much with preparing the Gold Coast to be a well-balanced producer capable of sustaining its own market. When the oceans were a British lake and destined to remain so, the wise rulers saw no harm in economic specialization, and thus Ghana depended on exporting cocoa for two-thirds of its foreign exchange. The new Republic of Ghana needed some of its profits to reinvest in the unfinished projects of modernization, and it wanted to diversify its economy in order to produce at least some of the goods it was importing for consumption, too. Some of these goods may have been fancy, but most of them were really simple things like soap and matches and candles and tomato paste. The new nation had what seemed like but really wasn't a lot of money saved up; it spent the money quickly

1. This celebrated case of economic initiative was documented in the work of Polly Hill, *The Gold Coast Cocoa Farmer* (London: Oxford University Press, 1956) and *The Migrant Cocoa-Farmers of Southern Ghana* (Cambridge: Cambridge University Press, 1963).

on infrastructure and factories and other things it needed, but the money was not enough. And cocoa could not finish the job.

Despite the continuing efforts of the Ghanaian government and other Third World producers of cocoa, even up to now the Western countries have never been able to maintain an agreement to help stabilize the price of cocoa, as we have many other commodities. I really have no idea what we tell their trade delegations. How crucial to our well-being is cheap chocolate? Maybe our speculative commodities markets need at least a few wild performers for the benefit of high rollers and their brokers. At any rate, gradually, from the late 1960s to the 1980s, the Ghanaian economy slid downhill. Ghana would borrow money and then be forced to sell future cocoa low in the volatile world market. Foreign exchange would become short. Ghana would be forced to borrow more money at higher rates of interest, but always too little and too late. Insect pests invaded the cocoa plantations: no money for insecticides. Oil prices doubled: no money to import gasoline or diesel fuel for transport. The cocoa was harvested and rotting because so many trucks were off the road: no money for spare parts. The trucks in service were breaking down at an alarming rate because of rough roads: no money for road repairs. Return to "no money for spare parts"; do not pass "Go." Ghana watched its cocoa production fall from nearly a half-million tons a year to well less than half of that. Foreign exchange went from short to scarce, and the local currency became worthless outside of the country. To keep the people at the minimal standard that had been established, the government continued trying to control prices and subsidize essential commodities, but less and less can never be more and more. Inflation ran wild, more than 100 percent a year. Prices increased from day to day. No one could save money, since tomorrow the money would be worth less than today. Whatever you had, you should spend it immediately. Because of shortages and inflation, traders were hoarding. Your money was not enough to buy something; you had to know somebody and be able to beg nicely as well. People who could afford it tried to buy commodities in quantity in anticipation of fluctuating shortages, and added to the problem.

The government should probably have devalued its money, but the move was difficult to think about. Since it would take more local currency to buy each unit of foreign exchange, the result would be inflation and increased cost for repaying its loans. Also, in a proudly emergent nation, devaluing your money is like admitting the failure of your policies and in Ghana was almost a prescription for a military coup. The soldiers took over in 1972 and, as they usually do, made everything worse. People used to say that the military government of General I. K. Acheampong was not so bad because the soldiers were not going around shooting people, but no one has calculated how many people died because so much was stolen and misspent that the government could not import many basic medicines or maintain many healthcare programs. When the soldiers took over, there was a very modest black market in currency. In the mid-1960s, Ghana had left the sterling zone and introduced the cedi, which was supposed to be roughly equivalent to a U.S. dollar. By the early 1980s, the official rate of the Ghanaian cedi was down to 2.75 per U.S. dollar, but on the black market a single dollar was fetching eighty cedis, then one hundred cedis, 130 cedis, and up, while the official rate remained unchanged. The overvaluation bred incredible corruption. If you could get something that the government imported at the controlled price, which was pegged to the official rate of exchange, you would be paying a fraction of the world market price. Carry it across the border to Togo or Côte d'Ivoire, greasing your way past police and border guard roadblocks, and you could make a handsome profit almost giving it away. You could sell it above the controlled price in Ghana if you made payoffs or sold it only to someone you knew. The soldiers would go around and confiscate hoarded goods; somehow, to no one's surprise, the wives of soldiers became the most successful traders in the country. Capitalism went mad. A lot of things just disappeared, and people were faced with the strange predicament of having money in their pockets and nothing to buy. And as for cocoa, since the government-operated Cocoa Marketing Board was paying in overvalued cedis and trying to squeeze a little extra for the country's own capital-investment needs, those enterprising Ghanaian farmers simply smuggled the cocoa out, too. There are no reliable figures, but a fantastic percentage of Ghana's cocoa was sold in Côte d'Ivoire and Togo. Ghana became one of the poorer countries of Africa. From a model colony in a storybook history of orderly Westernization, Ghana became a symbol of disorder, even to its neighbors. And now, the current observers are busy revising their predecessors' observations to demonstrate that the seeds of this deterioration were there all along, hidden in the apparent order. And while some talk about global systems, others talk of development in terms of decentralization, that is, smaller systems, and what they call "appropriate" technology.

Our heroine was somewhere inside the demographic statistics that issued from this process. Hawa's father was a national of Burkina Faso, which was known as Upper Volta between 1947 and 1984. He had come to Ghana for a better life working in the cocoa farms. Hawa herself grew up in Kumasi, capital of the Ashanti region, with none to praise her and few to love her. Later, she moved to Accra, and from Accra she went to stay in a provincial capital where she associated with some of the British hangers-on who had remained in Ghana after independence to help the fledgling country maintain its educational system and perhaps to avoid having to leave their bungalows and their stewards to return to a lower-middle-class life. When Ghana's economy began deteriorating in the early 1970s, she left Ghana for the neighboring Republic of Togo. In fact, many Ghanaians left Ghana during the 1970s. Teachers and health care professionals and engineers went to Nigeria by the thousands, to the extent that it might be said that Ghana's principal export changed from cocoa to educated people. They were accompanied by hundreds and hundreds of thousands of their uneducated countrymen who sought work as laborers in Nigeria. These Ghanaians attracted international attention in early 1983 when nearly a couple million of them were summarily sent home by the Nigerian government. Had Hawa gone to Nigeria, she might have been a face in that crowd. But as it turned out, the expatriate life in Togo was difficult enough. The Ghanaians in Togo had quickly aroused the xenophobia of the Togolese people, and she was caught up in that. After just a few years in Togo, she left that country, passed back through Ghana and went north to her native homeland of Burkina Faso in the mid-1970s. I mention all this background because little or none of it appears in the stories that follow. As far as Hawa thought about it, it was just that Ghana was spoiled, and she left Ghana for a better life, just as her father had long before gone there to find one for himself and his family.

As for Burkina Faso and Togo, two of this book's other settings, there was no decline from what had been because very little had ever been there in the first place. During the late-nineteenth-century rush to parcel out Africa among the European powers, these two countries were places where one wanted to be just so that someone else wouldn't be there. Burkina Faso was part of the vast area that France controlled. Togo was a narrow corridor through which the Germans pushed inland. After the First World War, France took over Togo from Germany, and both countries were within the French sphere. Burkina Faso was not ultimately constituted as its own place until 1947; before that it was an administrative extension of other parts of French West Africa. Both countries were really colonized almost as an afterthought. The colonial story was mainly one of the French building roads with forced labor and trying to administer taxes. They did well with the roads, as they always do. Today Togo exports phosphates and welcomes tourists. The people of Burkina Faso farm and raise livestock; the country has a few minerals.

One advantage of colonialism for the French was that a lot of French people could spill out of France and live in the colonies. Togo and Burkina Faso attracted a small percentage of those prototypes of sophistication whose hearts and minds and alimentary systems and gonads will forever recall *la belle France,* but whose children are known as *pieds-noirs* to indicate the contribution of the colonies to their aggregate bodily make-up. For the Africans, being a former French colony has several advantages that make the French look like good guys, chief among them the fact that the French franc (and now the euro) stood behind the currency. The trappings of a consumer society are everywhere. All the goods in these places are available at New York prices or slightly higher. In the 1970s, things seemed much better than in a place like Ghana. At night in the towns, the hum of the mosquitoes has been replaced by the buzz of the motorized bicycles. But all the French ever wanted from their colonized societies were a few good native Frenchmen to run the place. The countries are still poor. In the mid-1970s, when Hawa left Ghana for the French zone, the per capita income of Togo was less than $200 a year, and that of Burkina Faso was less than $100; during that time, in West African countries, annual growth of the gross national product on a per capita basis was less than 1 percent a year. Annual per capita income is less than $400 a year in Togo, $200 in Burkina Faso, and those paltry sums are very, very, very unevenly distributed.[1] The statistics are almost impossible to comprehend and are probably off-base somewhere. Don't go there with a few hundred dollars in your pocket and expect to live for a year. Maybe the majority of the people do most of their work without getting any money for it or telling anybody about it. They farm and harvest their crops and eat them. When you leave the showcase hotels of the capitals via the beautiful roads, you see them in their villages. Who is buying anything?

The View from Ground Level

For most Americans, it is difficult to imagine the many ways in which individual destinies get left in the lurch of events in the Third World. As

1. The figures in the text are based on 1974 information from the U.S. Agency for International Development, also showing the per capita income of Ghana as less than $300, cited in *The World Almanac and Book of Facts 1976* (New York: Newspaper Enterprise Associates, 1976), 681–82; also from *The World Almanac and Book of Facts 1993* (New York: Newspaper Enterprise Associates, 1993), 738, 757, and 805. Current online estimates vary. The online "Background Notes" provided by the U.S. Department of State (www.state.gov/r/pa/ei/bgn) show figures for Togo ($320) and Ghana ($350) as of January 2002 and for Burkina Faso ($230) as of November 2001. The 2002 U.S. Central Intelligence Agency's World Factbook (www.odci.gov/cia/publications/factbook) shows per capita income in Burkina Faso, Togo, and Ghana as about $1,000, $1,500, and $2,000 respectively.

much as we complain about our system and as much as our American system needs to change, our system is at least functioning at a certain standard and with the means for change in place. It developed over centuries. At some points there was great suffering attached to its growth, including incredible systems of exploitation and a very bloody Civil War. Some of our great-great-grandparents dealt with such times. Some of our grandparents and great-grandparents cut themselves off from their roots, or were torn off and cast away, leaving everything behind. For much of America's history, too, there was a frontier to attract those who spilled over the margins of our raucous society; for Europe's modern history, there was America. But it's all history to most of us now, brought to life on movie and television screens. Students who study history in books are supposed to understand concepts and accept the inheritance of the past; like their forebears, most prefer to forget it or deny its relevance. For personal inspiration, we rely on dramatists to give excitement to history and flesh out its myths, though the message is frequently that we are lucky to be living now and not then. We're there somewhere in history, no doubt, probably as the people who acquiesced to the pollution of the planet, but our lives run so smoothly now that our stories seem undramatic. These days, the gut-wrenching dislocations are happening in the Third World. Television lets us see a face every once in a while, for a few seconds of pathos inside a two-minute report; then the journalist cuts back to a more panoramic view and dispenses a dose of statistics. Moviemakers won't touch the real stuff, though every now and then a serious film from the Third World plays the art theaters in major towns.

In the case of Africa, it's hard to get your hands on a good slice-of-life drama. To us, apart from the nostalgic fantasies and unreal dreams of the Hollywood mentality, what's happening in Africa is all part of a distant history. The history of Africa as we see it now is a drama that occurs on the level of international processes and the efforts of the leaders and the powerful to participate in them. Not knowing the people who are struggling with the epic's day-to-day reality, we pay attention only when a situation reaches historic proportions, that is, through war or famine or pestilence. Such problems become global when they threaten the stability of nations, the diplomatic balance of power, or the flow of goods and essential commodities in the world economy. As far away and as poor as Africa is, such times are relatively few, and our own information brokers take care not to exceed a certain minimally defined attention span: a few statistics and some graphic images for three to five weeks, and then the whole problem disappears from our newscasts. If we had relatives in these countries, as we do for Poland and Ireland; if we saw the faces of the refugees, as we do for Central America and Southeast Asia; if there were large amounts of our national budget that needed justification, as for anything formerly raising the specter of Russia or currently raising the specter of terrorism; if the prices of our cameras and cars and sound systems and computers were at stake, as for Japan and Korea; if they were producing illegal drugs, if they were protesting our military bases or threatening our investments, if — only when our lives are affected do we want to know about the people whose actions force us to take them into account. Most of Africa does not have that kind of clout, and consequently we don't know much about it.

Indeed, the names of the towns and even the countries where the action in this book takes place are not in the common knowledge of most people in America. A lot of high-school students don't even know when the Civil War was fought or where Mexico is; we wouldn't dare ask them anything about Côte d'Ivoire. As for college-educated people, they may have heard of Ghana and Nigeria but not of Togo or Burkina Faso; they may know of Accra, Lagos, and Abidjan, but not of capitals like Ouagadougou (Wah'-gah-du'-gu — many people even laugh when they try to say it), Lomé, or Cotonou, and almost certainly not of towns like Kumasi, Tamale (Tah'-mah-lee), Bobo-Dioulasso, Banfora, Kpalimé, or Bolgatanga. Hawa's stories take you to such places and into people's lives in a way that statistics and analysis cannot. If we can see some real people who are caught up in the historical drama and represented by the statistics, we have a chance to relate to what is happening, not through statistics but through sympathy. That is why the strategy of this book is to focus on people's experiences. Hawa focuses on people's small problems and how they deal with them, recalling their conversations and their actions. For her and her counterplayers, the statistics are meaningless. What matters is getting by.

To an extent, moreover, the statistics are meaningless without the stories of the people. The people are the flesh and blood of our statistics and those broad social perspectives we love to discuss. The statistics and the analytic concepts we use to describe people's situations purport to represent their reality, but the standards by which we measure things hold assumptions about the relevance in their lives of different factors they do not necessarily consider. It is normal to claim that life histories help us understand history, as if stories of people are an adjunct to a history that is already clearly formulated. But how can we feel that we know what any historical period was like? With particular regard to the Third World, where different versions of history so frequently compete, we cannot easily move back and forth between an individual situation and its historical ground because nobody is really quite sure about what the latter is like. In such contexts, it seems almost an obligation to work from the experience of individuals to see the kind of world they inhabit.

We don't hear Hawa's voice in the accounts of the educated elites of her country or ours, but her stories add a human dimension to those accounts and perhaps represent another reality and another stage for drama and action. She is a good character to sit with us at the table of knowledge where we partake of reports and studies and other literary fare. In this book we will share her and her associates' perception of their historical situation and what they have to do about it. In the big picture, where history and money are being made, they are apart and away from the centers of power, out of it, utterly and thoroughly. The prefix "dis-," which dictionaries say means all of the above, attaches to their names with appalling reliability: disenfranchised and disadvantaged, disaffiliated and disinherited, discomfited and discredited, displaced and discarded, discussed and discounted, dispossessed and dismissed.[1] This book is the testimony of one person who is all of the above. Hawa is there among the people, fighting for herself and her family and her friends. But this book is not about her alone. She is unique and in many ways not typical, but there are many, many people like her, each with his or her own unique story. This book, the testimony of one, is a testimony to all of them.

These are the people who are last in line, those without the opportunity to participate in the universal grabbing. They have no choice but to manage with patience. Despite the chicanery at every turn, they hold strongly to a fragile fabric of social decency. Their approach to life is characterized by every type of exploitation but also every type of altruistic kindness. How else can one account for the survival of the common people? No economist has ever figured out how they make it from day to day. The per diem allowance deemed appropriate by the U.S. Department of State is several times the monthly wage of a well-employed worker, and more than half the people in a city like Accra are unemployed. It is a situation that would turn us into gunslingers, and instead, people somehow hang together and get by. The society may be disorganized, but the people are not in disorder. Under pressure from modern life, the old strengths of the traditional societies continue to support the social vessel. The extended family offers shelter to the castaways, and the mentality of the extended family reaches into the urban scene where people from different ethnic groups call each other "brother" and "sister." The traditional ethic of redistribution ensures that if there is little money to begin with, then at least the money that is there will move at an incredible velocity. Sharing is everywhere — sharing a room, sharing one's clothes, sharing food, sharing a cigarette, sharing a laugh, sharing a

1. I drafted this section of the introduction before the prefix became a well-known word in American slang, meaning "to disrespect," as in the expression, "Don't dis me," and that one fits, too.

moment in the evening breeze. Under the pressures of modern living at its worst, the inherited values of the people do not break, though they often bend.

In their own way these people can be seen as making history. The people in this book are denied the luxury of thinking about the broad sweep of historical processes. Their historical location is a continuous life crisis fraught daily with opportunities and difficulties; their decisions and attitudes are crucial to the quality of their lives, and they are the first to experience the validity or inadequacy of the values they bring to their social behavior. Hawa's stories are about survival and dignity, the antipodal elements of compromise. Her stories tell much about the life of young people in African cities and about the reasons why they run away from the traditional lifestyles of their families. Problematic status values, potentials for verbal and physical abuse, economic constraints, exploitation of labor and political powerlessness, human failings, the dilemmas of sickness and death: all these are the negative stuff of life both in traditional and in urban or modern systems. Erik Erikson, one of our leading thinkers on the relationship between history and psychological life, has written that people make history by acquiring and providing "a conception of truth in action."[1] To them, truth is what gives them strength as they challenge or come to terms with the limitations and possibilities of their situation. The millions of small decisions they make every day balance the big decisions by which we normally chart historical movement. The "dis" people have their views of the realities they face. They participate in those realities as they see them, becoming a part of them and shaping them according to their values.

How does knowing the people add to our sense of a history that seems to exclude them? What do the values at ground level have to do with the institutions of change? We ourselves view our cherished institutions as a reflection of our basic values, of course, but in the Third World, the institutions of Westernization were imposed by the designs of foreigners. Students of social change in the Third World originally assumed that broad historical trends would have an irresistible impact on indigenous people and traditional societies, often through gradual processes of assimilation and adaptation but occasionally through radical intervention, and we have seen much of that happen. The workings of Western institutions in West African nations have therefore often been perceived in terms of conflict between competing social systems and the networks of values, ideas, and meaning

1. Erik H. Erikson, "Psychological Reality and Historical Actuality," in *Insight and Responsibility: Lectures on the Ethical Implications of Psychoanalytic Insight* (New York: W. W. Norton, 1964), 205.

that surround them. Despite the obvious changes, however, it is not clear that Western role models and social expectations have penetrated into the hearts and minds of the people to any significant extent, and it is not even clear that Western role models have penetrated much into the very institutions of Westernization like the bureaucracies or the police. It was always evident that the institutions of the family and religion would be only somewhat affected by the changes of modernization and that they would continue to function with significant input from their traditional forms. It was assumed as well that traditional systems of exchange would function side by side with more modern forms. But for some time it has been suspected that even the Western institutions that were laid on top of the traditional systems, like the bureaucracies, were somehow partaking of "African" qualities and modes of functioning, though that suspicion was difficult to characterize and the extent of upward penetration was difficult to determine.

During the seven years I lived in Ghana, I often noted, in the many discussions about working conditions I had with expatriate Western colleagues, civil servants, development workers, and business folk, that there was often a lack of fit between expectations and events when such people dealt with administrative or bureaucratic problems. Standard literature on modernization offered little help in dealing with the frustrating interactional complexities of such encounters, a skill with which newcomers were almost invariably unendowed and which the older hands asserted could only be acquired as a matter of feeling and experience. In contrast, local people, whether or not they were successful in solving their individual problems, often seemed to have a very clear idea of the ground rules and necessary strategies for handling or pursuing similar matters. In many ways, it was acknowledged that the institutions of Westernization were functioning on well-established patterns grounded to a great extent on shared assumptions, and these assumptions were based on local, indigenous models of behavior; it seemed that the people who encountered each other in such contexts had redefined or modified indigenous roles to function within these bureaucratic institutions. When Hawa goes through gyrations just to get an identity card, or when she describes the ways of the police, among other examples, instead of watching her learn the ropes of assimilation, we seem to be getting a number of good looks at local customs. There should be nothing surprising about something like that, of course. We know already that many of our own institutions do not work according to their own rationales; what goes on in the nitty-gritty of the offices often has little to do with what an organization is supposed to be about. In a place like West Africa, where these institutions have been placed or forced on top of traditional societies, there is an added dimension with which only the old hands and the locals are familiar — interaction and values based on feelings and experience, that is, the realm of culture.

"Culture" is a very vague and plastic concept that refers to something we only see in bits and pieces, and that is why one cannot easily understand it by reading a manual. Who could even write the manual? Behind all of the development plans is the notion that significant aspects of culture can be operationalized, that there is a step-by-step program that can represent the workings of culture. So much of society is being organized around such algorithmic notions that many people assume that whatever does not fit can just be left out. But "culture" resembles "chaos" or "imagination," like a numinous idea that lets us know we don't have all the variables covered. One cannot pin it down, but one ignores it at one's risk. Although in some quarters, culture connotes symphonies and museums and poetry and other emblems of high spiritual attainment, for social scientists, culture's main connotations evoke ethos and character, referring us to the most basic feelings and experiences that people share when they are brought up within a particular way of living. Culture also lends a distinct tone and rhythm and style to the dynamics of interaction, and such qualities of people's lives are not easily categorized or compared. From the perspective of a person, social institutions merely articulate and display certain ideas that people have about themselves, about what it means to be a person and about how people should relate to one another. Institutions — political, religious, economic, kinship, and others — influence and instruct people in the ways of culture, but even when the institutions change, the fundamental features of a given culture somehow remain within its people and their means of communication. Historical changes can be dramatic in their appearance, but culture changes much more slowly and is somehow beyond the fray. The people retain their basic character throughout history, adapting their values to the changing historical scene and adapting history's new social forms to their values.

The process is so complex and difficult to comprehend that we usually can only talk about it by referring to examples. Indeed, the presence of culture on this level generally only becomes apparent when things that are supposed to be effective don't work. Sometimes it's a matter of limited resources, but quite often when efforts to change things fall short because "the people" lack understanding and commitment, the consequent grumbling is usually with reference to culture, to goals and values that the people do not believe in or share. The people are holding up the progress of the nation, but the people are the nation. How can we know about the type of understanding and commitment they bring to a situation? We can infer something about people's culture by looking at the institutions within which they live and work, but we cannot just look at those institutions and their official rationales and expect to understand their meaning to the people who are caught up inside them. We cannot just ask people, either. When people talk about their values, there is frequently a great deal of contradiction between what they say and what they do. Characterizing people's values is a risky enterprise that is usually conducted with inference and hindsight, and then one still must make a case, so to speak.

How appropriate for this book seems anthropologist Clifford Geertz's well-known phrase that a cultural form may be construed as "a story [people] tell themselves about themselves."[1] The values that preoccupy people's lives are like the major themes of a story. The sociologist Kai Erikson has suggested that these values are reflected in a range of responses arrayed along axes of variation, that cultural ethos is composed of the varied ways people respond to counterpointed but complementary tendencies, and that a given culture can be conceived "as a kind of theater in which certain contrary tendencies are played out."[2] As such, culture is an ambiguous moral space marked by both decision and drift. In their daily lives, people refer to their values with varying degrees of self-consciousness, and yet somehow they make decisions on the basis of their sense of what is appropriate. Their experience gives them their own sense of values, or ethics, and that sense is the foundation of their culture as they express it in their lives. Sometimes what holds them together is only a minimal level of common decency that is their share of traditional lifeways. Yet that heritage guides their interaction with one another on the playing fields of the particular institutional setup of their historical time. In the idiom of the street, the culture is where they're coming from, not where they are.

To understand the workings of culture on that level, in terms of people's sense of values, we can seek assistance in stories that let us watch people in action and see what is happening to them personally. Those who wish simply to see the people clearly have only the problem of spending the time to get to know them. It's not a small problem, though. The educated elites seem to have little access to the experience of the people; those who claim to speak for the people or represent them often seem transparently self-serving. The more familiar we become with the masses as people, the more irrelevant sometimes seem the statistical and historical descriptions through which they are generally presented to us. As we enter their world

1. Clifford Geertz, *The Interpretation of Cultures* (New York: Basic Books, 1973), 448.

2. Kai T. Erikson, *Everything in Its Path: Destruction of Community in the Buffalo Creek Flood* (New York: Simon and Schuster, 1976), 79–84.

more deeply, what recedes into the distance is not our ability to relate to them or understand them or judge them or accept them in human or personal terms; rather, what recedes is the shared conceptual toolbox that is applied and focused in the detached perspectives of observers, in the political ideologies of the powerful, in the economic plans of the money-makers, in the telephoto lenses of the journalists and social critics. That distance, the lack of fit between how things are supposed to work and how things actually work, the lack of fit between the official stories and the stories in this book, is a problem for those latter groups who are charged with making the stories conform. That distance has its own objectivity in the fact that most of what happens is beyond their reach. That fact links the perception that our social plans are shallow with a feeling that the metaphors of our understanding are a bunch of garbled babble.

In modern Africa, the people who are supposed to buy the stories of the elite are a diverse group caught up in the malfunctions and inequities and disorder of society. They are supposed to be in-between and are expected to choose. But what seem to be choices are not at all clear-cut. Instead of having a choice of either/or, people end up with neither/nor. They may be living in a city or working in the one of the political or economic institutions of the modern setup. When the system comes up short, the necessities and amenities formerly produced in the traditional way are not available. Neither is it feasible to ask people to go backwards. They cannot easily gear up to make soap out of plantain skins or lamp oil out of plant seeds. The factory is merely waiting for raw materials, and the ship is in port. They have forgotten how to grind their grains into flour on a stone. Faced with a shortage of flour, what would you do? Would you spend a couple of hours going around to look for it, or would you do without and find something else to cook? And if there were no rice or no yams? Even in the countryside, the farmers' children are in school and have no time to collect animal droppings for fertilizer. Would you keep your child out of school or accept a lower yield and then not be able to pay school fees? If the water pipe is broken, would you carry an extra bucket on your head from the pipe that works in the next neighborhood, would you keep a child out of school to carry water for the household, would you try to manage with less water, or would you sacrifice something and use some of your limited money to pay the person who comes around to fill your water-storage pot? At ground level, people are not in-between systems and choosing; they are inside a shifting maze of contingencies.

There is a word social scientists use to describe the kind of people you will meet in this book: marginal people. It is an interesting concept, but how can a person be described as marginal? A margin, the dictionary says, is a border or edge, something available beyond what is necessary, a limit or condition beyond which something ceases to exist or be possible. Despite the connotations, sociologists use the term to refer to people who live outside the mainstream or who live on the margins between social groups and hold allegiance to neither.[1] This technical use of the term is another piece of odd imagery, as if societies exist on flat pieces of paper and the mind of a person were a two-dimensional reflection. The term makes more sense in an unflattering way if we think about such expressions as the "boundaries" of taste or propriety, and then we locate marginal people beyond such boundaries. Whatever, for years marginal people have been a major attraction to social researchers. The idea behind the attraction, and one of the few generalizations that can be made about marginal people, is that because of their alienation, many of them develop a kind of sociological objectivity. Many marginal people are experts at recognizing variations in social settings, and they become extremely conscious about what is appropriate behavior according to the different rules of various situations. They are generally self-conscious about fundamental levels of social negotiation, generally aware of conflicting points of view and differing expectations as they move from one type of setting to another. Their designation as "marginal" implies that such is their experience or their interest. In all of this, they are somewhat like social scientists if one takes the view that most people apart from outsiders and social scientists do not have to pay overt attention to the unspoken rules of conduct that social scientists call the norms of behavior.

There is quite a bit of justification for looking at people who are "outside" of the system. Émile Durkheim, in his classical works,[2] even made the point that societies depend on various means like criminal trials and other types of proceedings to make deviance from group norms visible in order to help establish a consensus on what is and is not appropriate and acceptable. Although a rather peculiar perspective on the face of it, the point makes a lot of sense. Hawa certainly provokes some of that discrimination. Social scientists are attracted to outsiders and marginal people because such

1. Leo Spitzer, in his *Lives in Between: Assimilation and Marginality in Austria, Brazil, West Africa, 1780–1945* (Cambridge: Cambridge University Press, 1989), argues that the use of the term marginal as an analytic construct should be limited to people who orient themselves toward acculturation and assimilation into other levels of prevailing social hierarchies. To be marginal in that sense, the people in this book would have to be seen as seeking mobility through relationships based on other models than those customarily available.

2. Émile Durkheim, *Division of Labor,* and *The Rules of Sociological Method,* trans. S. A. Solovay and J. H. Mueller (1895; reprint, Glencoe, Ill.: Free Press, 1960).

people's lives take place in a realm where norms and their limits are often highlighted. Marginal people are of special interest when their lives or occupations are such that they move among various social groups in different social realms, when they live in a floating world of commercial and emotional transactions that take them into social domains that are inaccessible to other members of their class. We might assume that marginal people in Africa are particularly well informed about points of breakdown, weakness, and ineffectiveness in the institutions of competing systems. We might assume that the experience of the people in this book, who do not fit into traditional or modern systems, can tell us something about the kind of influence each exerts.

At a certain point, however, the notion of marginality breaks down. If self-consciousness and alienation are part of the human condition, perhaps we are all marginal to an extent. But a normal Westerner's situation is nothing compared to that of the "dis" people in Africa. Although they can be seen as in-between the competing realms of tradition and modernity, they are so out of it that they seem attached to neither. Their lives take place in what economists and social planners call the "informal" sector, which means that the statistics are hard to get and even harder to plug into the "formal" models of social functioning we have of both modern and traditional systems. Moreover, we would expect that being caught in the middle of conflicting values and always having to decide how to act would create a lot of anxiety and lead to confusion about one's identity. The social settings Hawa portrays are so diverse that it is never clear just who is outside of what.

Most of the "dis" people in this book, however, are extremely well centered, particularly our heroine Hawa, who reads the expectations of others, plays roles, mediates the disparate lifestyles of her pluralistic social environment, and still manages to manifest a sense of self within a number of social settings. Perhaps she has greater abilities than some of her associates in this regard, but she is like many young Africans who are not cut out for modern institutions and who at the same time are totally cut off from traditional supports. The situation should be debilitating and demoralizing to the people. But instead of being hung up between the two worlds, not knowing which way to go, they don't seem to give a damn. In a way, that is what is best about them, for it cheers them up. They know that they are on their own, that their hope is the very unpredictability of life's game, and that their strength is their adaptability and resourcefulness and perseverance. When the alienation of a significant number of people reaches such a point, social scientists are apt to use the word "sub-culture" to refer to the somewhat self-contained values and feelings that characterize what certain special groups of people hold in common. But there are very many people like those in this book, perhaps even a majority, and they do not isolate themselves or draw their own boundaries the way most people in sub-cultures do. Perhaps they are rather the typical people of West Africa, and the modernists and the traditionalists are the marginal people, the people whose dress distinguishes them at what is basically an informal gathering where disorder as usual is the wellspring of comedy.

If you want to see culture in Africa, you have to see it in the life of the everyday people. Once when I was planning to travel to Ouagadougou, I wondered aloud to a Canadian friend why I should even go, and he just said, "Well, people live there." We laughed at the weakness of the reason, but I went anyway. As usual, the people were worth a visit. To me, the people I met in West Africa were the best reason for the years I spent there, but they are very difficult to find in books or other media. In Africa there are only a few places where you can be a tourist and see culture in its monuments, and there are only certain occasions when you can see culture in its ceremonial manifestations. People on two-week trips try their best, but they fail. Asked about their trip, they are likely to talk rather about people they encountered. I spent part of my time in Ghana studying a traditional culture among a very thoughtful and conservative group of people in the north, and it was an inspiring and beautiful experience. But during the other part, I was hanging out in towns and cities like Accra and Tema and Lomé and Ouagadougou.

The young people I knew in those towns also spent a lot of time thinking about culture. Like Hawa, even when they were scrambling and looking to hook up, they typically sorted through their alienation with reference to concepts of how people should live together. They had an idea about a culture and a community to which they would wish to belong, and they tried to relate to such idealizations. They were even energized by that sense of themselves. In their perspective, there was little doubt that they were both modern and African in their living. They were more modern than the leaders, administrators, and other big people whom the youth somehow thought of as old-fashioned. There was likewise little doubt that they were the bona fide representatives of a truly African lifestyle. They gave respect to their parents and elders who lived within indigenous customs, but they thought of them as somehow mistaking the trees for the forest, occasionally missing the essence of their culture, in a sense, by being too caught up in its trappings. The older people were certainly typical of Africa, and they could be cute or endearing because of that, but in the perspective of the youth, the old folks were often confused when it came to seeing how to adapt the spirit of their lifeways to the changing times. Young Africans have little loyalty to aspects of the past that will only hold them in the past. On the surface, they seem to be without culture, but in their view of being African, they were constantly engaging African culture by asking what is right and wrong. To them, that engagement was an exciting and interesting aspect of their lives.

Social scientists who work in traditional African societies often befriend older people as those who know their culture and preserve it, because older people have experience, knowledge, and judgment. But older people I met there told me that it is young people who make culture, because young people are the ones who start things, and when the young people become old, what was new becomes old with them. One reason for believing that the marginal young people are carrying on a culture that is genuine and not spurious is that they do not make a point of claiming cultural authenticity in any kind of ideological or exclusive way, but when they get into disagreements or when they discuss the direction of their lives, their self-justifications and their understanding of motivations tend to be moral and cultural rather than psychological and pragmatic. They argue their cases with an appeal to basic assumptions about what is correct or not correct in human relations, or with reference to how people could or should do things in Africa. From ground level, in my experience, their marginality is only experienced as their poverty and their lack of a basis for self-advancement. They take it in stride: everybody knows that life is a struggle if you're not lucky. They are outside of institutional supports, to be sure, but that only makes them more dependent on fundamental cultural resources and what they see as the will to be true to themselves.

Culture is something that exists as an ambiguous and abiding challenge to the individual. Looking at the nature of culture's challenge to the self provides one way to think about the differences between the traditionalists and the youth in this book. The views of culture held by the traditionalists and the urban youth I knew intersected and diverged at several interesting points. The youth are not against traditional lifestyles in the same way as the bureaucrats and educated people. Most of the young people in this book, and certainly Hawa, understand and get along well with traditionalists if they want. Their differences are often related to general differences between young people and older people, or parents and children, in their respective positions on life's path. For the traditionalists among whom I worked, culture lets you know your limits, and it requires a frequently difficult mustering of commitment and acceptance. For them, culture involves a type of respect that looks a bit like fear. There are shared sentiments and shared beliefs, but what is underneath all of it is an idea that there are certain things one just does not do. The older people often told me, "What is forbidden does not walk": nobody sees it; if you do it, it is waiting for you in the form of trouble, when "Had I known" is too late. Such an attitude is often characterized as superstitious, but the traditionalists were actually rather sophisticated about the way this fear worked, for they knew that there was an element of sham involved. They compared the secret binding power of tradition to the tricks one could use to frighten children: "I have something in my pocket. If you don't watch out, it will catch you." They extended the metaphor by saying that their tradition spoiled when the children realized there was nothing in the pocket. They said that was when society changed from "What will make our way of living good?" to "Pour it down and let's fight over it, and if you don't get it, it's your luck." At worst, people without tradition present an image of selfishness; in more sympathetic views, they are to be pitied because they have nothing in front of them or behind them, nothing to their left or right, and they are alone. Young people everywhere probably seem self-centered to their parents, and the urban youth in this book certainly seem to have left many of the old ways; therefore, the elders' characterization of the youth as alone is probably quite apt.

In contrast to the traditionalists, one of the first things Hawa told me when we started doing this book was that when she was a child, whenever she was standing at the edge of what was forbidden, whenever anyone told her that people don't do this or that, she wanted to do it and see what would happen. She struck a distinctly modern note with that statement, and in a way she was right to think like that in anticipation of the modern life she was already choosing. African urban youth, like her, are particularly sensitive to the fact that the integrity of traditional cultures does not exist in the modern world or its cities, where it's everyone for himself and God for all of us, where the definition of self-centeredness has to be understood in a different context. To an old-fashioned moralist, self-centeredness is the root of vices like pride and envy; in the modern world, however, many ethical thinkers represent the existential dilemma of the individual as the problem of becoming centered to withstand the confusing anomie of mass society and the sheepish conformity that bureaucracies and ideologies encourage. On the other side of traditional lifeways is the political and economic culture of nation states and multinational corporations, a culture that the young people in this book experience as a matter of rich and poor, the powerful and the victims.

Unable or unwilling to believe in traditional rationales, the young people have to find themselves in the urban mix of African cities, where the wisdom of traditional cultures does not easily reach, nor, by the same token, do the taboos. Even the traditionalists will tell you that one town's taboo does not catch the child of another town. The taboos don't travel like that. If you come to enter the place where the taboos exist, then you are there, and you should watch your step; if not, they won't come out and chase you. When the young people gather in the towns, they do not think of themselves as being "at home." They have to find the authority of culture not through some science of comparative taboos but through a broad humanism that is liberal and universalist, and through a search for a type of common spirit, philosophy, or élan that is grounded in their experience and can be used to establish both personal boundaries and communal fellowship. Their identities evolve from that. For the people in this book, like everyone else, the essence of culture consists in being true to oneself, and culture is both born and borne in that dilemma. But compared to the West, the margins of African societies are quite wide; the draft manuscript of the modern system is sometimes barely scribbled on the page; the cultural issues are all the more acute.

The evidence of culture is everywhere within this book. Culture has its issues and its problems that affect the decisions and inform the discussions of the many people who play their parts in this book's dramas, but it cannot be easily seen. Like the unconscious mind that is the source of personal motives, culture appears in unconventional ways, as if by choosing absurd crises it could elude detection and continue its work. When I was in graduate school, one of my professors who had held a post at a Nigerian university during the first days of that country's independence told me a funny anecdote. I did not ask about a way to check the sources, but the anecdote concerned a series of letters to the editor in a local newspaper. Someone wrote a letter to the effect that now we Nigerians are independent and we have to make sure that our children are well educated. In order to help them in their studies, we should all pitch in and see to it that the children get a lot of sleep so that they will be alert in school, and therefore, we should not allow people to make noise late at night by playing drums or talking loudly or blowing horns. The response was a barrage of irate letters that maintained that the children also have to know that they are Africans and know that Africa is their homeland, and the place wouldn't be Africa if it wasn't noisy.

Cities as the Heavens of This Earth

I must have become an African when I was there. The place I lived was just up the street from an outdoor nightclub where live bands played till the wee hours, and I was always able to sleep all right. I moved back and forth from the serious traditionalists who set the rhythms of my research to the cacophony of Accra without missing a beat. As much as I had managed to adapt my being to the spirit of an ancient culture, I never felt out of place in towns like Accra or Lagos. I enjoyed those towns as I have never been able to enjoy American and European ones. The difference is the kaleidoscopic assortment of people who mingle there, as varied a group as one could imagine for any cosmopolitan place, but who seem to mix together more than in our type of atomized social world. I would meet more new people in a few days in Accra than I might meet in a year in the States, and then I would always be running into them because all of us were out of our dingy rooms and spending our waking hours in public places. Some people were going with the flow for fun and experience, and some were making contacts for survival. I met them easily because both conditions fostered a type of ambience that focused on sociability to an amazing extent. In a small bar, for example, someone entering will go around the tables and greet everybody else, "Good evening." This attitude comes straight from traditional lifestyles; in any village, one says good morning, good afternoon, or good evening to everyone one passes. In the cities, if you are walking down the street casually looking at someone, when you get to the point where normally you might avert your eyes, you'll see the person looking back at you, smiling, and nodding a greeting when he or she passes. People shake hands when they meet and hold hands when they walk together. They gravitate toward other people, and I remember being fascinated by that aspect of city life. I sometimes tested it in crowded places by staring at someone far across a room, and sure enough, that person would look up from the conversation and return my gaze. It was as if a physical network of tendrils connected the people who gathered anywhere.

Many of the people I knew were young like me. During my first year in Ghana, I was a graduate student who thought he had read enough books already and decided to drop out of the grind while he was there. At that time and place in my life, everything was data. Most of my friends in Accra were just trying to make do in the urban environment, usually because they either could not or would not fit into the more traditional lifestyles of their parents in the villages. They mixed peacefully despite their differences. They came from different ethnic groups and had grown up speaking different languages. They were of different ages and had different levels of education. The types of work they were able to do, if anything, were different and changing. Some were born in the city, but others had left their villages and provincial towns where the yoke of tradition was too heavy. They were struggling and suffering but I could understand their choice. They were people who refused to be peasant farmers or somebody's third wife. The attractions of a city can never be minimized when one considers the alternatives. If I knew I was probably going to be broke all my life, I'd rather live my life somewhere closer to the center of the action. Accra was their New World, their Yukon, their California. Like our ancestors leaving their original homelands for America or, once here, leaving for the frontier, many were misfits, many were seekers, many were free spirits. Most of the young people I knew were without jobs and without education or any means of self-advancement, but they felt little bitterness. They were open toward each other, perhaps because they had to be, as a cynical observer might say, but probably because they enjoyed being that way — always ready to get together and get something going. Their motto, painted in two parts on the front and back of busses and taxis, was "Observers are Worried; Believers are Enjoying." They were ready to believe in anything that would connect them with each other and with life on the rest of the planet, interested in anything new, anything "pop," anything "free," anything they called "Afro," which was their way of talking about the unique style they brought to the experience of it all. The main thing they had in common was their ability to get with what was happening at the moment and see themselves inside it, and that ability was enough to hold them together, at least until tomorrow, and they had a motto for that, too: "Who Knows Tomorrow?" The ambience of Accra and the West African towns and cities I know was well summed up in the words of an African American friend: "Lotta freaks, lotta fun."

In previous writings, I have described West African towns a number of times and a number of ways. One idea that always seems to help people recognize the kind of places these towns are is the observation that Charles Dickens would have felt at home in a place like Accra or Lagos. People create their own opportunities, like a jack-of-all-trades who can fix anything. Everyone has to find a way to survive, and the disorder of development provides the openings. A blacksmith can fashion bicycle peddles from recycled scrap or build hunting rifles from tubing, and a village hunter I knew used match scrapings to fire his gun. A motorcycle mechanic doesn't have a diaphragm for a carburetor: "No problem," he says, "it doesn't need it. The bike will run all right. They just put this thing inside so it will spoil and you will buy a new one." Need some cheap sandals? In the market, you can get sandals made from tire treads cut to shape, with rubber cross-straps fixed in place with bent nails. Ghanaians call them "Afro-Moses": the "Afro" refers to the locally gerrymandered solution and makes a joke on the poverty behind it; the allusion to Moses means that the sandals are guaranteed for forty years in the urban wilderness or forty thousand miles, whichever comes first. People need the guarantee: the Pidgin English expression "waka-waka" is used even in French countries to refer to the walking people do when going about dealing with their business. For the multitudes who do not see the benefits of the one-time investment in a pair of Afro-Moses and who prefer cheap disposables, there are people who actually make a living charging a few pennies for repairing rubber flip-flops. Africa: land of somehow. On a major road leading from downtown Accra to the suburbs, a young man is filling the potholes with gravel and sand; standing beside him is a sign that reads, "One-man contractor; donations accepted." Near the town center are letter writers with their old typewriters. Tailors and seamstresses who cannot afford their own kiosk carry their sewing machines on their heads giving door-to-door service. Runaway children push hand trucks at the stations. Even outside the markets, everywhere there are people who have something to sell, sometimes only one obscure thing, which they hold in their hands or place on a small table. Those not so fortunate hang around busy places, some waiting for an opportunity to carry something or clean something, others waiting for someone to beg.

It's urban poverty in action. Some readers may find that the stories in this book make them sad because of the way poverty messes up peoples' lives. On the other hand, some readers might be oddly disturbed by the way people in this book spend money. You may not get a feeling of poverty from these people, and in many ways they do not seem to be poor or obsessed with poverty. Yet you see their poverty from time to time, as when Hawa does not have forty cents for medicine, or when buying a bucket and a few pots is something to be shared among friends. Have you ever had to pack up your house recently? What the young people in this book own can usually fit into a large suitcase. It is important to understand that poverty is a factor somewhere behind everything that happens in this book, influencing the smallest details as well as the whole, but it is also important not to allow the effects of poverty to overwhelm your perception of where the people are coming from. You should understand their poverty as they do. They know they're poor: to them poverty is something like a sickness that imposes troubles and pressures. It is difficult for poor people to make long-range plans, and they take their problems and their pleasures from day to day, and in that regard they resemble old people as well as sick people. Because of their poverty, too, they have to do all kinds of extra things and take many extra steps to achieve a goal. Even your best Marxists sometimes have no patience to appreciate how much poor people have to do to get something together.

Poverty is about what is not there, and poor people are aware of what they do not have; when they walk into someone's room, they notice what is inside. They are aware of what they need to make their lives easier: anything cool. Poverty is hot like a fever, and everybody would like to be cool, that is, moving comfortably and without worries. In the West African idiom, when someone is "hot," it doesn't refer to being popular or on a roll; it can refer to being annoyed or serious or worried, but also when someone says, "I'm hot," he means he's broke. Yet if poverty is like a sickness, poverty is something that people deal with in different ways. Some people dwell on it and think only about it; some people ignore it and act as if they don't know they're poor; some people suffer quietly and take its problems unto themselves; some people react against it and try to collect damages from anyone and everyone. If you're a stranger among them, when they see you walking down the street, some of them are hoping that you're having a good time and will speak well of their scene, and some are watching your movements and wondering whether you need help. Although some are seeing you and thinking about food, most poor people in Africa harbor not ill will and jealousy but rather appreciation of your good fortune. A few may try to get their share by hook or by crook, though without being especially malicious. True bitterness and hostility reside within the ideological preserve of some of their educated or indoctrinated compatriots. In this book, the characters deal with their poverty on a case-by-case basis. It's always there and it's always bad by definition, and it makes them do some things that might upset some readers, but it doesn't always have the same meaning to the different people in the stories. It's a given, just a fact of life.

In the 1960s, the anthropologist Oscar Lewis wrote about what he called "the culture of poverty" as a common element of peasant and working-class life in much of the world.[1] He was trying to make the point that poverty affects people's lives so much that it overwhelms the cultural resources of a place; it determines so much of people's lives that it exhibits many of the characteristics of culture, even to the point that it instills lifeways and values that keep its victims and their children inside it in a vicious cycle. The notion of a culture of poverty was much debated and criticized, but a more interesting thing happened to Lewis's work. Lewis illustrated his ideas in the form of detailed life histories that depicted a number of Mexican and Puerto Rican poor people, and although the significance of poverty was evident throughout their stories, the magnificent spirit of these people showed through and caught the imagination of a large readership. The people in this book might not strike the same chords, but like the people in Lewis's books, they cannot be understood primarily in terms of their poverty.

1. Oscar Lewis, *The Children of Sanchez: An Autobiography of a Mexican Family* (New York: Random House, 1961), *Pedro Martinez: A Mexican Peasant and His Family* (New York: Random House, 1964), *La Vida: A Puerto Rican Family in the Culture of Poverty—San Juan and New York* (New York: Random House, 1965).

One thing that can be said about poor people in general is that they do not like to have someone's idea of poverty interfere with their idea of themselves as human beings. They know what's not there but they also deal with what's there. If you find yourself focusing too much on what's not there, remember that electricity and flushing toilets and supermarkets are recent inventions that even the rich and royal people of old did without, and no one makes much of that or calls them poor. What poor people in Africa don't want is a person who feels that he or she is better than others, who tries to show himself to be above them or who separates himself from them or who presses down on them. Most do not mind seeing a rich or powerful person if they have even a slight hope that they might have access to consumables or resources. Therefore, to be fair, we should consider the proposition that people who do not pity themselves for their poverty should also be exempt from our pity. What they have to do or think they have to do to survive is often lamentable, but to them, many of the consequences of their poverty are not sad but funny. Given the amount of attention they have to give their poverty, they have quite a few ways of dealing with it, and one of the more successful strategies in their repertoire of responses is to become very adept at laughing it off. They're not about to let their poverty spoil their life completely. Poverty, like any kind of problem, brings out the best and the worst in people. Poor people can be selfish, petty, and jealous about their lack of means, but poor people are often the world's most generous, and many of them don't mind spending their last penny to help a friend or to enhance a moment.

While I was with them, I was a believer and not an observer. I went along with the positive view, and I enjoyed the benefits of being positive. During my first year in Ghana, 1970–71, before I moved into town, I lived at the University of Ghana, seven miles outside Accra. I felt I had read enough of the books that were on the curriculum, and when I was not away in other towns and villages doing research into "culture," Accra was a place to have fun. My routine was to hang around the Institute of African Studies in the mornings, talking to colleagues and friends, or to relax in my dormitory room reading or writing, then hitchhike to town in the early afternoon. Unless I had to buy something, I needed only about two or three dollars for the day, one dollar of which was reserved for a taxi back to campus in the small hours. Once in town, I had a general walking route that would take me through several areas, and I would visit friends and let the day develop any way it wanted. In the quick tropical transition from harsh daylight to evening, the images of dilapidation, repair, and construction softened and faded, but the pace of life abated only a few steps. In the evenings, the streets were full of traffic. The petty traders were everywhere, many selling food or tea. People were on their way to visit each other. People were sitting outside and playing draughts or conversing or watching the passing scene. Actually, I went to Ghana partly because of a conversation I had had with a Ghanaian who was living in the States. He described Accra evenings by saying that many people go out "to refresh their minds." The phrase intrigued me for a few weeks while I was deciding to go there and see how my mind might be refreshed by the scene.

After my daily strolls through the town, in the evening I usually ended up at one of the bars or nightclubs with resonant names like Lido or Tiptoe or Metropole or Apollo. These nightclubs were outdoors, with metal tables and chairs partially under a roofed area and arranged around an open cement dance floor. I had early on befriended the people who watched the gate at these places, and I entered free, though I often had to wait outside for the right time to enter. No problem. Outside the nightclubs was another convivial scene. There were a lot of people hanging around enjoying the outside view while listening to the sounds from inside. People with small tables sold everything from kebabs to cigarettes to aspirin, and people with kiosks sold locally distilled spirits. At that time, a full shot glass — a "tot" — cost about a nickel. Two tots in a tumbler was a normal quaff, taken at a gulp. I would be hanging, perhaps chatting with one of the petty traders or taxi drivers or barhoppers or friends. The invitation to a drink was, "Shall we cut something small?" For ten or twenty cents, we sported each other to the stuff. I still can't believe how much I was able to drink in those days. Inside the club, excellent beer was about fifty-five cents for a 66 cl bottle, but people from inside also came out to buy the cheaper "hot" drinks or, if they preferred something "cool," to go around the corner to a darker spot in order to smoke marijuana, which they called "groove." On their return, people would tease them, "How you doing?" "Groovy," or "Coo-o-l," they giggled. Around the clubs in Nigeria, where capitalism was more advanced, the marijuana was sold already rolled; in Ghana the marijuana was folded and tied inside cut-up pieces of airmail paper suitable for rolling one cigarette. One "wrap" cost a shilling, just under a dime, and many groovers would nurse a drink inside the club and then step outside and rely on the marijuana to add a buzz to the evening. In Ghana, the marijuana sellers were not usually around the club; at a cost of about fifty cents, a taxi driver could be sent on a quick drive to get five wraps for several groovers and receive a commission for himself of one wrap from the seller and one from the buyers.

At that time and up to now, in French-speaking countries like Togo, Burkina Faso, or Côte d'Ivoire, the nightclub scene was annoyingly neocolonial. Instead of large open-air nightclubs that attracted a diversity of people, major towns in the Francophone countries had small European-style discos, indoors and air-conditioned. There was no cover, but inside, a 33 cl bottle of beer could cost as much as six hundred to twelve hundred to fifteen hundred or even two thousand CFA francs, about three to six to nine dollars depending on the exchange rate. Needless to say, the patrons were primarily European and Asian expatriates and members of the African elite. The whole scene stunk of class and threw patterns of sociability and conviviality totally out of kilter. The discos were often nearly deserted, though at several of them, drinks were cheaper by half and more people were present. Although there were some open-air nightclubs that functioned on occasional weekends with local bands, the main drinking holes for the general population were small bars with tables extending to where a sidewalk might someday be placed. You could go from bar to bar, corner to corner, to change views. In those bars, the large-size bottle of beer was about seventy-five cents, and of course, many people who attended a nearby disco but were serious about drinking would nurse a single small bottle inside the disco and then come outside to satisfy their thirst before going back inside to dance.

The drinking routine was for different people to buy rounds of several large bottles that were shared into the company's glasses; as soon as your beer was even slightly below the rim of the glass, someone would serve you and top it up. If you thought that you were already too loaded and wanted to stop drinking, you would leave your glass full, because if you drank even a last polite sip, someone would fill it up again. The cafelike atmosphere of the street bars was generally made even more typical by the presence of huge speakers that would blast popular African music onto the street. The sound systems were not up to the standard of those in the discos, and the records were sometimes scratchy, but at least the street bars had the advantage of never playing French popular music. For me, sticking my head into a couple of the dark discos and hearing Johnny Hallyday was about as far as I went into that particular scene.

I was into traditional African music, and my first requirement for urban nightlife was hearing the modern music that came from traditional beats and developed to suit the styles of the changing times. Inside the Ghanaian nightclubs, live bands provided the beat for the cross-section of urban life that congregated there. The first people I befriended were the musicians and the music lovers who were friends of musicians. From them, I met more people at the tables where we sat and talked. The ambience was clubby with the twist that all strangers were included. If I was sitting alone, it was commonplace for someone I didn't know to approach me and invite me to sit in company with him and his friends. I had traveled a bit before I went to Ghana, and I knew that going out alone is the best way to meet people; I always had the patience to sit by myself and wait for something to happen, and something always did. Somehow or other, I picked up the nickname "Psychedelic," and within a few weeks after my arrival, there was almost no place in central Accra where I could go and not hear a friendly voice calling me, "Hey! Johnny!" or "Hey! Psychedelic!" In addition to the sociability, the main difference between these nightclubs and the bars I knew at home was that the people were of all ages and social backgrounds. There were shortages of old people of course, and married couples were vastly outnumbered, but the young and middle-aged mixed together, and it was not uncommon to find a table with people in their twenties, thirties, forties, and fifties.

For the most part, I was with the younger set, and I was a "guy," a word that in the local idiom can refer to either a man or a woman, someone who is a friend to all, someone who is straightforward, someone who does not bluff, someone who can joke and hang with people. A guy is a believer, someone who believes in himself or herself and believes in others, someone who is prepared to get with what's happening. A guy has what they call an "easy" or a "simple" understanding, meaning that it is an easy matter for a guy to understand and agree with what someone is saying, at least for the moment. We guys shared a sense of togetherness as young people; we were in our teens and twenties and thirties but we called ourselves boys and girls, terms that in the context distinguished us from married people. My interest in the nightclub scene naturally extended from the music to the whole social atmosphere the music fit into and enhanced. I remembered teenage dances in the States where there were always people looking for a fight, bars in the States where I would have gut reactions to the ambient hostility, public places where people had to be sensitive to the space around certain characters. There was none of it in those African clubs, and yet the people there were so different from one another.

One thing that fostered the togetherness was the way that people just put aside many of the labels that we might ordinarily think would define their identity. For example, ethnic consciousness—what used to be called "tribalism"—is an obvious case: it was there; it was definitely a factor in the networking of the workaday world; it was often a factor in self-help associations in the neighborhoods. At the clubs, people from the same family or original hometown might sit together and converse in their vernacular. It was occasionally a factor in the many personal dramas that preoccupied people, and it was possible to find people who would talk about it privately. But I hardly ever heard people openly abusing each other about their ethnicity or publicly talking about "these" people or "those" people. There are over seventy linguistic groups in Ghana, more than two hundred in Nigeria. An African city like Accra is so pluralistic that people cannot be sure about other people's backgrounds and cannot allow their ethnic sentiments to prejudge a person who might become a friend. One evening I was in the company of an American radical and a group of Accra guys, and the American was talking against colonialism; he was evidently thinking to ingratiate himself and develop international solidarity while he delivered a speech about how much he liked the Ashantis because they had fought the British. I cringed because the group included not only Ashanti guys but also some Ga and Ewe guys whose ancestors had also fought the Ashantis. The potential discord was quickly glossed over, as usual, but whenever anybody at the university asked me what "tribe" I hung out with in town, I used to answer, "Apaches."

I was not being clever. Actually, during the period of time when I was in Ghana, a considerable number of young people in Accra called themselves Apaches. They evidently took the name from some movie in which the U.S. cavalry comes upon the smoldering remains of a wagon train, and the scout picks up an arrow, exchanges glances with the lieutenant, shakes his head, and mutters, "Apaches." The Apaches, as understood by uncertified Accra anthropologists based on the ethnographic accounts of Hollywood screenwriters, are generally quiet and understanding; they can sit and watch something for hours, blending into the scenery; they are individualists with a strong sense of interpersonal loyalty; they are true to themselves and they are prepared to die at any time; they mind their own business, and they don't like people who come around and make a mess. The urban scene is one in which people have to hang together and take care of each other to survive; they don't have time for "tribalism" unless it's going to help them or hurt them at a given moment. They try to avoid it in general, even to the extent of calling for themselves a celebrated heritage from thousands of miles away.

I fit into that spirit, happy that my own tribe was not much of a factor. As an American, I had to learn my share of tricks to avoid being typified by people who didn't know me, but by and large, I was just another one of the young boys who were there with no specific purpose apart from hanging. I was relatively passive in that regard, mainly because I was interested in the nightclub scene and thinking about it as an entry point for focusing on the music and the lifestyle of the urban setting. Thus, I did not choose some people over others; I decided to be friends with all of them, and I guess I became well liked because of that. During my first months, I had my share of guides who were masters of that particular social territory. I maintained my laid-back demeanor because many people opened up to me, and as I got to know more of them I learned a lot about where they were coming from in the scene. After a while, when I entered a nightclub after hanging outside for a while, I might already have greeted many of the people who were there. If the place was uncomfortably crowded, I might join a table; otherwise I circulated.

The main activities, as one might expect, were drinking, talking, and dancing, and it was through dancing that I came to know many of the girls. The bands played their music in nonstop sets; when one song ended, the drummer would add a coda that led into the next number. On crowded occasions, people would leave their seats for the dance floor en masse; as if being pulled by a magnet, they leaned out of their seats and were dancing by the time they stood up. To get a partner for a dance was simple: one could approach a table, salute the people with a greeting, and ask anyone who was not otherwise preoccupied. But since I was often hanging around just talking, girls who knew me felt free to ask me to dance if they had no partner. I figured they liked my style of dancing since I had been trained by a very cool guy from Newark whose revised moves had not previously made it back to the motherland. But probably what the girls knew about me was that I hung with the musicians and I was not a boyfriend of anyone in particular and I was not going to spoil anyone's game because I was one of the guys. Those girls who were regulars at a club would often sit together, and sometimes I sat with them instead of with other friends. If I had brought an extra dollar or two to town, I would buy a couple of bottles for the table; if not, one or another of the girls was buying. I suppose I had a somewhat privileged position because once I became known, it was general knowledge that I was not going to hassle anyone. The girls kept me dancing, which was good, and I enjoyed their conversation. The benefits of their friendship eventually extended to the point where I would often visit their houses during my daytime movements through the town. They also visited each other to cook and eat together in the afternoons, and I would sit outside with them while they cooked and we talked, maybe played a game of Ludo, and then ate.

I first met Hawa in 1971 when her boyfriend was a good friend of mine. Her place was also a popular gathering place that was close to the center of town. It was just up the street from an automotive shop owned by a Lebanese friend who had offered to fix up an old BSA motorcycle for me. We never got the bike on the road, but for a while I used to pass by there almost every day to check on whether or not he had found this or that spare part, and from there I used to go to Hawa's house, where there was often a group of friends cooking or hanging around. Urban housing for most people is typically a room or two in what is called a compound house. The house itself is basically a series of rooms off a yard, or compound. The kitchen is outdoors, generally in a shaded area of the compound, and the cooking is done on an open fire fueled by charcoal. One sits on wooden benches or stools or relaxes on a woven mat that is spread on the ground. People cook and eat together first of all because everyone knows that eating alone is a miserable experience. Second, the local food is usually a stew or soup that should be made in quantity, or at least in more than a single portion, and eaten fresh. Third, in Ghana cooking is hard work that is best shared: the stew or soup is usually served on a heavy paste made from some type of boiled flour or else on a starchy dough called *fufu* that is made by pounding cooked cassava, plantain, or yam in various combinations. Fufu is pounded in a large wooden mortar with a long wooden pestle, and although most women can do it by themselves, it is much easier if one woman turns the fufu while another pounds it.

As they cooked, the girls joked and talked about whatever — the events of the previous day, their plans for later, the films they had seen, their other friends, their boyfriends, their problems. Often they told extended anecdotes about themselves or things they had seen. The range of experience and people they described was very wide, reflecting the cosmopolitan scene as well as the fact that they were single. After all, one of the attractions of being single anywhere, for men and women, is being able to move with different people; a married person, as everyone knows, has settled down and sees less of life's diversity. When I met Hawa and began visiting her house on occasional afternoons, one of the first things I noticed was that she was very, very popular among her friends because of her storytelling. To me, her popularity suggested the notion that she spoke for her friends as well as for herself, that she was telling them the truth about themselves and the type of society they lived in. They gathered at her place and shared their stories, but she was the best raconteur among them. She could tell a story for an hour or more, holding them spellbound or making them laugh till they rolled on the ground.

When I returned to the States between 1972 and 1974, I thought about those happy afternoon conversations many times. I decided that when I went back to Ghana, in addition to continuing my studies in music, I would try to collect some stories from people in order to convey something about modern African youth and the type of lifestyle they have. I thought their voices would help me communicate some matters that were difficult to describe about the spirit that had attracted me to the nightclubs and other places where people relaxed and did their own thing. I thought to choose two young people from the people I knew, Hawa and an equally articulate and charismatic male counterpart, hoping to use them as a point of entry to discuss the pluralistic openness of the modern cultural milieu. When I did return to Ghana, however, I fell straight into my work on music. I continued working with contemporary and traditional artists, and I could never seem to get around to sitting down with Hawa or my other friend to tape-record their stories. The situation was complicated by the fact that Hawa had moved from Accra to Lomé, in the neighboring country of Togo. One of the traditional areas where I was working was just by the border, and I saw Hawa often during frequent visits to Togo because where she lived then was near a friend of mine. I often joined her and her friends to eat, and we all often met in the evening at roadside bars. I first suggested this project to her in 1975. I was more interested in her stories as vivid and intimate descriptions of the way people interacted than in her own personal story as such, though a life history seemed a convenient format. I told her simply that I believed many people in America would be interested in knowing how a young African woman felt about her life, and I expressed my conviction that she would be able to communicate effectively. She was sympathetic to the project, but a number of problems were occupying her attention, and she could not spend enough time with me for us to do any recording. For a while she was absent from Lomé and no one knew when or if she would be back, for she had accidentally stumbled into some serious trouble.

Meanwhile, my plans further unraveled regarding the man I had had in mind to complement Hawa. He remained a tight friend and was very close to me in Accra, but he changed the way he talked. His speech became so full of artifice that he no longer told stories as before. Indeed, he became less interested in telling stories. His focus on verbal agility seemed to overwhelm his narrative considerations, seeking rather to find expression in a kind of waggish jocularity that flirted with incomprehensibility. What happened was that he and some of his friends became enamored of Nigerian Pidgin English and began spending most of their free time in bull sessions that were oriented toward developing an argot of puns, multilingual phrases, fractured syntax, and deliberate mistakes that satirized semieducated usage of English. To them, Nigerian Pidgin was a model language because it raised linguistic ironies to new heights. He and his friends themselves had only primary or middle-school education, but they were incredibly alert to the ways in which concepts become twisted in translation and classes of words change from one language to another. In their pluralistic world, people are always learning other languages and making hilarious mistakes, particularly when they try to puff themselves up by using the language of the elite, English. In the way my friends used English, there was probably an element of parodied class-consciousness that poked fun at the elite and the bureaucratic pomposity of their speech, but the allure of Pidgin, with its odd personifications and strange metaphors, goes far beyond such inspiration. Nigerian Pidgin is particularly funny. Nigerian newspapers have humor columnists who write witty pieces glorifying Pidgin's descriptive power and flexibility; I remember one column I read in which the main character was explaining to a potential girlfriend that he didn't have a car, "I no be car-owner; I be leg-owner."

The Accra guys sat around and passed their leisure time sharing the latest samplings of such usage that their ears had collected and also making up their own examples. Their evening conversations were thickly laced with gradually built-up combinations of dislocated Akan Twi and Ga and Ewe as well. For example, my friend Santana, whom I will describe in the next few paragraphs, once saw someone wearing a shirt with the name of the Miami Dolphins football team. Such used clothing sent from overseas, particularly jeans and modern fashions, sells well. The local name for it is *buroni-wawu,* from the Twi *Oburoni w'awu,* in which one addresses the former owner by addressing the worn article of clothing, "White man, you died." Santana turned "Miami Dolphins" into *Mia-mia-odo-phians.* The Twi word *mia* means to squeeze and also to hug, and *miamia me* means "squeeze me tight," or "give me a big hug" or, in some contexts, "screw me." *Ɔdɔ* is the Twi word for "love," and *ɔdɔfo* is "lover." The suffix *"-fo"* indicates "a person who," and Santana also associated that syllable with the English suffix "-ians," or "relating or belonging to a group," to mean "the people of," as in "Philadelphians." The result, *Miamia-odophians,* meant people who really like to screw, and when we would go a nightclub and Santana would see a lot of girls hanging around the bar, he would say, "Yes. Those are the Miamia-odophians."

For another example, someone would take a Twi word like *ntɛm,* which means "prompt, hurried, early, quick," and add an "s" for the English plural and the suffix "-ment" to make an English noun. Then, when talking about a situation when he was extremely hurried, he would say, "The *ntɛmsments* were too much." Such mixed-language words followed each other so rapidly that even the people who could follow the allusions were always catching up with what had just been said and trying to slow the speaker down with interjected laughs, "Ha-ha! Yeah! The *ntɛmsments!*" They used English itself at one moment like James Joyce and in the next like an illiterate who had misheard what he was trying to say. A breeze would blow, and one person would take a deep breath and say, "Aha! Airfreshments!" Then another would say, "Ah-h-h! French air!" And everybody would fall out laughing. It was great stuff, but it was dense, and it lacked the extended dramatic thrust with which my friend had formerly imbued his stories about himself. While I joined in the laughter, I cursed myself for not having acted to record his stories previously when they would have been more presentable to people who are total strangers to the scene.

Since I had originally intended this book to be about both a young man and a young woman, I might as well tell something about the man who was intended as Hawa's counterpart, just to balance the view because there is no one quite like him in Hawa's stories. Santana was my friend's nickname. The nickname itself was a corruption of "Sartana," the main character of a popular spaghetti western entitled *Sartana the Angel of Death,* one of the many spinoffs of Clint Eastwood's and Sergio Leone's Man-with-No-Name films from the 1960s. The replacement name "Santana" pushed the name "Sartana" from popular consciousness in 1971 when the American musical group of that name played a well-hyped concert in Accra. For youthful Ghanaians of the moment, the name "Santana" was synonymous with a totally modern, do-your-own-thing attitude and style. "Santana" fit my friend well enough, and the switch became permanent. The film was popular enough in its time that a person could have the nickname Sartana the Angel of Death, and many people would understand the allusion. When the name Sartana changed to Santana, though, my friend also retained the epithet Angel of Death.

Santana truly deserved that nickname. He divided his time between Accra and a farm about thirty miles outside the city. Fed up with mooching relatives, he had built a rustic compound deep in the bush, where he worked sizable plots entirely on his own, living what he called a "heavy hippie life in the jungle." At night, he hunted with devastating effectiveness. He also caught live snakes barehanded, including cobras, for the zoology department at the University of Ghana. I met him during my first year in Accra, and he stayed with me in a house I was sitting for a generous professor who had traveled for the summer vacation. When I returned to Accra in 1974, Santana joined me in a small apartment I had rented in town. He would spend three or four days a week fooling around in Accra with me, arriving with bush meat from his hunting and sacks of food from his farm. He was still catching snakes for the zoologists, who paid him the paltry sum of two dollars each, but he stopped after I nearly opened a pillowcase he had deposited in the kitchen as if it held some limes or cocoyams when actually there was a deadly carpet viper inside it. After that he only brought the skins of dead snakes, which he sold to Hausa traders for making leather goods. Each skin, whether of a ten-foot cobra or a twelve-foot python, was accompanied by a fantastic story of The Big Fight between Santana and the snake. Santana normally did not kill snakes for fun, but when a snake moved into the compound and began eating Santana's chickens, it was war. Telling every detail of how he stalked and found and then chased the snake through the thatched roof of his house until the story culminated with the final blows of a machete, Santana would say, "Yeah, that snake had a very strong spirit!" Apart from his hunting, Santana also derived his epithet from his powerful hands, which were calloused from his furious machete farming into something like huge blocks of wood. On the very few occasions when Santana would get into a fight, the fight was over with one blow. I have never seen anything like Santana's hands. Everybody who shook his hand would jump back and exclaim, "Wow!" Then Santana would laugh and say, "Yes. I am the Angel of Death."

Santana did whatever he wanted, and he was such a funny and uninhibited guy that people knew him wherever he went. Everybody liked him. We were inseparable, but if we had not been around a particular area for even a couple of weeks, if I went there alone, the first thing many people would ask me, even before they asked how I myself was doing, was "Where's Santana?" He was a believer whose expressed motto was, "Do your own thing; no copyright." Fela Anikulapo Kuti, who sang mainly in Pidgin, had a song called "Gentleman" that went, "I no be gentleman at all; I be Africa man, original," and Santana boisterously upheld the message. One time when we were boarding a bus, Santana farted loudly, and an elderly man looked sharply at him. Santana said, "Yeah, na so we dey do for my country"; the old man said, "Oh? Where from you?" Santana laughed about the incident for days. A self-styled "original African man," he would fart and say, "Yeah! I dey!" meaning, "I'm here," an amendment of Descartes's philosophy into Santana's original African principle *Flato ergo sum.* He dressed in outrageous amalgams of styles, but his clothes were always clean and pressed, uniquely sharp, and he walked with a spring in his step. He wore wild hats because he neither cut nor combed his hair, and though his hair did not grow into dreadlocks, he was a Rastaman; as the song says, his vibrations were positive. His laugh was loud, and he was friendly to people. The only people who didn't like him were the occasional policemen or soldiers (whom he referred to as "government dogs") who tried to prevent the Angel of Death from doing his thing, but when we were together, we didn't get into trouble. I guess I may have protected him from unnecessary hassles from hustling authority figures, but all things considered, when Santana came to Accra, he came mainly as another fun-lover in a town of believers.

As I mentioned above, one of the delights of Santana's company was his use of language. It was not only I but everybody who enjoyed Santana's use of language. He liked to parody proverbs, and with an air of wisdom would say incomprehensible things like, "Yes, small boys are young because they are very little." He had attended only middle school but had an extraordinary vocabulary, and his interest in language extended to a mastery of American slang to which I was only occasionally able to contribute. He talked to anybody and everybody, from perfect strangers to his language-busting friends, making weird sense with references to things they could not possibly know about. For example, he had a bad tooth that could not tolerate cold. We were buying water at a busy kiosk that had some very frigid ice water, and Santana took a swig and shrieked, "*Ayi!* The thing is TOO HOT!!" As several dumbfounded onlookers stared, Santana set the cup on the counter and said to them, "Yeah, make I put 'am down so he go cool small." Anywhere and everywhere, Santana could always be counted on to enliven a scene by running his mouth and turning expressions upside down and inside out. He was usually equal to the challenge of explaining himself with further metaphoric dislocation, until his interlocutor, with brow twisted quizzically, would give up and laugh, saying, "Santana!" But Santana had more than his match among the Accra guys for whom such joking was their pastime. I enjoyed their use of language but I was not interested in presenting Santana as an example of that: it was Santana's personal stories that would have been worth sharing, for he had had many fascinating experiences at the crossroads of culture, and his positive attitude resembled and complemented Hawa's in many ways. I just missed the boat. By the time I became serious about recording his stories for this project, his language itself had become an obstacle that would have bogged most readers down even though it might have boggled their minds most pleasurably.

I decided to become serious about getting at least Hawa's stories. The next time I saw Hawa was in late 1975. She and some friends visited me in Accra when they were on their way to Ouagadougou. Their plans were to return within a month and then go to either Lagos or Abidjan. She failed to return as promised, and there was no word of her in Lomé. Finally, I traveled to Ouagadougou in mid-1977 to find her, a task that involved some tricky detective work. She was going under a different name, and of course, no one could be sure whether I might be someone whom she wished to avoid. After several days of inquiry, I was able to trace her and then contact her through an intermediary. She was happy to see me, and when I reminded her of our conversations of years before about recording her stories, she agreed to talk about herself on tape. We then recorded many stories from her life, sitting for hours at a time. The experiences she discussed covered the period of her life from the time she was around eight or nine up to her late twenties. The interviews were so extensive that I realized that I could forget about recording a male counterpart and could just rely on her stories alone. When we finished, I returned to northern Ghana to pursue my other research. In 1979 I went back to Ouagadougou again, and when I met her there, we recorded another series of tapes that added further material and bought her stories more up-to-date.

As it turned out, this book does not directly address my original interest in the public atmosphere of the African urban scene, but it will rather take readers more deeply into the private lives of the different types of people there. Perhaps it answers my interest more adequately, if indirectly, in the way it elevates the reality of their problems and the values by which they live. In retrospect, Hawa gave me what is probably a better solution to my original intention to describe the public places I frequented. After all, the public places are only the setting of the real drama, only the tables and chairs where the characters arrange themselves. From ground level, the setting need only be sketched, taken in with a glance before one starts dealing with the people. This introduction serves that purpose in part. In the stories that follow, you will hear next to nothing about modernization and tradition, Westernization, feminism, bureaucracy or economics or government, capitalism or Marxism; but you will meet urban youth and villagers, expatriate Europeans, men and women, farmers and contractors and civil servants and police, business folk and poor people. As for the type of values that sustain the people, your awareness of that will emerge gradually. There are no sermons, no psychologizing, no treatise on ethics. What is bad is simple and clear: abuse of position, lack of respect for a fellow human being, gossiping, small-mindedness, greed, jealousy, the usual stuff. There are some things people do in this book that are going to annoy a lot of readers. Accept these actions for what they are, but do not judge the people in Hawa's stories because of the failings on display. As Durkheim might have said, it is the bad things in life that give us the opportunity to know what is good and that give a storyteller the opportunity to show it.

Commodity Traders

Hawa's stories reflect the fact that life in African cities is laid over a traditional cultural background that stresses redistribution and reciprocity in economic life. Some social scientists argue that the most fundamental way to understand traditional societies is to think of them as systems of exchange in which anything that happens, even a funeral or (especially) a marriage, has features that make it look like a transaction. In a modern African city, when a money economy is laid over a traditional exchange system, people put values on all sorts of surprising things in surprising ways.

This situation led the Accra guys mentioned above to use the phrase "pocket lawyer" to refer to someone who continually becomes involved in disputes; a pocket lawyer is a person who acts as if he has a law degree and carries it around in his pocket in order to be ready to pull it out at any time. "Yeah," they'd say, shaking their heads after a stressful encounter, "That guy was another pocket lawyer." A place like Accra is full of them because ideas about exchange take many forms. Any marketplace has its rules, but I'm not talking merely about economic activity. In traditional societies where people are poor, exchanges of any type, even of gifts or greetings or smiling faces, bind people together into broader networks of relationships that have a real value. These relationships can be cashed in, so to speak, in times of need.

In Africa, money plays a role within many types of transactions where we would normally think its appearance inappropriate. If a new friend asks you for financial help, you might feel put off by his request; in many places in Africa, though, he might be thinking that since you two are friends, you would blame him if he didn't tell you his problem and give you an opportunity to help, because it would show that he didn't trust you or respect your friendship. Many of the problems that happen to the people in this book develop from exchanges that are misunderstood or go bad or because they get forced into an unforeseen situation of redefined obligations or relationships. But most of the time, people take a very positive view of how notions of exchange can get expanded into elaborate symbolic and institutional forms. They hold dearly to their ethics of interdependence and cooperation, and they believe sincerely that moral support is fine, but it is better to give someone real help. A day might come, they think to themselves, when they will also need help. They raise this orientation to the level of theology: when someone receives a big gift, he might say, "Thank you. I cannot ever repay you for what you have done, and so I can only pray that God will pay you back. May God bless you." A cynic might attribute this attitude solely to necessity, but it is still beautiful.

Ideas of exchange can bridge numerous ethical sensitivities, from the immediate to the multigenerational. For example, in many traditional societies of Africa, the same word is used for "stranger" as for "guest." Notions of hospitality are usually fairly elaborate throughout the world, but Africans pride themselves on being friendly to strangers. You can go to a town and have no place to stay: someone will just take you home, feed you, give you a place to sleep, and feed you again in the morning. There is no charge. That person will never ask you how long you plan to stay in the town. If you stay for weeks, it doesn't matter. Where is the exchange? If you ask him, even if he is a complete pauper, he might say that he hopes to travel to your hometown some day, and maybe someone will also help him like that; if he doesn't get the chance, he has children, and maybe one of them will someday travel to your hometown. Even if you are not at home, you have your family and friends, don't you? His children will not be strangers there. He believes it. What else might someone like that say? He is being righteous in the eyes of God, and God is marking it down. He is getting respect from his neighbors because they can see that he is someone who gives respect to strangers. He is getting respect also because he is showing that he can take care of a stranger. He is getting respect because even his neighbors are thinking that they might travel someday. At night, the neighbors will send food to him with the message that he should use it to feed his stranger, and the bowls will pile up in your room. You are getting these things against what? Only an idea. Your host must be getting something, because if you say you want to leave his house to get your own room, he will feel badly about it. Such multidimensional links between generosity, hospitality, greetings, respect, and exchange have been encountered everywhere in societies we call traditional, to the extent that social scientists sometimes see the whole complex as these societies' main characteristic. In northern Ghana where I did my research, people raised chickens but would not eat them; they would only slaughter one if they had a guest, or a stranger. When townspeople or villagers would greet their chief, they would give him some yams or poultry for the chief's household or in case the chief receives a visitor; when someone from outside came to greet the chief, the chief would give that person some of the food to take home and give to the people there. All these goods and services are circulating in a context of respecting oneself and respecting others.

The exchange factor in the lives of the characters in this book may confuse Western readers who think that putting some things on the level of an exchange somehow cheapens them. This idea of exchange presents a particularly thorny problem because Hawa and many of her girlfriends are often considered prostitutes in the sense that they have sex with men in exchange for money. However, readers should hesitate before calling these women prostitutes: the exchange of money or gifts for sex takes many forms everywhere in the world, and in Africa as in many places, it is somewhat difficult to draw a line somewhere along the extended range of people's sexual behavior and then to say that what is on one side is prostitution and what is on the other side is not. After all, even hardcore prostitutes sometimes just enjoy themselves for a night and merely say goodbye in the morning, and even the most straitlaced woman will occasionally look at her mate and wonder what she is getting from the relationship. A prudent opinion would hold that the women in this book should not be called prostitutes because the type of prostitution practiced in West Africa is different from the way we tend to think of it in the Western world, where it is by law an unacceptable kind of exchange and where it has been represented as a far-reaching symbol of the degradation of the self, the violation of the body, the mortification of the spirit, the exploitation of the powerless, the profanation of love, the corruption of the bourgeoisie, and the decay of society.

Hawa and her friends occasionally run into some tough spots and certainly are aware of their social position, but their obliviousness to most of prostitution's connotations indicates that it's probably better to say that they are not prostitutes, just because they are not attentive to many of the associations the term has for us. If they are indeed prostitutes, then their prostitution is semiprofessional or informal. The word the people in this book use for such women is "ashawo" (ah-shah′-wo), which is a Yoruba word that literally means "money changer," a person who exchanges money or currency. In the next few paragraphs we'll look in detail at what that word means. In her talks with me, Hawa was quite explicit that one should not try to generalize about ashawo women, but in the context of an introduction for Western readers, there is a need to talk about the ashawo life in general if only to help some readers get beyond an issue that is a potential sticking point. "Ashawo" is also a word used to refer to men who deal with ashawo women, and the ashawo man is the one paying. I also heard people characterize a man who doesn't pay as someone who doesn't respect himself and also as an ashawo man. Some people, like musicians, are adept at not paying, and they are also ashawo people. The word is not an easy word. Nonetheless, the most common use of ashawo is to characterize women who get money for sex. But in Africa, it seems that the negative connotations of the word might have less to do with selling sex than with other concerns because a great many men and women in Africa think about their relationships with one another in terms of exchange.

Their notion of sexual exchange has its broad and complex roots in tradition. In West Africa, giving somebody something shows that you like the person, which makes sense. Among the many things you can give a person, money is one of the better ones. You greet a chief or an elder with a small amount of money and some cola nuts or drink. In many traditional societies, even young boys start their friendships with young girls by giving a token amount of money they call friendship money. The friendship may or may not become sexual, but the money or the gifts that follow establish the relationship and show that the boy is serious about the girl. The friendship will develop with the boy giving the girl gifts that are within his means, such as a fowl or foodstuffs or money if he has any, and the girl will reciprocate by cooking food and sending it to her boyfriend's house. When children grow up and want to marry, it is customary in many places for a prospective bridegroom to pay money to the family of his bride or to buy many things and have them in place for his bride when she comes to his family's house; if he fails to spend something substantial, it shows that he doesn't respect her. When you follow the matter into details, the situation has its permutations: you might find that some poor people don't want their daughters to marry rich people, because if the marriage later runs into trouble, they might be reproached that they sold their daughter for money; the idea of the exchange is still there even when it is avoided. Of course, when it comes to a prospective marriage, parents make allowances for other people's means, and there is really no fixed price. The point is that even in situations like getting married, there should be something material to stand for the relationship, something for everyone to see. A married woman who can afford her own everything will expect her husband to buy her some cloth for her dresses at least once a year, and if he cannot provide, she may forgive him, but her fellow women will abuse her to her face and tell her that she's wasting her time with that man.

In general, people think about the connection between material things and relationships in terms of respect and in terms of demonstrating the benefits of what one person can do for another. After all, who is your better friend, the one who loves you or the one who helps you? Most people in Africa would answer that the one who helps you is the one who really loves you. Sex is not excluded from this general orientation: sex without exchange is exploitative. In one sense, being out front about it is a way of making sure that there is some sort of equality between the partners. For an ashawo woman in a land without alimony or community property, her deal is often better than that of a traditional wife, a sort of pay-as-you-go marriage. She might even call it such. There are many different forms of marriage, and the term is used in many ways. People joke broadly with the concept of marriage, often introducing a girlfriend or boyfriend as "my wife" or "my husband." Marriage is grounded in exchange, in the generation of family, in the binding together of lives, as it is here, but it is not a restricted realm for sanctified sex, nor can sex be monopolized in a polygamous household. Sex can beget relationships, and relationships are too important to be denied that possible channel. One can do it for fun, of course, but at a certain point, the perception is not that such fun is bad but rather that it is useless. In villages and backward places, some very young or vulnerable girls might follow a man to his room out of obedience because they are too timid or respectful to refuse. People whose eyes are open would disparage such girls as "bush" girls not because they had sex but because they have no experience and don't respect themselves enough to get something in return. In African societies, the issues around having sex do not present the same kind of moral problems as appear in the West.

Young people in African villages grow up in societies that have only rarely been noted for espousing elaborate ethics of sexual abstinence. The sexual freedom with which the youth conduct themselves is difficult to convey without the use of pejorative terms like loose, fast, and promiscuous. In their favor, it should be noted that many of them do seem to start their sexual lives a few years later than many Western teenagers, though some start earlier. That aspect of their lives must be accepted, and to counterbalance it, they have a heritage of strong family control. The family has been Africa's greatest institution, and sexual concerns are focused on consequences for the family, not on the soul of the person. Religious notions of hell's fire and damnation are alien. Evangelical Islam and Christianity have preached those latter concepts a bit, but presumptions of guilt attached to sex itself have not taken root in the fertile spiritual soil, and generally the religious focus has rather been on devotion and love of God. Youthful dalliance has remained somewhat innocent, requiring a serious response only when a consequence like conception comes to involve the family. For older people, female adultery is therefore also always a serious offense, as one might guess; female adultery exists but generally leaves center stage to male adultery, for the most part with unmarried women. All in all, the unmarried young are free in ways that we in the West cannot easily imagine, for they do not have to fight mental and emotional battles that even the most sophisticated libertine among us has at one time faced. They are not bothered by the heavy psychological residues that complicate our sex lives. When deciding about sex, they think mainly about two things, first whether they like a person and second whether they believe a person can help them, though either can lead to the other.

While most African societies are not known for having particularly puritanical sentiments about sex, there are some constraints. Few societies anywhere are prepared to deal with the delectation and disruption that can be caused when beautiful girls and fine young women are promiscuous inside and outside of their age group. Parents don't like to see their daughters having many sexual partners mainly because that kind of lifestyle can establish bad habits that will disturb a future marriage and, in a small enough community, reduce a girl's value as a potential bride because of conflicts about possible children. It is said that in traditional life, in the old days, there were severe sanctions that could be brought upon a man who seduced a woman who had been promised to another man. But it's always difficult to control kids anywhere. Village youth and city youth are the same in this regard: if they were reasonable and without passion, they wouldn't be kids. For young people, being open to chance encounters can signify confidence, can anticipate a game of exploration and pursuit, can demonstrate an aptitude for fun, can proclaim a hope for love. Love without memory is an ideal with some merit: sensualists fulfill the aspiration of poets to dwell in constant longing for closeness and to experience continually the pleasure of renewal, from one day to the next and to the next. Playboys and playgirls may not fully exemplify that spirituality, but they partake of it a bit, and they exult in themselves and their sociability, so that quite a few people fantasize about their lifestyle. Whatever the level on which young people approach sex, older observers have to try hard not to forget what it is like to be young.

In the past, the best way to control the girls was to engage them as children and marry them off as soon as they reached puberty. The boys were thus controlled by default. These days, in modern African towns, many girls are in school and the age of marriage has been pushed up. Currently the best way to control them is to provide well for them so they don't need anything from anyone. When a girl goes bad in Africa by sleeping around too much, people blame the parents for not taking care of her well. They assume that she is trying to get things that the parents have not given her. The corollary is that in towns and in villages too, young girls whose parents cannot help them enough, and whom no one would consider prostitutes, have relationships with men in order to pay their school fees. Remember the poverty factor, the maze of contingencies where people adapt their lives to a changing social environment. To many people, they're just girls growing up and trying to better themselves, and pandering themselves for an education is one of their options. When these girls become adults and find themselves on their own, they continue to assess their relationships with respect to tangible benefits. A working woman in a clerical or sales job might not think of asking for money as a straight exchange for sex, but once a relationship is established, she will ask her boyfriend to help her with some things that her salary cannot provide. Beyond paying entrance fees and entertaining her, he might see a lot of resources moving in her direction. Maybe she asks him to buy her some shoes she says she needs, or maybe she asks for help with her room rent, thus progressing from things to cash. If the man fails to demonstrate an interest in helping her, she will find someone who is more serious about her and her problems. If not, like a traditional wife, she might be abused by her girlfriends for being a fool for a man.

In Africa, no less prudish an institution than the Catholic Church showed itself capable of sympathy for the idea that amorous solicitation can be purified in the service of truth.[1] During the early days of colonial rule in French West Africa, European administrators used education to improve the situation of women, who were seen even by less than liberal minds as mere chattel in the traditional system. Many traditional Africans at first resisted the idea of Western education for anyone, and of course, they didn't want to spoil their daughters by educating them in the white man's ways, to say nothing of the fact that their daughters were valuable resources to the family, like money in the bank maturing. Nonetheless, there were administrative directives that the Africans could not ignore, and children were enrolled. The Catholic "White Fathers" who came on Christ's mission had a role in these early efforts to introduce change. The French administration was mainly interested in educating an elite group of followers who could help carry out policy, and therefore needed men. The mission schools were the more serious about recruiting women and indoctrinating them into enlightenment and Catholicism. One reason the Church needed to educate girls was related to the exchange of women. It was asserted openly that the missions had to develop a population of potential brides for male converts. By flooding the market with lovely Catholic girls, the missions could attract additional converts as well, since aspiring husbands had to embrace the Faith in order to get the mission-educated girls as wives. In the traditional system, one cannot get a wife for free, and there are a lot of men who despair of ever having the means to become a real person by marrying and starting a household. Some people who thought they could be clever and just go through the motions in order later to spirit their brides back into the traditional lifeways faced the shocking reality that the colonial administration would then intervene on behalf of the Catholic Fathers. In Dante's *Inferno,* those who give in to carnal desire occupy the second circle of Hell, just below Limbo where the poet saw the virtuous but unbaptized pagans, whereas the panderers are found much lower in the eighth circle where reside those guilty of various types of fraud. That makes sense to me, but it is possible to imagine the Fathers praying for the success of the policy by seeing it within a broader context of other intentions. We should extend ourselves no less when looking at the ambiguities of sexual exchanges in Africa.

Within a framework of exchange, it's not a question of morals but a question of strategy. Many women in Africa merely supplement other forms of income with what Westerners might call semiprofessional prosti-

1. See Elliot P. Skinner, *The Mossi of the Upper Volta: The Political Development of a Sudanese People* (Stanford: Stanford University Press, 1964), 167–71.

tution but what they call getting boyfriends. As for the "heavy" ashawo women who hang out at the international hotels and nightclubs, rather than simply providing sexual services for a fee, many think of a score as a steady boyfriend who could be a good provider, not unlike the kind of men we tell our daughters to look for. Ashawo women often attempt to develop long-term relationships that exchange emotional sustenance for general economic assistance, which takes such forms as capital or resources for trading, school or apprenticeship fees, or incremental investment in a house. Although there are some "real" prostitutes in Africa, particularly around port towns and in places where migrant workers live, most of the women in this book would sleep hungry before going home with a man they didn't like. Ashawo women are free: they go out in order to meet people, and they do as they want. A lot depends on how a man talks or presents himself. The women often have to be flirted with and propositioned in a context of having a good time and dealing with love. If the scales are equal, or sometimes just for the fun of it or for the hell of it, they will go with the feelings or the connection rather than hold themselves back. At other times, they'll refuse somebody they like, with or without means, because they don't want the bluffing or potential hassles the man might later bring to their normal routine. They're loose about sex, but not much more loose than many other women or girls around there or than many of the ones in Western countries.

The nightclub women bring assumptions about exchange from their cultural backgrounds, and the difference between them and other women in Africa has partially to do with their standards and with the frequency or boldness with which they are able to negotiate the monetary value of the various types of exchange that take place when men and women relate. A schoolgirl might be too shy to ask for money from a man; her silence will not prevent the man from charging himself, giving her some money, and telling her to buy something for herself or pay her school expenses. The schoolgirl is "making ashawo," but she would not be considered a prostitute or even a mistress. At the other end of the spectrum, many ashawo women see themselves in the same way as many single women here see themselves, that is, out there on their own. Some of the women who hang out in the international and local hotels and nightclubs are out there "for life," as they say. During the 1970s, many Ghanaian women traveled to other countries, partially because life in Ghana was difficult but also partially because they just wanted to see the world, and Ghanaian ashawos mixed with the locals throughout West Africa. The "ashawo" life exists along a broad spectrum of behavior and attitudes, covering a much broader range than the idea of "prostitution" implies here. One older Ghanaian man I knew qualified the term into ironic absurdity by referring to them as "demi-semi-prostitutes." The Accra guys like Santana looked at the traveling set and the hotel and nightclub people and did not call them "prostitutes" at all; they called them "roving ambassadors."

Let us again recall the poverty factor. Poverty always limits choice and limits options. One difference between here and there is that in Africa people are even begging for jobs as maids for thirty or forty dollars a month, and they cannot get them. Single women in America or Europe often have jobs that remove them to a greater extent from situations of dependency; when they do not, they also are forced into finding options, whether from the welfare system or from charitable institutions or from their boyfriends who buy things for them and their children or who help them in any number of ways. Such women are not particularly visible in the Hollywood films that play the movie houses in West Africa, but the ashawo women would understand them. The similarities are apparent, and the differences are mainly a matter of degree: resources are more limited there; grandmothers and mothers in the extended family provide foster homes for dependent children; the boyfriends are poorer, and one needs more of them. Other differences reach back into the realm of culture and touch the matter of style. Most of the Ghanaians I knew, both men and women, looked at the clothes and the bars and the cars and—above all—the attitude in American films and told me that the way we live looks like an ashawo life to them. The people they see in the movies are the really heavy ashawos. And that was before they could see music videos. On a more commonplace level, the Ghanaian women did not pattern themselves after the women in the movies, who were a bit wild by local standards. Everybody liked the Hollywood women who argued and fought back against the bad guys—"Yes, the girl *tried!*"—but the intense style was not theirs. Their issues were different: even the most hardcore ashawo would not feel the need to take a stand against being serviceable.

Looking at the way the women fall back on sex to help them in their lives, no matter how evident the connotation of dependence and exploitation, it is a mistake to think that African men and women are without models of feminine self-reliance and self-respect. Most of the men I knew said that quiet and obedient women can be good but one never knows what they are thinking. These men therefore said they prefer women who can stand up for themselves; such women are more interesting, more fun, more productive, more everything. And they have always been there. There has not been much attention given to African traditions that have myths and stories about roving princesses, women who set off on their own, or who become the ancestors of tribes or clans. These women are the counterparts of

African traditions of male adventurers, long-distance traders, or warriors who undertake their own travels, battles, and ordeals.[1] When Hawa becomes sick in Togo and tells herself that it is better to die there than to return to Ghana carrying the same plastic bag she had when she left, she is showing a sign of that mentality. She may not have been thinking about folklore, but stories of bravery and hardship are also part of people's self-image whether or not recollected from mythic history: once my family or my people were this or that, and I am from their line; if my life requires, I can also do what they did.

From another perspective, the domesticated men and women I knew grew up seeing many women in monogamous and polygamous households where everybody was happy and the living was beautiful, where the women shared work and good feelings. They grew up seeing women who expressed themselves and who were unafraid to show their strength. They grew up seeing some women who were enormously successful in business, who had large shops or who commanded fleets of trucks. But not everybody makes it like that anywhere, and not everybody is lucky in marriage. Like the men who leave traditional settings to go to the cities, the women are also dealing with a society that has created new opportunities to escape the problems that can arise in traditional life. In Africa, women's options are still seriously limited: although some elite women are able to reach high positions, the great majority are married and become homemakers; those who participate in economic life do so by looking mainly toward their marriages or sometimes toward their family connections for money to help them establish themselves in trading or business. Those who are removed from that general situation, in comparison with women here who also leave behind the typical family models, have even fewer options, and this book is about some of the options the African women do have and the price they are willing or have to pay in recourse.

It has been asserted by Westerners of all persuasions that despite a few exceptions, the situation of women in African societies is based on the restrictiveness of traditionally ascribed role models, that is, that they are powerless and exploited; the assertion is almost the same thing as saying they live a situation of marginality. If the women are marginal, it can perhaps be expected that many women will be included among the certain types of marginal people in any society who are adventurers or who are

1. For some comments on Sahelian traditions, see Paul Stoller, *The Cinematic Griot: The Ethnography of Jean Rouch* (Chicago: University of Chicago Press, 1992), especially chapter 8, and *Money Has No Smell: The Africanization of New York City* (Chicago: University of Chicago Press, 2002), especially chapter 3.

among the first to experiment with and develop new lifestyles to fit changing times. By the same token, and to qualify the above assertion, it should also be evident and acknowledged that many women in traditional settings reach maturity and achieve independence in terms that are meaningful to them. And if previously there were not women who stood up for themselves and acted in their own interest, then where did the current generation of tough-minded city girls come from? Did they spring out of the ground or were they dropped from airplanes? Most of the old people in the villages figure the latter. Moralists are perplexed, divided between seeing the ashawo women as confused hedonists or courageous rebels.

In these few paragraphs, I am providing some details about the cultural context of this book in order to make it more difficult to label Hawa and her friends as prostitutes. There are people like Hawa among us here, too, who are not prostitutes. But the independent women in Africa are among the vast number of unemployed, and someone without a job does not get a salary. Some have rejected the system, and some have been rejected by it. Still, as Hawa told me, no one says, "I want to be an ashawo when I grow up." The barebones background on Hawa is that her mother died when she was three, and she was raised by different members of her extended family. She was given in marriage at sixteen and divorced almost immediately, and because of her father's opposition to her divorce, she was forced to leave her family. When you read Hawa's stories, there may be questions, but the questions are presented as choices, and the choices people make are the substance of culture. Should the children be working? If not, how are they to be trained? Should Hawa have respected her various stepmothers and aunts more than she did, or did they cross the line into abusiveness? Was her defiance a cause or an effect of her difficulties? What would you do if you found yourself with a stepmother who was exploiting you while sparing her own children from work? After Hawa was married, should she have stayed with her husband? Would she be better off? Did her husband's eldest wife cross a line? Was Hawa's fear of that wife justified or an excuse? Would you have stayed in that situation? The issue is not what do you think of her but what would you do if it was *you,* and you saw your life stretching out before you like that? It's hard to say. Hawa was later reconciled with her father, but the family's own economic and social marginality precluded opportunities in traditional economic activities. Since her teens, therefore, she has maintained an independent lifestyle as a waitress and as an ashawo woman. A typical bad-luck story.

Human beings are such that when that kind of story is reality, somehow, wonderfully, a voice from somewhere appears and whispers, "Don't die now." If you have no husband or boyfriend, or you have no family willing or able to help you, or you have no money to become a trader, or you have no job, or you have no way to pay for your room or your food, there is little else to do except to go out and look for something, anything. Sometimes because of objective circumstances, and objective circumstances can be every day, the ashawo women go with men to whom they would not normally give a second thought, but then again, so do many women who are not considered ashawo. When they charge a man for sex, the charge often varies depending on subjective factors such as their feelings about the man or their perceptions about where the relationship might go. Some men with money in their pockets may want things to be straightforward and clear and over in the morning; others wouldn't mind finding a compatible girlfriend to take care of as a mistress; others cannot carry a girlfriend but will try their best to give something respectable, just to be nice and not with the idea of getting another chance later. The women, like the men who may be just scraping by, cannot know what or whom they will meet when they go out. Given the opportunity, many ashawo women hold jobs that reduce their dependency a bit and give them a few more options for day-to-day life, whether as waitresses or as hospital workers or as seamstresses or whatever, and many participate in trade. Perhaps as important, they depend on their friends, and they help one another. Most of the time, they get by. Sometimes, it gets really tough. But tough is not so bad if it gives them the chance to travel to someplace they would not have seen or to get something that they would not have had. As Ida Cox put it in a famous song, "Wild women don't have the blues."

None of the above realities tells us as much about their character as we might like to assume at first. There are problems with a model of marginality that portrays ashawos as deviants who have crossed boundaries of sexual conduct and mores. Since sex as such is not the problem because everybody's doing it, and the exchange factor is not the problem because everybody's doing that, too, then do they actually transgress social boundaries and bring social anxieties into focus? First, within the cultural context, the boundaries are not clear-cut. Basically ashawos are sexually active unmarried women in situations of dependence on men. That's a large group. Second, poverty and marginality do not in themselves turn women into ashawos. Similar situations of deprivation and alienation are so widespread that we cannot just point to such conditions as an explanation. By now, several generations of sociologists would be prepared to point out that if that were the case, why do only some women become ashawos only some of the time? By and large, in Africa, most people do not blame them and can understand the expediency behind their movements. Most people, men and women, get along with them.

It is also true in Africa that opposition and mistrust can characterize relations between men and women. These attributes are the counterpoints of the rationality and respect that normally underlie exchange. Perhaps the cynics deserve their share of the truth. On the negative side of this cultural axis of variation are stories of conflict and exploitation and, paradoxically, the reasons why some women see the ashawo life as an alternative of lesser ill. Let us follow that negativity. The name "ashawo" may carry a stigma of sorts, but the name only becomes appropriate at certain times and under certain circumstances. Various health ministries and agencies have no trouble classifying some woman as prostitutes for epidemiological studies. Police have no trouble when they are looking for an easy shakedown. Apart from the very few women who do sex work at such usual sites as ports, however, any stigma the ashawos bear seems mainly related to times and places when women are not under institutional constraints. These are the women who have divorced or left their husbands, the girls who are not under the control of their families, the girls who did not marry. The inference is that they are in their various situations because they don't respect the position of men and obey them. In that sense, their marginality means that their status—who they are—is not clear. Although they are entangled in circumstances, the basic problem with them is that they are free. Contemporary ashawos make do in modern contexts where they are seen as consumers and not producers, yet they are outside ideals of traditions that nowadays are and no doubt always have been part real and part nostalgia.

What does it all mean? Cut off from family, the ashawos have no real strength. Some like Hawa can talk well or appeal to cultural reason, but most get hassled and cheated a bit more than everybody else, and sometimes people say dumb things to them. But it's only sometimes. Sometimes a group of people only serves the occasional purpose of providing someone to blame. Maybe because the ashawos are isolated and defenseless, and there are a lot of them, they are an easy group to blame in a frustrated modern society that needs scapegoats and victims. The urban scene features many diverse and informal settings where social status has become vague, and ashawos are like magnets for pejorative expressions of class-consciousness. In an Africa traumatized by centuries of exploitation, the image of a society being spoiled is habitually and incrementally refined in multiple variations: the country is spoiled; the soldiers—or the Lebanese or the white people or the Nigerians or the whoever—are spoiling the country. As for the women, one constantly hears the reasons why the women have gone bad: the white people are spoiling our daughters; the Ghanaians are spoiling our Togolese girls; the Togolese are spoiling our Burkina girls. It's always something.

What makes the ashawo women bad in the eyes of some men? None of the reasons has much to do with sex. According to some African men who have a particular point of view, ashawo women are the worst kind: besides being harlots, they are unreliable, unrespectable, unrepentant, unrestrained, unregenerate, but worst of all, unaffordable. The ashawos in the upper echelon move with foreigners and the elite of the country, and the whole scene throws the structure of class or racial privileges into the uncomfortable light of the evening. Some of the women are totally out of reach. The ashawos who are called "heavy" are heavily into expensive things and deeply into their hustle, and their needs are thus too heavy for most men to carry. Sometimes the ashawo women don't mind telling that to a man's face. If a man believes a woman to be his social inferior, then oddly enough, in a way the problem is that of a commodity the man thinks should be cheaper. In the old days, he believes, if she was not the daughter of a chief or a big person, he could just call her and give her anything, and she would have been happy. But now her eyes are open, and he also sees that his standard does not measure up. Even in the most broad-minded view such a man can imagine, it's always at least partly her fault.

To add insult to injury, it looks as if the socially ambitious women are taking advantage of their ability to circulate in an open society and trying to arrange their own marriages. Some of them undoubtedly prefer a Western style of gender relations. A few ashawos even have the expressed objective of marrying a European man who can carry them out of all the annoying nonsense that goes on in a developing country. Some avoid friendships with African men, except when absolutely necessary. The international ashawos are relatively few in number, but many African women, including Hawa, do not particularly like African systems of marriage and can enumerate the problems. Marriage is beautiful when things work out, but what they often see in practice are the inconstant behavior of the men, the feuds with the rival wives, the minimal claims to property or inheritance, and the insecurity of child custody.

Some people have concerns about moving an ashawo woman into a relationship. Some people assume that ashawos, unlike good girls, cannot easily be placed into and controlled within long-term frameworks of potential exploitation like traditional marriages. Many ashawo women who later marry become good wives, but there is always the nagging thought that such women are not afraid of the ups and downs of independence. Many married women dislike them because the ashawos divert a man's resources from the women in the home. Some married women dislike them within the tangled web of their own jealousy, maybe because they themselves are stuck within the frustrating institution that marriage often is, maybe because an ashawo woman who marries their husband and comes to join the polygamous household will not give them the respect they are due as senior wives. In contrast, though, there are quite a few married women who will tell their husband to go and marry his ashawo girlfriend and bring her into the household so that she can help with the work. Many things are at stake when a woman enters a man's house, but sexual history is generally irrelevant. In both Western and African societies, it is extremely difficult to look at a group of middle-aged married women and know which among them had more sexual partners when they were young and single.

In summary, Western readers who are squeamish about the way Hawa and others in this book deal with their bodies and with gender relations should be alert to many subtle inconsistencies that make it difficult to criticize these characters' perspectives on sex and exchange in comparison with Western perspectives of prostitution. The comparison doesn't work, and the critique is irrelevant. Furthermore, the cultural context in which the characters function is quite complex. It's hard even to find a place to stand. Single life in the nightclub is just a different world from married life in the household. The traditionalists with whom I worked had a saying: "You use lies to catch a woman and truth to keep her." Pidgin English has a word that captures the ambiguity of the informal relationships of the nightlife scene. The word "boss" means to persuade or convince, to talk nicely with a purpose, sometimes but not necessarily with a connotation of insincerity. Given the possibility of good or bad intentions, the inference can run from confusing and tricking someone to calming someone down. You boss people to get them to go along with you when they're not sure, and you keep them moving. You boss children to make them happy when they're hungry or worried or angry. You boss someone with compliments. You boss someone as a gesture of support. You boss someone to be reasonable about something. You boss someone to take a lower price. You boss someone with a promise. It's all lies, sweet lies. There is another word that circulates in the scene: "shakara." Its usage was popularized in West Africa via a song by Fela Anikulapo Kuti. The word can refer to anybody, but it is certainly associated with the ashawo life, such that an ashawo woman is also shakara. "Shakara" refers to bluffing people and showing yourself to be more than another, or at a minimum, not giving respect to others. "Shakara" also refers to a person who is unreliable, who says one thing and does another, who lies. But a shakara person can be funny. Being shakara is not completely negative because in a partying social context of music and drinking and enjoyment, showing yourself is like strutting your stuff: it's nice. And in a market, too, it is important to make a fine display. In the ashawo life, there is another fine line between pretending and playing. All in all, there is less frustration than one might assume with a scene that most people consider to be something of a game called "Promise and Fail." They know that making a promise is bossing: it is expressed to enhance the good intentions of a plan, and they are happy when they are not disappointed, tolerant when they are. In modern life, love has no assurances, and flirting and seduction are not contingent on telling the truth but rather on self-confidence, risk-taking, and involvement.

Digression on the End of the World

Any talk that links sex and self-betterment in Africa no doubt strikes a sour note these days. The recent appearance of AIDS seems to pose a very real threat to the survival of humanity, striking us where we reproduce. AIDS, among a few other things, reminds us that perhaps we are not far from a day when fossilized footprints will be all that remains of our species. I must note, therefore, that the time period of this book is well before the recognition of the dread disease, during what we may view in retrospect as an age of innocence when love flourished in the Garden of Eden. During the 1960s and early 1970s, when most of the events in this book took place, no one had an idea about AIDS, and antibiotics and other successful treatments were available for sexually transmitted diseases — all the potentially devastating ones and most of the mundane ones as well. A generation of Western youth was joined by the mass media in promoting sexuality as an icon of freedom. The message is still out, to be viewed with the same indulgence we might accord a fanciful beer ad or a music video.

There are two relevant points to consider. First, my discussion of sexual mores and the ambience of exchange has been presented primarily for the benefit of Western readers. If one can simply accept that orientation and get beyond it, it will become clear that this book is not about sex or demi-semi-prostitution at all. Only a small fraction of the events in this book has anything to do with that aspect of Hawa's life. Hawa says that her personal orientation to sex is that she can take it and enjoy it, or leave it and not be disturbed. This book is about her and her associates and their relationships within family and friendship, and an amazing amount is about things that go on around food;[1] it is also about their ideas, their resources and their constraints as they dealt with the society they lived in. The second point

1. See Paul Stoller, *The Taste of Ethnographic Things: The Senses in Anthropology* (Philadelphia: University of Pennsylvania Press, 1989) for some interesting essays on this point.

follows from the first, in the sense that if we know them and the way they were, we can also get an idea about how others like them are likely to respond to or be affected by the epidemic. I will therefore note a few observations on the ashawo life and the relations between men and women in the late 1980s and early 1990s, when the presence of AIDS in West Africa became commonly known, and when I encountered quite a range of thinking about it among the people with whom I talked.

As a friend who works on AIDS for UNICEF wrote me, "We had warnings about [the AIDS epidemic], and supposedly knowledgeable people formulated strategies and communication which were supposed to reverse the tide, and that has been going on around Africa for about fifteen years now. The whole effort has been a remarkably resounding failure, and now a genuine holocaust is upon us. I believe these failures arise because we have set out to tell people what they should do. But most of those young women and men of Africa don't speak our language, and either we don't want to listen to them, or they don't want to talk to us. It may be the rank hypocrisy they perceive in members of the international jet set and beltway bandit crowd, coming in with talk about 'behavioural change communication,' suggesting changes in behaviour which simply don't take into account the realities of their lives or the nature of their dreams."

AIDS made its appearance in West Africa several years after it received media attention in Central and East Africa. There were those who said it came first from Zaire to Abidjan and the African Francophone countries. Many locals said it came from France and Germany and was brought back by Africans who contracted it there. Inside the various nations, no group is uncontaminated, but everyone seems to be able to point to the group that has it, a list headed by anyone who has ever been an ashawo. Many African governments, but not all, have launched aggressive information campaigns about AIDS, certainly more aggressive than ours, yet we complain that they don't give statistics to the World Health Organization because of their fears of scaring off tourists and investors. As usual, we need statistics, but nobody can really know how far the disease has spread. AIDS is difficult to monitor even in an environment with high-tech medicine and high numbers of doctors in the population. In Togo in the late 1980s, several doctors gave me wildly divergent estimates; the only one to believe was the one who said not to believe the claims of anyone. All in all, given their resources, some of the governments are not lagging. The information is out there in media from popular songs to signboards. What could be more aggressive? Well, maybe a lot. The governments that are doing something are not doing enough, and some governments are doing next to nothing. Or else nothing is working. In the late 1980s everyone knew about "slim disease" in East

Africa. Within a decade, South Africa's general seroprevalence rate went from less than 1 percent to more than 20 percent. Can anyone now quarantine such a percentage of a given population? It seems possible that responses will include some stigmatization along with criminalization of high-risk people like ashawos, and the police will be even more encouraged to extort money from ashawo women, though philandering men will continue to infect their wives. When AIDS first arrived in Ghana and Togo, I heard some people suggest that those who are seropositive should all just be taken on a big boat far out into the ocean and thrown overboard. After all, they had been warned, and they didn't mind. They have already committed suicide, so why let them run free in the society to infect others? Such a boat was only a fantasy, of course. Instead, as a short-term solution, it was suggested that maybe some of the victims and seropositives who were found could be locked away in guarded hospital wards to cancel their final flings. There were rumors of such measures, thought perhaps to be true but perhaps part of the fallout from the information campaigns.

The information, which is currently the only viable treatment in Africa, seems to be having some effect. In Accra, where formerly condoms were intensely disliked and the best form of birth control was thought to be D&C, one can see condoms in the wastebaskets at the hotels where the greenhorn ashawos do their business with African clients. On the expatriate front, even those wildest and craziest of guys, the male Peace Corps volunteers, use government-issue condoms. Many people are getting the message. The popular songs are interesting. "Love, Suffer, and Die," says one. "Solitude is the Solution," says another. In their music, African pop musicians typically focus on social problems and concerns, but it seems strange to see people dancing happily in nightclubs and discos to songs about AIDS. But again, it is only dancing, and in an urban African culture, when people meet at clubs to drink and dance, it does not necessarily indicate that the dancers will be going home together. As one musician said about the message in his songs, "The people get it first in the feet, and then it moves to the head." At least the songs are there. Another song is more provocative. The singer goes to visit his doctor friend at the hospital and sees AIDS patients. The doctor tells his frightened friend that AIDS is a sickness like any other, and whatever happens, one must die: if you drink too much, it's your liver; if you eat too much, it's your stomach; and so on. The singer gasps that he is going to abandon love, and the doctor replies, "If you give up love, then why were you born?" The songs inspire conversation and impart awareness. At table with me, an unmarried friend complained bitterly about the inaccessible escape of marriage, "You know, before a man and woman can marry, they have to be together for some time to know if they are the right size for each other, and by that time the virus will have passed." With us was a well-known womanizer who said he had completely stopped his old life: "What?! To die for pussy?! No, no, no!" But Santana was sitting there, too, and he echoed the doctor in the song: "Every death is death," he said.

The drug cocktail approach to treatment that currently seems to put HIV into remission is too expensive and too exacting to be available for the millions of seropositive Africans. If our treatment remains marginally effective, we can anticipate ugly debates about who will pay, or even whether to pay, for the treatment of our poorer fellow citizens in the Western world. The developed Western nations will reassert their own claims of poverty, and people in the Third World will be dying while some people in Europe and America will be saved. Western pharmaceutical companies will object to pirated generic drug treatments. Some public health professionals will say that drug treatment in the Third World is counterproductive: lack of compliance will eventually produce further drug resistance, and scarce resources would be better directed to prevention. The public health interventions in Africa will continue to focus on information and condom use. Some data indicate that many people have quite adequate awareness of the vectors of the disease yet still engage in unprotected sex; many other people claim to be abstaining from sex or drastically limiting their sex lives, and there is some evidence that they are sincere.[1] Much current research in Africa is still focused on tracing the progress of the epidemic: statistics, yeah. Information can only go so far, though. Even people here are only somewhat rational in dealing with risk. Faced with a choice of getting AIDS or not getting AIDS, everybody gets the answer right. But the issues surrounding sex are never clear-cut: we see all kinds of cultural factors at work in people's denial and excuses and contingencies and credibility. People in the West are not particularly conscientious about using condoms, and women here have a tough time negotiating safe sex. In the United States, making your boyfriend wear a condom means that you suspect him of having sex with other women; if he agrees, it means that his potential infidelity is acknowledged, and the whole relationship changes.

Condom use is rarely a straightforward negotiation. Why should we expect that empowering women to make the argument for condom use would

1. See, for example, Christina Linden et al., "Knowledge, attitudes, and perceived risk of AIDS among urban Rwandan women: relationship to HIV infection and behavior change," *AIDS* 5, no. 6 (1991): 993–1002; and Olaf Müller et al., "HIV prevalence, attitudes and behavior in clients of a confidential HIV testing and counseling centre in Uganda," *AIDS* 6, no. 8 (1992): 869–74.

be an effective intervention in Africa, where women are already operating from such a drastic position of weakness? In many places they still kneel down when greeting their husbands. One may or may not find fault with such customs, and they are undoubtedly related to women's vulnerability to AIDS, but we should wonder why it is more operationally feasible to affect cultural patterns of gender relations than to affect cultural patterns of educational access or economic opportunity. Many African AIDS programs focus on women partially because women are perceived as the victims in the sense that they are seen to have less responsibility than men for the sexual network in which they participate. It may seem logical to start with them when changing the equation, but many African women would recommend combatting the epidemic through educational and vocational training, through creating employment opportunities, and through targeting men and family elders as agents of information dissemination and behavior change. Is it the best one can do to focus on direct behavioral interventions that attempt to educate and encourage women to negotiate condom use with their freely philandering boyfriends or husbands? The descriptions and discussions of intimate male-female relations in this book indicate the extent of absurdity in such targeted empowerment efforts.

The scientists, however, will not consider the "stories" to be serviceable, claiming that there is no way for them to use what one might learn from this book. The scientists in charge of public health projects tend to think of ethnographers as people who, in Western contexts, observe how drug users handle their needles, or in African contexts, augment biomedical efforts by maintaining contact with high-risk groups to get people to come in for follow-up seroprevalence studies. The limitations of scientific procedures, which normally make for good science, are everywhere apparent as problems in this picture, from research financing to program implementation. In a marketplace of knowledge, the exchange motive is shameless or subtle or both. Drug manufacturers will hold patents and will justify the high cost of the medications to pay back the costs of research and development. Interventions have to be operational and therefore focus on limited objectives, however weak; they cannot in their conception address broader issues relating to women's economic and social vulnerabilities.[1] That would

1. An example of a population specifically identifying social and cultural factors as the most relevant means to prevention, while the researchers targeted women's empowerment is reported in Quarraisha Abdool Karim et al., "Women and AIDS in Natal/KwaZulu, South Africa: Determinants of the Adoption of HIV Protective Behavior," International Center for Research on Women Report-in-Brief (March 1994) and in "Women and AIDS Research Program: Second Phase," International Center for Research on Women Information Bulletin (March 1995).

be asking those in control of the knowledge about the problem to recommend choosing other types of professionals, maybe even from other institutions, to be service providers or to do phase two of the research.

An African proverb says, "When a river is dry, it is God Who is in shame, not the river." And truly, as for this case, God really should be ashamed. For poor and rich alike, sex is one of the most basic relationships between people. To the young in particular, if it is not the best thing in life, it surely is one of the better ones. And that great river of fine young people is now terrified of sex. Yet of course, people still go out, and the ashawo life is still there. Men and women — beautiful, handsome, pleasant, jovial, personable, sweet, cute, funny, gentle, charming — continue to attract one another. In an African nightclub, they are not forbidden fruits hanging on a tree; they are candy that jumps into your mouth and challenges you to spit it out. Young people — in every country, not only Africa — like sweet things; they always have trouble spitting out candy. Another African proverb says, "You don't gargle honey water to wash out your mouth." Those who are agonizing about the dreaded malady may go out to drink and dance and watch the people, but the thought of AIDS, which stifles temptation in some, inspires pity and incredulity about the behavior of others for whom the thought of AIDS has inspired bravado and recklessness. It is difficult to understand why the ashawos are still out there, yet every one of the women has a story or a reason. At the African bars, they have heard about AIDS, but while a few simply shrug their shoulders about having to make do, many still talk about trying to get vocational school fees together, and most will still portray the ashawo life as a temporary expedient before an eventual marriage. The river is dry, but it is God Who is ashamed.

All the reasons why women become ashawo are still there. In West Africa, quite a bit has changed, but the economic situation of the Third World is hardly any better than it ever was. These days, with so many men avoiding women, the ashawo life has become harder, though some men, Africans and Europeans and Americans and Asians, continue to chase the women. At the more disreputable clubs and hotels, the women are hanging about, desperate. Because of competition, some have become aggressive in ways one didn't see before. Some are so poor that they will decline a beer and ask for the money instead in order to go outside and buy food from a street vendor. As for the ashawos at the high end of the scale, once they have been there, with the fine clothes, air-conditioning, Black Label Scotch, and their dreams of a bourgeois life in Europe, does anyone expect them to agree to be selling ice water or bananas in the market? If the epidemic continues to extend, we will see many types of response from people who cannot just stop eating. Among them will be denial. There are those who simply don't mind the threat: their problems are too pressing for anyone to warn them about something that might or might not happen in five or ten years. Indeed, we have seen that response here among at-risk people with drug-abuse problems. The conditions of their lives already say quite a lot about the extent to which they think of the future or find it reasonable to do so. Most people respond to danger only to the extent that they feel themselves to be at risk, and then not even all of them respond. In West Africa, as the epidemic is still young, there are those who just refuse to believe it. There are those too who feel that they have no choice. The macho belief circulates among some people — men and women — that the disease cannot get *them.* Others say you only get it if you fear it, as if the virus conducts interviews. Others say that witches can make people get it; the corollary is that witchcraft medicine available from sorcerers can protect you from it. Some take it that they are probably already infected but don't want to know. For them life has become a Saint Vitus's dance to snatch a few moments of what they want before the inevitable. Stories circulate about a Chinese or Congolese or Tanzanian herbalist who found a plant that can cure the disease; no one knows how someone in a village without electricity has been able to do what all the world's doctors cannot. And who could have imagined the ghastly South African fantasy that sex with a child virgin could cure the disease?

The problem with AIDS is that the thing is hidden; no one sees it. An appeal to logic is not much of a solution when people are crazy with fear and desperation. Perhaps if the disease reaches a more visible level, and everyone knows somebody who is dying or dead, people's ideas and behavior will change. Perhaps AIDS will change the way people take care of their daughters. How will they do so if they themselves are sick? Or perhaps it will push many women into types of work that they will have to struggle to enter, or into markets that are already filled beyond the buying capacity of the population. No one knows how the situation will evolve. It looks as if AIDS has the potential to alter the life of future generations. But those who are there now are the lost generation. For them, it will be "Had I known," and it will be too late. At the moment, people who have only a little money to spend still go out to refresh their minds, to drink and dance, to be with friends, to watch people, to flirt, to hear music, to laugh, to meet people, to do all the things they did before — except one. The world of African nightlife seems now divided into two groups, those who have condemned themselves to death and those who have decided to go crazy with frustration.

We should not sneer at the twisted rationalizations of some members of the current generation. The women who are caught in this mess are responding with hope and patience to conditions of poverty, unemployment, social dislocation, exploitation, illiteracy, juvenile and gender vulnerability, and the rest of a long list of negatives. On the positive side of their struggle against necessity they exhibit admirable qualities: an indefatigable spirit, a playful attitude toward life, a willingness to take risks. But viewed against the vague context of AIDS, these qualities begin to look like foolishness, confusion, and philosophical I-Don't-Care-ism. We in the West cannot pontificate, either, for we seem to lack the capability and we most definitely lack the commitment to do much for Africa. People have to be dying in numbers, past a statistical threshold, before we respond to the visible symptoms of disasters there. In such times, we like to find out how the situation developed and why the situation is so difficult to treat. Our media focus on governments and groups that are impeding our relief efforts, without focusing on the role that the world economic system that supports our comfort has played in the genesis of the disaster or might have played in preventing or minimizing it. Our well-bounded and enlightened sympathy has at last achieved this compromise: we try not to blame the victims if we can blame their relatives and representatives.

But AIDS carries a personal stigma, particularly as long as it affects other people and other populations. The crux of the stigma is fear. We currently cannot cure AIDS, and its mutability makes it a very intractable problem. As the identification of those at-risk among us becomes more diffused, we are afraid for ourselves, for our lives and our ways of living. Still, Western popular culture elevates consumerism and youthfulness and sexuality. The spread of AIDS is abetted by both our culture and our nature. A species cannot abstain from sex, and in every culture and historical period, the institutions that channel sex and give structure to love have rarely if ever exerted their authority with total proficiency or without unforeseen consequences. At the moment, while the disease is still somewhat localized, we continue as before with slight modifications while we hope for a cure. The current treatment is so expensive that only people in developed countries can afford it, but maybe we will get a better treatment option. Failing that, we can hope that perhaps the virus will mutate into a more benign form. Of course, perhaps the virus will mutate into a hardier or more dangerous or more transmissible form. But it is not my purpose here to speculate: bouncing around the doomsday issue has merely the purpose, in a perverse way, of turning blame into sympathy.

If we think about AIDS affecting us as it has begun to affect people in Africa, and we ask ourselves what we would do or would have done along the way in our lives, it should be clear to most that there is no complete escape from risk. The risk exists on a continuum, a line on which every individual would move back and forth, making compromises with the chance of infection. In the perspective of the doctor in the song, AIDS is a sickness like other sicknesses. Ashawos and other women were dying young before AIDS appeared, of tuberculosis, of hepatitis, of infections, of complications from malaria and abortions and childbirth. Perhaps AIDS has only raised the ante, adding another risk, another means of personal catastrophe or untimely death. The attitudes of Hawa and her counterplayers toward their options, their bodies, and their lives may be horribly out-of-step in a world that has changed, and if one must judge them, at least they should be judged within the world as it appeared to them before AIDS. How could they worry about what didn't exist? Maybe some of them would have dealt with their lives differently. Certainly, though, the system has not changed.

Hindsight may make this book more of a eulogy than a celebration. It may be appropriate on some level to infer generalizations about the current generation and the current crisis. If so, I would reiterate my point that Hawa's stories from her life describe people in her culture and how they are. To understand them, we need to get beyond or at least temporarily suspend our own cultural ways of thinking about sex, prostitution, poverty, and relationships of exchange. Hawa's stories focus on their problems and their resources, and in that light, the book is populated by characters in whose feelings and thoughts we will have privy knowledge. As they deal with one another, we should note how they live with and take care of one another. They spend amazing amounts of time and resources helping mere acquaintances. Even when they are at their worst or their most foolish, there are boundaries on malice, cruelty, and violence. Their essential decency shines through in their compassion, their open-mindedness, their willingness to forgive and to share. If their circumstances and life choices would put them at risk of AIDS today, let us consider both their will to survive and their capacity to pity life's victims. We might therefore think of AIDS as only one dangerous snake among others in the dark, a symbol of bad luck on the ground they tread upon. It is probably impossible to forget about AIDS when thinking about African women, but there is one double-edged question whose answer is less than self-evident: if we were to pretend AIDS does not exist, as it did not when the events in this book took place, how much difference would there be?

Ethnography to the Second Power

Despite many sociological and cultural studies of the lives of African women, there have been very few studies focusing on the psychological dimensions of women's experiences in Africa.[1] Typically, scholars have had to turn to fictionalized portraits in novels and short stories, more often than not written by men. African women have been subjects in some ethnopsychiatric literature, and their frequent role as spirit mediums has drawn attention. Nonetheless, the primary focus of social researchers has been on social roles and social status, and by extension, social power. These issues have almost overwhelmed the complementary feminist issues relating to how women create various types of identities for themselves as they adapt and react to their circumstances. On the social levels at least, a relatively detailed picture has been drawn of the position of women in African societies, showing limitations in terms of ascribed status and access to resources as well as a general social distancing of men and women in terms of interaction, productivity, and institutional roles. Marriage and children have been the key elements of women's traditional roles and expectations. For both men and women, radical social changes have been reflected in changes in status and roles. To the extent that the old ways are not viable, people have had to develop new roles and new values without the benefit of adequate models. Some current research on African women has focused on situations in which women control institutionalized interaction or reverse the general patterns of traditional roles. Other work on status has turned the issue around and pointed out the disparity between women's frequently low status and the high degree of real influence they have, direct and indirect, in conserving the status quo or in exercising actual as opposed to ascribed control of cultural means.

Perhaps the most significant result of contemporary research on the status of African women is that we now realize how many factors determine their position. In Eastern and Southern Africa, where male labor migration compounds the restrictions of traditional roles, women have experienced more problems adjusting to social and economic innovation than has been the case in West Africa. In West Africa, there is some question as

1. There is a vast body of literature about African women. For more than 1,500 pages of bibliography covering one decade, see Davis A. Bullwinkle, compiler, *African Women: A General Bibliography, 1976–1985,* African Special Bibliographic Series, no. 9 (New York: Greenwood Press, 1989), with two successive volumes, divided between *Women of Northern, Western, and Central Africa* and *Women of Eastern and Southern Africa.* I need note specifically only that aspects of the discussion in the preceding section on exchange are presented in detail by Kenneth Little in *African Women in Towns: An Aspect of Africa's Social Revolution* (Cambridge: Cambridge University Press, 1973), and the point below about judging marriages on the basis of status is made by E. E. Evans-Pritchard in *The Position of Women in Primitive Societies* (New York: Free Press, 1965).

to whether the women's situation has deteriorated or improved. In some cases, women have often been able to expand traditional roles and increase their productive significance, though in some other cases industrialization has reduced the significance of traditional relationships and resources for women in households as well as for those who are branching out into business, and women have encountered new problems. Certainly, women traders still comprise one of the most productive sectors, if not the most productive, of many modern West African economies. By and large, however, men dominate most institutions, and male domination extends to many petty aspects of a woman's life. Thus, most studies of African women have been concerned with the ways in which women use traditional institutions and patterns of association to exercise their complementary functions in male-dominated societies.

While anthropologists continually make fresh attempts to respond theoretically to this imbalance, it should be noted that much of the contemporary scholarship on African women is equivocal. When we look at the situation of women in an alien culture, it is worthwhile to remember the difficulty of making cultural comparisons based on status concerns. Marriage, for example, is an intimate relationship that is difficult to evaluate on the basis of observations of work patterns and institutional roles; weighing the significance of various factors in a marriage is perhaps as much a moral task as a sociological one. Those who are reluctant to intervene in or who find it difficult to comprehend the continuing marriages of some of their own friends might regard some of the scholarly analyses of African marital roles as over-confident. While it is important to address the issue of male domination in society, it is necessary that research take into account what African women themselves say about their situation as a supplement to all research interpretations based on observations of activity or survey data. On that level, this book at least is Hawa's book in her own voice, recorded faithfully, transcribed carefully, and edited minimally. Perhaps more important, identity manifests not only a personal response to objective factors but also a style of living. Comparative categories disappear within the ambiguous significance of lifestyle and attitude: work is a pleasure for some people, and sex is an obligation for others; a strong family is a support for some and a prison for others; pride is a spirit and a sin. Sometimes, the more we know people, the less inclined we are to question them about their lives; we set aside whatever disturbs us, and we only ponder how the positive elements of their example can help us.

Doing research in Africa is complicated enough even when it's fun, but doing research on African women is particularly difficult. Those who have been able to do such research deserve credit for their achievement even if they themselves stress the unique people or circumstances that might have facilitated their efforts. In many African traditional contexts, women are reluctant to talk to outsiders, whether male or female, about the inner workings of their family and economic life. Even insiders have trouble knowing what is going on. With regard to the markets that the women dominate, I was told by a Togolese friend who had two master's degrees and a very successful business as an importer and distributor to market women: "The *Grand Marché* of Lomé is a special university which you can never understand. You can check all the classic economic laws, and you will never find any logic there. With ten Ph.D.'s in your pocket, you can never know whether what they tell you is 'yes' or 'no.' But they are making money."

At the other end, in the family contexts of many traditional African societies, there is no community property, and it is common for wives to hold their money separately from their husbands. The husband himself rarely knows how much money his wives actually have or even how much of the money he may give them for the household's food gets redirected to other purposes. In such contexts, if a clever man with a head for accounting continually asked his wife the prices of various foods in the market, she could leave him and everybody would understand. It is not likely that she will tell her money management secrets to a survey researcher. Outsiders like census takers cannot even find out from her how many people live in the house; she will say she doesn't know. Deference to husbands or family heads or senior wives is only one reason among many others in the general cultural background, where gossipy talking about other people generally implies either abuse or the malicious revelation of their secrets and weaknesses. On another level, in many societies, serious taboos and vulnerabilities are attached to asking about or discussing the mother's side of a family line. To get into details about such issues would take us far afield, in some cases into comparative religions and beliefs about the mother-child relationship, and in other cases into indigenous histories of secret tribal origins in migrations, wars, and interminglings. All in all, it takes a special person or a lot of time to understand what is going on with women in traditional contexts, and it is easier to get to successful women or disgruntled women or, in this case, marginal women like Hawa.

My main point here is simply that trying to understand the situation of women in Africa often involves more than just looking at the constraining character of social roles and status balanced against feelings and self-consciousness about gender and identity. What African women know about their societies goes far beyond those particular issues of feminist concern into areas of more universal concern; at the same time, both gender-related and broader types of data and the people who can give such data are often inaccessible. If we are looking for the deep spiritual or psychological forces that might be at work in the women's realm, and we reduce our focus to status concerns and power relations as the most significant means to evaluate a person's life, then we also tend to reduce the women who incomprehensibly put up with the African situation. When we rely too much on that particular lens, if the women say their way of life is fine, they appear pathetic and unenlightened; if they say it's terrible, they appear pathetic and miserable. There is no doubt, of course, that traditional roles and status hierarchies are aspects of life that almost all people knock their heads against. But as sensitive as we may be to the issues, who among us views himself or herself primarily in terms of social status? Most people would probably say that in their lives there is much more going on than such a narrow-focus lens can see. If one is not careful when writing about African women, one begins to sound like a self-assured development specialist planning to help them enter the advanced world of modern womanhood. It certainly would not hurt for African women — or men or children — to have a Bill of Rights to set standards for individualism and to protect them from getting pushed around. But there is an inherent dilemma and well-acknowledged burden in gender studies: the constructive advocacy that motivates the study of women's lives per se also tends toward politicized interpretations that inject an ironic element of moral smugness simply by virtue of focusing on our subjects' problems.

When Westerners look at Africa, we gravitate toward gender concerns. The obvious heritage of male domination and male-female role separation is one of the first things we see: to our eyes, it is clearly exploitative and grates against our patent values. Consequently, very few people, from colonial administrators to missionaries to anthropologists, have tried to defend it and maintain that whatever other elements or benefits there might be to the situation outweigh the accompanying inequalities. The situation is serious, and so is most of the writing that describes it or disputes it, though perhaps some of its redeeming features are hidden between the lines. The whole situation certainly doesn't look too good in this book, either. Indeed, it is easier to understand somebody like Hawa, who goes against the grain in many ways, than many of the women in traditional societies who find ways to cope within traditional structures. The fact remains, too, that it is easier to talk to marginal women who are in some ways outside the system, who have indeed increased their independence within one or more of its aspects or else who have a critical or negative view of it.

In general, even including the research done on modern women in African cities, the life histories that we currently have exhibit the same concern with status and power as most of the analytic studies: they deal with how women cope with traditional roles or with circumstances that develop out of the ways traditional roles are affected by the changing cultural scene. Hawa's stories offer a further dimension to the current trend that looks for situations where women stand on their own and stand up for themselves. Hawa's stories fit in and should be a worthwhile addition to this growing body of literature about new opportunities and new problems. When we apply the sociological view, we can understand her alienation because her "dis" personhood is accentuated by increased distance: she does not tie herself to one setting, whether static or changing, rural or urban, traditional or modern. The psychological level is more complex, however, because Hawa's irrepressible insistence on being treated fairly played a large part in her becoming an ashawo.

Understanding the positive nature of Hawa's commitment to her life is a bit tricky. Hawa is one individual making her own adaptation to social change. In building a bridge between past and future, she illustrates the hopes and needs of many people who are now also responding to the challenges posed by Africa's history. On another level, her character and intelligence have brought her to a position — evident in her values but not formulated as an ideology — that is far removed from the traditional ideals of many of her contemporaries. Actually, despite the obvious themes raised by Hawa's ashawo life, much of this book is about family relationships, about friendship, about children, and particularly about women and the way they treat one another. Many other women appear in this book, and by giving them their own voices in extended alternating dialogues, Hawa enhances her portrayal of them as real people. Many of Hawa's friends who have not achieved her degree of independence resemble the women portrayed in scholarly literature more than Hawa does. They act like many of the African wives who have been described, for example, as rationalizing and accepting the beatings or arrogant authority that some of their male friends occasionally hold over them. Several stories in this book portray the efforts and inability of Hawa's weaker and less resourceful girlfriends to pattern their behavior in ways that resemble Hawa's more independent ideas. Other women in this book are bitter or alienated or exploitative or aggressive. Some are jealous of Hawa, and some help her. While Hawa's accounts of these women are offered as interesting narratives, they also function as her own collection of case studies, conducted with detailed descriptions of the different perspectives of the female participants in various incidents.

In the stories that follow, Hawa moves with a kaleidoscopic assortment of people and gives us a panoramic view of contemporary African life. Her narrative tendency to show rather than merely to tell made her an excellent witness because she steadfastly avoided value judgments. When I attempted to prod her into moral judgments of the ashawo life by suggesting some popular biases, she immediately corrected me: "Some, maybe some, but not all. You can't say all." In assessing her own life and in providing background for her slice-of-life accounts of some of her less-gifted or more-alienated friends, she traced the life histories of a number of ashawo women. From spoiled only children to educated and rebellious bourgeoises to those left in the lurch of more localized circumstances like Akan matrilineal inheritance anomalies, Hawa was capable of understanding their motives and circumstances and of undertaking their advocacy, at least to the point of accepting the validity of their responses in their own terms. In so doing, she gave a tremendous amount of information. She did not focus solely on women: in her narratives, she tells us much about African men, those who are her male counterparts on the margins of society and those who are ambivalent about giving her the respect she demands. She also tells us how people help and exploit, use and abuse each other in order to survive economically in modern African cities. In short, she gives us a rich and complex view of her world, and what is more important, she gives us a positive view of it all, one that has depth because it does not flinch from conflicts or harsh realities, one that is inspirational because it retains humor, sympathy, and charm.

Many social scientists will classify this book as a life history, no doubt, and add what they like of it to the portrait they are continuing to draw of African cities and the lives of African women. Students of literature and history, on the other hand, may see it as an autobiography, an exploration of the meaning of the self. In a notably clear scheme for classifying the types of autobiography,[1] one literary critic has maintained that people who tell their life stories generally seem to be interested in one of three things: demonstrating the essence of the self in relation to nature, as in Rousseau's *Confessions;* demonstrating the historical continuity of the self in relation to broad cultural patterns and changes, as in the *memoirs* of great personages; or demonstrating the ethical integrity of the self in relation to social and moral law. Hawa's stories most closely resemble the third type of autobiographical focus, which literary critics call an *apology.* As with any type of autobiographical work, the extent to which Hawa justifies herself, the role of any such self-justification in maintaining her self-image, and the effect of her intentions on her recollections are aspects of her narrative that readers will perhaps wish to consider. To me, autobiography has an essen-

1. Francis R. Hart, "Notes for an Anatomy of Modern Autobiography," in *New Directions in Literary History,* ed. Ralph Cohen (Baltimore: Johns Hopkins University Press, 1974), 220–47.

tial validity merely as testimony, and a reader's engagement with issues of moral judgment does not detract from that validity but rather indicates that an autobiographer or a biographer has achieved his or her purpose of demonstrating the special interest due a particular life. It is, after all, the purpose of life histories to make readers briefly suspend moral and theoretical perspectives in order to challenge these perspectives with the circumstantial details of a life situation. Hawa's life history certainly provides a portrait of her times from her perspective, and as such, it has a certain value and intrinsic interest.

Within this book we can see the convergence of a number of issues on a single life, yet this book is not quite the same as an autobiography: Hawa was not telling the story of her life; she was telling stories from her life. To an extent, she was constructing her life out of the stories, yet she seems neither to see the elements of pathos in her situation nor to promote her own decisions as solutions. Autobiography is different from biography because many biographers demonstrate insight into the roots of their subject's life problems that the subjects do not themselves recognize. In biography — as in social science — there is often tension and even dramatic irony between what the biographer and we readers know about the subjects and what the subjects know about themselves. Readers of autobiography, armed with hindsight, therefore tend themselves to be especially alert to the evaluative task that a biographer would normally assume for them. For example, when we read about people in biography or autobiography, we see the connections between their troubles and their childhood experiences, and given a contemporary psychological orientation toward insight, we often and quite unreasonably expect autobiographical subjects to exhibit a degree of psychological sophistication that is supposedly a measure of self-actualization. In Hawa's case, readers will easily be able to connect her childhood experiences with her adult character, as when physical isolation triggers fears of being abandoned and forgotten or when she reacts strongly against certain predatory individuals. Readers will be able to analyze the themes of her relationship to her father. But Hawa does not make these connections explicitly. If someone were to say to her that the reason she enjoys exploiting certain people stems from her own childhood abuse, she might agree but she would also point out in her own way how emotionally authentic and morally appropriate her response to a specific situation was. She makes the connections implicitly and without analysis, and Western readers may find that her stories invite analysis yet render it somewhat irrelevant.

I believe that, like me, many readers will prefer to contemplate the situations Hawa describes than to analyze Hawa herself. In a strange way, she herself sometimes recedes into the background because of her focus on actions and conversations. When she was talking to me, I was absorbed in admiring her amazing memory for details, the objectivity of her perception of personality differences, and her ability to dramatize them. I was fascinated by her self-confident happiness and her ability to maintain her sense of humor. My experience with her storytelling is the foundation of how I understand what happened during our work. I took a detour later and found myself thinking defensively when I was challenged in several conversations about the typical vulnerabilities of life historical research, that is, the extent to which she may have been basically motivated to justify herself. Why is that issue important to some people? Is it the humanistic critics' version of the expertise of the development specialists, the protected interpretive space where significance is defined and allocated? In the end, in Hawa's case, the issue seemed a diversion. Although Hawa's autobiographical agenda—if classified as an apology—was focused on her ethical integrity as she moved through various social realms, my experience during the interviews was rather that I was listening to her tell stories, and I was thinking how smart and funny she was. In the stories themselves, she conveyed an abiding interest in seeing people and how they live in different places. Therefore, to my mind, Hawa was a storyteller with an ethnographic purpose. Her stories are not just a collection of self-serving anecdotes; they continually and cumulatively deepen into a serious and devastating critique of her culture, even while they entertain. It is that same mixture of philosophy and fun that we have become used to seeing in traditional African arts. In that regard, as we sat, basically she was trying to entertain us. As she told her stories, she laughed and I laughed. I laughed when I wrote them up, and I still laugh when I read them or think about them.

Much of the fiction that comes out of Africa as well as the majority of autobiographical work by educated Africans seems to have an ethnographic character. Some literary critics acknowledge that conjunction by talking of "autoethnography." Any autobiography or biography has a cultural location, of course, and many specifically address questions of cultural meaning. Autoethnography is distinguished by a sense that the author's experience as an insider imparts knowledge about a given culture (or an enveloping institution) and, frequently, that the knowledge about the culture is as significant as what happens to the protagonists. There is a premise that a reader can generalize about local culture from the author's experience or perspective. Furthermore, such works are specifically characterized by a concern for an audience that is outside that cultural or institutional milieu and by a self-conscious attention to conventions that can enhance qualities of credibility and realism. Sometimes such self-consciousness resembles a kind of defensiveness that weakens the genre and implies acceptance of external literary conventions over the voice of the author.

I would separate Hawa's stories from that genre because Hawa was not literate. I would also maintain that it is an advantage that her stories are uncompromised by many literary concepts. She did not see herself as writing fiction, even for a minute, nor did she see herself soliciting a literate audience or giving information that outsiders in particular might value. It is rather I who has addressed outside audiences with this introduction and with the many annotations about idioms and local references. She herself did not appear to be talking to a different audience from the one she was used to among her friends around the cooking pot. Nevertheless, Hawa's apparent lack of self-consciousness did not prevent her from touching concerns of great cultural depth. There should be nothing disconcerting about the vagueness of the issue of her purpose, particularly because her characteristic intellectual style—her genre of discourse, so to speak—shares much with traditional African oral arts based on interlocution and storytelling. Indeed, many of the stories consist mainly of conversations.

With Hawa, the movement of her stories led her back to her childhood, and from there to stories of village life. These stories along with her accounts of urban living ultimately formed a broad backdrop for a number of reflections—in story form—on the contemporary status of institutions like marriage and the family and of mores attendant on childhood, friendship, authority, sickness, and women. While we were doing our interviews, I was not aware of how much of a whole her stories were, though I had a sense that her stories about village life, about her family, and about witchcraft helped to contextualize her life choices. She had been all over the place, and her stories covered a lot of territory, too. People don't usually have the range of experience she had unless they look for it, but I was slow to recognize the extent to which she was a seeker driven by curiosity and a willingness to use her own life to gather material for her stories.

Why did she talk to me in such depth? In the isolated and nondirected format of our interviews, I provided Hawa with a different kind of opportunity from just entertaining her friends with one or two stories around the cooking pot. In our work together, she had an opportunity for a more extended, more concentrated and more ambitious period of in-dwelling and storytelling. Although the premise of our work was the production of a larger unity based on her experience, I just didn't make the connection to admit that she in her brilliance was also providing a broader vision that encompassed the whole text of her life as an ethnography and as a critique of her society. In effect, *she* took advantage of the situation. She used me as a way of fulfilling what she was already doing with her stories and what she had been doing all her life. Although I did not clearly see it at the time of our interviews, I believe now that she was easily capable of that kind of sustained focus.

I was doing a number of things right even though I did not fully appreciate the ethnographic aspect of Hawa's stories until I finished putting them all together. What is surprising, though, is that at the same time I was also doing intensive interviews that were explicitly ethnographic with a traditional drummer in northern Ghana, an indigenous intellectual in an ancient African state. His discourse was disciplined, full of proverbs, genealogical history, and other heady stuff. It was easy to imagine him taking control of the project. During that work, the drummer placed me in the position of an apprentice receiving his cultural knowledge as an inheritance of the tradition, and I was able to assume the role he gave me. With Hawa I was after her descriptions, which I recognized as ethnographic without necessarily considering them to be systematic at the time. For almost anyone, I believe, part of the difficulty in perceiving Hawa's ethnographic purpose is her nearly total reliance on stories. She might be easily contrasted to the traditionalists whom Western ethnographers seek out to open their eyes in their research. There is a sense of weight and seriousness to the traditionalists, a sense of "culture" in artifact and ceremony and any place we look for symbolic complexity. The art dealers, curators, and collectors who complement the academic search for culture also look to the ceremonial realm to authenticate an art object and increase its value.[1] Hawa does not rely on such realms to talk about culture, and her ethnographic potential was ambiguous even to me. Maybe she was just too funny. Maybe the state of the ethnographic genre was too narrow at the time. I received many more grants to support my work with the traditionalist than for my work with Hawa, and maybe that fooled me, too.

During the period when I was trying to get funding to work on Hawa's stories, my efforts to represent the work within conventional academic contexts were productive in some ways but also distracted me from remembering what was going on in the interviews themselves. I got caught up in the issue of self-justification and missed perceiving the type of intelligence that was at work. It was only when I finished assembling everything that I recognized her agenda to be more than an account of her experiences. Almost with a shock, I understood that there was a reason why I had

1. See Christopher B. Steiner, *African Art in Transit* (Cambridge: Cambridge University Press, 1994) and Sally Price, *Primitive Art in Civilized Places* (Chicago: University of Chicago Press, 1989).

chased her all over West Africa, from Ghana to Togo to Burkina Faso. Hawa brought a special dimension because she was a virtuoso storyteller. I knew some interesting people who could tell good stories but no one who was up to her standard; she was far beyond even Santana. Her virtuosity as a storyteller was a reflection of her perceptive intellect and her observational skills. I was following a deeper intuition about her, that she was a seeker as well as a storyteller. When all the stories were in place, I thought that she resembled seekers I have met in many places, particularly young ones, who plan their lives almost systematically to widen their experience of the world.

Hawa's agenda was her life and not the stories in this book. Perhaps I should have understood that about Hawa from the first, since I was also somewhat like that at the time I knew her. I only had my intuition as a bond of sympathy that went beyond judgment to an admiration of her intellectual style. I do not think that she would consider her success the fact she has had more access to the goods in a consumer society than most people in her country, and she has drunk a lot of champagne, eaten well, and had lots of laughs. I do not think that she would consider her marginality a curse of destiny because she never hesitates to move from place to place. Hawa's kaleidoscopic and panoramic view covers as wide a range of cultural experience as was available to her: good and bad, cities and villages, children and adults, boys and girls and men and women and old men and old women, marriage and independence, traditional religion and cynical skepticism, Africans (she speaks the language of her own people as well as Ashanti, Ewe, Hausa, Dioula, Mossi, Dagbamba, and Ga), Lebanese, British, French, Germans. As I have said, people do not usually have that range of experience unless they search for it. Like a typical ethnographer, as she observes each situation, she always asks why someone is saying something, and she analyzes the situations by looking at, or playing upon, people's intentions. Like an astute ethnographer, she searches for and dwells at the many points where culture becomes a problem. In this regard she shares the conceptual basis of the reflexive method, and she engages each diverse cultural arena with her perspective even while subjecting herself to the transformative potential of her experience.

Ethnography has been narrowly conceived but broadly defined as the description of culture, and in today's world there is no reason why we should not elevate certain types of work that formerly were subtly demeaned under the genre of life history or oral autobiography, a classification that reserves definitive interpretation or broader perspective to people supposedly better qualified than the indigenous authors. My work with Hawa convinced me that there are some life historical efforts that, by virtue of the subject's engagement with the challenges of a given cultural context, grow beyond the personal. Through extensive observation and deeply perceived experience, they achieve a level of cultural portraiture such that they can be considered ethnographies in their own right. How can we give a privileged position to one or another view? Does one need a doctoral degree, from a certain academic discipline, from a certain school of thought, in a certain decade? What do we think we need to know in order to think we know about Africa? Even in as small a literary realm as ethnography, there is no longer even a terminological center to struggle over. Under the pressures of social change, the defining images of traditional cultures have lost their influence, and countless people are struggling with cultural issues even while the perception of culture becomes more obscure. If we are going to avoid interpreting people's experience for them, we have to be more receptive to their voices and find ways to help their voices emerge. Still, many people who should know better, including intellectuals, have trouble accepting the relativity of knowledge. The indigenous universes of discourse are contained and limited with the prefix "ethno" to show that they are localized to a particular group. We have ethnobotany, ethnohistory, ethnocriticism, ethnomathematics. What shall we do with an ethnography done by an illiterate? It would be awkward to call it an ethno-ethnography, or an ethnography squared. Let us give it a positive designation and call it ethnography to the second power.

As I have noted, my initial experience of the interviews, enjoying listening to Hawa, should have been my key to understanding what was happening. It was when I thought I needed to *know* something that I began to ask questions about self-justification and rationalization. Such questions didn't lead anywhere except as ways to try to pick holes in the stories or in her character. Moreover, they obscured my acknowledgment, indeed even my perception, of her ethnographic purpose and control. In the same way, there can be no end to speculative assessments or conventional criticisms about Hawa's purpose or about my role in the interviews. No matter how much some people may wish to control for reliability or intention or any of the psychological factors at work, there is much one can never know about the process. As a process, intensive interviewing is easy to criticize. There will always be someone who will question whether the interviews are "untainted," implying that the subject's story has been corrupted or distorted by your biases. For example, you may have influenced the subject to talk about certain things. You may have chosen certain incidents over others. Your eventual assemblage of the subject's life story may not reflect what the subject initially intended when beginning to work with you. The subject is mainly engaged in an exercise in self-justification and the life history has limited relevance. The story has lost meaning in the movement across cultures, perhaps in your translation, perhaps in the extent to which you did—or did not—contextualize the subject's story within a broader framework. These criticisms have no answers. Raising such issues is often the main alternative to being personally receptive to the experiences the stories are conveying. The stories themselves are the key, and what is important is the way the stories resonate. One can share information about the context of the research, but the only thing that ever convinces anyone that the research was done well is the ring of truth in the stories.

If Hawa's storytelling was the medium of her ethnographic purpose, then what linked her to me was indeed the intuitive recognition of her vision that we shared, a sense of her life as a playing field of cultural observation. She knew of my interest in culture and she knew the way I was moving with the people in the society around us. In the urban scene, we were both "guys," "believers" with "easy understanding." What I assume, therefore, is that in some types of interviewing, shared intuitions have to be there in order to nurture the subject's unconscious vision and help the subject to articulate it. The particular demands of talking about one's life involve a journey of memory and self-discovery that can only be vaguely anticipated, and indeed, cannot be charted at the beginning. In such an intensely focused interview process, the sympathetic nature of the communication between interviewer and subject cannot be controlled, objectified, or clarified without interfering with the goal of the interviews to elicit inner experience. In intensive interviewing of the type that produced this book, getting the story is never simply a matter of placing a tape recorder in front of somebody and transcribing what the person says. Part of the process takes place outside the specific interview sessions, and part of it has already taken place before the first tape is rolling. Your subject talks to you only superficially because he or she trusts you as a supportive person who will not take advantage of the weaknesses or inadequacies the interviews expose. The more important basis of your subject's trust is the subject's belief that you *understand* what he or she is saying, can identify with it and affirm it. That is the wish being played out. That shared commitment to the subject's life allows the subject to maintain his or her voice even if talking to an eventual audience that is bigger than the two of you. Sometimes while you sit there with your mouth shut and watch the tapes spin and wonder whether you will have a big problem when you have to transcribe them, you are enabling the subject to dwell in memories and to decide what needs to be said when he or she also does not know where all this talk is going. But whether your relationship is characterized as a delicate presence or, more assertively, as a special type of mutuality that promotes the emergence of insight, you are not a passive listener.

There were thus several things I did right. First, I was able to recognize

Hawa. Even if I did not anticipate the full evolution of her discourse, I knew enough people and I knew enough about the scene to know that working with her presented a special opportunity worth exploring, that she had something of value to offer in her stories. Second, I was able to get Hawa to do the work. I nurtured our friendship and was on good terms with her and with people we both knew. I followed her for several years through several countries. I talked with her about what I saw in her, and I provided a situation in which she felt comfortable so that we could get started. I kept her talking while she found her own way into the work and developed her role in our relationship. Third, therefore, I gave up some of my control of the project and gave her room to change the dynamics — the flow and extent — of the interviews. Fourth, I respected the original inspiration and attitude that characterized the work, and I worked hard to preserve the style and substance of her discourse as her own. In doing so, I left open the possibility of my eventual acknowledgment of her control. Things always look easy when they are finished, but to the extent that my role is of interest, I would say that it required patience, discipline, and a thorough familiarity with the social territory.

Working with Hawa, I did not have the typical problem of helping a subject maintain an overview of the material, and I had little to do apart from starting her off. The stories had their own momentum. Sometimes in the middle of a story, she would laugh and exclaim, "Hey! How did you get me to talk about this?" Sometimes we would be talking about something, and she would say, "Hey, you reminded me!" But comments like that were mainly her way of acknowledging my presence as an audience. She was obviously ready. Once she got going, she supplied her own connections and talked nonstop. Since I had already heard some of Hawa's stories and since I already knew personally not only her but also about two dozen of the people whom she discussed,[1] I occasionally alerted her of the need to elaborate on some unmentioned points that were in our personal knowledge but would help answer the questions a strange audience might have, though such moments were remarkably rare. We spent a lot of time talking and telling stories without the tape recorder, and occasionally I asked her to tell one of those stories for the tape. Sometimes, too, she would say she didn't

1. Among people who are featured characters in various stories, in this book and its sequel, I knew Mama Amma, Limata, Jacqueline, Eddie, Frankie, Antonio, Zenabu, Woman, Yaa, and Vivian. I also knew a number of people whose stories are briefly told or who are mentioned incidentally in the text, including Agatha, Alice, Akosua, Apache, Auntie Dora, Steve, Hassan, Knock-the-Man-Down, Mahmoud, and Vélé. Identifying the several other characters I knew might reveal their identities.

think a certain story would be good for the work. By and large, however, I would maintain that she had already selected a large body of the stories by virtue of the life she had led.

It may seem natural that I did not ask myself at the time whether she had a big conception or a plan in her imagination. The stories were coming with diversity and movement, but the clearest evidence was the eventual completeness of the stories. Both times I sat with her, there was a sense of an ending when we reached a certain point, and we each said, "OK, that's enough; it's good." To an extent, the division of this work into two volumes reflects a natural division between the two sessions in 1977 and 1979. In the second volume, *Exchange Is Not Robbery,* Hawa has moved from Ghana and Togo to Burkina Faso, where she achieves greater control over her life. I shifted some of the first session's stories about village life in Burkina to the second book and a few of the second session's stories about Togo and about juju to the first book, but as a whole, the way she originally told the stories worked well for organizing them. In describing Hawa as a seeker with an agenda for her experience, I would not assert that she was an exceptional person in that regard. It is normal, I believe, to think about the completeness of one's life, to say that someone accomplished what he or she set out to do in life, or to talk about a life that was cut short or was unfulfilled. There is a saying that the work involved in a project expands to fill the time allocated to it, but I am also amazed at how often projects meet their deadlines so perfectly. There is evidence that medical patients get better in conformity with the timetable established for their treatment.[1] There was no apparent timetable when Hawa talked to me, but even though the stories did not come out in what would seem to be a narrative order, there was a structure to the emerging portrait of her life and times. I therefore assume that she had a larger conception, a sense of what could be or needed to be covered to that point, and a sense of when to stop.

Personally, I appreciated experiencing the freedom that Hawa projected as a human being and the reality with which she infused her stories. Hawa almost defines the meaning of self-actualization, but she is practical about her insights. She talks about having learned from certain experiences and discusses how people are influenced by circumstances, but she does not make "had I known" statements, does not make the same mistake twice, does not equate explanation of the past with justification of the present, and does not turn the insights of liberation into a whipping post. In short,

1. See Julius A. Roth, *Timetables: Structuring the Passage of Time in Hospital Treatment and Other Careers* (Indianapolis: Bobbs-Merrill, 1963). In contrast, people who suffer from vague character disorders can stay in therapy interminably, as Freud noted.

Hawa is prepared to take responsibility for her actions and her way of life, and she is concerned more with being good than being normal. If there are elements of biographical tension in her stories, then that tension is between what she is actually saying and the way she says it. She is as aware as any reader might be of the irony of her life; she sees it everywhere and thinks it's funny. For most of us, the autobiographical issue of self-justification should recede before a different issue, the incongruity between the whole tone of her stories and what we might know or feel to be true about the predicaments she describes. If we need a poignant picture of the situation, we can start with the image of Hawa as a little girl who wants to be free and feels that she cannot fit into the traditional roles and regulations of her world, and then we must imagine this little girl knowingly setting herself up for a lifelong struggle.

The Brer Rabbit School of Feminism

But what does her picaresque saga add? What kind of woman is she? In what ways does she represent something significant about African women and the cultural life of modern Africa? To answer these questions, readers might wish to think about the character and resources she brings to bear upon her situation. If we look at her in terms of poverty and powerlessness, hers is a sad story. Why, then, was she laughing throughout her recounting of it? A famous historian of African art, commenting on the finest forms of African sculpture, dance, and music, discussed "flexibility and balance as modes of iconic phrasing," which point to deeper expressions of African art as the incarnation of a philosophical attitude, "beyond the social turmoil we call experience," the ability to "move from one unstable setting to the next without a loss of humor (refusal to suffer) or composure (collectedness of mind)."[1] This description fits Hawa perfectly. If we are so much concerned with autobiographical issues in order to interpret her narrative as a self-justification, might we not miss the possibility that she is a verbal artist who partakes of this aesthetic sensibility? If we look at her in terms of canons of cultural authenticity, the shift from tragedy to comedy requires us to look more deeply at what she is making of the whole dizzy mess. In this introduction, there are some points that should be made at least tentatively to place her in a cultural context that looks beyond the negative and

1. Robert Farris Thompson, *African Art in Motion: Icon and Act in the Collection of Katherine Coryton White* (Los Angeles: University of California Press, 1974), xiv.

turns pity to a recognition of accomplishment. As her stories make clear, she feels that she has done well in the face of difficulties, living through them without a loss of humor or composure, refusing to suffer. She has enjoyed her life and she felt free to talk about it, and she enjoyed talking about it because to her, she was talking about her triumphs. Readers owe her that much, to see her as she sees herself, at least for a while, and much of the way we see her depends upon our ability to understand her world as she portrays it. Hawa's stories were told not to criticize her world but to satirize it. Satire is certainly appropriate in an age without reason or faith. But is satire more than cynicism blessed with creativity? What kind of strategy for living is satire?

Let us look first at her narrative style in its original context, that is, as an oral performance. During the interviews that were the basis of this book, even though she was drawing from her own memories, she behaved just like a traditional storyteller with a repertoire of folktales. Generally, I would turn on the tape recorder and begin a conversation about the last story she had told in the previous session. She would pretend to be annoyed while she arranged herself into a good sitting position and cleared her throat. Even though she was sympathetic to the goal of conveying her experience to a Western audience and she had agreed to the whole interview procedure, she usually had to be prodded into a story; she would laughingly say, "Oh, I'm tired," like a grandmother surrounded by toddlers. I would play the role and plead for just one more story, and then suddenly and energetically she would launch into a new vignette from her life. From that point, she was off and running. She avoided generalizations about her material, preferring rather to tell a related story. She did a splendid job of filling in the local references and the contextual background, though I will annotate the text from time to time to explain a few things that she took for granted, such as the international value of various currencies and some idioms and local references. The earlier chapters, of course, have more notes. Without seeming particularly self-conscious of the ways in which her storytelling was typical of oral art, she concentrated on recreating a dramatic elaboration of her material with a flair for the presentation of different voices, mixing other languages into her dramatizations of situations and immediately translating her characters' speeches into English. Her memory was truly impressive, and on several occasions when I lost track of things and asked her to repeat part of an anecdote we had already recorded, I later found that her second renditions were practically verbatim. In short, she focused on her stories in a particular way, and all things considered, her narrative technique was very much in the style of traditional African storytellers.

African storytelling as we think of it is supposed to be a dying art.[1] The image we cherish is an evening scene in a village. After dinner, the children gather around the wise old people who are relaxing in the gentle breeze. The traditionalists with whom I worked held that sentiment deeply. They prayed for walls. They had a proverb that drummers beat as a praise-name for a chief: "God should make the wall to be nice, and our elders will lean against the wall, and we the children will thank God." They had another proverb: "An exhausted old man, just leaning against the wall, is better than an old man who dies." I was told, "This is how we pray, that an old man, even if he cannot do anything, then may God let him lean against better walls, and we will meet him and hear something." The instructive talk of the elders concerns the history of the village and the customs of the tribe. It is there that children learn the proper way to deal with the problems of life. The highlights of the evening are fables with elaborate metaphors based on a cast of supernatural animal characters and wonderful beings like dwarves. The master storytellers are spellbinding raconteurs, pausing at just the right moments to elicit audience response. But alas, today the village is deserted, and the young people are now struggling in the cities. The old people are dying off, and soon no one will be able to tell the stories again. Yet do not despair: the new storytellers are there, and they are telling new stories for themselves. They are the people struggling in the cities, the young women sitting around cooking in the afternoons, the young men sharing the evening breeze outside a kiosk on a busy street. They debate and they joke, but they also talk to each other with lengthy stories that give instruction about the way things are and how to live in the world; thus at the same time, they maintain the role of that ancient art in their lives.

In Hawa's stories, character is the device that provides density and continuity to the events she selects. Her style is rambling and conversational on the surface, but the events are compact and well delineated. She gets to her point no matter how many details have been added for contextual elaboration. The part seemingly superfluous details play in her narratives reveals the mark of an accomplished storyteller. She relates her own lengthy history as a series of short, self-contained episodes. In her narrative development, she moves forward and backward through a variety of associations and examples. She makes extensive use of satire and irony. Like traditional African storytellers, she shows rather than tells. She takes roles and talks

1. This popular perspective was clearly presented in an article entitled "Traditional Tefle," by Janet Milhomme, in *The Christian Science Monitor,* March 14, 1988. The point noted below about understanding style as an elaboration of tradition is made by Bernth Lindfors in *Folklore in Nigerian Literature* (New York: Africana Publishing Company, 1973).

roles, using dramatization for vividness and contextual elaboration. Personality idiosyncrasies and tendencies become symbols of the people in her stories. The way she adds metonymic devices to broader metaphorical themes recalls the emblematic or iconic roles of animals in African folktales. She herself does not always hold center stage, and we see her in a cumulative manner; as her stories turn, so too does our view of her turn itself over and over. Her characterizations are cumulative as well, and she builds on our knowledge of them. If she is beginning a new incident, she paints the whole picture so that her audience will understand the incident's significance. To tell of a quarrel, for example, she will not only discuss the quarrel but will also show the origins of the quarrel by going back to the preceding events that are motivating the conflicting personalities. Once her characters have been established and typified, the character emblems become the basis for our appreciation of the dramatic encounters. With inexorable logic, a comedy unfolds, an ironic drama of proportion and distortion that aims straight at the satirical jugular of African wit. In her stories there are no well-rounded characters, just people who are parodies of their own idiosyncrasies, and she shows how all the consequences of their actions flow from their unbalanced characters.

A comparison of Hawa's stories with some aspects of folktales raises a number of issues. In comparing some of her narrative techniques to those exemplified in African folk tales, I would first like to recall a point made by literary critics: we should not diminish the achievement of artistic creativity when it is a response to traditional precedents; the important issue is how an artist elaborates on a tradition from which he or she has borrowed. This approach in literary criticism focuses on the processes by which tradition is transformed, and it complements criticism's (and social science's) more familiar tendency to examine the ways in which artistic forms articulate their historical context. In Hawa's case, the parallels between her stories and folktales are intriguing. Hawa is not utilizing folktales to write a novel or to be self-consciously creative. Furthermore, it is not important whether or not she is sophisticated about African oral arts. She talked and others listened, and the poignancy of her stories suggests that poetry comes from the heart and not the imagination.

There is a real problem in all of this, however. The similarity of Hawa's stories to African folktales is thematic as well as stylistic. In African folktales, generally speaking, the narrator takes the emblematic personalities of the characters and dramatizes them, but Hawa's stories reach beyond that stylistic element and exemplify one of the most common themes of African folk tales — the triumph of cunning over force, the small animal who outwits the larger or stronger animal. Sometimes the hero saves himself and sometimes he rescues potential victims, as Hawa does in her complementary stories of hapless friends. In a very real sense, Hawa is a kind of human trickster who resembles Brer Rabbit. The qualities by which we identify her—her resourcefulness, her courage, her verbal skills, her weakness portrayed in her childhood and in her tiny stature, her reservoir of loyalty to her friends, her mischievousness—become emblems of her life, the trickster elements that give continuity to her selection of events. The facility with which one can accept the familiar element of the trickster's reliance on expedience contributes another kind of tension to the moral ambiguity of Hawa's identity. The problem in viewing Hawa as a female trickster figure is that although many trickster folktales have a naive and comprehensible moral that everybody can see, in some folktales, tricksters do some really nasty things. The moral ambiguities of such folktales have been a stumbling block to literary critics, who have tended to respond by focusing on artistic techniques, and to anthropologists, who have tended to respond by focusing on classification and cross-cultural comparisons. Few people want to take the really ambiguous folktales literally as a reflection of experience, and they can avoid doing so by spinning elaborate interpretations. But Hawa is a real person, and her actions have real consequences for the people in her stories. In mythology, the trickster is usually the god who is closest to human life and to the ways of the world. Perhaps the style and form of folktales are closer than previously imagined to the lifestyles and lifeforms of the folk. Perhaps folktales are the repositories and vehicles of certain types of ethnographic knowledge. Perhaps the folktales are even more didactic than has been assumed. Perhaps, although sometimes life imitates art, art really imitates life.

In written African literature, though, we rarely meet people like the characters in this book. Generally speaking, when contemporary African novelists focus on small events, they maintain a historical consciousness. Early West African novelists were especially concerned with the effects of colonialism; the recent generation has been more concerned with alienation and corruption. Hawa's stories have no overt political orientation, and she does not exhibit the philosophical alienation of the characters we tend to meet in African novels. Despite her emphasis on generating plot from character and her straightforward descriptive techniques, there is little of the unifying philosophical, moral, and historical structuring of Achebe, Armah, Ngugi, Soyinka, or Ouologuem. Despite the humor, the complexity of action, and the emphasis on survival in Hawa's narrative, there is little of the fantastic prose and characterizations we see in the writings of Tutuola or Fagunwa. She describes the corrupting effect of neocolonialism without the moralism of expatriate writers; she might have owed a debt to Joyce Cary if she could have read him, for she seems to turn the naive faith of *Mr. Johnson* upside down. The common people of whom she speaks are also quite a far cry from those portrayed in popular African "market" literature with its sentimental and melodramatic clichés, and her experience and outlook certainly resemble none of the wayward heroines of that genre, including Ekwensi's much discussed models of the ashawo life.[1]

Hawa concentrates on small areas of experience. The important dimensions of her stories always focus on what people do to each other in face-to-face interaction. The larger portrait of life that emerges reveals a landscape of strange and funny people who are part of an unstable world. The historical situation is embodied in the characterizations of neocolonialist hangers-on whose elevated status allows them to let their quirkiness out of the closets, predatory police unhampered by civil accountability, and self-styled hustlers whose range extends from incredibly naive optimism to wickedly cynical manipulativeness. For all of them, from the most innocent villager to the most jaded expatriate, self-centered or opportunistic motives are ironically the foundation of gullibility and a potential for exploitation. Typically, relying on the interplay of conflicting motives and values, Hawa's stories move from stability to trouble and back to stability. The picaresque quality of her autobiography derives in part from the fact that Hawa does not see her life along Western models of a series of landmark events leading to growth and self-actualization. Life is not a matter of progress toward a goal but a matter of surviving by restoring the balance. In an unstable world, however, no condition is permanent.

Hawa's stories start with her either in a cool place or in search of one. If anything, perhaps, that condition conveys her truest image of herself. In one of the letters we exchanged, she advised me, "Be as cool as a snake." In her stories, she rarely generates her own trouble. Trouble comes her way. Hawa is ready to meet trouble head-on and work her way through it; once trouble comes, the complexity of the cool balance is revealed, but Hawa is never content to let something remain unresolved. Sometimes Hawa is in a nice situation, and a small problem presents itself in the form of a person or some unforeseeable circumstance; she begins to deal with it and a new factor enters, a consequence of the restorative action that complicates things way out of proportion to the original problem. Sometimes she gets caught in the middle of trouble that sweeps her up. Sometimes the trouble is the unintended consequence of her playfulness, for she makes fun of people who boast, who emphasize appearances or false values, or who

1. Cyprian Ekwensi, *Jagua Nana* (London: Heinemann, 1975).

abuse their position. Playfully, she befriends people whose stories she thinks will entertain her. When she does initiate her troubles she is not above poking fun at herself. By and large, the consequences of her mischief simply demonstrate tragicomic points about contemporary African life. Some situations can be terrible, with people doing or saying incredible things to one another, but most of the situations Hawa describes are quite benign.

When we meet Hawa after her mother's death, she is already a precocious and centered character. She is forced to center herself when she loses her mother, and she fights for self-reliance and commands respect. In her early childhood she is mainly fighting for herself, sometimes to defend herself against exploitation, though often her own mischievousness is at fault for her problems. When she grows up, she doesn't want to be dependent. She wants to achieve the stability that evaded her in childhood, but as an independent adult woman, this motive becomes a modest desire merely to be comfortable and have a nice place to stay. In her pride in her survival, she does not want others to see her problems, for her sense of justice would be violated by their knowledge of her failure or dependence. She knows that her main resources are her intelligence and will. When Hawa's lighthearted tales are not innocent, even when she plays deceptive roles to achieve her ends, she never doubts that she is different from the masks she puts on. The moral ambiguities of her identity in various incidents are submerged in the compelling circumstances of the situation. And in the balance, her ideals become pity, protectiveness, tolerance, and loyalty to friends and family. She consoles and advises others who are at the brink. Despite her insecure situation, she burdens herself with neither regret nor long-range plans. Daily life scenes and circumstances have immediate effects, and her imagination plays with what it is given. Always ready to take action and never willing to resign herself to her plight, she becomes a sharp observer of events and a witness on her own behalf rather than a creator of fantasies.

If there is an element of tension between Hawa's way of surviving and her desire to affirm the missing goodness in her life, she does not attempt to rationalize her behavior with an appeal to moralistic ideals or with complex observations about her own psyche. She throws everything onto the scales that measure the imbalances of the situation. She looks at the motives and strategies behind what people say and do, and she works through the reasons and the moves, step by step, as she or her protagonists sort out the proper path. She tries to demonstrate good character and often advises people on how they should behave, and her guiding principle and greatest virtue is her sense of her own integrity. But in her concern for certain social values, she knows that virtue in and of itself will not effect a solution. In Western literature, virtue is often portrayed as a kind of punishment, either as an emotionally indulgent consolation for powerlessness or as the ironic force behind a character's downfall.[1] But Hawa is no Clarissa. She relies on taking advantage of a situation, using her powers of observation to anticipate how circumstances will develop and using her intelligence and her verbal skills to manipulate the various characters involved. Yet she is also no Becky Sharpe because she is never maliciously exploitative, and she is prepared to stand on principle when norms of good behavior are violated. The moral ambiguity of her resourcefulness raises the question of why she doesn't become a criminal as a way of surviving, but she is no Moll Flanders, either. Hawa does not become a criminal because to do so would invalidate her way of surviving. Her emergence out of difficult circumstances is a source of great pride. Her stories are inspirational on that level, for it has been part of her struggle to show others that she can survive and remain respectful and happy, that one can maintain a sense of justice in the world if one understands that justice is often poetic.

There is a key to understanding the felicitous fit between the stock characters we know so well and the way they carry their emblematic qualities into an uncharted social landscape. The key is cut from the mettle of poor people everywhere, and it opens a door to a world where symbols weigh heavily on the scales of truth that measure the meaning of life. The world of the people in this book does not admit the weight of the hefty volumes of down-to-earth statistics that are the symbols we trust to calibrate existence and assess its qualities: symbolism in shantytown is not that grubby. In Hawa's world, base realities are sublimated and recrystallized through the constructive and transformative agency of symbolic processing. Would anyone expect the "dis" people to live in a world without such apparatus to play with? The circumstances of reality are the playing field of an experimental game where there is always a symbolic victory to be won.

Enter the trickster. A trickster plays games with a vengeance, particularly games where reality is not what it appears to be. Serious people like us hate those kinds of games. Our sense of ourselves is too pure, too refined. Weighed down by possessions and positions, we cannot attach something as deep and spiritual as who we are to a temporary and artificial symbol determined by chance or petty circumstances, an emblematic ball that can be kicked around the playing field by our counterplayers. We grasp so tightly to our limited perception of our realities and our identities that generally

1. See R. F. Brissenden, *Virtue in Distress: Studies in the Novel of Sentiment from Richardson to Sade* (London: Macmillan, 1974).

we have to be tricked into letting go.[1] The trickster's first task is to challenge us to accept the serious possibility of the game. If we agree to put ourselves on the line, the rules are simple: first, we have to want something, and what we wish for will stand for us and be taken at face value; second, whatever we want to say is our decision, even a joke, and we will be held to our words; third, the game must be played out, even when the initial decision leads to disaster. It's an archaic game whose image we hold to remind us that life can be war.

Hawa's life is a compendium of such symbolic games, a shifting complex of reverberating intentions knocking against one another, and playing them is a sport she relishes. Without them, living is food without salt. When she loses round one, she doesn't worry because round two is coming up, and the game has as many rounds as the one who seems to be losing is willing to play in order to tip the scales. Hawa is one player who does not quit. In the course of an evening, a week, a month, a year, or a lifetime, the game can turn things upside down and transform their meaning. She enjoys planning her strategies to extend the game and keep the ending open. In this book, she describes these games within dramatic narratives full of dialogue, but it would be too narrow to see the world portrayed in her stories as a stage where people are given their parts to play. Hawa herself did not accept the role she was handed. Although Hawa wrapped up a significant part of her life in her stories, she is not a playwright or a novelist tying up loose ends with an eye to the integrity of the presentation. There is no final curtain to Hawa's life history. Her story cannot be closed like this book. Hawa just stopped for a moment to tell me all this; she is still alive and will keep on going. She did not want to live out her character within the dramatic confines of poverty and powerlessness. She needed more freedom than that. In its context, her storytelling is a continuing part of playing the game and demonstrating its rules and its unpredictability.

It's not that Hawa and the people in this book take life as a game, but they do talk about it like that sometimes when there is a challenge. Whether about to make a quarrel or about to make love, they might ask, "Can you stand the game?" Hawa's world is full of people who are willing to play, and that is what people want: someone who can stand the game. Her environment thus has some advantages, because the people in it are not overwhelmed by forcefulness of character. Her world is full of counterplayers who are also not afraid to stand up for themselves. They know that when they put themselves out there, for whatever reason, there are others who will match wits or strength with them. They have an agenda and a

1. Carlos Castaneda, *The Power of Silence: Further Lessons of don Juan* (New York: Simon and Schuster, Pocket Books, 1987), 6.

framework in which they see themselves, and if they are aware of the unbalances in social realities, they are not looking at who has the power and the money with the idea of putting themselves down. They stay with their values and look for symbolic victories and poetic justice. When you move with them, you see a high degree of individuation and a kind of security about the self that probably has its roots in basic aspects of culture like the extended family and a number of sublimated symbolic hierarchies. You also see an amazing amount of interaction because people are into other people's willingness to become involved, and the scene is interesting because of their differences and the processes by which they relate to one another.

In the global-political view, Hawa and her associates are misfits passed up by history, but in some ways they are at its leading edge. It might seem too much to glorify them by saying that they are "[creating] order out of the disorder of the past,"[1] but somehow in life the philosophical is always mixed in with the practical. How are the people playing with the different ideas that surround them? How do they come together and communicate? How do they share a common ground in the face of disorder? Hawa's stories bring these questions down to the level of interpersonal action and motives. Hawa is as familiar with the ways of peasant villagers as she is with European expatriates; she has access to a broad span of historical experience, but she does not present it in statistics or in eloquent abstractions. The only thing she reads is people. In evocative terms that focus the world she knows through personality and personal intentions, her stories are all about strategy and contingencies, about the real stuff of everyday life. When people get together, they may begin with an analysis of who they are and where they stand in the social order: but then they contest it. They talk and put themselves out there. They try to find out where other people are coming from. They bluff one another. They call nicknames for one another, and they insult one another. They get puffed up and deflated. They expect things to change. They act as if they expect things to be a certain way. They mess with each other and cultivate uncertainty. They miscalculate and make mistakes. They hide their vulnerabilities and gossip about the weaknesses of others. They try to get into other people's business. They lie for fun. They die for pride. They do all kinds of things for good reasons and bad reasons and sometimes, it seems, for no reason.

It is very difficult to assess their situation judiciously because there is always an element of deception and bluffing in whatever is happening. Looking at them from far away, clutching our statistics and broadcasting our pompous pronouncements and relaxing in our easy chairs, we must none-

1. Erik H. Erikson, "Psychological Reality and Historical Actuality," 205.

theless contend with a fact of life that their experience tells them is true: things are not what they appear to be, and there is always another side to reality. In traditional African cultures, proverbs abound asserting that one cannot look at something—in different places it is a hand, a calabash, a honeycomb, the moon—and see both its front and its back. This philosophical proposition is articulated time and again by people in folk culture, and it stands them well in the modern world. Hawa does not consider herself a trickster, but she helps us recall the ambiguous truths that the trickster stories convey about the ambivalence of human existence and experience and about the affinities of laughter, indeterminateness, and play.[1] The trickster is a marginal god, a compendium of inferior and antisocial traits: clown, devil, thief, androgyne, magician and binder of spells, the breaker of taboos and boundaries, the source of sorrows and toil and mortality, the epitome of disorder. The trickster is also an archetype of heroism, creator of the world, benefactor of humankind, bringer of civilization, giver of fire, source of knowledge and skilled crafts and verbal arts, guardian of commerce, model for the shaman who would understand life's secrets. In African and African American culture, we know the trickster as Anansi, Eshun, Elegba, Brer Rabbit; in other cultures, the trickster is Loki, Coyote, Maui; we know the trickster figure best as Hermes and Prometheus and as the cold-blooded snake in Eden. This devilish, comic, and heroic character, watcher of the crossroads and unreliable messenger, is the god who appears at the end of an age to challenge the boundaries of the existing order. Hawa's connection to our world is not so much via an emerging order in modern Africa as via some things that have always been there in human experience and are certainly with us in our own world torn loose from its moorings.

Like all satiric comedies, Hawa's stories cannot deny an element of sadness that the world has to be this way, so hard, when people are so soft. Still, her stories prescribe the aesthetic antidote of humor and the refusal to suffer. She conveys an attitude that encompasses qualities of strength, adaptiveness, and tolerance within a kind of cultivated gentleness and lightheartedness. I have been happy to dwell inside the stories. Faced with the mess Africa seems from a distance, I catch a glimpse of that sweetness that I remember as part of life in Africa, a glimpse to make me less forlorn. That sweetness is an incredible achievement of the people there. And it is an achievement to capture it and give others a glimpse of it, as Hawa did.

1. On these trickster motifs, see Joseph Campbell, *The Masks of God,* vol. 1, *Primitive Mythology* (New York: Viking, 1959), 269–81, and vol. 3, *Occidental Mythology* (New York: Viking, 1964), 157–77.

We can understand Hawa as a representative of others at the same time as she represents them in her words. Even though they are a diverse group, she spells out the range of expectations of her counterplayers and how they respond in instances when norms of behavior either are unclear or are being violated. She thus consistently provides a definition of typicality against which to compare the motivations and behavior of not only herself but also the other people involved in her accounts who were less adept at mediation. And so if she represents them, it does not mean she is typical or atypical. In our beautiful world, there are so many stories, so many different types of people, so many ways of understanding. It seems misguided to present a life history and say the protagonist is typical. The details of any life will defeat such an assertion. Hawa herself is neither typical nor atypical: let us just look at Hawa's urban youth and say that she is an example, and a rather likable and articulate and good example. Whether we are thinking about Africa or about our own lives, she is a character worth keeping in mind. Sometimes people who used to enjoy Hawa's conversation and anecdotes would say, "There's no one like her." Yet I believe that if you note the way the people in her stories behave, you can say, "I know someone like that." But satire moves forward because of pettiness and maliciousness, and this book abounds in protagonists who serve the purpose of providing Hawa with adversaries. In such a world, it is worthwhile noting that Hawa is a model of how to be hardnosed on principle and then play softly in principle's application.

If you choose to perceive Hawa and her friends as objects of pity and sympathy, there is no problem with that: send your donations to an appropriate agency. You may find, however, that some of your sadness covers a wistful admiration and even envy of her. My own envy at first concerned the kind of intelligence she brought to the realm of words. She exhibits her way with words as a character in her stories, but more than that, when she was telling the stories, I noticed how the words she had heard stayed with her, and she just remembered them and brought them out. I cannot do that. I can summarize and analyze and reconstruct the main points of the conversations I have had, but I can barely remember the words of conversations I've just completed.[1] Hawa demonstrated a degree of attention to her experience that I wished I had more of, and when I listened to her, I was both feeling my own inadequacy to the task of describing her world and

1. This middle-class tendency is noted in William Labov, *Language in the Inner City: Studies in the Black English Vernacular* (Philadelphia: University of Pennsylvania Press, 1974). Hawa's sharp ears may also have derived from growing up in a multilingual environment and learning other languages.

feeling grateful for tape recorders. But there is yet more to it than admiring a storyteller's virtuosity. Many of my conversations will be long past and I will still be thinking about what I could have said or should have said. Hawa's awareness of the field of interaction is so broad that she is able to anticipate and control the movement of words, and she thinks on her feet fast enough to respond to an unexpected reply with an unexpected reply. The benefits of her control of words are both immediate and long-range. It is another point of significance that through words she is able to objectify and give order to her past by turning it into a story, a process through which she treats herself as both subject and object. This ability to perceive herself in stories is one of the important strengths she possesses, a strength we Westerners rarely appreciate and might do well to emulate if we could. It is her way of maintaining her identity and restoring to herself what psychoanalysis restores to its patients, "a productive interplay between psychological reality and historical actuality."[2] Before the age of psychology, we might have said that she is purified by truth and redeemed by the natural generosity of her art.

And then again, there is the matter of that historical actuality: what a world to live in! Certainly we must admire her good-natured and positive attitude toward difficulties that would drive us up a wall. Among her appealing trickster qualities are her love of freedom, her flexibility, her sense of humor. Above all, though, tricksters rarely get credit for their courage. It takes a lot of courage to stand up in the face of someone who can squash you, and Hawa does it all the time. In Hawa's stories, the moral focus on an individual managing to redeem her possibilities in an unstable world served to encourage her listeners, gathered around the cooking pot, to put aside their fears and participate in the struggle of life. In that original context, her stories are a gift. She is a spirit dwelling among untrodden ways, keeping hope alive, for them and perhaps for some of us. Who has the courage to join her? Who is prepared to accept the challenge of her playfulness? There are times in every life when Hawa's example might be an inspiration and answer a need.

By now, of course, Hawa is much older. This book is about her youth. I know what happened to Hawa. But there is no need to say it. If she escaped and found her dream, would it matter? If her life changed and took on the problems of maturity, what would that show? If she were still struggling and suffering, would anyone find a key to understanding her? Choose the ending you like. She is an example, and we shall leave her at the place we found her.

2. Erik H. Erikson, "Psychological Reality and Historical Actuality," 201.

PROCEDURES TO PROTECT IDENTITIES

Most of the names of people and places have been changed or switched. Sometimes I have simply deleted information that could indicate identity. Sometimes I have made up names, as with Tsukudu, the village supposedly near Kpalimé, and also with some of the nightclubs in Ouagadougou. Rather than think up new names for every place, however, and given the unavoidable problem of substituting one person's name with another's, I have generally used names of actual places. Since the names given to people or given to enterprises such as nightclubs or hotels or businesses are part of the ambience of a place, I have relied on my knowledge of Ghana, Togo, Côte d'Ivoire, and Burkina Faso to create a sense of place by substituting actual names for actual names. Drinking bars in West Africa do not have names like Ryan's Pub or T.G.I.F. or Boardwalk or Graffiti or Electric Banana, for example, which are local watering holes in my town. I have my lists of bars and nightclubs in Accra, Lomé, and Ouagadougou: Las Palmas, Weekend-in-Havana, Kakadou, Watusi, Pussycat, L'Abreuvoir, Tropicana, Café des Arts, Mini-Brasserie, Level Two, La Camionette, Santa Fé, Rama Palace, Flamboyant, Bataclan, Dessambissé, Palladium, Caban Bamboo, Cascade, Don Camillo, Tiptoe, Silver Cup, Metropole, Lido, Apollo Theatre, Playboy, Keteke. And the hotels: Ambassador, Star, Avenida, Continental, Ringway, California, Aams, Paradise, Independence, Tropicana, Miramar, la Plage, la Paix, le Benin, Camion Vert, Sarakawa, Ricardo, Royal, Oubri. I have used these names interchangeably, sometimes switching them from one town to another but more often just switching them around within a town. The substitutions within a country are done on the basis of comparable factors, so that although the name of place or enterprise may exist and may seem likely as a venue, that particular name probably does not represent the actual name of the place or enterprise depicted in this book. Where I felt it acceptable though, I sometimes used the actual name.

I have followed a similar strategy with towns and villages. The switching has been done on several levels. On the first level, for example, the name of a medium-sized town that is a regional administrative center has been replaced with the name of a similar town. Atakpamé, Kpalimé, Bassari, Sokodé, Sansanne-Mango, Dapongo, Lamakara are names of small towns in Togo; I have switched names within that class. Similarly, the names of the administrative centers of Ghana's nine regions outside of Accra are Tamale, Cape Coast, Koforidua, Sekondi-Takoradi, Sunyani, Bolgatanga, Wa, Kumasi, and Ho; I have also switched names within that class. Because I am familiar with Tamale, for instance, I switched the location of the British club to that town so that I could use neighborhood and suburban area names. On that second level, neighborhoods and urban areas were also replaced and additional switches were made, as for example in Accra among Adabraka, Asylum Down, Kokomlemle, Kaneshie, Jamestown, Cantonments, Osu, Tesano, Kotobabi, Accra Newtown, Alajo, Airport, Labadi, Mamprobi. In Lomé, where necessary, I have followed a similar strategy with Tokoin, Hanoukopé, Kodjoviakopé, Quartier Casablanca, and Quartier Bé. The discussions should make sense within their new contexts, though in some cases they may not. In one particular case, that of the villages in Hawa's cultural area in Burkina Faso, the information is intentionally impossible; I have just chosen some village names from a wide general area to stand for the actual villages she mentioned. In such cases, readers may assume that Hawa is not confused but that I have tried specifically to make things confusing.

All of the names of people have been changed. I have used local personal names appropriate to the switched setting, such as Ewe names in Lomé, Ashanti names in Kumasi, Dagbamba names in Tamale, and British, French, German, and Arabic names as appropriate. Finally, African personal names have then been replaced with other names in their genre, whether Akan day-of-birth names, Muslim names, French or English names, or surnames. For example, female Muslim names are Fati, Amina, Abiba, Miriama, Alima, Ramatu, and so on; female Ashanti day-names are Akosua, Adwoa, Abena, Akua, Yaa, Afia, and Ama; female Ewe day-names are Akɔsiwa, Adzowa, Abla, Akuwa, Yawa, Afiwa, and Ama. After switches to confuse the identification of place or language of origin, the names of people were then switched within those groups or local contexts. Therefore, Afia (Asante and Akyem) might become Afua (Akwapim or Akuapem) or Efua (Fanti) or Afiwa (Ewe).

In short, I have done my best to confuse any potential effort to identify specific individuals or places, and readers should assume that any name in the text is *not* the name of the actual person or place described. No character is pictured on the cover. Any identification or attempt at identification based on the names of places or persons in this book will result in conclusions that are purely coincidental and unintentional.

A NOTE ON THE TEXT

Hawa spoke ten languages, but because she was uneducated and spoke English as a foreign language, her stories required a degree of editing to adjust her language for this book, particularly her use of pronouns and tenses. Despite extensive grammatical and stylistic adjustments, the text of this book still preserves many conventions of Ghanaian and Pidgin English.[1] Akan is the most widely spoken indigenous language group in Ghana, and it influences the English of many uneducated or semiliterate Ghanaians, including Hawa, who is not Akan but who was raised in the center of the Akan traditional area. Ga, the indigenous language of Accra, also influences Ghanaian English.

There are shifts and borrowings in both directions between English and indigenous languages. In Ghanaian English, some English words have a more limited meaning and others have a wider or extended range of meanings. When I have retained Ghanaian idioms, I have provided footnotes to explain the particular use of various words or phrases. The annotations explain the first use of a given term or idiom, and the definition is repeated in a glossary for easy reference if there are later uses. In terms of syntax, particularly in speaking, there is a tendency to begin a sentence with an introductory noun or noun phrase, or sometimes an adverbial conjuction, that announces the presence of something. The phrase generally serves as an announcement of the main subject or object of the sentence, although sometimes it seems like a dramatic stage direction to focus attention on someone's speech or on what is to come. Such discontinuous sequencing typically establishes the main idea and then illustrates it. Occasionally the construction states the effect before the cause, indicating the significance of the introductory phrase. The convention thus initially places a pointer in front, setting a basic idea or condition, something to keep in mind when

1. Some of these conventions, with regard more to educated Ghanaian English than to Pidgin, are discussed in K. A. Sey, *Ghanaian English* (London: Macmillan, 1973).

hearing what follows. In preserving this aspect of spoken Ghanaian English, I have followed the introductory statement with a colon before the phrase or clause or sentence that elaborates the focus.

In general, Ghanaian English is quite clear, and Hawa's use of English is straightforward. Her speech lacks the verbose or artificial or even bombastic qualities that can characterize (and are often parodied among) educated English speakers in former British colonies. A mundane text that standardizes Ghanaian conventions would lose too much flavor and ultimately would lose its sense of place. As noted in the Introduction, I believe the text is not difficult, although it may seem a bit choppy before readers get into the flow of it. The first chapter or two are densely annotated and therefore offer a quick crash course in Ghanaian English. After that, the annotations thin out considerably, and I hope that the read will be smooth sailing. All in all, the syntax also preserves the style of a storyteller, punctuated with laughter and expletives and exclamations; thus, as it should be, the text is difficult to read faster than a person can talk.

I have used annotations sparingly to explain a few contextual details, but I have not used annotations to make connections beyond the text or to support the text. Readers who are familiar with West Africa either personally or through the ethnographic literature will be better able to recognize the references of some parts of the text that other readers might find surprising or questionable.

Regarding the pronunciation of African names and words, readers should try to pronounce all the vowels and consonants as written. For example, *kone* is pronounced as *connay.* In African or Pidgin words: *a* is short as in *bat; e* is like a long *a* as in *weigh; i* is like a long *e* as in *bee; o* is long as in *comb; u* is like a doubled *o* as in *boot.* The infrequent passages in African languages contain several phonetic characters: ɔ is a short *o* as in *ought;* ɛ is a short *e* as in *bet;* ɖ is like a Spanish *r; ƒ* is like an *f* pronounced with both lips, as if blowing out a candle; ʋ is like a *v* pronounced with both lips; *ã* is a nasalized *a.* Doubled vowels simply extend the sound of the vowel. Regarding consonant clusters in Asante Twi, *ky* is like *ch; hy* is like *sh; hw* is a slightly nasal *shw; gy* is like *j.*

PART ONE *Into The Life*

1 NOT BAD AS SUCH

: KUMASI :

Like a Letter

You know, I'm not bad as such. But when I was little, I thought my way was very bad.[1] My mother died when I was three years old, and my father

1. The story opens in the city of Kumasi in central Ghana, the center of the Akan tribal confederation (including Ashanti and other related groups) and also the second largest city in Ghana. Parts of the opening chapter also take place in southwestern Burkina Faso. The locations of the subsections are indicated.

Readers need note only a few points about the extended family system with reference to the terms used for relationships, because throughout this section particularly, it is easy to become confused about the way in which people are related. In an extended family, Hawa's "brothers" and "sisters" would include Hawa's father's children from women other than her mother, since in her culture, children remain with their father's family, and a father would have custody of a child from a divorced woman or of a child born out of wedlock once the child has grown past tender years. Also, in the Volta Basin, that is, the headwaters of the Volta River system, some people exchange children, so that for example, your brother will raise your child and vice versa, because it is believed that the child will not be spoiled as much as might be possible by a natural parent. Hawa's "brothers and sisters" would thus include as well any children from her father's family who might be living with him.

A major difference from Western kinship terms involves aunts and uncles. Hawa's father's brothers would also be called "father," or sometimes "junior father" or "senior father" had no other wife. He had children with other women, but my mother was the first wife of my father. I had brothers and sisters, and we all had to leave. We didn't live together. This one lived with the grandmother, and another one lived at the family of my father. You know, my family: they are very many. My mother's side is a big family; my father's is big, too. So all my brothers and sisters who were with my father, they just shared us like that. We didn't go together. So I had to be handed there, there, and there, to the families.[1] And no one could hold me.

Yeah, when my mother died and my father didn't have a wife, they sent the children around, but when my father married again, they came back. We were many children. The time I stayed in our house in Kumasi, we were about eighteen. But four were big girls, and they married, so we were fourteen children in the house. All of us were there in the house. The other children didn't stay with people. No, no, no, no, no! All my father's children stayed with my father.

Only me. I was not a good one, so I had to go around all the family. Only me! I used to go around. First I stayed with my grandmother in our village in Upper Volta.[2] She was my mother's mother. I was there until I was about four or five. Then I went back to my father in Kumasi. I was there for some time, and then I went back to Upper Volta. I was about six when I went to my village again, to my grandmother. I was a *small* girl.

---

or "small father," and so on, depending on whether they were older or younger than her father. Similarly, she would call her mother's sisters "mother." The words "uncle" and "aunt" refer to mother's brothers and father's sisters and their spouses. Hawa usually refers to her father's brothers and mother's sisters as such, showing their actual relationship to her, or as "uncles" and "aunts," thus adjusting her story to a Western listener; nonetheless, they would normally be addressed as father and mother, Papa or Mama. In the household, people are simply called "father," "mother," "brother," "sister"; it is not conducive to harmony to make a point of the distinctions. In the particular kinship system used in Hawa's family, she would sometimes also take and call her cousins (even children of her "real" aunts [father's sisters] and "real" uncles [mother's brothers]) as her brothers and sisters if they were living with her father, and as might be expected she generally addresses her stepmothers as "mother." People know their exact relationships, of course: the distinction of "real" mother or "real" brother is one way they might distinguish the nuclear part of the extended family. Thus, Hawa might say of a brother that he was the "same mother, same father" or "same father but different mothers." When a particular distinction is relevant, it is brought out.

1. the families in the larger extended family

2. Because Burkina Faso was known as Upper Volta when these events happened, I have retained the former name. Throughout this book, too, Hawa refers to the people of that country as "Voltaiques" instead of "Burkinabe." The term "Voltaic" remains in use with reference to cultures, languages, and peoples in the Volta Basin area.

Then they sent me back to Ghana, and I was staying with my aunts in Kumasi. My father was also working in the cocoa farms, in Brong Ahafo.[1] I stayed with him in the village there. I was always going around. And always: my aunts and uncles. Sometimes I would go to stay with them, and they would do me something,[2] and then I would say that they didn't look after me well, so I would make a palaver[3] to go and ask for myself[4] to find another place.

And they thought, all of them — they *knew!* — that I was a bad girl. I could not live in one place for one month: they had to send me back. And I thought it was because I was bad. Yeah, they said I was very bad.

But I didn't know why I was bad. I asked many questions. And anything I saw, when they said, "We don't do this," I wanted to do it and see what would happen. And all this was trouble for the families. So they had to send me like a letter. They would just post me: there and there and there. Yeah, this is how they were.

It was only one good family I found in my family — my aunt. She was very good. She didn't mind anything. She was in Kumasi, at Fanti Newtown.[5] That was the last place which I got to grow up.

My family was not all in Kumasi. They were in different places. I stayed in a village near Kumasi with my father's brother, with his wife. I stayed there for one month. They sent me home at twelve o'clock in the night! This woman had no baby, and every time[6] she liked to beat me. She wanted to force me to do things I didn't want, and one night she forced me to do something, and I said I wouldn't do it. Then she started to beat me. And I said, "Yeah. God knows. That's why you don't have babies." *Yes!*

Hey! She was very annoyed that night! She told my father's brother, "If you don't send this girl away, I must go away." So he could not let his wife go away like that because of me: they must send me to my father, in the night.

1. region of Ghana, west of Ashanti Region

2. do something to me

3. a problem, a case, a matter, a worrisome or troubling talk, a quarrel, an argument, a dispute

4. speak on my own behalf

5. section of Kumasi, near the central market. The Fanti are a major cultural group in the coastal area around Cape Coast and Sekondi-Takoradi. An area of a town would get such a name because it was a new part of town developed by Fantis who had come to live in Kumasi.

6. all the time; always

I had to stand on the car road in the village. I was crying, and she started abusing me that I was the last one my mother gave birth to before she died—and because I was bad luck, that was why my mother died and left me—because I am a witch, and I am a bad-luck girl—and that and this—I killed my mother. *Ha!* I was about nine years old.[1] And so when they sent me, we had to stand there up to one o'clock or two o'clock in the night before we got a taxi. Before we reached Kumasi, it was about two or three o'clock in the night.

It was my father's brother who sent me to my father, and he knocked the door. My father was sleeping. "Who?" he said.

"It's me."

"Yes?"

"I'm bringing Hawa."

"Who!? You don't call your name; you say you are bringing Hawa."

"It's me, Adamu."

Then my father opened the door. "What do you want in this night?"

"No, no, no, no! We can't help it! Hawa had some bad talks against my wife, and my wife is packing her things." Then: "You know, we are together for a long time; she shouldn't pack her things in this night time because of Hawa. So I must bring Hawa."

Then my father said, "OK. Thank you. You are a nice guy. I thought you are of the same father with me, and a different mother. But if you choose your own, it's OK. For me, I'm all right. I cannot kill her. I have already borne her.[2] I cannot kill her: she's not a chicken. If she's good, or she's bad: I like my thing." And so my father said OK.

Then this man wanted to sleep. My father said, "No, no, no, no, no. How she cannot sleep with you because your wife is going to pack away, I think if you sleep here, too, before you go home, maybe your wife will go away. So, bye-bye. See you!!"

Still, up to now, this man doesn't talk to my father because of this case. They had the same father but not the same mother. Since I was nine years old, up to now, they are alive, but they don't talk to each other.

Then I went to live with another aunt, and it was very funny. I lived with her for three weeks, then she sacked[3] me. She sacked me like a thief! *Ha-ha.* She had plenty of children, OK? But every time she used to beat

1. In American terms, she was eight years old. Age is counted from birth, so that a baby is one during the first year, two during the second, and so on.

2. given birth to her. The idiom is used for both men and women, so it is normal for a man to say he has borne his children.

3. drove me away; sack: drive away, make someone go away, fire (from a job)

fufu[1] by herself. She didn't want somebody to turn it for her; she didn't want somebody to pound it for her either. The fufu she will eat, she will beat it by herself. As for the rest, your own, you people can make it for yourselves. She would say, "Maybe you will sweat and your sweat will go inside." Or "Your hands are too dirty to turn it for me." So what she will eat, nobody will do it for her.

This woman was a very *old* woman. Every time when she beat her fufu and finished, she would relax for some time. Then I wouldn't say anything. I would put all her food for her in the room. When we beat our own and finished, then we would also put it in the room. So after resting, then she would wake up[2] before she would come to the kitchen to put the soup on the fufu.

And all this used to make me annoyed. You think you are neat. OK, we are going to see who is going to eat this one. So from there, before she would wake up to go and put the soup, I would change her own fufu to our plate, and I would put our own on her plate. *Ha-ha.*

So I think she had some sense, you know. About one week, when she beat the fufu, when I wanted to put it all inside the room, then she said, "Oh. Leave my own here." Then I left hers; I took our own inside. Then one day we took the same type of plate — the same color, the same size. She put her own inside one, then she put our own in the other one. Then she took her hand and rolled it on the fufu to press it down — down, down, down — with small marks on top of the fufu, because the plates were the same color. Then she told me to pack them[3] inside the room, and I packed them inside. Then I went and took a little of our fufu and put in the holes, and then I changed it to give her. I didn't know that she didn't put cassava in her own but she had put cassava in ours. This was the way she was going to catch me, no? So, when she put her hand and started eating, then she felt that this one is cassava, and she called us to bring our plate. So I took it there.

1. Fufu is a type of starchy food, eaten with soup that is poured over it in a large bowl for group eating. It is a staple food of Akan people. It is pounded with a heavy pestle in a large mortar. The ingredients are generally boiled cassava and plantain, but it can be made with cassava alone; occasionally cocoyam (a small tuber) can be substituted for plantain. Fufu can also be made from yam, and yam fufu is more common (and is preferred) in savanna regions where cassava and plantain are not grown. African yams are not the sweet potatoes normally called yams in America; they taste like potatoes but have a different texture. Generally two people prepare fufu, one pounding and the other turning the fufu in the mortar.

2. get up; stand up

3. gather; take and set down

Every time she used to make two balls of fufu, big ones, for the children. And every time, when we put the soup, I know the one from her. I will start with that one, and we will eat that first and finish before we are all going to start on the next one. So the time she called us, her own was already finished. Then she said, "Let me see." Then we brought it; we brought only one ball of fufu, the second. Then she said, "Where's the first?"

We said, "We have eaten it."

Then she said, "*He-ey!* You people eat like dogs."

So she just cut[1] a little bit and tasted it, and it was the same like what she was eating. Then she said, "Oh." Then we went out. She didn't say anything. She didn't ask me anything, either.

Then the next day, I thought in my mind that, hey, this woman is going to get my way and catch me, so I must stop for two or three days. So from that time, I didn't do it. Every day like that, I didn't do it. Then, one day I did it again. She didn't find out. The second day I did it again. The third day, she found out.

When she said we should bring our food for her to see, I said, "But why?! If you don't want us to eat, why are you calling us to bring the food to you again? I don't like this kind of living. If you don't want us to eat, don't give us! Every time we are eating, and then you have to get us up from the food to bring it for you to look at it. You know, if you are eating and you wake up and leave the food, then when you come back to eat it, you won't feel[2] it again. In my father's place, they don't do that. Why?! Because—because you think you are neat past everybody.[3] You are eating this fufu every day. You didn't die, no? Every time, I used to change your food, too, and we eat it. You eat what we pound, but you don't die. If you were going to die, you would have already died a long time." *Haa-hee!*

Then she said, "Go! Go! Go! Go to your father! Fucking girl! Fucking girl! That's why you cannot—to—to—to live with people. You don't respect. Go! Go! Go! Go! Go!"

Then I went out like that, you know. I didn't even take my things. I just went out, because from that place to my father's place was not far. I said, "OK. I will go to my father's house."

And you know, every time when I would do something like this, and they would sack me and I would come home, I used to be serious. Then my father would say, "Hey, Hawa, are you dead?"

1. took, pulled away a bit of it
2. have a feeling for; like; want
3. cleaner than everybody

"I don't want to talk. Nobody should talk to me. I don't want to talk today."

And my sisters, you know, and my brothers, when they saw me like this, they used to shout, "Eh! Hawa?"

Then I would say, "*Tsk!* I don't want that! Today I am serious." Then I would say, "*Tsk, tsk.* How they say that if your mother dies and leaves you, you will suffer, it's true. If suppose my mother was there, will I suffer like this?"

Then my father would say, "Who is talking there? Is it Mama?" You know, my grandmother's name was Hawa, so my father used to call me like that.[1]

Then I said, "Yes. It's me."

"What is wrong? Did your auntie say something bad?"

Then I said, "Eh-h. If my mother didn't die, do you think every fucking old woman that you say she is your sister, then I'll go and live with her? A fucking old woman!? I wanted to pound fufu for her, and she said, 'No!' She has to pound it by herself. If somebody is passing and sees this, it's a disgrace for us who are living with her. They will say that we don't know how to do anything. Our grandmother is old like that, and we let her to be pounding fufu. It's not good. I tried to change her food, and then she too, she wanted to bluff.[2] She just sacked me like a chicken! 'Go, go, go, go to your father!'"

Then my father said, "Don't mind her. So where are your things?"

I said, "I didn't take anything. I dash[3] them to her. Let her keep them." *Ha!*

Then my father said, "Mama, I don't believe these words. You did something bad."

"I didn't do anything bad! Because every time she thinks she's very neat. And then, me, I used to change her food, that's all that I did. But I didn't do anything bad." *Hee-hee-hee.*

1. This form of address is used routinely as a nickname. Among Voltaique peoples, children are sometimes named after their grandparents, and the parents would feel uncomfortable addressing them with the actual name of their father or mother; they would instead call the child "mother" or "father" or "grandfather" and so on, or sometimes, more indirectly, "the name of the mother," "the name of the father," and so on. Such children are also said to have "inherited" their grandparents, a term that sometimes refers to the personality or character or destiny of the child (or to the parents' hopes in that regard), in the sense that the ancestor has come back to the world in that child. It is also common for a diviner to help the parents know which ancestor has come back, particularly if there is a problem with a child, when it may be important to know more about such an inheritance.

2. to take oneself high, to boast, to present oneself as better than others

3. give as a gift; also, as a noun, a gift

Then my father asked me, "When you used to change her food, it's not bad?"

Then I said, "How can it be bad? All is food. When we eat, we don't die. And when she eats our own too, she doesn't die. She doesn't get sick, too. So what kind of bad did I do? I didn't put any poison in it."

So my father had to go and beg[1] this woman, you know, "Yeah. It's my baby, you know, it's my daughter."

And she said, "I don't want her. I don't want her to stay with me."

So my father said, "OK. Even she also says she wants to stay with me because you are bad."

Then this woman said my father had abused her. She said it's because my father used to talk about her in the house, and that's why I had a chance to say all these things. If it's not so, why should my father reply her like that? *Hee-hee-hee.*

They had this quarrel for about three days. My father wouldn't go there and greet her, and she wouldn't come to my father and greet him. Then my father's senior brother heard of this, you know, so he came and talked to them. Don't do that, you are the same family, you shouldn't be living without talking, and all this. So then they started to talk again. But every time, this woman used to say to my father, "I fear you." Then my father would also say, "Yes, I fear you, too." *Hee-hee-hee.*

She was an old lady, a nice old lady. But she was fucking! If you saw her, you wouldn't think that she could carry a pot of water. To take something heavy, she would say, "Oh! Come and help me. Come and carry this for me." But she could pound fufu with one hand! The way I pound fufu, she could do it. As for the food she will eat, she wouldn't want anybody to touch it. And this food, too, she would go to the kitchen by herself and cook it. And when she was cooking, she wouldn't cook with light. In the night she cooked in darkness, yeah, without any light. And she could see, too. I don't know whether she had other eyes in back of her eyes. Yeah. So I used to change her food every day. Why? You have been eating these things from the time you are young, and now you have become an old lady, but you don't want to eat the one which people make. You won't eat unless you make it yourself. So I asked my father whether this woman was doing that when she was young, and my father said, No. Then why? This time when you are coming nearly to die, and you want to be working. For what? So this one was what let them sack me from there. *Heh-heh.* Then I went back to my father again.

1. apologize; ask forgiveness, often with a sacrifice or gift. "I beg" means "Please."

: THE VILLAGE IN BURKINA FASO :

The Village of Don't-Go-There

Then my father said, "OK. If that be the case, maybe your grandmother is an old lady now, so she can take care of you." So he sent me to the village of my grandmother, in Upper Volta. She was my mother's mother, and I stayed with her. In that village, they had "Don't-go-there. Don't-go-there. Don't-go-there." And I didn't understand why I shouldn't go there. It's the land. Land is land for human beings. There is no land which they can say somebody cannot go to the land. So when they said that, *ah!* I wouldn't say anything, but in the night or in the daytime, when they go to the bush[1] or go to the farm, and they leave us small-small[2] children, then I would pack all of us and say. "Let's go."

They would say, "Hey! Here, they don't go there."

Then I'd say, "Fuck off.[3] If you don't go, I will go and leave you. What is there?!"

You know, at that place, they had some trees, and these trees make a seed which you can eat—it's red. And nobody would go there and take some. But when I thought of it, I thought, "This is good food. And they used to bring some from the bush for me." So when they were not in the house, if I was alone and I asked these children to go with me, if they didn't want, then I would go alone. Every time I went to get this thing and bring it, there was not one of these children who wasn't happy. Then I said, "*Um-hum!* When I bring it for them, they eat. Look at the foolishness. You don't want to go there. Then when I bring the food from there, you eat!"

So one time I went to some place, and it was very difficult. Hey, it was wonderful! There was a tree, the one we use to make soup with its leaves. It was a big tree. You could not climb on it until you passed from another tree behind, and then you could go up this big tree. And every time, when the village people would go to the bush, we children had to make *T-Zed.*[4]

1. any wild, uncultivated, or uncivilized area

2. The adjective is doubled for emphasis, i.e., very small.

3. Get away!

4. staple hot food of the savanna region, a pastelike starchy food made from boiled flour of sorghum or occasionally other grains, eaten with sauce or soup. T-Zed is a conversational acronym for T-Z, which is Hausa for "tuwon zafi," literally, a linked form of "hot (zafi) food (tuwo)." The Hausa term, shortened to "tuwo," is also commonly used by people throughout the region.

Do you know T-Zed? Hausa people[1] call it *tuwon zafi,* so we call it T-Zed. So, this big tree, when the *harmattan*[2] is blowing, all the old leaves used to fall down, and then the new ones would start coming out at once, and that new one is the good one for the soup. The leaves are like okra when you cook them. And I liked this soup! So I thought to go and get this thing, and then we will come and make this soup. My big sister was making the food,[3] so I told her, "Oh, I'm going to find some nice leaves, then we can make the soup with that."

And she said, "OK, if you can find some."

And I said, "Yes."

"Do you know where to find them?"

I said, "Yeah. I have seen some leaves: nice ones." I didn't tell her where. If I told her, she wouldn't allow me to go. So I went out to that place. I went on top of that tree. Then I took one leaf. The second leaf. Then: bees! Do you know bees? Who make honey? One came: *hhhhhh-hh-hh-hhhhhhh.* Then I said, *"Oh!"* Then I was taking the third leaf, and *o-ooh!* I didn't know where they were from. Plenty! They were biting me till I fell down from the top of the tree. When I fell down, then I started to shout, and these things fell all over my body, biting me. "Hey! *Hey-yy!!*"

Then my sister came out, and all the children ran to under the tree. They found me covered with these bees; they couldn't do anything, so they had to stand there and shout, "Help! Help, help!" And you know, these people who are in village, they are old. My village is very small. Yeah, there are only old, old people there.[4] Some of them cannot see anything.[5] And some of them cannot walk very well; they can only hold a stick and then shake. These old people came there, but nobody pulled me out. They just asked my sister to go and bring *pito.*[6] Do you know pito? It's like beer they make there. What are they going to do with pito? *Huh?* It was very hard! I was suffering, and nobody was touching me, and nobody was coming to me, too. They were all standing around me like this,

1. The Hausa are the major cultural group in northern Nigeria; Hausa traders travel and live widely in West Africa, and the Hausa language is a lingua franca well beyond the Hausa traditional area.

2. a dry dust-laden wind that blows south from the Sahara desert during late November, December, January, and into February. The word can also refer to the season.

3. The "food" is the starch or grain, the bulky part of a meal, i.e., the T-Zed or the fufu, so you eat the soup or the stew or the meat with the food.

4. The young ones are migrant workers or are working in towns.

5. Onchoceriasis is endemic in the area.

6. a fermented drink generally brewed over three days from malted sorghum or sometimes from millet, reddish-brown in color with a somewhat sour taste

and I was fighting to get myself out. Then my sister brought the pito, and they poured the pito down, *ta-op, ta-op, ta-op,* and then all these things just went away. Then they picked me home.[1] My eyes! For two days I couldn't see. All my eyes were closed, swollen up.

When my grandmother came, they said, "Ah-h, your child did that and this," and so, they must take one pot of pito — at our place when they say one pot of pito, it's the big one — and one sheep, a white one, and then four chickens, to go and beg this tree.

My grandmother did all this, and then she said "Ah-h-h. Why did you do so? Your mother left you alone: don't you pity for yourself? As a small girl, when they tell you don't do this, then you do it. So —"

Then I said, "OK. I won't do that any more."

"Or you want to go to your father?"

"No. I want to stay with you, grandmother. I won't do it again." So they left me. That case was finished.

Then: they have something they used to do, and it's only men who do this thing. If you are a child and you are growing up, they do it. I think it's their *juju*[2] or something; I don't know. If they want to do it to you, you will keep your hair without cutting it. Some of the boys keep[3] like that for one year; some of them keep two years. No knife or no blade can go in their hair, and their hair will grow up, and they don't comb it, either. So the time you start this thing, you must make all these sacrifices, and leave[4] your hair. Any time you have your money ready to make this juju, then you tell the big people so they will make this thing for you. It takes them one week to make it. This one week, you all go to the bush, and you don't go anywhere again. All the time, they make some small music[5] with a *tam-tam.*[6] And people don't see much. They sleep in the bush. Where they are sleeping, that place is where there are plenty of trees close together. They used to sweep under the trees, so the under is very clean. They sleep there about one week with this child, and they do their things.

1. took me home, carried me home

2. The word "juju" is still commonly used by indigenous people to refer to non-Christian and non-Muslim (animist) religious activities, or to the medicine given for herbal or magical treatment of sickness, or for animist religious or superstitious practices, or for the diety or spirit itself, or for the shrine of that spirit. It is no longer generally used by anthropologists because it has derogatory connotations, like the associated word "pagan."

3. stay, take (time); keep long: take a long time

4. let something be; also, let something go, stop doing something, let someone be free. "Leave me" means "Let me go."

5. a little music

6. (from French): drum, drumming

No woman cooks for them. It's only old men: they cook by themselves there.

And my grandfather was the chief for these things. My grandfather liked me, you know. So, *ah!* About three, four days, he didn't come home. And every time when my grandmother was going to cook, she would take dry meat, this smoked meat they make. And I didn't like it. If my grandfather was there, I used to get chickens and eggs and all these things. So I thought, "*Ah!* I am not eating well. I must go and find my grandfather." Every time when the men came home to take water, I used to see the road they passed. It was not far from the village. So one day I thought, "*Tsk!* The food they cook here, I don't want it, so it's better I go and tell my grandfather." Because every time, even if he was in the bush where he farmed, I used to go there and tell him, "They made this, and I don't like it." Then he would take me and we would come back home. So I thought, "Today I will go there and see him to talk to him."

When I went, they were many! I was afraid to go there. The place was round and open, and there were many grasses, so I hid under the grass, to wait and see if I saw my grandfather get up and pass somewhere, then I would call him. You know, I thought it would be easy to call him like that. *Heh, heh, heh.* So I was there in the grasses, and then I had to sneeze. Then I said, *"Ah-choo!"*

Then some people said, "No! Somebody is around here!"

Then others said, "Oh-h. No. Who can be around here?"

Then one man said, "OK. Let's wait."

And you know, when I sneezed, I was not all right: I must cough and this thing will come out. So I went, *"Ahem! Ahem!"*

Then: "Who is that?!"

Then I was quiet. If I was not a fool, I should have run. But I was just thinking I could hide myself well. And when I was hiding myself under the grass, this grass started to shake. Nobody talked again: they came, slow, slow, slow. It was very funny. You know, like a child when it wants to hide, I only hid my face! Then they came and picked me by my back like this and took me. "*Ah!* Whose baby is this?!"

Then my grandfather said, "Yes, it's for me." And then my grandfather started to cry.

And I thought, "*Eh?!* Today they are going to kill me, then? Because my grandfather is crying, so maybe I will be dead today."

So they talked, talked, talked, and then my grandfather said, "OK." He is the chief, and now the grandchild of his has gone against the law, so he knows what to do to beg them, and he is begging them that he will give them a cow, and this and that, and they should leave me. Then they said OK, and my grandfather took me home. When they finished this thing from the bush and they came, in about two or three days, then they did what the custom is to them, and my grandfather made the sacrifice and all that was promised.

Then my grandfather said, "No, no, no. If this baby lives here, we will never succeed. So it's better that they leave these children in Ghana. They can't stay here in Upper Volta, because they don't believe anything. It's better she lives in Ghana." So they wrote my father a letter to come and take me. My grandfather didn't say that I had done something. When my father came home to take me, they told my father that because it is the time when they are making their farms — and always from morning time to evening, if they leave me, I will be hungry — and I am too small[1] — and I cannot cook by myself, and all this — so it's better I live with my father.

Then I said, "No! Grandfather, don't say that! You must tell him what I did. I have done two things, and you didn't tell him. You just told him that you go to bush every time. But I'm not hungry, because my big sister is cooking."

Then my grandfather said, yes, it's not because of what I did. It's not because of that they are going to send me. But he thinks that when they are in the bush every time, to leave us children at home is not good. That's why he wants to send me.

Then I said, "No, Papa": I have done this. I have done that. I have done that.

So my father said, "Oh, it's OK." He will pay all the debt, this cow and all these things.

Then my grandfather said, "No. You shouldn't pay it, because I am for all of them. If she grows up, she shouldn't say, 'This is my father; this is my grandfather.' If she has something, she will give all of us. So if some debt comes, we shouldn't share it. If some debt comes, and she's with her father, he can do it. And when she's with me, her grandfather, if anything comes, I can't take a franc from any of you."

: KUMASI :

More Aunts

So my father took me away; he didn't pay anything. He gave me to my uncle in Kumasi, at Aboabo Number 1.[2] And my uncle's wife was a *bad*

1. very young. "Too" as a modifier normally means "very," without implying comparison or excess.

2. section of Kumasi

woman! From morning time, before you will eat: not until twelve o'clock. And we were selling things. Every time we had to carry these things and walk from Aboabo to the big market.[1] In my father's place, I didn't do all these things. But now I became like somebody who was learning, and it was very hard for me. It's very hard, eh? My life is very, very, very hard. *Ha ha ha ha!*

You know, this woman was selling things in the market. She used to sell groundnuts.[2] In the morning, she would make—I don't know what they call it in English—you know, when you go to the market, you used to see they put corn in something like a gallon container. It's not a bucket, but it's a tin[3] they use to measure and sell something, like the medium size of a tin of paint. They used to fill it with the groundnuts or corn or guinea corn[4] to sell. This thing full—two—she would get two full of this thing from the market; evening time, I would carry it home and cook it.

She's still selling her things in the market, but this time she doesn't have a helper, so she can't sell many things as before. That woman is still there in Kumasi, doing the same work in the market. She didn't die. But now she's suffering. She is very *bad* woman. Ah, that woman!

Look. The work I was doing when I was there: the first time, early in the morning, maybe about four or three o'clock, I would wake up and put the fire to the groundnuts. I would fry the frying one first.[5] When I finished, I would put the groundnuts for boiling on top of the fire of the frying one. Then I would make another fire for the hot water, for bathing. So before everybody would get up and take his bath and do everything, then I would go and wash the pans we were eating in. Then when I finished that one, it was that time I was going to the pipe to get water, to fill one big barrel. Then, when I finished all that, by then she would get up to wake the children and bathe them, and they would come and drink porridge. As I had finished all this, I couldn't drink porridge in the house, because before I would finish, it was the time to go to the market.

So I would come and carry the groundnuts, the fried one and the cooked one, to walk. I went by my feet, not with a car.[6] I had to walk.

1. The central market in downtown Kumasi is one of West Africa's largest markets; the "big" market in this context means the central or main market.

2. peanuts

3. generic name for a can

4. sorghum

5. Peanuts are fried, roasted, and boiled for different uses.

6. a taxi or minibus; transport

And she would take a car with the cola[1] and the cigarettes and these small-small things. She would carry them in a big sack, and she was taking a car with it. And I was also going to carry the food which we were going to eat for the whole day, on top of the groundnuts. And I had to go to the road and take water, one gallon of water, to put on top of it, because where we were staying in the market, we couldn't get water. If you went to get water, you had to go far. *Mm-hm.* I was still small, but I would carry all. At that time she had four children, and two were senior than me. One boy and one girl were senior than me. They didn't do anything. They didn't carry anything. The boy was in school, and every morning time, he would go to the school before we went from the house. And the girl was the first-born of the woman. Sometimes she would go in the car with the mother, or sometimes she liked to walk with me and tease me on the road. So, do you know what I used to do with her? Sometimes we would go to the road, and I would say, "Oh, I'm tired. Let's rest, just small."[2] Then she would help me to put the thing down. Then I would *catch* her, then we would *fight.* I would bite her! She used to beat me very well, so I used to bite her first-class, too. Before we would get to the mother, I had torn all the dresses.[3] As for me, if you are beating me and it's hurting me, I will just take the cloth anyway I can, together with all the skin. I was just like a wild dog.

And every time! The daughter for this woman passed me about by six years, but what the daughter could carry — the heavy one — this woman would make me carry it. And every time, I was sick: my neck would be paining me. One day this woman gave us things to carry, and she gave me one-half of a full bag of groundnuts, the fresh ones[4] which she used to boil and sell. When I reached the road, I was tired, so I threw it down. Then I sat on top. Then the daughter said, "Hey! Wake up. Carry this thing and let's go on." I didn't say anything. Then she left me and went home, and after, the mama came with her, and this woman started beating me at that place. *Ah!*

So I said, "What kind of bad woman are you? Did you think your daughter cannot carry this, or you cannot let us — when I carry a little bit, or when I'm tired — you cannot also let us change? Because what she's carrying is not a heavy load. It's this pan which we eat inside, and

1. Cola is a type of bitter seed about the size of a chestnut. In Africa it is chewed as a mild stimulant.

2. (adverbial): a little bit

3. clothes, any outer garment; applies to both men's and women's clothing

4. raw ones

a little cola, and the bucket we use to take water to the market. Why don't you give that one to me? You see that Kadija is grown up past me, but every time you want me to carry this. Is it that my father sold me to you to be a slave?" I asked her this question.

Then she said, "It's because of your mouth that you can't get any place to live."

Then I said, "Yeah. But I'm living in the world. No? If I talk bad, then God should take me away. I think I am good. That's why I'm living in the world. And even if I'm bad, and I cannot get any house to stay in, I can live outside. So leave me. I'm not going to your house, and I'm not going to carry this."

Then she was annoyed. The daughter took the groundnuts, and they went and left me. Then I walked home.

Then my uncle came. He used to pity for me. That fucking woman was his wife. Sometimes they would beat me, and when he came home, he would be annoyed. So he used to help. He is sick now. He was in the hospital, and that woman wasn't doing anything for him. *Ah!* She is *fucking!*

So when my uncle came home, I told him, "I thought you are my mother's brother. That's why they brought me here, not because of your wife. But what your wife is doing with me, don't you see it? You have nothing to tell your wife? 'No, don't do that, don't do that.' It's better you tell my father to take me back, because I don't want to be living like this. In my father's place, I don't carry things. I don't sell anything. But I am eating every day. If you cannot help me, then you can tell my father, 'No, I cannot help your daughter because she doesn't want to do things.' But what your wife is doing to me, I cannot do it."

Then he said, "What?"

"Every time when we go to the market, I have to carry the heavy load. And Kadija does nothing. And Kadija is my senior sister. She has to do something. When the load is heavy, she has to carry it, and then I will carry the little ones. But your wife doesn't want this."

So he called the wife and talked to her. "You know, this girl is a small girl. But she has experience.[1] Every time, that's why she used to ask people questions. And I think that she is some kind of old lady who has come to the family.[2] So you must take care of her. Don't do what you are doing."

1. intelligence; also, ideas, sense, wisdom
2. She has inherited the character or spirit of an old lady.

Then the wife said, "*Heh-h?* Why should you say that? What kind of a child who is a woman doesn't suffer? They say that if you are a child, and you are a woman, you have to suffer before you will know what to do when you marry your husband. But if you leave your baby girl like this, without training her, when she marries, she cannot do anything."

So I thought that in this case, I had to talk. "Do you know whether I'm going to marry or I'm not going to marry when I grow up? If I marry and I don't do anything, it's between me and my husband. It's not your problem. It's not—you shouldn't train me bad like this. You say it's because of marriage. If I marry, if I grow up and I don't do anything, and I'm very lazy, if I marry and my husband doesn't like me, and he sacks me, and I don't have a husband, it's OK. But not to be suffering like this. But why doesn't Kadija suffer? Kadija is not going to marry?"

Then she said, "Yes. Kadija is going to marry."

"Why doesn't she do the same work I am doing?"

"Yes, Kadija has done that for a long time. You are the one who hasn't done that before, so I want to train you."

Then I said, "No. This kind of training, I don't want it."

So then she said, OK, she wouldn't do anything. So what did she do? Every bloody Sunday she would bring their clothes. No? All these children — she had four children — with her and the husband — the dirty clothes which they used for the whole week. She would put it down and I would have to wash it. *Hm!* I would wash all this, and all my fingers would be hot from the Omo.[1] And I thought this was trouble, but when I put the wash on the rope, then this woman would come and say, "Look here, and look here," and she would put it back in the water. *Ey!* This mama is not a good mama. What kind of mama is this?

I did that for about three weeks. The fourth week I said, "No. This thing, I won't do it." I just took all of the clothes — they had a big washpan — and I put all inside the pan, the white dress with the blue and all, and then I put water and put soap on top, and I just turned it —*sh-h, sh-h* — and then I put it all outside and put it on the tree.

Then she came: "Look here. Look here."

Then I said, "Look, Mama. The way I wash, if you are not satisfied, you can do it by yourself."

Then: "*Huh?!* You are telling me this —?"

"Yes! Because I am tired. This is what I can do."

"Ah, Hawa. Don't do that. You know, I like you. I know that you are a

1. a brand of laundry detergent

nice girl. And I like you. You shouldn't do this. A small girl shouldn't reply to the mother's mouth like this."

"*Eh?* I'm small, but I can reply something which I cannot do, you know. Because I think this thing is heavy, every week. You say you won't make me carry heavy things. And that time, I liked it. But the way I am washing, I think it's better even to be carrying timber. Yes! Pieces of timber, if you make me carry it, it's better than what I'm doing every week."

Then she said, "OK." So when my uncle came, they had to tell him, "This girl doesn't want to do anything. She's very lazy. Even to wash the clothes, too, she doesn't want it."

Then my uncle said, "No. You know, to train somebody is little by little. You shouldn't train somebody to know everything in one day. It is very hard to be training somebody. You have to take patience, a little bit, small-small.[1] Then she will know."

Then this woman said, OK, she won't give me anything. I won't go to the market. I would be in the house. But every time: I had to carry water to the house. We had two *big* barrels, and I had to fill them full with water. If I went with a bucket, I think twenty buckets could fill one barrel. And to go and take water in Aboabo Number 1, there was a small hole: it was a small well they dug, and you took the water from down. And the people used to fill up the place, and you would have to wait before you can fill your bucket. And so sometimes I would get water to fill one barrel, and then I would think, "*Agh!* One is OK. Even I am tired; I have wasted about four or five hours to get this one barrel, so if I want to do the two barrels, maybe I will take twelve hours. And there is no need. This water can reach us for today. And there is also some small water in that other barrel."

When I did that, *oh-oh!* This woman didn't like that way, either. When she comes, she has to look at both these two barrels. If they are not full up, *agh!* Do you know what she did? She didn't beat me again, because I told them I don't want beating. So: ginger. Do you know ginger? Ginger with this white pepper: she would grind them together, then she would put it in my eyes. *Ah-h! Twe-e-a-a!*[2] *Shit!* My life was hard, eh? Yeah, that was a *fucking* woman! Now, every time she sees me, it's, "Oh, my daughter," and this and that. But still, if I remember what she did to me, even if I was going to give her something, if I remember this, I won't give. I will

1. (adverb): little by little, bit by bit
2. (Asante Twi): *Tweaa* is an exclamation of disgust.

take my thing back. Sometimes now, if I see her, I used to dash her something—the day when I forget of this, then I will dash her. But sometimes if I want to give her something and I remember this, I will say, "No! This bad woman like this. The way she treated me, if God didn't bless me, I would be dead. Does she want dash from me now?"

This woman put the pepper in my eyes two times. Then the third time she put pepper in my eyes, she said that I shouldn't go to the toilet either. So I didn't say anything. Their bed was there, like this, and she would make something like a mat beside the bed for me and the daughter. Then when we slept in the night, she closed the door. And I wanted to shit, because this pepper was in my eyes. I didn't say anything. I just went—I was twelve years old when I did this—I just went to the middle of the room, like that, and then I *shit.* When I shit and finished, then it was *smelling. Ah!* I couldn't sleep. And all of them were sleeping. And I knew that if they saw this shit, maybe the next morning this woman would make me eat it. So the best thing to do: I opened the door. When I opened the door, then she heard the noise, "Who?"

Then I said, "I am going to piss."

"Who?"

"It's me."

Then she went back to sleep. When I opened the door and went out, then I closed it back. Then I went. I started to walk. From Aboabo to Old Tafo.[1] It's very far. Old Tafo and Kumasi, I think is three miles. And then Aboabo will also be three or two-and-a-half miles. So I walked that night from Aboabo to Old Tafo.

And you know, when I went home to my father, I was crying, because on the road of Tafo, there is a cemetery there. No light. No anything. I had to pass this place to come home. Then my father said, "No. You alone? It's not true. Somebody brought you."

"No, Papa. I came alone."

"What?"

"Ah! This woman put pepper in my eyes, and she told me don't go to the toilet. Night time, I was feeling pains." I didn't tell my father that I shit—*hee-hee-he*—in the room! You don't see? It's very funny. I didn't tell him anything about my shit, you know! So: "I felt it was paining me. I could not sleep. So I thought it's better if I leave this woman to come back home. Because I don't want the way she treats me."

So my father said, "OK. Come and sleep."

1. section of Kumasi

Then he opened the room, and he started to cry. "Oh, God! What are you doing to this girl? What are you doing to me? I don't have any best family to look after this girl for me."

Then I said, "No, Papa. You shouldn't mind. God will look after us, eh?"

Then my father said, "Yes. OK." Then he took me in his arms, and when he was dreaming, I slipped through, and he put me down, and I slept.

About eight o'clock, I saw my uncle! When I saw my uncle, *aassh!* I went out straight. I didn't want to hear this nonsense. I shit! I know that I shit! This—*aagh!* I shit because she put this thing in my eyes from eight o'clock and then she told me to sleep with it. It's pepper. Yeah, and it's hot, too. So when my uncle came, and I knew that he was bringing this talk, I just went out, to this place: Amakom.[1] Every time when my father was going to work, he would give me two shillings, so when I got my two shillings, then I saw that my uncle was just coming to meet my father. Then I just went out. I took a trotro.[2] I dropped at Kumasi; I took another trotro to Amakom. My father's big brother was there.

When I went to him, he said, "Eh-h? Mama. I haven't seen you for a long time. Why? You don't want to come and greet me?"

Then I said, "Oh, yeah. You know, I was in my uncle's place. Then I wasn't happy. So now I have come home; I have the chance. When I was there, I had no chance to come and greet you. That's why. That's why today when I went home, I have tried to come and greet you."

"It's OK. I'm going to work." He was a collector at the Wa station.[3] So he said did I want to come with him?

Then I said, "No. I want to stay here." I knew that if my father heard of this shit, he wouldn't like it. If I was at home, too, he would beat me. *Hee-hee-hee.* Yeah. You know, it's not good to put pepper on babies and say don't go to toilet, but I shouldn't shit inside the room, too. I was not a child at that time. I was twelve years old. Yes. I knew that something is bad. So by all means, if my father heard this case, he would beat me. So I said, "OK. I will stay with your wife till you come back."

So when my uncle came and told my father that I shit in the room,

1. section of Kumasi

2. a privately owned, inexpensive bus. The name derives from "tro," meaning threepence, which was the former fare; the driver's mate would collect fares, saying "Tro, tro."

3. the station where transport departs for Wa, a town in northwest Ghana. In large towns, there may be a central station, or lorry park, and various other stations at the outskirts for places on particular roads out of the town.

then they were looking for me, and *oh-oh,* they didn't see me. And some of the girls said, "Oh, I saw her passing there." And some of them said they saw me in a car, going to Kumasi. Then my uncle and my father went to work.

So I stayed with my father's brother's wife up to six o'clock when the husband came home. "Mama! What did you do at Aboabo?" Do you know that my father passed at his work place?!

Then I said, "Ah! I didn't do anything. Because my uncle's wife put pepper on me, then I could not sleep with it. So I shit in the room."

"Oh, Mama! Why did you do that? You are not a small girl now to shit in a room."

Then I said, "Yeah. This woman said she's wicked. So I want to show them that—I want her to be a latrine boy for me. To clean my shit! Before I leave her house, she has to clean my shit. Because what she was doing to me, even it's better if she told me to clean her shit. Yeah? So I want her to clean my shit last."

Then he said, "Oh-h-h. Because of that you came here?"

"*Noo-o.* I just felt to come and see you. Oh, *pfft!* Even when I shit, what will they do to me? My father will beat me. And if he beats me, he will never kill me, you know. So I just came to visit you."

Then he said, "Do you want to stay with me here?"

I said, "Yeah. If you like. I can stay with your wife." Now I am going to make my own arrangements! Now it's not my father who takes me some place. It's not anyone who takes me: I take myself.

OK. Then we were there. And this woman too was *another* fucking woman. Every time, she ate fufu, like an Ashanti.[1] You are not Ashanti. You are Voltaique. And Voltaique food is T-Zed. And every time you want to eat fufu. Morning time, you cook food: *aa-oo, fufu-o, aa-oo, fufu-o.*[2] Evening time, two times a day: fufu. And you know, to pound fufu is hard. Then I thought, "Here, too, when I look at my hands, it's not possible." Then I asked her, "Eh, Mama, why do you want to eat fufu like this every time? When I went to Upper Volta, I never ate fufu for a good three months when I was living there. I didn't see fufu there. How did you learn to eat fufu? When you came to Ghana, then you got to know fufu?"

Then she said, "Why should you ask me this question?"

I said, "Yeah, I want to know. Because when I went to the village where you are from, I didn't see anybody beating fufu. Every time, they

1. major cultural group of central Ghana; major subgroup of Akan cultural area
2. The *-o* at the end of a word adds emphasis.

make T-Zed or rice or other things, but not fufu. Who taught you how to eat fufu?" *Heh-heh.*

Then this woman said, "Hey! What are you trying to say?"

I said, "No. I want to know the way you like fufu. You know? Every day: fufu. Every day: fufu, like this. Because I thought I'm getting tired. Look at my hands."

Then she said, "So? You don't want to do anything?"

I said, "Yes. I want to do things. But not every day. You know, even you yourself, when you are here, it's not every day you feel like cooking. Sometimes you will like to cook, and sometimes you will feel too much tired to cook, or you will feel too lazy to cook. As for me, I can cook, and I can do things. Yes. But it's not every day I used to feel that. Sometimes I feel to do hard things, and sometimes I don't feel to do hard work like this."

Then she said, "OK. If because of my fufu, my fufu, you are saying so, then every time I will beat my fufu for myself, and for your father,[1] and I will leave the yams like that for you."

Then I said, "OK. I'm all right."

So from that time I didn't eat fufu for one year, because every time, I didn't want to beat the fufu. So they would leave my yams for me, then I would eat that. I was about three months with them, and even when I went back to my father, I didn't eat fufu again. I thought it was very good for me because I don't eat fufu, so even if you are making your fufu, I don't have to help you to beat it. You just give me my yams with the soup, then I am all right. So I was there with my father's brother and his wife: this woman was also doing that every time, every time.

Then one day I went to where my father was working. He gave me four shillings, and I brought this four shillings and I hid it. And this woman saw this four shillings, and she asked me, "Who is this money for?"

I said, "It's for me."

"Where did you get it?"

I said, "Last time, when I went to my father's work, he gave me, and I wasn't hungry, and I didn't buy anything. I think you give me a lot of food; I don't need to buy anything. So I want to save it."

Then she said why didn't I give the money to her, but I saved it for myself. Look at the case like this! "Yes, you are a bad girl. You are a bad girl. That's why you cannot live with anyone. Why should you get money

1. In the extended family, she would call her father's brother her father.

from outside, and you come and hide it in the room? What do you need money for?" And that and this and that.

I said, "*E-ey,* Mama. Why do I want money? You don't want money? Are you sure that if you get this four shillings, you won't like it?"

She said, "Yes, but a small girl like you, if you get money outside, you should show me."

"No, it doesn't need showing to you. Because it does not belong to you. It's for me. Ah! When you get your money, do you show your husband that 'This is what I have,' or you go and show your mama, 'This is what I have?' This is not the way you do."

Then she said, *"Eh?"* and that this four shillings was for her, that I stole it from her.

Hey-y-y! Then I vexed. I started: *ta-ta-ta-ta-teh-teh.* "Fucking woman," I said. "Don't you know that I know your village? I know all your family. Poor family like you! You want to tell me that I am stealing? If I want to steal, I will go and steal from the rich people, not a poor woman like you. If it's not because of my father's brother, you — in your village, your sisters are there — all their cloths are torn. Don't you think that I saw them? When I went to Upper Volta, don't you know that I saw your sisters? They take needles and sew their underpants before they go to bring water. And you, you think that now you are in Ghana, you have got a good man, he's looking after you, he's giving you a double cloth to tie,[1] and you are — are —You say I am a thief? If I want to steal, I will steal from better people! Not from poor people like you."

So I talked this, and she was annoyed. She beat me. And I took my four shillings, and took my taxi! *Ha-ha!* Yeah, when I was young, I suffered. I *suffered!* So I took a taxi back to my father. Then I said, "Look, the four shillings you gave me is the thing that brought me problems now."

Then he said, "What?"

"This woman saw the four shillings. I hid it under the table. Then she saw it. She asked me. And I said that you are the one who gave me. Then she asked me why didn't I show the money to her. So I'm a thief. So I was hot. You, you are my father. You know me. I stayed here. When I was here, if I wanted something, I asked you. I don't steal. I know where you put your money. You used to have plenty money, coins, in your room. But I never take it. So how can this woman call me a thief?"

Then he said, "That's all?"

1. Instead of just wrapping herself with one cloth, she has two cloths, to wrap one over the other.

"Yeah, as for me, I have abused her. Because I know the family. When I went to the village to be with my grandfather, they told me that this woman, this is the family of this woman. So I told her all."

Then my father said, "You told her all— of what?"

"Yeah, I told her all, how she's poor, and all her families are poor. Even they cannot get good food. Even her sisters in the house, they don't have good underpants. And all this. I told her."

Then my father said, "Oh! Hawa! You want to kill me." So now what should he do?

Then I said, "No, Papa. I want to stay with you. I don't want to go anywhere. I don't want to stay with anyone. I want to stay with you alone. Don't take me to any family."

Then he said, "No! It's not me who took you there. It's you who went by yourself!"

"Yes, but this time I don't want to go by myself. And I don't want you to send me to somebody." So I stayed with my father.

Then my aunt: she was in Abidjan,[1] and she was married to one French man. She had two children with this man, one girl and one boy. And—I don't know what her trouble was in Abidjan—she told her man that she was coming to see her brother in Ghana. And when she came, she got a Lebanese man. This Lebanese man had a big shop. So I think this man was a good man, and my aunt didn't want to go back to Abidjan again. She wanted to stay in Ghana. This Lebanese man gave her money to sell cloths[2] in the Kumasi market. Even still she's in the Kumasi market now. She's selling cloth. This Lebanese man left; he is no more in Ghana now. So he gave her money and she was selling cloths and all these things.

And when she came, *oh-h-h,* she liked me. When she came first, she stayed with my father in the same house. She left the French man in Abidjan to come and see my father, yes? Then she forgot that French man. But she used to go and see her children, and sometimes the children would come to Ghana when they had school holidays. So she was taking care of me. And I liked the way she was. She didn't tell me: do that, do this and that. No. Every time, she would give me. If I was hungry, I'd say, "Aunt, my head." Every time, if I was hungry, I had a headache! And she knew what my tablet was. So she would make quick,[3] preparing soup, to

1. capital of Côte d'Ivoire (Ivory Coast)

2. normally refers to African wax-print cotton cloth. Saying different "kinds" of cloth refers to different patterns or sometimes different countries of origin.

3. hurry

cook something quick-quick-quick and give me. When I ate and finished, then she would ask, "Are you all right now?" And I would say, "Yeah."

So I liked her. The time she came, for about three months, she was living with my father, and then this Lebanese man took one flat for her to live there. And then I went with her and lived there. She had a houseboy; we didn't do anything. Even my clothes, I didn't wash them. It was this boy doing everything.

And every time, this Lebanese man used to take us with the car and we would go to the market. My auntie was selling the things, and she took me with her. Sometimes I would go under the table to sleep. The time I wanted, she would wake me, "Won't you wake up and eat?" I would eat, and then I would go back under my table. Or sometimes, the women who were selling cloths, they had small children, so I used to go from place to place to play with them. And I was free. And this was my *la-ast* place where I stayed and grew up.

A Brief Adolescence

When I grew up, I was fifteen years old. Then they started: *"Hey!"* My father told my aunt, "Hey, we have to watch her well. Because this girl, when she was a small girl, she had a mouth. She talked a lot. And so now-now,[1] she is growing up. You shouldn't let people spoil her." And all this. So my aunt has to take care of me, not to let me go out in the night, and all this. *Shit!*

When they told my aunt this, she called me and said, "You see, your father told me this and that, but I don't want to be forcing you. So you must know the way you walk. If you need something, you should ask me. I will give you money. You shouldn't go and be taking money from somebody."

Then I said, "Ah! Auntie! Why are you telling me this?" She didn't want to tell me the truth, you know. "How can I take—? To borrow somebody's money? Or what?"

She said, "No-o-o. Because there are some girls: some boys used to like them, and because of money they go with them."

Then I said, "A boy can like me with money?! Is that boy rich more than you?! You are selling cloth. Nobody is rich past you. And somebody will be giving me money? Every time, you give me new clothes. What do I need money for?"

Then she said, "OK. You are a good girl."

1. just now; at this very moment

So, do you know one funny thing? One boy, an Ashanti boy, was living behind our house. And every time this boy passed, he used to call me his wife. You know? And I liked this boy's way. Then every time, when I was grown up a bit, I used to sell cloths for my aunt; I used to go to Kejetia,[1] where the lorry station is. These village people would buy from me, and if you wanted two yards, I would know the way I would cut it, leaving a little bit, so that a small part would come to be my own. Before I would finish one piece of cloth,[2] maybe I would get one and a half yards out of it. And that was my profit. These village people didn't know the real two yards, so I used to steal from the bottom.[3] And you know, when I got these pieces, what did I do with it? I would go and give this boy! *Ha!* Then I told this boy, "If you finish your school, are you going to marry me?"

And he said, "Yes."

And I said, "OK. If I also grow, I am going to marry you." This was the way I was doing.

Then my aunt, coming to some time — I don't know — when some people get old, and some people have money, they don't know how to make accounts. So whenever we came from the market, my aunt could make accounts ten times, and she still didn't know how much it was. Then she would call me. How she was counting, if she wanted to make her *real* accounts, she used to make the money two-two. Ten cedis[4] like this, she would make it two-two, two-two, two-two.[5] Then she would think she has the ten-ten cedis, ten times or twenty times. That was the way she made her accounts. She didn't know that this ten-ten cedis, five times is one hundred. No. She didn't know all these things. She could make it two-two-two-two. And the one cedi was also two-two-two-two-two. So when we would come from the market, she would say, "Oh,

1. section of Kumasi

2. A "piece" is twelve yards: a half-piece is used for women's traditional dresses with skirt, blouse, scarf or head-tie, and waist-wrap; two yards is used by men for shirts.

3. the underside (when folded)

4. Decimal currency was introduced in 1965, replacing and phasing out the Ghanaian pound that had replaced British West African currency in 1958. One New Cedi is one hundred pesewas, or ten shillings. The New Cedi was aligned with the U.S. dollar but has been progressively devalued. The old or Nkrumah cedis were originally valued at eight shillings and fourpence; for ease of calculation, the New Cedi was introduced in 1966, valued at ten shillings, with two New Cedis being a pound.

5. People who grew up counting money in pounds often continued grouping the money in twos. For example, if two cedis is one pound, then two ten-cedi notes would be ten pounds.

Hawa, today I am tired; I have a headache. Will you come and make my accounts for me?"

I would say, "Yes, aunt." Then I would come and make this account. Maybe I would take about five cedis out. Then I would go and give this boy! *Ha!* I took this money: I didn't eat with it; I had nothing to buy with it. We had everything in the house. So if I just wanted to spoil it, or what, I don't understand. If it's now when I have my sense, I wouldn't do this foolish business. So: yeah! I gave this boy many pieces of cloth to make shirts. I gave him a lot of money from my aunt. But he didn't do anything with me. But then, from the first time when I was getting to know him, it came that every time I was going to him, I used to find a woman in his room. Then I started to become jealous. Yeah! A small girl of fifteen years. *Hee-hee!*

So I said, "*Eh-heh.* Kwabena, is that the way you are? I'm trying to give you money to go to your school and finish so that we are going to get married. To give you cloths, to make a shirt to go to school. When you finish, we are going to get married. But when I give you all this, you are giving to other women."

Then he said, "No-o-o."

"OK. How many cloths did I give you?"

He said, "Oh, you gave me about twelve cloths."

"Where are the shirts?"

Then he said, "There are shirts here!"

"These shirts are six, so where are the rest?"

He said, "Oh, they are with the tailor—"

Then I said, "If you don't bring the shirts, it's finished!" By that time I was getting my sense back a little, you know. "This is foolishness. I can't do this monkey business. Ah! 'Monkey dey work; baboon dey chop.'[1] Who is a monkey? I don't do that!"

So we had to leave each other. I didn't go to him again; I didn't give him anything. And every time he saw me, "Oh! My wife! Oh-h-h."

And I would say, "No! It's finished. Because I am not a fool. Do you think that if my aunt catches me stealing money for you, she won't beat me? She will beat me! And she'll beat me for nothing. You are taking it for other women. I won't give you anything again, and it's finished."

"Oh! But you can come and greet me."

1. Pidgin English proverb, referring to exploitation. Literally, the reference is that a monkey works to get food from a tree, and a baboon comes and eats it.

chop (Pidgin): eat, consume, use, spend; also: kill; chop money: money for cooking or food

"No! I don't want to greet you even. I don't want to see you. If you are passing here, don't greet me." *Hee-hee.* So that's the time I grew up.

Then they said I must marry, and all this. So I had to go back to my father's place to make this *amariya,* this Muslim marriage. The Hausas call it *amariya,* and you the new wife, you are the *Amariya.*[1] That is their marriage. To put this black thing[2]—I don't know the name in English—on your feet, and then putting this thing on your head,[3] the veil, and then they play the tam-tam: *gbong-gbong, gbong-gbong, gbong-gbong. Ha!* That's the marriage. If they are going to give you to a man, or if you choose a man to marry, then they keep you in a room for about one week! But this time, they don't keep like that. The first people, who were good, they could keep like that. The first people, too, when they were going to make you an Amariya, and you didn't go with any man before, you would get many things, gifts from your family or from your husband's family. They do all this at the father's house, so they took me back to my father's house.

When I was at my father's house, every time, I used to go to cinema. In the night, eight-thirty, I'm in the cinema. In the day, twelve o'clock, I'm in the cinema. It was an Indian man who had this cinema. And one of his small brothers, every time he would buy me chewing gum, and candy, and I would enter the cinema free. *Hee-hee-hee.* So one day he asked me, "Ah-h, when you finish the cinema, where are you going?"

I said, "I'm going home."

"OK. I can drop you home in my car."

Then I said, "OK."

Then: I didn't know how to drink, you know. So we went together, and he passed his house and gave me Coca-Cola. Then he dropped me home. The first day, he didn't say anything. The second day. The third day: he took me to his house again, and he gave me Coca-Cola. I went to piss, and he mixed whiskey in the Coca-Cola. Then he put the glass on the table. So when I came, I was drinking, and I smelled the scent: it was changed! But I didn't know. I thought, "Ah, maybe it's the scent of this Coca-Cola." I drank the Coca-Cola, and I thought, "Ah! This Coca, it's a drink."[4] I didn't finish the bottle before I got *dru-unnk!* And this man did something with

1. The Amariya is the most recently married, or newest, wife in a polygamous household. The word can also refer to a woman without cowives who was married in a Muslim ceremony, since she is still the new wife, or to the ceremony itself.

2. henna

3. West African Muslim married women generally do not cover their faces but only wear a scarf.

4. hard liquor

me. He made love with me. And I hadn't made love before. So, *ah!* Before my eyes opened, before this drink was going away small-small, I was feeling pains. I said, "Ah! I cannot stand well when I get up. My waist[1]— *Ah!! What did you do with me?!*"

"No, I didn't do anything with you. Because you drank this whiskey, that's why."

Then I said, "Who told you to give me whiskey?"

He said, "Yeah, I thought it's good. If you drink a little whiskey, you will be happy."

Then I said, "No." I went to the toilet and I saw that it was coming blood and something like water. Then I came back and said, "No. It's not true! You did something with me! If you don't tell me the truth, I'm going to tell my father!"

Then he said, "*O-o-h-h, no-o-o.* This thing that you did, you shouldn't tell your father." And that and this.

Then I said, "OK. Now I'm sick. I cannot go home. I cannot walk well. When I go home, and they ask me, what should I say?"

Then he said, "No. You can tell something to your father, that—ah—maybe you are sick in your stomach, or—ah—you have some sickness in your waist." Then he asked me, "Have you passed menstruation?"

I said, "Yes." I had passed menstruation by then.

So he said, "Ah, OK. You can tell him that when you passed menstruation, you had waist pains."

So I took it like that. This man showed me experience.[2] When I got home, they said, "Where did you go this long time?!! Where did you go?!!"

"I went to cinema."

Then: "Why didn't you come after the cinema closed, not now?!!"

Then I said, "Yeah, after cinema, I was feeling pains in my waist—because I have—I have menstruation. Then I was feeling pains—I cannot walk fast—to come home—and I haven't got money to take a taxi." *Heh-heh-heh.*

So: my father didn't know that I had done something like that. And from that time, I was afraid of men. I thought that every time, if you make love, you will get pains. *Hee-hee-hee.* I was about fifteen and some months, and getting to sixteen years, I didn't go with a man again. It was my first time, and from the first time, I stopped up to sixteen years. I was afraid. And this Indian boy, every time when I would go to the cinema, when he would tell me to wait for him after the cinema, he wouldn't

1. lower back and hips
2. taught; in some contexts, take advantage of, cheat

know where I passed to go home. I ran. Because I was afraid. *Hee-hee.* He made me feel pains. Yeah.

Junior Wife

So then they came and made me this Amariya. After these sixteen years, they brought a man. They were going to make me Amariya with him. He was a young man, but he was a bit grown. Maybe he was about twenty-eight, or something. He was not too old, and he was not young, either. I was sixteen. Then my aunt talked to me a lot. She said, "This boy is rich." He's that and this, so if my father tells me to marry him, I shouldn't refuse. If I refuse, what my father will tell me, it will be bad for me after, and so I must agree with my father, and all this.

So I said, "OK."

They made me Amariya to this man, and this man had two other wives, and I was tired. I had thought that if you marry, you are free. I didn't know that in the Muslim way, if you marry somebody who has a wife, you are a slave. *Yeah!!* It's *true.* Because: everything! You are the young one: you have to do it. I am the one who is cooking. I am the one who washes this man's clothes. The first wife: I am the one who washes her dresses. As for the second wife, I didn't do anything for her, but the first wife of my husband, I had to do everything for her.[1]

Then I thought, "Ah! I thought if you grow up and marry—" One day I thought of this. That day I did a lot of work: I washed many things, then I started cooking, then I went into the room. As for me, my groove:[2] even if I was married, I smoked. I went inside and smoked some groove, and then I started thinking, "Ah! Look at the way I suffered when I was young! I thought if I grow up and marry, I will be free. And now I'm a prisoner. Or a slave. To some people. What I don't even do in my family, I am doing for some people. No. I don't think I can stay."

When this man came home, I told him, "Did you marry me, or did you buy me to be a slave for you? I want to know."

Then he said, "What question are you asking?"

"No. I want to know. Because I think this way is not the way to marry. My big sisters have married, and I go to them all the time. And I didn't see that they are suffering like me."

1. It is customary for the Amariya in a polygamous Muslim household to be in a position of subservience to the other or "senior" wives.

2. marijuana

Then he said, "No-o-o, you are young. You are the last woman, and you are the Amariya. You have to do this, do that and that."

"*Ah-hah!* Is that the way? Then what time am I going to leave doing this?"

He said, "Yes, if I marry another woman."

"*Ah-hah!* So I have to wait until you marry another woman? Maybe it will take you ten years to marry another one before I will come and shift, too. I cannot stay with you."

Then he said, "OK. If you like, I will get one room for you. You can cook by yourself. And then you can cook for me and you, and the other women will cook their food."[1]

Then I said, "If that, then it will be better. If it's that, I will accept. But: to wash your first wife's dresses, I cannot do it. OK?"

So then he took a room for me and him, and he gave the first room to the two other women.

Then I thought I wouldn't be washing things, you know, because I already told him that I could not wash the first wife's things. Then one day I was doing washing, then the first wife brought her things out. She said, "Sister Hawa?"

"I'm not your sister. You know? I'm not your younger sister to do this business for you."

Then she said, "What?!! *What?!!* What are you saying?! I didn't hear it. Repeat it again!"

Then I repeated it. I said, "Yes. I'm not your younger sister to do this fucking work for you every day. I have been here two months. Every day I have to wash your things. Why? Are your hands cut off? Can't you wash? Or do you think my family brought me here to be a slave for you, or to be a washboy for you. If you want a boy, you have to tell your husband to get you a boy. I can't do it."

Then she said, "*Oh-Kay!* We are going to see who is going to live with this man. We will see."

"Hey! You can live with your man. I met you people together. And I can fuck off even today, if I like."

1. In a compound house, the man has a room and each wife has a room. A new wife may originally be placed in a room with one of the senior wives. Wives generally cook in rotation for the whole household, and a wife sleeps with the husband on the day she cooks. By separating the wives' cooking, the husband is releasing Hawa from cooking for the household, but he is mainly preventing the wives from quarreling by suspecting or accusing their cowives of putting something in their food. Nonetheless, this kind of preferential treatment for the Amariya would be likely to provoke jealousy from the senior wives.

Then she said, "OK. I think that will be better for you, because you cannot live here to control people."

And I said, "You can't control me, too! We married the same man, no? The way he fucks you, it's the same way he fucks me. So you can't tell me this."

Ba-ba-ba-ba-ba! Ba-ba-ba-ba!! "You don't respect." And that and this. "If you play with me, I'll beat you." And that and this. But she didn't beat me. There were many women in the house, and they separated us.

So I went inside. I had many things; I could not carry them. These our people, they are fools. If you marry, they bring you big, big pots like drums, with mirrors, packed all full of clothes, and many cooking pans, and this and that. So I went inside. Which one can I take? I took a small bag, and I put three cloths inside, and I closed it. Then I went to my father's house.

I said, "Hey, Papa, where you gave me, I cannot stay. I'm coming to tell you the truth. And whatever you do, I won't go back. So if you people like, you can go and take your things."

Then my father said, "No. It's not possible. In Muslim marriage, you cannot leave like that. Two months: you cannot leave the husband. Even if you don't like him, you have to be patient for three months."

"*Heh?!* To be a prisoner for three months? Or a slave? I cannot do it. If God will punish me, let Him punish me. Or if you want to punish me by yourself, you can punish me. But I'm not going back."

So: we were in the house in the evening time when this man came. I think the wives told him what happened, and they saw me take my bag and go out, and since morning I didn't come. So he came to my father's place. He came and met me. Then he started: he's coming to beg — and that and this — his wife — he talked to the wife — and she wouldn't do that and this again. And so he told my father.

Then I said, "Hey, father. I talked to this man about this palaver first, and he said, 'No.' That's why he took one room to give me to live together with him. Then any time, when he means to sleep with the other woman, he can go with the other woman and sleep with her. But the room where he and I live, all his things and my things are there.[1] And I talked all this. This is the palaver: I told him I cannot wash the first wife's things. And he said, OK, I wouldn't have to do that again. But the first wife brought

1. Normally, the husband would have his own room, and the wife who cooked in her rotation would go to his room to sleep with him. For the husband to be keeping his things and staying in the Amariya's room would also provoke the senior wives.

the things again today, and then she told me I have to wash them or we can see. *We can see!* We Africans, if somebody tells you that you can see, it's very hard, because that person can make some juju to kill you or make you crazy.[1] She is the first wife for him. I cannot challenge her. When she tells me I will see, I don't think I should step in that house again. If I go there again, then I will see! What am I going to see?" So I asked my father this question: "This woman says I will see. If I go there again, and something happens to me, what are you going to do?"

My father said, "No, she cannot do anything to you."

Then I said, "No. Whether she can do something or she cannot do something, I am fed up. I cannot go there again."

Then my father said, "*He-ey!* If you can't go there, then you can find where to live. You cannot live with me."

Then: now it's between me and my father, you know. Yeah! Then I said, "OK. If you don't want me, I can go away. I don't care. The people who don't have a father: did you hear that somebody hasn't got a father, and some animal ate his meat?"

He said, "No." Then he asked me, too, "Have you heard someone who hasn't got a daughter, the animals ate his meat?"

Then I said, "No-o. It's finished. You looked after me; you tried. I thank you very much. Because you took me when I was three years old, you suffered with me. And now I have grown up. I can feed myself; I can look after myself. So this is it. Bye-bye."

Then I took my bag again. *Ha-ha!* I went to my aunt. Then my aunt said, "You can stay with me, but I am afraid of your father."

I said, "Why, aunt? You're afraid of my father? My father can kill you?"

"No."

"Then why?"

She said, "Your father will say it is because maybe I didn't marry; I have no husband. That's why I just follow Europeans.[2] That's why I want you to spoil like me. So they will come and say something against me. Then maybe I wouldn't like it. He's my brother, and maybe we — we are going to get some bad talks against — you know — against your father or

1. Hawa is saying that the senior wife threatened her with juju. The words "We will see" mean "We will see the result," that is, no one will see the juju at work, but once it has finished, the people involved will look at what happened but may only suspect that there was something behind it.

2. generic term for white people, including Americans

against me. So it's not good. Whatever the man's wife says, you should stay in the house with him."

Then I said, "Yeah, aunt. But I cannot stay with him. What my father has told me, the words he told me, I don't want to stay even with him. So I can't. If you don't like me, I can go."

Then my aunt said, "No-o. It's not that I don't like you. So, stay."

Then because I had gone there, she had to go and talk to my father, you know. Then my father said, "Oh? It's not my palaver. If something happens to her, it's your problem. If you like, you can take her. It's not my problem. My hands are not inside. I have washed my hands *and* my feet out of it. Yeah, she — she told me i-if people don't have a father — eh — th-there's no animal eating them. And I know that if you haven't got a daughter, too, animals don't eat you. So as for me, God blessed me: I have many daughters and sons. So if you like, everywhere, she can go. But as for me, I don't want to hear anything from her."

Then: how to go and take my things from this man's house? Three weeks. Every day, my aunt would say, "What are you going to do with your things?"

And I would say, "*Ah!* The people who took it there, they can take it back. It's not me who carried the things there, no? I didn't carry it by myself. The way you people managed to carry the things there is the way you're going to manage to bring these things home."

So they left these things there one month before they went and carried them. And when they carried them, I didn't want to touch any one of them. I thought maybe that this woman could put something inside, you know, like juju. *Heh-heh-heh.* Yeah? So still, now, these things are full up in[1] my aunt's room in Kumasi, and I didn't touch any. Only these three cloths that I took out from those things were the ones I used to find[2] something for myself.

I stayed with my aunt for about one and a half months, and then, she was also becoming fed up, because every time my father was saying that and this, that she wants to spoil me, and this and that. And my aunt said, "Look, I am not sacking you. But I will show you the way. How you don't want to live with your father, and every time I have trouble with your father, I don't want to talk much. If you want, I'll give you money. To travel. Travel to where you want. If you have money, it's not hard. You can go to Accra.[3] You can go anywhere you like. Or you can go out of Ghana. I can

1. fill up
2. to look for; to get
3. capital and largest city of Ghana

give you money that can be sufficient to do that. Because your father is — every day, what he's talking, if one day I don't hold my heart, we are going to say something bad, and it's not good for the family."

Then I said, "OK."

So: this was my life when I woke up, when I started my life; that's the way I suffered. Yeah. I suffered, no? I suffered a lot. From the family. From all the places I passed.

My auntie gave me two hundred cedis. Two hundred cedis! I'm telling you that that time was not like now when you cannot eat with one hundred cedis.[1] That time, you could take one cedi and cook. This Nkrumah cedi: you could take it and cook very well. Food! *Eh?* I had two hundred

1. The devaluation of the cedi proceeded slowly in official trading, radically in black market trading. Eventually, the currency was floated under a "structural adjustment" program of the World Bank. For people using hard currency converted at the black market rate, prices and inflation were somewhat consistent with the world market, but because the government did not devalue the cedi to reflect actual value, the currency became seriously overvalued. The actual value of the cedi, and by extension the actual cost of goods in hard currency, could only be known via the black market rate.

In 1970, the cedi was trading at 1.15 to the dollar officially and 1.50 unofficially. Major problems developed during the Acheampong regime. In 1974 a dollar bought 1.80 cedis; in 1976, 2.80 cedis; in 1977, when much of the interviews took place, a dollar bought 4.00 to 4.50 cedis; in 1978, 7 cedis; in 1979, when additional interviews were conducted, the figure was 12–14 cedis. By 1981, a dollar bought 38–40 cedis; in 1982, 75 cedis; in 1983, 130 cedis; by 1988, the number had risen to 200 to 300; in 1996, a dollar bought 1,600 cedis; in 2000, a dollar bought more than 5,000 cedis; in early 2001, a dollar was about 7,500 cedis.

The two hundred cedis Hawa was given by her aunt in the late 1960s could be comparable to $600 to $800 today. In 1971, when I knew Hawa in Accra, a bottle of beer was fifty-five pesewas; an orange was threepence; a trotro ride across town might have been sixpence; a short taxi ride from one area to another cost two shillings. In contemporary Ghana, the costs would be in the thousands of cedis. Now nobody can dream about dealing with pesewas or pence, let alone shillings or single cedis. The result is that the prices Hawa gives will seem absurdly low, with things thirty years ago appearing to cost thousands of times less than current prices.

With regard to the high levels of both inflation and overvaluation, one therefore has to think about the cost of goods and services in hard currency terms such as dollars. The following inflation factors indicate the turn-of-the-millennium value of a dollar from the time period of this book: 5 in 1968, 4.5 in 1970, 3.6 in 1974, 3 in 1977, to 2.5 by 1979. For a rough calculation of cedi values, one can divide the black-market value of a dollar in cedis into the inflation factor. For example, in 1974, a dollar bought 1.80 cedis, and a 1974 dollar was worth about $3.60 in 2001, so a cedi was worth about two 2001 dollars. By 1977, in 2001 terms, a cedi was worth about seventy-five cents. From the late 1960s to the early 1970s, when Hawa was in Accra and Tamale, therefore, one cedi would be equivalent to between two and four dollars, after adjusting for inflation.

cedis. Since in my life, I didn't have money in my hand like that. Then I took my way: Accra!

2 THE LIFE

: ACCRA :

Paradise Hotel

I went by train to Accra, you know. At that time, I don't know anywhere. So when I reached Accra, I asked a taxi driver, "Do you know a cheap hotel where you feel I can get a room for two cedis a day?"

He said, "OK. I know a hotel—Paradise Hotel: many girls from Kumasi are living there."

Then I said, "Ah, it will be good, because maybe I will know somebody there." Yeah. When I went to Accra I didn't stay with somebody. I took my own room, two cedis a day. And I knew one girl staying there: Ramatu. She was a Hausa girl. She was from Kumasi, too.

Do you know Paradise Hotel in Accra? You pass Apollo Theatre,[1] going, near to the big gutter.[2] Paradise Hotel is there. There were many girls there. All the house[3] was full of girls.

When I was living there, every time this Ramatu would come and talk to me. Or I would go to this girl, and we would talk together. And every time, we would go out together. Ramatu would say, "Let's go to the Labadi Beach;[4] let's go here; let's go here." And she would tell me, "Accra is like

1. Accra nightclub
2. an open drainage ditch. A very large one runs through the area.
3. the whole house
4. section of Accra on the coast

this. Accra life: you shouldn't be free with these boys who stand outside Lido[1]—these boys who used to find women for men—because they are very bad boys."

We used to go out every time together. And there was no trouble when we went together. I thought everything was OK. I had no problems; I had nothing worrying me. And I felt it was OK. And true, it was not so bad. The way she showed me was not bad, and I was not free with those bad people, and I was all right. You know, when I got to Accra, I was a big guy.[2] *Hee-hee-hee.* I had two hundred cedis. *Ha-ha!* I enjoyed. Every day, I would go to Lido with Ramatu.

And at that time I used to put on African dresses: every time I wanted to tie[3] African cloth, up-and-down.[4] *Hee-hee!* And Ramatu would say, "No, no-no-no-no. You shouldn't tie cloth. You should put on some jeans, or you should wear some hot pants, or a swimming dress." Swimming dress! I was ashamed to wear it! My dress will be up, and people will see my thighs? *Ha-ha!* Then this girl would say, "But look at me! I wear it! Look! Look at everybody here!"

Then I would say, "No-o-o-o. It's not good to do so. If you are a woman, to show your thighs to men to see, you know, it's not good." Every time, I wanted something like a cloth to cover every place of me, here. And Ramatu would wear a small minidress, and I would say, "*Eh! Ramatu!* If you are bending, they are seeing your pants!"[5]

And she would say, "Oh-h, but this is The Life, you know." The Life!

So: I was following Ramatu every time. To the beach. To Star Hotel. To Ambassador Hotel.[6] To afternoon jump[7] sometimes. To Metropole Hotel.[8] And I used to see the girls and the way they dressed. Then I said, "Ah! If it's bad, they wouldn't do it. I think it is good things they are doing, and so I also must go and find some material to sew some hot pants, and some trousers."

And the day when I put on trousers, *eh-heh!* I thought, "*Eh-h,* yeah. It's

1. Accra nightclub, frequented by Europeans. It closed in the early 1970s.

2. a person, man or woman, who is modern and can deal with The Life

3. to dress in African (wax-print) style. The verb refers to the final piece of cloth that is wrapped around the waist.

4. an outfit that uses the same material or cloth for blouse and skirt, or shirt and trousers

5. the normal (shortened) way to say underpants. Long-legged pants are normally called trousers.

6. state-operated hotels in Accra

7. afternoon dance

8. nightclub in central Accra

good." I was looking in the mirror, turning myself. *Ha-ha! Hey!* If you don't know something, it's hard! Yes? So I said, "*Aah!* It's fine. I didn't know that trousers are a very nice thing." That time they had some trousers called skipants. I bought three at U.T.C.[1] Every night, oh! Now I knew how to put on these things. I didn't want African cloths again! Every night I have to put on trousers or a minidress or hot pants, and I am the chief with my big hats and—yeah—I didn't know these things, but now I know—*ah-hah!*—it's this and that and this. *Eh?*

So Ramatu showed me The Life. Yeah. The first time, when I came to Accra, it was Ramatu: every time we used to go together.

And at that time too, I had a lot of hair, and every time I used to tie it.[2] And when I went to Lido, I saw the women loosen their hair, and I thought, "Eh-heh! This is The Life! The good life!" *He-hee-hee-hee!* So then every time I used to braid my hair, and there was one girl—Akua—she has died—she used to call me "India Girl" because of my hair. "Hey, India girl. Hey, India girl!"

Then I would say, "Hey!"

It was because of Ramatu that I found everything easy in Accra. You know, at Lido, sometimes the Lido manager—he was called Hassan—he didn't allow the young girls to come into Lido. And then they used to sit outside. And the young girls, as they have told them they are too small to come in, they get some boys to help them, and some of the girls and boys do this. But when I went to Accra, because of this Ramatu, I used to enter Lido every time. I just had to find my gate fee. When we would go, Ramatu is in front, and we enter together. She had a friend, Mahmoud, the brother of Hassan. Now he's in Lomé.[3] You know Knock-the-Man-Down, that Hausa boy who used to watch the gate at Lido, to let you pass inside: this Mahmoud is the one who took Knock-the-Man-Down to Lomé. Mahmoud was a friend to Ramatu, and we had no problem in Lido.

And Ramatu found me another friend. He was also Lebanese. Now I think he's in Kumasi. He was called Richard. Every time he used to drink much, and if he was driving his car, he would say, *"Kiriam bom bom, kiriam bom bom."* Kill him, boom boom. So we called him, "Kiri-am, Kiri-am." I was a friend to that man, and Ramatu was a friend to this Mahmoud. Every time, we had an appointment to meet in Lido. Yeah. When-

1. United Trading Company, a major department store and trading company in Ghana

2. In local styling, hair can be braided but is more often wrapped with black thread.

3. capital of Togo, the country to the east of Ghana

ever we went to Lido, we would just enter. I had no problem of someone to tell me I'm a young girl or all these things.

Cheap Money

You know, the time I reached Accra, I knew something about men, because that Indian man spoiled me, and then I made Amariya. So I knew something about men, but not too much. When I was from my husband, I was a greenhorn. *Ha-ha!* It was in Accra that I came to know more. And I was getting more money there. Every night. At that time I didn't know to hold my money well. I used to spend! Then I got someone as a friend, an Ewe[1] woman. She was from Ho.[2] She was working at Ghana Airways. She was called Victoria. I stayed in a house with her, and she told me, "You see? At this time, you are young. That's why you are getting money cheap[3] like this. You should save some in the bank. It will come in future that you won't get like now."

Then I said, "O-o-oh, *pf-ft!* You shouldn't tell me this." If I got my money, I would go to U.T.C. or Kingsway.[4] I would buy better shoes, better dresses. Buying clothes! Every time, every day, I had to go shopping to buy something. Every day! There was not one day I wouldn't go shopping — unless the day I didn't have money. Whenever I had about twenty cedis, or thirty cedis, I had to go to the market and buy something out of it. I didn't have any money saved.

Then one day the police people came and arrested girls. They arrested girls, and I was among. I had only fifteen cedis. When we went to the court, they fined everyone thirty cedis. *Ah!!* I had fifteen cedis! Then I thought, "Suppose when this woman told me to hide the money, if I was having some now, this case could not come so."

And so all the girls paid, and it remained three girls, and we hadn't got money. I had fifteen cedis, but I didn't have thirty cedis. So they brought the prisoner car to take us. Then I started to cry. All my body was shaking. *"Yee-e-eh,* I'm going to prison. If my father hears this, it's a big disgrace. He told me to stay with my husband. And I refused. And now I'm going to prison! *Eh-h-h." Hee-hee.*

1. cultural group in southeastern Ghana and southern Togo; pronounced eh-ʋeh

2. town in southeastern Ghana

3. easy to get

4. Kingsway, U.T.C., and G.N.T.C. (Ghana National Trading Corporation) were the main department stores in Ghana.

Then I saw one woman, and I asked her, "Where is Auntie?" I used to call this Victoria "Auntie." "Where is Auntie Victoria?"

And this woman said, "Oh-h. Yesterday Auntie Victoria went to her village." The same night they caught me, she went to the village! And she hadn't come back.

So then I said, "Oh-h. Will you please lend fifteen cedis to me to pay my court case? If Auntie Victoria comes, I will take my money from her." You see how I was? I didn't have money with Victoria, but I said I had money with her: "I will take *my* money from her and pay you."

Then this woman said OK. The full thirty cedis, she paid it. Then they took me out. So I went with this woman home. And I said, "OK. Maybe Auntie will come this evening, then I will take your money for you."

That very day, I was very lucky. In the night I went out. The time they caught us, I was with somebody, and I saw that man. That man said, "What did they do?"

I said, "They fined me thirty cedis; then I had to borrow money to pay." So that man gave me forty cedis. The morning time, I returned this money to that woman.

And so that time, too, I thought, *"Ah!"* I moved from Paradise and went to stay with this woman, Auntie Victoria. When I went to stay at Auntie's place, the thing that moved us from Paradise was a woman they used to call Fada Doumbaya. An *o-old* lady: every time she was on the street going up and down, on the main road. This woman came and caused trouble at our Paradise, and all the girls beat her well and then put pepper in her eyes. So the police people came and arrested all of us to court, and everyone had to pay five cedis each. And it was the Paradise manager who made a witness for the woman, so every girl hated the house, and everybody moved. You see? We are staying in your house: if we do something bad, you cannot be a witness against us, because we are paying you. *Um-humm!* So we all left the house. And I found a room at Auntie Victoria's place. And that girl, Ramatu, she went back to Kumasi.

I stayed at Kokomlemle,[1] near Silver Cup nightclub. That house was for one Mr. Prempeh: he had a big provisions shop in Lagos Town.[2] He stayed upstairs, and Auntie Victoria and some other Ghana Airways women were staying downstairs. And I was in the servants' quarters[3] of that house. When I left Paradise, that was the first place I stayed in Accra.

1. section of Accra

2. section of Accra, now called Accra Newtown. The reference to the neighborhood as Lagos Town is similar to the name Fanti Newtown.

3. generally a separate small building behind a house

: TEMA :

The Price of Tea

You know, from Accra, I used to go to Tema.[1] The first time, I went with some girls. One was called Mensah. The other one is dead—Janet—she died in Tema. We went to Tema to enjoy the life of Tema. When we went, we knew one girl in Tema—her name is Abena, but she was called Aba Warri. She was the only one we knew, but when we got there, we didn't find her.

Then we met some boys—they were cooks—and they told us we could stay with them until the next morning when we could go to find this girl. So we put our things there. In the night time we had our baths, and these people led us[2] to go to El Paso. It's a nightclub. And these boys thought they had also got some women: they knew that if we didn't get anyone, if we would all come back home, then they would share us. OK.

So we went to El Paso; we didn't know anybody; we didn't see Aba Warri, too. *Ah!* What could we do? Then I asked Mensah, "What can we do now?"

Mensah said, "It's nothing. How these boys have pity for us, I think if we go back there, they will give us a place to sleep." We stayed at El Paso up to the closing time, and we didn't get anywhere to go, and we went back to these boys' rooms to sleep.

When we went, these boys were living together. They were friends, but their quarters were in a line. The one with the first room, I think he was Frafra,[3] and the other one was Kanjaga,[4] and the other one was Ashanti. Then the first one said, "Eh—it is not good that—ah—you—all of you people cannot sleep in my room. If—tomorrow morning, if my master sees three girls come out of my room, he will ask me. He will sack me—and this—and ah—so you have to sleep there. And you have to sleep there. And one of you will sleep with me."

Then I said, "Ah! I don't understand this. It's the same quarters; it's the same line. Or every morning your master comes and checks your room? Is this master your husband?"

He said, "No-o. You know, in Tema here, when you are a cook, you

1. Ghana's main port, a medium-sized town just over twenty miles east of Accra
2. accompanied us; dropped us off
3. small cultural group in northern Ghana, around Bolgatanga
4. small town in northern Ghana; also, the Builsa people from the area near around the town

shouldn't bring many girls to your quarters. The white people don't like it. They say the girls will steal from them and go."

Then I said, "*Um!* To live with you here for one day? So we can do this? In the night when you sleep, we will go to your master's room, and then go and pack everything that he has inside?"

Then he said, "No-o. You don't understand me. What I mean, I don't mean that you are a thief. But, if the white man sees you three girls in my room, he wouldn't understand."

Then I said, "OK. Mensah, how do you do this?"

Then Mensah said, "OK. Which room can you sleep in?"

Then this boy said Mensah can sleep there, and Janet can sleep there, and I can sleep with him here.

Eh-heh! Nothing to say? Then—I'm waiting to see what you are going to do now. So Mensah went and slept there, and the other girl went and slept, and then I and this boy.

Then he said, "Oh, you are nice girl, you know. I like you."

I said, "Huh?"

He said, "Yes!"

Then I said, "Yeah, but—in my country, you know, you don't see a woman for one day, and then you like her and then you sleep together and make love together. If you have patience, sometimes you can get me. But today, *tsk-tsk.* Because in my country, my mother didn't show me this, eh?"

Then he said, "What???"

Then I said, "Yeah, I'm telling you the truth. We don't do this."

So, you know, he was trying to force me and all this, and I said, "*No!* If that will be the case, I can go out from your room now!"

Then he said, "No-o, don't do that. Sleep. I won't touch you."

So I slept; he didn't touch me. The next morning I woke up, and this boy had gone to the kitchen. Then I went to these girls. They were drinking tea, talking. But as for me, this boy didn't give me tea. So I said, "Hey! You people are lucky! You have tea!"

They said, "Yes. Why? You didn't get tea?"

I said, "No. This boy didn't give me tea."

Then they said, "What? For what he didn't give you tea? Go to him and ask."

I said, "No. Did you people go there and ask before they brought you?"

They said, "No. We didn't ask, but this boy just gave us tea."

Then I said, "OK. You are lucky, then. Should I drink some with you people?"

Then: Mensah is a very bad girl, you know. She said, "No. You must ask your man."

I said, "Who is my man? He's not my man!"

Then she said, "Ah! When you think your eyes are open, you want to close your vagina." *Mensah!! Shit!!* She's still in Tema now. She said, "If your eyes are open, then you want to lock your vagina? You can't get tea in the morning. Who is a fool, that they fuck her and give her tea, then she will give you to drink? We won't give you."

Ho! Then I said, "Then you people must pay me. Because I am the one who paid to come here — two shillings each, to come to Tema. I have forty pesewas with you people. And the taxi we took to go around-round-round, we shared it together, and I paid. And so you people must give me two cedis, one cedi each."

Aah! Mensah caught me! She's a very tough[1] guy, you know. She beat me well. Then I was crying. I took my bag, going to the town. When I got to the town, then I started to ask girls, "Do you know Aba Warri? Do you know Aba Warri?" They showed me Aba Warri's house. When I got there, yeah! She was in! She was very happy, too, because whenever she came to Accra she also used to lodge with me.

Then I was there with Aba Warri, and these two girls were there with the cooks, and they turned to be like married women; they didn't come out. These boys seized them[2] not to go out. Yeah? So: now everyday they will get this tea. When it's fresh, they get tea. They ate my two cedis, and they beat me on top.

The time when I went and met Aba Warri, she was conceived.[3] So one day she said, "Oh, let's go to cinema."

Then I said, "As for me, I don't feel cinema. But if you like, I can give you money to go to cinema. After cinema you can meet me at El Paso." So I gave her money, and after, she came and met me. We were sitting. I asked her did she want to drink beer. She said no. Even now, that girl still doesn't drink beer — only Coke and Fanta. She said she wanted Coca; I said, "OK, you take one Coca." We were conversing, then I saw these two girls, Mensah and Janet. They were there, calling me, "Hey! Hawa!"

Then Aba said, "Who is that?"

I said, "These girls, I don't know them."

"They are calling your name."

"Yes. They can call my name if they know me from someplace. But I don't know them."

Then these girls came. "Hey, Hawa!"

I said, "What? Am I owing you?"

1. heavily built, heavy-set, thick and large-framed; strong
2. took possession of them
3. pregnant

"Oh, is that what you are going to tell us?"

Then I said, "Yes. You have had luck. When we came, you got a husband. And you took your morning tea. And you beat me on top. What do you call me for? I don't owe you!"

Then Mensah said, "No-no-no-no-no. You know, we have some story to tell you."

Then I said, "OK. Say your story."

"You know, these boys, we — we — we — if we — they don't let us to go out. Even if somebody — if we talk to somebody in the quarters, then they start to be jealous."

Then I said, "Yes. Because you told me you are not a fool to close this thing and sleep hungry. But I am a fool. I close my key,[1] then I sleep hungry, then morning time you don't give me tea. So it's lucky for you. It's good! If this boy doesn't love you, he won't be jealous. He loves you! Maybe he's going to marry you."

"*Aie!* Northerners![2] Do you think I can marry a Northern boy?"

Then I said, "Ah-h. But you can drink a Northern boy's tea. Or a Northern boy can fuck you? The way an Ashanti can fuck you to sweet[3] you is the way he fucks you to sweet you, no? And in the morning time, he serves you good tea! It's *good!*"

Then Mensah said, "Because of tea we came here?"

Then I said, "Ah! I don't know. I think it's because of tea you people came. Because when I didn't come here because of tea, I didn't drink it. I didn't allow, and I didn't drink tea. So I thought you people came to Tema because of tea."

Then she said, "*Eh-heh!* That's the way you are going to talk? When we said we were all going to come here: we said we haven't got money, and you said you have money. But when we don't fuck with these boys, how can we manage to eat?"

Then I said, "OK! It's a good idea! Yeah? You can stay with him, too. You can get some things from him. Maybe if his madam is going to Europe, she can give him some shoes and some dresses, and then he can give them to you."

So this girl and I made a palaver again. She beat me the first time, no? From the quarters, now she has followed me in the bar too, to beat me

1. lock my vagina

2. people from the savanna area north of the coastal forest, about 150–200 miles inland, i.e., northern Ghana, or the Northern Territories when Ghana was the Gold Coast colony; people to the north of the Akan traditional area; also sometimes applied to Muslims and people from northern Togo, Burkina Faso, northern Nigeria, Mali, etc.

3. to please; to be sweet or good to

again. Then she said, "What you are saying is foolish! If you say those foolish words again, if you repeat it again, I will slap you."

Then I repeated it again. Then she slapped me. And Aba was conceived; she could not fight. And she is also small like me. So Aba didn't say anything. Aba just got up and went and called some tough guy, and this guy just came and took Mensah like this and—*tipp!*— outside. Then he pushed the other girl. He pushed her once; she fell down. When she went to get up, she fell down again. Then they went away and left me.

So we didn't talk to each other again. They were there till Mensah found an English old man. This man said he could look for a room for her, and he would pay everything. So she found a room, and these two girls were staying together there. The keys were two: Mensah gave one to the other girl—Janet—and she took one. They were there about one month, and then she had trouble with that girl, too, that she is not a fool to rent a house for her, and she doesn't pay anything, she just sleeps inside free, and morning time she doesn't want to give money to go to market and cook. So she must go out from the room. *Ha!* So this girl Janet also went out, and then she came to us.

Janet's Baby

Then I said, "Oh-h. Aba, to take this girl: as for this girl, I know her. She doesn't talk. She's very quiet. She's not like Mensah." So we stayed with this girl, and then this girl also became conceived. *Hoo-oo-oo!* Another problem! This girl wanted to cause abortion. And I was afraid. Aba too was afraid. Then we told this girl, "No. Don't do that. You know, if you are young, you should give birth quick, and then after, you can enjoy your life better then. Because abortion, if you make abortion, maybe the time when you will like to get a baby, you cannot get." We used to talk like this to this girl, you know, as advice. So this girl left the stomach like that.

She was staying with us, and it was another problem. Every time this girl wanted to eat, she had to vomit. Yeah, she was always vomiting. So she didn't go out. Morning time, if she wanted to eat something, she must come to us. We are the husband now. She would say, "Yeah. This is the palaver when I wanted to cause abortion. Even, since morning, I didn't eat anything. And I have no money. And night time, it's not possible that I go out. So if you people know that you are going to take care of me, I will leave this thing.[1] But if it's not so, I'm going to do it."

1. in this context, to keep the pregnancy

And we were afraid that if she would do it and die, we would have more problems. And so: we had trouble. Every time, the day Aba got small money, she must give her. Or if I got money, I would give her. We did so until this girl came to have the baby.

And when she had the baby—she was a fool! She didn't know the one who conceived her.[1] But when she gave birth to the baby and she looked, the baby resembled one of the friends. So now is the time she's going to find the father of this baby. She said she got this conceive[2] from Accra. But first time, she didn't tell us. When she had the baby, then she remembered. She was a fool, no? So we had to take this baby to Accra to find the father. *Uh-huh.* To get some money, you know? *Hee-hee-hee.*

So she took this baby to the father. It was one Lebanese man. We all went there. When this man opened his door, he said, "Yes? What do you want here like—" *Hee-hee.*

Then we asked him "Do you know this girl?"

He said, "Yes. I knew her a long time ago, about ten months or eleven months ago."

Then we said, "Yeah."

"But it's a long time when I saw her."

Then we said, "Yes. She has conceived; she says you are the one who conceived her. And this is the baby. So we are coming to ask you whether it is true."

"Kus-um-mak! Shar-mu-ta!!"[3] *Ha-haa!* Yeah! Then: "Afia?[4] You bring this baby for *me-e?!* It's for *me-e?!*"

Then we said, "Yes. But you can just look at this baby's face." You know, if you are young, too, you are a fool. This case: we must go and find somebody, some grown person, to go with us. But we small-small girls, we were trying. We thought when we took the baby, this man was just going to give money! You know? *Heh-heh.*

Then this man said, "No! No! No! No! *Kusummak!* Go! Go go go! You want to give me this *kusummak* baby. You think I am *kusummak* to have *kusummak* baby?" *Kusummak*—yeah, it's the words of Lebanese. I think it's like bastard or something. Yeah.

Then he said, "How many months a woman takes a conceive?"

Then we said, "Ah! It's nine. Some women take nine months. Some women take maybe ten months before they have a baby. But you con-

1. make someone pregnant; also, become pregnant
2. pregnancy
3. (Arabic): Your mother's cunt! Bitch whore!
4. her day-name, from the day of the week when she was born. Many people have both a Christian name and a day-name.

ceived the girl, because when you knew this girl, it's when she was conceived. And she didn't come and tell you. When she had the baby and finished, we didn't see somebody who can look after the baby. That's why we are forcing you to take this baby."

Ah! Then he said: if we don't go out now-now-now, he will let police people lock us. And at that time we were afraid of police. *Hee-hee.* It's not now: when a policeman tells me "Shit!", I tell him "Shit!" But before, whenever we heard the name of police, *aayesh-sh-sh.* So we went.

When we went home, then we sat down and we were thinking, "How can we do this thing? What can we do about this thing?" Then this girl also knew a woman from Auntie Victoria's house. She was also an Ewe, and she was also working at Ghana Airways. And Janet was an Ashanti girl, but she was from the same town with this girl. So we said, "We'll go to Auntie Vivian and see."

So we went to Auntie Vivian, and Auntie Vivian said, "Oh. It's not any heavy case." She will take us to the man and see what this man is going to say.

Then we went there again. Ring the bell. This man comes out again. When he comes out, then this woman greets him. Then he says, "Wait. I'm coming."[1] Do you know this man went inside and made telephone to Kotobabi[2] police station? So they came and carried all of us to the police station at Kotobabi. With this woman! *Hee-hee-hee!*

This Auntie Vivian was living at the same house with Mr. Prempeh. Nkrumah-time,[3] I think this Mr. Prempeh was taking care of something for the government. So he was another big man. So the police people took us to police station and put all of us in cell, with this small baby—*hee-hee!*—about three-weeks baby. We were all in cell. Then this woman asked the police people that she wanted to telephone her brother, to ask him if he can come and bail her. So they gave her the telephone, and she telephoned Mr. Prempeh, and Mr. Prempeh came there with his car. Then Mr. Prempeh asked what was wrong. We talked. Then this Lebanese man too talked.

Then Mr. Prempeh said, "No, it's not possible." He started to fuck[4] these police people: "So you people think—this baby—they say every baby, it's the mother who knows the father. Even a married woman. Some married women can give birth to a baby which is not for the husband. But the woman will know who conceived her. So if this girl says this man

1. I'll be right back.
2. section of Accra
3. when Kwame Nkrumah was ruling Ghana
4. verbally abuse

conceived her, maybe it will be true. Because he is young, he is a fool. He doesn't want the conceive. Then if she takes the baby to him, if this man doesn't like it, he can tell her, 'No, it's not for me. I don't want it.' Simple! But not to ring police to come and catch people and lock them! And then *you!* You are African! And a Lebanese man lies to you with his ten cedis or twenty cedis, to lock your sister Africans! Do you think this way is better?"

Then this Mr. Prempeh talked-talked-talked-talked-talked. So the police left us free. Then when they left us and finished, then Mr. Prempeh told this Lebanese man, "Yeah! You! You will look after this baby! Otherwise, you will leave Ghana. You're going to leave very soon if you don't look after this baby." So we were happy. Then he asked us the man's house. So we took him to the man's house, to know the house. And we took him to know this man's workplace, to know that he had a big store for material. So Mr. Prempeh knew all these places. Then we went home. And we didn't know what he talked to the man, but every month, this man would bring thirty cedis for this girl to look after the baby. Every month.

Then, this baby had six months, and this girl went away with the baby. To Akosombo.[1] When she went away to Akosombo, then this man was free. If this girl was not there, who was he going to give this money to? And when she went to Akosombo, they arrested her. She went to prison, six months, and left this baby with some woman as a baby nurse. The baby nurse: every month, ten cedis; six months, sixty cedis. No? When she came out, she didn't have sixty cedis. And then this woman said she was going to take this baby for the sixty cedis! *Hah!?* Did you ever see sixty cedis have a baby? This woman said, "Ah! If you don't pay, I'll take your baby to pay my sixty cedis."

Then this girl didn't have money, so she came back to Tema again. When she came to Tema, she found a French man. This man was a good man. This girl told him her whole problem, and this man gave her a hundred cedis to go and pay and take her baby. So she went and paid and took her baby, and she came and lived with this man.

Then this man went on leave to France for three months. And this girl took one African boyfriend. The father of this boy had a big factory, but this boy was a crazy boy! One day, they said they were going to Cape Coast.[2] They hired a taxi, and this taxi had an accident on the road. And

1. small town in southeastern Ghana, site of a large dam on the Volta River that formed Lake Volta

2. town on the west central coast of Ghana

that girl too had conceived again about three or four months, I think. When they got the accident, they didn't have any wound. Nobody — nothing cut anybody. So they thought they were all right. They came back to Tema, then in about three days, she said, "Ah! I'm feeling pains, I'm feeling —" They took her to the hospital, and they had to make her an operation, and when they made her operation, then she was dead. And she left the baby, this fine baby. Yeah. Janet. The family came and took the baby to their village. They are from Brong Ahafo.

You know, I don't like drinking *akpeteshie*[1] too much, but that day — *hey!* When I was in Asylum Down,[2] if it was raining, sometimes my friend Jacqueline would say, "Let's cut this thing small." Then I would tell her, "Excuse my face, because I don't like it. As for *agbã*,[3] I don't know how to drink it." But the time when I drank agbã was the time when this girl was dead. Janet, when she died from the baby in Tema, she was a good friend to me. *Mm.*[4] That day I drank agbã more than one bottle, but I didn't get drunk. It was wonderful. Then I drank more — more beer — but still — I felt to be drunk, because the girl was a nice girl, you know. But I wasn't drunk. *Ha!* So: The Life. The Life is hard.

The Problem of Being Small

All the time I was at Tema, I was still staying at Accra. Always, I had my room in Accra. Every month I would come back to Accra to pay my rent and then go back to Tema. Tema was good then.

Yeah, Tema. When we went to Tema, you know, that time was the time when this Afro-wig came in, and so every time I used to put on Afro-wig. And then one day I cut all my hair, to be very nice, all cut down, to be a Myriam Makeba[5] or something. I thought it was nice. Then I put on my shoes, these tall shoes, and I wore my dress, and I went to one nightclub — I can't remember the name. It was one African man who had it. He was married to a English woman. Any time when I went there to enter the club, *ah-ah-ah-ah!* This English woman would say, "No. This girl

1. (Ga): Akpeteshie *(akpɛtɛshi)* is locally distilled spirits, usually made from sugar cane or palm wine. Akpeteshie was illegal during colonial times, and the name has two applicable Ga meanings, one from "hide-out" and the other from "lean over or against."

2. section of Accra

3. (Ewe): akpeteshie

4. yes

5. a close-cropped Afro hairstyle resembling the way Myriam Makeba, the famous South African singer, wore her hair. The style was often worn by schoolgirls.

is under age." And you know, those like this woman are the big women in Tema, in these nightclubs. So the day I cut my hair to be short, when I went to that nightclub, she sent to the police station to report to come and catch me because I'm under age, I shouldn't come to the nightclub. So—*whew! Hey!* In Accra I didn't used to go to the police station, but in Tema—*aaah!* Even if I'm in the house, they will come and arrest me! People will give complaint and they will find my house to arrest me.

So they arrested me to the police station. When they asked me my age, anyway, I lied. I said I'm twenty-two. Yeah? Then, I didn't have any papers to show that I'm twenty-two. So they looked at me with my short hair, and they said, "You are lying. You are fourteen years old."

I said, "Ah! How can I be fourteen years old? I have married! I have left my husband now, it's two years. Eh? I had twenty years before I married. I have twenty-two years. You are not the one who borne me; you cannot say my age."

They said, "OK. Whether we are the one who borne you, or we are not the one who borne you, we know that you are not twenty-two years. You are under age. So you must go to *Nkwadaabɔne.*"[1]

Hee-hee! You know Nkwadaabɔne School? The prison for the children? Yeah-yeah. So they said they must take me there. And this nightclub, the director was called Mr. Annan. Mr. Annan came and said, "No. This girl is not underage. I know the family." So he also came and lied and took me out.

Married without a Ring

Then one night I went to my El Paso, and I saw these Japanese people[2] plenty. Then I saw this girl, Aba Warri. I said she was conceived the time I went to Tema: she was conceived with some Chinese man. So if the ship came, all the group, she would sit with them. So when I went, I saw them, and she said, "Oh, come and have a seat." Then I sat down. This was the day I was going to meet an old Holland man. He was called Henrik. He was looking at me, and he called me; he said, "Come." And I went.

He said, "So you are going with such people?"

I said, "No-o-o-o! I'm afraid of them. But because of my girlfriend, I'm sitting with them."

Then he said, "Look, if you want to be a nice girl in Tema here, don't

1. (Asante Twi): literally, bad children; from nkwadaa (children) and bɔne (bad)
2. used to refer to any Oriental person, including Chinese

try to sit at table with these Japanese people. If a good European man sees you with these people, he will be afraid of you; he will never call you."

So I said, "Ah! Because my friend is sitting there, and then I'm alone, I feel to sit there to converse."

Then he said, "OK, you can sit with me here." So we started talking, talking, talking, talking, and then he said I should go and know his place.

Then I said, "Where."

He said, "BBC."[1] And this BBC, they used to arrest girls there. So I said, "I'm afraid."

Then he said, "OK. Tomorrow I'll come and take you in daytime to go and know that place."

Then I said, "OK."

So the next day he came and we went to BBC. He said, "Here is my house. If you like, you can come and live with me here."

Then I thought: Eh! To live very quickly like this? I'm afraid. I don't know this man's character. Maybe he will say, "Come and live with me," and in three days then he'll say, "Pack off!" So I don't want this life.

So I told him, "No. Where I'm living is good for me." I told him I could be coming to him any time, or every day if he wants, but I didn't want to bring my things here. We lived about one month, and after I saw that he was a very nice white man, then I said, "OK. We can stay together." So I brought all my things from Aba Warri's place.

I stayed with him three months, and every time, it was trouble. It was funny, you know. I was living with this man in that area, BBC, and I had a small dog. I called this dog Ashawo.[2] *Hee-hee!* I am an ashawo who has a dog, and so I'm also calling the dog Ashawo. Yeah. Then every afternoon, Ashawo and I would go round to take a breeze. This man was working at the main Tema harbor. And every afternoon about four o'clock, when I would take my tea and finish, then I would go around these bungalows with my dog.

So one day I was going round, and I saw two men. They were running. I thought they were going to pass by. Do you know they were running to catch me?! Police! They were C.I.D.;[3] they didn't wear any police dress. They just ran and came and hooked me like a thief! Ah! I didn't understand this! Then I said, "*Eh!?* What's the matter?"

Then one man said, "Yeah. We heard of you."

1. section of Tema. Tema is a planned community; the name of that area is derived from the contracting company that built it.

2. a "loose" or "free" woman

3. Criminal Investigation Division; detectives on the police force

"You heard of me that I'm doing what? You heard of me that I'm killer, or I'm a thief?"

Then he said, "OK. Let's go. If we go to the police station, you will say what you are."

OK? So we went. You know, that time, I had not much experience, but I knew something better by that time. So I was with my white pants, with my dog and chain. Then they took me and the dog and all to the police station. *Hee-hee-hee!* And this dog was a very fucking dog. *"Rf! Arf! Arf! Arf! Arf!"*

Then they said, "You," and they put us behind the counter, me with the dog.

So I said, "OK."

They said, "*Eh-h-eh.* Didn't you hear that they don't allow the girls to go to BBC?"

Then I said, "Ah! Why don't you people allow the girls to go to BBC?"

They said, "Yes. They don't let ashawo girls to go to BBC."

Then I said, "OK. Is something written on my back that I'm ashawo? Or front? Why should you say that? I'm living with my husband."

"Where is your ring?"

And I also said to the man, "You there, do you have a wife?"

He said, "Yes."

"Where is your ring? Have you a ring?"

He said yeah, as for him, he married in African way. And I said, "Yes. I, too, I married like that. Yeah, I'm a Muslim. We make Amariya; we don't make a wedding with ring. So we don't need a ring."

Then he said, "Who—who made you Amariya?"

Then I said, "OK. You give me a telephone. I will call the man."

Then they gave me telephone; then I called Henrik. When this man came, *who-o-o-o!* He was an old man, you know. *Tall* like this, and everybody knew him in Tema. When he came, they said, "This one made you Amariya?"

I said, "Yes. It's not possible?"

Then they asked him, "Did you make this girl Amariya?"

He said, "Yes."

"Where?"

He said, "Kumasi." I had told him my story that I came from Kumasi. He didn't know even my parents, but he used to ask me the name of my family, you know, and I used to tell him.

"What is the name of the mother?"

He said, "Miriama."

"And the father?"

"Issahaku."

Then they said, "How long did you make the marriage?"

He said, "Ah, it's about one month now when I made Amariya. Before, she was with me one month. Then I took her home to make Amariya."

Then they said to me, "And you—you make Amariya; then you are putting on hot pants?"

Then he said, "Yes! I'm not a Muslim. But the family wanted me to make Amariya, to marry her in their way. And I thought it's hot here in Tema. I told her to be putting on what she likes. Even I don't want her to put her hair with this *mayafi;*[1] I don't want it. But I have married her with the family. If you like, I can telephone the family to come down here."

Then they said, "If you are sure that you married her, then we are going to leave her. But you must tell her to don't go around the bungalows in the daytime."

Then he said, "No-o. She has nothing to do in the house. Every time she sleeps. We have a cook; we have everything in the house. And she's tired. She must go somewhere. She can take a walk—as exercise. I can't lock her. She's not a prisoner. She must go where she likes in the afternoon." *Hee-hee.*

Then these police people, they looked at this man and laughed, "You!"

So they left me. Then, Henrik worked in daytime for one week, and then one week in the night. Every month he worked two weeks in the night, and two weeks in the day. So when he was in the night work, I could go out alone. When the driver took him to work, he brought his car back, and this driver would take me to Top Hat.[2] There was some nightclub upstairs to go to dance. Yeah. Any time, I would tell the driver, "You can come back at one o'clock and pick me home." And I was alone, and I could enjoy how I liked. I could sit with people, but I didn't go with anybody. But if somebody called me, I could sit and drink with that person.

Then one day they came and arrested all the girls. And I was among again. This was the second time since I was with this man. *Hee-hee!* This Amariya is an in-trouble Amariya. Yeah? Then they took us to the police station. The ones who collected me first time were from BBC police station, but the second case, they brought me to Community One[3] police station, in what they call Community One. The time when they were taking

1. scarf or veil worn by married Muslim women
2. nightclub in Tema
3. section of Tema

us with the car, this driver just arrived to collect me from the nightclub, and I said, "Ah, you'd better to go back to the harbor and tell Henrik that they have arrested me again." So he went to the harbor, and this Henrik came with two other guys; they were three. Yeah, they came because they were friends of Henrik, and they liked me. We were all in the same flat. There were three bedrooms, and everyone had his room. So when they heard this, they all said, "No, no, no, no. It's not possible; it's not possible. They cannot arrest Hawa; they cannot arrest Hawa."

So the three of them came, and they said they are coming to see Mary. Yeah, Mary. Sometimes when I was in Accra, they used to call me Mary. How I was moving with Europeans, I also had a European name.

And then the police people said, "Who is Mary?" Then I came out.

Then this one policeman was Ashanti, but we called him Alhaji.[1] So Alhaji said, "So, all these three, tough, tall men, they all came for you, one small girl? To see *you?*"

Then I said, "Yes. Why?"

He said, "So all of them fuck you?"

Then I said, "Why should you say things like this? So unless they fuck me before they will come and see me?"

He said, "But why?"

I said, "Yes, they are my husband's friends."

Then: "You say your husband. Who is your husband here?"

Then Henrik came and said, "Me." *Ha-ha.*

"Yeah? It's your wife?"

He said, "Yes."

"When did you marry her? You didn't tell us that you married? No?"

Then Henrik said, "Yes, but it's not your problem. If I tell you people, you have not got any help to help me. So there is no need to tell you people before I marry."

So they said, "Are you *sure* that it's your real wife?"

Then he said, "Yes."

"So why did you let her to go out alone, and walk in the night?"

"I couldn't let her sleep. The time when I go to work, at six o'clock in the afternoon, it's not time for her to sleep. And she will be in the house from six, and she has nothing to do. She can go to some places, to listen to music, to take a bottle of beer, or something like that, to be happy."

Then they said, "We Africans, when we marry, we don't allow our wives to go out alone."

1. honorary name for a Muslim who has made the pilgrimage to Mecca

Then he said, "Yes, I have married an African girl, but I am not African. So I do as we do in our country."

Then they said, "You have to keep your wife well. We are leaving her for you, but you have to keep her well."

Then he said, "I'm keeping her well! When she came here, did she tell you that she's hungry?"

"No."

"But why? What kind of well can I keep her? The way I keep her well is like that, to leave her free to be free. Then she'll be happy to live with me."

So the police people left me. *Ha-ha.* So we went.

So Tema: I did something small in Tema, too, with the police. *Twe-a-a!* Alhaji used to say, "You, you, you, you! If I don't jail you in Tema here, I'll leave police work."

And I would say, "If you play with me, too, they will take your dress off."

Ah, Alhaji! Every time I go to Tema, I used to ask of him. They say now that he's not in Tema. I want to see him again, but I don't see him. I think they transferred him to some country.

And this Holland man, I stayed with him three months, and then I went away. I went away by myself. You know, it was something funny I didn't see before. Since I was meeting people to live together, I haven't seen anything like this. Every night, when we would sleep, I used to dream of him. When I saw him in the dream, all his body was a snake, and his head and his face was Henrik! *Hey!* Every night I had to shout, "Henrik! Henrik! Henrik!"

Then he would wake up. "What?"

If he asked me, I didn't feel to talk. And my body was shaking, and I would think, "No. This may be some witch, some kind of witch from Holland." Every night, I will dream. There's a *big* hole, and then I will see the snake coming. When the snake is coming near the hole, then I will stand near the hole, then the snake is coming up under to push me to fall down the hole. Then when the snake gets up like this, then I see all the head, and the face is Henrik. But all the body is a snake. *Ah!* I dreamed of this for about two months. Every night when I slept, I saw this. Then I said, "No. I must leave." Even I left some of my dresses at his house. Until today. He has gone away. I think maybe he has dashed the dresses to somebody. Yeah. Every time he used to come to Accra, "If you don't like me, come and pack your things."

And I said, "I don't want the things. I give them to you. If you take another girlfriend, you can give her for dash. I don't want it." I was afraid to live with him; that's why I left him. I went back to Accra. Hey, the world is hard.

Reflections: After the First Year as Ashawo

By then I was about seventeen, or seventeen and some months.

Yeah. So when I went to Accra, my fi-i-rst boyfriend was Lebanese, at Accra. When I left Accra, the second was that Holland man at Tema, when we stayed together.

And then after, I got one Italian. After I left Tema, I got one Italian man who used to come from Akosombo. Sometimes I used to go to Akosombo for one week, and then I would come back to Accra. Sometimes he would come to me in Accra, pick me, and we would go round-round. He was the one who was paying my room. And every time he used to send me money to eat. If I needed something, he bought it for me.

Aah-h-h. So, I didn't find it easy, but anyway, it was not so bad too. Some people find it difficult more than me. Yeah, Tema was very good. At that time Tema was nice more than now.

That first year, when I was in Accra, I didn't think of anything of Kumasi. Sometimes if I saw some drivers from Kumasi who knew my family, I used to ask them how my families were feeling. But I didn't have any feelings to think of them. What was I going to think? My father said, "Go! If I have no daughter, nothing can eat me." And I also said, "OK. If I have no father —" So I pretended that I had nobody. I didn't think of any of my family at that time. Only my aunt: sometimes I used to think a little bit of her.

Sometimes I used to write a letter to her,[1] and tell her I'm in Accra or I'm in Tema. And sometimes she used to write in a letter and ask me, "When are you going to come to Kumasi?"

And I would reply her, "Yeah, I don't know yet. I didn't make up my mind yet. If I make up my mind to come, I will tell you."

Sometimes I used to think about how I didn't know the life I would be living. As for that one, yes. You know, it's not that I used to think about it, but sometimes if I would smoke groove, then I used to think, "*Eh-h.* So: so the world be? If somebody told me that I will be free like this, without any trouble, I wouldn't believe it." You know, as for that, I used to think like that. Because first time, I thought I would be in trouble until my end. But I just stayed OK. And by then I thought, "I'm free. Nobody tells me this; nobody tells me that. And not any one day I will wake up and I don't have money to eat. Or if I feel like doing something, I don't think, 'Oh-h, I will wait, and tomorrow I will have money to do it,' because every time I have small money to do my program, whatever I like. If I want something,

1. communicate by mail. She would dictate, and someone would write it.

today-today I can go and do it, today-today." So I used to think, "Yeah, I didn't know that my life will be free like this."

The time I was coming from Kumasi, and the way I came, I was thinking that I was going to suffer more than that, you know! I was thinking: "Whether it's life or death, I'm inside it. I will go and leave this country, this world." This is what I thought. "Now, I'm going to Accra. I don't know anybody. How can I come to be living in Accra?" And then: "I haven't known Accra before. The way people talk about Accra, it's big, and all this." Then I thought, "Ah! I'm going to be suffering more, more than Kumasi."

But something said, "OK. You are in suffering, or life or death, you are in it. So you must go. And see."

And so the time I reached Accra and I was staying at Paradise, that was when I and this girl, Ramatu, would go out together every time. And the way she showed me was not bad. There was no trouble, and I thought it was OK. I had no problems and no worries. So I was all right.

3 PROBLEMS OF SELF-EMPOWERMENT

: ACCRA :

Repaying Rough with Rough

You know, our life, our ashawo life: we used to see some bad things, too. Especially, from some of the men. Some of the men are bad, and you won't know. Will a bad man tell you that he's bad? If I am bad, do you think I will tell you I am bad? Somebody who can say he's bad, he's not bad. The real bad people don't talk anything about bad. *Ha-ha!* A bad man will never say, "I'm bad!" *Ha!* If he tells people that he's bad, people will fear him. So he will hide his badness. He won't tell you. It is when he has done something to you that you know that, yeah, this man is a big crook. *Ha-ha!*

A killer. Don't you see that killers, when they want to kill people, they boss[1] them first? Do you know what is "bossing"? If you are walking a long way to some place, if you get somebody walking with you and talking, then he is bossing you. Yeah. You are walking like that and then conversing and—*ha!*—you are there. That is what bossing means. And so a killer: he will boss you, and then you will get belief that this man cannot do anything bad. After, when he gets you to the corner side, then his eyes start to change. *Ha-ha!* "Do you know me?"

Now, if somebody does you something wicked, what do you think? Won't you reply him? As for me, if you play me a way like this, I will want to reply you a heavy one—past yours. As for me, I do so. Because I like good friends. I don't like—*ha!*—I don't like friends who see you, and then they like you, and their mouth is smiling: they have a smiling face, and they don't smile inside. If you do that kind of way to me, I will know who you are. *Ha!* I have to treat you badly, too.

So this is the way. Even some of the men used to play some ways. Sometimes someone won't want to pay. But you must pay me the money I want. We are not friends. You call me one day; I go with you. You must know that it's not because I love you that I follow you. It's because of money I am following you. Yeah? So you must pay me the way I say. If you don't pay me—*ah!*—as for that one, you can beat me or you can do me anything, but I will spoil plenty of your things. *Ha-ha!* Yeah, I will do much. I will try my best to do something which will hurt you. Yeah? I will think: this thing, I'm going to spoil it—maybe it cost more than what I want from you. If you like, we can go to police station. If they put me in jail, it's your luck. I don't care. *Ha!*

You know, I'm not rough. If things happen like this, I will talk to you, for understanding. Slowly. "You must understand me. This money you are giving me, I don't want it, because—although we are many girls, but everyone according to everyone's price. You can see some material—you will get it for two hundred. You will go to some shop, maybe the same material is there, but it's five hundred. So you cannot take me as the others. So please, respect yourself. What you are doing, I don't like it."

1. to talk nicely or gently to, sometimes but not always with a connotation of insincerity. Other meanings of the word are: to trick, to persuade or convince, to cool someone out, to calm someone.

Then if you want to make me—*pa pa pa pa pa!*—like you are somebody, then that is the time I will say, "*Ah-hah!* This fellow doesn't want respect. OK, I will show him that I am a bastard more than him." Then I will start to do my foolishness.

You know, there are some people, when I used to talk like this to them, they will say, "OK, I understand you. But please, I have not much. You can take this. Any time when I see you again, I will give you the rest." I won't worry about this.

But when you say this, there is someone who won't understand. He wants to show you: "Hey, who do you think you are? *Hey!* What is inside of you? Do you think I went inside of you to take a diamond? Or you have a golden key?"

And this time is a time for me. You have given me a free chance to spoil everything in your house. Yeah, I will spoil something. I will say, "OK, the money you gave me, I give that back to you for dash, for your repairs."

"Repairs? What?"

Then I will say, "OK, you wait. I will show you something to repair now." And I will just get some machine, or if I see what is big or important for you, then I will break it. I will say, "OK, you can take your money—if this money can repair it, take it and repair it. This machine is not a human being; I am a human being. I don't know you. You don't know me. I don't know whether you are a correct man or you are not a correct man. If you are sick, I am going to take care of myself. Maybe I will have to go to hospital. And so what you are going to do with me? I did it. You can beat me for that, but I have done what I did. And if you beat me, too, that will not repair this thing." *Ha!*

Then, sometimes, they used to beat me. *Hee-hee!* Yes, sometimes they used to beat me.

The Lebanese Twins

Twe-a-a! Yeah. Accra! Look, one day I went to Asylum Down with Lebanese people. They beat me; they tore *all* my dress. But what I did to the house, any time they see me anywhere, they used to say, "This girl is a very wicked girl." I *did* them! I did much business to them.

These Lebanese people were twins. I didn't know. They resembled each other. If you see the one, you will say it is the other one. OK? Then one came and carried me. We went home. When we finished making love, he said he was going to the bathroom. Then I also went into the bathroom. When I came back, he lay down on the bed. I didn't know it was the other one! The first man just went out, and then maybe he told his brother, yeah? How he resembled, I couldn't know. And they had been doing this thing to girls, not me alone. So when the other one also came, then he started. *Ah!* But we just made the love; it's not quite five minutes. Why is this boy doing so? So I said, "Oh, but won't you rest? Won't you let me rest a little?"

He said, "No. Because, you know, our big brother — my big brother is going to come with his wife, so we have to finish everything quickly, then I will send you home. I don't want my big brother to meet you here."

I said, "OK. Then I accept." But then, the perfume they used was not the same scent. So I said, "Oh, but why are you doing so? *No!* I don't want this!"

Then he said, "Why? Hawa, why?"

Then I said, "Oh, but you are not — you are not the one who brought me."

"Yes, I'm the one who brought you."

"No! You are not the one!" So I forced him to get him out of me, and then we started fighting. *Ha!* He wanted to force to use me, you know, because he already started using me, and he didn't discharge before I forced him to get him out. So we started fighting in the room. Then he held my neck. The way he held me, I thought he was going to kill me. So I got my knee up to knock him in the stomach. Then he bent down. Yeah, I gave him the knee in the stomach, because the place he held me, all my eyes came out! I am going to die! I have to do something to defend my life. So I lifted my knee, then I gave him —*bang!*

Then he said, *"Oo-o-o, kusummak sharmuta!"* Then he bent down.

And I said, "Yes." Then I got up from the bed. I held his back here. I wanted to press him like the way he pressed me, but he was a man, you know: he was strong more than me. So I was forcing him, and then the way he was talking loudly, the other one entered, and he just picked me by my back like this and threw me. Then my head knocked the wall. *Whew!* And that time my eyes became red.[1] Then I thought, "Yeah, these people, I will have war with them today." Then I shouted, "OK, pay me! Pay me, pay me!"

Then he said, "Why should I pay you? I want to make love with you — you don't allow me. How can I pay you?"

Then I said, "But you made once."

1. I was angry, wild; I was serious; I saw red.

Then they said, "Who will pay? We are two."

Then they both became one as if—*Good God!* It's—*ahaa!* The girls had been talking about these people, but I didn't know them. Many girls had been giving their complaint on them in town, you know, but I never saw them together before, so I didn't know. So I said, "*Ahaa!* Is that so? Today I have seen you people. I have been hearing of you people. But for me, nobody will fuck me free-o. Even pure white people—English people, even they were holding Ghana, but they didn't fuck me free-o. And Lebanese? Africans like me?[1] You try to teach[2] me? No!"

Then the other one came and gave me one slap, fine![3] So I fell down. You know, it was very funny. I fell down. I lay down about two minutes. And I was thinking, if I get up, what should I do? So I lay down quietly. Then the other one said, *"Kusummak sharmuta."* He started to speak this language, the Lebanese language, and *pa-pa-pa.* Then when I got up, I took a bottle, so he thought I was going to knock him with the bottle. So he pushed me again, then I fell down. Then: they had a big radiogram.[4] So then I got up, at once, and just went to the radiogram with the bottle. *Bang!* This thing broke—some of it broke, and some of it didn't break. Then it was like I was crazy. That day I did something like somebody who is crazy. I went outside, with my underpants. I didn't wear any dress. I got outside. The house, I think it was a new place. They were making it nice; they were making some cupboards, and all this. So the carpenter had some wood outside. And when I got down there, I picked up a stake—it was not heavy. Then I got something—it was iron. Then I came—*poom, poom, poom.* Then the other one laughed. He thought I was going to the bedroom, because the other one was in the bedroom, and he thought I was taking this iron to meet him in the bedroom. I just went straight to the radiogram. *Tcha! Ha!* Before they held me to beat me, these things—*Whew!*—all spoiled. They had one cupboard—I just pushed the cupboard and all fell down, all the glasses and the plates. I broke many plates.

Then: what will they do to me to hurt me? I wore a dress, and my dress was inside. So they took my dress and tore it to pieces, so that I could not go out with my underpants. It was about half-past one in the night. But then I went out like that, too! Then I said, "I'm going to bring

1. an abuse to the Lebanese, many of whom are multiracial, but the reference is to the negative attitudes of Europeans regarding Lebanese

2. cheat me; show me experience by taking advantage of me. The idea of teaching is opening one's eyes to something the person didn't think about or know about.

3. an affirmation: yes, a big slap

4. a radio and record player in a console

police to you people! You don't believe me—you wait! You will see who I am!

So I went out from there to my house. At that time I was staying in Asylum Down, and my house was not far, so when I went out, I passed some corner ways.[1] Then I saw one girl I knew, and she had put on a dress and covered it with one cloth.[2] At that time they were arresting girls, so every time the girls used to dress nicely and then put cloth on top of their dress when they were in the street. Then I called her, "Adwoa. Come." Then she came. I said, "Look at what these Lebanese people did to me. Give me your cloth. I will come back just now and bring it. Or if you like, we can take taxi together." So she gave me her cloth to cover myself. We took a taxi to my place. I got my own dress. Then I went to Adabraka[3] police station.

Then, you know, Ghana police, they are funny. French police, in this kind of case, they are very good people for it. But Ghana police! When I told the first policeman, then he asked me, *"Nti wɔmo mmienu nyinaa no dii wo?"*[4] So both of them fucked me?

Then I said, "Yes."

Then he said, "*Ah!* It's not a shame for you to come and give this complaint?"

I said, "What kind of shame? It's my business. This is what I'm doing. I have no work to do. This is what I'm doing to pay my rent, and this is what is keeping me in my life." I was serious. And these police people were laughing at me, you know.

Then they said, "OK. How the two of them fucked you—how much do you want from them?"

Then I said, "OK, you: you think. If you are me, how much do you want from them?"

The one policeman said, "If it's me, as you are saying they are young people, you can take twenty cedis—ten-ten cedis is OK, because it's only one-one."

Then I said, "Yeah, you are joking. Ten, ten cedis—if I am sick now, can that ten cedis take care of me in the hospital?"

Then this policeman said, "I didn't talk about your hospital. I'm just telling you because you said they are young people."

1. shortcuts or indirect ways; backways, as behind or between the houses
2. wrapped an African cloth around the dress
3. section of Accra
4. (Asante Twi): So the two of them both fucked you?

"Yeah, they are young. I am not old, too." So we were talking this, and these people took it like a joke. But then the Inspector[1] came, and this Inspector, I knew him because he knew my father from Kumasi.

When the Inspector came and met me, then he said, "Hey!" He used to call me Issahaku. Every time he didn't call my name; he took my father's name and called me. Then he asked me what happened: "Hey, Issahaku! *Na adɛn? Yie akwadaa yi deɛ, woyɛ patapaa dodo. Ɛyɛ deɛn?*"[2]

Then I started to cry: *"Boo-hoo."*

Then he came and held me. He said, "Oh, tell me what is wrong with you?"

Then I was crying, *"Eh-h, eh-h-h—sniff.* You know the Lebanese people are trying to teach me, and they beat me. *Sniff.* Even my neck is paining me, the way they held me. And I came to give complaint. And these people are laughing at me-e-e. *Eh-h-h, eh-h—sniff."*

Then he said, "No. This girl, she doesn't make — she doesn't want palaver. So if she says something happened to her, she is serious. Before I can see her in police station, if she's not — if she is not saying something — if she made some palaver and she's not correct inside, she wouldn't come to police station. So you people must follow her and go and see." So he gave me one policeman.

Then when we went there, these Lebanese were not there. They ran away — they went out. So the policeman said, OK, as they are not there, then tomorrow morning I must come back to police station and give the complaint. So we took a taxi again back to Adabraka police station. And from Adabraka police station, I went home again. Then I went to Playboy,[3] and I saw them there. Then I said, "*Ah-hah,* now they are doing the same business." So I got a taxi back to Adabraka police station. And when I went, these police people were not there. The Inspector was alone.

Then he said, "OK, I'm going with you." So the Inspector himself, he went with me. When we went to Playboy, we didn't see these people again! *Ha!* We had to go to their house. And when we went to their house, they were very foolish. They had put on lights, so when they heard a car come, then they got up and switched off the lights. And when we were knocking, they didn't mind. Then the Inspector started, "It's police knocking your door! If you don't open, then I will break every place." So

1. An Inspector might be the senior duty officer at a neighborhood police station.

2. (Asante Twi): Hey, Issahaku! But why? Hey, as for you (this) child, you're so aggressive. What is it (with you)?

3. Accra disco

they came and opened. When they opened, they made their faces to look like some people who were asleep for a long time, and they were still feeling sleepy. You know?

They opened the door, yawning, "*A Yallah?*[1] Why? Why?"

Then the Inspector said, "Do you know this girl?"

Then the one said, "Yes, I know this girl. Come and see — this girl! — come and see what she did to my house. *Kusummak sharmuta!* Come and see!" *Ha-ha!*

So this policeman went inside; he saw all this thing I did. They just went out and left it; they didn't pick up anything. Then they were telling him, and the Inspector said, "Yes. Do you think in Lebanon, can you get a girl to come and sleep, and you are two brothers, and both of you two will use the girl, without giving anything?"

Then the one said, "No, because my other brother was about to use her, but she didn't let him to use her. Then she started to fight with him."

Then the Inspector said, "In Lebanon, you people can do that. Here is Africa. We Africans, we don't do that. Even, if we are twins or if we resemble each other, I will never want my brother to sex a girl I sex. So this girl has suffered. You people have to pay her."

Then he said, "What am I going to do with this?! *Kusummak!* She can take this thing and go and sell it!"

Then the Inspector said, "If you would have paid her, she wouldn't break these things. I know you have wounded her. You beat her. You are two men. To beat one girl, a small girl like this, you don't pity? As a man, giving blows to a woman, don't you think maybe her body can be spoiled more than — when she's going to hospital, it will cost more than this radiogram? Or do you want me to take her to hospital? Then the paper they will give her, I will come and give you."

"OK! I don't care! You can go to hospital." So we went to hospital. Korle Bu.[2] We saw a nice doctor. The Inspector knew him. Then he wrote me many, many, many, many things, that one bone of me here is broken, and this and that.

Then we went back to Asylum Down, and the Inspector said, "OK, can you sell this radio and buy a bone for her?" So they had to pay sixty cedis in police station. Then I gave the police people twenty cedis. *Ha-ha!* I took the forty.

1. (Arabic): Oh God!
2. major teaching hospital in Accra

Deviant Sex

I don't usually do things like this, but if I see that you want to show me that you are—you know—that you are somebody, then I used to heat. If you talk to me slowly, I will understand. Even, maybe the person will never find even a cedi for me, but the way he talks to me, I like it. Then I will just leave and go. But I won't feel it if you do me like you are trying to fool me. How can you fool me? You see me like a fool because every time—*ha!*—I will never be serious with people. Even if somebody is telling me something serious, it used to make me laugh. I will start to laugh, and then people think that the way I laugh is the way I am a fool. If you look me in that way, I used to be annoyed.

So this kind of case, sometimes I used to get it. Yeah, there are some times, you know, some of the whites are fucking. Especially, there are many people, white people, who are foolish. He will take a girl home, then he will tell her to suck him. This case: I was having many, many people in Accra with this case. Every time, I will carry them to police.

You know Tesano:[1] many white people are living there. There is not one good white man inside Tesano. The Tesano police station, they know me like—*ha!*—like the police station is my house. Every night, two o'clock, I will go to the police there.

Somebody will come and carry me from someplace, "Let's go to Tesano." When we reach there, I will take off my dress; he will take off his dress. Then he will say, "Do you know French love?"

And I will say, "No, I don't know. What is French love?"

"But you say you are from Upper Volta."

"Yes. I am from Upper Volta, but I don't know their love. Because I grew up here. I didn't go there to make love with any Voltaique or French man. So I don't know."

Then he will say, "Yes, French love is to suck a man."

Then I say, "Ah."

Sometimes, you know, if I am drunk, if someone says this to me, I will look at him, then I will laugh. *Ha!*

And you know, some people used to say, "Fuck off!" *Ha!*

Then, there is somebody who will just open his gate and then push you out now-now: "Go away!" And in Tesano at night, you can't find a taxi.[2]

1. suburb of Accra

2. Because the area is residential, it is rare to find a taxi cruising; at that time, the area was on the outskirts of Accra, with little traffic on the main road through it.

So in my way, I will never walk and go home, because I am afraid if I go to some corners, a policeman will catch me too, and I will have another trouble.

So in Tesano, there was an embassy there. I don't know the country whose embassy it was, but every time, police people are there, guarding that house. So when someone pushes me outside, I won't say anything. I will take my dress, and I will tear it by myself, tear it all. Then I will walk. When I am near to the police people, then I will start crying: *"Boo-hoo."*

"Who is that?"

Then I will start, *"Oh! Oh! Awurade! Awurade, mɛwu o!*[1] *Eh-h-h. H-h-hm." Ha!*

"Who is that?"

"It's me, Papa."[2]

"Who are you? Where are you from?"

Then I will come, *"Boo-hoo."*

"Where are you from?"

Then I will be crying, "I am from Kumasi."

"But why are you here?"

"When we were coming with the car, the car was broken down. So there was a car, and a white man was inside. He said he will give me a lift. He said he will take me to Accra. When we came now, he took me to his house. Then I said, 'No, I don't want that, because they sent me from Kumasi. I never made love before.' Then this man said, 'If you haven't made love before, then if I make love with you, you will conceive.' So he said he will put his prick in my mouth. Then I said, 'No, I didn't do this thing before.' So this man beat me. Look at how my dress is, Papa. *Boo-hoo!"*—*Ha-ha!*—"Look at my dress! Oh! *Mama-a-e-e!*[3] Oh!" *Ha!* So this policeman will take me to police station to lodge the complaint, and then they will give me a policeman from there to the man's house—straight. And then you are going to pay! *Ha!* You are going to pay.

Then one time, you know, it was funny. One police man asked me, "You—every time you come from Kumasi, and every time in this Tesano here, you have your case. Where is your valise?"

I said, "Oh, but, when this car spoiled, I know the driver. He is from my father's house, so I told him tomorrow to bring me the valise, because

1. (Asante Twi): Oh! Oh! Lord God! God, I'm dead.

2. Traditional African wisdom calls for young people to consider any old person as a parent; Hawa is addressing him as a child to an elder, as in a courteous traditional context.

3. Mother!

I have a lift, because I can't sleep here in bush like this, so he told me to go, and tomorrow he will bring my valise for me." *Ha!*

I think I went to that police station about six times. After that, I knew that these police people were going to get my way, so if somebody wanted to take me from Lido, I would ask him, "Where do you live?" If he says Tesano, I will say, "No, I'm not going." Because I know I have been there many, many times. Yeah, I knew many, many, many houses there, and all these people, I had gone to police station with them. So I was afraid. Maybe I will go with you, and you are not a correct man: you are like them. Then I will be going to police station again, and these police people now know me. So now they will also start to think, "This girl, every time she says she is from Kumasi, and every time, every time, we see her." So I didn't want to be there again, to get another trouble to go to the police there.

And you know one funny thing? If these police people went to the man I was charging, they didn't ask where he picked me from, whether from Lido or some place. They never asked this question to the man, because they thought that many white people are doing this to African girls, to be sucking the girls, or to force the girl to be sucking them. You know? Suppose someone is not good to sex a girl, especially. And then some Europeans do it because maybe they have some medicine, and after, they can wash their throat with it, without any sickness. But if you do this to an African girl, it's not good.

So if the police go there, the only question they will ask: "Do you know this girl?"

You know, one bad man, when we went to his house, they asked him did he know me, and he said, no, he doesn't know me. Then I said, "Don't you know — don't you think that, now-now-now-now, some girl went out of your house?"

He said, "Yes, but I just saw you. I don't know you. I brought you here to make love. You said you don't agree. I said, 'Go away.'"

Then they said, "How can you send her away like that? You brought her to make love with her. Then she is not agreeing with you. Then you send her out in this place. In Europe, can you do that?"

Then he didn't have anything to say: "Hey! In Europe, if you bring a girl and she doesn't want to make love with you, she can find her way."

Then they said, "No. Do you think Tesano here — it's one-thirty in the night, and you are sending this girl to go away — somebody can come and catch her somewhere and beat her, or somebody can wound her, or somebody can kill her. If she doesn't want, then send her back with your car. Why didn't you send her back with your car?

Then he said, "*Ah!* But she didn't agree with me! How can I waste all my petrol for her?"

Then I said, "Why—why shouldn't you?!"

Then they asked him, why didn't she agree with you?

And then he said, "Yes, because—it's because according to the way every man likes to make love."

Then they said, "Which kind way[1] did you want to make love with her?"

Then he couldn't talk again. Then they asked me, what did he want to do with me?

I said, "Yes, he told me to put his prick in my mouth. I said I can't do that. Then he wanted to fuck me where I'm sitting. And I cannot do that, and I never did that. So I cannot accept, and I told him to take me back. And he said 'No.'"

So the one policeman told the man, "No. You are not all right. You have to come to police station, anyway. She has lodged your complaint there. So you can go to police station and judge your case—whether they will leave you free there. They sent me. I am not a judge. I am not an inspector. The Inspector sent me to bring you." Then this man got up. When we went to police station, they asked him for his passport. He didn't bring his passport. They had to go back home and bring his passport. And then they asked him whether in his country, they can do that and this.

And he said, "Well, in my country, when you take a girl, if the girl is a harlot girl, then she hasn't got a husband, and she is doing this as a business. So if you take her, anything you ask her to do, she will do it, and then she will charge you. She will charge you the money, and if you can pay her, you can do whatever you like."

Then they said, "OK. When you took this girl, did you ask her whether she is a harlot woman? Or she is doing this business or she doesn't do this business?"

Then he said, no, he didn't ask me.

Then they said, "But why? Maybe this girl thought you are a nice man; you are going to give her a lift. Or you are a nice man; maybe you want to go with her to take one drink. We Africans, we do that sometimes to the girls like this. When we see a young girl, even if we like her, we don't follow her for one day; maybe we will take her to drink with her. And the second or third or fourth—some people do about one week before they

1. (Pidgin): which kind of way; also "what kind way" or the answer "some kind way." The phrase usually is meant to question an unacceptable or unknown alternative, for example, "What kind way is this?"

press the girl—and this girl will not refuse. Maybe this girl is very young; she doesn't know anything. When you asked her to go with you, she thought that maybe you are taking her to some place to drink." Then this man could not have much to say again. So they said, "OK, her dress is torn. She hasn't any dress." And one policeman went to the quarters behind there and brought me a cloth from his wife.

Then the man said, "God! I didn't touch her!"

Then they asked me, "Ah, so somebody beat you on the road?"

I said, "No, not somebody. He is the one who beat me. Even he threw me out." *Ha!* I was serious. You know, in things like this, I don't laugh. I like to laugh always, but not if I want to do something bad, eh? If you see me, you will say that this girl never laughs. *Serious!* If this man wanted to look at me, I didn't want to see his face. *Tsk!* I turned my face.

Then this man had to pay. They asked me, how much did I buy my dress? I said, "I bought it for thirty-six cedis in Kingsway. It was already made. It's not sewn here.[1] But it's not *buroni-wawu*."[2]

Do you know buroni-wawu? These second-hand clothes they are bringing from Europe, yeah? That's buroni-wawu. It means the white man died. They say if the white people die, then they send the clothes to us to buy. *Ha!* Because if they die, nobody in Europe wants to take the dress. It's old and the fellow is dead, so they must sell it as buroni-wawu, because it's good for us Africans. So that's why we are calling that type of dress buroni-wawu: we say that if the white people die, then they leave their property and nobody wants it, then they carry it to Africa to sell to us. *Ha!*

So: then these police people said, "OK, after you pay for her dress, then you must give her money, to get a taxi to home." So he paid for my dress, thirty-six cedis, and then he gave another ten cedis for my taxi fare. The police people led me to the road. They waited until they got a car for me, and then I went away.

So after about four or five days, I saw this man in Lido. *Ha!* They were three men together. And you know, I thought the other one said something about me, that he liked me or something. I don't know. Then this man said, "Hey, this girl! You don't know her! She's a bloody fucking liar. If you take this girl, you will have trouble. One night she didn't let me sleep for the whole night."

So one girl was sitting with them. Her name was Constance. Constance came and told me, "These white people, one of them likes you, but the other one said he knows you. You are a bad girl. What did you do to him?"

1. It is factory-made, European style.

2. (Asante Twi): *Buroni-wawu* is a noun form, from *Oburoni w'awu* (White man, you died). The pronunciation is "broni-wawu."

Then I said, "Which one?"

Then she said, "My man."

I said, "Your man? He's your man?"

"Yes, he's my boyfriend."

Then I said, "*Ah-ha-a-a-a!* So you are the people who take the prick like a chewing stick!"[1] *Ha-ha!* "You are the people who are spoiling these people! Wait, I will show you. You, Constance. *Ah-hah!* Is he your man? Then he is telling you I am a bad girl. Why don't you ask him what I did to him?"

She said, "He didn't tell me what you did to him, but he said one night you didn't let him sleep for the whole night."

So I asked her, "Do you think he was making love with me for the whole night? Why don't you ask him?" You know, if I was the one, if I had a friend, and my other friend told me, "This your friend is bad," I would ask him to understand why he's saying my friend is bad. *Hmm?* Yeah? But she didn't say anything, and she just came to me. So I also replied her, "It's your man. Your *man!* So you are the people who are doing this business here. I will let people know you now." *Ha!* She couldn't say what these people talked about me, you know, so she just went out from Lido.

Then these people were there. Then I went and said, "Hello, mister. How are you? So you got a girl who can suck, or who you can use her ass, no? You are a nice man. And the girl, too, is also a nice girl. But I don't think that she is a Ghanaian, because Ghanaian people don't do this." *Ha!* "So you are a lucky man today to meet Constance, you know. And you are talking about me."

Then he said, "No, no, no! Go away! Go away! I don't want to talk to you!"

Then I said, "Thank you. Even I don't want to talk to you. But I want you to know that we are not the same. You see, Constance is a very beautiful girl. Look at her: she has a nice waist; she has a nice face. Then you see me: I'm very ugly. And my head: everything I do, it's ugly things I used to do. I don't do something nice, because I'm not nice. So the next time, if you want a girl, look at the one who is beautiful like Constance."

This Constance, the one I'm talking about, she is a nice girl. Now she has gone to Switzerland. Some man took her from Lomé. Some man saw her at Hôtel le Benin, and then just like that, he said, OK, he will make everything for her, and then he will take her to Switzerland. Yeah, I think

1. the indigenous toothbrush, a small piece of hardwood used to polish the teeth. One chews it for a while, and then the fibers become like a brush.

she can do this work well, so she got a husband to go to Europe. *Ha!* Oh, yeah? But she's foolish. *Ah!* To do this fucking, fucking business like this? *Shit!*

So after I went away from this man, then I had to tell all these boys in Lido that Constance used to suck or that they fuck her ass. I said it. And then every time she passed, we used to make rough.[1] Even, the time when I went to Lomé, she was also there. If she saw me, she didn't talk to me. She was living with one friend of mine, and I also got a room in that house. And then, when she saw that I came to live in that house, she just left. She told the friend that she was going to Accra for one week; then she went for about three or four months. She didn't come back. And the time when she came back, she said it was because this man was making the passport for her, so she had to stay in Ghana to make the passport.

This man from Hôtel le Benin was a tourist, you know, these people who used to come for holidays, from Europe, in Togo. Yeah. He could not stay and wait for her, so he gave her money to make her passport. But every time when he sent money, he sent it to Togo, then she would come and take the money and go to Ghana to make the passport. And when she finished the passport, then to make a visa and all this, the money was finished. She spent the money by heart.[2] So she borrowed some money from one girl named Yaa. She borrowed the money from the landlord of Yaa in Accra. Then she went to Europe. And what she did, that is what let Yaa to come and remain in Lomé, because the landlord told Yaa, "I didn't know this girl. Because of you, I lent her the money. And this girl went to Switzerland. She didn't come back to pay me my money, so you have to pay." So Yaa said she would come to Lomé to find money to pay this debt, and if this girl comes back from Switzerland, she can pay the money to her. But when she came to Lomé, she didn't get the money, and then she conceived! *Ha-ha!*

Yeah? Constance was very bad girl. But very nice and beautiful. Oh! A nice girl like this, and she was doing this fucking business. It's shit! If I was beautiful like that, even I would tell people to fuck my feet. And pay me! *Ha-ha!* You are beautiful, and then you will put this fucking thing in your mouth? *Phoo!*

Mm? So in Tesano, I have done that way until about the sixth one, then I stopped. The sixth one, by then these police people got to know me well, you know, because this thing, I didn't take time; I didn't make it in months and months. Maybe I will make this trouble: one week after, I'm

1. quarrel
2. senselessly, roughly, carelessly, without sense of purpose

there again, or three or four days after, I'm there, in police station. Then these people got to know me, so I had to stop my business there.

Really Deviant Sex

But even in Nima[1] police station, I had two cases like that. There was one Lebanese man who stayed in Nima. A tall guy! And this man — Oh! — if you saw this man, you wouldn't suspect him that he can do something like this. He knew me because of one of his friends. The friend used to take me every time, and this man also got to know me. I used to go to his house with the friend, and we used to eat together. He had a nice house. I thought he was a nice man, too. Every time when we went there, he used to make jokes, and all this.

So every time, if he saw me, "Oh, Hawawu,[2] what will you drink?" And so we were nice together. Then after, the friend left Ghana, and this man was also trying to follow me.

So one day he came to my house in Asylum Down, and he said, "Oh, tonight I want to come and take you out." Then I said OK. And he said, "OK. Prepare about nine-thirty." So at nine-thirty, we went to Continental,[3] to the casino. You know, these Lebanese people like these games. Yeah. So when we went, he told me to drink anything I wanted. He gave me a place to sit, and that he is going to the friends, and they are going to play lottery or some things like that. So I said, OK. I was sitting there drinking up to one o'clock. Then he came and said we can go home.

Then I thought he was going to drop me at my place. I thought that he invited me because of the friend. He didn't tell me anything that we should go together or something like he wanted to make love. So I was ready to go, then when we were coming, he passed Asylum Down, and then I said, "Oh, won't you drop me?"

And he said, "Oh, but don't you want to go with me?"

Then I said, "Hey, what about your wife?" I knew the wife, with two children.

"Oh, my wife has gone away. There is nobody in the house. We can go."

Then when he was trying to talk to me like that, I thought, "Ah, it's money I'm searching for, no? We don't search for brothers or friends. So, ah, I can do with him." So I said, "OK."

1. section of Accra
2. diminutive of Hawa
3. state-owned hotel in Accra

Then we went. This tall guy—*ayay!* This business, we dey see something inside, only we no fit leave-o.[1] *Ha-ha!* When we went, he said we should go and bathe. So we went and bathed together, and he said he wanted to bathe me. Then he was bathing me. He put soap all around my body, then he put much soap here, and he wanted to put his finger in my ass. Then I didn't want that. So I said, "Oh, what are you doing?"

He said, "Oh, wait, I am going to wash there."

Then I said, "No! This is not the way. You are wounding me."

He said, "Why? Didn't you do this before? This small finger? And what about when I say I will fuck you there?"

Then I said, "That way, no. I never did that."

He said, "You lie!"

"How can I lie? If I didn't do something, and I tell you I didn't do it? If I can do something, it's OK. You are going to pay, no?"

Then he said, "Yes."

Then I said, "I didn't do it before, so I cannot. I don't want it." Then he didn't say anything. So we finished the bath. Then we came. We lay down, you know. When we lay down, he started the same way. *Ha!* He used his hand, and then he wanted to put it there. Then I said, "No, mister. If that will be the case, you had better drop me at home."

Then he said, "Do you think I can get my car out at this time?"

"Why? Why can't you get your car out?"

"If you want to go, you can go. But my car cannot go out at this time."

Then I said, "*Ahh?* You are one of the ministers? So your car cannot go out at this time? And your car can go and bring some girl at this time?"

Then, he just started: *Ch-ch-ch! Ka-ch-ch-ch! Slapping* me, eh? He just started beating me on the bed. Then I didn't say anything. I got up and took my dress. You know, the way he slapped me was very hard on my body, but I knew I could not cry. If I cry, there is no Mama, no Papa: who will take me out? So I must be quiet. Then I took my dress, then I said, "OK, thank you very much." He said I should look on the table: there is money there; I can take what I want to go and take taxi. I said, "No, I don't want anything from you. Thank you very much. God will bless you."

He said, "*Kusummak sharmuta!* 'God bless me'?!" Then he came and kicked me out.

Then I said, "Yeah, this is what I want: kick me out!"

And by that time, the housegirl woke up. When the wife went, this girl was still staying there. So the way we were talking loudly, this girl came

1. (Pidgin): This ashawo life, we get troubles in it, but we can't get out of it.

out, and then he told her, "Akosua, Akosua, go and sleep!" Then this girl went back.

Then I thought, OK, now I have got a witness; I must go to police station. I didn't say anything to him. I went to Nima police station, and I met police.

They said, "What is wrong?" When I went there, I didn't cry; I didn't do anything, but I was serious. "What is wrong?"

I said, "Ah, I came to lodge my complaint."

"What kind of complaint do you have?"

I said, "I was in my house, and somebody came and invited me to go and drink. And that man, I know him as a friend's friend."

"Who is this friend? What kind of friend?"

I said, "As my boyfriend's friend. He invited me to go and drink. He came to my house and told me we should go out at nine-thirty. So at nine-thirty I was ready. Then he took me to Continental. At Continental, he give me excuse, that I can drink what I want. So I was there drinking up to one o'clock. Then he said we should go home. So when we reached my place, I said, 'Oh, but won't you send me to my house?' Then he said, 'No, we can go to my house and drink. From my house to your house is not far. I can take you there after.' So we went together. When we went together, this man said, 'Oh, you know, I like you,' and that and this. The friend who was my friend has gone away; he's not here again, so I also thought, 'I am a girl. I have no husband. Nobody promised me to marry me.' So I thought I must do this fucking business for my money. So I agreed."

Then these police people said, "You *agreed?!*"

Then I said, "Yes, I agreed. Then he said we should go and bathe. When we started bathing, then he started to put soap in my ass to put his finger. Then I didn't want that way, so I told him that I don't want it. He didn't say anything. We finished our bath, then he said we should sleep. Then we went to the bed. And when we lay down, he started doing this thing again. Then I told him, 'No, I don't want this thing.' Then he just started beating me, up and down. Even he was beating me heavily, and the housegirl woke up. Many people in the area woke up. So I don't understand this. So I have come to lodge the complaint."

Then one policeman, he was a very, very, very good man. He was from Osenase[1]—a short man, at Nima police station. He said, "*What?!!* You people are disgracing us! A white man?!"

1. small town in south-central Ghana

Then I said, "It's not a white man. It's a Lebanese."

"*What?! Lebanese?!* Let's go, let's go, let's go." *Ha!*

So we went to this Lebanese man, and the way this short man acted, this Lebanese man was afraid of him. But if they say you will leave this short man with this tall Lebanese man to fight, maybe this Lebanese man can beat him like his own son. But he was in uniform. The Lebanese man could not touch him. So when we went there, this policeman knocked the door —*kpam kpam kpam*— and this man didn't mind. Then he took the police stick, and knocked again: *ke-ke-kem-kam, pah pah, pah!* And then this man said, "Who?"

"It's police." So this man came out and this policeman said, "Get on your dress! We want you at police station! Do you know this girl?"

"Yes, it's Hawawu. I know her. She is a friend of my friend."

Then, "OK. She is calling you in police station. Let's go."

So this man got inside and dressed up. And we went to the police station. Then this man, you know, he was also trying to be clever — very, very clever. So he said, yes, he knows me because of the friend. The same thing I said, he said the same. He knows me because of the friend, and the friend has gone on holidays. So he thought I'm feeling lonely because — when the friend was there, we used to come to his place and eat, and he also used to bring his wife with his two children to our place and eat. So when he saw that the friend has gone away, maybe I am feeling lonely, so he came and invited me outside, to go and have a small drink. But when we drank together, you know, a man and woman matter, you know — it's — it's different — then he changed his mind — that he would like to make love with me. So he brought me home — and when he brought me home, he wanted to touch me, and I said, "No, I don't want that." Then when he touched me, then I said, "No, no, no, no, no."

Then these police people said, "Yes! It's correct for her to do that. If that is the way, it's correct. Because of your friend, you know her. Yes? Even, we Africans don't follow our friends' friends."

So my own talk, what I said about my ass, he didn't say anything about that. So they have to take the charge he gave to himself to get him. Yeah? He gave his own sex charge. As for me, I said he was putting his hand on my ass. But he didn't say that. He said that he touched me, then I said no — and then he asked me why I came with him — and I said, yes, because I thought he is a nice man to my friend, so that's why I went with him, and I didn't know that he was going to do something like this with me — and he said, OK, if that will be the case, I should go out — then I said I wouldn't go out — I'll let him carry me with his car — and he said the car could not go out at this hour — so he was sleeping, and then I started troubling him — I didn't want him to sleep — then he was annoyed, so he started beating me.

Then the police people said, "No! But you are not all right to beat her. When you came and invited her to go out, did you tell her, 'I love you. After we go out, we will go to my house'?"

Then he said, no, he didn't tell me.

"But she had to do that because you haven't promised her. So you mean that, when you were drunk, then your mind changed?"

Then he said, "Yes."

"Ah, then this girl is correct. But it's not good like that — the way you beat her. And then you pushed her out."

"No, I didn't push her out."

Then I said, "Yeah, your housegirl was there. Even your housegirl woke up, and you told her to get back inside and sleep. If you like, we can go and bring the girl."

Then he said, "No, no, no, no, the girl is a housegirl for me; she has nothing to talk about here."

Then they said, "OK, so what this girl said is true? You were doing all these things to her. This girl said you wanted to force her in her ass, and she didn't agree."

Then he said, no, he didn't want to fuck my ass, but as for him, every time he used to feel for a woman, he used to feel to put a finger on her ass. *Ha!* It was funny! *Ha-ha!*

So they said, "No, in Ghana we don't do that. In Ghana, if you do something like that to a woman, it's not good, because the Ghanaian women, they don't treat them in this way. If they treat the girls in Europe in that way, but in Ghana, Africans don't treat their children in that way. So you have wasted her time. Suppose somebody went with her, she knows what she will get today, so you had better give her something. You cannot do her like this, beating her like that. Maybe she will feel pains. Maybe, now, she's half drunk, so she doesn't know what she is doing, but in morning time, she won't feel all right, so you must —"

Then he said, "OK, OK, OK! So how much? How much do you want me to give her?"

Then the police people said, *"Ahaa!"* Then this short man said, *"Hɛɛ, buroni wei, ɔpesɛ ɔkyerɛ ne ho paa!"*[1] Do you know what is *"kyerɛ ne ho"?* It means that the white man wants to show himself. So this short policeman said, "This white man wants to bluff: *ɔpesɛ ɔkyerɛ ne ho.* Yeah, he wants to bluff. A Lebanese like this, even he is not a pure white man. And he comes

1. (Asante Twi): Hey, this white man wants to bluff too much!

to the police station to bluff like this! OK!" Then this man just took the pen from the other one, and he charged him: *ch-ch-ch-ch.* Seventy cedis!

Then he gave him the paper, and then this Lebanese man looked at him and said, "But why? Why? Everybody knows me!" They knew him because he was the director of a small factory near to the Nima police station. Then he was trying to prove his work,[1] and this and this, and he is not a stranger to come and teach himself, seventy cedis without a fuck, without anything.

Then this policeman said, "OK, if you don't want, you don't pay the seventy cedis. Tomorrow, you people are going to the court. OK?" You know, he was a fool. Instead of paying the seventy cedis, he had to pay eighty cedis, because these police people were annoyed. They said, "Oh, if you want to talk this": then they started, "OK, tell me and I will take your statement, and tomorrow you come at eight o'clock in the morning, and we will go to the court."

Then this man could not stand this. He started to shake, because many people would hear of it, and the wife just went away about one week before, eh? And it's a disgrace for him. So he had to call the short policeman to beg him. Then the policeman said, "No, no, no, no. Hey, this case — no, no, no. The Inspector has already heard it. I cannot do anything about it. So if you want, you can see the Inspector. If it's OK with the Inspector, or maybe you can see somebody to see the Inspector for you." So the man had to pay eighty cedis — they added ten cedis for the Inspector — to close the case. *Ha!* Yeah?

And from then, if this man saw me, he said, "Thief girl." He called me a thief girl. But I am not a thief, yes? I said, "It's your way. It's your way. You made me." First time, we were *very nice* friends with that man. The wife was very nice — oh, a beautiful woman — and every time, when we went to them to eat, or they came to my friend's house to eat, every time, she used to say, "Oh, I have a younger sister; she is called Hawawu." She didn't call me "Hawa"; she called me "Hawawu." She would say, "You are my younger sister. When I see you, I used to remember my younger sister." She was a nice woman. And then her husband did this foolish business. *Ha-ha!*

So then I used to think whether, when the wife was there, he was doing this thing to her. And then I thought sometimes that some of the white people don't do this, but if they have a wife, they used to think that maybe, if he makes love with a girl, maybe he will get some sickness. Then he will try to change the way, when he gets feelings. You know? I

1. show what he was doing in Ghana

thought a lot about these things, and then I asked one French man, "Do you French people like these kinds of things?"

He said, "Yeah, as for French people, it's their life. Even if you're married to your wife, you two will do this together. You know, you can suck your wife and your wife can suck you. It's their life."

Then I asked him, "What about the other people?"

He said, "Some people too, why they do it is, when the wife goes away, maybe the wife won't keep away a long time. So he's afraid that maybe he will make love with somebody and he will have a sickness, and the wife will come, and then he will give that sickness to the wife, or something like that. So he feels that this place, nobody used to make love there, so if he does it like that, he cannot get any sickness."

Then I said, "*Ah-hah!* To get this thing in your mouth! I will go: *'Gug-gug-guggh-gug. Aach-cha!!'* I will bite it! It's also a sickness! If your wife comes, then what are you going to say? *Ha-ha!* It's very foolish, you know. Yeah? It's very foolish when they think this way, to do this, because somebody can just bite you. When she bites you and your wife comes back, and you have got this sore, you cannot make love with your wife. What are you going to tell your wife? 'Somebody bit me'? Or 'I fell down'? You didn't wound any place, but only that place got a wound? What can go inside there and cut that place?"

Then he said, "Yes, what you say is true. But you know, people who do it, they don't think—they don't think of this before doing it." *Ha!*

Wounds

So this way, this *waka-waka-waka,*[1] it's hard. No? Look. One time I went with somebody who was staying at Cantonments.[2] OK? Then I also had a promise with another man to meet him, and I didn't want to miss that promise, because I trusted that fellow; sometimes he used to give me a lot. So I didn't want to go any place, but, I saw this way—I thought it's a job, you know, a quick job to go and do and then return back. So I went to Cantonments to the man's house, and then we finished everything. I took my bath, then we went to take his car. The car tire: one was spoiled—*gbang!*—it could not go, and there was no other one to put on the car. So what shall we do? Then he said, OK, he would lead[3] me to the road to get a taxi.

1. (Pidgin): to walk and walk, i.e., to be going around or carrying on with a job
2. section of Accra
3. accompany

Then we went to the road. Oh, we stood there for more than forty minutes. Not any taxi was coming. Then this man said, no, if that will be the case, I shouldn't mind; I can come and sleep till morning time, then I can find my way. So we went back to the house. Then I didn't feel happy because I thought I had to meet that other fellow. *Ha!* So I said, "No, OK, if that will be the case, I will go alone."

Then he said, "Can you go?"

I said, "Yes." Then I went out. When I was coming, then I heard these policemen coming with these big shoes: *Kro, kro.* I just *jumped!* I had some power, you know. I don't know the way I had the power. I just made like this: "Hey! *Tcha!*" And then I jumped into the bushes. So: there were some small flowers, these flowers with plenty thorns. *Shit!* The next day I could not bathe. When I bathed, it was like they put pepper on my body.

So when these police people came, they felt that they saw somebody on the road, and he jumped to the side, so they started to put their lights to watch in those flowers. And I was there. So what I did: I was having a white dress, and I knew that they would find me out with the torch,[1] so I removed all my dress and lay there in the bushes like that. But they were also afraid, so they didn't get near to the flowers. They just looked somewhere to point their light. A small hole was there, and I lay down. If a snake was there or a snake wasn't there, I didn't think of death at that time. *Ha!* They searched around that place; they didn't see anything. Then they said, "O-ho? If the fellow wants to kill himself, let him kill himself. Let's go. It's not we who killed him." Then they left. When they went forward a bit and passed, then I came out.

When I came out, I saw a watchman.[2] I didn't know the road. The road was like this and like that.[3] Then I asked the watchman, "If I want to get a taxi now, where should I pass?"

Then he said, "Oh, do you see that light over there?"

I said, "Yes."

He said, "Yeah, if you go, then you pass right. You are going to Star Hotel. It's not far. You can get a taxi there. But in this area, you cannot get a taxi."

So I went out and walked, walked, walked, walked. Then I saw a light of a car like a Jeep police car, so I had to dodge[4] into the side again. Then

1. flashlight

2. a private watchman guarding a residence. Many bungalows in residential areas have such an employee.

3. curving and branching this way and that

4. elude, avoid

they came and passed. When they passed, I saw them: it was a police car. Jeep — a black one. Then I said, "Ah! So this road is only a police road. What shall I do? To go to Star Hotel and take a taxi, what shall I do?" That time, I didn't put on a cloth. I only put on a dress, with no cloth to put over it. So then I started to think, what to do? This road, if I pass, police will pass or a police car will pass, then they will see me without a cloth, in this type of dress, and they will catch me. And I didn't know how far to the Star Hotel. So if I didn't have some way to help myself, then always I would be going into the flowers and these things would just cut all my body. That time I already had *plenty* of marks on my body. But I didn't see these marks yet, until the morning time.

So I went to another watchman again. I said, "You see, even if you don't believe me, I can deposit something for you, to just give me one cloth. Tomorrow I will bring it back. Even if it's torn, if it's torn — a piece of cloth like this, you can just give it to me."

And this man said, "What do you want it for?"

I said, "No. You know, where I am, I have wounded my foot, and then blood is coming out, so I have to get something to tie on it. If it's not so, before I get taxi, I think I will waste much of my blood."

Then he said, "Let me see."

Then I said, "No." You know, it was something funny. I thought that when I said "blood," he wanted to see the blood. So I had to change, and I said, "No, it's not like blood and it's running, you know, but, I was seeing a car come, and the way the car was coming, I thought the man who was driving the car was boozed. He was drunk. So I jumped in some place and — like something chooked[1] me. I don't know if something bit me or something cut on my feet, but the way I feel, I am not feeling all right."

So this watchman was a nice man. He said, "No, I don't want anything from you. If the next day you are all right, you will bring my thing back. It's OK for me like that." But he didn't give me a cloth: he brought out some plastic, and then, he tied it! *Ha-ha!* He tied my foot! Oh, very *strongly!* Because if something bit me there, the poison cannot come up, so he tied it well for me. *Ah!*

Then I was walking: I could not walk; this thing was paining me. I said, "*Ah! What a bloody hell!* What kind of fucking man like this?" I needed something so that I could put something on my stomach and tie it, and then I could put this dress on top, so if the police met me, they would see that I was a conceived woman, and they would leave me. And this man didn't give me. He just gave me some plastic like a rope and then tied my foot, *very* tightly. Then I was walking away. And all the time I was

1. (Pidgin): stuck, pricked, stabbed

walking like this, I said, "*Ah! Oh!* Everything they give you is luck. Or is your luck like this?" So I was walking like that.

Then this police car: *Whoosh!* "Hey! *Bra ha*—Come here." Then I went. "*Wofiri he?*—Where are you coming from?" When they talked Ashanti, I made like I didn't understand. Then they said, "*Na! Hyie-e! Ghanafoɔ, wɔmoyɛ bad-o! Wokyerɛ sɛ wonte kasa, na wonenam ha sesɛ berɛ?* What the hell?! Ghanaians are *bad!* So you mean you don't hear someone speak, and you are walking here on this road, at this time?"

So then I started, *"Ni, ina jin Hausa. Ni, Asante—um!"*[1]

"Ah! Mpepefoɔ nkwadaa! Nkwadaabɔnefoɔ nyinaa!"[2] You see? *Pepe?* Northerners. They said, "Pepe, they are very *bad* girls. You see the way she is acting; now she can speak Hausa." Then one man said, yeah, he also can speak Hausa. He was a Kanjaga man. He asked me, "What is wrong?"

Then I said, "Oh—you know, my—I'm living here with my husband—he is a cook. He went out. And a scorpion bit me. You know? A scorpion bit me. So I didn't see my husband—he didn't come. And this—I am feeling pains. So I went and knocked the room of the master. The master could not wake up. So I want to get a taxi and go to hospital. That's why I'm walking here." *Ha!*

So they had to take me, to drop me at Star Hotel to get a taxi to go to hospital. Free charge! *Ha!* It's a police taxi. I didn't pay for it! So when they got me to Star Hotel, oh! I was dropping, and as girls are fools, one of my friends saw me, and then she was calling, *"Hey, Hawa!? Hawa!"* I didn't mind her; I seemed as if I didn't see her at all. These police people are there! Let them move their car before you call me! And you want to shout. But these people didn't ask me my name, you know, so they didn't know I was the one the girl was calling. Then I went and entered taxi.

I took this taxi to Lido. When I got to Lido, they said, "Oh, this man was waiting for you. Just right now, about two minutes ago, he just left." *Aaagh!!* What foolishness did I do?! This man—the man I went with—he gave me thirty cedis: suppose maybe if I slept there, he would have given me fifty cedis. I left that place and suffered like this, to come back to Lido. The other one I wanted, I also didn't see him. I lost twice. So these thirty cedis: I have to be drunk with it in Lido before I can sleep well. *Ha!*

It's a very foolish business that we do sometimes, you know. *Ha-ha!*

1. (Hausa): Me, I hear (speak) Hausa. Me, Asante—no!

2. (Asante Twi): Ah! Northern children! All (of them) are bad children! *Mpepefoɔ* (singular, *Pepeni*) is a name used to refer to Northerners, people north of the Akan cultural area.

So I started calling drinks. And I'm very funny. Sometimes, if I am drinking, if I am getting drunk, then I will see all the friends, and I want to buy them something. I finished that thirty cedis there. Then I was just thinking and thinking, "Yes, this money: if I don't finish it, maybe I will die. I don't know. This is a very bad-luck man —*ah!*— he is bad luck — because I went with him, and after, when we were coming, he dropped me back to his house. The tire was burst. When I went to the road, I have to dodge to the grasses — and *all* my body, and that and this."

You know, when I got to Lido, they said, "Hey! *Adɛn? Adɛn? Wodeɛ hwɛ! Mogya ɛba ha!*"[1] These girls said, "Hey, you should look! There is blood on you! What is wrong with you? Somebody beat you?" Then we went to the toilet and got the toilet roll, and then I rubbed all that place, you know. *Ha!* All that time, I didn't feel pains.

The next morning, when I went to the bathroom —*whew!* I could not bathe with a sponge. When the soap went inside my body, *she-e-e-e!* I didn't know that I was wounded like that. Because it was night, and I think I was worrying: all my money is somewhere. So I didn't feel the pains. But the next morning, I felt it. And this thirty cedis, too, I didn't have twenty pesewas of it *Huh?* Even twenty pesewas, I haven't got it in my bag. I spent it. And I haven't got any money. So I just lost like that — two places. I lost here: I thought I was playing a good game, because maybe if I get this thirty cedis, and then I will come and meet this man, maybe — yeah, that man was a good man. He was not living in Ghana, but he used to come. Every time, when he came he was in Ambassador Hotel, and any time when I would go there, he used to give me maybe a hundred cedis, or two hundred. So I thought, "Ah, if I go to him, then he will give me hundred cedis, and then this thirty cedis, I will spend it for food and this in the house." Then I didn't get anything. That thirty cedis which I could spend in the house, I spent all in Lido. And the next morning — *ha!*— when I searched my bag, I just saw some old tickets from cinema. *Ha!* And some fucking, fucking things like that — some papers, addresses, and this. So I was *very* annoyed. Then I could not go to bathe, too. When I went to the bathroom, then this thing *hurt* me. So: *ha!*

What No Girl Says

Ah-h-h, yes. We have palaver from this life. Trouble. But some people think that we girls used to enjoy every time. Sometimes, you can enjoy

1. (Asante Twi): Why? Why? You yourself look! Blood has come here!

some place, and sometimes, at some place too, you will be hot like a pepper. A pepper. A pepper is not hot, you know: there is some place you will stay, some place where you can cry and call your God to take you out of this business. And then tomorrow, if you come to some place, you will forget about what you suffered yesterday. *Ha!*

Yeah, you can see some people outside, and you will think they are enjoying, but they are suffering. Isn't it? Every time, when you see girls in Lido, or some nightclub, you will see the girl dressed nicely, and she's dancing, she's happy, and all this. But that very night, maybe she's going to suffer, the very night when you saw her with her man. Maybe that night, she will go with somebody and she will suffer just like that.

So I think that we girls who are doing this ashawo business, though, we take our life like that. You know? You can die at any place. Something can happen to you. Don't you know that? Yeah. Suppose when I jumped in those flowers, something bit me or something did me something there. It is in the morning time that they will come and find me, and it will be too late. Do you know that? But if you see a girl in the nightclubs, you will say, "Ah! This girl! Ah! This girl." You don't know what is the problem she has got.

Some people say that this life, it's unto us. It's unto us? Yeah, it's unto me, but sometimes it's not on me. Sometimes it's not on me, maybe. Before when I was growing up, I didn't feel like doing all these things, you know. There is not any girl who will wake up as a young girl and say, "As for me, when I grow up I want to be ashawo, to go with everybody, to do this and this." Not any girl will think of this.

Butterfly Wings

Maybe before when I was growing up, I thought—*ah!*

At first I was very funny in the house, and they used to laugh at me. Every time when I saw somebody making the husband food, then I used to say, "*Ey,* what time shall I grow, too? I'll make my husband's home like that and that and this." We had one Amariya in our house, and this Amariya was a heavy groover.[1] She could *groove!* The husband was a driver of a trotro in Kumasi. When I was living in my father's house, they rented one room. When the husband would leave in the morning, he would leave some money there for her to cook, but when she woke up, she would just take some money and go outside and buy some food and

1. also, groovier: marijuana smoker

come and eat. When she finished eating, she would bathe and put on all this eyes' pencil, and then she would go to the market and make the shopping and come and put it down. Then she would have a heavy groove. She would sleep. When the husband came, he had to come and cook. Then sometimes the husband used to think to force her, you know, because you cannot be married and then you will do two jobs. You work in the day with a car to find money for the woman, and the woman cannot cook. So sometimes he would come: "Amariya, Amariya!"

"Hmm?"

"*Yaya ne?*[1] What? Won't you cook?"

"Ah, driver, excuse me. A nice thing, ah-h-h, I have it, I have it, a thick one. I cannot cook."

"But didn't you wash my clothes, too? Look, I left this for you in the morning time to wash."

"Ah, the time when you were putting it there, when you were talking to me, I think I was dreaming. But when I woke up, I didn't watch there, so I didn't see them. But, this time, I cannot wake up. Please."

So this man will start cooking, you know, in the kitchen. Then, he used to call me his small wife. I would bring him water and help him because he could not cook well. Then I used to sit down, thinking. I would say, "Ah! What time am I going to grow up and then I will take this man from this girl?" *Ha!* So when I was growing up, because this man was calling me his wife, I thought that if I grow up and I know how to cook, I will take him from this girl. This was my mind how I used to think. And I used to tell my sister that I'm praying to God to let me grow quick-quick.

Then my sister said, "What did you see and you want to grow quickly like that?"

And I said, "Look at the way the Amariya is treating the husband. Do you think it is good? It's not good. She doesn't cook for the man. The man must go to work, and then close maybe at seven o'clock and come and start cooking in the night. Everybody has eaten, some people are sleeping, and he is starting to cook. It's not nice. So I want to grow up quickly and then I will get the husband from her."

So my sister also was another funny guy. So she said, "Do you want to grow up tall or —"

Then I said, "No, but, a woman doesn't — whether she grows tall or she doesn't grow tall, it's your brassiere that is showing something, you know, so if you have breasts, then you have grown up."

And then she told me, "Do you know where I got my breasts?"

1. (Hausa): What's this?

I said, "No."

"From butterflies."

Yeah! Every afternoon time, when they put out water, if it was dry season, where there was water, then these butterflies used to come to this thing. Then we would find some stick and whip them and kill them. Their wings. She said that if you rub the wings here, you will grow hair, and if you rub the wings on your breasts, then the breasts will come. We would take their wings and rub here to grow breasts and rub some here to grow hair. Every time, that was our business, in back of the house! *Ha, ha, ha.* We killed *more* butterflies — to get breasts, oh, and get hairs on your vagina, showing that you are growing up, because if you are growing breasts and you don't have this hair, you are nothing, so you must take this thing and rub the two places. Rub here and rub here. And she was *helping* me! *Ha!*

So every time we used to do this in the house to take this man from that Amariya. But the time when I started having breasts, and I started to know what is shame, then I didn't want this man again. But when I was young, I was thinking of marriage and all this.

The Man with Four Noses

Yeah, but my first husband was a man with four noses. *Ha-ha!* Yes, when I was small, I was very, very funny. *Ha-ha!* There was a man who had four noses. It was very funny, eh? *Ha-ha! Ha-ha!* He was African, but I thought he was a *Kwasi Buroni.*[1] Oh yeah? I saw he was black, but I didn't see somebody like that before. The way his nose was, my mind made up that an African man cannot have this kind of nose. Unless a white man. I was young, and I was thinking that only the white people had that, so I had to call him Oburoni, Kwasi Buroni, because of the nose. I used to see white people with long noses, so maybe it's possible for them to get four noses, and so I thought he was a white man. But he was not a white man. He was a black man, an Ashanti man. *Ha-ha!*

You know, I think it was some sickness, but I didn't know about these things. On his nose, one thing came out like this, and it was swollen up

1. (Asante Twi): name for a white man; from "oburoni," white man, and "Kwasi," Sunday-born because on Sundays, the white people would get dressed up. The locals joke that Sunday is the white people's name-day, so they address whites as Kwasi (for men) or Akosua (for women). Kwasi Buroni's wife or sister also has a full name: she is Akosua Mensah; "Mensah" means that she is the third-born of her siblings.

like a boil, but this thing never went away. It was a long time I knew this man, and then the other side too came up. But there wasn't any hole, nothing: just behind, and then it came from the other side, and it was a bit big, and it came from behind again. So it was something like a boil. Yeah? It was a sickness, but the first time, when I didn't understand all this, I thought it was a nice thing. I thought every boil was a nose! *Ha!* So every time when he was passing, I liked to look at it. I would say, "Eh!" Then I used to think some things: "Ah, this man is African? No! It's not possible." But his color was black. The nose, I never saw an African one like that, so always I used to think this man was a white man.

He used to come to our house, with one policeman, to collect *lampeau.*[1] And when I saw him, I ran inside the house to call my brothers and sisters to come and see. I whispered, "Some white man is coming. He's a white man." Then my big brother came and said, *"Pffft,"* and then he went back. So I ran with the other ones, and we were standing by the door. So when this man came, I saw that he was going straight to my father's door, and I ran quickly, and I whispered, "Papa! Papa! Some white man wants to see you." So my father came out. Then he met this man, and they talked about the *lampeau,* and then my father entered the room to take money to pay.

So when my father left me and this man on the veranda—with the policeman—I looked at him, and I said, "O-oh-h." He was sitting down like this, you know, and I was trying to point my hand to the nose, to say that it was nice. Then this man slapped my hand. So I said, "Oh-h, why? Your nose is nice, you know. You are a white man? Are you a white?" *Ha-ha!* Then my father heard my voice, so he came and sacked me. *Ha-ha!* And then, I wasn't satisfied, so I went and stood by the gate. I knew that this man was coming out, and my father would not follow him outside. So I was standing there waiting. When he was coming, I said, "Hey, *Kwasi Buroni, wodeɛ, wo hwene yɛ fɛ o.*" I was talking to him in Ashanti, saying, "Hey white man, you, your nose is nice. As for you, you have four noses. It's nice, eh? I like you." *Ha!*

Then this man was annoyed, so he had to return to the house and tell my father to give me a warning. Then my father beat me for this, that I shouldn't say things like that. He said it's a sickness. So I was crying, "*Eh-h-h-h*—I—oh, but I didn't—I thought it was a nice thing. Because even if his nose is lost, he has another nose! He has no worries. Even if this one is not there, he can rest at night because he has four noses." I didn't think whether a hole was there to make it a nose which can breathe. I don't

1. (French): head tax, a tax levied per person in a house

know what kind of sickness that was. There is some sickness that just cuts the nose off, and the nose used to be lost.[1] I used to see all these things in the market. There was a man in the Kumasi market, and all the bones from the nose were outside, and the nose was not there. You couldn't look at him. And he was begging, begging people for money. When you saw him, *ooh!* It was very pitiful. But the sickness with this man with the four noses, I didn't think it was a sickness. I thought that how some people didn't have a nose, that this man was lucky, because if he lost his nose here, then he had another one, so he wouldn't worry. *Ha!* But it was a bad sickness: this boil didn't have a hole, and I think he couldn't breathe, too. Yeah. There are some bad sicknesses, and that one was a bad one. But when I was very young, I didn't understand these things. So that was my first husband. Yeah. *Ha-haa!*

: ACCRA, TEMA, TAMALE, LOMÉ :

Case Histories

Then when I grew up, they didn't give me to the correct man. Maybe if they gave me to a correct man, I don't think I could do this work. Yeah. And the time when I refused him, if they had patience with me to say, "OK. Rest and choose the one you want," maybe by this time I wouldn't be doing this; maybe I would have married. But my father had no patience, and I also was not patient, so I had to go out from his house. And when I kept myself for about one year, then I thought, "Maybe I'm all right past these people who married." You know? *Ha, ha! He, he!* Yeah. I thought I was better than them, because when I wanted to drink beer, I bought my beer. When I wanted food, I got it. The time when I was married, I didn't know what is drinking, and I didn't know what is beer.

You know, I think that when you start this ashawo, you used to think that it's better than marriage. When you start it when you are young, too, because you have no experience for money, to keep some down, I don't know why, but you used to get money more. When you start it and you are young, and you don't know anything, you used to get money just like that. And you don't know how to spend it. When you get it, you just think, "Tomorrow I'll get more. If I finish this money, then tomorrow, if I haven't got money, I can go to this man and ask him. He told me that any time I am short, I can ask him." And then you continue, you continue.

1. leprosy

And then it comes to the worst. The time when you want to leave this ashawo life, it's not possible! *Ha-ha.* You cannot leave it.

So sometimes it's not the fault of us girls; it's the fault of the family. Yeah. You know my friend Mama Amma.[1] As for Mama, when she told me her story, I can understand her. Mama is from Kumasi. Her mother was in Kumasi. Mama was born alone: she has no sister; she has no brother. She was the only child for the mother. And when she was in school, she used to go to dance. In Africa, if it's not now that we are free, if you are still in school, you will live with your family. You cannot go out after eight o'clock or nine; you must be home with the family. And if you are going to cinema, maybe one of your brothers or one of the family is going, and then you will follow him. You can't go alone. But Mama was alone. And if she did anything, the mother didn't hit her. You don't see that her name is Mama Amma, but we call her "Mama, Mama." Because she was the only child for the mother, the mother was calling her Mama. So when she would go out and come back home, then the mother would go to her, "Oh, Mama. Oh-h, Mama, where did you go? I could not sleep. Oh, Mama, don't do this thing to me."

And Mama said that when her mother told her that, then she would say, "Hey! Look at this old lady. You think I won't go out and dance rock?![2] I'm a student. I don't know how to dance rock. I must go and learn rock, you know, Mama."

Then the mother would say, "No, but if you are going, you can come home early."

Then Mama would say, "OK, tomorrow I will go, but I will come early." And next day when she goes, she will keep late past the day when her mother talked to her. And every time, the mother used to talk this and that, begging her. So this dance Mama was going to, she found a good friend, and she didn't feel for school. And she was growing up, and the mother didn't want to say something to her that would make her annoyed to go away and leave her. So anything Mama did, the mother wouldn't say anything, you know, like to give her advice, that what you are doing is not good, and that and this. The mother didn't do it.

So Mama had her friend. She said that boy was called Kwame. Then the boy went down to Tema, and he wrote her a letter to come to Tema. And she also wrote him and said, "Ah, I cannot come. You know that I'm in school."

Then this boy said, "OK. Then the time when I will come to Kumasi, I'll come and see you." And that boy came to Kumasi, and then Mama

1. The name in Asante Twi would be Maame Ama.

2. dance to rock music

started. Every day when Mama's mother knows that Mama has gone to school, Mama is with this boy. So this boy and Mama made one mouth[1] to talk to the mother that, OK, he likes Mama and he thinks he's going to be married with Mama. So now he's working; he's a cook at Tema. And the white man asked him if he had a wife, and he said yes, so he wants to take Mama to Tema, and show his master that this is the wife, and then he will bring Mama back.

When they went to Tema, Mama didn't come back, and they wrote a letter to the mother that Mama is going to school in Tema. But Mama didn't think of school. *Ha!* She was in love. When she told me this story, I said, "Yeah?!" The first time, how she was going to start, and how she ran away from the family, you know, this was the story she was telling.

Then she was there with this boy, and every time she was OK. And you know, it was foolishness. This is why when many of the girls do these things, I understand some of them. This boy just took Mama as something. Every time, mistake or no mistake: *kah, kah, slap, slap.* You know, sometimes if I say this to people, they say I'm funny, but this is African love. You know, when African lovers are living together without fighting, people will say, "You people don't love each other." Every time they have to blow each other:[2] *brrm, brrm. Ha!* Yeah, if you are married to your husband, and he has been beating you every time, and you go and give your family the complaint, do you know what they tell you? They will say, "Yes. Love is war. Love is: you call somebody to come and make war with you, so it's because your husband loves you very much — that's why all these things are happening." Yeah?!

So Mama got fed up from these beatings, and she said, *"Ah! Awurade Nyankopɔn! Me Maame! Me Maame a wowoome, wonni meho agorɔ.* God, God in heaven! My Mother! My mother, you gave birth to me, you didn't play with me. And then some fucking boy like this, every time he has to beat me." The last day when she was going to see this boy, this boy beat her until she got blood on her mouth. Then she said, "Ah, my mother who gave birth to me, even she never touched here before, and then because of love I'm following this boy to do this to me. He will give me — *sniff, sniff.*" Then she said she went to the mirror, and she looked at herself and said, "Ah, I'm not beautiful, too. If this boy wounds me, where shall I get another nose or other eyes? With my two eyes and with this my ugly nose, this boy is doing all this. If I get half of this off, what shall I do? So the best thing: I have to leave this boy."

She thought of this, and she didn't say anything to the boy. The next

1. agreed; said the same thing
2. give each other blows

day she said she was going to market. She knew some friends in town, so she went to them and told them her trouble, that this boy was doing these things to her. "*Ah! Maame Ama, wo maame a w'ahwɛ wo kama, na w'aba abɛtena obi nkyɛn, na ɔrebɛsɛe wo. Hwɛ w'ano!* Mama Amma! The way your mother looked after you well, and then you come and live with somebody. He's going to spoil your life. Look at your mouth!"

Then Mama also looked at the glass and said, "Yes, I have to leave this boy." Then she said, "If I leave him now, I have no money. What can I do?"

And one girl said, "Oh, you can leave the boy and come and stay with me."

And one girl also said, "Oh, even if you want money to go back to Kumasi, I will give you money. To go back to your mother and go to your school, it's better. But to stay with a stupid boy like this, to be beating you every day, it's not good."

Then Mama thought she could not go back to Kumasi, to the school. So she had to leave the boy and come and stay with the other girl. And then this boy followed Mama and the girl to the house and beat the two of them together. *Ha! Ah!* So the good friend had to tell Mama, "OK, if that will be the case, then I'll get you some money to go away from Tema. You can go to Accra, and this boy cannot do anything to you in Accra."

And Mama said, "I don't know anybody in Accra. How can I go to Accra? How can I go to Accra like that?"

So you know, these girls were having somebody like a father in Accra. He was called Steve. Do you know that Steve? I think he was an American. So when Mama said she didn't know anybody in Accra, this girl said, "OK. Accra and Tema are not far. I will take you to a house and you can be free there. You can do everything, and this boy cannot even dream to come there." Then Mama said this girl brought her, and when they went to Steve's place, there were many girls. They were all happy in that place. And then Mama lived there. And she didn't see this Kwame again, to come and beat her. *Ha!* And Mama was free. But from the first starting, you see, suppose this boy—eh? Don't you think that if this boy was serious, maybe this girl will now be with him as a wife? But how he was not serious, she had to leave.

So we girls, we are bad. But sometimes our boys too, our men too, they are also bad. They treat us badly. And some of us too, it's from the family training: the family is bad, and then we leave. I told you that no girl will choose to grow up and be ashawo. A girl will not even look at it.

When you're in the house with your family, you used to see some nice things. How marriage is, especially in my father's house, when they make this Muslim fasting and finish, the husbands used to buy some gifts for the wives, some nice things to give them as gifts like a Christmas for them. When you are a child and you are in the house, you will see all this, and you will also think that if you grow up, if you marry, you will get a nice man to do all this for you. You wouldn't think to become ashawo.

But if they treat you badly in the marriage, you have to come back. And some people, the family doesn't treat them badly, but they follow the bad boys.

And yeah, some schoolgirls even make it: they follow men to pay the school fees. Especially these Ashantis, *mm?* Ashantis, as for me, every time I used to say what they do is correct for them. Ashantis don't take the properties of their father. If you give birth with an Ashanti, and you have married her, when you people are living together, the child is for you. But if it's coming that you are dead, your child cannot take your property; if you have a sister, your sister's children are the ones who will come and take charge of your property. So these Ashanti girls, some of the fathers look after them in school, and some of them refuse, because you are for your mother. Why should he follow himself to pay your school fees? And then maybe the mother doesn't have anything, and her brothers don't mind her. What shall you do? You have to do this business to pay your school fees. *Hmm?* Some people do that. And especially, I think, the Ashantis: as for them, I understand them.

And these Northern girls, they too, many of the families are poor, and I think it's coming that some girls think it's a nice thing, or some girls think, "Well, I would like a nice dress; I saw one of my girlfriends wearing a nice dress yesterday." Maybe in the family they didn't buy anything for her, so she must try herself to get that kind of dress. And what shall she do? If she's in school, she cannot do anything like work, so maybe she can go to somebody, and then she can get that money to buy something nice for herself.

But it's not everybody. *Ah! Some!* Not all: some. I cannot know the life of everybody. But some: some of the people, when they give you their history, what made them to be making ashawo, what made them this or that or that, then you can know. But you cannot know all of them. And you cannot ask all of them a question. "What are you doing that for?" Unless you get the person who is free with you, then you can talk to her some matters, or questions, or you can say, "I was like this before. And then you, you were like that. But I don't understand why you are making this ashawo, and that and this." And maybe if she's a good person, she will tell you her problem, what brought her to make this life.

In my country, in Upper Volta, especially in Ouagadougou,[1] there are many, many, many, many, many, many Ghanaian girls making ashawo.

1. capital of Burkina Faso, the country to the north of Ghana

You can see that in Ouagadougou they don't respect Ghanaians now, Ghanaian girls. For what? There are many of them. They just leave their husbands. They say, "I'm going to greet my mother," or "I'm going to greet my brother in my village." She will go to Ouagadougou. She's in Ouagadougou. And such kind of woman, when you see her, you will ask, "Oh-h, Auntie"—you know we used to call the married women "Auntie"—*Yie-e, Auntie, na wobaa ha dabɛn?* Hey, Auntie, so when did you come?"

"Oh, I just came here two or three days ago."

"But why? What about your husband?"

"Oh, he's there. I just told him that I'm going to greet my father in my country[1] or my mother or my mother's sister in our country. He doesn't know I'm in Ouagadougou here." What does she mean? She just told the husband that she's going to greet her family. You have a wife, and if your wife is from Kumasi and she tells you, "Oh, you know we have been here where we are living for a long time, so I want to see my family. I want to see how they are. So I want to travel to Kumasi to see all my families," then you will just say OK. You will think she's going to Kumasi, but then she will go back to Ouagadougou. And some of them, they are good. Some of them will stay two months, three months, and when they come, they just buy things. When she gets money, every time she will buy nice, nice dresses and all, and then she will go back to the husband! And some of them, maybe some people will see her in Ouagadougou, and when she returns back, she will not have a chance for marriage again. So she has to go back to Ouagadougou again. *Ha!* Yeah!

There were two Dagbamba[2] girls who came to Ouagadougou together. One girl was called Zara, and the other girl was called Fati. They said that now Fati is in Savelugu.[3] Fati came with a *small* baby; even it was in Ouagadougou that this baby started to walk. One day I asked her, "Oh, Fati, but why? Why didn't you let your baby grow and then give it to your mother before you came?"

She said, "No. I didn't want to give my baby to my mother before I came. I didn't come here to be ashawo. I was an ashawo for many years, and I think I got about three Singers"—Singer machines, you know, to sew. She had three. And then she wanted to have a baby, and she tried but she didn't get. She was in Ghana, and she went round-round-round-round, and everywhere they told her that she should go to this village

1. her traditional area or her hometown or village
2. large cultural group in northern Ghana, around Tamale and Yendi
3. small town about fifteen miles north of Tamale

or that village, and they will make juju for her to have a baby.[1] And she tried all: it was nothing. Then she met one small boy. This girl was older than this boy by seven years. They became friends; then this boy was ashamed because everybody knew this woman was an old lady.[2] So if she was going to this boy, she must hide herself, and this boy also must wait until the people in his house sleep before he could bring this woman inside. Just small-small like that, then she conceived. This boy didn't work; he was only a farmer to get food in the house, but he had no money. Then they had their first baby. All this girl's dresses which she was having before, she used them to make trousers for this baby boy or shirts for this boy. Then she didn't have any cloth again; all her cloths had become old. She had to sew them, patching them in some ways to get something to wear.

At that time she was in Ghana, and she was a girlfriend to that Zara. Zara was married to a soldier. So one day, Zara said, "Eh, my sister is in Ouagadougou. She used to bring many things—big, big bags and big things—and we are here suffering. Ah! Fati, as for me, I'm going to leave the country, because—because I think my husband is letting me suffer much, and he doesn't give me anything. He's a soldier man; he has money. As for you, your own case is better. You know that your man is a farmer; he cannot get anything, but he can get food for you people to eat. But for my own man, he's a government worker, and every month they pay him. But he doesn't want even to buy me a cloth. So I'm tired. The cloths I brought from my mother's house[3] are getting old. So I will go to ask of my sister in Ouagadougou."

Then Fati said, "Ah, if that will be the case, I will follow you." This is how the friends are! Some people go by the friend's way, you know. So they made an arrangement together, and Zara was in Tamale,[4] and she came to Savelugu. The family of Zara was at the back of Kumbungu.[5] If you pass Kumbungu, there is another village called Voggo. It's a small village. I have been to that place, but it's long time; maybe now it's not the same. Zara told the husband that she was going to Voggo, and the husband gave her thirty-six cedis to go to Voggo to see her family. That was the charge for her from Tamale to Savelugu to Ouagadougou. And she is still in Ouagadougou now.

1. Many local shrines are known for their ability to treat infertility.
2. People would criticize or abuse him.
3. I brought when I was married
4. major town of northern Ghana
5. from Tamale, on the other side of Kumbungu, a village northwest of Tamale

She has a driver of this big, big truck. This man is going to Kaya,[1] Bobo,[2] Abidjan, and all these places. He rented her a big room and—oh!—he gave her everything: only a fridge she hasn't got. She has a very big record changer. She didn't tell the husband she was leaving him or she was going to go to Ouagadougou; the husband thought she was going to her village. And now I think she's about seven or eight months in Ouagadougou. What will the husband think about? By all means the husband will hear that the wife is in Ouagadougou. But she didn't tell him she was leaving the marriage.

And this Fati who came with her, she is a Dagbana.[3] How Dagbamba are, if you marry a Dagbana girl, if she has a baby with you, and you are a Dagbana, you won't worry. Even if this woman goes out to another country, you wouldn't worry because if Dagbamba have a baby and the baby is young, they don't make love. They wait until the baby walks before they make love. But if a Dagbana girl goes out with your baby and the baby doesn't walk, if she makes love with another man, she cannot come back to you. If you like, you can take your baby. But if this woman has made love with another man, if she comes back to the father and makes love with the father, the baby will die. So Dagbamba are like that.

This Fati stayed in Ouagadougou four good months, and she didn't make love with anybody. She just served in the bar, and anybody who said he wanted her, she would say, "No, I have a small baby. I cannot make love with a man." She was just like that every time. Then she returned to Ghana. The day I was asking of her, they said she went back to the husband, and they conceived again. She wanted to have babies because she walked a lot of places, but she didn't give birth. Then when she went back to her house, they were abusing her, "Hey, you just want to make ashawo; you don't want to have a baby." So now when she started to get babies, she closed everything. She forgot about ashawo; she forgot about everything. And she's serious to be married. She went and stayed in Ouagadougou four months working in a bar. Every month they pay them eight thousand francs.[4] With this eight thousand, she will buy one piece

1. small town north of Ouagadougou

2. Bobo-Dioulasso, the major town in western Burkina Faso

3. singular of Dagbamba

4. 8,000 francs CFA, Francophone African currency indexed to French francs. CFA stands for la Communauté Financière Africaine. 50 CFA were previously equal to one French franc; in 1994, the currency was devalued to 100 francs CFA to 1 French franc, or 1 centime. In 1999, CFA francs were pegged to the euro at just under 656 francs per euro. In this book, U.S. dollar prices for CFA therefore directly reflect the prices for French francs. In the 1970s, with the dollar generally between 4 and 5 French francs, CFA varied between

of cloth for herself and some small-small clothes for the baby. And after four months, she will go back again.

You know, I asked one girl, "So Fati, she is in Savelugu now?"

The girl said, "Yes, she is making *adeɛ-yie.*"[1] Do you know *adeɛ-yie?* The tailors who don't know how to sew a full dress, but if you have some place cut, they can patch it for you: in Ghana we used to call them *adeɛ-yie,* that they can make something well. So Fati is at Savelugu, and she has now conceived a girl with the husband, and every time she carries her machine[2] to make *adeɛ-yie.*

Then I said, "It's nice." So some people are serious. You know, I think that as for her, she started with this ashawo, so she knew The Life. But if you don't start with this and you don't know The Life, if you go away to join it, you won't go back. They were two who went. Yeah? Both of them thought to go and get many things to come back to their husbands. And the one remained in Ouagadougou. But Fati, when she meant to do something, she was serious, and she came back. And the other one who wasn't serious is now in Ouagadougou. She has a *tall* Mossi[3] man. This man is *very* tall, and this girl is short like me. She's staying with the man there.

Sometimes if they are sitting, I say, "He-ey. Ah, so you are with this man? Are you fit to carry him?"

Then she will say, "Why? Why? But you know, we don't carry them like a load." *Ha-ha-ha!* She is still there, but this other girl came back to the husband who will give her a nice pregnancy.

So it's according to everybody's men, you know, according to their men — the men you met before, or what your man makes you to do. Some girls do ashawo because they think it's life, because they see ashawo people wear nice dresses, and they think, "Ah, if I am ashawo, I can also dress nicely," and they jump up[4] to become ashawo. And some people, they have a program before they become ashawo. So it's not the same. You cannot say all of their lives are the same.

You can find some rich children, and the parents do everything for their children in the house, even in Ghana. You can find one rich man's

---

200 and 250 to the dollar, only occasionally pushing 300 or above. Generally in this book, one can use 250 CFA per dollar to calculate amounts.

1. (Asante Twi): ɔyɛ-adeɛ-yie; she is doing (making) something well, i.e., she is doing patching. Such tailors and seamstresses can be seen carrying their sewing machines on their heads and going around to houses.

2. going around to houses or to the market, carrying her Singer machine on her head

3. large cultural group in Burkina Faso, centered around Ouagadougou

4. get up quickly (without thinking)

daughter in Lido, and she's boasting, "My father is this; my father is that." But why don't you live with your father? She doesn't want it because she thinks the father is a big man, so she can do this thing freely, and nobody can beat her, and nobody can trouble her, and she thinks it's a good life.

Do you know Cynthia Oppong? I think I have heard that she has gone to America, but I don't know what country of America. She was at Lido before. A very black girl. She was the daughter of one army captain or lieutenant or something. It was one boy called Sammy who spoiled her. She was in a boarding school, and this boy Sammy was the boyfriend of this girl. The father was making trouble with Sammy, so Sammy took Cynthia to Kumasi, to hide her. The way some people used to run away to marry with the girlfriends, Sammy and Cynthia made this way. But they didn't marry. Cynthia went and found another thick friendship in Kumasi which was thick more than Sammy, so she had to shit[1] Sammy, and then Sammy also got another girlfriend, Rose, a half-caste[2] girl. When Cynthia shit Sammy, that she has got another good man, then Sammy also said, "OK. I won't take any black color again; I'm going to take black and white, and bluff Cynthia."

And then Cynthia also shit everything and went to Togo. When she went to Togo, she also got someone of the same color as what Sammy got in Ghana, a half-caste boy, and she had a baby with this boy. In six months, she threw the baby at this boy and said, "Oh, I'm not a woman who can marry. I'm not going to marry you. But the baby we have, if you like the baby, you can have the baby; if you don't like, then I'll take the baby for my mother." So this boy took the baby to his mother. And Cynthia flew away — to Lagos. From Lagos, I heard that she is in America now. She got somebody to fly away with.

This girl could smoke and smoke groove. She will come into the nightclub and she will start to loosen her buttons, "Who can help me?" And she will look in everybody's eyes. "Can you help?" If you are looking at her, then: "Can you help?"

Then some people will say, "Oh, Cynthia, what are you doing? No, it's not good."

Then she will say, "OK. Many people are saying it's not good. So I will close it. But anyway, excuse me, you know. I'm Cynthia Oppong." *Ha-ha!* Because the father was one of the army people, these soldier people, a thick man there, so every time she wanted to call the name to show the family,

1. get rid of, ignore, dismiss, snub

2. a light-skinned person, of mixed race, generally African and European; half black and half white

that she is from the top family. *Ha-ha.* So in Lomé when we met her, we used to call the full name, "Hey, Cynthia Oppong, Cynthia Oppong."

Cynthia had a small dog, and any time she went out, she put this dog under her arm. The dog was for the father of the baby she had. She would put the dog here, and then this girl would go — Look! Lomé is not big, *hmm?*— but this girl would go with taxi, up and down, up and down, up and down. Then she would go to the husband to take ten thousand. Then this boy got fed up.

So what this boy did: he had a car, and he had every drink in the house. We called him Onassis. Every girl liked Onassis, and he was lucky with girls, too. So he said, "Ah, why should I be cool like that to this girl? Because it's Cynthia Oppong? I am also Onassis. So we are going to show." When the boy drank and thought of this, he would say, "No! I'm going to find this girl!" And he would take his car, round-round-round-round-round, to every nightclub.

Everywhere Cynthia was going, too, she had this dog. If she was going to the nightclub, this small dog was here under her arm. *Ha-ha!* It was funny, you know. So when she was coming with her dog, then sometimes, "Hey, Cynthia!"

"Warf, warf, warf-warf!"

Then she said, "*Sh-h-h.* Shut up." Then this dog would shut up.

So this boy would be going round-round. Whatever place he would meet Cynthia, he would say, "Cynthia, oh, please. Let's go home."

"Why? I'm not going. You are with me, no? You are with me!"

Then he would say, "What are you telling me? You see, the baby is crying. Let's go home."

"What? But this is a baby also!" Then she would press this dog, you know. "This baby is also a baby; it's a small baby dog, so it's also a baby. I'm with your baby, so you must look after my baby, too."

So this boy would start: *Tchak, tchak, slap, slap.* And Cynthia would say, "If you beat me, I will kill your dog!" *Ha!* "If you beat me, I will kill your dog!" And then she would start to squeeze this dog, and the dog would be shouting, *"Hayii, hayi-i, hayi-i-i!"* You know, she hadn't got strength to beat the boy, so she would beat the dog and squeeze the dog, and then this dog: *"Hayii! Hayii!"*

Then people would say, "Oh, Onassis. If you don't pity for the girl, you should pity for the dog. It's a young dog. Don't do that."

Then Onassis would say, "OK. Let's go home."

Then Cynthia: "I won't go. You are forcing me, so I won't go home again. It's finished. You can go and get my baby for me and come and take your baby."

Every night they were like that. *Ha!* Every night! And after six months, Cynthia gave this baby to this boy, that if he doesn't want the baby, she'll take the baby to her mother. And this boy said, "OK. I want the baby." So he took the baby, and Cynthia went to Lagos. And from Lagos, I heard that now she's in America. I don't know who took her, but they said some man took her from Lagos to America. So now she's a big guy. It's Cynthia Oppong, you know! *He-he-he! Hee-hee! Oh!*

So some people join The Life like that, and some people have a program before joining this kind of life. Some people, the time they will start this, they aren't happy. They are not happy to join it, and they force to join it, and maybe the time will come and they will be all right with it. And some—*ha!*—some of the girls just see it as a nice life, so they have to join it.

Look. I think Cynthia was living in a nice house, and the father also liked her. You know this *apɔtɔyowa,*[1] this small mortar we grind pepper in. If you give pepper to Cynthia to grind in your *apɔtɔyowa,* she's an Ashanti, but for her to grind this pepper, she will grind it from now until tomorrow morning. She does not know how to grind it. When she was at school, she didn't do anything. At the father's house, they had a cook, they had everything, and she said that if she came home sometimes and she felt like to going to kitchen, the father would call her, "Cynthia! Why are you going to—all this smoke—to smell this smoke? Come here." Then when she came, then the father would give her a pen with a book and say, "You have to do your studies. It's better for you not to go there." Then when the food was ready, they would just ring a bell—*Pling, plang, plang!*—and Cynthia would come and sit down and eat. She was living well, isn't it? But she saw the girls with this kind of life, and she thought it's good, so she said, "I must join them."

So you cannot say everybody's life. You cannot know everybody's life, to know how they joined this. Some people join it because their way is not good. And some people think it's the good life. And then some people play, and they also come to join it. Yeah?

1. (Asante Twi): mortar for grinding small vegetables

PART TWO *With the British in a Provincial Capital*

4 THE CHIEF OF BAGABAGA

: ACCRA :

Nigel's Courtship

Then: I was at Accra and I got a man. Nigel Manners. *Heh-heh-heh.* The first time I saw him, I was at Lido. Lido was closing up. I just came out, and I saw somebody with a Vauxhall. I saw the license number: it was an AT number, so it was from the North.[1] Then this man called me. He had a big voice, like a soldier: *"Hey?!* Hey?! My dear, come *here!"* Then I went to the car. And he said, "Can't you find any place to drink?"

And I said, "Oh, I can't find any place. But if you like, we can drink at my house." This woman where I lived had a fridge, so every time I used to put drink in her fridge.

So he said, "OK."

So we went to my house. Then I was staying near to Silver Cup. When we went there, we had two bottles of beer, and then he said he won't drink more, and we should go and I would know where he was living. I went with this man. He was living at Cantonments. You know, it's a very funny story. Nigel Manners! *Ha-ha!* He was staying with one of his friends. The

1. The license plate letters showed where the car was registered.

friend was a Scottish man. When Nigel would go to Accra, he used to lodge with that man. So he was in Tamale, but he came for a conference in Accra.

So when we went to this place, I slept there. The next morning, this man gave me these Nkrumah cedis. Do you know the Nkrumah cedis? Eight and fourpence, no?[1] One cedi was eight and fourpence, I think. He gave me one Nkrumah cedi! And all this money was *coins!* What a bloody hell! An old man like a grandfather like this? *Tsk!* "*Hey?!* What are you doing?"

He said, "Ah! Ah! My dear, I have nothing. It's all my last money. But you know, I like you." *Ha! Ha!* "You shouldn't worry. I'll get something for you, and then I'll come to you evening time."

So I said, "OK, but it's best you take your cedi. I don't want it." So he dropped me at my place. He said he would come evening time that day, Sunday; he didn't come. I was waiting for him on Monday—he didn't come. Eh? So this old man is a guy?[2] You know? *Ha!* This was what I thought. Uh-*huh!* He's a guy old man. I said nothing.

Tuesday, he came about ten o'clock. He told me that he had a lot of work. That's why he hadn't come.

When he came, I had just dressed up. I was going to go to Lido, but you know, when he came, Lido became something like I didn't want to go there again. *Ha!* Because I had many people who I knew, many friends and girlfriends, and if they knew I was with this kind of man, I wouldn't be happy much. So I told him, "Let's go to Star Hotel. It's better." *Ha!*

He said, "OK." Then we picked one of his friends, and we went together to Star Hotel. Oh, we were enjoying: he bought many drinks. We left Star Hotel about two o'clock or half-past one.

Then I thought, "Ah, maybe today, this man will pay all, because the first one he didn't pay, and so this is the second one. Maybe, how he is an old man, he will be a nice man." *Ha-ha!*

So we went and slept at his place there, and the next morning he told me he was going to Tamale. So he had to bring me home. So he said, "OK. Let's go. I'll drop you." I thought maybe when we reached my house, he would give me something, you know, but when he got to my place, what this man had to give me—it was all coins, eh?—twenty or twenty-two pesewas. That Nkrumah money he brought, it was making about two shillings, or twenty-two pesewas. These coins?! *Ha-ha!* Then I took the money and threw it in his face. Then he said, "Oh, Mary. You know, I haven't got much. Here is not Tamale. I live in Tamale. I am a teacher in

1. in terms of the former British-based currency
2. in this context, a hustler

the Training College. I haven't enough money. I have spent all my money, and I cannot get any money until I go back to Tamale. So I am going away today. So you have to give me your address; I can write you and send you something."

I was annoyed! I don't need the way he is talking to me. So I said, "I haven't got an address. And so what shall you do now?!"

Then he said, "Oh! Try to find an address for me."

You know, I wasn't happy to give him my address, because I didn't have much belief in him. So there was one Ewe woman where I was living. Auntie Dora. She was a hairdresser. She was there. I told her, "This man said he wants my address, but this kind of people, I'm not sure of them."

Dora said, "Never mind. If you want an address, I can give my address to you to give him."

Then I said, "No, this is not your business. Why should you put your mouth inside? This man has to pay me. I have slept with him two times. Why? I'm not making a credit for him to go to Tamale to pay. No!" *Ha-ha!*

So this woman said, "OK, how much do you think he has to pay you for the two days?"

I said, "OK, I don't take it to be serious. He's a grandfather, you know. I can call him a grandfather, so even if he's not nice, he must give me sixty cedis or I will take the car key. I won't give this car key to him. Then I have to sell this car, and I will take my sixty cedis and give him the balance."

So Dora laughed. "Do you think you can sell this car easily?"

I said, "Yes!"

"For what?"

"*Ah!* For what?? This man went with me two times and deceived me and told me that he's going to Tamale to send me money. Do you believe this?"

So Dora said, "OK." To cut the whole case short, she will give me the sixty cedis. She will lend this man sixty cedis to give me, and then she will give her address. If this man is good, if he will pay her, she likes it; if he doesn't pay her, she also likes it. *Eh?* She didn't know the man! I don't know why she did this. So this woman gave me sixty cedis. I didn't care. I took my sixty cedis, and this woman wrote her address for this man. When this man went to Tamale, in about three days we had a letter from Tamale. He was sending a check—150 cedis—that we should go to Barclay's Bank near the Circle[1] to collect the money. So this woman took the sixty cedis out and gave me ninety cedis.

1. roundaboat at a major intersection in Accra

Then this man had sent me a chain with this money — a gold chain with a Lebanese cross. He said he had put my name, and God will bless me, and God will help me on the road to come to him in Tamale, and all this. Then I said, "Ah, what a bloody hell!" Ninety cedis to take me from Accra to Tamale! It's not possible. It is not enough. Ah! That ninety cedis — *abi!*[1] The same day I got this money: *Ah!* U.T.C.! Kingsway! I didn't bring any balance[2] home. Even I didn't bring one cedi home. Yeah? I spent all the same day. So I just spent the money and then I didn't write again; I didn't give any answer.

Then Dora said, "Did you give an answer?"

"Yeah. Yeah. I replied." But it was a long time — about one week — and Dora didn't get his reply, so I said, "I don't know what this man is doing. I have given a reply, but he has to reply me before I go."

So this man was waiting long, about one week, and he didn't get any reply, so he wrote another letter again, to ask me whether I'm coming or I'm not coming. Then I replied and said, "Ah, well, the money you have given me is not enough. The money I'm paying for my room, even you know that I pay sixteen cedis a month for my room. And you sent me ninety cedis. And then I have bought many things which I didn't pay for. Even my furniture, you know I told you that I didn't pay for it all. I paid half, and then they gave me the furniture. So I have to pay all. I cannot leave all this debt here and then come to Tamale." That was how I replied him.

So he sent Dora two hundred cedis to give me. OK. The two hundred cedis, I waited about one week, then I replied him that, "Yeah, I have finished all my debt, but I have to get some money to pack all my things to Kumasi, you know, to hire a car, because to take all these things to Kumasi, I must get a special car to hire." So then he sent more money again, another two hundred cedis. And this was the money we were going to fight for. *Ha-ha!* That two hundred cedis, oh, in about one week it was also getting finished. When I started to go inside that money, too, that woman was annoyed. She was a nice woman. It was left sixty cedis, and then Dora refused to give me that sixty cedis.

I said, "Ah, why? When this man came here, I was the one going with him. If I have my money, I have to spend it. You can't seize this money. You are not my sister; you are not my family."

Then this woman said, "No! You must go to Tamale."

1. (Yoruba, also Pidgin): or. The word is used for emphasis, like saying, "Or what?!" or "Isn't it?" or "It's true, or am I lying?"

2. change

"I won't go. Is it a force? I think you like this old man. If you like him, you can go with him: you're an old lady; you're good for him. You can go to stay with him if you like. I will give you a chance. I will never tell anybody that he was my friend before you took him from me."

Then this woman was annoyed. So she said, "OK, we are going to see the way you are going to leave Accra here."

Then I said, "OK. You can't do anything to me. I'm paying my room. You cannot sack me."

So this woman didn't say anything. Then the next day when I was sleeping, she brought the police! Early in the morning, they came and arrested me. *Ha-ha!* They took me to the police station. You know, I didn't understand why they arrested me. So they took me to police station, and then this woman came. She said I am the daughter of the younger sister, but the younger sister has married to a Voltaique. That's why they gave me all these marks on my face.[1] But now she thinks I want to be an ashawo — she doesn't want it. I have got somebody who says that he is going to marry me. He's going to stay with me; if I am good, he will marry me. And this man was sending me money every time. And I was eating the money, deceiving the man, and I wouldn't go to the man, and all this.

So! This is a case for police? Yeah! Adabraka police station! Then Dora said that if I don't want to go to the man, then it's better they send me back to my mother at Kumasi. She doesn't want to see me in Accra. *Eh!* What kind of fucking case is this?! And then, you know, I was very short. If anybody saw me, they would think that I was very young, too, so I was afraid. At that time too, they used to catch girls and send them to the school for bad children, Nkwadaabɔne. Yeah, it's for the children who they send from the family to keep them there like a prison, but you can learn things there. So I was afraid to go to that house.

So then the police people said, "If you don't want the man, we will send you to your mother at Kumasi. If you don't want to go to your mother, then you better go to the man. Otherwise we are sending you to Nkwadaabɔne. Which one do you choose?"

In Kumasi, too, I had trouble with my family. Since I left Kumasi, I didn't go back there. So I didn't want to go back to Kumasi. So the best thing: "OK. I will go to the man in Tamale."

So they reported[2] me. You know, it was like reporting because it was two police women who took me to Accra station and found a big truck. Then they put me inside, and they gave a paper to the driver that he

1. cicatrization or facial scars to identify cultural or family heritage
2. in this context, took into custody

shouldn't let me drop on the road. So always I was in front with the driver. *Ha-ha!* Everywhere we reached, in the night or in the daytime, this driver had to be a watchman for me. *Ha-ha!* And then I had a small pussycat. I liked this pussycat, so when I was going away, I took my cat and put it in a sugar carton. I made holes in the carton, and this cat was with me the whole time from Accra. We made four roads[1] on the road to Tamale. The first day we slept at Ho. The next day we slept at some village—I forgot the name—it was also an Ewe village. The third day we slept at Bimbila.[2] And from Bimbila, we came up to Yendi.[3] And this driver was telling me some story again, that he was going to Bawku,[4] so I have to follow him up to Bawku, and then when he's coming from Bawku we will pass Tamale. Then I said, "No! I'm tired from this big lorry. So I would like to take a car from here."

Then he said, "Ah, but the police people gave me your papers."

Then I said, "Did I steal? I didn't steal. So what kind of papers can police people give you? On my papers they told me to come to the North. And from here to Tamale is not far. I will join a car[5] by myself, and I will go to Tamale." So this driver had to find another truck, to give the same papers they gave him at Accra, to give to that driver to watch me. *Ha-ha!* Yeah? By force, eh? This was force! That woman is still in Accra. Dora. Every time when I used to go to her, later, the time when Nigel started building a house for me, sometimes he used to go and greet her, and he would say she's his mother-in-law. So this woman used to say to me, "OK, now, when you get this house, are you going to give it to me?" *Ha-ha!*

The Two Wives of the Chief of Bagabaga

So when we got to Yendi, this driver gave the papers to another driver to take me. That man took me to Tamale, and he also had to find a taxi driver to put me inside, to take me to Bagabaga,[6] to the Training College. And this taxi driver didn't know that place. We went round-round; we didn't see anybody. Then we saw some laborers who used to pick up the

1. four days; four drives or itineraries
2. small town southeast of Tamale
3. small town sixty miles east of Tamale
4. small town in upper northeast corner of Ghana
5. board a passenger vehicle
6. suburb of Tamale

grass on the road. I said, "Stop." Then he stopped, and I said to the laborers, "Oh, I want bungalow number two."

And they said, "Oh, this is it on your left." We were just standing in front of number two when we asked, and they said, "Look there."

And then I saw the number. "Oh. It's here."

So when we got to the house, the driver stopped. I took my things out, with my small pussycat. I knocked the door, and a woman opened the door. She said, "Who do you want?"

"I want Nigel Manners."

"Nigel Manners has gone to work. He's not in."

"Please, can I keep my things here?"

And then this woman was looking at me. "OK, if you like." And I got my things inside.

Then I asked her, "Is it possible to telephone Nigel in his office?"

She said, "Yes."

"What is the telephone number?"

She said, "I don't know. You can find it."

So the Bagabaga telephone, the times they're in the office, if you wanted to telephone, you had to telephone the school office before they could telephone to town for you. So I just picked up the telephone, and then somebody answered. "Hello? Hello?"

Then I said, "Is that Nigel?"

"No, Nigel—it's not Nigel. I'm the messenger."

Then I said, "Please, I want to see Nigel."

So he called Nigel, and Nigel came, and I said, "Oh, I'm arrived, but I don't see you at home."

"Who are you? Mary?!?"

I said, "Yes."

"Oh, wait! I'm coming!"

Mm-hm. You know, when he was in Accra, he used to put on trousers and all this. So when he was coming home, I was watching the window. He was with big knickers,[1] like a skirt. You know? "Is that Nigel? It's not him." *Ha-ha!* And his stomach was *big!* It was big past the time I saw him in Accra. Then I said, "What the hell? Is it the same man, or it's another Nigel?!" *Ha-ha!*

So he came. "Oh, Mary!"

And I said, "Oh."

"How was your journey?"

1. wide-legged shorts. Women's culottes are also called knickers.

And I said, "I have suffered on the road, before I arrived."

So this woman started, *"Mmm-m-m. Oh-o-o-o-o."* This woman didn't like it, because he had already told her that he has a girl who is going to come from Accra, so this woman must leave the house. And this woman wasn't happy. And so he didn't sack her at once. He said we would all live together. And I said I didn't care. So we were two. Then he gave a room to this woman, in the quarters behind the house.

Every night, we would go to the Gymkhana Club,[1] and we were two women, with him. And then every time, he wanted to be big. "Hey! Hey, hey! My dear! Hey!" Then when we were drunk, he would hold this woman and hold me, too, and he would call the barman. "Hey! Yakubu! Come and see! Do you know the Bagabaga-Naa?"—Do you know what is "Naa"? In Dagbamba language, it means chief, so he's the Bagabaga Chief—"Hey! You see?! You think I'm a fucking man? You think fucking Nigel Manners is a fucking man? Don't you know that fucking Nigel Manners is a rich man? *Eh?* Bagabaga-Naa! I have two wives! Eh, my dear? Look at my small wife![2] Look at the big one!" *Ha-ha!* Yeah.

We could stay at this club up to six or seven o'clock in the morning, drinking, and then we would come home. This woman too could drink. Every morning, when we came home, before we would sleep, we had to drink in the house again. So sometimes I would sleep about seven o'clock or eight o'clock. Then, after about one hour, this woman would come and knock the door. *Pom pom pom pom. Pom pom pom pom.* "Mary! Mary! Mary! Mary!" Then I wouldn't mind her. Even if I heard, I didn't mind her. Then she would say, "Oh-h, will you please open the door for me? I want to take my tea."

Then I'd say, "Ah! What a bloody hell!" This woman was troubling me. Every morning time, I couldn't sleep.

"Open the door; I want to take my tea."

So I used to tell Nigel, "Hey, Nigel. Open for your wife. She wants to take tea. I'm not a maidservant for your wife, to be opening the door every morning. So you go and open the door."

And Nigel told me, "I will open it," and that day, come and see. *Ay, ay, ay, ay, ay!*

This woman wanted to beat me. "You are the one who is giving Nigel bad advice." And that and this. "I thought you are my small sister—that's why I let—Do you think Nigel can bring another woman to sack me to the quarters, and then I will stay there? I will beat that fellow! But I

1. a British colonial drinking club
2. junior wife, the one most recently married

thought that you—I think—I will take you like my small sister. That's why all these things—I don't mind—and then—you know, you are trying to give bad advice to Nigel." And that and this.

I didn't say anything. No. She was abusing me for the *whole day.* I didn't say anything, because I knew she was strong past me. She's my mother, so if I play, she can beat me like a daughter. And so whatever she said, I didn't say anything. I went inside and I turned on the record player to play music. She came and stopped it. She said, "Yeah, Nigel bought this for me. It's not for you." And that and this.

And so when Nigel came home, I said, "Ah, so this changer is not for you? And then you are bluffing that you brought it from London."

He said, "It's for who?"

I said, "It's for Elizabeth. Elizabeth told me that you bought it in London for her."

Then Nigel was annoyed. He said, "OK, Elizabeth will never enter here again."

Then I too said, "I won't touch this player again." So he has to go and buy me a new player, if he wants me to stay. So we went to the town. Near to Rivoli Cinema there was a Lebanese shop, and this Lebanese man was selling players and such things. We went there, then Nigel bought me a record player. Then: I didn't want all the old records, too; I wanted my own records. So he bought records for me, and then he bought me one foot machine for sewing.[1] *Hey!*

So now I have brought trouble to the house. This woman was with Nigel for three years, and Nigel didn't do anything for her! Then he just gets me for about two days, and he bought this record player, and he bought a sewing machine and all this! And so now, every time, this woman had to come and cause trouble with me.

Then I was fed up. You know? I didn't tell Nigel anything; I didn't tell her anything. One morning time, Nigel went to work, and I packed all my things. I left his record player; I left his sewing machine. I didn't want anything. I just packed what I brought from Accra, then—*pap!*—I went back to Accra.

Then he was writing me, "Oh, Mary, come! I have sacked that fucking woman."

I said, "Oh-h!" I didn't want to reply. If I saw a letter from Tamale, I didn't even want to see what is inside. Then: I was staying in my house in Accra, and he sent the school driver there. I think the driver was coming to do something in Accra, and Nigel gave him the address, and this driver

1. a sewing machine that uses a foot pedal to operate it

came and found my house. When this driver came, I was out. When I came back, they said, "Oh, your man has sent a driver from Tamale to pick you up."

Then I said, "Me? I'm not going."

Then this driver came back and met me. He said, "Eh, ah, Nigel said if you don't come, he will go back to London."

I said, "Ah! He can go back to London. I'm not the one who brought him. It's not because of me he came here. He came to do his work. When he knows that now he has money from Africa, and he wants to go back, he can go back. It's not because of me he's here."

Then this driver said, "No, madame, don't say that." This driver was trying to boss me.

And I said, "Hey, my dear, you cannot boss me. I'm not going!" *Ha-ha!*

So this driver went away. About three days, a teacher came, Mr. Bedu. Mr. Bedu came, too. "Eh-h, the Principal said I have to bring you." And that and this.

And then I said, "No. I'm not going, Mr. Bedu."

He said, "Oh, if you do so, it's not good. This time, our Principal is worried. Even if you come to the office, he shouts on people. He didn't do that before. So if you do that, he won't work well."

And I said, "Hey! You people cannot boss me. This man has married in his country. Even his wife is in London. He doesn't have a broken heart. What about me? How many days did I stay with him, and he got a broken heart to spoil his work? Maybe he wants to go away. I'm not coming. Nobody can boss me." So this man also tried for two days. I said I wouldn't go, so he went back.

After about one week, Nigel came by himself. When he came, I was not in the house. In Kokomlemle, you know, there is a wooden house—Apache House—they used to sell groove there. Do you know Apache? I used to leave my house every time to go there. When I grooved, then I would sleep there in the daytime. So I was smoking groove, eating a lot, and then I covered my head and slept on a table. Then Apache said, "Hey, hey, hey." I woke up. Then he said, "Somebody wants you."

I said, "Where is the man?" When I took the cloth off my head, I saw Nigel.

"Oh! Mary!"

And I said, "Don't touch me! Don't talk to me! Get out! Fucking man like you. You want to marry two? Look at the man who wants to marry two. So you think I'm a fool? Don't you know that if I want to marry a man your age with another woman to be two, I would have married a long time ago? Or do you think there is not any African man who is rich like you, who is old like you, who likes me? It's because I don't want the trouble with two wives. That's why." *Ha-ha!*

He said, "Oh, no! I have sacked Elizabeth." And that and this. "Let's go to Tamale. Even we can go — if Elizabeth — if you like, you can leave your everything. We will go and you will see if she's there. Then you can come back. I can pay your in-and-out transport. Then you can come back."

"No! I won't go."

Then Mr. Prempeh, the house owner from the house I used to stay, when Nigel went to look for me, he had sent Nigel with a small girl to look for me at Apache House. So they went and called Mr Prempeh, and he said, "No, Hawa, I know this man from Takoradi.[1] When he came first with his wife, he was a good friend of mine. So if you like, you can go and see if that woman is there, and if you aren't happy, then you can telephone me, or you can write me with the address. So you must go. You are my daughter, and if I see that something is going to be good for you, I cannot allow you to refuse like that." So I must go with this man!! OK? Now, this is another old man who is begging me, so I shouldn't say no. So I said I will go and see.

So when we went to Tamale, Nigel had already sacked this woman to the town. This woman was not in Bagabaga again. But every blessed time when I didn't go to town with Nigel, when Nigel went alone in the night time, when he was coming, he's going to bring this woman — and they are both drunk!

"*Eh!* Mary! Come and see that fucking Elizabeth! *Eh?* You see Elizabeth loves me? I told her Mary is in the house: she never minds. She's coming to greet you. Eh, Mary! Come and see! I brought Elizabeth!" Then I would pretend I'm sleeping; I wouldn't mind them. And every time he was doing this thing.

Then one day, Nigel told me he lost his money. And you know, I don't like this kind of thing. You know? You're living with somebody, and he tells you he lost his money. It used to pain me! It's not my business, stealing from people I'm living with. So this thing *pained* me. Then I said, "No. Nigel. I think that when you were here with Elizabeth, you haven't lost your money before. And now I'm here, and you lost your money. It's best if I go away. I don't want such things."

Then he said, "*No, no, no, no!* Eh, Mary! I know Elizabeth is a big thief. Every time she steals from me."

"How did you know that? You are still with her every time. You said you don't want her in your house; and you used to bring her from town."

1. major town, former main port, in southwest Ghana

He said, "Ah, it's not me. She loves me. When she sees me anywhere, she wants to follow me. It's OK. I'm not making love with her, so it's OK." *Ha-ha!*

I didn't say anything. So one Wednesday, we went to the Tombola[1] at Gymkhana Club. Do you know that Nigel took his pistol? We played Tombola. When Tombola finished, I used to joke with one Swiss man. They called him Fritz. So when we finished this Tombola, Fritz and I were playing and joking, dancing. And Nigel was drunk. Then Nigel said Fritz was carrying me, dancing and all this. Then he said, "Eh? My friend Fritz! Come here! Today, you know, eh, I'm going to kill you." *Ha-ha!* Nigel was very funny, eh?

Then Fritz said, "I will beat you like my own son!"

Then I said, "Oh, Fritz, don't do that."

Then Nigel said, "Eh? You think a fucking boy like you is fit to beat a captain — a British Army Captain? You think you are fit to beat me? Eh? Ask German people what I did with them. And you! Small boy like you! Fuck off, my boy!"

Then this Fritz was annoyed. So he got up to get to Nigel, and then Nigel ran to his car to take the pistol. So when Nigel brought out his pistol, everybody saw the pistol with Nigel, and then everybody had to run away. Because he was drunk, too.

Then, there was one English woman — even I fought with her one time — called Evelyn. Evelyn said, "No! Mary! Go to Nigel!"

But I was afraid, too! So I said, "Hey! If I go there, he will shoot me."

And she said, "No, he won't shoot you. You are living with him. You are a woman. You just go to him."

Then I got up, and I said, "Hey, Nigel, don't do that! What are you doing? Let me see your pistol." Then he gave it to me. Then I took the pistol. "Let's go home." He said he wouldn't go. So I just left him like that. When I took the pistol, I went away and left everybody. I walked. I walked from Gymkhana Club up to the petrol station before I got a taxi, and I went home. And when I left Nigel, Elizabeth was in Gymkhana Club. Yeah, I left that woman and Nigel.

So I was at the house. I couldn't sleep. This thing was worrying me. I thought, "What kind of stupid man am I coming to live with? To disgrace people in public like this?" So I was in the sitting room, going up and down.

Then I heard his car coming, so I switched the light off. Then, when he came: "Eh? Elizabeth! Eh? You fucking woman! Oh, what do you want

1. a game like Bingo

from Nigel? Eh? You think Nigel can make love with you? Eh, my dear, Nigel cannot make love with you. Eh? You think my Mary is not there? I have my Mary. I cannot make love with you. You know, eh? Elizabeth, you know, I'll tell you something: when I bring you here, Mary doesn't like it. You shouldn't come to me again. Eh, Elizabeth? Eh? You can go home."

You see the thing?! *Ha-ha!* How can this woman come like that? Look, her house is in town. And Bagabaga College, to walk there in the night, about two or three o'clock? It's not possible.

Then this woman said, "I won't go anywhere. I will sleep here. Or else, you will drop me with your car."

Then he said, "*Eh?* Nigel Manners's car cannot go out now. I cannot take my car out because of you, Elizabeth."

Then he came inside, and then this woman wanted to enter, and he pushed her and closed the door. Then I came and opened the door. I told this woman to come in, and she came in.

So, every time, when Nigel was drunk, whether it's four o'clock or it's three o'clock, he had to take tea with sandwiches before sleeping. Yeah! *Ha!* So he told me to bring his tea. So I made the tea for him, then I went and slept. So when I slept, it was air-conditioned, and that time, it was a little cold, so I put a blanket on all my body, then I covered my face. I was making as if I was sleeping. I was watching them. I thought maybe they would do something, or something like that, and I would get my excuse to go my way. So they were in the sitting room. Then Elizabeth said she wanted to go toilet. Then she came, "Oh, Mary, Mary, Mary!" She was shaking me.

Then I said, "*Mm-m-m.* Auntie Elizabeth, *m'ani kum.*[1] I'm feeling sleepy."

So she left me and went to the toilet. Then she came back to the bedroom. Then, we had a kind of dresser; it had two sides. On my own side, I put my creams and my everything on top, and then Nigel also had the other side. And whenever Nigel would come from Gymkhana Club, he would put all his money in this dresser. So this woman opened the drawer slowly, and then she took the money. She didn't know how much; she just took it and folded it and put half of it inside her bra like that, and then the other half inside the other side of her bra. Then she went into the sitting room.

Then I got up. I put on my nightgown and went to the sitting room. I said, "Auntie Elizabeth."

1. (Asante Twi): my eyes are tired; I'm sleepy.

"Yes?"

"What you're doing is a disgrace to me. You are disgracing me."

"Oh, Mary, what?"

I said, "No, the money you took from Nigel—you know, if you want money from him, you should ask him. He will give you. You know Nigel: he's not somebody who you will ask him for something, and he won't give. Every time when you come to Gymkhana Club, I used to tell him to give you money. Even I used to help you to get money from him. But if he puts his money down like that, and then you take it, then you are putting me in trouble. You shame me, because when you go away, Nigel won't think it's you who did it. He will think I am the one who did it."

Then she said, "What did I do? What did I do?"

Then I said, "OK, can you tell me that you didn't take any money in the room now?"

So she was trying to challenge me. And then Nigel said, "OK, it's no palaver. I fucked you, Elizabeth. I fucked Mary. It's no shame. Elizabeth, take your dress off." *Ha!*

So Elizabeth was going to talk something—*kpam, kpam, kpam.* Then Nigel went and brought the gun. He said, "Eh, my dear? Pull off your dress, or else I will shoot you. You know me? You know fucking bastard Nigel Manners? I can shoot you!" So this woman was shaking, you know, so she took all her dress off—the money she took was 150 cedis.

Then Nigel said, "I don't want it. Take it. And go out. You won't sleep here. It was your last chance for you. I thought—I had pity for you. Because you see that Nigel Manners is a fucking drunkard; he hasn't got any experience, so every time you have to steal from me. When you came here last time, you took my money, and I told Mary. Mary was annoyed, and she wanted to go away. So from today, go. I think if you are coming here, Mary won't live with me. So from today going, it was your last chance I gave you. Don't come here again."

You know, you think she wouldn't come again? What thing did she do? If we saw her in Gymkhana Club, I would say, "Oh, no, Nigel, don't do that. Buy her a drink." So Nigel would buy her drink. OK?

And when we were going home: "Oh, can I come to you people tomorrow morning?"

And we would say, "Yes, you can come, morning time or afternoon, or daytime."

Then, whenever she would come, Nigel had gone to work. He left me alone in the house. And I used to like sleep. So I would close every place and open my air-conditioner. When Elizabeth knocked, I wouldn't open. So she wouldn't know what to do.

Then, Nigel didn't go to work on Sundays and Saturdays, so every Sunday morning, she would come and knock the window—*pom, pom, pom, pom.* "Hey, Nigel! Good morning, Nigel Manners! Good morning, Nigel Manners! With your conceive[1] and your wife and your everything." *Ha-ha!* So one morning time, Sunday morning, she was coming to knock the door. Then, I didn't know: I had made this pepper with ginger water—you know, we women used to grind pepper with ginger to pump and douche, or to pump and go to toilet. Yeah, so I finished making this water and I put it into the rubber thing, and then I put it on the table. Then I was going to the quarters to wake my small sister: my younger sister had come to be living with me. I was going to wake her and then I would go to the bathroom to pump. So Elizabeth came and passed to the back of the house to start knocking the window. So when Nigel just opened his eyes, he saw this rubber, then he took it—*pssshh*—he sprayed all the window. Then the pepper got in this woman's eyes. "*Oh-h-h!* He's *killing* me! He's killing me! He's killing me!"

Oh! Many people ran to the house, shouting, "Hey! What's wrong?"

Then Nigel said, "Hey, Elizabeth, fuck off!" *Ha-ha!* As for Nigel, he didn't have any word apart from "Fuck off!" So: "Fuck off, my dear, eh! You are a fucking thief-woman, eh! You thieved from me; I didn't say anything. You are coming here every day, you say my conceive! And *your* pepper, too! So you'd better to go with your pepper." Then from that time, this woman stopped coming to us.

So that's the way I met Nigel, to come and stay with him. *Ha-ha!* Yeah. I think I stayed with him for a long time, about a year and some months. It was a long time. At first I didn't like him, but when I came back, I thought, "Ah, he's a nice man. He's *free.* He's a free man to live with. Without trouble and all this talking." If he was drunk, that was the only way I didn't like. But he was helping me. When I came back, at that time he asked me whether I had a bank account. I said, "No, I haven't got a bank account." Then he went and opened a bank account: two thousand cedis for me. At that time, two thousand cedis was a lot of money. Yeah, after he opened this bank account for me, I thought, "Oh. He will be a good man if I stay with him, because he's free, and maybe too I will get something from him."

That time, too, he gave me a job in Tamale. I was supplying bread and meat pies to the school. I was drinking every night, but I had three children with me, and I was paying them. There was one girl who was conceived, and then another girl—they said she's now dead—and then my

1. your fat stomach like a pregnant woman's

sister, too. And my sister knew how to do all this: I taught her how to do everything. So I was free every time; they could do it. Before I would wake up, even they had already taken the bread to school. Early in the month, they would pay me, and I would buy flour, oil, corned beef, butter. Then I had to pay these three girls, and then the rest was for me. So the balance I used to have in a month, as profit, it would be maybe a hundred cedis. And even sometimes Nigel could help me to buy the provisions, and I wouldn't pay him back.

But oh-h-h—ha! I didn't suck him well.[1] It pains me, you know. That time, I didn't know anything. I didn't know much about money. Even if I got two hundred cedis, I thought it was money. Yeah, it's this time now when I know what to do with money. *Ah!* When he went, we shared his things fifty-fifty. *Ha!* And I was foolish, too. That time, when I was with Nigel, I was starting to see my family again, and I was trying to help my family. Every month I used to send about two hundred cedis to my father. And that time my father was strong; he was working. But I had to pity him. He had so many children, and they were in school. And then I had one sister and one brother with me. My brother was at the Training College. It was Nigel who paid the school fee. And my small sister also started school. Nigel was the one who looked after her, too. But that time, I didn't know money. If I knew money, I wouldn't have done all the foolishness I did. If I had saved all that money, I think that by now maybe I would be somebody, too. I would have money to do something better. *Ha!* But I didn't save. If I had money, I used to give it to my father, or buy them things. I could buy them corn from Tamale—about six bags[2]—to send all to them, with yams—many of them. I used to buy many things to send to them not to suffer, because Kumasi was very expensive more than Tamale at that time.

Jack Toronto

So when I was staying with Nigel, my sister and my brother also came there. When my brother was at the Training College, I had the canteen of the school. We had provisions inside. I gave my brother that canteen to keep.[3] Some of the teachers could credit things there, and at the end of the month, they would pay. Everyone had his book, and if he credited some-

1. get much; consume all, as in sucking the marrow from a bone
2. large burlap sacks, fifty or one hundred kilos each
3. manage; hold

thing, they would write what things he credited and then the money. Then, I didn't take the money every day. I would wait till the end of the month, and everyone would make his account: all these people would pay. Then we would know how much profit we got, and we would go and get more goods to put in the store.

So Nigel was going on leave, for two months. And I was living alone at Bagabaga, in the bungalow, with my sister and my brother, and these girls who worked with me, and the watchman. These two months: the first month, my brother made a good account; the second month he didn't make the account well, and then he told me that the teachers didn't pay him yet, and that and this. And I thought that maybe because Nigel was not there, you know, because Nigel used to pay the teachers. If you were owing something to me, I would give Nigel the paper so that he would take that money out of your pay before he would give you your balance. Nigel would tell you, "You owe Mary this. Here is your book." So when Nigel was not there, and my brother told me this, I believed that maybe because Nigel was not there, these people had already taken their pay, and maybe for them to pay their accounts would be hard for them. Do you know that they had paid all? And my brother spent the money.

And then, my brother knew how to drive, and when Nigel was leaving the country, Nigel told my brother that if the car was kept in the garage, it would spoil, so he should take the car out whenever I wanted to go to town, and he could drop me. And every night, or sometimes, it was one of Nigel's friends who used to take me to cinema. This friend was a Scottish man named MacIver. Any time MacIver took me to cinema, my brother would take the car out and close the garage. When I would come home, the garage was closed, and I thought the car was inside, and maybe my brother was asleep. My brother was staying in the quarters there, so I didn't knock his door in the night time. So you know, if we went to town like that, then he too would go to town with the car himself and be picking girls.

So one night, I was in the house when I heard shouting in the quarters. When I went, it was three girls. They were fighting. My brother brought two girls from the town, and he came and met one girl waiting for him. *Ha-ha!* So these girls started fighting. Then I said, "Hey! Kofi, what are you doing?"

Then he said, "Fuck off!" *Ha!* Everybody learned how to talk like Nigel! Yeah? "Fuck off! Don't tell me this. What am I doing? Did you see me doing some palaver?"

Then I said, "Oh, but you must talk to this girl. We are not alone here. Nigel is not here. If we are making annoyance like this, if Nigel comes, the teachers will give him a complaint that we were disturbing them. So I don't want these things."

Then my brother said he would beat me that night. *Hmm!* My senior brother! He wanted to beat me, but then the watchman said, "No. No. It's not possible."

So I left him and went and slept. Then the next month, Nigel came before the ending of that month. And my brother made the accounts of that month for me, and he said the teachers didn't pay him again, so the money was short. So when Nigel came to pay the teachers, I told Nigel, "But these people have owed me too much."

Then he said, "How much?"

I said, "I don't know; I have to ask my brother to bring their books."

But when my brother brought all the books, they had paid all. Then I said, "Ah, Kofi, you told me that for about three months, these people didn't pay all the money, but all is paid off."

Then he said, "Do you think I'm your laborer, to come and work for you to find money?" My own brother — oh! One mother, one father! I thought he was suffering in Kumasi, so I wanted to help him. But he wanted to bring me down. *Ha-ha!* Yeah.

Then Nigel said, "OK, what did you do with the money? Tell me the truth."

Then my brother said Nigel shouldn't ask him that question, that it is a foolish question he's asking. "Why should you ask me what I'm doing with money? You Nigel, what are you doing with money?" Look at things like this!

Then Nigel said, "Yeah. I work. I work, suffering myself, to get money to spend. But you don't work. Your sister is helping you. It's your younger sister, so you must help her too."

Then Kofi said, "Yes, that is not your lookout. Before you came from London, we were not eating sand. We were eating food. Even if you leave my sister today, we can go. We are poor but we can eat the same food we are eating here."

So Nigel said, "No, this is not possible." He said he was going to take this boy to the police.

Then I said, "No. Because of money I won't take my brother to police." Then I said, "Nigel, do you know that blood is thicker than water?"

He said, "Yeah? Are you telling me?"

Then I said, "Yes. You cannot take my brother because of money to lock him in prison or in the police station. You will get a bad name. So the best thing, if you think my brother cannot live here, I will send him back to my father. That's all. You cannot take him to the police station."

So we made a time to send this boy, but then Nigel said, "No. We cannot send this boy. I will leave him to go to the school, but he cannot keep on the canteen again. So we must find somebody to look after the canteen, and this boy should continue his schooling." So my brother was there until he finished his schooling, and then he went back to Kumasi to find something to do. My own brother—*hmm.*

That was my brother, Kofi. At that time, people called him "Jack Toronto." Jack Toronto. They had some paper which came to Ghana; they said it was one schoolboy who made these papers because he hadn't anybody to look after him in school. So he took some sense to make these papers, as a joke, and then he sold them. They called it "Jack Toronto": "Hi, man! *Alomo-e. Alomo dada dada.*"[1] It's something like a joke. My brother was the first fellow who brought these papers from Kumasi to Tamale, and he used to give it to the friends to read, and then they would start laughing. So everywhere he went, "Hey! Jack Toronto! Jack Toronto! Jack Toronto!" All Tamale people were calling him Jack Toronto.

And he was bad boy. Do you know what he did? When Nigel came from leave, he brought me many dresses. My wardrobe was full up. This boy used to steal my dresses and give to the girlfriends. *Ha-ha!* Yeah. Shoes and everything, he used to steal them from me. Sometimes I would want to put on a shoe, and I would look, "Eh? But I thought I had this color. Where did that shoe pass? I don't remember well? Or-r-r-r—what? This is not the color like the one I'm thinking."

Then one day I went and saw one of my blouses with my shoe on some girl in the market. She didn't know me. I called her, and then I said, "Where did you buy your shoe?"

She said, "Oh, I have one boyfriend at Bagabaga, at the College." She said the boyfriend had one friend who was European, and when the man was going on holidays, this boy told him to buy these shoes, with this blouse, too.

So when I went home, I said, "Hey, Kofi, what you are doing is bad." Every morning when this boy was going to school, Nigel would give him five cedis. He didn't sleep in the school; he slept with us. Five cedis! That time, you could do something with five cedis. And this boy didn't have pity for me, that he could just take my dress to go and dash girls. So I said, "Kofi, every morning when you are going to school, how much do you get?"

"Five cedis."

1. girlfriend; old girlfriend; from a Highlife song. *Alomo,* which is Ga for "girlfriend," has become part of general Ghanaian vernacular. *Dada* is Twi for "former."

"Then why? What do you want again? If you have a girlfriend, you should show me. If you want, and you take one girlfriend, I'm all right. Tell me, 'This is my girlfriend, sister.' Whatever the girlfriend wants, I can do it for her. Then you can stay with her alone. Why should you carry my things to town to give to all these girlfriends?"

Then he said, "Oh, but you have all of these things plenty! What are you doing with them? Some of them, you don't use them. You just take them to go and give to our sisters who are living under the cocoa trees. They are making farm work. So if I give it to my girlfriend, it's bad?"

"Why don't you ask me? You must ask me. The one I don't like, I can choose it for you. But sometimes you will take the one I like."

"OK, OK. I won't do that again. Then tell me what one you don't want."

Then I said, "No. You can't force me to tell you what I don't want. From today going, you shouldn't enter my bedroom again. Don't enter my bedroom again." So from then, every time I would go out, I would close my bedroom. I didn't leave the key. My own brother — from one mother, one father. If suppose we had different mothers, I would say it's because he's not my real brother. But this one: we were from one mother, one father, and he was playing a *bad* game, a very, very bad game. I had plenty of wigs. I lost some of them; I don't know where these wigs passed. *Ah!* What kind of brother is this? When this boy was not there, when I was alone with Nigel, I didn't lose my things, because our houseboy was afraid of me, and he could not take my things like that. At first I used to think that maybe, because my brother had come, this houseboy was trying to do these things. If I didn't see that shoe in town with that girl and I asked her, then I was thinking it was the cook. And I didn't want to give the complaint to Nigel, either. If I said it was the cook, Nigel would go and sack this poor cook, and maybe it wasn't him. So I had to keep quiet, before I got to know this thing from that girl. When she told me, then I knew that it was my brother who was doing all this.

So Africa: it's hard for us. You will see somebody let his family suffer, and maybe he has some small money, but his family is suffering. You won't understand, but it's not his fault. Now my brother has changed his mind, but if he was like the first time, I think I wouldn't help him in any way. But now he used to think of me if he has something. Even he used to buy some things for me. If I go to Kumasi, he will say, "Ah, we have a new cloth which came, and many people wear it, and its name is like this. Will you like it?" If I say, yes, then the next day he will go and buy it for me. *Hmm.* Yeah. But before, at Bagabaga: no, no, no, no!

Roads Not Taken

And so Nigel also did something. Yeah. I don't know how much money this man was collecting in a month. I never asked him. He had a wife, Josephine, and the wife had two children with another man, and that man was dead. Then she married Nigel. She already had two children, and she didn't want a baby again. So she had no child with Nigel. All that Nigel did, he said he took care of one child of his sister. The sister died and left one baby boy, and he was in school. Nigel was the one who was taking care of that boy. And I think the wife was a little bit rich, because the first husband died in the last war, so he got some insurance or something from the government. So she was also a little bit rich, the woman. She was a dance teacher in London, and I think she also had some money, so she didn't worry about money from Nigel too much. So Nigel always spent the way he liked.

And what let me leave Nigel was that Nigel went to London, and he didn't come back. I was staying with him up to the time he went away to London. That was when I got my passport. When Nigel went to London, he was telling me, "Try to have your passport and come." He gave me letters to go the passport office, and it was those letters they took to make the passport for me. And so I had a Ghana passport—an international one.[1]

And then, when I finished the passport, I wrote him, and he sent me one thousand cedis to go to British Embassy and get a visa. And then he could send me the ticket. At that time, my small sister was living with me. So I was going to take her to Kumasi, then I would do all this for the visa. If I could go to London, I thought it would be good. Then I told my father, "Oh, Papa, I have a passport."

So then he said, "Oh, let me see it."

I showed it to him, and he said, "But this is a Ghana passport. Why didn't you go to the Upper Volta Embassy? Where are you going?"

And I said, "Oh, I just want to have a passport because it's nice. Sometimes I would like to go to Lomé or Ouagadougou. It's good if I have a passport."

Then my father was very foolish. He said, "No. You can't travel with this passport." He just took the passport from me. He said I'm not a Gha-

1. a passport that is valid for travel for all countries. Some travel documents were valid only to specific countries.

naian, so I shouldn't have a Ghanaian passport. He just took the passport from me. And he burned my money: I deposited two hundred cedis to have the passport, and he said no, and then he burned the passport. He said if he gives me the passport, I wouldn't give it back; I would keep it.

I was annoyed with my father for about six months. I didn't go home again. When I came back to Accra, I stayed six months. I didn't write them; I didn't go to them. *Ha! Hm.*

And you know, the time Nigel wrote me to come, he was very funny. He said, "When you are coming, you must buy me some whiskey from the plane, and King-Size.[1] But I am in hospital. I am taking a rest in hospital."

And he died in the hospital. After two months, when I didn't go, I had a letter from MacIver, the other friend who was at Bagabaga, too, the one who used to take me to cinema when Nigel went on leave. He wrote me. He said, "Ah, Mary, Nigel is dead."

So: Nigel. You know, I liked him somehow. Somehow. I liked him the way, you know, the way he helped me in my problems. When I was with him, I had no problems. If I had any problems for money, then I will have the money. Every time, I used to go to Accra—with plane. When I go to Accra, I don't stay with anyone. I'm in Ambassador or Star Hotel. It's all his account, and I don't worry. I can go to Accra for about two or three weeks with my girlfriends, going up and down, spending, drinking, dancing. So I liked it! Who doesn't like to be free? *Ha!* Nobody in this world who has a chance to be free will say he doesn't like it. So I liked it. I liked him in that way, you know.

Sometimes I would tell him, "OK. Yeah, I want to go to Kumasi." He would telephone to City Hotel.[2] The director there, Nigel knew him well; he was his friend. "OK. My wife is coming. You have to give her a room. And then after, you should make all the bill and send it to me." I would eat there; I would do everything there. I don't know how much they charged for a room. But all my bill, they would collect all, and then they would send it to Nigel, and he would post them a check to take their money out. And so that time, I was not suffering.

And that time, it's very—I was very foolish, you know. Because that time, I didn't know what is life. If it was this time, I think it would be better, because now I have experience a little bit, and I can do something with money. But that time, when I had money: *whew, pish, pish!* With the friends: "Oh, let's go. What do you want? Today we should just go and bluff. Everybody shouldn't go to anywhere. I can give you people what

1. a brand of British cigarette; Rothman's
2. state-owned hotel in Kumasi, like Star or Ambassador in Accra

you can eat tomorrow morning." We would get *drunk* at Lido. I have many pictures in Accra. You will see me with a group, and the bottles are full-up on the table. That's why this time I hate to see bottles on a table. Sometimes we would leave beer and go away. And every time when you see a group like this, I am the one who was buying. I alone, I have to buy for all of them. And then I will bring a photographer to take our picture, and I will give everyone one, one, one, one, one, one. I was foolish. I thought this was the world—I thought I was enjoying—I didn't know I will come and suffer later, you know.

I told you Nigel built me a house, no? Yeah, that house, the land is not for me myself. Nigel was not the one who got the land. The land is for my father at Kumasi, at Old Tafo. And what made Nigel build the house was, one day, we went to Gymkhana Club. And there were some girls—you know, he used to chase some girls there. When I came, he was afraid, and he didn't approach these girls again. And when these girls saw me with him, they used to be jealous.

So one day, I and one girl fought because of him. This girl said that Nigel should buy her a beer. And he said, "Oh, go and ask Mary. If Mary allows me to buy for you, I will buy it."

Then she said, "Who is Mary?"

Then I said, "Yeah, I'm here. I'm Mary. I'm not tall. I'm not fat. But I'm the one who controls him. If I don't say it, he won't buy it."

Then this girl just came and hooked my dress up. Then we started fighting. When they separated us, then that Swiss man who I said Nigel brought a gun to shoot him—Fritz—Fritz came and beat this girl well for me. So I liked it. Then when we were going home, I didn't sit in the front. No. I went to the back seat. Then Nigel said, "Why don't you come in front?"

I said, "Leave me." Then I started to cry from this nightclub up to the house. I said, "Yes, it's because I have a poor family. Suppose my family was better, I don't think I can live with you, an old man like this. Every time, to be suffering in the night, and people will be beating me like this and that." And then I was crying.

And you know, he was drunk, so he was also stupid a little bit. Then he said, "Eh? Eh, my dear? You want money? Eh? So? Because of money you are with me?"

Then I said, "Yes, what do you think? If not because of money, do you think I can live with you? You are my grandfather, you know. Even you are not my father's size."[1] The time when I was living with this man, he

1. age; also, in other contexts: standard, status

was *fifty-two years old! Ha-ha!* Yeah, he was fifty-two years old. So every time, whenever he said something, I would say, "Aw, fuck off!" *Ha!* "You are my grandfather," and that and this.

So he went to the office. You know, they had their savings there from the school. All the school money, they used to save it some place in the office. He went there and brought some money in a sack. That money: suppose I carried it, maybe I'll be rich. Or suppose I carried it, maybe I'll be dead. Maybe I'll be dead. I don't know. He brought some money, I'm telling you, that night, I was nearly crazy in the room. Then he said, "OK. Mary."

I said, "Yes?"

"You are poor?"

"Yes."

So he brought all this money to me. He said, "OK, you said you are poor. What is money? This fucking thing—these fucking cedis? Fucking Nkrumah papers? Take it, my dear. Take it and do what you want."

So I looked at this money. No? My sense said, "Oh, you can take this money and go away. Because this man is a drunkard. Before he wakes up and he will know that he has lost something, you are far." So I brought out one box. I had a small box, an iron box. I brought this iron box down, and I packed all this money nicely, ten, ten, ten, ten cedis—I packed them nicely—*fresh* ones! *Ha-ha!* I packed them nicely, then I took dresses, about four, and put them on top, then I closed the box. Then I said, "*Tsk!* I'm going, I am going to go." I took a telephone to get a taxi. It was four o'clock. No taxi. They didn't agree: there was no taxi. *Ah!* OK? So I had to stay up to the morning time.

Then something came to me and said, "No. This old man, when I came here first, he asked me whether I have got a bank account. He opened a bank account for me, no? Then after he was good for me. My family: I have two people in school—he is the one who is paying their school fees. And he's nice to me. Maybe if I take this money and go, they will arrest him as a thief, to put him in prison or something like that. It's not nice. God will punish me." I thought of these things first. Then I sat down. And, you know, when I sat down a little, I opened the box with the money, then—*sniff!*—I smelled it. You know? Its scent was *nice!* Then I said, *"Yee-ee-a!"* I was nearly crazy that night. Then I started drinking, and playing loud music. He was asleep. When he was sleeping, he didn't hear anything again, because he used to drink heavily. After five o'clock, getting to five-thirty, then I said, "No." I was broken down, because I had drunk a lot. Before I went to sleep, I took this money and put it back in the sack he brought it in, and I put it in my wardrobe and closed it.

The next morning, he didn't go to work. He woke up around two o'clock in the afternoon. All that he had to do in the office, the messenger brought it home, then he signed. From the office to the house was not far, so he could keep three or four days like that. Hey, in Tamale, they were *free.* When I met him in Accra, he was a bit serious, you know, because when they went to Accra for business, they didn't drink much. But Tamale! *Ha!* He drinks; he doesn't go to work; he's in the house. Even one week, maybe he wouldn't go to work. In Tamale, he was free. Everything they wanted, the messenger would bring it home and then he would sign the papers. He didn't used to go to office. So when I put this money in my wardrobe, and the next day when he woke up about two o'clock, he didn't ask me anything. I didn't tell him anything. The second day, the same. The third day. Then I said, "No, I must ask this man. Or he wants to trick me, to know what I am?"

Then we were eating. So I said, "Nigel."

He said, "Hm?"

"Today, will you go to your office?"

He said, "Yes."

"Are you OK in the office?"

He said, "Yes."

"You didn't lose anything?"

He said, "No. What is wrong? Is something wrong?"

"No. I'm asking you whether you lost something."

Then he said, "No, I didn't lose anything."

I was going to tell him, but you know, the first time I was very funny. Things like this, when I was going to say them, then I would start crying. I started: tears.

So he came and held me, and said, "Mary, what is wrong?"

And I said, "Because I told you my problems that I'm poor — so you know that I'm poor — so you're trying to trick me to know my mind whether I'm a thief or I am not a thief. I already told you that if I am a thief, I wouldn't come and do this fucking work — I wouldn't follow you. I would follow the thief people, to do this burglar work and gain more. But even if Elizabeth steals your money, and you tell me that your money is lost, it pains me. I told you this. But why should you take money like this to me?"

He said, "What kind of money?"

Then I brought the sack. When I brought the sack, he said, "*Jesus!* I brought this here?!"

And I said, "Who brought it? Who had your office key? Is that your office key?"

He said, "No! Who brought it? I don't know, Mary. Do you think I'm the one who brought this here?"

And I said, "Yes! Do you remember Wednesday when we were coming from Gymkhana Club, I was crying that I am poor, and all this, and you went and carried this money from your office?"

Then he started to cry, too. He was crying heavily. He said that suppose this money was lost, he wouldn't be troubled much, because he had worked in the school for a long time, and nothing had been lost like that. But the messenger would be in prison for this, because the saving box key, they have only two — one with him and one with the messenger. And they wouldn't believe that he was the one who did this, so by all means they would say that this boy did it. And he would also say yes, because he didn't know the time he took this money out.

Then I said, "What? It's because — you know — you just want to trick me, because I told you I'm poor. But I'm not a person like this."

Then he said, "Oh-h, no, no, no, no, no. What do you want? Do you want me to get you an estate house[1] in Tamale?"

"I don't want to be in an estate in Tamale because I'm not Dagbamba; I'm not from here."

Then he said, "What do you want me to do for you?"

Then I said, "If you can help me in a good way — because my father has some land in Kumasi, and they haven't built on it. He hasn't got money to build on it. So if you can make it for me."

And he said, "OK." After one week, he bought cement. You know? What they use to make the blocks. And zinc and everything. I sent it to Kumasi. Then they started making these blocks.

Then for about one month, my darling didn't say anything again. And I said, "Hm! *Uh-huh!* Now I know your way. Do you think this cement and zinc can make a house? You have to get some tiles, and all this, you know?"

He didn't do it. So every time, I used to press him. When sometimes they would talk some bad talk in the Gymkhana Club, about Africans, then I would say I was going to report him to the ministries. *Ha!* "Oh? My dear, eh? If you report Nigel, who can build your house?"

Then I would say, "The house is not building.[2] It's better they report you: you have no benefit here."

"Oh, oh. Tomorrow we will do it!" The next day, he would send something to Kumasi, to my father to go and buy all these things. And small-

1. An estate is a residential or suburban area, normally of one-family bungalows.
2. not getting built

small, he finished that house: eighteen rooms. It's single rooms, the African round house. They made it that way. Now, my father is living in my village, but my brother is taking care of it. Every month, we take the money from the house.

So Nigel also tried. You see, he was there at the school a long time. He said he had kept long in Africa, so he would like to go to London. The time he went on leave, he came back from leave in about one month, and he said he had made an application to get some work in London, so if he gets a reply, he will go back to London. We were there about one month, and then he said, "Ah, I have got a reply, and I have got nice work, so I have to leave." And even the wife had died about six months. When he went to London, he wrote me that now Josephine was dead, so I had a free chance to come to London, so I must get a passport. That was the time I started making my passport. And then he too didn't keep long. When I got my passport, then he wrote me that he was in the hospital resting. I thought that he was sick, but he didn't tell me in the letter; he just said he was resting in the hospital. So: after, they wrote me that he was dead. I don't know if he knew he was sick. Maybe he poisoned himself with the drink. Some people used to do that. Yeah, one man died in Tamale like that. He was a Scottish man.

You know, Nigel also gave me his car, his own car. When he was going, we had to go to the police station and make the transfer paper, that he was leaving me this car. It was a private car, and I didn't know how to drive. My father too didn't drive. It was no use to take it as private car. So we painted it "Taxi." This taxi was an old car. My father got a little out of it, and then every time, he had to make repairs, repairs. So he had to sell it. And then, when the house was finished at Kumasi, we rented it, and the people inside paid every month. And so when he sold the car, then he added the small money he got from the house, and he made a deposit for a new car. Now they have finished the debt of the new car. They bought another taxi with the money, and now, they're running the taxi. *M-hm.*

So my family: maybe I have done well for them. Maybe. Some people, when you do much for some people, they don't see it. You know? Some people can say, "Ah, she has tried." Or some people can just say, "Oh, what did she try?" But as for my father, he thought that I did a lot for him. Every time he used to say that suppose all the children for him, if they tried like me, then he wouldn't be suffering. If they tried like me. You know, you have to do something for your parents. So, maybe I have tried.

And since then, I haven't lived with any man who did what Nigel did for me. I've met many people, but I haven't met somebody like him. He—

anyway, he was very funny. Yeah. In Tamale, when he was drunk, he was funny. *Ha!* Yeah. If you haven't got a heart, you know, if you have a quick temper, you cannot live with him, because every time he will make trouble with you. If he is drunk, what he is saying is bad talks. Oh, yeah. But I didn't care about all this. When he tells me something I don't like, I will just say, "Fuck off!"

And he would say, "Eh, eh? My dear, eh, eh? You are telling me to fuck off? Eh, you are telling your Nigel Manners to fuck off? Eh? In London, ladies don't say that to the husbands." *Ha-ha!* Yeah.

Then I would say, "Yes. Here is not in London. Here is Africa. I can tell you to fuck off." *Ha-ha!*

And then he would start singing, "Fine, fine woman; fine, fine woman-o; you no savvy nothing; I will send you back to your fafa." *Ha!* He was very funny, eh? Ah-h, Nigel was funny.

5 FUCKING ENGLISH PEOPLE

: TAMALE :

William and Abena

So: Nigel. Yeah. You know, in Africa here, many girls must follow men for money, to get something for themselves. But the first time, when I was with Nigel, I had no experience to keep money. I just—*pfft-pfft*—spent money like that. Nigel: I stayed with him a long time. Oh, yeah. Sometimes, when I was in Accra, I used to be with a friend for some time, but you know, when I was in Accra, I could be with people for a few days or some weeks, but always I was not staying there. Sometimes, half of my things are in my house, and half of my things are in your house. Maybe it will be two or three days before you will see me. I will be in my house, or

I will go with my friends to some places. But when I was with Nigel, I didn't know anybody else in Tamale as a boyfriend, so even when I would go to anyone's house to visit, I still did my everything at Nigel's house. But when I was in Tamale, I had plenty of friends.

Yeah, let me tell you. The first time when I went to Tamale from Accra, I didn't know many girls there, but I got to know some of the African girls who were staying with these British people. We were three. All of us three, we knew each other at Accra, not to go round-round together, not as friends, but I met them first at Accra, and I used to be seeing them sometimes in the town. So when I was in Tamale, we met and saw ourselves there. The one girlfriend was called Gladys. She was married to a Lebanese man. The other was called Abena. Gladys also knew Abena from Accra. One time I saw Abena in the cinema, so I started telling Gladys that I had seen this girl in the cinema, but as she was not my good friend in Accra, we didn't used to talk to each other. So then Gladys said, "She is a good girl. She is my friend, too." You see? And at the same moment we were talking this talk, we were going to the market, and when we entered the market, we met the girl there. So we all became friends.

The boyfriend of Abena knew her from Accra, and they were together for about three years. I think they went to some places before coming to Tamale. He was working at one of the companies in the town. He was British. When I met Abena in Tamale, we were living in the same area. The man was living in a bungalow on the Bolga road,[1] and they had a small road you could join from there to Bagabaga.

Abena used to come to visit us every time, but we didn't go to her. She was coming to my place at Bagabaga. Gladys would come, and Abena would also come for the whole day. Gladys's husband had a shop, and when he closed the shop, then he would come and look for Gladys at my place. Abena too, when her man closed from work, he would also come and find her in my place. So every time they were coming to me. You know, as for me, I'm free.

So these girls, Gladys and Abena, when we met in Tamale there, as we knew each other from Accra, we were happy. We were good friends, walking together. We would go to our shopping and our everything together. So cinema: when we would go to shopping, we would have to pass to look at the picture to know what is on today. And if it was a nice film, all of us will promise, "Ah, tonight I will come to the cinema."

But whenever I would go, I didn't see the one girlfriend, Abena. I saw

1. the road to Bolgatanga

the boyfriend, every day. Then, ah! What can it be? Then I said, "Ah!" One day we went to one nice film, and then the next morning time, Abena came to me, and I said, "Ah, Abena. Yesterday you missed something nice, something good!"

Then she said, "Where?"

I said, "At the cinema."

She said, "But I was there," and she started to give me all the story of the film.

Then I said, "What the hell?! I saw your man; I didn't see you. Or did your man tell you?"

She said, "No, no, no, no. You know, my man has a wife in London. So he doesn't want to walk with me, for people to see him that he is walking with an African girl. So any time when you see him upstairs,[1] I'm downstairs. Every time we go to cinema, then after cinema I have to wait for him on the road, before he will come and pick me."

So she was telling why they don't sit together when they go to cinema. OK? She was living with this man. At first when she was with the man, the man didn't have a wife. Then he went on leave for three months, and he married. He left the wife there, and he came back. Maybe the wife will come, or the wife won't come. Nobody knows. So he told the girl that now he has to change his life — they shouldn't go to cinema together — in Tamale there are many people who know his wife — they will write to the wife — and all this.

So when this girl was telling me, then I said, "Ah! This man! Oh, no! Look. Don't try to be a fool. Don't you think my man has a wife, too? He also has a wife! Even they wrote his wife. His wife came and met me here. She had nothing to do to him. Even if they write this man's wife, and because of that, the wife will say she will divorce, or she will come and kill you in Africa here, she can't do anything. So the way this man is taking you, he's teaching you. He doesn't want you to know how to spend money. If you know these things, or you like these things much, every time you will be asking him for money to buy them. That's why."

And I told her this story.

I was with Nigel in Tamale when Nigel's wife came and met us. We didn't know that she was coming. She didn't write any letter. Some people wrote a letter to her, "This is what Nigel is doing." And she also had a big heart, so she didn't write any letter: she just came like that.

And then, the day when she came, I was afraid, but this man *fucked* her. Shit! "What a bloody hell? To come to me without writing? Yes! Here

1. in the balcony

is Hawa! Is she the one you want to see? She is here! Hawa! This is Josephine. She has come to see you. Josephine, this is my girlfriend."

You know, that day I was ashamed, and I was afraid, too. I thought that when we sleep together, this woman will shoot me. The time I was a kid, they told me that if you go with a European and he has a wife, if the wife meets you, she will kill both of you together. So that night, I didn't sleep the whole night! *Hee-hee.* I was afraid.

And we even came to Gymkhana Club together, to drink together. All three of us! Yakubu was there. Yakubu wondered![1] Yeah. We two women, we were at the back of the car, and then Nigel must be a driver for us. *Hee-hee.* This woman was to sit in front, and she said "No." Then she and Nigel asked me too to sit in front. Then I said no, too. How can I sit? You are the Madame: you have to sit before me. But I was thinking: maybe I will be sitting in front and then she will punch my back!! *Ha!* So we two both went to the back of the car. We went to Gymkhana and drank. And everybody said, "*Eh-h-h!* Nigel! What you are doing is not good!"

You know, these English people, they are very fucking people. They talked about me, that I'm this and that. But the wife didn't say anything. She stayed one week, then she went away. She said, "OK, Hawa, you watch my husband for me. I think you can take care of him well. Because he's so stupid. He drinks much. If he is doing something foolish, you should stop him." Then this woman went. When she went, she gave me a *nice* dress, a nice one. She made it by herself. She was a good tailor. In London. Yeah.

So when this girl, Abena, was telling me all this, you know, *ah!* Then I said, "Oh!"

So it came to a time when this girl was telling us *all-l-l* her problem. OK, we used to go to shopping, to get some new dresses, to get some shoes, to get some Cutex, and some lipstick — some things like that. But if you asked this girl, "Wouldn't you buy some of this? It's a nice thing," then she would say, "No, my man doesn't like it."

Mm-hm. And so, then we used to ask, "Why doesn't your man like it?"

She'd say, "If I dress like this, my man will say I'm ashawo." And her hair, the man didn't like it when she would plait the hair. He said it's ashawo. Every time she should look like a student.

So from this point, what this girl was bringing out, then I thought, "Ah, if this girl doesn't get sense! This man is teaching her! So I have to give her some experience." *Ha-ha!* So this is the time when I told her, "Look, this man is teaching you."

1. was surprised

Then she said, "Oh, my man is not good. He doesn't want me to tie my hair, because if I have plenty hair, maybe they will call me ashawo, and I should put on this, and I shouldn't put on high shoes, and—"

Then I said, "No. My friend, this man is teaching you. He doesn't want you to know money. He doesn't want you to know how to spend money. He's teaching you 'don't-do-that.' The next time when he tells you 'don't do that,' do it—and see."

So I thought I was a good sister to give her advice. But then, this girl was stupid. I was thinking she was a nice girl, so I would try to change her mind to know that this man was teaching her. You see? But that was how I got her problem. She was stupid. When I gave her advice, she went and told this man *all* that I had been telling her. *Um-hum! Ha! Ah!*

So the man got annoyed. "What kind of girl is this? Hawa? Trying to spoil my girl? I will see her."

So the next morning, seven o'clock, we were inside. We were coming to table to eat, then this man just walked up to our house and knocked the door: *boom-boom-boom-boom.* So Nigel opened the door. "Ah, good morning, Mr. William."

Then this man had a big voice, "Where is Hawa?"

Then Nigel said, "What? What is wrong?"

Then he said, in his big voice, "I want to see Hawa."

Then I said, "Yeah. I'm here. What?"

He said, "Look. You are fucking. If you are a fucking girl"—*ha!*—"If you are a fucking girl, you don't think of yourself? You shouldn't tell all these things to my girlfriend like that, because the girl loves me. I want to tell you today. You don't know where I met Abena. You know, I met Abena, it's a long time, it's about three years now. You just found Nigel about two months, so you think you are high. Because Nigel is a fool. He's a fucking old man. He gives you money to do whatever you want." *Ha!* Then: "Don't try to spoil my Abena for me. What did you tell her yesterday?"

Then I said, "What did I tell her?! Yes! What I told her is true. Because I'm African. If I see a kind of African and she is fooling herself like this, too. One man like you, you are not the size for Abena,[1] and then you say she should follow you because of love, I think, the way I don't follow Nigel with love."

Then Nigel said, "Yes! Yes! Hawa doesn't follow me with love. Money cannot buy love, but money can rent love!" *Ha!*

1. You are not up to the standard for Abena, i.e., you don't have the money to take care of her properly.

So my man, he was strong, you know. Nigel. This man just came there to fuck me off. And you know, Nigel didn't need things like this. When this man told me these fucking things, that was the time when Nigel also put his mouth inside. So he just came out and said, "Look, you shouldn't treat this girl this way. She's a — they are all Africans. Hawa can show her some experience, because they don't live with us free. You say you have married. You won't marry her. So because of money, they live with us." *Ha-ha!* You know, Nigel was trying to tell him the truth, what he should do but he didn't want to do it. "If you don't like the girl, you should let her go. You shouldn't do that to a girlfriend." So Nigel just shamed him like that. He said, "Yes. What Hawa is telling her is correct. Because she's African. When she sees this African girl living with a white man that is not correct living, she must tell her."

Then Nigel said, "Abena is eating every day in my house. So from today going, she must pay for what she eats here. Because, I don't want — you say Hawa's spoiling her — maybe it's because she is giving her food. Suppose you were feeding her well, she wouldn't come to my house to eat. Then, she can listen to advice also. So: if you don't want this, then you must pay for what Abena eats."

Then he said, "How much?"

Then Nigel said, "OK. You take it like: African food is very cheap. She ate here about two weeks now. So, you know yourself."

He said, "Yes."

"OK. You yourself, make account. Two weeks: how much?"

Then this man said *he* doesn't know how much I have spent to get my food. So Nigel said, "What do we make it? We must make all our accounts: fifty cedis! Yeah! For two weeks! Yeah, we won't take it to be much. Fifty cedis only."

Then we sent a letter to him. And William said he wouldn't pay this, because, every time he gives this girl food in the house, so if she doesn't eat in the house and she comes to me and eats, then this girl herself should go and pay the bill.

So Nigel said, "OK. If this will be the case, Hawa will come to you and eat, too."

I didn't like the idea, you know, but Nigel just told me. "OK. You just make a quick way. You are not going to eat, but you should say you are coming to greet her." So when the girl came to me, I told her that I would be coming to greet her, to know her place.

So one day we were in the house. Then Nigel said, "You won't eat in this house today. Let's go to Abena's house!" *Hee-hee.* And then, nine o'clock in the morning, he carried me with his car, and he dropped me at

Abena's place. Then Nigel told this man that, oh, he's going to Kumbungu, so I'm alone in the house, and that's why he brought me here to talk to Abena. He didn't talk about food.

So, we were there. Twelve o'clock. *Bing!* Then this man said, "You must go to the quarters! Some people are coming to me!"

What the bloody hell! When I'm in the house, and Abena comes to me, even a thousand people can come to Nigel, and Nigel will never tell us to go to the quarters or to go to the toilet. And this man said, if we don't want to go to the quarters, if it's hot, we can go to his bedroom, but when we hear that somebody is going to enter the bedroom, we must hide ourselves in the toilet. Then I said, "No. As for me, I won't do that."

So Abena got up and went. And I was sitting there. And he was trying to force me! And I said, *"He-e-ey!" Ha!* This man, I dealt with him before. I said, "Hey! Don't try to force me! I won't go anywhere. If you want, you must take me back to my house. Because when Abena comes to me, you know, Nigel used to drop her. But Nigel has traveled; he's not there. So if you don't want somebody to see me in your room, you should take me back with your car."

He said, "But these people are *coming!* Oh, Hawa, *please.*"

Then I said, "I'm not 'please.' First time you are forcing me, and now you are asking me with 'please.' These people, are they eating people? Or if they come and meet me here, they will say something about—"

"No-o, you know, I have big problems—and my wife—her friends are coming here. If they come and see, they will write something against me." And that and this and that.

"Uh-huh! Is that the way? But I'm not among. And these people: many people know me here. I'm living with Nigel. If they come and see you with me, it's nothing."

Then this man started, *"Ba, ba, ba-ba."* And then these people came. *Ha!*

"Oh, hello! Hello!" And then, some of them didn't like it. You know, English people are very wicked. Some of the women squeezed their face[1] and made their face so. I didn't care. I lit my cigarette, brought my leg to cross my leg. Then I said, "Hey! *Hey Abena!* Won't you come?"

Then this man looked at me. He wanted to tell me to shut up, but these people were looking at him, so he was just standing like this. And I was laughing. So at the last minute, I left them. Then I went to the quarters. I said, "Oh! Abena! How can you be a prisoner like this?" You know, I didn't stop from what I told her at home. The first warning is not a warn-

1. frowned; tightened their faces

ing; the second one, too: I wanted to say it again. "Why do you want to be foolish like this? When you come to Nigel, don't you see that plenty people come to Nigel. And I don't go anywhere. I sit on a stool, and we talk together. They talk to him, and whatever they talk, if I'm living there, he never tells me to go out. But why you are living like this? You think you are a small girl? You are not a small girl. This man knows you for about three years. What did you get from him? Won't you leave him and go and find another man?" That's what I said, in the quarters.

So, I vexed.[1] I passed from the quarters. Even I didn't tell the man anything. I just passed from the quarters, then I went out. I got my taxi and went to my bungalow, and then I told Nigel what happened. Then Nigel said, "Let's go." *Heh-heh.* My Nigel was another foolish man, you know. "Let's go there! What a fucking bloody hell! This fucking man, he thinks he is the best man? He thinks he's an English man? This man is from bush![2] He's not a real English man. Fucking man with a long legs!" Because this man was very tall! *Ha!* So we went there.

"William, William."

"What?" He had this big voice, you know. "What should I do for you? Nigel, you want to trouble me. I don't want that. Even if you want Abena, I can give you her things, together with Hawa's things. Why?"

Then Nigel said, "But, you can't do that. Abena comes to me. If people are there, we eat together with Abena. Why should you sack Hawa?"

Then he said, "I didn't sack her, but I told her to give me excuse, and she refused. And these people met her."

Then Nigel said, "OK." Then, "Did she eat?"

Then he said, "No, she didn't eat."

The Nigel said, "Hey, William. You must pay the fifty cedis. You must pay the fifty cedis. We are all coming here to find money, you know? I'm also from London to come and find money. And you are from your village, too!"—*Ha!*—"To come and find your money. How can I be feeding your girl?"

Then: Abena was very foolish, stupid. So she came and announced these topics again which I told her. She said, "*Um-hum.* Even if I am foolish, it's true. What you told me is true. Since I stayed with him, three years, he didn't get me anything. You just came here two months, and you have two machines, you have that and this, and that. You told me all. But I'm foolish, because, if you love a man, they say you are foolish. William, I love you. That's why you think I am a fool. Hawa came here about two

1. I was annoyed.
2. an abuse, that a person has no sense or manners

months now. She met me here in Tamale but now she has two machines and she has that and this and you don't give me anything and now I can see what Hawa is telling me is true."

He said, "Who told you that?"

I said, "Yes, I told her that she is fool. Because, first time—you go to cinema, you don't go with her. You have to go to a different place. And after cinema, she has to wait for you on the road. OK. And when she is here with you, she doesn't put on a high shoe because it is costly. If she's going to buy it, you are going to buy it for her, and it's costly, so you don't want her to do it. So you say, 'If you do that, you will be ashawo.' So, suppose she's not ashawo, where did you meet her?"

He said, "Lido nightclub."

Then I said, "Lido nightclub! Which people are there? The married people?" *Ha-ha-ha!* "The ashawo people! They are the ashawos. At Lido nightclub, if you find some girl there, you must know that she's ashawo. You should let her enjoy herself, because you are not going to marry her. You have a wife. And you have to give her something so that when you go away, she will remember you. She will say, 'Ah, first time I met one man, and he was that and this, and he is the one who gave me this.' She will remember you. But when you treat her like this, it's not good."

Then we talked, *o-o-o.* Nigel said something, I said something. William was annoyed. Then, he had a parrot. This parrot, since we knew this parrot, until this man left Tamale, this parrot had no hair. He said they brought the parrot when it was baby. It didn't have hair. Any time when one hair comes out like this, this parrot would eat it. And so every time, it was like a chicken when you take all the hair out. Then the parrot also started talking, saying, "*Quago, quago. Kak kak, kak kak, kak kak, kak, ka-kak.*"

Then Nigel said, "You see, the way you are bad, you have a parrot who has no hair but he can *talk!*"

So we left this man and went away. And this man was annoyed. You know, in the Gymkhana Club, sometimes when we went, we met this man. He wouldn't say hello to us. He was *annoyed.* He used to come to the Gymkhana Club alone. You would never know that the girl was staying with him. So from there, this man didn't talk to us, and we didn't talk to this man. Our friendship was finished, with that Abena, and with this man also. Before, this man used to come to us every day. From that time, no friends. *Ha!* No understanding; no friends. Yeah, so all this is why I don't like to give friends advice. You will be getting problems inside. *Ha-ha!*

Reflections: Property and Family

So: many girls follow men for money, in Africa here. Yeah? But me like this, I think that now — all my life for some years, I've been going around like this: I have no property. Before: I used to think of marrying. If you find a man you like, and you want to stay with him, you can do it. Yeah. Sometimes — before, I used to think of this. But now, at this time, I don't have that idea. Even I think that later, if I can become a little bit rich, to get something better to do, then I think I can feel myself all right in my life. I don't want all these problems — to marry and then tomorrow is like that, and after tomorrow is "Yeah, yeah." Hey, African marriage is hard, eh? Ah, well — to us, as a Muslim, our marriage is hard. To marry a Muslim, and then you are in this Muslim marriage, it's hard. It's prison.

OK? Then what is my trouble? When I think of marrying, what is my trouble to be married? OK, maybe now, I make up my mind to marry: maybe I will see some boy, and he loves me, and I love him. Then we make up our minds to marry. Maybe we will marry for about one or two years. He will want another woman to marry again. OK? Then maybe, in that first year when we marry, we have nothing. We are suffering together. And then we are trying to get small money to save for our children after. Then he goes and takes another woman, too. That one too will bring babies out. And then: who is the property for? If I am dead, maybe my property is for my children. And maybe these children are very small, so it's the father who is going to take care of this property until they grow to reach it. And then, when they are growing up, maybe the father too will die before they grow up. Or when they grow up, and their father is in life, maybe he will give this property to them; but if it's much money, maybe he won't give it to them. He will put it in his account, that all his children are for him, so if he dies, it's this one child who going to take charge of this money. And maybe you, the one who suffered, your children won't get anything. And so what is the meaning of marry and suffer? For what? Everybody is suffering, and maybe your children will come and suffer more than you. Is that it?

Yeah? I know that. Why can't I know that? Look: among my father's children, eh? My father's children: we have one senior one inside of us, *hmm?* Every time, we all, we all know that if our father is dead now, this boy is the one who is going to take the property of our father. And this boy is a dangerous, secret boy. Nobody knows what he is doing. And we thought — if our father is dead now, if this boy takes the property, we will be coming to more suffering. Every time we used to think this, every time, all of us. Even sometimes we used to have meetings about these things. If our father is sick, seriously, you know? *Ha-ha!* Then my senior sister will say that, "Hey, Hawa."

And I will say, "Hey, *tsk,* the way old man is now, ah, well—"

"But we are going to suffer after."

Then I will say, "Why?"

"Don't you think—if our father is dead now, and we are coming to this house, do you think this boy will allow us?"

And I say, "Ah, if he doesn't allow, too: everybody will find his way. This is it. That is all."

All of us, we are afraid of that boy. He is very bad: he doesn't talk. But the way he plays his ways, he's a very wicked fellow. So we all, we know what things we are doing for our father. So: this house we have, the land is for my father. But I told him to make my name on the house, because I know that if he doesn't make it so, if now-now he's dead, this boy will take that house. But if it's my name on the papers, he cannot take it from me, because it's for me. Yeah, I have to do so. I told my father that when he's in the world, I don't want money from the house. I don't want anything from the house. But he must know that if he is dead, the house is for me. But he can take that money when they rent the house—the small-small money they get inside it—he can take it because now he cannot work and he doesn't do any good job. And he doesn't get a pension. He doesn't have anything. He just forced his strength himself[1] in his life. He didn't do any government work, that they will say that they will pension him or something like that, so he has nothing like that. So this is the pension: I gave it to him. But he must know that if he is dead, then the house is for me. But now when he's in life, I don't want any penny of the house. I don't want penny of it. He can take that money and keep up the small ones, the young ones with him, and the wife, to look after them with that money. So every month, when my brother collects the money from the house, he has to take that money and post to my father in our village.

But you know that if our father dies today-today-today, even if I am not there—ah, if I'm here, as we are talking, maybe he's dead today: then all these families will go there before me. Before I will hear of it, maybe it will be two or three days or one week. Then I will go there. These papers for the house, they will be my business, no? If it's not so, if it is something like this happening at my back, then before one week when I go there, they will share everything for themselves. They will say, "*Pffft!*

1. used his own strength and willingness to work to live his life

Oh, Hawa—*pff*—even she goes round and round, she doesn't come to us. She doesn't worry about this thing. So let's share it." And they will do it, I know. So I don't want anything from there. Only what I have suffered for is my own. So I told him to make the papers in my name. And the taxi too, is for me, but I don't spend that money. Every time, they have to keep that money in the bank; I have one bank book from there. *Mm-hm?* Oh, I don't take care of it, but I thought, last time when I went, I don't know, but I thought my brother too was spending some of the money. So, whatever they say they get from the taxi, then I say OK. But the house is mine.

The last time when I went to Kumasi, I asked my brother, "How much do you think that this taxi can make a month?"

He said, "Oh, some months you can make one thousand cedis a month, some months you can make sixty or one hundred or two hundred cedis." He was telling me some story like this.

So I said, "OK, anything you get, you just keep it in the bank."

So then he told me that the car spoiled. They bought this, they bought that part, and they received this, they had to take this money and do that and go there and do that. So the money in the bank there, I don't mind it. Yeah, the time when I saw my bank book, it was a long time ago, and I think I had about three thousand cedis and some hundreds, about five hundred, or something like that, in the book. But it's long time. We must have got more than that. They are spending it off, you know. Because they didn't suffer.

Yeah, they didn't suffer to get it. They don't know the way of getting my cedis: to be in Bagabaga. "You fucking girl, you sleep in Bagabaga, eh? You think you are big woman, eh, Hawa? Be careful. Fucking small girl like you, eh? You want to control Nigel Manners?" *Ha-ha! Shit.* Oh yeah.

All that and—you know, my heart is like a stone, eh? All this doesn't press me, you know. When Nigel says that, I will say, "Do you think so?"

He will say, "Yes."

"Eh? You think so? You think I am a very fucking girl? A stupid small girl, yeah?"

"Yes! You are small girl, and you don't understand."

I will say, "Yes, thank you." Sometimes I will say "Master." I used to call him "Master," you know, and all this, yeah: "Master doesn't spoil anything."

Yeah? So as for me, I thought, suppose my brother was a good man to look after this taxi, we could be buying more, more, more, more. Then we could catch about four or five taxis. I thought it would be better. And then, what I am thinking: if I have enough money, I would like to have a small house, a portable[1] house, for me alone. Like a flat, you know, and then if I am coming or going, there is nothing to worry. I will live alone quietly. Then I will get something to do. If I have money, I will get something to do, some things to sell, not to be going out to — all my life, you know. I will be living, resting, thinking — having better things to do, at that time. Ah, well — if we have the money, we know what to do. But when we don't have the money, every time the blame is like that.

Power Show for Cigarettes

Yeah, I used to remember Tamale, because in Tamale, I was with these fucking English people every day, every day, night and day. You know? So I studied them well there. In Accra, I didn't have time. Even if I was living with somebody as a friend, sometimes I would go to town to meet my other friends and go round. But Tamale, every day, in the daytime at my house, they used to come in, maybe two or three, and we would start to talk. Or sometimes somebody would call me on telephone, "Hawa, come and see something." And I would go. Some of them wanted to know how to make palm soup:[2] they would buy the palm nuts and then they would call me to come and show them how to make it. All this.

I was good to them, but still they talked about me. And you know, I was serious. If they said something and I was annoyed, I wouldn't laugh at that. I used to be serious. But sometimes, if they were talking something like their own joke, they used to make me laugh. And sometimes, they used to talk something which they thought, *ah,* maybe they can make me be annoyed, because they knew I used to be annoyed quickly. Sometimes they used to make something like that, and then I would laugh at them. *Ha!* Yeah.

The first time, when I went to Tamale, when I came from Accra, I didn't like Tamale much. I didn't like it much because, every time when we went to Gymkhana Club, I wasn't happy. To be with these old, old women, you know, these English old, old, old, old women: as for them, everything they saw was not nice for them. Every time they talked about people too much. I didn't like them. Every time we went to Gymkhana Club, and I didn't like there.

1. small, easy to carry, manageable, i.e., not expensive; sometimes applied to people, meaning "cute," as in "a portable girl"

2. soup made from oil palm nuts

But that first time, Tamale was swinging. Now, it's making quiet.[1] By this time, Tamale is quiet, but first, it was not quiet like now. There were some Russian girls: they brought them and put them there, and they hadn't got husbands, so every night, they used to make a dance at Katanga Rest House. Every night, you would see plenty people in that place, drinking with these girls, or at Gymkhana Club. Now, because there's not any good place, all the girls went away. But that time, Accra was not the only place in Ghana: they had some thick girls in Tamale. When I went to Tamale, then later, when they used to make dances at all these different places, I didn't used to go to Gymkhana. Sometimes I could go alone to dance or I could go together with Nigel. Yeah. Nigel used to dance, too, with his conceive! Yeah. Hey! He liked Highlife.[2] *Eh?* When he danced, he had a big ass—*ha!*—and when he danced, shaking his stomach in Highlife, people liked his dance. *Hey!* What are you talking?! Nigel?! *Ha!* He danced nicely. *Special* Highlife. Yeah, his dance was nice!

So the first time, when we were going to Gymkhana Club, I didn't like the place. But when I started going out to outside dancing, I liked the town. I used to make some kind of friends at the dance, girls, and we would drink together, dancing, laughing, doing all these thing. After, when the dance closed, I would take a taxi to go to Bagabaga. So at that time, Tamale was good.

I didn't go to these nightclubs every time. Sometimes I would go to Gymkhana, and when I was going there, some small-small thing would come. Some women are very, very bad—these English. They would make as if they liked me. Every time they saw me, "Oh, Hawa! Yesterday we did this. Why didn't you come?"

Then I would think, "Oh, maybe these people are right[3] people." Don't you know that they were left? They were not right at all. *Ha!* But we were together every time.

The English women: *agh!* Always this—you should know that, especially, if it is an African girl who is walking with a white man, and they go to a place where there is no other African woman there, or not any African woman is with a white man, then all these women will look at you. And by all means they will talk about you. They have to talk about you. Some are looking as if they like you, but they don't like you exactly. She will smile to you, but you don't know what she's saying to her heart. The English women: they can talk about people!

1. It's quiet.
2. popular dance of Ghana
3. good, correct

I even fought with one. How we fought: OK. You know, at that time there was Tombola in Gymkhana. Every Wednesday they had Tombola, so every Wednesday, we used to go to this Tombola. And sometimes I used to win their big money, and there was one woman who started to be jealous from there. An *old* lady! I thought she was feeling like doing something to me, but I didn't talk to her. I didn't say anything bad to her so that she wouldn't get a chance.

So one time I won the Tombola, and this woman said, "No. We are doing this Tombola by luck. We don't do it by juju! That's why we don't believe much in Africans to come and join the nightclub. He shouldn't bring this girl, if she's making juju, and then she's coming to win our money every time."

You know, this woman was just shouting in front of people. There were many people. That time, Gymkhana Club Tombola, outside and inside will be all full up. Many people were there, and this woman was just shouting. So that day, I didn't take the money I won. Nigel went and collected it for me. I said I didn't want it. I was crying. I was feeling pity that day.

But the day when we were going to get trouble, it was because of cigarettes. They brought cigarettes like the way they brought it.[1] And that time, they used to be short of it in Tamale. So they were bringing some cartons, and at that time I was smoking 5-5.[2] She also smoked 5-5. And the 5-5, they didn't have it much. They brought the 5-5, and then it was left with one carton, ten packets. Then Nigel told the barman, Yakubu, that he shouldn't sell it again, that he would pay for all and give the ten packets to me. Then that woman also came to buy that cigarette, and Yakubu said, "There are no cigarettes. They are finished."

Then she saw the carton, and she said, "But what is this? But there are cigarettes in that case."

Then Yakubu said, "No, that is for Madame. It is Master who said to keep it for his wife." You know, Yakubu used to call Nigel "Master." So Yakubu said, "It's the husband who brought it for her."

"Which Madame?"

He said, "Ah, Master's wife."

Then she said, "Which wife?" You know? *Ha!*

So I was sitting. There was one table where we used to sit every time. At that time, when Gymkhana was Gymkhana, that table was the table for Nigel. If they knew that Nigel was going to come out that night, and

1. by allocation of limited supplies from the distributor
2. a British cigarette, State Express, also known as 555 or 5-5

somebody came, they would tell the fellow that nobody should sit at that table. Where we were sitting, anything that would happen at the counter, you would hear it. And this woman also knew the cigarettes were for me, so she just turned her back and she was just talking.

She said they should give her cigarettes to buy, that she is also a member — there is not any way to be keeping it for Nigel's wife — so she doesn't need all this fucking thing — what! — how long did I know 5-5 before knowing how to smoke it? You know? She was just talking some things like that.

And you know, I didn't want to talk, but the thing was making me hot. So I said, "Hey, Nigel, did you tell Yakubu to keep the cigarettes for me? Let's give it to the woman to buy."

Then Nigel said, "No. Why?"

Then I said, "I don't want the topics she is making."

He said, "What's wrong with you? She said it but she won't get it."

Then I said, "No, you must give her the cigarettes."

So Nigel got up and collected all the ten packets and came and packed them on top of the table in front of us. *Ha!* Then I said, "OK, she can come and take some of the cigarettes and smoke. I'm nothing. Even, before I grew up, I didn't know how they make the tobacco plant, to make all these fucking 5-5. Without any 5-5, I think I will live in life. So if she can't live in life without 5-5, she can come and take it."

So she said, "Hey! Who are you talking to?"

Then I said, "What are you? Who do you think you are? You think I can't talk to you?" *Ha!*

You see? Because of the first thing she had done to me about the Tombola, I was hot, too. And then the second time she came and talked about cigarettes like this to me. So I was annoyed. She was trying to bluff herself.

Then this woman turned to us, and then she came and stood in front of us, and she asked Nigel, "The cigarettes are for your wife?"

Then he said, "Yes."

She said, "Are you saying 'Yes'? So she's your wife?" *Ha-ha! Ah!!*

Hey! This woman: I looked at her! Then I thought, "Yes, I'm going to know these people now." But you know, this woman was the first woman who liked me. Every day she used to bring her car to our place. Every four o'clock, she would come and take tea with me. Then I thought, "Oh-h-h-h-h, that's the way."

Then Nigel said, "Yes, she's my wife."

She said, "Oh? Now you are a pure African. So you forgot Josephine in London, and now you have got another wife here."

Then Nigel said, "Yes, it's possible. Maybe even Josephine knows this, because Josephine has come and met me with her, and she had nothing to say, and she went back. So Josephine knows about this, so she's my wife."

She said, "Good God! But Nigel, I'm going to tell you: these cigarettes, we have to share them."

Then Nigel said, "Oh. Yeah. But you cannot share it fifty-fifty; if you like, she will give you two packets."

Then she said, "And so you think this fucking girl is better than me?"

I was there! I didn't go anywhere. I was sitting there. Then I thought, "No, this woman, today, if she will beat me, it's better." Because what she was doing, many people were starting some things: you know, British people, when they see something like this, they just start scratching each other. Maybe they pass their feet under the table, scratching their feet, and raising their eyebrows. Yeah. Man, they are *shit! Ha!*

So when I started this thing, I looked, and when I turned my head, I saw people were making a face. So I thought, "*Aha!* Today I must make my show, because if I leave this thing, I have lost my chance. People are starting to look at me, so I have to do something." *Ha!* So I was serious, because this woman *fucked* me, *two times.* The first one, I didn't say anything. I just looked at her. And she repeated again. Why? *Ha! Ah!* How can she fuck me like that? So when I thought of her, I thought, no, I must reply her. If I don't reply her, she will take it far. Yeah, she was the first woman who showed me something in Gymkhana Club.

Then I said, "Look, if you are talking to me, you must talk slowly. You know? Here is not London, anyway. You are in Africa. I can't talk this way to you in London. So you must be careful." *Ha! Hee-hee!*

Then I looked at this woman. I said, "OK. Go and take all. The whole carton: I give it to you. Even Nigel has already paid for it. Don't pay anything. Take it. I dash it to you. I don't want it. I'm so fucking, I shouldn't smoke 5-5. If I'm so fucking, then this 5-5 is not a good cigarette for me to smoke. You are my grandmother, so it's better for you to go and take it. You are my grandmother, and you are smoking 5-5. I shouldn't smoke it. So you are not abusing me. I'm so fucking to smoke it. Go and take all. I give it to you."

Then Nigel looked at me. "Eh? Eh, my dear? You! You feel to talk so?" *Ha-ha!*

Then she said, "Hey, Nigel, you'd better tell her. Here is Gymkhana Club!"

Then I said, "Yeah, it's Gymkhana Club, but the land is for Africans. We didn't refuse it to you. You are the one who built the house, but I don't think the land is for you. You are not the one who built the land. So it's for us, all of us, not for you alone."

Then: "Hey, Nigel, this girl doesn't respect. Don't you bring such girls like this here to disturb people."

Then I said, "You go and have your cigarettes, Grandmother. Grandmother, go and take your cigarettes. It's finished. I don't respect, and I have said what I am going to say, and it's finished. I won't say anything again. So just go and have your cigarettes."

This woman *boiled* up! "*Shit!* What are you talking about?!" If not because of Nigel, did I talk to a white before? And how much about a white woman?

Then I said, "*Good God!* This woman!" I slapped her mouth. I got her. First I gave her a dirty slap. Then she wanted to hold my dress. Then I said, "*Fine!* You want to hold my dress? I will show you how to hold a dress. I won't hold your dress."

And you know, she had very lovely hair, long hair back to here. So I just got her hair. And squeezed it. *Ha!* I was just taking her around, you know. Anyway, I didn't beat her; I didn't fight her. You see? When I got the hair, I made so. Then she said, *"Oooooooooo!"*

Then people were trying to separate us. They thought if they squeeze me well, they will get the hair, the place I was hurting her. But if you hold here strongly as if you want to break my bone, I also have to pull this hair out. So you know, they were separating us, but the way they separated us was some kind of *kɔnkɔnsa* way.[1] Some people were holding me very strongly, so that I would feel pains and leave her. But this was the case, and I was wounding her more.

So when they separated us, then this woman wouldn't take any of these cigarettes. *Ha!* She wouldn't take it! She refused: she wouldn't take anything, even one packet. She just went to the table and took her bag, and then she called the husband and they went off.

So that week, I came to Tombola but I didn't take the ticket. I said I wouldn't play. Then the people were saying, "Oh-h, don't! Play! This is past things. It's your luck. Maybe some people have their luck. Some people don't have. There is some month when you are lucky." And what and what.

I said, "No. Me, I won't play Tombola again. You people can chop your

1. in this context, roundabout, fake, bullshit, indirect. Kɔnkɔnsa (Asante Twi) refers to talking about people, often in a manipulative or distorting way, or to gossip that causes trouble between people. Gossiper: kɔnkɔnsani (singular); kɔnkɔnsafoɔ (plural).

money and go to London and build a money house. I don't want a money house. You people need a money house, then you come from over a thousand miles away to come and find money in Ghana. Not me." *Ha!*

Cool-Catch-Monkey

So that time I was getting a time for them — a tough time, too. I used to give a tough time to all of them and their men. There was another English woman, Evelyn, and that time, Evelyn was good for me. Every time, she used to come to my place, or sometimes she would make a telephone that I should come to her. She was near me, too, and so sometimes I would walk down there. Sometimes the husband would come and pick me. Any time she had a party, she used to invite me and Nigel. We ate there, and they also used to come and eat with us. So I thought she was the first friend I got. Do you know, she was also like that! She was just blowing bubble gum, you know, this thing children used to play with. Yeah. She saw me like that.

So, I didn't know. One afternoon, we went to Gymkhana Club. There was one man. His wife had three boys; they had no baby girl. He used to bring his children to Gymkhana Club every afternoon. There was tennis, and these things the children could play on. Every Sunday or Saturday afternoon, if you went there, you would see plenty of them with their children. The women are playing tennis; the men are playing the darts or the billiards. So one day we were sitting and drinking, and these children were playing with one half-caste boy. The half-caste, the father was Scottish but the mother was a Ghanaian. These four children, the half-caste together with this woman's three children: they were going to play on these things for the children.

So they went and met some African man's children who were just living behind that area. Sometimes they also used to go and play there. These African children were playing there, so the children — because they were white — they came to force the African children to get down and give them the way. And these African children were grown a little bit past the white children, and you know, Africans too, we don't like these things. So one African child wanted to show that Africans too have bones, so you can't do this to me, and he beat one small boy — the white one. So this white boy came back to the mama, crying, showing the mama how the other children beat him. Then the mama didn't mind him; the mama was conversing with others, and so she didn't listen to the baby.

Then Evelyn just answered, "What is that? What is that?" You, Evelyn! You don't have a child, like me. You have nothing, like me. Then you are trying to do these things. And I thought that if these children were all white and they fought together, who would like to beat his baby because of your baby? And these African children, their mother was not there. But because they were Africans, the people just got up and caught these boys and: *s-s-s-s-s!* And they said, "These fucking cool-catch-monkeys, where are they from!?"

Yeah, that time they used to say this "cool-catch-monkey," or "coal-catch-monkey," something like that. Cool-catch-monkey.[1] In Gymkhana Club, sometimes when these English people were sitting together, they used to abuse Africans. But if they said, "Black monkey," they used to get trouble for that. "Black monkey": any kind of small baby can understand it. Especially me, when I heard this, then I would say, "I am going to report you. I don't care who you are." So they changed their words if they wanted to abuse Africans. They made their gang and brought this talk so that we wouldn't understand what they meant. They all made one mouth to be saying "cool-catch-monkey" instead of "black monkey." Every time, they used to say that.

So I didn't know it. Then one day I was talking to Nigel, and I said it: I thought it was something like a joke, you know, so I said, "Hey, you cool-catch-monkey?"

Then he laughed. "Do you know what we are saying with this 'cool-catch-monkey'?"

Then I said, "No."

"Every time, when we say, 'black monkey,' everybody knows it. Now you people know it, and if we say 'black monkey,' we have troubles."

Then I said, "Yes."

Then he said, "So this one you said, you said it to yourself, because I'm not African. Do you know meaning of this 'cool-catch-monkey' we are saying in Gymkhana Club?"

Then I said, "No."

He said, "*Black* monkey."

So at the club, Nigel used to be with them, and they would talk all this

1. I had not heard of this phrase and have not learned its logic or allusion to post-colonial Ghana. I have heard two proverbs in Ghana that link "coolness" and monkeys, though whether Gymkhana members would have come across them is obscure. Dagbamba say, "It's cool for the monkey; that's why it carries its baby on its back." The image is that of a monkey carrying its baby, but if the monkey is frightened or disturbed, it will throw the baby down and run away. Akan say, "Softly, softly, catch the monkey," that is, go gradually to get something or someone.

thing nicely. But in the *end,* when this fucking man got his beer, he would tell me *all* that they were doing there. So: if this word comes in this way, I should know that they are talking about Africans. *Ha!*

Ah! I don't know what kind of sense they were taking to say this word. When they were using the word, then they would turn and turn and be saying it. And you know, they were very funny. If they wanted to talk about you, they would look at your face. Yeah. This one would look at you so, then that one would make so, then they would turn, make so, and then they would look at you so. So every time, when I sat with them, I looked at everybody around. My eyes used to go around and around. *Ha!* So if it came like that, then I was already boiled up—I knew that something was going to come out. Always, if it was like that, my eye used to go fast. Then my drink: I used to drink it fast. Small time, I would puff my cigarette. Small time I puff; then I'm sweating; I am waiting for what you are going to say. Then I'm thinking of the reply to give you.

Ha! Then any time they said this word, "cool-catch-monkey," I used to heat like hot water, because—*ha!*—Nigel told me.

Gymkhana Club! Sometimes, they didn't like to see me there. Sometimes in Gymkhana Club, when they came and met me there first in the club, they would stay, but they wouldn't stay long, and then they would go. Because what will they talk? If they sit together, they haven't any talks. Their only talk is about Africans. Always. English people never make three together, and they won't talk about Africans. In Africa here. I don't know their country, but here in Africa, never. They will start. They cannot sit together to say something better, apart from things about Africans. Yeah, always. They are like that. *Ha!* I don't like them. *Hee-hee!*

So every time, I had to make trouble with them. The first time, I was shy. I was giving them some respect when I came. Then, I was a bit shy. But the day when this woman came and talked about the cigarettes, I said, "No. These people, I will start to fuck them." *Ha!* Yeah, the way they talked to me, I thought they took me as a friend, nicely. I didn't know the way they took me, I must try to show them too. So anything you say, I will just listen. When you say the case and finish, then I will answer you. If I answer you, too, then I will look at you. *Ha!* I want to look at you like that. Then you will watch me well-well. The next time, if you see somebody like me, you won't say those words in front of him.

So from that time, when we went to Gymkhana, then I started making them hot. That time, the first Regional Commissioner was a friend to Nigel. His wife was a half-caste woman. Sometimes this man used to come to our house and drink with Nigel. So any small thing, I used to say, "I will go and report you." *Ha!* That time, I had this Nkrumah C.P.P. cloth.[1] I had different-different kinds of colors. I was a kɔnkɔnsa C.P.P.[2] I didn't go to their party meetings, but I am a complete C.P.P. member in Gymkhana Club. You would say something small, and I would say, "Yes. Now I know you people. I know all of you people. I have started to know you people now, from now going. I have been watching you people one by one, but the day when I'm going to do something to you people here—*ee-e-e!*—in Tamale here, you will doubt. You will know that Africa is good, but Africa is hot."

So if I talked this, then they would say, "Hey-hey, Nigel. Why should you bring this girl here? This small girl, and you give her a chance—" Look! Oh, they didn't know. I am short, but I'm not small.

And sometimes, you know, when they thought they were talking to Nigel to tell me to stop it, that was the time when Nigel was going to be fired up, too. He would say, "But why? Yes? She has a right. It's her right to say that, because even it's true. Those people are good, because in London, you can't get any corner to talk about a British fellow and somebody wouldn't reply you. So you know, as she has been with me a long time, and she has been conversing with many English people, now she knows our tongue. So anyway, if you people have to say something like that, if she hears it, she is right to say it. Even if it's me, I can't stop her to say this."

So they too, they would be annoyed with him. Sometimes, because of me, we could be coming to the nightclub, to Gymkhana Club, and for about one week, Nigel wouldn't have any friend. Nobody would talk to him. If he saw someone, he'd say, "Eh, eh, eh, my friend, come here." They would just look at him—*ha-ha!* Yeah, the fellow would just look at him and then—*shit!* You know? They didn't mind him.

So that day, when Evelyn started to talk this "cool-catch-monkey," you know, I was annoyed. She was talking about the club, and it's for them, and that and this—and no African man pays to be a member of the club—and they are the people who made the club—and African babies should not be going on their babies' thing—and that and this.

Then I said, "Oh, Evelyn, why do you say that? Don't you know that it is not good?"

1. Convention People's Party, the political party of Kwame Nkrumah. Associations often have special wax-print cloth designs. A cloth for a political party, for example, might feature a picture of the leader, with a motto above and the name below, with the name of the party worked into the surrounding design.

2. literally "gossip C.P.P."; in this sense, bogus, just talking it or showing off

"Oh, they are fucking cool-catch-monkeys! And they don't understand." Even I was the one talking to her: she still didn't listen to me. "Fucking people — black monkeys."

Then I thought, "No! This woman!" So I didn't want to talk much then; I thought that to shout much will be very annoying for me, so I went to the toilet. I got up and went to toilet. When I was coming from the toilet, then she also was going to the toilet. Then I said, "*Ah-hah!* Now we will see! Cool-catch here! If here is for you, you will go and leave the house for me. It is for me, too. Ah! I leave you your house." So I caught her and we started fighting. And you know, the way I held her — she also had a lot of hair, long hair — oh, it was very nice. *Ha!* When I got that hair, then I put her down. I didn't want to beat her, so I just held where she couldn't get a chance to shout. And then we were fighting. The chairs and the table in the toilet were breaking, and then one woman came and saw it, and then she shouted, and they came and caught me.

So Evelyn's husband was called Roger, and Roger was another *fat* guy, and very tall. The way he was, if you saw him, you wouldn't think he was an English man. He was very tough. He just got up, "Good God!" Then he wanted to beat me because I disgraced the wife.

And you know, my man, Nigel, he was not strong, but he had a mouth. Nigel had a *hot* one. But he was not strong. If Roger would give him a blow, *tsk,* Roger would kill him. So if something like this came, Nigel wouldn't say anything. He would just sit down. Unless the thing passed before he would talk. But if the thing came like this, he didn't want it.

Then this Swiss boy, Fritz, said to Roger, "If you beat this girl, I will beat you, too."

"Why?"

"It's their palaver. It's two women. If two women fight, men shouldn't come inside. What are these girls to you? Your wife said something she doesn't like. If your wife went to the toilet and she didn't say anything, this girl wouldn't say anything too. So you can't beat her."

So that day I was very happy! Then it was finished. I came and sat down, and these people left: Evelyn and her husband went out.

Then: "*Eh? Eh?* Hey, Hawa, that is war. *Eh?* My dear, you want to start?"

Then I said, "Yes."

"Yakubu, eh? You see my wife is strong? She beat Evelyn. *Eh,* Hawa, you are strong!"—*Ha! Ha!*—"Yeah, you are good boxer. You can save me? Hey, Hawa, you see?"

Then I said, "Fuck off." I was annoyed! *Ha! Ha!* "You! You were there when this man got up. He was going to beat me. You didn't say anything. And then they are not here, and now you try to make your mouth. Fuck off. Why? When Roger was going to beat me, you were here, no? But what did you say then?"

Then he said, "Oh-h?"

"Now you say you're better because they have gone out. Fuck off!"

"Eh? You think Roger can beat you? Oh, my God! I was waiting! If he touched you, I would take him —*pfft*— out this window!"

Then I said, "Fuck off!" *Ha-ha!*

"Oh, don't you know? You think fucking Nigel? With this long muscle? Big muscle like this?" Then he made his hand like this, you know, and when he made this, then the muscle made so. Yeah, then he made that thing, and he was saying, "Eh? You think this thing is a fucking thing? Eh, my dear, if I pick Roger, I will throw him out this window." *Ha!* These people had gone, and then he was making mouth! *Ha!* When they were there, he didn't do anything to show that. When he saw that they have gone, he could talk anything, but if Roger was there, Roger would beat him. Nigel knew it himself, so he wouldn't allow that.

One day, Nigel let one man hold him, just hold him like this. That day, oh, I pitied him. Then they held his hands like this. And I said, "Oh, oh, this my old man, they are going to kill him in front of me."

But his mouth wouldn't sleep. Anything he saw, he would talk about it. Look, some people would do their things. If Nigel was there, if he came back to sit, he would tell me, very quietly, "Hey, Hawa, you see this boy, Roger? With this girl?"

"Yes."

"Do you know why?"

"No, I don't know. Why?"

"You think this fucking boy—you think this fucking boy likes this girl? No, my dear, this fucking boy doesn't like her *at all.* Do you know why?"

And I said, "No."

"Because this girl has money. That's why this boy likes her. That's why—"

Ha! You see, Evelyn was older than the husband. *Ha!* Evelyn had money. She was a nurse. So he was telling me that the husband didn't like her. Roger didn't like Evelyn. It was because of the money of Evelyn. That was why. *Ha!*

So, if Nigel saw anything, he would come and talk it. Any bloody, fucking thing.

Nigel's Mouth

There was a girl, an African girl. OK? This girl was called Confort. She was married to one man called Stephen. Stephen was Scottish. They had three children. OK. Her husband was one of the people who was building things, and every time, he was staying in the bush. Every week, maybe he would come home once. And this girl was living in town. She had a baby about seven months old, but every time, this girl used to go around the town. If she saw somebody she liked, she would bring him to her house, because the husband was not there. And Nigel was seeing all this thing. So Nigel thought it was easy to make kɔnkɔnsa. But it's not easy for anyone. When the husband came to Gymkhana Club, we were drinking. Then this girl went to the toilet, and when she was coming, she passed outside. There was a man too who came from his place and went out to meet the girl. I saw this girl going outside. Nigel also saw. Then Nigel said, "*Eh, eh, eh?* Hawa, *eh,* you see? You see Confort?"

And I said, "Where?"

"She passed there. *Eh,* my dear, you think you can do that? Hawa cannot do that. *Eh?* Stephen—you are a fool." *Ha-ha!* "You see Confort?"

Then Stephen said, "Confort has gone to toilet."

"No, my friend, go outside and you will see Confort."

Then Stephen said, "And so what?"

Then Nigel said, "Eh? You don't know? If you go anywhere, you see that boy who went out: he used to go to Confort. Every time I see this boy with Confort."

Then Stephen said, "And so what?!"

"Eh, my dear, because you are fool. Oh? You cannot fuck, so you take your wife to everybody to fuck, to give you a lift because you haven't got a car, eh?"

Ha! This man got up and—*unnk!*—he just took Nigel and he threw him like a piece of bread. Then I said, "Yeah. Today is today. Mouth pass man."[1]

Stephen was shaking Nigel like that, and Nigel's shirt came off, and plenty people came: "No! Stephen! Don't do it, don't do it." And they took Nigel's dress from Stephen.

So then Nigel made like a fighter, "Stephen, prepare your dress. You fucking boy. You think you're fit to beat Nigel Manners, eh? Eh? Confort,

1. (Pidgin): The mouth is more than the man.

fuck off. Fuck off. Plenty people fuck you, eh? Yesterday you made telephone for me to come to your house. I told you, Hawa will beat you, eh? Fuck off. Fuck off." *Ha!*

Hey! Ha! Then all the people were quiet. Then everybody said, "No, Stephen, don't touch him, don't touch him." Because everybody knew that this man is not strong, and he was a very fat man. If you beat him, maybe you will kill him or something. He used to talk things, but if someone was going to beat him, then all the other people would separate them. Then Stephen took his wife away.

That night, we didn't sleep the whole night. "Eh, Hawa, you think this fucking Confort is a lady? Fucking, fucking woman like this? And Stephen is a fool. Eh, Hawa? You think an English man can do that? That fucking Scottish. The fucking Scottish." *Ha!* "With their skirts!" *Ha!* "They can do that. Do you think Nigel Manners can do that? *Tsk!* Fuck off, fuck off! Fuck off."

You know, when he was drunk, he called everything together. Even if he was talking to you about somebody, and you were answering, he would tell you, "Fuck off" too. Then he would talk about you, too. *Ha!* Even Yakubu: when all the people were gone, and it was left with me and Nigel and Yakubu, Nigel would talk. And every time, when it was Yakubu and Nigel, Nigel would talk to Yakubu, and then Nigel would come and start to abuse Africans. Then he would ask Yakubu, "Yakubu, is it true? Africans do that? Can Nigel Manners do that?" Then Yakubu would just laugh and say, *"Yes! Master!"*

Yeah, Nigel's mouth was too much. You know, the first time, there was one Canadian boy, and this boy was a teacher in the school. OK, every time you saw this boy in the daytime, he didn't wear a shirt. On the bicycle, coming to the market for shopping, he just had some shorts, with a kind of knife like Frafra people have, hanging on his belt. And he would pass Gymkhana Club and take one drink before going home, with all that he had from shopping on the back of his bicycle in a basket. So one day Nigel was sitting down and looked at this boy. It was Saturday. And Nigel said, "Look, do you know, here is not California. Here is a British Club. I'm telling you. Why should you come inside without a shirt? You want to show us a knife? I have a pistol; I don't show it to people."

This boy was looking at Nigel. Then he took his glass to drink. You know, Nigel was lucky. He used to meet people who have patience. So this boy took his drink, and Nigel just took the glass from him and put it down. "I said, look, go and put your shirt on before you come and drink. I know that you bought it. But here is not in your country, to come and stand here with your chest. You want to show us you have a big chest?" *Ha-ha!*

Then this boy didn't talk. Nigel put the glass on the other side of himself. Then this boy went behind Nigel and took his glass again. And Nigel took the glass from him again. So this boy was boiled up! And then he took the knife — I don't know, like magic — he took the knife like this and said, "Can I show the knife? Can I show the knife?"

Then Nigel gave the glass back to him. He said, "Yeah, I see it." *Ha!* He was afraid. "Yeah, I see it. I see your knife. Drink your beer and go. But next time don't come here like that."

But Nigel wouldn't be quiet, too. He came and sat, and he said, "*Tweaa!* Do you think this fucking American boy can kill me? Suppose I had my pistol here, my dear, eh? I will kill him. I will finish him just now. A fucking army captain like me? Don't you know that I went to war before in Britain? *Tweaa!* A fucking, fucking small boy like him. To show Nigel Manners a knife?" *Ha!* You know, when you do something to Nigel and he looks afraid, he will be talking about it for the whole night. When he's drunk, when he sits down a little bit, then he will start again, "Ah! *Tweaa!* You see this fucking thing? This fucking small, small boy like this. Trying to show me this knife? My dear, you see? You are the one who doesn't let me. You think if I come here alone, he will show me the knife? I will fucking shoot the hell — kill the fucking boy!" *Ha!*

So he was just like that. At Gymkhana Club, *all* the people got fed up with Nigel, so he didn't have a friend. But sometimes, you know, at first, what they had at Gymkhana Club: if any white stranger came to the Catering Rest House,[1] he would come to the nightclub. And the ones who were working at Wa, and all these places — you know, there were some white people working there — when they came, they came and lodged at the Catering Rest House. In the night, as they felt this club was for white people, they used to go there. If Nigel met a kind of person like that, then he would get a friend to talk to. But the ones who were working in Tamale, because of me he didn't have a friend. He lost all his friends, because, you know, I didn't care. I know that Nigel was a drunkard. Number one: Nigel was a drunkard. OK? Number two: he also gave me the way. At first, when I was with him, when I didn't know his character, even the friends could say something which I knew that I could reply to, but sometimes I used to feel that this man, maybe if I reply it, he will say I have disgraced him. So if the people left, I would tell him, "Look, this person,

1. state-owned hotel in Tamale

he was saying so, and he said so, and I overheard it. If not because of you, as for me, I would have given him a reply."

He would say, "What! Why didn't you give him a reply? Is he my father? Even my brother, if he tells you something you don't want, you should *tell* him. In London this is the way we do."

So from that time going, I didn't fear in front of him. I didn't feel shame too. If you say something, I will just fuck you off. And sometimes, you know, when Nigel didn't drink, he used to be ashamed to follow me. Sometimes he used to tell me, "No, you shouldn't say that. He didn't say anything bad."

And I would say, "OK, together with him, you and him both: fuck off." *Ha-ha!* Yeah, the two of them, they can fuck off.

So I think that sometimes, if Nigel was drinking, even if I said something to his friends, then he will be behind me, every time. But if he wasn't drunk, if I said something against a white man like that, I think it used to pain him, or he used to feel shame. I don't know. At that time, he didn't want you to be saying things straightforward like that. If somebody does something to you, you know, like maybe somebody will tell you some topics, and you don't like it, you also have to reply that fellow something. Yeah. But when he wasn't drunk, I think maybe he was feeling something like, "This fellow is my friend or something like that. We are all white." But if he drank, he didn't mind about white, or anything. If he drank, he would say, yes, what I said is true. But if he didn't drink, and if he didn't agree with me, I would fuck them all together. *Ha!* I would mix with Nigel, and then I would fuck off all of them together. If we were in the house, then I fucked them together, then I would leave them together. Maybe I would go to sleep. I would say, "Yeah! I'm going to sleep." Or "I'm going out. You people can say whatever you like. It's in back of me, because you can't say it in front of me."

Then I would go out. Then when I came back, Nigel would say, "Look. But this thing, I know that what you said is true. But, you know, every time I follow you, so sometimes I should follow my friends, too, a little bit. But if you want to fuck them, if you want to disgrace them, then don't put me inside."

Then I would say, "You, you want it. You asked for it. Why don't you keep quiet then?"

He would say, "No, but not every day I will keep quiet and you will be abusing them, you know." *Ha!*

So he was just somebody like that. So that time, when it reached like that, then we were all right.

A Beating among Friends

So every time, Nigel used to do these things to the people in the Gymkhana Club, and they never let somebody beat him. Only Ian. Ian wanted to beat him, but he didn't really beat him. Ian just pushed him and Nigel broke his head,[1] but nobody beat him. *Ha!* There weren't many people in the Club that day; if there were many people, they wouldn't allow it. We were just three there. With Yakubu, we were four. Then Ian did that to him.

Ha! You know, Nigel was drunk, so he sat back on the chair. Nigel always was sitting like that, and he told Ian, "Hey, my dear, fuck off. You fucking Scottish — eh? You forget your skirt?"

Then Ian said, "Hey, Nigel, don't tell me something foolish."

Then Nigel said, "Oh, oh? My dear? Oh Hawa, you know this man? You know Scotland? They used to put on skirts like a woman. Have you seen that before?"

Then Ian kicked the chair, and then Nigel fell down. So when Nigel fell down, he was wounded. Yeah. His head was broken. Yakubu was there. So then I held Ian, no? And Yakubu had to watch Ian. I went out to bring police, and when I went out, I met Lawyer Owusu and another friend. They came with their cars, and then they took Nigel to hospital. And I also went to police, and then they took Ian and kept him in police station.

So when they sewed Nigel's head and finished, then his eyes were opening. "Hey, Hawa, hey, my dear, come here." Then I went. Then he said, "What did I come here for?"

And I said, "Don't you know that you were wounded?"

Then he touched there, and he said, "Yeah? How did I do that?"

I said, "It was Ian."

"Ian? That fucking Scottish?"

I said, "Yes. But I have locked him in police station."

He said, *"Good God!!!! You have what?"*

I said, "Yeah. I took him to police station. He's in police station now. Tomorrow we will go and see him."

Then he said, "What tomorrow? The way you got him in, you must get him back, my dear, eh? You fucking —" *Ha!* "You fucking girl, don't you know we are from Europe together? Do you want to spoil my people's

1. got a cut on his head

name? You want to give them a bad name in prison? No, no, no, no!" *Ha!* "The way you got him in, you must get him back in that way."

Then I said, "Eh? So that's the way?"

He said, "Yes." So then I had nothing to say. I went to police station with Nigel together with Lawyer Owusu. And we took Ian to drop him at his house. And Lawyer Owusu dropped us at our place, too.

So I was annoyed with Nigel in this case, you know, because he shamed me. So I didn't talk to him. Then one day we were sitting, and he said, "But why? This time you don't talk to me?"

Then I said, "Yes, because, you know, I'm a fucking foolish girl, you know. If it's not so, I wouldn't live with you. If I'm not foolish, I wouldn't live with you even for one minute." *Ha-ha!* "So I know that I am a fucking foolish girl in this case. I don't want to talk to you because, even if I talked something good for you, you say I did bad. So if you want to talk to someone, it's better you go and talk to your Ian."

Then he said, "But no, Hawa, look: you know that Ian is an English man. Though we can play, we can make some jokes, but—*tsk, eh*—you know—he's British also. You don't think Scottish—Scottish—you know, Frafra, and Accra or Kumasi people, they are *all* Ghanaians. And so we are the same. If we are playing and he is drunk, and he does something to me, you shouldn't take him to police station. So if you see white people making their palaver, don't try to take the other one to police station. If I want to take him, if they finish everything with me, then I can go and take him. But not you to take him. You are not correct to take him to police station."

Then I said, "Oh. Thank you. I didn't know. You have taught me sense. So the next time, if I see somebody who wants to kill you, I must leave him to shoot you."

Then he said, "Yes. If—if he's a white man, it's not your palaver."

Then I said, "If he's African?"

"Yeah, maybe I don't understand, so you can beg for me. But a European, we understand each other."

And I said, "OK. One day will come to you." *Ha-ha!* Yeah.

So every time I used to give my friends that advice. I will say, "Eh, if you see some white people, and they take guns to shoot each other, you should just give them the way. The one who wins, it's his luck." Yeah? You know, I thought I did something good; I didn't know this man was going to fuck me like that. Suppose I knew, even I wouldn't take Ian to police station; I wouldn't shout for people to take Nigel to hospital. I would just sit until people came and met him and carried him. *Ha!*

Yeah, Nigel had a mouth. *Ah!* He could talk things about people! Every time, he wanted to say something about what he saw. Then he would come and talk.

Then I would say, "Yes, I know you people." All English people are like that. When an English person says something, then he will make his face to the other ones like this. Then he will say, "Did you see—?" When they say yes, then he will start to tell the story. *Ha!* They will ask you to see the thing first, then they will give you the story of it. *M-mmm?*

You know, the white people I used to meet in some of these places, like that Dutch man in Tema, they weren't the same way. No. You see, as for them, the way they were living, they didn't have a group, where they could meet in a group to talk. Yeah, they didn't have it as—we will go to this man's house party, or something like this, and you people will mix up, or you will go out to the nightclub and meet them with their wives. Many of them hadn't got wives. So they had not much of a group. Yeah, everybody would go out with his girlfriend, and then, they wouldn't make a party to call each other. Those people who came there, I thought they were coming to work hard, so they didn't bring their wives. So you know, always, before you will see these people talking, the way is if there are plenty of wives among them. Especially these English people, if you see the ladies, the old, old ones—especially the old, old ones—*hey!* They can talk; they can abuse people at any time. Yeah, Tamale. I used to think of Tamale and these fucking English people. Yeah, when I stayed with them, I studied them well.

PART THREE *Into The Life Again*

6 AVOIDING THE LIFE

: ACCRA :

A Ghanaian Boyfriend

When I came back from Tamale, at that time, every month Nigel used to send me money. Before he died, he stayed at home about four or five months before he was dead. He used to send me money every month. So I thought I was all right at that time, you know. I thought, oh, every time I can go out with this money, to buy drink for my friends and all this. And then, at that time, I started to get some kind of character: I thought to change my life. I didn't want "just-because-of-money-I'm following-you." Yeah. When I was getting this money always, I used to think, even if I don't follow someone, at ending of the month I will get the money to pay my rent.

So at that time I didn't have a man every time, and I changed my mind that even to go out every time, I didn't want it. So that was the time I changed, you know, to be sitting quietly, to be looking at what was going on. Yeah. I was fed up. Not that I didn't go out, but I just didn't feel to go out and drink with the friends, and all this. I thought it was just wasting of money. So I was just hanging quietly in the house.

And as for boyfriends, I didn't look for a boyfriend. I didn't find any white man, and I didn't take any African man. On my own part, I have only had one Ghanaian boyfriend.

You know, the African men, how they treat the women, it is difficult for me to know how all of them are. I cannot compare them, to say they are good or they are not good. You know, by all means, you cannot find that all the people are not good. By all means, some of them are good, and some of them are not good. But there are some ways some of them have, if they don't have good character.

Look. Maybe the man will see a woman today. He will be running after the woman every time, every time. When he gets the woman, he will have some days, or some weeks, and he will start to become fed up with that woman, and he will start chasing another one. And I think this trouble used to be a big problem to many girls. Maybe the men are not good to keep long with them. There is one girl called Agatha. Agatha went to Lagos, and when she came, she bought a television for her boyfriend. But this boy left Agatha and went to engage another girl. *Ha!* And now Agatha is just like somebody who is not correct.[1] Every day, she is drunk. Day and night, Agatha is drunk.

And then number two: there are some of them, when he gets the woman, he wants to get everything from her. These young boys, this is what they try to do with the girls. Maybe he thinks, "OK, this girl is also a hustler: she always goes out nights, so she can do everything for me." You see? Some of them used to like girls because of that.

And some of them, they are very obedient. Maybe he doesn't want to take something from the girl because he thinks that maybe later he will have trouble with the girl. But you know, it's funny: that kind of girls and boys used to quarrel all the time. Blows, every time there are blows. And "You took this and that from me," and that and that. And what the girl was doing, she will be doing it, and after, if they have a problem, she will talk and let everybody hear what she was doing for the boy. So it's a disgrace for them, for both of them. But the girl wouldn't know that. And then tomorrow you will see them together again. See?

So all these kinds of things, I think it's teaching—as if somebody is teaching you. Many of the girls are doing that. They get these boys who are just living from them. I don't know. Maybe she loves the boy, so anything the boy asks her, she feels she must force to get it for the boy. She doesn't think about anything. She just thinks to get a nice boy. He will come in his guarantee, and you will also be in guarantee.[2] And maybe, if they live together and she is forcing, even something that is costing heavily, she doesn't mind to buy it for the boy. And then everybody will say, "Ah, this girl is the boy's friend." You know, some girls used to be happy like that.

1. who is mentally disturbed; mad

2. a thick-soled shoe or platform shoe; high-style shoe; i.e., they will be looking smart together. The shoes are called "guarantees" because the soles will not wear out.

And I wouldn't do that, because I know what brought me. When I went out from my father's house, I didn't think, "Oh, I'm going to stay with a boyfriend and then I'll be getting money for him." No. I thought maybe I would be getting some good man who will look after me. I didn't think I would get a good man to look after him. So *ah-ah.*

Then some of the girls, too, the family wouldn't like what they are doing. But sometimes, in some ways, the family used to like them a little bit, because if they have problems, the poor people, maybe she will be getting. A girl like that, maybe she will help the family. You see? And that kind of girls, they cannot do all these things for a boyfriend, because always she will be thinking hard. Maybe she will be thinking, "I'm in this now because if some trouble happens to my mother, I can help her. My mother is an old woman; she hasn't any job to do; she is in the village." Many girls used to think of this.

But many of the girls, this thing used to happen to many of them: some girls think their family is rich, and she has just come to this ashawo for life,[1] for making her whole life to be happiness. She doesn't look at her back.[2] What she gets is for her alone. You know, some girls think they are better, that they have some money, so they want to keep a boyfriend, to keep him and cook for him and buy him clothes. I used to see this kind of girl.

But as for me, I don't try it. Nobody ever did that to me, and I don't try to make a boyfriend. If you try it, you will get it. But I didn't try it. You see what I mean? If you try it, and you are giving the boyfriend everything, it will happen to you. But maybe I want something from the boy. I don't want the boy to fuck me off later. Maybe I will be falling in love sometime. But not yet. I don't know yet. I am not ready. *Ha-ha!*

So the time I came from Tamale, I had this small problem. I was just fed up. You know? Something just came to me that I was fed up with everything. OK? And it's funny. That time was the only time I had a Ghanaian boyfriend. He was called Eddie. Yeah, when I came back from Tamale, I kept a bit long, getting to one year, before I knew Eddie. The family was from Brong Ahafo. Eddie was the first and last Ghanaian boy for me to take. First and last. *Ha-ha.* Yeah.

When I was going to become friends with Eddie, Nigel had gone to London for some time. First he went and came back. When he came back, then he packed all his things to go forever. Even he got work to do there. That was the time he started falling sick. He wrote me he had teaching work at some kind of school. It didn't keep long when he got sick. Then

1. for enjoyment, for experience
2. the people following her or dependent on her, i.e., in the family

they wrote to me. One of his friends working at the Training College, a Scottish man, wrote a letter to me when Nigel was dead. After I got the letter that Nigel was dead, I didn't keep long before I stayed with Eddie. Maybe one or two months.

You see? The time Eddie started following me, Nigel was still in life, and every month he was sending me money. So at that time I thought that if I stay with Eddie and he can give me everything for food and he can pay my rent, then if I also get the money from London, I can save some of the money Nigel is sending to do something with it. OK? But it didn't take a month and Nigel was dead. So when I got the letter that Nigel was dead there, all my program which I had planned was just like that.[1]

Then I thought: this boy used to help me, so we can stay together. When he met me, his work was to sew chair cushions. He was supplying them to the Lebanese shops. And when we were together, I was also working this work with him.

You know, the way I got a boyfriend is *funny*. I met Eddie in Playboy. That is the place we met.

The first day I met Eddie, he said we should go to his place. Then I said, "OK, you should give me fifteen cedis. I am going to buy cigarettes and come." So he gave me the fifteen cedis, and then I took a taxi, and I went and slept. *Ha!* The next day I didn't go out. *Ha-ha!* OK. The third day, I didn't go to Playboy. I went to Tiptoe.[2] Then I saw him there. I said, "Oh-h, I'm coming. I left my girlfriend outside." When I went out, I went to Playboy. *Ha!* From Playboy I went home. OK. Then, for about three days, I didn't meet him again.

The fourth day, I went to Makola market[3] and bought crab to cook, and I was trying to find a taxi to come home. There was a taxi which stopped. Eddie was inside. He said, "Hello, Madame. Can I drop you?" *Ha!* I didn't say anything. I went inside the car. He said, "Hey, as for you, you can dodge-o!"

I didn't say anything to him. So he said, where am I living?

I said, no, they should drop him before dropping me. I didn't want him to know my house.

He said, "Oh, I'm just going to drop—"

I said, "Yes, I know. But I don't want you to know my house. It's better. I have a boyfriend. I don't want trouble."

1. just nothing, just left hanging
2. Accra nightclub
3. large, central market in Accra, now disbanded

He said, "I'm not following you to your house."

Then I said, "No. They have to drop you before they drop me."

So they went and dropped Eddie before the driver came back and dropped me. But he had paid for the taxi. *Ha!* He didn't say anything. But when I wanted to pay the driver, the driver said, "Oh, the man has paid."

So that evening I went to Playboy. Then I met him again. And he came, "What are you going to drink?"

I said, "Guinness."

He bought me two Guinness. Yeah. I drank two Guinness. Then I told him I was going to lead my girlfriend to some place; we would be coming back. That girl was called Felicia. Felicia and I went to Lido. We were in Lido for some minutes, and Eddie also came. He said, what would we drink again? We drank Star beer there. I and Felicia, we drank two bottles each. You know, he couldn't ask me any question, because I didn't give him face.[1] The way I was looking at him, he was *afraid* to ask me. OK, after the two beers I told Felicia, "This boy wants to trouble me. So me, I want to go home and sleep. If you want, you can go home. There's nothing here today."

Then she said, "Oh, I will stay small."

So I said, "I think I will be going home.

Then he said, "Should I lead you?"

I said, "No, I don't want anybody to lead me."

"To lead you to see your taxi off."

And I said, "If it is that, it's OK."

So we came out. And he paid the taxi money. Then he said, "Do you have cigarettes?"

I said, "No." He bought me cigarettes, one packet. *Ha!* Then I went home and slept.

The next day, I think there were some drivers he lied to them to show him my place. About two o'clock he came there. You know, they were selling beer inside the house. When he came, he didn't ask of me. He just went under the mango tree and took his beer and was sitting there. And I didn't know that he had come to the house. I was passing to the toilet, and I saw him. Then he said, "Hey, Madame! Are you staying here?"

I was annoyed! *Ha!* I said, "Is this your lookout?"

He said, "Oh, no. But it's not trouble."

Then I said, "Why did you ask me that?"

He said, "Oh-h, I beg."

1. respond to him, acknowledge him; also, give respect to him

So I went my way. I went to the toilet. When I was coming back, he said, "Oh, can you come and have one glass with me?"

I said, "No, I won't drink."

So he drank his beer, and when he was going away, he paid for two bottles of beer for me. He told the girl to bring the beer to me. When the girl brought the beer, I said, "Where is the boy?"

Before I went out, he had gone away.

So I remember: every time when I met him — oh, I knew Eddie more than two good months, and I didn't know his house. He knew my house. He didn't go into my room. But every time when I met him with any of my girlfriends, he would buy us drink as we liked. I used to tell my friends that I have a stupid man, you know, so let's go to this place: we will find him; he will get us drink. *Ha-ha!*

And Eddie didn't know anything: he didn't complain. Only once, we were sitting down. We all grouped for a photo. I have the photo. I was in a group with all my girlfriends, with Eddie, and one other boy, and Eddie's old-old girlfriend. He had a baby with this girl, and this girlfriend was a very funny girl. She was called Gifty. So every time, always, we used to drink Eddie.

You know, before he got me, something just came to my mind that I was fed up. The way this boy was doing, he was a good boy any time. Since the time he knew me, he used to give me money. He hadn't asked me any question. I didn't give him face. So I thought, "As this boy is afraid of me like that, that kind of boy is good. He is not someone, if you say 'one,' then he will say 'two.'" *Heh-heh!* So I started to be doing everything with him.

I was with Eddie for about seven months. And what made me to get fed up with him: he had two children, one girl and one boy. He brought the girl to be living with me at Asylum Down. How the mother liked me! Gifty: that was the mother. The girl had been staying in village with the grandmother, and when he brought the girl, mosquitoes had spoiled all her skin. So I knew one doctor at Asylum Hospital; I was taking her there. He was an Ewe man. He was the brother of the woman whose house I was staying. So if they had something, he would bring the medicine, many different kinds for the children. And then I would give him about two cedis; it was plenty for him. So I looked after this girl well, and the mother liked me as a sister.

But what made me annoyed to be fed up with Eddie was that, look: these two babies had different mothers. Every month, these women would come, and he would give chop money for the children. And then I got fed up. It wasn't that I didn't like him to be giving the money to the women. But how these women were, I didn't feel it. So I didn't go to his place again. I came and stayed at my place in Asylum Down. Then he followed me, and locked his room. He didn't—*ha! Shit!* He didn't give up his room. Every month, he was paying for the room, but he didn't stay there. He packed all his things and came and stayed at my place. Then I said, "OK, if you want to stay here, if your women come here, I wouldn't mind. If they come and collect their money, this is not my problem. I know that, by all means, I can get my share, too."

You know, when I was working with Eddie, if we got a big contract, sometimes we could be sewing the chair cushions up to four o'clock in the morning. He used to get a big contract — maybe four hundred, even one thousand cushions. And he wanted to finish this work in two days. He had two electric machines. When he took one, then I would take the other one. So we were doing it like that, and before he would sleep, maybe it was four o'clock. And when he got to sleep, then these women would come and start early in the morning, about five-thirty or six o'clock. *Kon-kon-kon-kon-kon-kon:* "Eddie, wake up! Wake up! Wake up and give me money. Your child has lost his shoe." And what and what.

You know, as they knew I was with Eddie, I thought they used to do something like that to make me annoyed. But I didn't care. I used to wake up and open the door, and tell the woman to sit down. Then I would wake Eddie. Eddie could hear, but he wouldn't mind them. But as for me, if there was some noise, I couldn't sleep again. So it was better I would wake him to see the woman.

So the time I went to my place, and he packed his things and followed me there, then I don't know how the other woman knew my place. The other woman who had one child with him was a Ga[1] woman. They called her Esther. Her baby was a boy. One day, that woman came to my house, early in the morning, about six-thirty. She said, "Eh, you think you can run away? Even if you go to any place in this country, I can see you. I know. People told me you are staying here. Why? It is two months now, and you didn't give my baby chop money?"

So I said, "Look, Eddie, wake up and pack all your *nyama-nyama*[2] things, with your nyama-nyama woman. Get out. Here is not your house. All of you people."

Then the woman wanted to talk. "You know, Auntie —"

1. cultural group in Accra area. The pronunciation is nasalized as "Gã."

2. (Hausa): general word for anything of low quality or messed up; pathetic, lousy, cheap, poor, dirty, messy, run-down, worn-out, torn, nasty; literally, a pile or assortment of unrelated "stuff"

Then my landlord's daughter, she just put her mouth inside. She said, "No! No, I don't agree! You come and teach my small girl like this? No! No! Go out! If you are Eddie's wife, if Eddie goes to his house, you can follow him. Don't follow him here."

When this woman put her mouth inside like that, then this Esther was afraid. So she went away. When she went away, then I said, "No, Eddie, pack your things. I'm fed up. I can't help it again, so it's better you go."

But Eddie didn't want to go. I was telling him to go away for three days: Eddie was still there. He didn't say anything. He was still staying in there, working there, sleeping there. So one day, I was fed up. He was working outside. So I put his portmanteau and all his things outside, and I locked my room. I told him that I was going out, and he should pack his things to his house. Then I took my key. I went to Achimota.[1] I stayed three days. When I came back, Eddie was still sitting there. *Agh! Oh, what!* You know what finished between us? I said, "Look, if you don't pack your things now, I am going to bring police. You know, we didn't make any marriage. You don't know any family of mine. We have met each other. I thought we have understanding, and that's why we are staying together. But if you don't have understanding, you should go your way. It's finished. I don't want you in this house. Here is for me; it is not for you. If I say 'Go away,' you must go away."

Then you know, he had told my landlord's daughter that he would give her money to build one room for him at the house, and this woman told me all. Then I said, "No. Auntie, I don't agree. I have brought him. If he was a good man, I would say yes. But I don't know. How I am finding him, maybe I will yes, yes, and then sometime if I am not here, he will come and do you something, and you will say 'because of Hawa.' So no: I don't want that. Make him go his way."

So I called the old lady to talk to him. I used to call her "Mama." So then Mama went in and talked to Eddie. Then Eddie was crying. And Mama was crying. *Ah!* These people! So I said, "But Mama, what are you crying for?"

She said, "It's very pitiful. Somebody's son."

Then I said, "Somebody's son? I am not somebody's daughter? If it's you, would you agree to that? You wouldn't agree, Mama."

Then she said, "No, he won't do that again."

Then I said, "Mama, whether he does it or he doesn't do it, I don't want him again, because I am fed up. This is not the first time. I have been telling him every time, you know."

1. suburb of Accra

So it was coming to end then, me and Eddie. And he went his way. He packed his things and went. This case was what let us finish. You see, the time when we used to sleep, we used to sleep late. So if you want something like that, you should come around ten or eleven o'clock, huh? But early in the morning? Maybe I have got up from this work to sleep at about four o'clock. Then you will come and knock my door and start shouting. "Wake up! Wake up!" Maybe if people are outside, they will come and start looking, as if somebody has stolen something. And maybe I have slept by four o'clock, and I have only had a little bit of sleep. At six o'clock or five-thirty, I can't help it. I didn't say not to give the money to the children, because if I were the mother, too, I wouldn't allow it. If I have a child, and I know the father, he will feed the baby. I knew that what Eddie was doing was not bad. But I didn't want the women to come at the time they used to come. So I told him to tell them they could come about ten or ten-thirty or eleven o'clock. But they wanted to show that they have their business to do at that time, so they have to come at six o'clock in the morning. And then I couldn't help it. That was what I didn't want. Eddie and I were all right with the work. It was only that case which let me get fed up with him. Since that time, I didn't have another boyfriend.

Reflections: An Independent Life

You know, if I go to some place and I see the people and how they are, then that is all that is in my mind. To see if they are good or bad, it's good for me. And you know, to go someplace and find a friend is not something hard. If you know the way to keep yourself, you can stay with any kind of person, even if that fellow is not your friend. Somebody will like you; you can stay with him. Or sometimes, if you are quiet, and this fellow doesn't want palaver, and he's also a very quiet guy, you can stay with that kind of person. And if he is doing something you don't like, sometimes you won't say anything, because you are staying with him. So in this case, for me, I find it easy to stay with a friend. You can do me many, many things: I don't mind. Even it will come from you yourself, that you will become ashamed, "Ah, I have treated this girl in this way. She didn't say anything. I have treated her some bad ways, and she didn't mind. Oh-h, this is a shame to me." And so every time, I find it easy to live with a friend, because, if I know that I am with you, and you do me something, I don't care. I will just be laughing.

Suppose I had a lot of money, I would travel more, just to see different people and their life. Now, I don't want to be in one place. I want to be traveling. To me, this time, how I have been traveling, I would like to travel even more. When I travel, if I just find a new place, and I don't know the place, then I have to stay and know the people from that place. And then maybe if I know their life, I will be liking the place. So always, I used to force to stay. Even, in some places I used to suffer, and I know that if I go back, maybe I won't suffer like that. But I will say, "No. I won't go back. I must see what they have here." And sometimes, in some places, after I enjoy a little, then later I will suffering, suffering, suffering, suffering. And so one funny thing: if I get to some place and it's nice, if I enjoy for two or three days, then I will leave the place. When I see that I am starting to enjoy some place, then I say, "No, I don't like it again." *Ha-ha!* Oh yeah, it's funny, eh? Sometimes I used to do that.

Yeah? *Ha!* Oh-h-h. Some people, if they want to leave some place and go to another place, they used to sit and think—and think—that maybe if they go to that place, they will be better than in this place. Oh, yeah. But as for me, I don't think things for a long time. If I think to do something today, if I don't do it tomorrow or the day after tomorrow, then I won't be happy. So every time, when I want to do something, maybe the same day I think of it, then I will do it the same day. I don't think two days. Sometimes I will sit down and remember I have something to do—I have to do it. This is the way I used to do my things. So I usually have one-day programs, then I will say, "No. This place—*tsk*—I won't sleep in this town today." Then it's coming like that, you know, and I will just go away. I will think, "Ah, if it's good, or if it's bad, I will see it." Then I will go away to some place. *Ha!*

If I had money, I could do whatever I liked. I could be traveling. Or I could get a small shop and sell some things, and I could put one of my sisters inside of this shop, so if I was going around and around and I was short of money, I could come back and I would have money. You know, if you're traveling, you also spend money. But if you have money and you are spending it to travel, I think, and if you are traveling and some place is good for you, you can also get something more from that place. You can still be going to clubs and all this, to get some money while you are traveling. You know, the rich people who think they are rich, do you think they don't want money again? Even if you are traveling and you have money, you must try to find other money, too. Because money, when you think it's plenty, it is going to finish every time you go anywhere. You will spend for transport. You will go somewhere: you will spend. You must know that it's going to finish, so you must try to find more so that your money doesn't finish. Some place won't be good and you can be spending, and maybe you can keep back half of your money, to get your transport back, and to be well.

To be traveling to other countries — to know how the people are living, too — it's good. Even if you spend on that, you will understand: you have traveled; you know that place; you went and you spent your money. But the first time, I didn't travel. Just Ghana. And then the money I got from Nigel, I spent — all.

And so this time, if I get some money, then I will find something to do, maybe to be in the market to sell things. Yeah. But I don't want to be selling some things — some dirty, dirty things, you know. If I get a place for selling cloth, if I get money, I can do that work. Or shoes or blouses. As for that work, I have feeling to do it.

But if you have some money, you have to be growing it. Not to say you will just spend all of it. If you start to spend it, don't you think it will finish? So you have to take that money to find more money. Yes. How I am, I think maybe I can be selling some things at some place, or if I can get a small shop to be selling things inside. Maybe. But not to have it and then to say, OK, I can spend that money? No. If I spend it, then it's finished. Then I haven't got anything again.

So if you are looking for something, you shouldn't feel bad about that. At all.[1] For example, when you are going to start something, maybe you will start it small-small. And what you get, you can use it to get more things to sell. If I have a chance, maybe, to ever have a lot of money, maybe I will be getting to some place, small-small, something like the people who are selling cloth. It will also be good for me. It can be nice, if you can sell more and then get more, you know, to be buying and selling. But as for starting it, you know, you can't start it complete: you can't just start with everything full up. You have to start small, because I think that in everything, you have to know the inside before doing it. So you have to take your time, small-small, starting with small things. Before it's getting to the middle, maybe by that time you will know all the business, so that you can get profit like the others.

And so I'm thinking, if I have money, this is what I'm going to do, too. But if you don't have money, you can't do these things. You know, I can't know the money I need. *Ha-ha!* I can't know. Because I think that to sell cloth, it's better when you have a passbook[2] to buy the cloth from these big stores. And a passbook, I can't know how much they pay to make it,[3] but I think it will be some heavy money. And then, when you get the passbook, you have to have some money to deposit; then, if the cloth comes,

1. not at all; an affirmation, from *koraa* (Asante Twi)

2. an allocation book to obtain imported (often scarce) goods from major trading companies

3. issue it; pay to make it: bribes on top of whatever fees and deposits are involved

then they can supply some to you. Some people can get the passbook. Sure, if they have money first, then they will get it. But if you haven't got money, you won't get it. Any business, you won't get it. If it's farming, if you get some land to make a farm like this palm oil plantation, in three or five years to get the palm oil, you need money. Yeah, but to get land in Ghana, to get some land like this, at this time, you have to know people. Yeah. You have to know people who can help you, the big people or the good people. In Ghana, at this time, if you don't know many of such people, and you just go and enter the ministries or you see somebody to ask for something like that, somebody can deceive you and take your money. And so that one, too, to do it, unless you get somebody to be front of you. As a girl like me, if I enter a place like that, they will just say, "Ah! This one is meat who has brought himself; let's cut it and eat." *Ha-ha!* Yeah. It's so.

So all that I'm struggling for now is only to get some money to do something better. I don't have an idea of marriage. When I think that I haven't got my property, then I can't have somebody to live with, or to be married to him. So I don't think to marry. No. To get married now, I think it will be trouble for me a little bit. *Hmm!* It will be trouble for me, yeah? We girls — or me — I can't say everyone, because maybe, maybe people think that the young girls who are following men, if they are doing it small-small, and then they don't grow in this life for a long time, if they can get married, their own case is better. But we — when you do this life for some years, and you want to get married, you must know that, "Yeah. I'm going to get married, but I know what I am going to do. I already have some money to do some business." You cannot stay and wait for your husband every time.[1] In Africa here, it is not possible. *Ha!* Because everybody is crazy now, eh? Girls and boys: everybody is fighting for his own. So you must get something for your own before you can do that. Then even if your husband is not all right,[2] you will be all right.

Because now, our men, too: *hmm!* It's hard-o. *Abi? Ha-ha!* Our men in Africa here! It's hard. You are a girl, hmm? Then you do this ashawo life. Then you go and marry somebody after. Oh, if the person likes you, and you like him, it's OK. But sometimes, the way people will talk about you, that fellow won't like you again. I have seen some women — many, many, many — in Kumasi. When they married, they thought that to be married will be good to them. They are tired of this life. But they won't stay with the husband for a long time, you know, and people will be talking, "Ah, so

1. to provide the capital to start trading or to start a business
2. does not have enough money to help you

you are the one who went and carried this ashawo to your house. Hey, this girl, I knew her in this place before. She was like this, she was—" And then the husband will get fed up, because everybody is talking about his wife like that. So some people don't like that, and then they leave you.

If you have nothing, and then you go to marry, it's the same. You make ashawo and you are going to marry, or you are poor and you are going to marry. It's the same way. When you are ashawo, it's better. Your other ashawo people can abuse you. So it's better to make your ashawo life. Do you follow me? In Africa, we Africans, especially we Africans like this, eh? When you make this life before you go to marry, then maybe you have got your money and you are doing some work, or you are selling some things. If it is that one, I think you will be all right to rest. You know? But now, I have known how to spend money. Yeah? And I have not enough money. Then I want to marry. Maybe that man will not have enough money. You know? But if you have been doing all this ashawo life and by then you have got some money to work, then when you marry, you will be all right with your husband. The girls who have their money to do their own business, and they don't need anything, even people are afraid to say it; people are afraid to say that you were ashawo.

But if you haven't got money, maybe the man who has the money to marry you, you won't like him. And you shouldn't be married because of money. No, I think you must marry somebody you like, or somebody you love. Then maybe you can stay with him and be correct.

You know, if you haven't got something and that fellow also hasn't got anything better, then every time, you people can be happy, but you cannot be happy much. And then the man, also, will start to hear of you, "This girl is like that. She is like this. She was doing this work." You know? And then some people will say, "Oh, if he was not a stupid man, how could he be married to this girl? This girl who walked and ran through all this work. She knows everything of it." And maybe the person himself, if he doesn't have, if he's very poor like you, then they will say, "Ah, it's because of this woman whom he married. Because he took such a woman, that's why he's getting broken down." And this and that. They will talk about you, and then they will start to talk about him. And maybe this man, if he doesn't have his own experience or sense, he can leave you.

There was a girl who went from Kumasi to Ouagadougou, and I saw her in Ghana. When she was at Ouagadougou, if you saw her, you would think she was half-caste. She put on that cream[1]—plenty. People thought that she was half-caste. But when I saw her in the market in Ghana, if she

1. skin-bleaching cream

didn't call me, I wouldn't know she was the one. She was very black.[1] Then she was telling me that she had a baby, and the baby was about six months now. So what she wanted now was that if this baby starts to walk, then she will go back to Ouagadougou, because the husband has left her. People told the husband that the girl lied and gave this baby to him, that the baby is not from him, and all this. And this man took it so; he said, "Eh, you brought the conceive from Ouagadougou. This is a conceive from Mossi people. And then you came and gave it to me. So now, I have come to know all your secrets. So I don't want to live together with you, because my family doesn't like it."

So as for me, I'm not thinking of marrying now. Unless I get something first. If you haven't got money, or you haven't got some work to do, even to get children without any marriage would be a problem. To give birth just like this? As for me, I don't want just to have a baby like that. I think if — the time I get a good husband, and we stay together — if I have a baby, and after, if we leave our marriage, I know that this baby is for this man.[2] It's OK for me. But in this way, as an ashawo, to have a baby? No. I don't want it, because I don't have any good person if I have a baby. Some people can give a baby to the mother, you know, and then if she goes away to anywhere, maybe for some years, without coming back, she knows the baby is with her mother. But I have no mother. Only my stepmothers are there, and their children also have children. Won't they look at their own? Or they will look at mine? It's not possible. This is my case: the time when I don't have to be going around like this, maybe I will have children. It's not good to have a small child everywhere you go, and he is following you. It's another problem. And I don't like to spoil babies.[3] Yeah, you know, you can be taking something to take care of yourself. If you know that, you don't need things like spoiling babies. If you are making this ashawo life, you must take care of yourself in it. It's possible to get something to take care of this. It's not hard. It's not costly, too, to do that.

Yeah, if, suppose I had money — as for me, I don't want to live in a hot country like Upper Volta. I want to live where it's cool, like in the area of Kumasi, or some place out in the country, you know. Always, I don't like the capital towns. I want out-of-the-town. Yeah. Someplace like village places. You can be there very quietly. Not to look much: you don't see many things, too, you know. You look as if you don't know anything. And

1. The skin-bleaching cream has the reputation for causing skin to be darker after a person stops using it.

2. In most African cultures, the father has custody of the children.

3. have an abortion

that kind of place, I think, it is good for the poor people. You don't see; you don't hear. *Ha-ha!*

But to be rich, I don't think of it. I see that the really rich people, they are suffering, sometimes. *Ha-ha!* Yeah? Yeah. I think so. Look, we know a man who's a *very rich* man, and every time when he meets people, he talks about money. And then I wonder. *Ha-ha!* I wonder. You know? Sometimes, they will bring the letter for the school fees of his children: "Ah-h, where can I get this money to borrow." All this money, and then I wondered. I used to look at him. He's a Ashanti man. He has about three or four upstairs buildings[1] in Kumasi. The first wife has a car. And then the other car, he keeps it for the second wife. When they are going to market, the driver must take them and wait for them to do their shopping and then bring them back. And he has a car himself. He has got a big cocoa farm in a village. And still, when they bring the letter from the school: *Ha!* How to take that money out and go and pay the school fees of the children? It pains him. And so he used to ask, "Ah, if suppose I can get a good helper who can lend me money to pay these school fees. After, when the cocoa comes, then I will pay." All these houses—what do you do with them? He has a downstairs at Kumasi, at Brababume.[2] There are some white people who are living there. All this rent, when he collects it, he cannot pay his children's school fees. So he wants somebody to lend him money for one year. When the cocoa will come, then he will pay the fellow. So the rich people, they have problems. So if you are too much rich, too: *tsk!* Your problems are many!

So I'm not thinking that I'm going to become rich. Ah, well, I'm not thinking of that, but maybe if God gives me luck—all is luck. But I don't think of the way that maybe, later, I will become rich. Or maybe, later, I'll be poor more than now. I don't know. But every time, I'm fighting to become rich. *Ha-ha!* Yeah. As for that, *mais oui!*[3] *Ha-ha!* But every time, I just want to become some kind of a woman, you know. Not much rich, and not poor too: medium. *Ha-ha!*

1. a building with more than one story; also, a "story" building
2. section of Kumasi
3. (French): but of course!

7 WITH JACQUELINE

: ACCRA :

To Go to Togo

Ah, well. So when Nigel died and I also took Eddie and left him, I went back to The Life, but I changed. I think the thing that was different, was because I—first I had thought that I wouldn't come to this life again. You know? So when I was coming in again, I was feeling shy. That's why I left from Accra to go to Lomé. I was feeling shy when my friends saw me. "Ah-h, we thought you had married." *Ha!* You know?

So when I started to come back in this life in Accra, I said "*Shit!* I'm not going to stay here."

If all my friends saw me, "Hey, Hawa! Why? You are in this town?"

I would say, "Yes."

"It's a long time. Hey, did you travel?"

I'd say, "No, I'm in town."

"Accra here?"

I would say, "Yes."

"Ah! Accra is big-o."

Then another one will say, "But we haven't seen you for some months."

I will say, "Yes, I'm here."

So I saw these things. It was teasing, you know, something like they were teasing me. And I didn't feel happy. That's why I left to go to Lomé. After I left Eddie, that was my last time in Accra. I was fed up. I didn't want to go out to start this life again in Accra, to see the friends, and all this. I just took about one month at Accra. I went to Tema for some days, then I came back to Accra, and then I went to Lomé.

I went to Lomé with one friend, Jacqueline. Jacqueline was a friend to me for a long time. She is a Krobo.[1] When I came to Accra, the time when I was going to start this life, at Paradise, Jacqueline was friend to one girl,

1. cultural group in southeastern Ghana

and she used to come to this girl in Paradise. So we came to know each other there. Then the time when I went to Tamale, I didn't see Jacqueline again for about one year. And when I went back to Accra, we met again. She also was living with one English man at Legon, and this man had gone away. My man had gone away about two weeks, and this man from Jacqueline had also gone away, and he was not coming any more. So at that time, Jacqueline was living at Apache House, in Kokomlemle — that bloody house. So: we have not seen each other for a long time, and then, both of us, our husbands have gone, you know, so we have to become good friends again. OK?

And the way we made our plan to go to Togo: she brought some talks, you know, about Abidjan, and that and this. "Now Ghana is spoiling. You can't get money. There is no money in Ghana. So if you want, we can go on trek:[1] Abidjan, or Lomé."

And I said, "*Heh!* For me, I have never traveled far away. And I haven't got any car. So we have to try for Lomé. But later."

First, I wanted to go to Tema. "This time, if you want to go out of Ghana, you can't get money, so if it is traveling, I want to go to Tema."

Then she said, "To go to Tema, it's also Ghana. Let's go to Lomé. It's better. Lomé is also a good place."

"Ey! Jacqueline, but to go to Lomé, I don't know anybody there. It's a French country. I've never been to a French country like that, you know, without anybody."

So she said, "Oh-h. I know somebody. When we go, we can stay with this man — a very nice man."

So one day I told Jacqueline, "Let's go."

And she said, "Tomorrow." Tomorrow, Jacqueline will say, "Tomorrow." Hey, every day: tomorrow, tomorrow.

Then I thought, "If I don't wake up and go, it won't be better." *Ha!* Because I was suffering, you know. So one day I told Jacqueline, "Yeah, Jacqueline, can we go today?"

She said, "Oh, tomorrow."

Then I said, "OK. If it's tomorrow, then any time when you're ready, you can meet me in Tema. You can meet me in Tema and we will go together, because I am going to Tema. I wouldn't like to sleep in Accra here today."

"O-oh, wait, I'm going to take my dress[2] from the tailor."

I said, "OK. You'll meet me in Tema. I won't wait for you to go and

1. travel; from the colonial notion of going into the bush
2. waiting to get my dress

take anything. Because it's too much. Every day: tomorrow, tomorrow. So if you like, we will go to Lomé. Or I will go to Tema, and the time you're ready, you can come and pick me in Tema."

So she said, "OK, we are going together." To Lomé. She will leave the dress with the tailor. When she comes back, then she can get it. OK?

So we took a car. I had my thirty-five cedis. *Hee-hee!* I thought this thirty-five cedis is big money in Lomé. Yeah? I didn't know it was small money. We went to Lomé station and took a car, three-three cedis each. At that time, they were charging three cedis.

: LOMÉ :

At Podo's House

When we got to Lomé, we changed a little of our money to Togo money[1] to go and eat, and then when we finished, we took a taxi to this man's house, the man we were going to live with. He was called Podo.

Oh! That day, when we reached there: "Hey! Jacqueline! Jacqueline! Hey, Jacqueline!"

Ah! I was happy. I said, "Yeah, he's a nice guy." *Ha!* Do you know this man was a *big drunkard?!* I didn't know. Jacqueline knew this, but Jacqueline didn't tell me. So we were together with this man a few weeks. And then, when I would go out and come in the night and I wanted to sleep, he wanted to romance me. And I didn't want this. Every time, when he did this, I would make, *"Pffft!"* Then I would get up; I would put my cloth on the floor; then I would sleep. When I would sleep on the ground, he would follow me there again! Then I thought, "Ah! What kind of man is this?" So I told Jacqueline.

And Jacqueline said, "Oh-h. It's like that. Even he cannot fuck. He has no prick. He's just making you like this to hold you."

Then I said, "I don't want the scent of akpeteshie. It used to worry me."

So in this case, Jacqueline talked to this man. "You shouldn't do that." Then he was annoyed. He waited until we went out, then he closed his door and locked it. He didn't come home. When we came home, we didn't know where to find him. We had to sleep in front of the house, by the door of the room. So we were there in the night: heavy rain! *Hee-hee.* All the place was full up with water. We were sleeping. We didn't hear anything. It was raining, and then I was turning myself, and I said, "Eh!

1. CFA francs

Why? Did I piss or what?" Then I woke up. All my dress was full of water. "Hey, Jacqueline! Wake up! What is this?"

So we had to wake up. So! That day, *hah!* I don't think that day—*agh!*—I thought, "Now, if I get back to Ghana, I won't go out of Ghana again." We were sitting like that, then it was cold. And all our clothes were wet. We had to sit like that up to five-thirty in the morning. Then this man came and opened his door. Then we went inside and changed our dress. Then even to go inside, he said, "*Tsk!* Don't take your wet dress to my room! Don't wet my room for me!"

So we didn't say anything. We changed our dress. Then we washed the one from when the rain beat us. Then we hung them to dry. Then, the sister of this man came and talked to him, you know, that what he was doing is not good, and that and this, and it's not right to live together and do that, and all this. So we were still there. We were not happy, and we didn't get the key, too.

Then I caught fever. When this rain beat me, I got fever. And this fever was a fever in which I used to see people. I used to see people with white, white, white dresses. And every time I would say, "Hey, hey, hey, Jacqueline! Look, look, look, look!"

"What?" She didn't see anything.

I said, "Hey! You don't see a *tall* man there with a white dress?"

Jacqueline thought I was going to die, because they say if you are going to die, you used to see ghosts. Then: *ha!* Jacqueline used to cry. And I thought my sister was feeling pity for me, you know. But night time, she would go out, and before she would come, maybe it was evening time the next day. And Jacqueline also had a friend, Yvonne. Yvonne would give her nothing, but every time she liked Yvonne. She would go and sleep there and then walk and come home![1] *Heh-heh.* Yeah. So: when she goes out in the night, unless the next day evening before she will come home. I could be hungry. I had my small money, but to get somebody to send to buy me food, it was not possible, because I didn't know anybody and at that time I didn't hear[2] the Ewe language. And Jacqueline said she hasn't got money, and every time I had to spend my money. Do you know that Jacqueline also had some? A ten-cedis note. She hid it from me. She hid it under the table of this man, but it was funny, because this man also took that ten cedis and went and spent it. And every time, the people in the house would say, "No, Jacqueline, what you are doing is not good. You brought this girl and she's sick, and if you go out, you don't come."

1. because he did not even give her money to take a taxi
2. understand; also, speak

Then these people were talking to her. So she also went and brought some doctor to give me an injection. This injection, they said it was a Nivaquine injection.[1] A *fucking* injection: you will scratch every place! So they gave me this injection. And those people also made medicine from a tree — nim tree — and took the leaves and boiled it to give me a bath and all this.[2] Then one other woman, too, she said she can give me some medicine; she also mixed some tree leaves and the skin of trees and cooked it. It was bitter: if you saw it, you'll think it's coffee. *Black!* Then I was drinking that, too. I suffered to go to Lomé, eh?

Then I thought it was a bit better. But Jacqueline is Jacqueline. We were still there. And whenever we saw this man: his eyes were red.[3] Because if we didn't move from that house, he wouldn't be free either. So Jacqueline found one boy, Joe. This Joe was driving a car. So this Joe said, "Oh, you people can come and live with me." He was driving this turkey-tail car. You know these people who are selling the turkey tails?[4] He was driving the car full of turkey tails, and every time, this boy used to go with this car to the villages, and sometimes for two or three days, he didn't come to Lomé. So he gave us his room, with record player and everything.

Then, you know, it was funny. The day when we were going to take our things to leave this drunkard's house, then this drunkard said we shouldn't go away, because we came here because of him, so if we want to leave him, we must leave Togo and go back to Ghana, not to go and live at somebody's house. So he wouldn't give us our things. We had to leave many things there, and then when we wanted to come back to pick all these things, before we got those things, even we had to bring a man to accompany us. When we went there, this drunkard said, "If you are — you — you should enter this room and come out and see something!"

Hey! Then Jacqueline said, "Let's call Yvonne."

Then I said, "O-oh, b-but, J-Jacqueline! Eh? Slow! This country is not for you."

Jacqueline said, "What?! This foolish man?! Stupid man?!"

But then this drunkard went and took a knife, you know, and he said he will chook us. He was shouting, "Enter! Enter the room and come out! I will chook you people *basabasabasa*."[5]

1. chloroquine for treating malaria

2. a treatment for malaria, bathing and inhaling vapors; nim tree: *Azadirachta indica*

3. He was annoyed; he was serious.

4. a popular food from roadside vendors

5. (Asante Twi): disorderly, helter-skelter, messed up; i.e., he will make a mess of them

So when this man brought a knife, then Jacqueline said, *"Sh-h-h!"* She didn't say anything again!

Then I said, "Now, talk. You say he's a foolish man. Tell him now!" *Ha-ha!*

Then Jacqueline said, "*Sh-h!* You too, stop. You don't see him bringing a knife?"

Then I said, "*Uh-huh!* You are afraid!" *Ha! Ha!*

So I ran to call one friend—Maurice. Then Maurice came, and Maurice talked to this drunkard, and Maurice said, "OK. If these girls come, and they say it's because of you, and then they think that they are not all right with you, then let them go. Anywhere: they can go. It's not—you are not the one who paid their transport. You can't seize their things."

So he said, OK, we can go and take our things. Then we said we were afraid. This boy must follow us. So this boy followed us inside the room. Because we were afraid that maybe we will enter and then he will come and meet us with this knife, and he will kill us. So this boy entered and then we packed all our things, and then we went to that boy, Joe. *Ey! Hmm!*

The Turkey-Tail Man

When we reached Joe's house, I said, "Even this is a better house. They don't bluff. Look at the nyama-nyama house for Podo, and then he is bluffing. Look at a fine house like this: a nice breeze, with a big watch." You know, they hung this thing, and every time if it's twelve o'clock, you must know the time: *kling-kling.* "A fucking dirty house like that, and Podo is bluffing with it!"

And Joe told me, "Jacqueline is my girlfriend. You can live with Jacqueline without any mix-up. I think she's a good girl, and so, I can give you this room to sleep in. And even, I used to travel every time, and so you can stay with her here."

So now Jacqueline was madame, no? This boy Joe, his sisters were cooking for us. We didn't do anything. Every time, we put on the records; we didn't buy anything. He had this record by Charlotte Dada: "She Does It Cool." It's *co-o-ol!!* And Jacqueline liked this record. The things we did were only grooving, and eating, and then in evening time I would go out, and Jacqueline would sleep with her boyfriend. Sometimes this boy would travel with his car, and we would go out together, and come. Sometimes if this boy traveled, Jacqueline didn't even want to go out. She said that if she goes out, some people will tell this boy that she has gone out, and this boy will leave her. *Ah-h-h.* So I used to go out alone. And so every time we were just in the house. We enjoyed. Jacqueline didn't go out; I would go out alone. And every time, this boy's sisters would cook good food for us. From the time we stayed there, this boy didn't give Jacqueline any finer thing, but we ate well! We could take our baths, we could do everything there. OK.

Then, one day we went shopping — it's very funny — and we met one boy from Ghana. You know, after California Hotel,[1] there are some boys repairing motors.[2] When you pass California Hotel and you are going, the small petrol station is here and the fitters[3] are here. This boy could ride motor! They called him Small. They said that there were two of them doing this work, and one was dead by accident, motor accident: a car knocked him and he fell down.

So: one day this boy Small came to Lomé. He was a friend to Jacqueline in Accra. We were going to our shopping in the market, and we met this boy, and he said, "Oh, let's get to a bar, and then I will get one bottle for you people." We went to Bar Senegalais.[4] We ate: this boy paid. We drank: this boy paid. Then from there we went to Royal Hotel.[5] Do you know it was this boy's *last* money he was spending for us?! Then: his money was finished. What can he do to get transport back to Ghana? Then he said, "Jacqueline, you know, the money I brought, it has finished, and so if you can give me three cedis to go back to Ghana?"

Then Jacqueline said, "Oh, I have no money, but, I think I will take you to my boyfriend's house. I'll tell my boyfriend you are my brother, so that he will give you a place to sleep. Then tomorrow I'll get money from him to give you for transport."

Then this boy said, "OK."

When we went to Jacqueline's boyfriend's house, this boy Joe was also coming from traveling. So we sat, and Jacqueline said, "Oh. Ah — this boy is a — my brother — my younger brother. He has come from Ghana, and then I met him in the market, and it's night, and we can't find a car for him, so I want you to give him place to sleep. Then, tomorrow morning he can go away."

Then Joe said, "OK." He said we should sit down; we should eat: he's coming. Then the sisters brought us food, and we were eating, and this

1. small hotel in Accra
2. motorcycles
3. mechanics
4. small restaurant in Lomé
5. small hotel in Lomé, where many Ghanaians lodged

boy went out. When this boy came back, he came and called me and said, "Hawa."

I said, "Yes, Joe."

Then he said, "You see, I think I must tell you, because when you people came here, I liked you very much. You are a quiet nice girl. Don't let people say that I told you people to go out. But I have taken this key from Royal Hotel. I paid for three days, to give this key to you people to take the stranger[1] there, together with you people and the stranger to sleep there. And so I cannot help with boys, because you know in Togo here, everybody is afraid of Ghana boys. Maybe I will let this boy rest here, and then my sisters, you know, they don't sleep in the house, and even they don't close their doors, and something will get missing. They will say that, 'Yeah, it's Joe who went and brought his girlfriends and their brothers to come and steal.' And so the best thing: if you people live here alone, I like it, but now if I take this boy to sleep here, tomorrow you people will bring another boy again. And so I don't want all those things. And so you must tell Jacqueline that this is the trouble."

He didn't tell Jacqueline! I was the one he called and told me, and then he gave me the key. Then: how can I tell Jacqueline this? I came out and said, "Jackie?"

She said, "Yes."

"Come." Then she came. I said, "Jacqueline, did you hear what Joe said? Joe brought us a key from Royal Hotel. He said that we can go there with our stranger. Because he doesn't want to have strangers in his house. He likes to have stranger girls, but not stranger boys." Yeah. I just cut it short, you know; I didn't want to say all of what this boy said.

Then Jacqueline said, "Joe told us this?"

"If you don't believe, go and ask him. He's there. Here is the key, too." Then I started to pack my things, you know, because I didn't want any long talking.

So I was packing my things and Jacqueline said, "No, I don't understand this." Then she called this boy inside, and then she started making a palaver. *Kra, kra kra krakra.* And this boy said this and that.

So I took my bag and left them. I got to the Royal Hotel and asked for Room 3. They showed me Room 3. I put the key in the door; I opened it;

1. visitor, guest. In many African languages, the same word refers to stranger or guest; you would call your visitor a "stranger" even if you knew him or her very well, and you would introduce the person to your friends as, "This is my stranger I have brought to greet you."

I put my things down. I was there about fifteen minutes when Jacqueline came with this boy, Joe.

Then Joe said, "Every time I will come and see you people. When you need some food, if you don't see me, you can come to my house. Even if I am not there, you can ask my sister. She can supply you people with everything you want." Then he left.

So: we could not just sleep, so I told Jacqueline, "Let's go out." Then Jacqueline said no, she wouldn't go out, she was thinking.

So I said, "Ah! Whether you think, or you don't think, this thing is finished. This boy doesn't like you again."

Then she said, "Why should you say so?"

So it turned to trouble between me and Jacqueline because I told her that this boy doesn't like her again, whatever she did. Then she started crying: *Ehh-h-h. Mmm-m-m.* She doesn't know what bad luck is for her this year—her mother is dead, and every time, where she goes is not all right for her—and they said that if you don't die, you can help your daughter or your son, but her mother just died for nothing—she doesn't help her in any road—and that and this—and that and this. Jacqueline is funny, eh?!

So: *shit!* I went out and left her. When I went out, I didn't come back to sleep at Royal Hotel. I got somebody to go to Hotel de la Paix,[1] and I slept there. Morning time, I had six thousand. I was happy. Jacqueline had nothing. And this boy Small still had not got transport. So I said, "Jacqueline, this boy is going to sleep here today, too?"

She said, "Aah, I don't have money. How can I give him?"

And I said, "OK, I'm not giving you free. But I will give you one thousand to give this boy to make transport, and after you can pay me. I don't do this free, eh?" Then she said OK, so I gave her one thousand. Then I still had five thousand, and this boy Joe had paid three days for the hotel. The hotel was one thousand for a day. So I went to deposit three thousand again for the hotel, and it was left with two thousand. I thought that we don't get money every time, you know, so maybe if I go out and use this money, then maybe after we come, we won't have money for the hotel, so it's not good. So I deposited three thousand for the hotel and left two thousand for me and Jacqueline to eat and all. OK?

We were in this hotel for two weeks: sometimes if she had money she paid; sometimes if I had money, I paid.

1. international hotel in Lomé

8 A BAD SICKNESS

: *The Treatment*

: *Love and the Banana*

: LOMÉ :

The Treatment

I was in the Royal Hotel when I came to have a *ba-a-d* sickness. Again! Apart from the fever. I came to pass menstruation, but this menstruation lasted three months. *Three good months!* There wasn't any blessed day when I didn't see blood. Every time I went to hospital and they gave me an injection, that was the day I would bleed more. I thought that all my blood would finish. *Ah!* And people were telling me that a doctor can't get the medicine for this sickness, so I must find African medicine. And I didn't have anyone to ask. Everybody said, "Go back to Ghana. You will die here. It's not good."

And do you know what? Jacqueline went back to Ghana! Yeah, when I was sick, she left me in the hotel and went back to Ghana. And then I was alone.

That was the time I was coming to be friends with Mama Amma, when I was sick. I knew Mama Amma in Accra, but we were not friends like now. Before I went to Lomé, Mama had been in Lomé, and she was at Lomé when I got there. When I saw her there, I just said, "Eh! Mama, I have come here." And the time I was sick at Lomé was the time when we were coming to be good friends. One day I was sitting in front of Royal Hotel, and I saw Mama pass, and I called her.

She said, "Um-hmm. I saw you have some trouble."

So I told her all my problem. "You see now what is with me? Yeah, Mama. I've had menstruation for about three months now. It doesn't stop for any medicine."

Then she said, "You don't know Togo! Togo is like that. It's somebody who did you.[1] We have one girlfriend who had the same thing. You can go to every doctor: they can't do anything with it. But I know a boy called Brazil. He's a musician. See him."

This Brazil used to come to Royal Hotel, but I didn't know his house. So I said, "I don't know his house."

1. did this to you, i.e., made medicine against you

And Mama said, "OK. Tomorrow morning I'll come and take you there."

The next morning Mama came and took me to Brazil. This Brazil's father was Togolese and his mother was from Dahomey,[1] and he took me to a Dahomey man. And this man said, "Bring two hundred francs."

Two hundred! I didn't have even two hundred! I had three good months without going anywhere. Even to eat was hard. I had a big flask and I used to boil tea and fill it. Maybe for four or five days, it was my food. Tea! No milk. And sugar, only if I asked somebody to buy me sugar. Just like that, and I was living. *Heh!* And I didn't want to go to Ghana either. If I would go to Ghana, I could get some money; I could just go to the bank and get money to spend. And I wanted to go. But if I thought about it, the way I came out of Ghana, to come out with this small rubber[2] bag and then go back there with this same bag again? No. I thought, "No, I won't go. I will stay here and die. It's good when I die in Togo. In Lomé." That's what I thought.

So when we went to this Dahomey man, he said I should bring two hundred. *Ah!* How could I get two hundred? Then I told Brazil, "Truly, I haven't got a penny."

Then Mama said, "Oh, for me too, today is not good. I have only one hundred."

And then I said, "No. Keep your one hundred. If I'm going to die, I must die. If I'm going to die, this man will take the two hundred and I will still die."

Then Brazil said, "No. I have two hundred."

So Brazil gave the man two hundred, and this man brought a mirror, just the small one we look at our faces with. He put it down and he told me to put the two hundred on top. I put the two hundred on top, and he put some powder on the mirror, and then he rubbed it together with the money, and then he took the money. And he said, "Look inside the mirror." And I looked, and he said, "Do you see something?" I didn't see anything. And he said, "All you people are how many in the hotel?"

And I said, "We are many."

"Do you know all of their names?"

I said, "I think I can remember some of their names, but I can't remember all."

So this man said I should start to call the girls' names. And when I

1. former name for Benin, the country to the east of Togo. Dahomey also refers to the traditional state of the Fon people, Dahomey, in Benin.

2. plastic

called every girl's name, I looked on the mirror and I saw a picture like a photo, just standing on the mirror. Yeah, it's something like belief, you know. And I came to one girl called Love. I think now she's in Cotonou.[1] She's a very *smart*[2] girl, very fast. I liked her a lot. When she came to the mirror, she was making something like snapping her fingers and dancing.

And then this man said, "Yes. This is the girl who did you."

I wondered! I wondered because when I was sick, every morning, sometimes this girl would ask me, "Have you milk?" I would say "No," and she would buy me milk. And she would buy me sugar to make my tea. And now this man was telling me that she is the one who did me to pass menstruation like that. These Dahomey people say the thing is in the hand, that if they make it, they put it in your hand. If you don't want someone to play with you, you touch her with this, and it's finished. She will be in menstruation, and it doesn't stop. If she doesn't find medicine, she will bleed until she is dead. So I wondered. How can she make me like this and then spend on me? But this man said she was the girl.

Then I said, "OK. What shall we do now?"

He said, "I will give you something to bathe in." And he said I should go and bring a certain African pot, the clay one they cook in.

"How can I get the money to go and buy this thing?! I don't even have two hundred francs to give you! Can I get money to buy this thing?"

And he said I must bring it along with five hundred francs, and he would go and buy the things to make the medicine for me.

And I didn't have money, so I said, "OK, Mama, let's go." And Mama followed me back to the hotel. When we got there, I said, "Mama, I think you must go home. Any time when I find the money, I will go and find the thing for the man."

At that time the fellow who had the Royal Hotel was a Yoruba[3] man. I went to him and told him, "You know, these days I can't pay my hotel bill because I am sick. And I went to someplace, and they showed me something to do. But it's about one thousand. If you like, you can give me the one thousand." That time I had three full pieces of this African cloth, and so I said, "You can take this cloth and keep it; then you give me one thousand. If I finish, I will pay you and take my cloth back."

And he said OK, he will give me the one thousand, but he doesn't want the cloth; I can keep it.

And I said "Thank-you."

1. major town of Benin
2. fast, quick; fast-moving, on top of things, hip
3. large cultural group in southwestern Nigeria and southern Benin

I took five hundred to go and buy the pot, and I took it together with the other five hundred to this Dahomey man. This man said I should come back at four o'clock. Four o'clock I called[1] Mama and we went. Then he got some leaves, and then he spread the leaves and put them in water in the pot. You know, this is why I believe a little bit of African medicine. He cut a big hole in the bottom of the pot. He was holding half, and I was holding half. Then he was putting water, and the water was coming out the hole. Then he was talking, some kind of Dahomey language—I don't know what language he was talking. If he put water, then the water would come out. Four times. Then the fifth one, the water started to fill up the pot, without coming out the bottom. So I was looking at it.

Then I said, "*Hey!* Mama!"

Then Mama too said, "Hey! This man is *strong!*"

We looked under, and we saw the hole, and we saw the water, but the water didn't come out. I put my hand inside to see whether he had put some mirror there, but when I put my hand, it was water. But this kind of water didn't come out. Then the man said I should take this water to the bathroom[2] in his house and bathe with it. So I went and bathed with this water. When I came back he put down a broom, and he said I must go on top of the broom. I stood on the broom, and then he took some threads, and he gave me the threads to tie around my waist.

And when I did that, he said, "Go. Three days, you come back."

Ah! When I got home I started to *bleed!* It even passed the way I used to bleed. I was afraid, and I started crying, *"Yee-i! I die finish![3] Hey Mama! I'm finished!"*

Then Mama said, "Let's wait for tomorrow."

When I bled like that, the next day I didn't see anything. And the next day, too, I didn't see anything. Then I said, "Ah, well, maybe it will be all right."

On the third day when I went to the man, he said, "Oh?"

And I said, "The first day I had much bleeding, but from yesterday up to today the third day, I don't see anything at all."

Then he said, "OK. You know what you will do? You must bring me five thousand francs. Five thousand, with two chickens, one red and one white." Five thousand with two chickens!

1. went to get

2. In houses without running water, the "bathroom" does not have a toilet but is rather an enclosed area with a place for water to run outside the house. One bathes from a bucket, using a smaller container to wet oneself, then soaping oneself, then rinsing oneself with the remaining water.

3. (Pidgin): I'm dying, I'm dead.

"*Ey!* Papa! You don't pity for me? How can I get that five thousand?"

So he said OK, if I don't have the five thousand, I must say to his juju that I will bring the five thousand but today I don't have it. But I should know the time I'm going to have it. I should say the truth always. If I don't say the truth, this thing will come back and nobody will be able to cure it. *Ee-eh!* What day should I give now? Then Mama said, "Oh, it's nothing. You can give two weeks. Even if you don't get it after two weeks, if I get it I can lend it to you, then you can come and pay." So I gave two weeks. Then we went back home.

Then, this thread. You know, if I don't pay this money, the man cannot cut the thread. It must be on my waist. But to go with somebody to see this thread on your waist, he will suspect that you have juju or something, and he will be afraid of you. So I couldn't go out. I stayed home for one week. Then, one day we were at the hotel, and some Nigerian people came there and stayed at the hotel. The one man said he was a contractor, and he came to me and said he liked me and this and that. We drank up till midnight, and he said he wanted to go with me. Then I said, "Oh, I am in menstruation. Today I cannot sleep with a man. Maybe I will finish tomorrow or after tomorrow."

Then he said, "OK. Take five thousand and go and eat."

EEE-ey! I had the money! It was left only with the two chickens, right? So I was very happy that day.

Early in the morning about six o'clock, I ran to Mama. She was sleeping. *Tat-tat-tat-tat-tat-tat!* "Hey! Mama! Mama! *Mama Mama Mama Mama!*" *Ha!*

Then Mama said, "Who?"

"It's me! Mama!" Then she opened the door. I said, "Mama, I have the five thousand, but I don't have the money to buy the chickens."

Then Mama said, "OK. Take one thousand." I took the one thousand, and I went and bought the chickens, then I went and gave it to this Dahomey man. And this man cut the thread. So that time I was free.

Love and the Banana

Then this man said, "OK. Now, what do you want to do with Love?"

I said, "Oh? What should I do with her? This girl has done good to me when I was sick. Maybe somebody made me like this, but I don't believe it's this girl. So I don't want to do anything with her."

Then this man said, "The way you say you don't believe, I want to show you something. You will see that Love will suffer in Lomé. If you want, you can take your eyes and watch."

"OK, but as for me, I don't want you to do her something bad."

Then he said, "No! I'm not going to do her something! I'm just going to show you a movie. OK? Something like comedies.[1] Eh?"

Then I said, "OK."

It was about three days and Love conceived. She used some medicine to take it out, and everybody thought she was going to die. We carried her to hospital that very night. Then she was in hospital. Nobody was going there because none of us had money to go and greet her.[2] So, that finished all right, but she also didn't have money to pay the hospital and come home, so she had to run away from the hospital in the night and leave everything there.

That very day when she came home, she went to Pussycat[3] and some thief boys beat her and took her wig and tore all her dresses off. *Ah!*

Then I went to this Dahomey man. I said, "No! This girl! What you are doing, if you are the one doing it, you must stop. I don't want to see her like that in this world. Yesterday she went to the nightclub and they beat her, tore her dresses and wigs and left her in the gutter. Even her pants, she didn't have them."

Then this man said, "You say you don't believe, so I also wanted to show you."

Then I said, "No. If that is the case, then it's OK. This girl, I like her a lot, so I don't want you to do something bad to her."

Then this man laughed. "OK. I will leave her. I won't do anything."

Getting to one week—*ah!*—the police people caught Love. When they took her to police station, they said she must pay five thousand. And she didn't have the five thousand, so they just kept her there. It was this Yoruba man whose hotel we were staying who was the one who went and paid the five thousand to take Love out from the police station.

Then Love came to me. She said she was in Cotonou for three years and she had two babies with one Dahomey boy, then she ran away from this boy to come to Lomé. Since the time she came to Lomé she didn't have any problems. And now all this. And she told me she went to some place and they told her that I was the one who was doing her like that. *Ah!*

"How?" I said, "What did I do you?"

She said, "Yes. I found out. They said that you are the one."

So I went back to this Dahomey man and said, "Look, this thing you are doing, I don't want it. This girl has come and given me warning. She

1. short subjects or ads or diversions before the main film at a movie theater

2. The "greeting" is a presentation, in this case money to give her as a gift to help her with her expenses.

3. discoteque in Lomé

said that they say I am the one who is doing her. She has been in Cotonou and all these places. Don't let her come and kill me here. I told you to leave this girl alone. If you are the one who is doing it, then leave her!"

Then this man said, "OK. I will leave her. But I want to show you the last point. It's something very nice!" Then he gave me a banana. You know, it was very, very funny. I still have interest in this banana. He said, "OK. I want to cut everything short, and so when you take this banana to the nightclub and do something, everything that I have been doing to Love will go away." This is what he told me, but I didn't know that he was going to disgrace her. He told me that when I go to the nightclub and I see Love dancing with somebody on the dance floor, I must put the banana down and press it with my foot. Yeah? It was just a banana like any banana.

That night I put the banana in my bag and went to Pussycat. Love was there dancing with some white man. Then I didn't know what was going to happen, but I thought that when I pressed this banana, it was going to be something nice. So I put the banana down and pressed it with my foot. Then this girl started to *shit! On the floor!* In Pussycat! Then everybody started shouting, "Hey, hey!" This white man left Love on the floor and went and sat down. Love was standing there. She was wearing trousers, and they were all full of shit. Then she ran outside. Everybody was following her, saying, "Hey, Love! What is wrong with you? What is wrong with you?"

Then I was afraid. I picked up this banana quickly and went and put it in the toilet and pressed the water.[1] *Ha!* That very night I took a taxi to this man and said, "Why should you do that?!"

Then he said, "Yes. It's finished now."

And from that day, until I left Lomé, I never saw Love with my eyes again. They said the next day she left Lomé for Cotonou. If you ask Mama about this case, she will tell you. I never saw this girl again. I heard that she said she was going to Cotonou, and I don't know whether she's in Cotonou or she's in Ghana or she's somewhere. I don't know. This banana was a very big disgrace for her in Lomé.

And so from there, I thought, if I'm sick, I don't want to ask who made me to be sick, but I just want to be cured of my sickness. Yes. It was a very big disgrace for Love. *Heh, heh, heh!*

Yeah, so it was in Lomé when I came to have belief in this thing. In Accra my friends used to tell me, "Let's go to this place; this man is good." And all this.

I used to say, "Oh, what is good: it's good if the money you are going to

1. flushed the toilet

give to these people to chop, for them to lie to you, it's better you buy a fine dress and fine shoes. You will get somebody who likes you."

Then this Dahomey man showed me something which I have believed. I used to have belief about their things, but not to make them myself. I just thought: maybe. Then you know, when this thing finished, I thought that maybe it's like when you do bad to somebody, and God is going to punish you. And if God doesn't do anything, it can come like that. Maybe it's like that, and this Dahomey man has been doing that. But I didn't think that this man and this banana could do all that. And so I think maybe it was true that this girl was doing me bad, eh? That's why God agreed to see these things.

If it's not so, I don't think that this man, or this juju, can work like that. You know, where this man was living is not a nice house. An ugly house, dirty, and all! So, I wondered. Why don't you let this juju find you money to prepare your house nicely, you know? *Eh-heh!* This is what I say. This man: where he's living is not a nice house; it was a very dirty house. And this juju you have can work like this? Why don't you let it find you some big money to make a building, a big nice house to live? They can kill somebody with it, but they cannot find money with it? It's not possible. I think that if this thing works truly, if I have something like this, I will find money with it. I won't do people bad. And so this sickness, I thought that when he did the thing for me, gave me three days and then it finished, I had belief that he had juju and his juju was working. But I didn't know how the juju can take care of the sickness, and the juju cannot take care of the master to get the master money.

Heh-heh! Yeah, he took my five thousand, and I think that this five thousand didn't do anything for him. When he does the same thing to everyone to have five thousand, five thousand, from everyone, if he's saving the money well, he can do something with it. So I don't know what such people do. Or maybe he gets five thousand in a year: maybe the five thousand, in the whole year it was only this five thousand he got from me, because he cannot live well with that to make his house fine.

PART FOUR *Juju*

9 THE SHEER UBIQUITY OF IT

: THE VILLAGE IN BURKINA FASO :

Issahaku's Medicine

You know, as for juju, or as for medicine, I think that some of the people who have medicine know the trees. They know that this tree and that tree, if you mix them, you can make something. Even my father knew much about medicine from the trees, but he didn't have juju like the other ones. The other ones say that the juju shows them the medicine.[1] But as for my father, if somebody is sick, my father can find different trees: you know, this tree is doing this; this tree is taking care of this sickness; and all this. Yes? My father was doing it, and many people came to my father for that when they were not well. Or if somebody cannot do anything with woman, or when he sees a woman he has no feeling to make love, and all this, my father knows all these trees to make medicine for them. Sometimes if you went to my father's place in the village, you would see plenty of people, the place full up. What they want: the men who cannot make love with their wives, and these things. And my father made medicine for them, and then, it was true. You know, if he makes it for one and it doesn't work, then the other one won't come again. So I think it's true, that what he is doing to them is working for them. So every time if somebody has a problem like that, he would say, "I'll go and see Issahaku."

1. through divination

Christmas for a Juju

And so, even in my country, they have juju. *Oi!* They have it plenty. You know, I didn't stay there much, and I don't know much about their juju. But in my village, they have something, and they believe in it. Every year they make a Christmas[1] for it. If you go to Upper Volta, you can see it. Even if you don't go there, maybe you can see it. I think I saw it in some picture in a hotel. They have a kind of dress that is like something they make rope with. They make part of it with wool, and then they can make part like a statue. Some people used to put it on, to put all this thing on their body. Then they put something like a statue that you can buy from these traders by the hotels, a big statue. I don't know the name of this thing: some of the white people buy it as a statue. They can make some like a cow; they can make some like different things. Then they make a hole inside to put it on your head, and you can put it on like a mask. Someone puts it on his head, and then covers all his body. You can see somebody like a statue. You know, they have a big one: someone can put it on his head. It's tall. And this thing is juju in our country, in my village.

The time they're going to make the Christmas for this thing, every year, they have to go to where there is a river. In my village, we have a river; it's not a big river but it's not small. It's there. Every year they go there. The men sleep at that river for about one month before they will come home. Every night, this thing is coming there. *Heh!*

One time I went to my village because of this thing. My brother in Ouagadougou asked me that since I have been going to our village, did I ever meet this thing? I said, "No." So he told me, "OK. Let's go and see it." And he said he would show me the day they are making these things so that we go there. The time they had done eighteen days, then my brother said we should go: it remained two days and the men will come home.

The last day when they will sleep at the riverside, they will come home in the evening time. You will hear something like the ground is going: *DUMM-M HUMM-M UM-M.* And then, you know, it is so much interesting when you hear that: this thing is making like something in the ground. I don't know whether they make a big hole and then what! *Ha!!* So: everybody must be quiet. If you have a light in your room, you must switch it off. Even an oil lamp, you must switch it off. This thing doesn't want where it's light. And this thing, they call it the *chef du village.* That

1. make a festival

is the name they give it: chief of the village. They say when he comes home, he comes to the village to watch all around the village, because of the witch people. They say that it's the witch people who go out in the night to find people to kill. If there are witch people in the town, the time they go out to kill somebody or do something, if they meet you they will kill you too; the next morning they will find that somebody is dead there and somebody is dead there. The chief of the village will come and go round and meet the witches. They want to spoil the village; they want to do the village bad: he will kill them.

And the next day, you know, it was very good. A *good* dance! They put on all of these things and: come and see people dancing! They were making some very funny things. *Ha!* Yes, I have interest in their dancing. And they said you shouldn't put on a red dress. The *chef du village* doesn't want red, something red. When they dress with the mask, all the things they put on and wear on their skins, they dye the color red, but it's not too much red. And so they don't want somebody to challenge them with red. They hate red! When you put on red, you will see that they will come and beat you. Yeah! So: when they said this, I didn't believe, you know, and I put on a red blouse and came outside.

Then they started: *kikikiki kikikiki!* Then my brother picked me up, "Go, go, go. *Go!!*"

I said, "Eh? Why should I go like this?"

He said, *"Go-o!"* Then when I was going, I saw this thing following me. *Heey!* I fell down three times before I reached home! You know, I was afraid, because it was a human being, but the way he dressed up, you wouldn't know that it was a human being. I think they have small-small holes in the mask to see. *Um-hm!* So, if you see them, you must be afraid of them a little bit. So I saw this once in my village. And they say it's juju: the *chef du village.*

And all these things, some people believe; some people don't believe. Ah, Africa! We have many problems. Everyone with his problem, you know.

In Tamale, they too, they have something when you steal something or you lie on somebody. If you say to somebody, "You did this," and he says, "It's not me who did it," then you are forcing him. If he takes you to someplace—I think it's Pong Tamale[1] or some place like that—then they will call the rain. Rain! They will call rain for you. You will see a cloud. When the rain is falling, this thing makes *prrrrr,* like a fire, like electricity.

1. village twenty miles north of Tamale, site of a rain shrine

They can kill you now-now-now with it. In Togo too they have the same thing. In Togo if you see these women who used to put the white marks,[1] they are the people from this juju.

: LOMÉ :

The Keta Girls and the Seaman

The Lomé one, I saw it. Near to the harbor in Lomé, there are some girls who live in these grass rooms. If a ship comes, the seamen come to them. There were two girls who came to Lomé. I think the one girl was Anwona,[2] you know, the people from Keta.[3] She was in Lomé, then she went and brought the friend from Ghana; they stayed together, two girls. And then, every time she was losing her money. Then she told the friend, "Ah! My friend, when I was by myself in Lomé, I didn't lose anything, but since you came here, I used to lose my money. So I don't want this way. If you want something, you must tell me."

And this girl said, "No-o-o! I haven't taken anything."

Then one day the girl lost a thousand francs. Then she said, "Ah! This thousand is not plenty money, but I'm not going to give up on this. I will find my one thousand." So this girl got up and went to see these juju people.

You know, in Lomé when it's something like this, they will bring something and blow: *prum prum prum.* And they will say, "Somebody says his something is lost. His one thousand is lost. The person who took it, he must bring it to the juju house. If you don't bring it, then give it to the owner. If it's not so, we are giving you three days." They come to all the areas[4] to say all this.

Then this girlfriend who came also said, "OK, I don't care. I will not do anything. I didn't take this money. What should I do? My friend just wants to do this so that she will make me afraid." So this girl was annoyed: she went and got her own room, and left the friend.

Then one day there was a ship, and she went with some man. If you ask all of the girls, even Mama Amma, everybody went there to see this. But as for me, I don't like to see a dead body like that. Mama said, "Let's

1. painted lines on face, limbs or body; worn by cult initiates
2. (Asante Twi): Anlo Ewe
3. small town in southeastern corner of Ghana
4. neighborhoods or sections of a town

go," and I said, "I'm not going." When this girl brought this man, then they were sleeping together, and it started raining. This rain, it fell heavy, but it didn't stop. Before it finished, then it started falling heavy more than before. In the night. All these juju people, nobody slept: *"He-wo-wo-wo. O-oooooey, O-oooooey —"* They were in the rain. And so, this girl slept with one seaman, and he was a white man. And they said that if the seaman was an African who understands, the time he got the scent of the rain, he should have gone out. This thing came to the room three times. The fire just made: *prrru-cha!* Then it went inside: *prup-prup.* Then it went out, like electricity. When it went out, then it came back again. Three times. And I think, you know, when it's raining, this is the time when some people feel to make love. So these people were making love, and this thing came, *prrrurr.* Then *pffft:* both of them, the two. And then it moved a coconut tree, and this coconut tree fell on them. And this house: it was like somebody took the house and threw it away and left the place with their bed and everything. They didn't have anything on, and they were there, dead under the coconut tree.

Then these juju people got up, singing, *"Oo-oo-oo-oo."* All of Lomé! That day, oh, it was a show, eh! This thing let people see a show. It was very hard that day. They said, "Yea-a! The rain did some bad at some place. Some people did bad." If this thing is coming, the people don't know where it is happening, but if it happens, now-now-now, they will go and find the place with their white dresses. Then they went to the harbor, and the ship's captain wanted to take the white man from the girl, and they said, "No, it's not possible. Even if you bury him here, you must pay some money. Because this is our power which made this thing. And so if you take him free, you will see the results." These people talked to the captain, and he understood them, and he gave them some money, and they buried this man in Togo. So the juju killed this white man. Ah! You know, I thought maybe the time when this thing was coming, and it was not getting a chance, because he was on top of this girl, so this thing didn't know what to do, so it had to kill him with the girl.

And you see the girl who took the money? It's something like me with this sickness. I told you that I don't have belief in these things. So if I don't believe, then I think all this is shit. Yeah! She too didn't believe that something can do that. But when the thing happened and these juju people came, they said, "Yeah. This is what this girl did and then this happened, because this rain cannot kill like that, by heart, without any reason." It's their juju; they are the people who control the thing. They look after it, and if you don't do something against it, it cannot kill you, and so it has done it.

And because of this kind of case, you see, many people are afraid of stealing. In Togo, too, the real Togolese[1] used to fear each other. If they get some way of stealing, they can do it, but with the Togolese who know, some of them are afraid. *Eh? Heh, heh, heh.* Ah, Africa!

10 WITCHES

: THE VILLAGE IN BURKINA FASO :

Witchfire

So all these things: Africans, they believe in it! You know, we the children at this time, especially, many of us don't believe this. But still now, there are some children our size[2] who are in the village: they believe it. They believe it, even today. *Yeah!* They really believe it.

You know, I don't believe it. But sometimes, too, when you go to the village, especially something like our village — look, in the village, they don't have light.[3] Sometimes, if they show you something in the night, you will be afraid. You will believe it. You know, I didn't used to believe in them, but anyway, in the village, *hm?*

I have a younger brother. He's a ruffian. He's a bad boy. If I go to my village in Upper Volta, I sleep in that boy's room. He will sleep on the

1. Ewe people; people from Lomé. The description implies the people at the main or initial point of historical contact that eventually became Togo, that is, the indigenous people of the coastal capital and not those from the northern or more provincial regions.

2. age

3. electricity

floor, and then I will sleep on the bed. And his wife will go and sleep with the mother. *Ha!* So every night, I don't know what he used to look outside for. Whether he's going to piss, or something like that, I don't know. So one night, we were conversing nicely, and we all fell asleep. Then he woke me about one, or half-past one. He said, "Sister, sister."

Then I said, "Yes."

He said, "Can you wake up?"

Then I said, "Why?"

He said, "Come and see something."

So I just got up from the bed, and we went out. We have a *big* tree outside of the village. The skin of this tree can make you *itch.* It can scratch you if you play with it. Where it gets you, you can get a knife and cut that place, and it will still be itching you. He said, "Look at the top of this tree. What do you see?"

You know, I was seeing something like small balls of light, small-small. This tree used to make some big, round seeds. When it is grown and dry, they used to cut it. Inside there is some food they used to eat. It's white.

So I said, "Ah."

He said, "What are you seeing?"

I said, "I'm seeing the seed of the trees."

Then he said, "How do they look like?"

And I said, "They are white."

He said, "No, it's not that one. In the morning, look at this tree where you see the seeds, whether they are white or not." But morning-time, when I looked at the tree, it was not the same thing. The color was yellow. So when I saw it in the morning, I said, "OK."

Then he asked me, "Is this white?

Then I said, "No. But what do you want to say?"

He said, "Yesterday, didn't you see many witches on this tree? The small-small things you saw, white: that's the witch light."

So I used to be afraid, but I used to want to watch and see it. So once, in back of our place, they used to plant crops there, yellow corn and some things. And our house is just in the middle. If you see it in the rainy season, you will see it like some village which somebody made and then planted things around it. So one night I was about to go and piss. And as this boy had been telling me this, I had mind of it, and I used to be afraid a little bit when I came out in night time to piss.[1] The way they build the

1. A village house is a collection of round rooms like huts, and one urinates on the ground outside a house.

house, there is no gate you have to pass before you can go out. They just build the rooms one here and one there, and there are some places between. So when you get outside of the house, you can look everywhere. So I was squatting down to piss. I didn't finish pissing, then I saw something just like some fire that went *swoo-osh,* like a bird, you know. Then I *shouted! Ha-ha!*

So my father came out. Then he said. "Why?"

I was shouting. I shouted and ran to the room. Then I woke my brother. I said, "*He-ey!* This is a witch, yeah? Today I saw a witch."

And my brother said, "What is it?"

I said, "I have seen the witch! She had a big ball like this!" It was just like a ball which babies play with. It was round, but this fire was going along.

So my father came to my brother's room and said, "What is wrong?"

Then I said, "Papa, I have seen a witch. So my *heart.*" *Ha-ha!* You, know, my heart was just going: *Kikikiki.*

So my father held me. Then he said, "Oh-h, *tsk.* It's not a witch. Maybe it was some farmers who used to go to find honey at this time." You know, at our place, they find honey in the night. Sometimes you see some people go to find honey after twelve o'clock in the night. They are afraid the bees can bite them, but in the night time, the bees have all slept. So these people go with the fire and then get the honey. So my father was saying it was those people.

Then my brother said, "You lie! No man can find honey in this village, in town. We go and find the honey in bush." So my brother was making me more afraid!

And my father didn't want me to be afraid much. Maybe I would become sick. So he was trying to boss me that and this. He said maybe the people were going, that it was night and there was no moon. It was darkness. So I could see their lights but I couldn't see the fellow.

I said, "No! I was seeing the thing! It was just like this. I was watching it! Ah! I don't understand. What is this?"

When the fire went up, there were some small-small sparks, as if you take some firewood from the fire and go out and the breeze is blowing, and the small ones are dropping. I saw the thing like that.

So my father said, "No, this is the people who are going to find the honey. Maybe they got up early."

Then my brother said, "You lie!" When my father went to sleep, then it was the same thing: I couldn't sleep. Then my brother said, "He lied. Papa lied. It was a witch. But you wait. I will *show* that witch person who is coming around this house. I will *see* him." *Ha!* That boy is a *bad* boy.

: THE VILLAGE IN GHANA :

Babies as Strangers

You know, among my father's children, we are four children who when they borne us, they said we are the children of a juju. We didn't know: that is the story our father told us. We were born in Ghana, and I think I was about six years old, from the time I was born: they didn't put a knife to my hair, and they didn't cut my hair, and they didn't comb it. My hair used to be like this Bob Marley.[1] I was having it. Then they used to get this Ghana *kobo*[2]—the penny, the old, old penny which has a hole on it—they used to get them plenty for me, the white ones. They would just take some of my hair—as they didn't comb it—it would come long, and they would tie the penny inside of the hair so that the penny would stay there. I was having these pennies in my hair when I was six years old. I was seven years when they took me to the juju's place, and then they combed all of them out, before I started to get my own hair to comb it. But before, we were four of my father's children who were from that side like that. We all were growing up without combing the hair. They were bathing us and washing the hair, but they didn't comb it.

Yeah. There are some jujus: they can say someone is a child of them. Sometimes, if somebody doesn't have a baby, she can go and beg the juju to have a child, and they used to say that the baby is a child of the juju, and they give the child the name from the juju.

We Africans, you know, we have some interest in these things. They used to say, if you have much belief in your juju, it's just like these politics people, or maybe somebody's witchcraft, or somebody's this and that.

1. name for a hair style with dreadlocks, taken from the name of the Jamaican musician

2. British West African currency, used in Gambia, Sierra Leone, Nigeria, and Gold Coast from 1907 through 1958, had different coinage with holes: penny, half-penny, and one-tenth penny. Hawa's classification of "white" and "red" reflects the fact that tenth-pennies, half-pennies, and pennies were coined at different times in bronze and in copper-nickel. Kobo is now the name for 1/100 of a contemporary Nigerian naira. The word is borrowed from the English "copper" in Hausa as well as Krio (the creole language of Sierra Leone) and was also widely used throughout West Africa in Pidgin. My Dagbamba teachers in northern Ghana told me that when coins initially replaced cowrie shells, they used the word kobo as a name for the penny, which was one hundred cowries. In Asante Twi, similarly, a penny is kaprɛ. When the Ghanaian pesewa replaced the penny, some people used the various terms interchangeably. Holed half-pennies and pennies were common souvenirs people gave me when I first went to Ghana in 1970.

Some people have juju in their house, for the family. There are many people who have interest in this juju, and every year or any time, they used to sacrifice things for their juju. So in this case, it can become something like: as this thing likes you much, the same way as you like him, then he's going to give you a daughter or a son. Even you can get babies by yourself, but he would just like to give you his own, as a gift. And they used to say that the baby is from the juju. You see?

So we just came like that. My father said we were gifts to him. We didn't know. They said when they gave birth to us, then—you know, I don't know whether it's all of Africa, but at our place, when they get a child, before they will make the name of the baby, they have to go to some places to see how this child has come.[1] Did he come to live, or did he come for what? There are some children, they say they come for life. And there are some children, when they come they want to get problems. All this, you know, many people have belief in it.

So since your wife has had a baby, she will try to run to a juju man. Some of them have these white cowrie shells—the one some girls used to put in their hair—some people used to throw these shells and tell you what is going to happen. And some people just use sand: he will pour it down and then write something on it in Arabic, and then he will bring something and he will tell you what is going to happen, and that and this. And many people have belief in all this, all the time.

So always, especially our people, when the wife has delivered a child today, if it's not too late, the husband has to go to these people to see what kind of child the wife has delivered. If it's very late, then the next morning, he has to go there to see what he has: is this a good child, or is this a troublesome child, or is this child going to live in life, or it is not going to live in life? And some people, they used to tell him that the child is not going to live, so he will ask what does the baby want before living life. That's why sometimes, you can see a small baby: they will put something on his neck. Sometimes a ring on a string around the neck. Some of them put a ring on the hand. Some of them get something different. This is what the baby is asking for. If the father doesn't do for him, he will go back: it means that he's going to die. So if the father gives the baby what he wants, then he will stay in his life.

They do that in many places. At our place, too, we have the same thing. So we four, when they gave birth to us, they said it's the juju that

1. through divination, to look at the child's destiny or character. The souls of the children are at some place, and they choose to come or are sent to be the babies who are conceived.

liked my father, the way my father has behaved to him, so he doesn't know what to give my father, so he will give him his children. So we were four of us like that.

The Witchcraft of the Senior Mother

You know, my father's senior wife, they have been calling this woman a witch. It is coming from this juju, the juju that brought us. Apart from my mother, my father married two other women, and as my mother is dead, he is left with these two wives. They are sisters. We have this at our place: one man will marry sisters. *Ha-ha!*

When we were growing up in Ghana, the senior wife was sick for about six to eight months. She was always sleeping. She couldn't wake up. And then it was fucking: she was *smelling!* When you would go to the room, you couldn't breathe. You know, she was sick very seriously. She could not sit. Always, she was lying down. And all the flesh on this place, on her waist and bottom,[1] was chopped off.[2] Yeah?

So this woman, before she was going to be all right, one night she called my father. You know, we didn't know about this, but my father used to talk to us about this woman, to be careful with her, and what he had seen with her. He said one night the woman called him to beg him that he should take her to the juju, to the juju's place. So my father said, "Why?"

She told him, no, she can't say anything. If my father gets her to the place, she will tell him.

And that juju, too, they don't take a person there in the night time.[3] The juju doesn't want you in the night. He wants day time, for everybody to see you. So my father said, "OK, if that will be the case, it will be tomorrow."

So the next day, my father went and saw the juju man, that he will be bringing his wife. She has a problem. She said she can't say it to him. She wants to come and say it here to the juju.

And the juju man said, "Ah." It was Saturday when the woman told my father. Sunday, he went and saw the juju man. The man said, "Any-

1. buttocks

2. eaten away by sores

3. Different shrines have their own protocols and etiquette for supplicants, such as particular days or times, or sometimes require that a supplicant be accompanied or led there by a householder from that town or village.

way, this place, if your wife has a real problem that she wants to tell this juju, you know, Sunday is not the day for this juju. It's Monday. So if you can be patient, Monday you can bring her, early in the morning."

So the Monday, my father took her there. That juju was from Brong Ahafo, from the road to Brong Ahafo from Kumasi. Do you know Bechem?[1] It was from Bechem-Ahenkro[2] in the Brong Ahafo area. But this man brought the juju from there, and he was staying in the village where my father was farming in the cocoa farm. It was a small village on the road to Brong Ahafo. It's a little bit far from Kumasi.

My father said the reason why he left the house in Kumasi was because of the witchcraft of his brothers. They were witches, and that and this, and that was why he left. Then he stayed in that village. And that time we all were there. When he went to that village, he saw this juju there, and he said this juju doesn't like any witch. So if you put *all* your body to the juju, the juju will look at you. A witch cannot touch you. So my father was going to that juju to be helping him for his life, or to be helping him because of his children, so that any witch couldn't chop them. And that is the juju where they brought the four of us. They said that we were the children of that juju.

So the senior wife: when they took that woman to that juju's place, if the juju catches you as a witch, you will be sick and sick and sick and sick. There is not any doctor who can take care of you. You will be going to doctors. They will be giving you injections, but you will never, never, never feel all right. You'll be sick all the time, until you have said what you wanted to do before you had this problem.

So they took this woman to talk to the juju there. It was Monday. They were playing gungon.[3] That juju, they used to play on gungon, the Ashanti gungon: *gun gon gón gon, gun gon gón gon. Hey!* I used to dance this dance! If you saw me dancing this, you would like it. The chief of this juju liked me very much. He used to call me his wife.

So these things: the juju used to come. I don't know how, but to us Africans, we used to say the day they are going to carry the juju, or to bring the juju out, the juju can choose somebody he likes for that person to carry him. Then that person who will take this juju and carry it, he has

1. small town on the road to Sunyani, about thirty miles from Kumasi

2. (Asante Twi): *ahenkro,* from *ahenfoɔ kuro,* literally, royal town. The spelling is often Anglicized as *ahinkro* on maps. The suffix usually indicates a suburb or a village linked to a town.

3. a large double-sided tom-tom, with a snare, beaten with a stick

some thing to carry it, and you will see the person is very tall. So the way he can dance, he can't go fast.

Yeah. I used to look at this juju man every time when we went there. Every Monday when I saw the gungon: *Kaɛ!*[1] I was the first person there. And every Monday, too, they used to cook cocoyam fufu, with groundnut soup, but they didn't put pepper in it. That juju didn't eat meat. Fish: they would make the sauce with fish. And *all* the children in the village would go there and eat. And a special child for the juju, he can go inside the room of the juju: the food that they put in front of the juju, he will eat that one. So I used to eat it a lot of times! *Ha-ha!*

The time when this juju caught this woman, by that time we weren't grown up. We didn't know anything about it. It was only that my father used to tell us a story to be careful of her, because of what he had seen with her. And he said that when he took this woman there, and the people came to beat the gungon, the *first* person's name the juju called was my youngest brother. That boy is a strong boy in the house. I think he's also a witch. *Hee-hee!*

So you know, this woman said that the first time when she married to my father, then she thought she was in love with my father. But since the younger sister has come, and she gave her to my father, my father didn't want to mind her again. So that was why. And she said she was not born in witchcraft. She wasn't born as a witch. But one time, she bought the witchcraft. You know, some people can be born in the witchcraft, and some people can *buy* it. Her own, she *bought* it. She was not born in it.

She said because of this, when my father got the younger sister, my father didn't mind her much again. That's why, when she went to her village in Upper Volta, she took her younger brother. She had her village there. So she went and took her younger brother to give to buy the witchcraft. And they killed the younger brother. The younger brother wasn't sick before he died. He just came out, and then he said he was feeling headache. Then they said he should sleep a little bit, and maybe it will go. He went inside. That was all. The younger brother died. She was saying this in the juju's place. She took that younger brother and exchanged for the witchcraft, you know, just like you give something to me, and I give you something. Then when she came back, it was about three or four months' time when she started her sickness. And then the juju man asked

1. (Asante Twi): an exclamation of objection, rejecting a situation or statement as useless. In this context, its use is an affirmation, as in "What?! You lie!"

her: why did she want to buy the witchcraft? She said it was because when my father got the younger sister, he didn't mind her. So she wanted to kill my father. That's why she bought the witchcraft.

So then the juju man asked her, "You have children with your husband?"

Then she said, "Yes"

"If you kill him, what are you doing?"

She said, if she killed him, she knew that among all the children of the husband, she knew which ones are good and which ones aren't good. And she knew the ones who would come and challenge her about the property. So she would finish all of those people. If she kills our father, then she will be frying us one by one. *Ha-ha!* Like fish.

So then, the day when she wanted to go and kill my father, when she went, she took my brother, Kofi. You know? My brother—one mother, one father. She said Kofi was a horse for her in the night. A horse. *Hey!* So because of this thing, Kofi doesn't want to see this woman's face. That's why he's always in Ghana. He doesn't go home. Kofi said that the day the woman dies, he will come home, or the day the woman divorces my father, he will come. But if this woman is there, he can't stay with my father. *Ha!* So she used to turn this boy into the horse to go and eat.

So she said that the night when she was going to kill my father, she told all the witches that she would bring a cow, you know, which was my father. Then when she went to the place she was going to get my father, she saw this small boy, my youngest brother, the one I'm talking about. At that time this boy was a baby. I think by then I was walking, but this boy, he didn't even know how to *crawl.* He was *small,* about two months old. They had just given birth to him. But she said that the time when she was going to kill my father, she saw the boy standing up there, with a big club. This thing, the watchmen used to carry it. It's a stick, and the head is big. Many watchmen, the people who are watching places, they used to hold that type of stick.

So this boy was with that stick the time when she wanted to put the thread[1] on the neck of the cow. You know, they say that the witches, when they are going to kill somebody, they can turn you into a sheep or a cow. It's not your own body. They say they used to get your soul to turn you into the sheep or to turn you into the cow. So she was coming to put the thread on her cow when this boy knocked her in her back with that stick, and then she just felt weak and fell down. So then she was sick, and she was like that all the time. And then the boy took the cow from her

1. to tie it. A witch uses thread or string instead of rope to tie and lead it.

and then went and took Kofi — my brother who was the horse — this small brother took him home. This small boy, he didn't walk yet. He did these things.

She talked all this at the juju place where she went, and they gave her some water of the juju to drink. And then they asked her to bring all her witchcraft to this juju's place.

I don't know now: suppose I knew that juju is still in that village, I would wish to go there one day. When I went to my village, I asked my father. Then my father said that maybe the owner of the juju has died. Then I said, "What? And you didn't die yet?!" *Ha-ha!*

If you go to this juju's place there, you will see many beads. Those Ashanti women used to give some beads which are costly. You will see that thing. You will see gold — many, many gold earrings, necklaces, and everything. If you are a witch, and this juju catches you, maybe you have been killing people to sell their meat to the witches like you, to get money and buy some things. This juju will take all of it from you. If you don't bring all of it out, the juju will kill you. So they asked our mother to go and bring her witchcraft.

So from then, my father didn't love the woman again. But he couldn't sack her. I think he is also afraid of her. He said where this woman got the thing, he wondered. What made him wonder was that this woman could keep this thing in her wardrobe. She was staying with my father with the same wardrobe. If something happens, maybe she will just open the wardrobe and take something. But he was opening this wardrobe every time, and he didn't see these things, the gold and beads and these things. And when she took the things to the juju, the juju took everything from her. So it meant that she was no longer a witch: she didn't have the power of the witchcraft again, because the juju has taken the power. She can be a witch, but she can't do anything. When the juju got these things, then in one month's time, this woman was all right. And my father sent her back to her family.

And you know, this woman was very clever. She just said, "Eh-h." I think she was making an argument with my father that if my father sends her alone, it is not correct. If he's going to send her away, he has to send both of them, because she had brought the younger sister. If he's going to divorce the senior wife, he must divorce both of them. So the family brought this problem. So my father said, oh, he doesn't want to divorce the younger one. So he will take her like that. And he got her back. That's why she's there now.

But even my father says that sometimes if he is asleep, when the woman troubles him, he says, "Ah! I say: go to your father's place! And let me sleep! Even I can't sleep in the night. Sometimes I used to be afraid of you!" *Ha-ha!*

You know the village door: they don't have an actual door. Some people just used to put these heavy mats against the door of the room. So my father said that sometimes in the night time, some old people used to wake up thinking a little bit. So if he hears that something is making *ss-s-s-s-s,* then: *gai-i!* He will put on the light. Then he will say, "Come. I'm here. You think you are up to me?" *Ha-ha!* So when he used to have a problem with her, he will say, "No, no, no, no, no! I can't sleep. This time your thing has started coming again. Because I left this juju there, so you want to start again. Every night you have been coming out and going in!" *Ha-ha!* He himself used to be afraid of the wife.

: THE VILLAGE IN BURKINA FASO :

Belief in Witches

So, this witchcraft, I think it's there. It's just like something we Africans believe. As for you people, you don't have belief in it, so you don't see it. But us: we have belief. Every time we used to see some things.

The witchcraft, they have old woman, old ladies, and they have young ones, too. Even they can catch a *small* girl as a witch. You know, there are some people who used to sell medicine in the market, these African medicines. Some of them are taking care of sickness, and some of them are taking care of witchcraft. So Africans, we used to have belief in all these things. Sometimes. In our place, too, I think so. They have belief. That is why sometimes they can bring dwarves to call a person who is far away. And the witchcraft, too, they have belief in it.

Sometimes somebody can die by his own death. But somebody can die by a witch, too. That's why, at our place, if somebody dies like that, and they don't understand, they have to go and find out. So you know our place: if somebody has died, I think they all are witch people, so they know if you died by a witch or if you died by your own death. So if somebody is dead, they won't bury the person yet. They will go and find out what killed him: whether it is his own death, or if somebody killed him, or if some witch killed him, or if somebody poisoned him. At our place they have this kind of things. They will go to the juju man, and they will throw this thing down — like how I told you they throw the shells or the sand — and say, "This man was dead by a witch," or "This man, it was his own death," or "Somebody didn't like him, and he made poison or he made his juju to kill him." These things, we have it in our place.

So our place—where they do this thing, you know—if there was somebody and he wasn't sick, it can be that somebody will be dead, just now. Maybe he goes out, and he's feeling headache. He will just come inside, not quite ten minutes, and he's dead. If this thing happens, if he is a young, strong man, or a young woman who is strong, they don't understand. They have to find out why he is dead like that.

So when they go to these juju people, the juju man will say what killed him. What the juju man says, this is what they take. If the juju man says a witch killed him, even somebody can be dead, and they will go to the juju, and he will say it is his own mother. *Eh?* You have wasted your time for a good nine months, and your baby, maybe he will grow up to twenty or twenty-two years, and you will kill him. Have you seen something like that before? But they will put it like that. If they say the mother is the one who killed him, they will just come out and go straight to you that, "You killed your son, so we don't want you in this house. Pack your things." Our place, they have people like that. And the old lady is just going away to suffer, you know.

Befriending a Witch

Oh! We had one in our village. She was from a village near our place. I ate with her a lot of the time when I was young. When I went to my village, I asked my father. My father said, "Oh, she is dead a long time."

So I said, "Oh-h." I went to the place where I used to eat with the old lady. I just went to stand like that and look at the place. You know, she was a witch from some village, and she had many children. They all were dead like that, without any sickness. He goes out. Maybe he's in the school. He comes from the class. He has a headache. He goes inside. *Pop!*

She had about twelve children. All the eleven died. It was left with one. The one who was left, he was a farmer. He stayed in the village and did farm work, so he used to get a lot of food. And this man had three wives, and he had about eight children. These eight children, all of them died like that. So he didn't have any child. When the wife gave birth, in about one month's time, *poom:* it's finished. So he went to these people to find out, and they said, "Ah, it's your mother. She killed all your brothers. And she knew that if she killed you, she wouldn't get any more. She will be suffering, because she is owing a debt." They said every time the mother was getting the children to pay her debt: she would go and meet her fellow witches to share the meat. You see?

So this man, when he came home, he said, "Ah well, I can't help it, because all the eleven brothers have died, and I can't get a child too to be my brother, so this fucking old lady, she has to get out from the house." So he just fucked off the mother like that.

From our village to their village, it's about eight kilometers. The mother walked from there and came and stayed at our village. But she didn't have a house. She was staying some place a little bit out of the village. Where we used to go and throw the dust[1] from the village, that was the place she stayed. She didn't have any room there, but she got cartons from the dust heap and made them like a room. She had about two cooking pots, and some small-small things. She used to cook there and do everything, and she was sleeping there, like somebody who didn't have anything. I was very sorry for her, you know.

So the time when my father took me to my grandmother, when I would go to throw the dust, I used to see this woman. Then I said, "Hey! Grandmother. What are you doing here?"

Then she laughed, "Ha ha ha ha ha!! Here is my house. My daughter, why?"

Then I said, "But why do you want to stay here? Wouldn't you like to stay with my grandmother?"

She said, "No! Your grandmother doesn't like me. Not anybody in this village likes me. Everybody doesn't like me."

Then I said, "Why?"

She said, "I don't know."

"And you don't have children?"

She said, "Oh no, all my children have died, so I haven't got any place. I haven't got any family."

Then I said, "You haven't got brothers either?"

She said, "No."

So every time, before I made friends with her, this was the way we used to talk. And every time, when they would give me the dust to go and throw it away, I would go, and when I would come home, I would forget all the things which I went and threw the dust with. I wouldn't bring anything home. I would just stay with this woman. We would go to the river, and I would fetch water with her. And we would be talking, you know, coming home, cooking, and then I would eat and finish before I would go home.

If I came home, my grandmother had finished cooking. Then she would say, "Hey! You, this girl, I don't know what to do with you. Since morning time! Do you know what is the time now? It's afternoon. You, now you are coming home!"

And I would say, "Oh-h, you know, I have met—I have a girlfriend."

1. trash

Then she said, "Where did you see her?"

I said, "There's an old woman. She is sitting near the dust. She is a nice woman. Grandmother, wouldn't you like to live with her? She's living there. Maybe night time an animal can come and catch her."

Then my grandmother said, "Ah-h. It's a big animal. An animal can't catch her. She is a *big* animal."

Then I said, "Why? She is *not* an animal! She is a human being! I was talking to her."

Then she said, "Do you know why she came to stay there?"

Then I said, "No. She told me she had children, and all of them have died. All the family has died and left her. It's very pitiful. So let's have her, and she will stay here with us."

She said, "Look, she is a witch! She killed all her children! She had twelve children: only one is left. And the one who is left, he has given birth to about eight children by now, and he doesn't have them again. When he went to the juju man, they showed him that the mother is the one who has been doing that. That's why the son sacked her. It's not that she doesn't have people."

I said, "Oh-h, they lie! But I have eaten with her just now."

Then my grandmother said, "You have eaten a human being!"

And I said, "*Kaɛ!* I didn't eat a human being." *Ha-ha!*

This old lady cooked fresh meat. Sometimes she used to get fresh fish. I don't know how she got them. And she had a small cooking pot, the one we Africans used to make. I don't know how this woman got her food. But I saw that she used to get fresh fish—big ones. And the flour and seasonings, I don't know how she got them. She cooked T-Zed, with fish soup, with the dawadawa[1] and other seasonings. I liked it. I used to go and eat well there.

But this time, when I think about it, it's *fucking! Ha-ha!* This time, if she gave me that kind of food, I wouldn't eat it. But then, I used to *like* her food more than my grandmother's food.

Interlude: A Special Child

You know, my grandmother used to make special soup for me. Sometimes she fried chicken or sometimes guinea fowl—about three—they fried them in a big pot and kept it. And if I was going to eat, even if my grandmother had something to do, she had to sit down with me so that I would

1. a seasoning, used mainly by people from savanna regions, prepared from the seeds of the dawadawa tree, *Parkia clapertiniana,* a type of locust tree

eat and finish before she went to any place. If not, the other children would come and take the food from me. And I too would give them some, and it would finish quickly. They would be killing fowls and killing fowls and killing fowls, and they would finish all the fowls in the house. So I was a chief! *Ha!*

When I wanted to eat, even if my grandmother was doing something, I just said, *"Eh-heh. Boo-hoo.* I'm hungry. *Boo-hoo,* I'm hungry. *Eh-h-h."* Then my grandmother would say, "OK, OK." Even if she was cooking, she would leave the food on the fire. Then she would come to sit with me. *Ha-ha!* She would put the food on the plate, then she would sit down, and I would eat and finish. Then she would cover the rest and carry it in, and then go back to do what she was doing.

Why did they do that for me? You know, my mother was dead when I was three years old. OK? And we Africans, when a woman has left a child and the child is very young, they don't want the baby to be feeling pity for herself: she doesn't feel happy; she's always crying. Africans say that the soul of the mother used to come and see the baby. And they say if the mother sees that the baby is suffering, she will take the baby away. It means the baby is also going to die. So every time, at our place, if there is a small baby, about two or three years old, if the mother dies and leaves her, they used to spoil the baby completely. They don't want her to make, *"Aha-a, eh-h-h."*

Ah! I was up to twelve years—I still used to sleep on the mat and piss. Piss! *Ha-ha!* Sometimes I used to know that I was feeling to piss. I won't call my grandmother. I won't want to wake her. I will just go behind the children who are sleeping there and piss near them. Then I will come back quickly and sleep at my place! *Ha-ha! Ha! Hee-hee-hee!* Yeah, and come back to my place, my dry place, to sleep. And sometimes, when I sleep, it makes me like dreaming that I'm pissing in a gutter: it's just my bed. I was pissing on top. *Ha-ha!* Morning time, when they see my mat, then my brother will say, "Hey, Hawa has pissed!" And I will start crying, *"Ah-h-h-h." Ha-ha! Hee-ha-ha.* Then I will start to call my mother, "My mama, come and take me! I'm suffering! All of them, they can piss and they will lie on me that I have pissed!" *Ta-ta-ta-ta!* Then my grandmother will come and beat the child who said that I am the one who pissed. They know that really I'm the one who did it, but they can't say it! You see?

So this is the way, in our place, when somebody is dead and leaves the small child. They used to give the baby the chance. They don't want her to be crying, or they don't want her to be looking too much sad. They want every time to be happy for the baby, so that if the mother's soul comes home to see the baby, she will see that the baby is all right, she is happy, and the people are looking at her well, so that she will live in life.

So in that case, too, when your mother is dead: I don't know whether if you are grown up, they do this thing, because I didn't ask exactly to know. But when my mother was dead, they had a pot—you know, I was very young, but I used to remember these things. Sometimes, some nights, if I sleep, I used to think of all this. They had a small pot. They put water in it and put some leaves on it, and put it top of the grave of your mother. *Early* in the morning, they will carry you and go and bathe you on top of the grave. Yeah. They were doing this to me. I remember this.

But that time, when my mother was dead, I didn't exactly know that my mother—I didn't have feeling like my mother was dead. I thought maybe she had traveled. I didn't know that she was actually dead or something like that. So that time I didn't know that it was the grave of my mother which they were bathing me on top of it. It was my brother who let me know the grave of my mother, my senior brother, because that time, he was grown up.

Befriending a Witch (Conclusion)

So this old lady who was living in the dust heap, they started to stop me from going there, but I didn't stop. When my grandmother stopped me, they didn't give me the dust to throw away again. So what I did, early in the morning, you know, African children: when you wake up, you take the kettle with water to go outside and wash your face. And sometimes, if children wake up from sleeping, they are very funny. Sometimes I used to just carry this kettle—*ta-ta-tn-tn*—and then I would go and sit down. The kettle is front of me, and I will sit on it, and I will be washing myself like that. Then I will be watching the house. If I see that somebody doesn't come from our house, then I will leave the kettle there, and go to this old lady. *Ha-ha!* I don't wash my face. I will go to the old lady *straight.* When I go, I will say, "Hello, you are there?"

She will say, "Yes."

I will say, "Ah."

She will say, "Yesterday evening, why didn't you come?"

I will say, "Ah, no, yesterday evening was night, and it was dark. The moon didn't shine. That's why I didn't." Sometimes I used to go to her in the night time, when the moon was shining. *Ha-ha!*

You know, the time when I was growing up, when I started to be strong with my father, my father said, "Yes, your grandmother was telling me that you were a friend of a witch. Maybe she gave you a little bit!" *Ha-ha!* "You have a small witchcraft, too. She has given you. This old lady cannot leave you like that. She will give you a small one."

Then I said, "*Mm.*"

So I was just going there every day. Then my grandmother was sacking me. When I came home, she didn't want to beat me. But she would be shouting on me. At that time, I was about six to seven or eight. So when she was doing all this to me, when she did it a little bit and she started shouting on me too strongly, then I would start crying. Then she would come and say, "No, don't do that. You see, it's the witch people who killed your mother. Don't be a friend with a witch. I don't want you to walk with this woman. Don't try to do it." You know, when my mother was dead, too, they said it was a witch who killed her. It was the senior brother of my father who killed my mother with witchcraft. And then he killed all the three sisters and brothers.

And what let me stop going to this woman was that after a while I had a problem with her and we left our friendship. What made me have the problem was my small brother. I have a *small* brother; he is the son of my uncle. And this boy is a *witch!* As for him, he doesn't hide his own. He was small, a child. He was a baby. And he used to say the things he did in night time. When we would go out to play, he used to say: Yesterday night, we have been to that place, and we did that and did that and did this. He was just talking, you know.

So once I told him, "You know, I have a friend here. She used to cook good food, more than grandmother's one. But grandmother is trying to be jealous. The way I eat with this woman, I don't eat grandmother's food. So she is telling me that the woman is a witch. So if you want, we can go together. You shouldn't tell anybody. Only we two. You shouldn't tell anybody about what we are doing there, so that every time we can go there. She used to get fresh fish. Sometimes she used to get good meat. And she used to get chicken."

But you know, *shit!* I want to vomit. It's now I know the way she used to get the chicken meat. You know, the chicken which is dead and then they throw it on the dust, she will clean it fine and cook it. You will never think that it's a dead chicken. I used to eat this kind of things with this woman. Only God didn't kill me. I was supposed to die. It's a big poison.

So: *ha-ha!* I told this boy about this woman. And once, we went there. When you would go inside her room, you had to bend down, because it was only a carton. I was small, and I had to *bend* before getting inside. But she herself, when she was going inside, she would crawl, and then she would get inside. Inside was big a little bit, but only how to get in was the problem. So when we were going, then I was in front because she was my friend, and I was bringing my brother to visit her. So we went, and I told her, "This is my younger brother. I told him about your cooking. You cook nicely. So he wants to come and eat with you every time."

So she said, "Oh-h-h-h, my grandson."

Then my brother said, "No! Don't touch me. What are you cooking there?"

Then this old lady hadn't made any fire, and she said, "What am I cooking? I'm going to prepare now to cook, but I didn't cook anything."

So this boy is another witch boy. He is a bad boy. He said, "You lie. What is this?" He was pointing to some place, and that place which he was showing was just some dust. You know, this woman didn't have anything, just the dust which she was sitting on.

So I told this small boy, "Go out! I don't want to see you here. You are a liar. Every time you used to tell me that in the night you go there and go there and do that and do that. Then you come to laugh at this woman: 'What is she cooking?' Every time I come here, if she is cooking, I know when she's cooking."

So the small boy got up from the place and cried back to home. Then he went and told my grandmother that when we went to that old lady, the old lady was cooking some meat of a human being to give me, and he was saying it, and then I was telling him that I didn't see anything. So I sacked him. So my grandmother had to come straight to that woman. They told her to go out from the village. Yeah. They sacked her. They said she was trying to give me a witchcraft.

Ah! You know, after she went and was gone, one day we went to throw the dust. And I said, "Oh-h-h, this woman has gone. My good friend. They sacked her because of me. May God bless her. Oh-h."

Then one girl said, "Eh, now that they've sacked her, it's good. Look! All these chickens are dead. They are in the dust. Before, when she was here, she would chop *all.* She chopped human being's meat, so she cannot stand without any meat. She used to take all these dead chickens.

Ha! So that was the way I got to know that—*eh!*—the chickens which I was eating with this woman—they were *pfttt*—dead! *Shit!* I have been eating the chicken which they throw in the dust, from this old lady. I didn't know because she made it nicely, and put some oil on top. *Agh!* I didn't know how she got it, but I used to eat with her every time. Every day.

Revenge of a Bedwetter

You know, I told you that I used to piss on the mats of my brothers and sisters. One day I pissed, and they turned it to that boy I sacked from the old lady's place, and then he made them sack the old lady from the village. I used to sleep at the right side of my grandmother, and that boy used to sleep at the left side. So night time, when I was feeling like pissing, I woke up. But to call this old lady to take me outside to go and piss, I didn't feel it. So I just got up and passed beside the feet, and then I passed behind and went to that small boy's place and pissed, and then I came back to my right-hand side to sleep. *Ha-ha!*

And every morning time, in the morning time, that boy never pisses, so in the *whole* house, among all the children in the house, he's the chief. He used to abuse everybody: "Get away! *Pff!* You think I piss in bed like you?"

So that day I put him in trouble. And that was the *same* night when my grandmother had said, "From today going, someone who will wake up and his mat is wet, or his cloth is wet, we are going to take him outside and *all* the children of the village will come and shout on him that he has pissed."

So they got up: this boy's mat was wet. My grandmother was annoyed! But if it was my mat, she wouldn't say it aloud. Nobody would hear. She would call me and say, "Look. Now you are not a baby again. Look how your mat is wet. Do you want that?" Then I would just make my eyes like I was going to cry, making *eh-h-h, eh-h-h-h.* Then she would just whisper to me, "Don't cry! I'm not going to tell anybody. But don't do that tomorrow." *Ha-ha!*

But the other children, *"Ay-ay-ay!"* She would shout, "Go outside!" All the people would hear.

So the morning time when we got up, this boy's mat was wet with two girls, two small girls. All of us, we were about eight or nine children with her. All of us, she was our grandmother. As she was old, sometimes some of the sons gave birth or some of the daughters had babies, and she just used to keep them. She used to be happy with babies.

So that day we had three people who had pissed. This my piss, I had pissed on this boy, and the other two girls, too, were pissing. So my grandmother said, "I swear, today I won't leave you people! Why? Grown children like you! I have been washing your smelly piss like this. And your mothers and fathers are someplace enjoying their life. *Ah!* Today I won't leave you people."

So she got the mats. *Ha-ha!* The mats we were sleeping on are those soft mats they used to sell. In Ouagadougou we used to get some for three hundred or four hundred CFA. So this old lady was annoyed, and she went inside and took a knife and cut a hole in the mat and put it over the head like it was a smock, just like a dress which they sew for you. They were three. Two girls and one boy. And she took a calabash and poured water on them, and pushed them outside. Then she called me.

You know, I told you that my name is my grandmother's name, the mother of my father. And she was my mother's mother. So at our place, how they are, she used to call my other grandmother her friend. So my mother's mother used to call me "my friend." She didn't call my name. She used to call the name "friend." She said, "My friend. Follow them! Follow them! Shout! Call everybody to shout on them! Look at these grown children like that!"

But you know, I was laughing because that boy was not the one who pissed. *Ha-ha!* So I went outside and started shouting: "These children: they pissed! These children have pissed! Piss-pots!" We used to call them piss-pots. Piss-pot!

So: we used our hands and were pushing them. They were crying. There are some children who have grown more than you, so you can't say you won't go. They will push you to go around the whole village, for everybody to see, so that you will be ashamed and you won't piss again. *Ha!* So I was in front of them, shouting. Then, if you wouldn't go, I would say, "Hey, if you don't go, I will beat you! You pissed yesterday. Why did you piss?"

And this boy, I was older than him, but he was stronger than me. I think I was one year older than him, but he was a strong boy. He could beat me to hell. *Ha-ha!* When we reached some place, if I said, "Go, go!" then this boy said, "Shut up! Hey you! You are not pissing? Maybe you are even the one who pissed on me."

Then I said, "*Oh-h-h!* You pissed! *Oh-h-h!* A big boy like you. Aren't you ashamed for that? You pissed!"

Then he said, "*Ah!* I will beat you just now."

Then I said, "Why? Why? I'm the one who did it? Go and beat our grandmother. She's the one who put you in this mat. It's not me."

So that boy: I pissed on him. And I was always fighting him, so I think he also thought—he felt that this piss, he was not the one who did it. So he was thinking that by all means, maybe it was me. That's why he was about to make trouble with me. So we shouted on them around all the village, and then we came back to the house. Every time, when they would go to play outside, "Hey! Piss-pot! Piss-pot!" *Ha-ha.* So they had this mat.

Then once, this boy, there was something like we were having an argument. You know, always, if there are children, when the children meet, we used to converse. So I used to like to show them that I know everything, more than anybody. *Ha-ha!* So I am the chief. And this boy always used to challenge me. He was trying to tell me that because I was born in Ghana, so I thought my eyes are open more than everybody. But if my eyes are open, they're only open for myself. It's not for anyone. As for him, I cannot show him anything. And I said, "Get away! Your eyes open?"

Then he said *"Pff!"*

So I told him, "Get away. You think your eyes are open? You were born in this village! This bush! Maybe your mother gave birth to you in the farm. They don't want to tell the truth. Do you even think you were born in a room? Your eyes are open? How much are your eyes open? Your eyes are open like what? You: they borne you in the farm and they brought you to the town. Now you see a small village, and you say you are captain. *Pff!* Your eyes open! Do you think, me, Hawa — do you think somebody can come and piss on my mat in the night, when my eyes were open like that? I used to piss everywhere on the mats of people. *Ha-ha!* Because I don't want the old lady to suffer to be waking her always to take me out. Or if I walk out and the breeze has blown me a little bit, maybe if I come back, I won't sleep in time. So that's why I used to piss on you people's mats. So your eyes are open! That day I pissed on your mat. You are not the one who wore the mat to go around all this village? Did you see that they put it on me?"

I wanted to show them my eyes are open proper![1] *Ha-ha!* You know, if you have too much heart, to be annoyed to say much, too, you used to spoil your way. So, OK, this boy went and told my grandmother. So from that time I had to take care of myself, because they knew many children who had not been pissing when I was not there. But when I come, all of them will start to piss on their mats, because I used to go and piss on them. So from that time I had to take care of myself. I didn't piss on their mats again. Every time I had to call my grandmother. I used to piss about four or five times before daybreak, and that's why I didn't want to wake her. I used to like to piss on their mats, because I knew I didn't want to go outside. I would go about once or twice, and then —*ha-ha!*

You know, when my mother died, they took me to my father's, but I didn't stay long there. They brought me back to my grandmother because at that time I was so young. My father didn't have much trust in his wife to take care of me, so they brought me to my grandmother. I was very young. And then I told you that I went and saw this thing in the bush and they sent me back to my father again. Then after that, I went back again, and the next time when they took me, when I started to piss on the people, at that time I was a bit grown up.

1. really, well; generally used simply to emphasize a verb

11 CHILD OF THE GOD

: THE VILLAGE IN GHANA :

A Wonderful Man

You know, I told you that when I was a baby growing up, I had something with my hair: they didn't cut it, and they didn't comb it, so my hair was just growing out. I had my hair like that for about six or seven years, so I was a bit grown, and I think I can know a little bit about my hair. I told you this.

When I was born — OK — you know, sometimes we Africans, especially the Muslims — many of them, if they have a baby, they used to go to the maalams.[1] Do you know what is called a maalam? That is somebody who knows much as a Muslim. They used to go to the maalams to see how this child is coming: if he is coming in a good way, or he is coming in a bad way. Yeah? So I think, when I was born, they looked into it, and this is what they found out. I don't know about the time I was born, but this is what my family told me.

It was not a maalam who told them. When they borne me, we were in the village where my father was working in the cocoa farm. It was an Ashanti village, near Kumasi. There was a man who had juju in this village. This man was a friend to my father, a very *close* friend. My father didn't like him much, but this man liked my father. When I was growing up, I *liked* the man. He was *black.* They called him Kɔmfo Manu. *Every* time, he would come to the house. He called me his wife, and I told my father that if not this man, I wouldn't marry anybody in the world.

So when they borne me, my father went and asked, and they said there are some children that they should not put a knife to their hair. And these children, I have come from that side. This kind of children, too, there were many of them in that village. So when they said that, then my father said, "Ah! As for me, I'm a Muslim, so what does this juju want from me?"

1. (Hausa): Muslim scholar or cleric

And this Kɔmfo Manu told him, "This does not mean that you are dealing in juju. Maybe the juju just likes you, and he gave you a child of his." You know? So my father had to get up. He didn't like this man much, but this time he had to be a friend with him, to tell him the story, how he had his daughter, or his son. Yeah, so we were four with this in our family, but we were two who kept our hair a long time. The other one was also a girl: she was about four years old when they cut her hair off.

This is my first starting I'm telling you: when I came, how they borne me and found out about this thing. Yeah?

So when they had us like that, and my father was coming to be a friend to this man, they used to make this juju's things on Mondays. When I was *small,* very small, they used to carry me there. I didn't know anything. My mother used to carry me to that place every Monday. Even if you don't eat, at that place, they would cook fufu. Sometimes cocoyam fufu with groundnut soup, and with fish. This juju didn't eat meat. Only fish, dried fish. Then, they would get the groundnut soup, and even the small babies, about two weeks, if she was the baby of that place, at two weeks time you would take her there, and the baby would eat some of the soup. Every week, you would start going with the baby every Monday, to take her there to visit the father. They said the father of these children is the juju. They said—I don't know. *Ha-ha! He-hee!*

So we were going there when I was little, and they were putting all this groundnut soup in my mouth. At that time my heart didn't know that I was chopping. And when I was getting a bit grown, and started talking, I started it with this man, with his children.

He had a *nice* children! And, you know, it was wonderful! I think in my life, I haven't seen somebody like that. He had more than forty children. And any son or any daughter of his, if you saw the child, you will know the man, and you won't ask any questions. They all resembled him. *All* of them! *All!* It's wonderful!

He was an Ashanti man. He was from Brong Ahafo. All his children—girls and boys—they were more than forty. He had about six or seven wives. The ones he had divorced—*pfft!*—I think they were more than ten. And then the children of girlfriends. But all the ones he brought home, they were his children, and you couldn't doubt. You couldn't say anything. Even the voice: if you didn't see the man, and you heard the big son in the room, talking, and you knew this man, you would think he was the one who was inside.

My father used to say, "This man: Number One. He is proper ashawo, Number One." He had a daughter from an ashawo woman. She didn't want to marry, to suffer. He took his baby. He kept it with him.

So if he would make a friendship with you, and if you tell him, "OK, I have conceived for you."

He would say, "OK." He would look at you. Then he would say, "OK, if you love me, we will get married."

Maybe there were some women who didn't want to marry. She will say, "I'm not ready to marry."

Then: OK. Even he took some of his children—three, four months old—from the women, and he kept them in his house. And he wouldn't give the baby to the other wives, so that maybe the other wife will be giving him milk, or something like that, because this baby is too young. He will keep his everything by himself. He will say that maybe the other wife doesn't like that baby, or the other wives will poison the baby. So every food of the baby, he will make it by himself. And then the food the wife will give him, he will eat with the baby. If he's going to work, he will carry his baby away.

He was a wonderful man. He had about forty children. And, you know, it was wonderful. His *first-born,* if he showed you his first-born and you saw the boy, you would say that the first-born was the father of the man. He looks very, very old. The first-born is *rich.* But I don't know why he became old quickly. He just grew up. He has a face, an old person's face. If he is walking with the father, in the village, people used to shout on him, "Hey! Don't you shame? Aren't you ashamed? You are walking with your father? You are the one who borne him!"

Yeah, so this man was a *nice* man. Every time, when he's working, he's *smiling.* So I liked him. Every time, when he came, he used to put me on his hip. He just picked me up on his hip like that and put me there, and he would be walking with me through the whole village. I used to like it. Then if we went to some place, I didn't keep my mouth, too. I could speak like something. So he would say, "This is the *last* woman I'm going to marry in my life. When I marry her, I won't marry any woman again."

Then they would say, "*Ay-y!* Can you wait for this girl?"

Then I would say, "Why not? He's waiting for me. That's why he's carrying me every place."

Then sometimes we would go to the wives' houses. You know, Ashanti houses: it's very nice if you go to the village. If they are married, village people, it's not necessary to go and live with your husband. You can stay at your parents' house, and your husband will be coming to you. And all the houses have names there. So maybe you have one wife from Mr. Boakye house, and then one from Mr. Asare house. This is what they do in the village way, Ashantis. I remember all this thing. I was there when I grew up. So if we went to any of houses for the wives, then he would call them. He would tell me, "You see? This is my wife."

Then I would say, "Uh-huh? Eh? This big one is your wife?"

Then he would say, "Yes."

I would say, "Oh, then I wouldn't like to eat."

Then he would say, "Why?"

I would say, "Oh, you bring me to your wife to eat, because I can't cook." You know? Just a small girl! It's jealousy!

He would say, "No, I'm keeping her as a wife, just to be cooking for you. If you grow up, I will *sack* her."

Then I would be *happy!* So I would be eating your food, and the next time, if I met you on the road, I would tell my friends, "Look, do you think that my husband has married? He is taking her to be a cook, so that I will eat, and when I will grow up, then he will sack her." *Ha!*

You know, in the village, we didn't have a water pipe; we would go to the riverside and bring water. And if I had a bucket, I couldn't lift it to put on my head and carry it. So then I would talk. I would say, like somebody who respects, very quietly, *"Auntie, mepa wo kyew, wonsoa me kakra?* Auntie, please, can you help me a little?" Some people would help me easily, and then there was somebody too who would just take it as if she's annoyed and put the bucket on my head—*kak!* Then I would say, "*Pfft,* upon all, you are cooking for me! They will sack you away!" *Ha-ha!* "Let me grow up. You see how I'm starting to be carrying this small bucket?" Oh! I was just a baby! "I will be carrying the real bucket. They will sack you, and you will see."

I used to do this thing to this man's wives at the riverside. *Ha!* So when the man came home, then I would say, "You see? You see? You say you are taking her like a cook. But she's not like that. She's jealous. When she met me on the path, when I was going to take the water, I asked her, 'Auntie, I have given you a full respect to—you know—to help me to carry my bucket.' She just took it and knocked on top of my hair. She doesn't want me to growing fast—tall—so that I will grow quickly. She's knocking my head, to make me be coming short. Did you see that? I won't eat in her house again!"

Then he would say, "Which one?" *Ha!* He would make like he was annoyed with her. So I *liked* this man.

Pennies in the Hair

So all that time when I was young, we were with this juju like that. OK, if they have you like that, as you are a daughter for this juju, then they do some things. You know, we Africans, as a little baby, when you are little, you have soft hair. Your hair is curly but it is very soft. So every time, they will bathe you with a sponge, and they just put a towel to dry it, and they don't put a comb inside. If you do it like that, every time it will be coming. If you have plenty of hair, it used to grow just one-one, and then be hanging, just like a small Bob Marley.

So the babies of this juju, you can have some people for two years before they will cut their hair, some of them three, some of them four. And the heavy one will be up to maybe seven years. I had my own hair like that for seven years. OK.

And all this time, if you have this hair coming long, if it starts dropping small-small, they used to put pennies inside it. You know, at that time we had a penny with a hole in it. They were two, a red one and then something like a white one, like silver. They will squeeze the hair and put it inside the hole of the penny and then turn it so that this penny can't get a chance to fall. Isn't it? It's always inside the hair. Yeah. So always, if this hair is growing, this thing is hanging.

I think maybe it is for the people to know where the children are, because sometimes, if you are in back of the house, you know, when you are running, the money is touching. Or maybe you have a child who is playing outside of the window. If he has this hair, when he's doing something, the money is touching, and you will hear some noise.

But as for me, I didn't used to like it. I used to chop them. When I would run, my hair was making this *"Chang, chang, chang, chang."* Sometimes, you know, the women like to relax in the day time or something like that, and if they hear this noise — if she has a small girl, and she hears something like that, she thinks maybe somebody is beating the girl, or maybe somebody's doing something to her. Then she will shout and get up and come out. Maybe that time is the time you are enjoying yourself. You see? So this is why I used to chop this money.

You know, my mother, I think when she used to see the children like this with these pennies, she used to like them. So when she got one, and they said it's this kind of baby for the juju, she liked it. She didn't care to spend maybe forty pesewas on pennies in my hair a day. See? She would just ask people for these pennies. The way I was, I didn't used to like the red penny. So that one, if she put it in my hair, then it was not one minute: I was just going to toilet and then it's lost. This is what I was doing. I was going to remove it and then chop it. Then, if she asked me, I would say, "When I went to toilet, it fell inside. So it means that my hair doesn't like the red pennies. Only the white ones."

So they used to give me plenty. Even one lock of hair, I used to get about two or three pennies inside. So when I got this thing, then we went outside. OK? This place was a small village, but they had Yoruba people there selling things. You know, the Yoruba know how to find money. This Yoruba woman used condensed milk to make toffee. The condensed milk—they have one with a lot of sugar inside—she used that one to make toffee. On top of all these sweets, she made her own, too, with condensed milk. So you know, this sweet with the milk is good, huh?

So this Yoruba woman used to make it, and I *liked* it! OK. The way I liked it, at that time I didn't have much experience, but if I had experience, I would have stolen *a-a-a-l-l* of everybody's money to buy this thing. You know, the people in the village, I think they used to get the money cheap.[1] Because they used to throw it down. They didn't hide it. When we came to Kumasi, everybody was trying to hide his money, but in the village, if you go to somebody's room, you will see these two-two shillings and shillings and then sixpence and pennies—*plenty!* Lying there. And he leaves it. Even the door, he doesn't lock it. He goes to the farm to farm again. That time, we didn't know how to use money.

It was Kumasi when we came and we knew how to use money. So at that time in the village, they also had their chance to leave the money free. *Ha!* I didn't know how to go and steal the money. I could go the room and see this money. Even if I took some, they wouldn't know, because they were just putting them there. When they had coins from the market or from the town, they just put it in some place. And they were just throwing it. If you picked something from inside,[2] they wouldn't know, isn't it? But I didn't have that sense at that time.

So instead of going and taking this thing, I used to cut the pennies from my hair to go and buy the toffee. I thought that this is mine, so if I chop it, that's not a problem. Sometimes if my friend didn't have a blade, I would go and find something which could cut the hair. Sometimes, if I had one that was a little bit long, it could come to my mouth; I would just cut it with my teeth. I would chew my hair—*ke-ki-ki-ki*—and it cut, then—*pfftt!*—I was going for this toffee.

This Yoruba woman was cutting it into pieces, two for a penny. And maybe these two pieces, we will be about ten or eight or six who are going to chop it. So every time, I am the owner: one for me and one for all of you people. And I am going to be watchman.

I would go to you. "You see? *All* this is for you." Then I will hold it like this, then you will bring yourself. Yeah! Then I will hold the toffee. Then I will say, "OK, if you chew it, you shouldn't swallow. You should wait for

1. get it easily. In this case, they didn't regard the money.
2. from among

all of everybody to be chewing it." And now the manager has come: I will take my own, and then I will say, "*Ss-s!* Wait." You will wait, and then I'll chew *all* of my own, and when it becomes like water, then I will say, "OK, everybody can chew his own." Then we all will be chewing. Then I will say, "OK. One, two—" and when I say "three," then everyone swallows. *Ha!* You see? So this is the way I used to chop my pennies. And *all* these friends I had, because of this, they liked me.

So you know, in the morning time, sometimes we African children have some funny things. You wake up, and you don't feel awake. Or you think you are awake, but you didn't wake up. You used to sit down—in some kind of sitting. And especially, as for me, they said I was an old lady.[1] When I woke up in the morning time, when I was young, I used to be difficult. I didn't want to talk to anybody. And I didn't want anybody to talk to me. When I would wake up from the room, the time when I started to have sense a little bit, I would just carry my piss-pot, the pot which they piss inside. Everyone has his own. But I didn't actually piss in this piss-pot in the night, so when I wake up in the morning time, I will carry this thing and sit on it. I'm going to toilet. I can sit on this thing more than two hours! Maybe I have finished the toilet, but I'm sitting on top of it. And this smell is coming in my nose, and I wouldn't mind anybody. But if it's not my stepmother or my father or my senior brother, the one who I said is the first-born of my father—if not these three people in the family—nobody can get me up from this thing. Any other person who is going to try to force me and get me up there, I will cry and start throwing the shit, and then—*ha!*

You know, I didn't know my real mother. When I was young, in that age, I think it was my stepmother. The one I liked much, the one who was taking care of me much, was the younger wife of my father. So if she came, she would say, "Oh, mother,[2] why? Wouldn't you like to wake up and wash your face? See: all the children are coming out. And a grandmother like you: you are sitting on top of this piss-pot. Aren't you ashamed?"

Then I'd say, "But you didn't give me the water! You didn't give me the water!"

So she will say, "OK, come, I will give you the water."

So as for her, I would go with her. Or my father, I would go with him.

1. because she had the name of her grandmother, or she had "inherited" her grandmother

2. As she had the name of the grandmother, her parents addressed her as "mother" or "mama."

Or if it was the first-born of my father, I would get up. But all the rest, even the first wife to my father, if she came and then she talked something like that, *pfft!* I will get up from this piss-pot and take it and throw it on her. *Ha!* So, if I was sitting like that, they have three people they can go and ask to come and beg me to get up from this thing. And when I was on this, sometimes, all my friends would come, "*Afia,*[1] *Afia. Womm'yɛn nkɔ? Hwɛ! Alatani no abue store no; ne yere wɔ abɔntene.* Afia. Wouldn't you let us go out? Look! The Yoruba man has opened the shop; his wife is outside. Why you are sitting like that?"

Then I will look at all of their faces. I will get up and take the shit and then throw it at them, so everybody will run away. So when they go away is the time maybe my mother will come and beg me, to take my bath, that she will make me a nice bath, and get me a dress. Then at that time I'm happy. So then all the people I sacked from the place, I'm going to call all of them again. I will go to your house and say, "You came this morning, so when I threw this piss-pot at you, with shit inside, you were annoyed?"

Then maybe you will say, "Why should you do that?"

Then I will say, "Why not? Did you see me in your house early in the morning? Have I seen you without drawers before? Without any pants?"

Then maybe you will say, "No."

"But why should you come and see me like that? And you were asking me to go out. What did you think?"

You will say, "But—oh why? You should tell us. You shouldn't throw the shit on us."

I will say, "Yes! You want the shit. That's why you came the time when we are shitting. And you came there to ask me to go out. So it's better. To chop the shit is better. But now I'm ready. Let's go."

And they wouldn't be annoyed, you know! They would be following me. So we would go. And this Yoruba woman was also a bad woman. The first time, I used to go in front of her and be biting my hair to get the penny for this toffee milk. So I think maybe my mother gave her a warning about the way I used to cut this thing. I don't know. So then when I went there, if I went with my penny, she wouldn't sell anything to me! She said, "No, I won't sell to you." Everybody can come and buy, but as for me, she won't sell it to me. So that time I also had my way. I had many girlfriends, isn't it? We will go to your house, and we will be sitting there playing. If your mother has a kitchen knife, or if we have a piece of blade,[2] we can bring it, and we will cut about two pennies. Then we

1. (Asante Twi): name for a woman born on Friday
2. razor blade

will send one girl with it. I'm not going myself. If I go there, they know me: they won't give me. So OK, I have a messenger. We will send for it. If I cut two pennies to buy toffee, then one penny is for me, and the one penny is for all of them.

Yeah, and my parents, I didn't tell them I was spending these pennies. Sometimes they asked me in the house, "How did you manage to lose this?" or "This penny is not there," and that and this. And sometimes if they bathed me, they would see that the hair was cut off. It's not that it fell down.

You know, this kind of hair is wonderful. If they don't cut it and they don't comb it, when they bathe you and they finish, if they put the towel inside to dry it, some hair can just fall down with the penny. But I used to cut it, and if you see it, you can see that it's cut, isn't it? And I used to say that it fell. Then they will say, "This place has fallen. It's not the same thing like here. Here is cut."

Then I will say, "Maybe in the night time, when I slept, some rat or something came and cut it."

So they got me, you know. They got to know that I was eating this money. Seven years! What?! Can you keep my hair without combing it for seven years? And be putting more and more pennies inside? You know, if you have this hair, the day when they are going to take it all off, they buy some sheep — many things — some animals — chickens — to kill for this juju, to dash the juju. And *all* the pennies in your hair are for the juju. OK. But they had only the dash my father gave them. They didn't have many pennies from my hair. I was eating them. But as it was the money of my father or my mother, I didn't think the juju would do bad to me. So when they got me cutting my hair, I didn't mind. But in my hair, this juju didn't have profit on it. They kept my hair for seven years! Seven good years, without a comb. You can bathe inside, but you can't comb it. And you can't put blade on it. You can't cut it. But when I was growing up, I was cutting it, and nothing happened to me. I was cutting it with all the money. And I was chopping the money.

So the time they make this thing and comb your hair, then all that hair they take, and the pennies, they keep it at the juju's place. So they kept my first hair there. You know, I told my father, "You people."

Then my father said, "Who people? You came on your own way."

I said, "I'm not coming in my own way. I came like the others. But you people believe that — you people say I am a juju baby, and you keep my hair there. But the day God will ask me about my hair, I will ask you. He is the one who gave it to me."

So they keep it there. They take the pennies out, but they keep the hair. Maybe by this time they threw it somewhere. Maybe it is already finished. The pennies are for the people who have the juju. The masters of the juju. They will spend it. Or do you think if they get these pennies plenty from your hair, do you think they will keep it? They are going to spend it!

I think they used to see that if you are one of the children for this juju, when they see that maybe you are lucky — in your family they used to give a lot of pennies in your hair — then they will want you to be keeping long with the pennies, so that they will get plenty of pennies. But they were not lucky with me. I was getting pennies — many. Every day. From my mother. This woman didn't have anything to do. When she wakes up, early in the morning, there was one women who was selling cooked rice. At that time, you could buy rice and beans for a penny. Every morning time this woman would wake up and wash her face and go to this rice woman with her shilling-shillings, and tell her that, "If you have forty pennies, you should send your baby to bring it to me at home." Then she will come back home to prepare. So before I get my bath and do everything, they already have *new* pennies which they have brought to the house. And I was chopping them!

Interlude: Village Playtime

So when I was growing up like that in the village, morning time after my bath, they would give me food. You know, in the village, we don't drink tea. Early in the morning, before they take their baths, they put some yams on the fire, with this stew, *kontomire.*[1] Some of the mothers who feel for the babies, they will take plantain, the one you ate yesterday: she will just put it on fire. Before she finishes bathing you, this thing will be ready, and they will put it in your hand. This is your first breakfast.

So as for me, every time, when I was small like that, I didn't have time to sit and eat. You will give me my food on my plate, and I will carry it. When I want to eat it, I will put it down and then take a little and put it in my mouth, and then I will carry my plate away again. I will be walking. I didn't want them to see me because I used to get food from our place and then go and share it with the friends outside. If they saw me, then I wouldn't get anything.

So to go outside, I had to dodge. Maybe you give me the food, and you say, "Sit down here and eat." Then I will cut small. Then maybe some of my brothers or sisters are sitting outside behind the door. So when I cut

1. (Asante Twi): stew made with spinach leaves

my own small, and put in my mouth, I will tell them that my own is better than their own. And maybe the other one will say, "You lie! My own is better than yours."

I will say, "OK. Let me see."

Then I would be carrying my plate to that place. OK? I will get up from each of them, and from there I will get somebody and ask him, so I will be making my way small-small to go out.

So every morning time, when they give me food, my mother used to say, "Sit down." Then I will sit down. Then she will give me. When she gives me, she will say, "Eat and finish before you go out."

Then I will say, "OK."

You know, when I was young, I didn't feel eating alone. If they gave me something on my plate, if somebody didn't eat it with me, I didn't feel it. And I didn't want someone from the same family. I didn't want all these children from our family to eat in one place. But the others from outside, I was all right with them.

So when they would give me the food, I will eat small-small, and then when I get out, if I call you, you will hear my voice in the house that I'm in back of the house. I will say, "Come." Then maybe I will show you the plate. So they will come, then I will share all. Yeah. Then I will say, "You see my own is small."

You will say, "Yes."

"See, I had it but I gave all to you people. My own is small, isn't it?"

You will say, "Yes."

I will say, "OK. You know what you have to do? I won't go back home. You take this plate. When you go to the house, the first left on the veranda: you put it there. When they are calling me, don't answer. You just run and come." *Ha!*

So I vanished. OK? Maybe I can go out from the house about eight or nine o'clock. Before I come back, maybe eleven or twelve. I'm always busy with my friends. We will be eating toffee. After, we will go to get plantain. You know, in the village they have plenty of plantain. They have everything.

And you know, it's very funny. As we were boys and girls, we tried to act as a husband and wife. *Ha!* Small children! And I don't think many people do this now, but in Africa, we children have some things. It's very, very wonderful. Now I have grown, and when I see children doing this, I used to be annoyed. You are with your husband, OK? All the children, boys and girls, they mix together, and maybe this boy or this girl will say, "This is my husband." And then it's like that.

You know, the children will pick the tins they throw in the dust and try to learn how to cook in tins. So you will come, and then we will joke, and we will bring all these kinds of things to be cooking but not really eating. We don't eat it really. But we make all these things. Maybe we will take sand and make sauce. And then you will go and bring it for your husband. The way you have to bend down:[1] when we were like this, we used to learn all this outside. When you bring it to your husband too, you also know that this food is not food which someone can eat. So you will take it and then put it in the sauce from the sand and be tasting—*nyum-nyum-nyum ts-ts-ts*—and then throw it.

You know, we took the sand from the ground and made the sauce—boiling the water and putting the sand in a tin and mixing it. And maybe you have some plantain: you will cook it in another tin. OK? You are not really cooking it. You are just taking it to your husband. Yeah, and the boys were also playing. The boy is not going to eat it and swallow it. He will just take plantain from here into the other soup and pretend to be tasting it, and then he will throw it away. Then he will take another one. Then all will finish. Then he will hold your two tins for you. Then you will walk and go and take it. And then you will say, "Hey, as for me, my husband has eaten all my food today!" *Hee-hee! Ha!* You know?

Sometimes, in Africa, when the farmers are in the farm, the women used to cook from the town and take the food to the farm to give the farmers. And sometimes they will send the children to carry it. If you are growing up a little bit, as how I was getting grown up, I had younger sisters, and we used to play this. If we go out, then I will say, "*Tsk,* don't play the fool with the food for your father." You will tell the other babies like that. "Today, if you go, if you waste time on the road again and take the meat from the soup—you will see!" You know, we used to see all these things from the ones who used to steal.

So somebody is there. Maybe she is the only one in the house—one woman or maybe two, and the others will go to the bush. And the children are also in the house. So she knows that she is going to cook in the morning and the evening.[2] If she cooks the day food, like the twelve o'clock food, if there are some children on the house, she will send you with this food to go and give to the people in bush. OK?

Some children, they will carry it the easy way, to go and give to the people, and they will like it. And some children, they will get to the road

1. In many savanna cultures particularly, a young person or a wife kneels or squats when greeting or serving an elder or senior person.

2. Evening is late afternoon; in tropical areas, the sun sets quickly and there is not much twilight. The wife who "has cooking" will cook all the house food on her cooking day; she cooks lunch in the morning and dinner in the evening (late afternoon).

and put the food down and take all the meat from the soup. Some of them will eat even the T-Zed! You know how they would eat the T-Zed? When the women cook the T-Zed, because the people in the bush are many, they can't get only one pot to put all of it inside. OK? They will put it in maybe three or four pots. Then they will get a big calabash and put all together. That time it is a little bit cold. So if you want to take one ball like this, you can take it out from the others.[1] It's not hard, and it's not too much pressing to each other. They can take it one by one. So some of the children, when they get to the road, they put this thing down and then take the top one up and eat the one under, and then cover that side where they ate so that you can't see. There are some children who are doing that. So the old people used to talk to the children about that.

So when we would also go out to be playing, you know, we would start playing, and say, "If you don't take it to your father straight, and he comes and tells me that this is what happened, I will *kill* you!"

"Yes, Mama, I'm taking it. I wouldn't touch it."

"Be a good girl, huh? You have been saying that, but you people are like that: you have been saying 'Yeah, yeah, yeah, yeah, I won't do it,' but then you will do it."

Then, you will come and tell the other friend, "As for me, I am tired. I have cooked for my husband. My daughter has taken it, so I'm tired. Even I feel like sleeping."

And the other one will say, "Are you sleeping? Why you are going to sleep now?"

"Yeah, because I have been doing a lot of work to cook for my husband. He is in the farm; he is farming. And then to do all this thing for him, I am tired."

Then you know, the boys too, they used to come. When they come, maybe he will just lay down on the sand. He doesn't have any cloth, or maybe he will get a small piece of cloth, and he will just lay down. You say, "What are you doing? Are you sleeping?" *Ha-ha!*

Or maybe you will also be lying down, and he will say, "Are you sleeping? As for me, I have gone to farm, and I am not tired, and you are in your house, just to make this small food, and you are tired like that. Wake up! Give me water to bathe!" You see?

So you will get up and go and carry the sand in this small thing and come and put it down for him. *Hee! Ha! Ah! Shit!* So he will just take a

1. In some places the T-Zed is not just put as a mass into the pot but is formed into separate portions, small balls about the size of a lemon or an orange; as it cools, it hardens slightly, and the child can separate the balls.

little of the sand and put it on his feet, and then he's finished bathing. He's bathing himself with *more* sand! *Hee!* If he goes home, they will have to bathe him for a thousand years! *Ha!* It will never come out! So we would do these things, and we were happy with each other. *Ha-ha!* When you are children, it's *nice.*

Return to the Village

You know, this Kɔmfo Manu, the master of the juju, I told you how we were when I was very young. But later, when I grew up, he tried to talk to me once. I was *annoyed!* Even now I don't want to see him. But when I was young, I liked him. Even now, he's a *nice* man. But, you know, it is very foolish what we Africans do, eh? You know me. They have borne me in front of you, and then I can grow up in front of you. OK? I was about thirteen years when we left that village to Kumasi. But before that, with *all* these things, this man was with me. Sometimes they would take me to our village in Upper Volta, and they would bring me back to the same village. Just like that. I was going up and down. And every time I was meeting this man.

So when I grew up, I was up to — up to maybe nineteen. So then, since I was thirteen years, I hadn't been there. Then I told my father, "No, I want just to go and visit the village and see how this man is." And that time too, I had a ring. It was from this thing, this juju. I had removed all. I didn't want it. *Ha!* They gave a lot of problems. And this my ring, I had lost it. I don't know how it has lost. So I told my father I have to go to the village, and that and this.

So my father said, OK, if I can know the road. Or he can accompany me, or if I want, one of my brothers can lead me.

Then I said, "No, I want to go alone."

So when I got to the village, *nobody* knew me. But some people saw me, said, "Hey, this girl looks like Issahaku — Issahaku's daughter." Then some people said, "Oh, no. She wouldn't have breasts by this time."

So I was hearing things like this, but I didn't mind them. When I got down from the car, I walked to the house where my father was living before. He had rented a house in the village. I went to that man's house, and the man had died. And *all* the children didn't know me. Only one daughter was there who was clever. She is also Afia,[1] so I used to call her "my namesake." When I went there, she was also *grown.*

1. Friday-born, like Hawa

I said, "Ah! This girl resembles Afia." When she was young, she wanted to get a mark.[1] And in Ashanti, many of them, if they got this wide one or a round one, it is not from cutting. They have a tree. If you cut the tree and then get the water from the tree and put it, then after tomorrow, that place will burn. It burns and becomes something like a sore. When it finishes, you will have the mark. Some people, if they don't have good skin, it goes inside, then if it finishes, it becomes round. She just wanted to get a small mark; she wanted one point. Maybe she took a stick and made it, and then this thing became big. So this girl had this mark from the time she was young. Then when I saw this girl, she resembled Afia, but she looked fat and very tall. I didn't believe she was the one. Then I said, *"Auntie. Wo ho yɛ?"* I called her, "Auntie, how are you."

And she heard my voice, and then she said, "Hey! Namesake! You are calling me Auntie today! *Hey!*" So we were happy.

So she said, "When did you come?"

I said, "I'm just coming. And where is your father?"

She said, "Oh. My father has died, about two years ago."

O-o-o. It was very pitiful. So we got to the town. At that place, there's no drinking bar. I don't know whether maybe by this time, maybe they will have one, because now every place is starting to open. But that time they didn't have a bar. So we went to an akpeteshie house,[2] and I don't like to drink akpeteshie, but I cut[3] akpeteshie there. I cut a very small one — sixpence — and even I didn't finish all. Then I said, "You know why I have come here?"

Then she said, "No." Then she said, "Where is your father?"

I said, "My father is in Kumasi."

"So you came here alone?"

I said, "Yeah, I felt like seeing you people. It's a long time since we have seen each other."

So she had one brother who was called Kwaku. Then she said, "Let's go to Kwaku." You know these people who are buying the cocoa — Cocoa Marketing[4] — he was the big man in that village. He was the one who was looking after the whole village. So we went to him. Then when he saw me, "Hey! Afia, Afia! *Ey-y! W'anyini o!* You have grown! Hey!" Yeah.

1. cicatrization, a decorative scar

2. the house of someone who makes and sells akpeteshie. There would be a small area for taking a quick drink.

3. drank

4. The Ghana Cocoa Marketing Board, since reconstituted in various ways, was a government agency responsible for cocoa at the time.

Then I saw that this boy, too, he was *big.* So I said, "Oh, is that so?"

So he had a wife. Then he called his wife: "Abena! Abena! *Bɛhwɛ bɛhwɛ bɛhwɛ bɛhwɛ bɛhwɛ!*"[1]

And that girl also came out. She knew me; I didn't know her. It was the same village where they borne all of us, but I didn't know her. Then: *"Yee-e-e."*

Then he stood, and he told her. "Don't you know this girl? She was the one, when the father was at our father's house, this girl used to like to talk. Every time, you would see Kɔmfo Manu putting her here on his hip, going around the village."

Then she said, "Hey! Is this the one?"

Then he said, "Yes!"

Then, you know, he was talking like that, so—*ah!*

Then I said, "Oh, I have come to greet to you people, because I think it is a long time since I saw you people."

Then he said, "Hey, when you came, did you see your husband?"

I said, "Who?"

He said, "Kɔmfo Manu."

Then I said, "Yeah, it's because of him I came, but I haven't seen him here."

Then he said, "Oh, he has just come from here, just now. He just came and took his money for his cocoa. Hey! Today, he will marry you. He will do everything. He had plenty of money here today."

So I said, "Oh, shit! You think I came for this man's money?"

So from there, this boy served us beer. He had a fridge. He's a big man; he had a fridge and everything. I took about two beers there. And from there, then I said, "OK, I wouldn't like to be drunk. So I have to go. What brought me here is to see my husband. So I want to see him. Whether we will do our marriage, or we will marry, or we are going to leave one another and then I will find another husband."

I just joked for this boy like that. And this boy said, "Are you going to marry this old man?"

Then I said, "Oh, but yes, I think the old men, they are the good ones, you know."

So we just talked like this. Then we left. I went to the man's place, Kɔmfo Manu's place. And when I went, I went with the girl, Afia. Then when he saw us, he said, "Oh-h!" That girl also was Friday-born, like me, and she was also the same name as me. But she had three weeks: they borne her three weeks before they borne me. And she was also a daughter of this juju. So we were good friends.

1. (Asante Twi): Come and see!

You know, this juju they have, which they said we are children of this juju, it is two jujus. The two: there's one woman and one man. There are the children who are from the man: they are called Tingó. The children who are from the woman are called Dahiri. So me, they called me Afia Dahiri. And her, they called her Afia Tingó. You see? So we are the same people, but only Dahiri and Tingó.

So when this man saw us, he was happy. So he said, "Oh, what should I get?" He went and brought one bottle of Schnapps.

Then I said, "You know, I don't drink spirits."[1]

Then he said, "What do you drink?"

I said, "If you can get some cold beer. But Schnapps, whiskey, and all this, they don't work on me, and akpeteshie."

He said, "Oh, rather than to get you akpeteshie, it's better to get you palm wine."[2] This man couldn't get beer for me. So he just brought a big pot of palm wine. *Ha!*

Then I said, "Hey, Afia, *ɛnnɛ yɛbɛware o.* Afia, today we will marry." And you know, I thought that he took me like a friend's daughter, that he is going to enjoy seeing me or something like that. But what I was thinking when we were young, that we would marry, I didn't have that mind when I came back. But I think he had this mind when I came back. So I said I was going to lead the girl back home, that I was going to the girl's place and sleep.

Then he said, "No. You know, this girl has a boyfriend. They are going to marry. You have come. As your father knows me, I know you. They borne you in my house. You have grown up, so I don't want you to have any problem in this village. Maybe you wouldn't be happy to go and sleep there. And maybe some people will be disturbing you. You can have this room and sleep inside." And all this.

So you know, I liked it much. So we went to this girl's house. We talked and we went to the brother. The brother Kwaku was a *big* groovier. The sister didn't smoke, but he smoked. When I led her to the house, then I said, "Afia, can you get me something?"

Then she said, "What is that?"

Then I said, "Ah! So you didn't change your life? So you don't smoke cigarettes?"

She said, "No."

I said, "Oh, then I can't talk about this thing for you."

Then she said, "What is that?"

Then I said, "Oh, it's something serious."

1. hard liquor
2. the sap of a type of palm tree, which rapidly ferments into a slightly sweet drink

Then she said, "OK, my brother Kwaku smokes cigarettes, so if it is a serious thing, you can see him."

So I went to Kwaku, then I said, "Kwaku." You know, Kwaku was a friend to my brother Kofi. They were the same size, so they were friends. So I said, "Kwaku."

He said, "Yes."

I said, "You know, I don't hide anything from you. I can talk to you as I talk to Kofi, because you are my senior brother also. You know something?"

He said, "No."

I said, "Look. When I left this village, I have grown up in Kumasi. I learned how to do some *bad* things. I don't want to hide it. When I was coming away, I didn't bring some. If you have some, you can give me."

Then he said, "What is that?"

I said, "Indian hemp."[1]

So he said, "Oh, is this all that you want?"

Then I said, "Yes."

He said, "This is not hard."

Then I said, "OK, if it is not hard, you can bring some." And he brought a *big* one[2] and put it on the table. Then I said, "Yes."

He said, "If you go to my Papa's cocoa farm, I *planted* it *many*. And I told these people —" You know, as he was the manager for these people, for the Cocoa Marketing Board, he gave it to the laborers who were working in the cocoa farm, to plant this thing plenty. Then he was telling them some story — a different story about these things, that this thing is a flower. But this flower in Europe is costly. It costs a lot of money. So he wants to try it in Africa here, and if it is good, you know, they will be getting some business from it. So these farmers were looking after this thing very *nicely!* They didn't joke with it. And then he is the Cocoa Marketing Board director. What could you say? He knows everything.

So he had this thing, and I said, "Bring me small-small." Then I told him, "OK. I'm going to sleep."

Then he said, "Why don't you sleep here with me?" He just said it straight. "Why don't you sleep with me?"

Then I said, "What? What do you think? Sleep with you? And your wife?"

He said, "Oh, no. My — my wife wouldn't mind. We have many rooms."

Then I said, "*Ah-hah?* Sleep with you? If I want to sleep with you, would you like it?"

1. marijuana
2. a lot of it

He said, "Why not?"

And I said, "*Aha!* But we are different, you know. Ashantis and Pepe: we are different. Because I don't think Kofi will see Afia, and Kofi will ask Afia to come and sleep with him."

Then he said, "Why? If Kofi likes?"

Then I said, "Kofi wouldn't like it. So you shouldn't like it too."

Then he said, "Oh-h. Don't do that. That was in the olden days," and that and this.

And then I said, "Oh, you are the olden days, or you are these days. But I am the olden days. Take it like that."

So I just got annoyed. I didn't finish. I was going smoke much, but I was just fed up. I just wanted the way to go away, so I just said, "Oh, because of this fucking thing, you can take it. Tomorrow if you like, you can take a car."

You know, it's very funny. In that village, they haven't got a police station. If somebody does you something bad, before you will go and report him in police station, it is almost forty or fifty miles before you will get to the police station and report the fellow. And they will come from there and catch the fellow. *Ha! Hee-hee!* So that village, no police. So I said, "If you like, you know, I'm not going tomorrow. I'm going after tomorrow. So you can go. Tomorrow, as you have your car, you go to Bechem police station and bring police. Come and arrest me, that I smoke *wee.*[1] And the one who gave it to me, and the way you planted it under the cocoa of your father, you will cut all before you go to the police station. OK? Take your fucking things. You think when I'm taking drugs like you, that I am a drugger like you? Then I can do anything you can do?"

So I threw his things on him. And then I told the sister, "I didn't know that you brought me for your brother." I was feeling this thing! "Your brother was trying to tell me his foolishness, so I'm going."

From Frying Pan to Fire

So I thought I was proud. I was going to have a nice place to sleep, isn't it? Getting to this man's house, "Oh-h, why did you keep long like that? Why?"

I said, "Oh, you know, I was talking to my girlfriend." Then I said, "Oh, but you know how I have kept long from here, I made a lot of

1. marijuana

friends who didn't know me before. So I had to introduce myself to them and have some conversing."

Then he said, "OK, OK. This is your room."

This man showed me the room nicely. He showed me many things, like if you go to meet somebody, and it's his place, to show you how the room is nice. He said, "This is your room. If you like this, you can do this, you can do this."

I thought he was a nice man, and he gave me a nice place. So I said I wanted to sleep. So I was there, but I didn't feel like sleeping. I was on the bed lying down and thinking how I came from Kumasi, and how my father said I should come with one of the brothers, and I didn't come like that. And I came alone, and then I saw the place. And anyway, it was not so bad. This man is a very good man, a gentleman. He has given me a room like that. I was happy.

And you know, the door of the room, when I wanted to lock it, there was no key. So I didn't think this was a problem. I was laying down, thinking of all these things. Then I heard somebody. I didn't hear the feet of the person, but I heard the person move, and open the door very *slowly*. Then, in my heart, you know, I was about to laugh. But I laughed inside of my heart, to say, "Eh-heh! They say—they say that I'm the juju's baby. And I am sleeping in the manager of the juju's house. And the witches are coming to eat me. I am all right. I want them to eat me in the house of juju, because he is the one who brought me. They say he's the one who brought me to the world, so if somebody can come and chop me in front of that fellow, I like it." You know? I was thinking of this, huh?

So when he opened the door small, then he closed it back again. I think he went back to his room, or what. I didn't know. Maybe he didn't see me moving, and he thought I was sleeping nicely. So he went to his room and made ready, and then he was coming now. So when he came and opened the door, I was acting like I was sleeping, but I was not asleep. So when he came inside the room, then he locked the door with a key.

Then I thought, "*Ah-hah!* When I was searching for the key to lock this room, I didn't see it. So this man has the key." So I was thinking that this man is going to cut my head. I thought he was going to kill me, because he is a juju man. So what I was thinking, "Oh, OK. It's because, as my father's wife had this problem"—I told you that they said she is a witch—"OK, if this thing can catch a witch, and then they can catch somebody, and kill him, I want to believe in this, so I won't say anything." So I was thinking all this. And then all this time, I was calling the name of this juju in my heart, you know, because I had belief in him. This time I don't have much belief. *Ye-ay!* But first time: I had belief! If you talked something about this juju, I wouldn't agree. But now I have had my experience to change my mind. So I was calling the name of juju, "Oh, Dahiri, oh Dahiri, Tingó, Tingó." In my heart, this is what I was calling. "Look at this manager of you people. What is he going to do with me?"

And this man closed the door softly, and then he was coming to the bed, going around the bed. Look: I was looking at the other way, so when he came, he had to pass and look at me. I was closing my eyes. And you know what was funny? This lamp, the kerosene lamp, is not bright, so sometimes we tease with it a little bit. If I make like this with my eyes, you will think I have closed my eyes, but I will be looking through my eyelashes. So I was looking small-small, and when he was going away to turn, then I was looking at him, to see whether he had a knife. You know, this was what I had in my mind.

Then he came and passed in back of me, and then he lay down on the bed with me. I didn't say anything. I was just as if I didn't feel anything. So I was lying down, and I think he also was thinking or something. He was lying down about five minutes. Then after that, he started to take his leg and touch my feet, for his feet to touch my feet. I made as if I didn't feel anything. Then he started making something like touching me, and I gave a slap—*pak!*—like I thought he was a mosquito! I just did this like I wasn't thinking about anything. But I knew that there was somebody in the room. I meant that I should get his hand and knock it, but that time he was smart, so he took his hand and I knocked my feet. Then I said, "*Mmm-m-m. Awurade. Ntontom nie.* Oh, God. There are mosquitoes." Then I turned, so he was at my back. OK, I have fixed him now. So in this way, I got to make *"Ee-eh,"* but he was also trying. He didn't want me to know what he was doing.

But, you know, one thing I used to think: the men used to think that if a woman is drunk, she doesn't know anything. They think there are some girls who can drink, and then they can sleep with them. If they say this to me, I don't believe it. However you slept, or whatever you drank, will somebody get you to make a love with you, and you won't know? Maybe there are some girls like that, but I don't feel that it's true. Whatever I drink, if somebody wants to touch me, I will get to know.

So the way we drank and I came home, maybe he thought I was drunk, so he was going to just get me in a cheap way. So then I turned my face to him. I didn't touch his body, and I didn't open my eyes. I just turned. So I was free on the bed, and I was making like I didn't know that somebody was in the bed. I already knew that there was somebody, but I wanted to see what he was going to do. The time when he started touching my feet, this was the place when I thought that maybe this man just wanted to get me in some way like this, to chop me.[1] So *pfft:* I was waiting. I turned my face to him, and he started on my arm, touching it and making so. Then I slapped that place. *Tchak!* And he moved his hand. I didn't get him. Then I turned, and I slept on my stomach. I used to sleep like that. So then I started snoring, *"Hh-hm, hh-hm."* Then I started making like I was dreaming. I started talking in my sleep. I said, "*Mempɛ saa, mempɛ saa. Adɛn? Medeɛ mempɛ saa o, mempɛ saa! Adɛn na woha m'adwene saa?* I don't like that! I don't like that! Why? As for me, I don't like that! Why are you disturbing me? Why are you doing all this? What is all this?" You know, I was just saying something like this in Ashanti. So he just drew himself back. When I said these things finish, for about ten to fifteen minutes, this man was there. He didn't say anything. So, after that I didn't say anything again. Then I became like normal. I slept, breathing heavily.

I was just doing this for about one second. Then he thought, "Ah, as she has finished the talking, she is drunk; she has slept." So he started moving my cloth, you know. How I slept, I just had one cloth to cover myself. And if I sleep alone, I used to put my cloth around me, and then I sleep on top of it. So before he could take this cloth, as I had covered my head, maybe he would start from my head or from my legs before he will get it off. But if he started in this middle, I have slept on it, so I would feel some movement. So this man was taking this cloth small-small from my feet. Small-small. Then I let him to reach my knee, *"Bue![2] Ɛdeɛ bɛn nie?" I shouted!* "What is that?!"

So this man said, "Oh, Hawa, Hawa, Hawa."

And I shouted, "Who is that?" *Ha-ha!* "But who is that? Who? You people are going to kill me now?" Then I got up from the bed. I took my cloth and covered myself. I said, "Who is that? Who is it? Are you going to kill me?" Then I made like my body was shaking.

So this man said, "Hawa, it's me, Kɔmfo Manu. Kɔmfo Manu."

I said, "Where is the light?"

Then he went and put the light on.

Then I said, "Why?"

Then he said, "You know, since you were young, I was falling in love. I think I love you. So as you have grown up, and you have your own experience, and you came back to me, I thought your father knows everything."

1. to have sex with me
2. (Asante Twi): an exclamation of distress or shock

I said, "*What?!!* My father knows what? Did my father chop your money?"[1]

He said, "Oh, no. We are not talking about money. Don't shout like this. It's night. You know, here is a village, so in night, if things happen like that, it's going outside. So—"

So I said, "Look, I have respected you, as a friend of my father. You get back to your room and sleep, or else I will take my bag, and I will go to my girlfriend to sleep. When I came, I didn't come to you straight. OK? I came to visit you people because it's a long time since I have left this place. And you gave me a nice room, as a friend of my father. I take you like my father. But I don't have any mind to come here and have something like this with you."

Then, "You want to disgrace me?"

"Hey, look at this. What kind of disgrace is inside of this? We are two, talking about this."

So he said, "Oh, I don't believe you can do this to me. Your father is a nice man. He is nice, and you started bringing a problem." And this and that, and that and this.

And I said, "OK, if that will be the case, my father—he told me everything. When I came in the world, and they said, maybe you thought my mother was going to borne a girl. Maybe you are a witch. You knew this, so you think you could make me a baby of your juju. And then after, you will come and chop me. You have this juju. We call you the father of the juju. OK? So if the juju is my father, or my mother, you can be—you can be—as you know that this thing has come from your family—and—and you have me as a daughter of the family. So it's the same thing. So don't try it."

"Well, I was about to do you something good when you are going."

Then I said, "No, I'm not coming here to do good. I'm not coming here to do bad, too. But the way you are taking me, I don't like it. If suppose, as I have come to you, you tell me, 'OK, Hawa, you know, the way we are, and that and this, so I'll give you one room if you like. You can sleep inside, and I'll come and see you later.'"

Then he said, "But you came here with your girlfriend. I couldn't get the time to talk to you."

Then I said, "OK, but then the time when I came, when you opened the door for me, and then you showed me all these things, and said how I can use the room, that is the time when we were two. You can talk to

1. Have you given my father money to marry me?

me to see if I'm all right with that. Then I will come and sleep. If I'm not all right, I will sleep at that girl's place. But never mind. Even, it's two o'clock or three o'clock. I can go back to that girl's place and leave your room. Because I don't want to put you in a problem. I don't want to make you ashamed, too, because you are my father."

So this man said, "Oh, never mind. You can sleep. I won't say anything. I am going to sleep. Good night."

And I said to him, "Good night." Then he went and slept.

Reckoning with the God

So the next day, I went to greet the juju. And there's a nice thing, you know? This juju takes cola. Cola. If you are going there, you can carry any kind of cola—white cola, or the red one, or any different color. If you go there, you will ask, and you will talk on the cola. Maybe you will say, "Something is following me," or "Some bad luck is following me," or something like that, so the juju should show you the signs. You talk on this cola, and you give it out, and then you break it in two. You know the cola has a mouth,[1] so if you squeeze it, it breaks into two. Then they will squeeze it together, and the word you will say, they say it, and then be knocking it down,[2] and then lift it up like this, and let it go, and it falls by itself. If you haven't any problem, it can fall and open so that the inside of the cola will come out. If both sides are outside, it's good. If both sides are turned down, it's good. So all open or all turned. But if you have a problem, when the cola falls, the one part can turn, and the other part is up. It means that maybe you have some problem. So you have to be serious, to ask, so that they will be asking many things, and that and this. So if it comes to the point that this is happening to you, they say it, and then they continue to throw this thing.

Yeah, so I had my cola for more than two hours. If it falls, the one part is open, the other part is closed. Then I asked these people, "Can I see the manager?"

Then the manager was busy in a room. So they said, "Why?"

Then I said, "No, you know, I came straight to him, and I have slept in his house. I don't know what happened, and then this my cola doesn't work. Since I have known this thing, if I was coming here, I don't have a problem like that. So I have to see him."

1. an indentation
2. knocking it on the ground

So they said, “But this place, anyway, you know, people don’t used to see him here. So if you want to see him after, you can go and see him in the house.” And that and this.

So it was very funny. They didn’t want me to see the master, isn’t it? Then I was there. You know, when I was young, they said I used to do the dancing of this juju very nicely. And many people in the village took it that this thing, this juju, could be coming to me. Any day I went there, they said this juju used to carry me, that I could dance. Everybody would be tired, and I wouldn’t be tired. I would be dancing, sweating, and I would start shaking. You know? They said it was really the juju making me do that. I used to think so, but now I think it was because maybe I used to like the way they dance and go around. So when I was young, I did this thing many times.

So I was sitting, then I thought, “Ah! What is wrong? Oh-h. This man has taken me in a bad way.” You know, I told you that first time I had much interest in this thing. So what had this man told this thing, what bad thing to come out, or what has happened that this cola doesn’t come correct? So when I started thinking this, I was sitting like that, you know, and watching. They were telling me that there were many people that day — so I should give the chance to the others — because my cola didn’t chop[1] — so I should wait for the Monday coming. But I didn’t want to wait to the next Monday in that place. So I was worrying, then I started looking up, up, up, up. Then, something came to my mind that I should challenge these people.

So do you know the way I challenged them? I didn’t challenge them with talk or something like that. I was looking up, then I started making my eyes like this, blinking them. Yeah. I was looking up. I didn’t look at anyone’s eyes. I was looking like this. Then I started blinking. You know, how I had watched these people, when they say that the juju comes on them, they can act any way, but the *first* act is from their eyes. So I knew all this, and I started to make these tricks. So I made my eyes like that.

Then one man was talking, “Look.” Many people were bending down. Then I was blinking. Then another one said that, “Oh, no, no, no, no. Leave her. She is not well. See what is happening to her.”

So that time, they brought some water of this juju — they had it in a small-small pot — and they were *pouring* it on my head. Then I said, *“Ah-h-h-h.”* You know, I was becoming like somebody who is cool, somebody who doesn’t talk. And then I started grinding my teeth, and then I started groaning, *“Ow-w, ow-w.”* You know? And then the manager, they had said

1. My cola was not clear.

I couldn't see him, isn't it? But this thing has come. So I have to see the manager. He is the one who can cool these things down. *Ha-ha! Hee-hee! Oh!* It's very nice, huh?

So then, it's very *small* place, just a small round house. OK? The door is very small, just like the size of a window, up to down. If you are going inside, you will have to be on your knees before going inside. So if you come there to throw the cola, the people who are following this juju, the people who have belief in it, when they come, they don't actually go inside. They will sit kneeling at the door, and they will give their cola. If you are the son of the juju or daughter of the juju, you can go straight to the room. You have no problem. So all the people who were outside the door bending down and waiting to see the manager, when this thing started, then they gave me chance. I wanted to see the manager because I didn't understand my cola. So I started forcing, and then he came.

You know, when I started, when the thing was coming, I just *acted* it. It's not like this thing was taking me, but I started acting it that this juju has come. But you know, I think that when I did this cola to take it to the manager, and then this thing came, I don't know the time when I finished. When I did this thing, they had to get the manager. And then they had to get the people who will beat the *tam-tam,* the drums, because the people who are beating the drums, they are not serious. They are just for the weekend. But if something like this happens, they will come, and they will get more people to change, because they will drum and then change to others. It's because you will dance, and you will never be tired, so they have to change the drummers. You know? *Ha! Hee!* This is the case.

So the women: if you are a woman, if this happens to you, they will get the women to come and tighten your cloth well so that your cloth shouldn't fall. You know, if this thing happens to you, you won't know if even your dress falls off. You don't care about anything. You can be stupid.

So they got these women to come and tighten my cloth well, and then I was shaking my head. I didn't talk. I was chewing all my teeth, you know. *Hee-hee-hee-hee. Ha-ha!* So they tightened my cloth nicely, and then they looked for the musicians, and then the man himself was coming there, the manager. He had a tail of some animal. I don't know what kind of animal, but it was not too big. It was not a cow. He had a small tail. It was a white one. They were putting this thing in the small pot. They have different-different kinds of pots, and different-different kinds of water in the pots, with some leafs inside. This is the juju. They have some to care for the sickness of some people. They have some for if juju falls on you. If it falls on you, when it happens like that, they say that the juju likes you, that he loves you, or something like that: they have that kind of water. OK. And they have a kind of water, if you are a witch, to wash off your witchness. They have different kinds of things, just like drugs, like a hospital.

So they were putting this tail on the water, putting it on my head, and then singing, *"Na-o-o, na-o-o."* It was very wonderful, and it was very funny. This man did everything. But this thing never stopped. He talked everything, and this thing never stopped on me. If this thing comes to you, they have many words. He said everything that he could say. They had many numbers of the drums. They can play, and you will dance. If they finished the number, they have some words to beg, for the juju to leave you a little bit, and then he will say all this. *All* the people who were beating the drum were tired, but Hawa didn't get tired.

So these words, now he has looked for the words, and he has found out there was not anything to say. So he had to say the truth, that maybe, yesterday, he had been trying to do something with me, and then I didn't agree. That's why. Maybe that's why this thing happened, or that's why the juju is annoyed with him. If it's because of that thing, the juju shouldn't be annoyed. I haven't agreed with him, so it's finished. He doesn't think of it again: he has tried once, and it's finished. It's his first and last.

Then I came and lay down, then I fell. *Hee-hee-he! Ha!* When he talked this thing and finished, then I fell. I think it was the way I danced heavy. I was too much tired. So when I fell, it was just like I had fallen asleep. I don't know the time when they took me home. The time when I got to wake up, it was about five or something to five. We had been there from eight-thirty in the morning, and then I was doing this thing up till two o'clock. On Mondays, if you go there, they normally close about eleven or half-past ten in the morning. So I delayed them up to two or something like that, before they took me home. When I woke up, I was asking them, why is my dress wet like this? Where is my cloth I tied on my dress? Then I saw that they had tightened there strongly, and then I hadn't got any dress. So I started asking, "Where is my dress?"

So the man came to me. He said, "Oh, your dress?"

Then I said, "Why should you come? You didn't knock the door."

Then I held the cloth. Then he said, "Your dress?"

I said, "Yes."

He said, "What happened?"

Then I said, "What happened? What happened?"

Then he said, "Not anything happened. But you are asking me of your dress. Yesterday you have sacked me here, so you can ask me of your dress?"

Then I said, "This house is for you. I went to throw my cola this morning. I didn't see you. My cola didn't chop. And then I don't know the way you people brought me here without any dress."

Then he said, "Look, Hawawu, you know, I have done bad things. So I have begged your mother and your father,[1] that they should forgive me, and they forgave me. So you also should forgive me."

Then I said, "What bad thing did you do?"

He said, "You know, *all* these children for the juju, I didn't try anyone. But I have been trying you. But what happened to you today, I can't say it. And it's not a thing to say. If it happens to you, they can't say it in front of you. So I can't say it. But I think you should forgive me, because I have begged all your people, all your family, your mother and your father which is the juju, to forgive me. And that is the time when they gave you to me to come and bring you home to sleep. So when you wake up, there is no need to hear all of this. So you just forgive me. I won't try it again. I know that you are my daughter."

So I said, "OK, if you are my father, then you have to find me my dress."

Then he said, "Yes, it's with my wife." So he called the wife, "Abena."

She said, "Papa-a."

"Fa akwadaa n'atadeɛ no brɛ no." He said, "Bring this — little child — bring her dress for her."

So the wife brought the dress. And he said, "Abena." You know, she was the first wife. I think he loved the woman, too. And the woman had *very nice* children with this man. She is copper, and this man is black, so these girls look like chocolate. They have chocolate-color. So he told her, this is what I have done yesterday with Hawa, and this is that what happened today. And he said, "You know, I have trust in you. You are the only wife of mine to whom I can say my secret. So I wanted you to beg her for me."

Then she said to me, "Oh, Mama, it's nothing, you know. The world is like that, the way it can turn. So this is nothing to me. But you shouldn't let your father hear of it. If your father hears of it, it will be a very big shame for him."

So I said, "OK, my father wouldn't hear anything. It's between me and you. As for me, I have forgiven. As you say that my family has forgiven you: if you are daughter of someone and then somebody has done you bad, and he comes and apologizes to your father and mother, and they forgive, then it's the same thing they have done for you. It's the respect that they give you. So what you said, I have heard it much. And I will forget it. I won't say anything. My father will never hear of it."

But I *lied-o!* My father had to hear of it! Because the thing pained me.

1. the juju

So the day I got to Kumasi, *ah-h,* I didn't even go home: I went to where my father was selling his things in the market. I had brought many, many, many things: plantain, banana, cocoyam. I brought all these things in bags. From the station I brought all these things with taxi to my father's place in the market. Then I told my father, OK, this is the case, that we should send these things home, because I have been to the village. I have spent five days there, and it was nice, but I don't want to go home before telling him the story of his friend. So he sent one of the boys. You know, my father used to have boys to carry the cola. He is an old man; he can't carry it. So he has got people to do this work. He is only there to be changing the money.[1] So one of the boys took the taxi with all these things.

Then I said, "*Ey!* Papa!" You know, when we left the village and came to Kumasi, my father used to give me the story of this man—how he did this and that, and how I was young when I was following this man, and he was joking with me about his wives, and all this. So I said, "Papa, but why? You have been telling me this man's story. I thought he is a very good man."

Then my father said, "Yes. Did he do you some bad?"

And I said, "No, he didn't do me bad, but he was trying to do bad."

Then my father said, "What kind bad?"

Then I said, "No. Is this your friend?"

He said, "Yes."

"But do you trust him? That he is the one who brought this juju in this village?"

Then my father said, "Yes. I met him there with this thing. And many people believe him. He tried to catch me when I borne you people."

I said, "Oh, uh-huh."

"I know him and he hasn't done any bad to me. What did he do to you?"

Then I said, "No. He also has done me good. But you know, he made me afraid a little bit."

He said, "How did he make you fear?"

Then I said, "When I went, you know, I went to the house where we were lodging. The houseowner has died, and the daughter was there. And the daughter is the one who showed me all the people I wanted. And Kɔmfo Manu said, OK, if that will be the case, as this man is dead, leaving the children, and maybe some of them don't know me, they wouldn't give me a nice place to sleep. So he gave me a nice room. But night time, when I slept, he came inside the room, sleeping in back of me, trying to touch

1. making change and keeping track of the money

me. I don't understand this. So what is all this? If this man's daughter comes to you, can you do that to her?"

And my father said, "What?! Are you crazy?!"

Then I said, "Why am I crazy? I'm asking you whether if his daughter comes here in Kumasi to you, can you do it?"

He said, "What?"

I said, "Can you go and sleep with her and start to be touching her?"

"Did he do that?"

And I said, "Yes!"

"Did he do that?!"

I said, "Yes!"

My father was annoyed! He said, "Let's go to the village." *Hee! Ha-ha!* I couldn't go with this old man.

Then I said, "No."

He said, "What! This man did that to you?"

Then I said, "Yes!"

"And what happened?"

Then I said, "I just talked to him. I thought he was like my father. I didn't know that he would do things like that. So he said that I should leave it. It finished, then he went away. This is all that happened. But I didn't believe: the way you talked about this man to me, I didn't believe that he could do things like that."

So, you know what my father had to do? My father is another man. The time when this man said that we were the children of this thing, this African juju, they made something like a talisman to give to my father. Because of us, isn't it? So that thing, my father was carrying it everywhere. But the time I told this story to my father, my father took two weeks and went to the village. He didn't tell me the day he was going. He went and told this man, "OK, this is what you gave me to take care of the children. But now, as you are trying to be falling in love with them, I think it's better you keep it, and take care of them. But if one of my daughters or my sons has a headache, I will come and ask you, because you are a witch." *Hee-ee-ee!* My father is a very funny man. "So you take your things and keep it, but any one of them, if he has a headache, I will come and ask you." So because of this problem, their friendship was finished.

12 BLACK POWER

: THE VILLAGE IN BURKINA FASO :

Calling the Lost People

Yeah, so these things in our place, I was telling you I didn't believe it. But about two years ago I have seen something. And since I went inside, I have belief in it.

OK. These things in our place: for example, they used to search for people. If you are at the age to be grown, you can go everywhere you like, isn't it? But at our place, whatever the age you are, if you are some place, if they don't hear of you, they have their kind of way. Many of us do these things. They don't hear of you; you don't write letters; you don't do anything. So they have belief in this, because if they do this thing, maybe—nobody knows—maybe it's the time that God is going to say that the fellow should come, or I think it is their *power.* As for me, I believe that it is their power.

At our place, there is a man. He is a dwarf. They will go and tell this dwarf man, "We have somebody in the family who has traveled for two years. We don't hear anything of him—no letter, no anything. Nobody has said that he saw him. So we want you to help us to know. If he's in life, or he is not in life." OK?

They are going to tell this dwarf man, and he will come. He will give them the day, a special day to come. So that day, when he comes, all his debt—what he will eat, where he's going to sleep, wherever he's going—all this debt, they have to take it.

Then they will get a room for this man to do his work. But, you know, in the village everybody can come inside the room. They don't pay any half-penny to go inside. It's a free gate. It's inside a dark room. It's not a room with a straw roof; it has a flat mud roof. So in night time, if there is no light, it's *very dark!* Even in day time, there is no window: it's very dark. In day time before you will find anything in it, there must be a light. And how much about night time?

So we all went inside. They got light, full light, for the whole place. Everybody sat down nicely. They started singing, and playing some kind of music with calabash. Nobody danced. People started singing, singing, singing, singing. To make their singing, it took them maybe about one hour, playing this thing and singing.

So you see? This dwarf man will come out like this. Maybe with some kind of nyama-nyama dress — all is torn. Then he will come and sit near you. Yeah. That time, the light is on. So the time when the light is going to go off, it just seems like some breeze. Maybe he will open this door and some strong breeze will come, and he will have some candle here, and then it's off.

Look, this man, when they are going to start the whole show, he must be there. OK? But some people who will like to be getting a good place to sit near him, they used to come early. So maybe if you are early, you will see him coming. He hasn't got any ring; he hasn't got anything. Yeah, that's the master of the dwarfs. And when he's coming, he wears something like our old, old things. They used to put something in front here, and tie it around. And he will wear a small fugu.[1] And he is like somebody who didn't bathe before. And he's coming. He will come and sit down like that. With that *small-l* fugu. The fugu all is torn, but there are many — what did you call it?—*gris-gris.*[2] It's black power. Yeah. You will see big, big ones all around. This is what he has on his fugu. When he comes, he sits down. Then they will play the music about one hour. The light is on.

So, they just do something. I don't know how they do it, anyway, but I think they do it. You will see something will be like wind. I don't know. At that time we didn't know much of trickish things. Maybe if it was this time, I would know. They will blow some air. This air will come just like a breeze which has come from outside. And the light they had lit will go off. *Uh-huh.* This is where I started to believe these things, you know.

When the light went off like that, then these people started. You will hear somebody beating *bom-bom-bom-bom,* and then you will feel that the floor is shaking. I don't know. Maybe they have some stone or some iron. It is this time I used to think of it, but before I believed this thing. You will see everywhere is shaking, just like you are in disco and they opened the speaker very high, it used to kick. They make this thing: *kung-kung-kung-kung, kung-kung-kung.* You know?

Then, it will take some time, then you will hear some voices which are like — what do you say?— some voice that is not small, but it is somehow quiet. And it is growling, like something very big, *"Gr-r-r-r."* And the

1. a type of smock sewn from strips of cloth; also, batakari
2. amulet or talisman, usually sewn with leather

dwarf who has come, they call him the Master. The one you saw in the day time, that is the Master. As for him, you will hear his real voice. But this voice of those people, some can come there and make a kind of squealing, *"Fee-e fee fee fee-e!"* You know? There are different-different kinds of voices!

So the first one came, and he said, "Ah! Ah! Ah! You are calling me! You are calling me! I'm there. What do you want from me? What do you want me to do for you? Night like this, wouldn't you sleep? And you are trying to disturb me. Can I disturb you like that?" You know? *Ha! Hee-hee!*

So, when you hear this, *hey!* It's *beautiful,* eh? And the man — the Master — he said, "Yes, I have called you."

Then the voice said, "What do you want me for?"

Then the man said, "This is what they brought for me, and I don't know my back and front." You see? He doesn't know what is in the back or what is in front, if he continues, if he's going to be going straight. He doesn't know what is happening in front of him. So then he said, "I know that you are my father."

Then the voice said, "No! You are my father!" He is challenging! "Because if I was your father, suppose, you can't call me at this time. You are my father. I want you to tell me what you want."

You know, they used to say something sharp-sharp like this. So the man said, "OK, I want you to help me with this problem."

Then he said, "OK." They gave him the fellow's name. And there is someone, they will give the name of the village, the place maybe somebody can see him. Maybe somebody was just from the village, and came to Ouagadougou, and maybe I saw him once there, and then I go to them and tell them he's in Ouagadougou. But maybe he's no longer in Ouagadougou. OK?

So then in this case, for example, they will say, "OK, we say we have seen him in Ouagadougou, and his name is that and this. If you are clever, I want to see your clever work. Try to find him even if he's not in Ouagadougou. Find him where you can find him. Because you have already heard his name. By all means, if he's living in Ouagadougou, if he has lived in Ouagadougou, by all means, if *all* the people can't know him, choose one inside who can know him, his name."

So this thing will get up. When he goes away, no light again. Then this calabash, they have been *beating* it inside — *tun-tun tun-tun tun-tun tun-tun, gudugu gugu.* You know, at our place they don't have drums. This thing they are doing, there is some kind of the calabash you buy, but they don't make any design on it. They put empty pieces of cloth or some clothes or something inside, to fill the calabash, and turn it with the back down. If you beat it, it has some sound. Haven't you heard it before? Yeah, there's something inside so that it can make the sound. If you put the calabash alone, you can't beat it like the way they are beating it. You think it won't break? And then they have this thing: *all* the men have something like a rattle. They have that one, with the calabash. And they blow a flute, but it's something like a whistle. They have that one. But they don't blow it all the time. They have a time to blow it. It means that he's coming back, and he is near to the town. So he will give a message to come and tell them that he is coming, with the fellow. So that time, you hear *"pee-e-e."*

When they start, *"pee-e, pee-e, pee-e, pee-e!"* Then all the calabashes will be hitting *more!* That's the power, you know. Then somebody will say, "Hey, hey, hey, hey. My master, I'm tired! My master, I'm tired! The place is very hot. I have tired myself. Oh, my master, help me!"

Ha! Then the calabash will be going down,[1] for them to listen to the talks. So the voice will say, "I have brought him, I have brought him, I have brought him. But I want to come and give you the message that I have brought him. But I have left him at this place. I'm going to bring him now."

So he will go off again. So that time, the calabash people will start again, with this whistle. So the one who brought him, he wouldn't say anything again. Then the fellow will come, like somebody who has come from many miles. Then he will start only with heavy breathing, *"Heh-h, h-h-hm-hm. Heh-h, h-h-hm-hm."*

So if you hear this like that, you will *die!!* You will *collapse! God!* This was the place when somebody touched me. *Shit!!* I think somebody was sleeping, or some people used to go inside like that, and as it's dark, you know, to wait, to wait, to wait—some people used to fall asleep. So I think maybe somebody slept, and his hand touched me. *Wow!* I jumped up and ran out of the room! *Wow!* Can you? In the dark, nobody is there, and then you have been hearing all these fucking things. And then after, this *"Hm-m!"* You will hear this: all the room is *"Hm-m-m."* You don't see the fellow. There's no light to see anybody's face, to see what he's doing. Whether he is near you, or he's not near you. And somebody is touching you like this? *Wow!* I jumped up and ran away. *Ah!*

So I was sitting there up to that time. You know, this thing, I had heard of it. They gave me the story of it before I went to see it by myself, and I saw up to that point, but I didn't finish all. So this is the *whole* story I'm giving you. OK? Because I didn't finish it. But the ones who finished it, they came and told me what happened.

1. reducing its volume

So: then you will hear, *"Hm, hm, hm, hm."*

And some, when they do this, then he will say that, "I want water to drink."

So you will hear that. You hear the water: *glug-glug glug-glug glug-glug glug-glug.* You don't know where the water is from. But a very easy one: when this man is going to do this thing, he doesn't have anything with him. But maybe, you know, some people can see in dark. I don't know. Maybe when they shut the light off, he can find all these things around him. I don't know. Because I didn't stay for the end, too. So when they are in this way, when this person does so, you will hear the pouring of water.

So the one the dwarf brings, he will take some drink. He will ask for the water. And you will hear the noise—how they pour this water—*glug-glug glug-glug glug-glug-glug.* You will hear the noise. Then he will drink and say, "Thank you very much. Thank you very much. What did you call me for?"

Then the dwarf will say, "Ah, but why? You leave all these your families home, and you wouldn't write, and you wouldn't give any message. They don't know where you are. So we are trying to find you, to see what is happening to you."

And the fellow, if he's in life, if he's alive, he will start to make "*Mm-hm, mm-hm.* So? They want me?" He will ask whether the family wants him. It's just like he went to the court, you know, and somebody is judging the case between the families. So he will ask him, "Do you think they like me? And I have been away so many years like that? They don't search for me? It is this time they feel like looking for me?"

Then the dwarf will say, "No. They care for you, but they don't know the way to find you. They have been trying to search for you. But they don't have a correct person to find you. That's why they don't find you. So now they have got a correct person to bring you back home. So they want to know where you are living."

You know? It's very interesting, eh? I believe these things sometimes. He will show the place he's living. And then, he will say, "You know, by all means, I can't sleep here, as I'm living there. Maybe I will come home."

Some of them, they can give a date. "I will come home in about a week's time." And in a week's time, he will be there.

And some of them will say, "If they want me truly, let them follow me. This is the name of the place I am. If they ask of the name of the place, they will get me." And then the family will go, and they will get the fellow.

So at our place, they believe much in these things. Somebody can be dead. You know, I think death can come any time, but at our place, they don't take it so. Somebody can just die. He's not sick, he's not anything, and he will die like that. They wouldn't agree. They will go to this dwarf, and the dwarf will call the soul of the person, and the soul of the person will show the one who killed him.

And then, sometimes if he sees the fellow, they will say that maybe this fellow can't do him bad like that. But the one who died won't go alone: he will carry the other one with him. By a week's time, you will see that the same fellow whose name they called there, he will die. I don't know whether they kill them by witchcraft. The fellow will die, and they will say, "Uh-huh! He killed that fellow. That's why he's dead, too. Because that day the dwarf was saying it."

So that night when I went inside the room, I didn't sit inside until they finished it. That was my first and last. I was afraid. So I didn't try for it again. But the people who looked at it, you know, they were telling me this story, that this is what was the ending of this dwarf.

The Master of the Dwarves

I have one of my uncle's sons who likes these things much. And I think he may be one of the witch people, because every time, when he hears of this thing, he will go to it. And every time, if I'm in village, I'm his *bes-s-st* friend. So he has *much* interest in this dwarf, and he used to give me the story about it. So this type of thing, I think it is the olden days when they learned it. And they like it, because they think it is doing good things for them.

You know, this time it is very difficult. We the ones who are coming, we don't have much belief in it. But the real people who have belief in it, the juju people, it used to work for them. Yeah, all this is juju. Maybe they have built something like a shrine, and every time they will kill chickens and cows and sheep on it. OK? That is their juju. That place is just for some of them: they build it, and they believe in it. Every time, they have been doing all the sacrifices. So it's their thing. And if they ask this thing to do something for them, they see the thing clearly. It will come the same as they want. So they have belief in it.

But anyway, the believing is not that you say, "OK, today-today do this for me," and the same day the juju will do it. They have patience for this. Maybe you will ask for something, maybe some people will ask for one week, some people try for three or four days, before this thing will happen. So they have belief on this thing. OK?

And some people — these dwarf people, as they used to say, "the real one"—the one I saw when I went inside and I shouted and came out of the room: he is the master of the dwarves. He knows the dwarves. They say he was a boy, a little boy, about eight to nine years old. And they used to send him to the bush with the sheep or the cows, following them in bush like the cowboys.[1] So once, this boy went out with the cows. All the cows came back, and this boy was not there. They were praying all over the country to find him. They didn't find him. They went to the bush side to find him, and everywhere near to the village to look for him: they didn't find him. OK? Then it was just like, well, maybe some animal ate him. You know the village people took it like that, so they forgot about him. And this boy, before he got back home, he was about twenty-four or twenty-five years old. He was getting to be a man. Or I can say he was a man. Even I think that he was getting to the old age. So when he came home, he didn't talk to anybody.

And he had this bag like the one the Tuaregs[2] use to put water inside. In our country,[3] every man has this thing. And this man had this thing. And he came home. And, you know, he is not very much tall. He was a very short man. But he was lost for some years. So when he came, he went straight to the house. He didn't talk to anybody. Everybody was greeting him. He didn't answer anybody. And the way he wanted to put this thing he was carrying, he didn't reach the place well. So he took a stone to stand on and reached some point there, and then hung this thing there, and then he came. He didn't talk to anybody. Three days: he didn't take any water; he didn't take any meat; he didn't talk to anybody. Everybody who was talking to him: he's looking at you, he doesn't say any word.

So, in this case, after four days, this is the time when he started to talk. He said, "Well, there are some friends I have met, and they have been enjoying me much. So I liked them very much, and I wanted to stay with them. Maybe they have been coming to me—but anyway, they sent me back to see you the families—so—as they know that you people have been looking for me, they want me to show that I'm really in life—I didn't die yet—so they brought me back to say hello to you people."

So OK. From there, as they have been seeing these things, then everybody had to bend down, and call the boy their father, or their master. *Hee-e!* It's funny! So that is the way they have it. So any area of our place

1. children who herd cattle
2. nomadic people from the Sahara desert area
3. traditional area

there, any small village, many people, when they have a problem, they used to invite this man to come.

And this man, sometimes, if you want something, you know, that you want to see him so that he will do something for you, you must say it before one week, because every time he is busy. He hasn't got time. He has a lot of work. People have been calling him over and over.

Yeah. So the time when I also was inside the room with that man, that was the time I believed it a little bit. And after, my uncle's son believed it, so he could tell me the whole story — a *nice* story. Even he is the one who told me the story of this man, and then I went there.

: THE VILLAGES IN GHANA AND BURKINA FASO :

Showing the Power

So at our place, we have these things like that. But the one where they will dance and fall,[1] like in Ghana and Togo, I haven't seen that one at our place. The one I told you about in the village near Kumasi, when they borne me and I had this thing with my hair, that juju is the same thing like they have in Togo. There are people like that who dance and fall, but they don't have a special one like that at our place.

But our place, too, they have different ones. Especially these masks. There are some people who go inside the mask and dance with it. But the one at our place, you will never see even his hand. *All* is mask. You wouldn't see the foot. It's very beautiful. They *dance!* They dance *good!* And then after, they also do something, you know, like the kind of this thing when you want to show the juju.[2] But they don't fall down. He can dance some kind of dance, and this dance can't stop, and he will continue. And these drummers have to change the music, and then he is dancing. Every time, too, when they change the music, the feet are going by the drums. Yeah. They have this kind of thing. They have a lot of plays — different-different kinds of beating the tam-tam. Some places have a lot of dances. But we don't have this falling down.

Yeah, but you know, if you feel this thing, at the *same* time you are doing the thing, you wouldn't know what you are doing. I don't know. I think the meaning is that it is the power. It is the power which they say for any kind of juju. OK? There are different kinds of juju. You know, Af-

1. become possessed
2. make the juju manifest or demonstrate its power; enter possession

rican way is not one way. They have maalams: maalam people, they don't deal by juju. OK? They deal by Allah. They deal by God. You see? These juju people: they are not Christian, they are not Muslim. They just believe on their juju. Their juju is their God. But they don't have much things with the maalams. The Muslims don't have much of this kind of life. OK?

But the juju people have this kind of life. It is their God. So every time, the juju has to show them something, that, "I am God of you people." This is why he comes: somebody will be dancing, dancing, dancing, dancing, and she doesn't know what she's doing, trying to chew her teeth and tear her dresses. That's why, if they see somebody fall down, they used to take off her dresses. Do you know why? Maybe you will spoil the dress. Somebody can just catch this thing and tear it by her teeth, trying to bite it. She knows this cloth is costly, but that time she says she doesn't see it. So she will spoil all her dresses from her body. So the best thing, to wear your nice dress tomorrow, if he catches you, the people who are there will take off your dress, so that tomorrow you will have it. Because they know that you are going to do this thing, but tomorrow you will regret. Uh-huh.

So this is the way they have. They think this is their God. Any time, when they will be playing this music to him, he has to act, and show the people he loves and show the people he likes much, the people who have been following him. This is really what he wants. He has to show them that if he does that with someone, you will see that they take the fellow to the room where the master is. And then do you know what they do? Some people used to put some water on their hair, and then—yeah?—that is God-water. He likes you; he asked you to drink this, or to come and take this blessing. So the people the juju likes, they are in front of it.

They are showing the power of the juju. They don't call something like a name of the God. They don't call a name of God, but they are showing. Some people say that when the people are playing this kind of music, they can ask, "Juju, show your people you love." When they start this drumming on the tam-tam—*kugun, kugung gung*—they are asking the juju to show his love, or to show the people he loves. So that is the time you will see: when they start this drumming, they have some drumming which they start playing and these people will start falling down. So he will start to show his lovers.

Yeah, as for the master of the juju, and the people like that, the juju can come to them sometimes. Because the place where I was with my hair, where I said that I was a daughter to the juju, I saw the way the juju can come to them. He can come to the master, but the master doesn't fall down. But he can dance. And the way he dances, he doesn't move to there and there. He is at one place, turning like this, just like this — maybe for about three to four hours, he is in one place. You will see him like this: *ss-ss-ss-sss.* He can dance. He doesn't fall down. No, no, no, no, no, no. He will *never* fall. If you come to look, if they don't play the tam-tam, he stands and makes so: *sh-sh-sh.* And if they start it, then he will be doing fast dancing with the feet. God! You will see him like this. They used to wear something like this kind of Dagbamba short smocks. And then they have many of these things I said Hausa people used to sew — the *gris-gris.* They have them plenty, plenty, different ones in back and in front. And it is heavy. So the time he is standing, all these things are there. This dress is just like — if you can get a photo of this, it is *very* nice. And he will never fall down.

So I think, I don't know: the Ewe people's one, I don't know it much. Maybe they can catch the masters to do the same dancing. But this one I saw in the village in Ghana, he will only dance. The master will never fall down. He will be dancing, dancing, dancing. This man can dance and dance and go inside of the room and bring this — the *ol-l-d* gun, which they put some gunpowder inside,[1] they make *BOOM!* Then the fire will go off. *Po-bum, po-bum, po-bum.* He is shooting the witches. So when he shoots that, by about the next week, you will see many people becoming sick. They will be *sick:* the witches who are about to kill the people or who used to chop the meat of people, he will shoot them.

So then the week after, many people will come to that place with their sickness, and then be trying to beg the juju to forgive them, that last week he has shot them. "You can see my here.[2] This is the place I have been shot." And they show, and you will see the mark, from the wound. So why don't you believe this? Huh? They used to show the mark. And they open their mouths: "This is what we were about to do, but we saw that this time you are serious to take care of the town. So we are begging you to forgive us. I will never go there again. I will never join the group again."

Then people from the juju will say, "OK, if you feel like you are not going to join the group again, you should give the spirit you used to go out with in the night. You should give it to us. We will keep it." If you do that, then they will believe you. They will never believe you like that until you give out your spirit.

So somebody will go to his house: he will find some calabash, sometimes red oil, and some kind of hair of human being, or the head of some-

1. like a musket
2. see the place I am pointing to

thing, or some bells. And some of them go to the houses and bring this kind of beads. You want the big-big ones, well, this is what they buy with it. And they put it inside for them. So if you go to that place, you will see many beads and many gold earrings and chains. Yeah. You will see all of them hanging there. It is the witches: maybe somebody will take her witchcraft and kill her daughter. Or somebody is poor: she will kill her son to sell his meat and buy something to become rich.

They will collect all the witchcraft. If you go to the house of this juju, ah! They have long, long, sticks like from our gate to this side. Long, long, long ones like that. *Oh!* The time I was there, I saw it was more than fifty, and all were full up with different kinds of beads, and gold. *Ha!* Yeah, these things: *all,* they kept them there. The master doesn't want it for anything. He just keeps them there. You can see some gold, nice ones. Some of them are very old, so they don't know the years they have. These beads, some of them are there: the rain has been beating them, and then the thread will be getting tired, and maybe one night it will fall down by itself, and morning time they will get it for the children to make it again and put it back there. Nobody wants it. This man doesn't want it. It is for the juju. The juju is carrying all their witchcraft, and keeping it at his place, so that in night time they don't get power to go out.

Yeah. And you know, people believe in these things, and people have been going to this place every time. Even *I* had belief on it, because when they said I was from there, as the daughter of this juju, you know, if it was not for the time I went to the man's place and he tried to do his stupid thing, I liked these things much. But since the time when he was trying to do that stupid thing to me, that's why I hate it. So now, I don't believe it. Because in my sickness in Togo — anyway, I had been to many doctors. They didn't take care of it. But some African man took care of it, and then it was OK. But still I don't believe it.

PART FIVE *The Life in Togo*

13 A FAST BOY

: *The Rich Biafran*
: *Frankie and Antonio*
: *Frankie's Game*

: LOMÉ :

The Rich Biafran

You know, the sickness I had in Lomé, and the time I was suffering from my sickness, it give me the sense that it's better not to go around. If you can get somebody, one person who can take care of you, or if you ask of something you need, and maybe he can help you, then it's better. That time, when I finished my sickness, I had some different sense which was coming to me. So I had to find my way: I shouldn't be living like how I have been hanging, you know, every night, to go here and there, every night. So from my sickness, I had this experience, this sense, to change my mind. I mean, every time to be changing men — the time when I had the sickness, and I became well, I didn't feel like the first time when I used to go out alone. When I went to Lomé first, I used to go out alone every night. I would go. But the time when I got sick, before I became well, I thought that to get a friend is better. Suppose the time when I was sick, if I had a friend, maybe I wouldn't have suffered like that.

Then, I got one man at Royal Hotel. This man was a Biafran,[1] from Nigeria. He was from Lagos. He stayed in Lagos, but he used to come to Lomé. He had a big transport[2] company in Lagos.

1. from eastern Nigeria; also refers to someone from the Ibo cultural area
2. trucking

OK. How I saw this Biafran man, he had a girlfriend in Royal Hotel. OK? This girlfriend was just next door to me, you know, so we were together. Any time when this man saw me in the bar, he used to buy me a drink. At that time I used to like Guinness. This man used to buy me my Guinness any time, and this girl became annoyed that this man wanted me. And actually, this man always had been telling me that he wanted me. Then I would say, "No, you are the friend to my girlfriend."

But it's a funny thing. This girl said, "Eh-h-h, Hawa, I didn't know that you are like that. I didn't think that you would do this and that to me. Even this man was spending money, and that and this. So when you see it, your eyes are wide on this man." When this girl got annoyed, to say she suspected me in this way, and as I didn't do the thing and she was telling me this, I also got annoyed. So then I had to do it. I said OK, if that will be the case, from this moment, any time the man will come here and he will ask me, I will go with him. I told this girl so. So I started.

So the next morning the man came to Royal Hotel. He asked us what are we going to eat. I said, "No, I'm not going to eat. I just want drink."

And this man told me that there was nice food at some place. If I like, we can buy food for this girl here, and we can go to someplace to eat. So I agreed with him. He bought the food for this girl, and then he told us to go to one hotel in Lomé, Forever Weekend. So we went there. This man ordered food: he didn't eat. He drank; he didn't eat. So we ate at that place, and he came back with taxi and dropped me at Royal Hotel. That was my first day to know him. And he gave me ten thousand. *Hey!* Somebody who invites you to restaurant and you eat. He doesn't ask anything of you. You know? Then he gives you ten thousand. OK. This man, I will start to chop him. This is how I made my mind.

So from there, if this man came, this girl can come to the man. The man will buy anything—whatever this girl wanted—for her. Maybe this girl will ask for some money. Maybe the amount she will ask, he wouldn't give her the same amount she will ask. Maybe he would give half of it to the girl. And as for me, this time, I have somebody who will pay my hotel and everything. So I have to go to the upstairs. At Royal Hotel, that time I was living in a five hundred CFA room: it was a very small room; besides the bed, there was no place to sit. When this man came, I went to a two thousand, five hundred room. It had a fan, and it had a toilet. And this man was paying. So I was very happy to meet this man, and I was very happy with him. Sometimes if he came, if he got drunk, then I would take him to my room to sleep, and then I would come back down and stay there and drink, just putting all the receipts on his account. He is going to pay. I was very happy that time with this man, because since I knew him, he never asked me for sexing. And he was giving me a lot of money. OK?

So that time I was starting to be happy with him because I was getting a lot of money. Any time, I would tell him I'm going to Ghana to see my family, and that and this, and he would give me maybe fifty or sixty thousand. Then I wouldn't go anywhere. I would be staying in Togo for two or three days. Then I would come. I would show myself to him that I have come back. But I was all the time in Royal Hotel. I knew the time he used to come, so that time I would vanish from the bar. And you could tell him that I'm in town, but if he came to my room, I was not inside. So I was *happy* that I had got this man.

Then the time when I was very *much* happy, this was the time I met Frankie with this man. Frankie came in. And Frankie started to shit my way.

Frankie and Antonio

Frankie! You know Frankie already. Frankie grew up in Lagos, because his mother had stayed there, but all the family was from Togo. Frankie knew this man from Lagos. I knew Frankie from Togo. The time when I knew this man, that time I didn't know Frankie. I used to see Frankie but I didn't know him to be friends with him. I didn't talk to him before.

So one day, this man came to me at Royal Hotel and saw Frankie there. And Frankie saw this man. So he went and greeted the man, you know, as, "Hey, master, when did you come here?" And this man was also talking to him. They came as friends, as old friends, that they knew each other in Lagos, and they have come and met here. I think this man knew Frankie at Fela's house.[1] So they started their friendship again. And that time, I wasn't free with Frankie, because I didn't know him.

Yeah, Frankie. Before I knew him at the Royal Hotel, he was having a girlfriend, one Fanti girl from Cape Coast or from Swedru or something like that. This girl was called Saha. This is the girl Frankie used to come with to Royal Hotel. So once Frankie came to this girl with his friends, some copper-colored boys, you know, some half-castes. They came to this girl, and they brought one tape, a small tape, and left it in this girl's place.

1. Fela Anikulapo Kuti, a leading Nigerian musician. His house and adjoining nightclub in the Surulere section of Lagos were a meeting place for many diverse people who were friends or followers of Fela and music.

And when they went away, police came and arrested this girl with the tape. Then the girl said that one half-caste boy gave it to her, then they went and carried the half-caste. And Frankie went out from this problem. Eh? Frankie wasn't inside. But he was the one who let the girl know these boys, so that they could keep something like that in this girl's room. Did you think that they wouldn't arrest Frankie himself? But that time, he was quick, and he acted as if he didn't know these people. So they put these people in jail, and this girl, this Ghanaian girl, a poor girl, a small, very small girl — Saha — they sent her to Ghana that they have deported her. The police people took her to the Ghana border at Aflao[1] and left her there.

So this was the time when Frankie thought that, OK, if that will be the case, he will start going around. And that time, Frankie didn't speak French. He spoke only English. He couldn't deal with these Togolese girls. He was only dealing on the English way, with Ghanaian girls or someone who could speak English. That time, Frankie looked like a different person. Nobody believed Frankie that he is a Togolese. All the boys didn't believe him. So he was living with this Ghanaian girl, and every time he was dealing with the girl.

And when they deported this girl, Frankie got another girlfriend. That girl also had a trouble. They brought her a nice suitcase, a nice one which was costly. And then this girl went out and brought some man, and the man said this box is for him. Just like that! She went out. Maybe somebody wanted to follow her and come, and then he came and saw his suitcase in her room. Then he said, "*Ah, bon!*[2] So, you are the one who has my suitcase."

Then she said, "What? What your suitcase?"

And this man said, "Yes, this is my suitcase."

"How is it for you? You are the only one who they make this suitcase, for you alone?"

Then this man just opened the suitcase to show that he cut it someplace and wrote his name there. So he just got it and said, "Look. Do you see? Do you know my name?"

Then the girl said, "Yes."

"If you can read this. I don't think this box is for you. Where did you get it?"

And this girl started shaking.

1. border town in Ghana next to the Lomé border crossing
2. (French): Oh, good!

So Frankie was with gangs in Lomé. But they never got Frankie. They got the group and they didn't get him. He was just lost like that. There was some big trouble, that some girls went and took some money, with Frankie's people, and this money was for one French man. So the girl ran away to Ghana, and they were looking for these Togolese boys. And Frankie got lost. He was smart. Frankie went and stayed with one Italian man. Now that man is dead. Antonio. He was the one who opened Disco Uno in Lomé.

But first time, Antonio didn't have money. He was like a hippie. He stayed at the seaside, just near to the beach. He was a *very short* man. This Antonio was a tailor, sewing dresses, and many of the European women gave their materials to him to sew dresses for them. He had one machine. Yeah, he could sew nice dresses. That time it was not costing much. Many, many women used to go to him. So when Frankie was wanted by police, he went and stayed there with Antonio. Yeah. It was through Antonio that Frankie learned to be a tailor. So when Frankie was wanted, and he and Antonio were in that place, you know, nobody thought Frankie was there. Everybody thought this Italian man is a nice man, a very quiet man. Nobody thought Frankie could be living with him. So Frankie was free there for six months. And that's the place he learned tailoring. And from there, he got to know all these French women, and different kinds of women. That was the place he knew them, from Antonio.

You know, this Antonio was a groover, too. He smoked. And I don't think this Antonio liked women. Well, I don't know his life, but he liked African boys. He didn't used to deal with the women. Anyway, I had one girlfriend who went and slept with him. So I don't know. But the time Antonio was in life, we didn't used to see this boy with women. I used to go to Antonio's place because I also had one friend, an Italian man who was staying with Antonio the time he opened the nightclub. And the time I had this Italian man, I didn't really meet any girl with Antonio in his room. He had his place. He had some kind of flat. It was very nice. Anyway, he hadn't got a chair. He just made something like a hippie's way, you know: "Let's sit on the floor." In the sitting room, he had some pillows, heavy-heavy ones. I used to count them. He had thirteen pillows, round-round ones. And every one was covered with African cloth. If he had Ghana cloth, if he brought it from Ghana, then on that side of the pillow, he would write, "This is made in Ghana." So all these pillows: "This is made in Holland"; "This is made in Togo"; "This is made in Benin"; "This is made in —." You know, Antonio was a *wonderful* man! Before you would go to his room, you would pass some ropes hanging: you pass Antonio's room and then go to the next room, and it was the same like that.

So I and this Italian man used to go out. We didn't stay home. Maybe from Disco Uno, we would go to another place. Maybe before we came back to Disco Uno, Antonio had closed and gone home. And then we would come home. And any time, when the nightclub finished, you would come and meet the room-light of Antonio on. He didn't put any bed there. In his spare room, he didn't put any cot there. Maybe he was with one boy, and in his room, no bed. I think he had about twenty mattresses covering all the floor of his room—no bed. So he was like that. But in daytime, if you would go to his place, you would see *many girls! Beautiful! Beautiful women!*

So first time, Frankie was with this boy, Antonio, and I don't know, but to my mind, I think that Frankie also tried that way at that time. Some of my girlfriends wanted to tell me something like that, but I used to swear, "No, Frankie doesn't do that!" Because of the respect Frankie used to give me, I didn't want to say yes. But maybe. I think so. So in this case, when Frankie was there, he was very smart. If the women would come to Antonio's shop, the way they would play with Antonio, Antonio wouldn't give them face. Then Frankie would answer. You know, this is the way he got his chance to be smart. As Antonio couldn't do with the girls, so Frankie tried to catch all the girls that followed Antonio. Maybe Frankie would say, "OK, evening time we should meet at this place," and that and this.

And then some women used to bring their problems. Yeah, some women used to come and tell Frankie the way they wanted to catch Antonio, and Antonio cannot be caught. And Frankie would say, "Oh, as for me, if I talk to him, he will listen, he will listen. I can help to let this man have understanding on you," and that and this. When they are there like that, Frankie will be starting so. And I think these French women, how cheap they are, Frankie can boss them and get them in this way. And you know, sometimes there are some kind of women who can say "that and this": they bluff themselves or something like that. But Frankie used to *coo-ol* them. He gets that kind of women *easy*—without no anything.

And then Antonio came to open Disco Uno, and Frankie couldn't get his chance again. So Frankie had to follow other ways to try to look for customers. So in this case, Antonio still had his tailoring. He used to cut his dresses to make them in a hippies' way. He would take different, different, different kinds of pieces of cloth to make a nice dress, *nice.* Many people liked it. And that time, people would buy from him.

Yeah, and the time when Frankie started, when Frankie knew how to cut all these patterns and sew the dresses a little bit, then Frankie copied all the patterns. And Frankie was giving the things at a cheap price. Frankie was free with these women. Maybe they will go to Antonio and find a dress for ten thousand. When they come to Frankie, they will find it for three thousand. So this is the way he started catching them. And Antonio's market fell down.

So Frankie got his chance from there. This time Frankie has a big studio. You know where he got it? He caught a nice Italian woman. She was the one who started taking Frankie's dresses to Rome. When he started to get these women from Antonio's place, he got this Italian woman, and this woman was working in Togo. I think, when this woman saw Frankie, she thought he was a nice boy. So she followed Frankie, and then she came and seized Frankie not to sew the dresses and give them to the people cheap. So when Frankie sewed the dresses, she would put them in a parcel to go to Italy, and then her people in Italy would send them the money back. This woman was making that arrangement for Frankie. So Antonio got to be annoyed with Frankie so that they were no more friends. First time, when this man opened Disco Uno, Frankie used to go there every day free. But in some months, when Frankie started all this sewing, if Frankie came to the disco, he had to pay. If he would come, he didn't talk to Antonio at all, and Antonio didn't talk to Frankie.

Frankie's Game

So the time I met Frankie, Frankie and this Biafran man started their own friendship again, and they were together. Frankie was not free with me; I was not free with Frankie. That time I didn't know him, and he also didn't know me. And so, what to do: I think Frankie was thinking he will be doing the best thing for him himself, or this man, so he was trying to show this man, when he has a girlfriend, how to do with the girl, and that and this.

Then, one day, this man came. He said, "Take five thousand and pay your room. Then you can pay your food with this." But before, this man didn't give me five thousand. He would pay the rent — the rent and all the receipts. He told the manager he was going to pay the rent, and they would put it for him. Then if he came to me, maybe he would give me twenty thousand or thirty thousand. There was no account of the room inside. This was where I was going to get Frankie, to know that he is a bad boy. Since Frankie was walking with this man, sometimes he would come and tell me I should take five thousand. Sometimes he would come and tell me, "Take twenty-five hundred, and pay your room. Today I haven't got money; I have to go to bank to get some and come." That and this. And maybe he wouldn't come back to the Royal Hotel till the next day, or something like that.

This was the way I got to get this idea: "This boy is spoiling this man." Yeah. Frankie was spoiling him because he was trying to show him experience. He was trying to show him sense. You know? He was trying to show him sense that this is not the way they spend here for the girls who are living in a hotel. Maybe he would try to tell the man that I'm not here for him alone, or maybe if he goes away, I can get another man, and that and this. So this man started to change his life. So that time, I had to heat on Frankie.

And this man was also a drunkard. It's very funny: he was a drunkard, and if he drank, sometimes he used to get a feeling to tell me the truth. You know? Sometimes he used to bring Frankie's palaver, that Frankie said he is spending much, and it's true, when he looks at his account, he sees that he is spending much, and that and this. So Frankie is a good boy. He's going to have Frankie as his secretary. *Ha! Hee!* He was telling me this.

So when he was telling me this, I had to get annoyed with Frankie. Isn't it? That is the time I thought, "Frankie: *aha!* This boy is trying to do his best." But I thought he is clever. And I am not much clever, you know, but I have to try to meet him. I should just try to meet him. So I said, "OK, if this will be the case, I will fix this boy."

So one time this Biafran man said I should cook for him. You know, he could say that he's hungry, but if you bring the food, he wouldn't eat. He told me he doesn't eat in restaurants in Lagos. Always he used to eat at home. So he said he was hungry because every time, if he goes to the restaurant, if they serve him, then he sees the food, then he's full up. So he doesn't eat in Lomé. He doesn't like to go to the restaurant to eat food. So he asked me to cook for him.

OK. I'm staying in hotel. Number one. I haven't got cooking pans. I haven't got a cooking pot. I haven't got a coal pot[1] to fire the charcoal. All the things for cooking, I haven't got. So I told him, if that will be the case, if he wants to be eating here, I can do it, but it is very expensive to buy all these things. So this man gave me forty thousand to go and buy all these things. OK.

1. a small stand for charcoal cooking, sufficient for one pot

I took five thousand to buy all that I wanted. I bought two cooking pots, four plates to eat inside, a coal pot, and a half-bag of charcoal. And this man went and told the manager of the hotel that he is going to marry me, so he's taking me to Lagos. So when he's here, he doesn't eat, so the man should get a place for me to cook. So at the back, where the wife was cooking, they gave me that place. I used to cook there.

But I could cook for this man, and he wouldn't eat. When he came, he would take one spoonful, one and two, and then he would say, "Ah-h, beer." He just wanted beer or whiskey, so he would say, "Go and bring me one bottle of whiskey." Sometimes he would say, "Bring Passport."[1] I will bring it, and I will serve him in a glass with plenty of ice. He didn't drink the whiskey with anything. Plenty of ice: no water, no anything. And he would say, "I'm OK, my dear. I'm OK."

So the time when he knew Frankie was also the time when I started cooking for him, and when he was coming to eat, he came with Frankie. And I looked at this food. I looked at Frankie. I looked at this man. Then I was asking myself, "Should I give them this food? Should I give them this food?" Then I said, "OK, the way this boy is, I will serve them both."

So when I served them—*oh!*—Frankie ate well. This man couldn't eat much—one, two, finish. And then he drank whiskey, and then he went to sleep. So when this man slept, it was left with me and Frankie. Frankie ate *nicely!* Then I said, "Hey, my brother."

He said, "Hey, my sister. Take care of my master. He's a big man! He has a big transport in Lagos. I first knew him at Fela's house. But I was not close to him, but—"

Then I said, "Ah, is this the case? He's a big man. But he is not a nice man, even if he is big in Nigeria. He is not big here in Lomé."

And he said, "If you know how to hold him, he will give you."

Then I said, "What? This man doesn't give me."

Then he said, "*What?!* You don't hold him well."

Then I said, "Ah! What should I do for him? I have been cooking for him. He says he can't eat in restaurant. I have been cooking for him here. How do you think I should hold him?"

So Frankie didn't answer. Then I said, "Hey, Frankie, look. You have been holding this man. I know what he was giving me. But I thought that since this man got to know you, he's changing his life. But to me, you know, I think we are both suffering, both of us. We both are fighting for ourselves: you are fighting for your life; I am also fighting for my life.

1. a brand of Scotch

Maybe I'm older than you. I don't know. But I think that if you know that in this world, we have to fight for ourselves, then why do you do that?"

Then he said, "But I didn't do anything.

Then I said, "Yeah, you did something."

Then he was trying to challenge me. And this man was sleeping, and he was turning. So I said, "OK, let's go to the bar, because maybe the way we are talking, maybe he can't feel like sleeping."

So we went to the bar. Then I said, "What are you going to drink?" I bought drink for Frankie. I knew that this receipt, I was going to give it to this man, so I didn't worry. Then I said, "You know? I think the way you are, you are very smart. I like the people who are smart like you. But the way you are doing, I think it's not nice. We have met one another here. If not because of this man, maybe I will meet you, or I won't meet you. You know this man from there. You are not a friend to him, but when you came here, you people have become like friends. Or brothers, I don't know. But you shouldn't close my chance."

Then Frankie said, "No! I didn't do anything bad."

And I said, "Look, Frankie, you see. I can tell you the truth. This man is a drunkard. Every drunkard, any person who can be drunk any time, you know, he doesn't hide anything about himself. He hasn't got a secret. All what you have been telling this man, this man has told me."

Then Frankie just sat, very quietly. I said, "*All* that you were telling this man, he has told me. But I don't want to take any action against you, because I know that you want for yourself, and I also want something. But you shouldn't close my road. If you try to do that, this man will shit you. If I try to do what you are doing, this man will shit you. If you like, let's bet." And I gave my finger to Frankie to bet, but he wouldn't hold my finger.[1] So that was the place I was going to get him to pull all his secrets out, you know.

Then he took some excuse that, "Ah — no — you know, I think the first time when I was seeing you with this man, I thought you are Ghanaian, and these Ghanaian girls are very bad. Even in Lagos we have many of them," and that and this.

So I said, "OK, I'm not Ghanaian. I'm Voltaique. So what do you think?"

And he said, "Ah, yeah, I'm also Togolese, but I was born in Ghana, and I grew up in Lagos."

Then I said, "OK, I'm also Voltaique, but I was born in Ghana, too. So we are both travelers. But if you come back to our place, I think you are

1. lock pinkies to make the bet

from the same French-speaking country. Any time we meet, we speak the same language. But we were lost, and we grew up at another country."

So he said, OK, if that will be the case, that and this, that and this.

Then I was *annoyed* with Frankie that day, because he had tried to tell me all his secret, that he thought I was a Ghanaian, and this and that. And Frankie had been following a Ghanaian girl—with his French thieves! He will steal, and this girl will be getting troubles with the police. Maybe he was trying to take me like her. He was trying to take me on this way, isn't it? So when he didn't get me, he had to get annoyed and tell this man something against me. So then, from this time, I was annoyed with Frankie. Frankie was trying to talk nicely to boss me, so I just fucked him off, and then I left him in the bar.

Then I went and woke this man, "Go with your secretary. I'm fed up. Because you have a good secretary who can save your life, who can save your money, too, and then he will come to get double money, so you can fuck off with him."

Then this man—you know, when somebody is drunk, and he has slept, he feels to sleep. When you wake him, he is just yawning. So I said, "*Hey!* Fuck off with your Frankie!"

"Who is Frankie? Who is Frankie?"

Then I said, "Who is Frankie? Don't you know Frankie?"

He said, "I don't know Frankie! I know you!"

Then I said, "You know me? How do you know me? Frankie has been telling you things? To pay my hotel bill and then to leave me nothing for eating. I'm all right. Frankie told you that I have plenty of boyfriends, isn't it? I am not here for you alone."

I just pulled this straight to the man, to know what Frankie told him. You know, this man didn't tell me all these things. He just told me that Frankie said he should take care of himself. But I wanted to put all this for him, so that if Frankie said it, he would also say it. And he said, "Yeah, yeah! Frankie was telling me this. But I don't listen to Frankie." You see? *Ha!*

Then I said, "OK. You had better get up from here. Frankie has been telling you, and you don't listen to it. So why did you pay my room bill, and you don't give me chop money? From today going, if I see you with Frankie, it is finished between us. I won't talk to you anymore."

So this man was still with Frankie. But if he was coming to Royal Hotel, he wouldn't come with Frankie. And I think this man didn't give money to Frankie as before. OK? So then Frankie had to find his way to come and boss me, then we would be friends. So one day, this man came there. I think he came with Frankie, but they didn't enter together. So as this man came in, then he gave me ten thousand to pay my room and then he went. And he told me that he would come back twelve o'clock. He went, and in about five or six minutes, then Frankie came.

And Frankie said, "Hawa — in Lagos — I think — in Lagos, I was living with Fela. I knew the way of the girls. So in this way, you know, I like it very much as you are from Upper Volta — you are not Ghanaian — I think that if we are together, it's nice with Lawyer." We used to call this man "Lawyer." His name was there. I don't know his name, but I gave him the name of "Lawyer," so everybody called him "Lawyer." If you asked him any question, he would give you an answer. So I called him Pocket Lawyer.[1] So Frankie: "You know this Pocket Lawyer — he can talk, he can say anything, so — but I think as you have much experience, I think we can help this man — and just — you know, also to help us for some few times."

So I said, "Uh-huh. Now you have got your sense. So how can we help this man? How can we do this man to have in future, or to have our time keep long with him?"

He said, "You know, I think this man loves you much. And he's telling me — this man was telling me that, since he knows you, he hasn't had sexing with you. He doesn't mind the girls. He says there are some girls who just come to him first time, and they just need sexing with him. And since you have been coming, you don't ask for sexing." Look at this! Do you think I'm going to ask this man for sexing?! "And the way he likes a woman, a woman who is like that, and maybe after, she will love that fellow, and maybe he will be marrying that girl. Because he knows you like that: you haven't had any sex with him."

Anyway, the man — I knew him for quite some time — oh, I can say more than four months. He hadn't asked me for sexing, and I didn't ask, too. He thought that he was waiting for me to ask him. You see the way he was? The man had said that when he wanted to marry, to make a wedding with a woman, it's not possible to sex, and that and this. Then I told him that he's Christian, and we are Muslim. So if we want to be getting married, you don't make sexing before getting married. We were understanding ourselves. Then Frankie was telling me all this.

Then I said, "Yes, you know, as for our place, when you are going to look for a woman to marry, you shouldn't sex her before you marry, because in a Muslim way, and Muslim custom, we don't sex before getting married. So this man, even he asked for marriage, that we are going to get married. So this is the way we are."

And actually, I didn't usually stay with this man at his hotel. He was living at Hotel Miramar. And I was staying in Royal Hotel. OK? Every

1. He acted as if he had a law degree in his pocket.

time, he would come and drink and do everything. If I wasn't fed up, if I felt like sleeping and relaxing, then I would follow him to Miramar. I would sleep there. I would give time to the taxi driver who was going to drop us to come and pick me in the morning before we would pay him. And the taxi would come and bring me back to Royal Hotel. And this man, when he finished from Miramar, he would go to book all of his business and finish, and then he was coming to Royal Hotel to have a drink, and we would drink together.

When we would go to the bed, we didn't have sex. Sometimes this man will be drunk, you know. Sometime he will fall down with all his clothes on. You have to remove his shoes. And every time, he liked a room with two beds. If you remove his shoes and you see where he is, maybe you can't sleep there. You will leave. Sometimes he wouldn't get drunk like that. He will cover you. He will make you nice, putting you on your bed, and say, "Don't be annoyed," and that and this, and he will go back to the other bed and sleep.

And one funny thing: he told me, "You know, I don't want to spoil you." And me, I didn't understand him. That time I thought that maybe he thought I was very young.

So I said, "What do you mean, that you don't want to spoil me? Do you think I'm too young for you?"

Then he said, No, why he said that he doesn't want to spoil me, maybe if he makes love with me, if he makes sexing with me, maybe I won't feel to follow any man again. So that's the meaning that he would spoil me.

Then I thought, "What? So you mean that you know how to make love more than everybody in this world?"

He said, "Not so."

Then I said, "Why?"

Then, you know, this man couldn't talk. Then he laughed. He looked at me and laughed, "Ha-ha!" Then he went to his bed. He said, "Come here." You know this Nigerian English. "My dear, come here. Come. Come here."

Then I went. Then he said, "Will you play me romance?"

Then I said, "No, I can't."

He said, "Why?"

I said, "Because we Muslims, we don't play romance with boyfriends. When we start, when we get married, we can play romance."

Then he said, "No, I want to show you something about why I can't spoil you for the others." You know, I don't even know whether this man could sex. But he had a very *heavy* prick. This thing, if you took it, it was not strong, anyway. It didn't get up like a man. But when I tried to hold this thing, it was just like catching hold of my arm. Then I said, *"What?!"* So this is what he has!

Then he laughed, "Ha-ha, that's why I don't want to spoil you, you know. So the time we get married, then I will know you are for me alone. So that nobody will—" *Ha! Shit! Uh-huh.*

Then I said, "Yes. Because at our place, before getting a girlfriend which you mean to marry, until you know the family, before getting a sexing with you." He can't know my family. And he wanted to know, but you know, I can't take him to my family. So we were just like that, together. And so this man, since I knew him, he didn't take a sexing with me.

So I was with this man like that. He was giving me any time. Any time when this man met me, or any day when he was in Lomé, every time, the day I don't sleep with him, he could give me about twenty or ten thousand. But if I go to sleep there, at this man's place: forty thousand, or thirty thousand, or sometimes fifty. The day he would go to bank to come and make his budget, you know, that time I would get more money. And sometimes he would give me a check. Then that time I didn't have a *carte d'identité,*[1] too, so I would give it to the band boys—the boys who were working in the bar—to go and collect it for me.

If you wanted to take him to the room, if he didn't drink, he wouldn't go. Up till the time he got drunk, then he would say, "OK, let's go home and we will eat something." So we would go. And you will give him a chair, and serve him at table? No. You should bring the chair near the bed. He will be sitting on the bed. So maybe he has one spoonful, two spoonfuls. Then he will ask for Passport. You bring the Passport with plenty of ice, and pour it inside. I used to make it like that, so that water would come inside, and he wouldn't get drunk. But when he got it, then he would drop the glass, *pom!* Then he would fall down. Sometimes, if you didn't take care, he could break the table. So every time, I used to take care of it. If I saw him, and I knew that if he finished this whiskey, he was going to sleep, then every time, I would be sitting at the one side, so if he was going to the table like that, then I would start to draw the table back. Then—*pom!*—he would fall back on the bed. And maybe I would get up and pull his shoes off, to let him have a nice breeze on his feet and everything. Then sometimes I will take his shirt off, but I didn't try to take his trousers, since he showed me his—I had touched this thing of his, so I didn't want to take off his trousers. But this man, good God!

Then Frankie told me that he had a white woman. I didn't believe. Anyway, I don't know whether the woman just liked him because of his money, or the woman had many boyfriends to sex outside with them. But I don't know whether this man could sex a woman.

1. (French): identity card

But he used to smell of drinks. If he was talking to me, the way I was getting the scent of these drinks, I didn't feel it. I would close my eyes. And so always: cigarettes. I will get about four packets. Every time, I was smoking.

You know, when I met him, he used to go and come, go and come. Sometimes he would stay in Togo about one week, or two weeks. Maybe three weeks. Sometimes he could make one month. Then he had a program with this VW company, and he made one and a half months in Togo. We were together. So I think from the time I knew this man, before we went to separate, it was maybe five or six months, together with him.

And if he came to Lomé, he wouldn't go out. If I wanted to go out, he used to give me money for that. You know, after Frankie showed me, and I showed him, we became friends. The time when Frankie and I were all right, any time I felt like going out, I used to tell Frankie, "As for me, I would like to go to the nightclub today, because I don't want to follow this drunkard."

So Frankie would say, "OK. Tell him."

And I would tell him, "OK, I would like to go to the dance."

Then he would say that I should go with Frankie, because Frankie is his secretary. You know? So I should go with Frankie.

"OK."

"Do you want money?"

Sometimes, he would give us ten thousand. Sometimes he would give us fifteen thousand. And any kind of amount he gives us, I know how much I'm going to give Frankie inside of it. If I got ten thousand from him to go to dance, when we got to the gate, I would tell Frankie, "For me, I want to go inside here, anyway, so if you can change your place to go, I don't want to go inside here with you. But I can give you money to go."

Then Frankie would answer. If I got ten thousand, then I would give him two or three thousand. If I got fifteen thousand, I would give him five thousand. That one, as for that, I was good. But sometimes, when I thought about what Frankie had been telling this man, I used to reduce the price and come down. *Ha-ha!* But sometimes Frankie used to boss me. If Frankie bossed me well, I could give him five thousand. But if he didn't boss me well, maybe I would say, "OK, your master has given this amount. And I don't care. You can tell him anything tomorrow, and he will come back and tell me. But we are still here. We will meet again."

So anything this man gave me, I would give a little bit to Frankie. And when this man went to Lagos, me and Frankie, we both knew the time he would come back. But if he went away, as I was alone, Frankie thought that I was one of the girls, those who can go with master and boy. You know? So he was trying his best to catch me: "You are beautiful," and that and this.

"Hey! Don't touch me! Don't you know why I like you? Because I have one son. He is also called Frankie. That's why, when I saw you, your *name.* My son hasn't grown like you, but maybe he will be half of your age. I like you for your name. So I don't want to take anybody who is named like my son."

So Frankie and I became friends like that. And this was the time when Frankie used to call me Mama Hawa, and I called him my son. We started it from that time, up to now. Frankie had a French girlfriend, and she used to call me Frankie's Mama: *"Maman de Frankie."* She used to write me postcards: "Maman de Frankie." She didn't call my name; she only knew me that I was Frankie's mother. *Ha!*

You know, at first I didn't like Frankie, but I think the way he is now, I like the way he is. When I first knew him, Frankie was like a crook. The habit[1] he had from Lagos was some kind of habit like these crooks, these boys who can steal, and that and this, small-small things. And the money this Antonio was giving him, Frankie would just spend it. He would go out with his friends. So he was having this life. When Frankie was living with his family, if you went to Frankie's room, you would pity. The room was very small. And he didn't have a bed. But the way I like Frankie: his way is very *smart.* He's *fast.* Every time when he was going to have trouble, you will never find Frankie inside: they will arrest all the group; Frankie alone will be out. OK? And at the same time, as he didn't speak the real Ewe language, it's now he is speaking the language. Before he didn't speak French, he didn't speak Ewe. He didn't understand much of these languages. Now he speaks them completely. So this is the way I like Frankie's life. And Frankie was sewing my dresses free; I didn't pay anything. Even I could wear a dress, and some girl would like it. If I took the girl to Frankie, maybe he would tell the girl five thousand, or four thousand, or three thousand. And he will sew my own for me, free.

Then this Biafran man went away. Any time he was in Lomé, he would spend his money. But if he went away, I wasn't getting. I was writing him. He gave me his address. I would write to him, and he would write to me back that he couldn't send me money, that if he wanted to send money — this is why I called him a Pocket Lawyer — in Lagos, if you want to send money to the French country, they wouldn't allow him, because he was a business man. That's why he didn't send me money. *Ha!*

1. way of living, character; also: culture

And when he went away, then I got a man from Austria, and I was staying with that man in a village. So when I got that man, then this Biafran man also came back. Then I was in that village, and some people had to go and make kɔnkɔnsa that this time I had a white man. So when I saw him, the time he went and come back, it was too late: they had already spoiled him. When I said something, he said, "Hey-y, you are a white man's wife."

Then I said, "Who told you this?"

But I tried, you know. I have tried. I got a little from him again. So: "Who told you this?"

He said, "Somebody told me."

I said, "It's Frankie who told you this?"

He said, "Not Frankie." He didn't want to prove Frankie again, because maybe Frankie told him not to tell me anything again. So I agreed like that with him.

So at that time I was not living in Royal Hotel again. I rented a room, near to the cemetery near to Royal Hotel. There is a cemetery behind there. The house was for one fucking, crazy inspector, police inspector. I went and stayed at that man's house. I had a small girl for a maidservant.

So this Biafran man, I tried to get him for the last show. I brought him to my place, and I cooked him red plantain, making a stew in oil, a nice one to eat. And I knew the time this Austrian man was going to come back and pick me to the village. So I had to make a way with this Biafran man. As this Biafran man was a drunkard, maybe he could tell the Austrian man that he was my boyfriend. So I couldn't keep him there up to the time the Austrian man would come back.

So the time this man ate this nice food, then he said, "Oh, that's why I like you. But people —"

Then I said, "Yeah, you are listening to people. You are going to spoil your chance."

So I said we should go to Royal Hotel, me and him. I knew that if this Austrian comes back, if I'm not there, he can stay with my small girl in the house. So then I got that Biafran man. It was his *last* show. He gave me forty thousand, because I said that tomorrow I have to go to Ghana and tell my family that I have some man whom I'm going to marry, and that and this. Then he said, anyway, suppose it's tomorrow, he will go to bank, but he hasn't gone to bank yet. The money he has, if he gives me, it can't be enough, but he can give me this forty thousand for my transport. Anything I spend there, if I come, I should tell him. So I took the forty thousand and came back to the house and met my Austrian man and went. *Ha!*

14 A NICE PRISON IN TOGO

: LOMÉ AND KPALIMÉ :

Django and the Fucking Germans

And so that was the time when I met that Austrian man, and I stayed with him at a village. Ah! What do you call the name of that village? It's near Kpalimé.[1] It's where they were cutting trees. But where we were living really was called what? I forget the village's name. Tsukudu! It was Tsukudu! We were at Tsukudu, and from Tsukudu to Kpalimé I think is about two or three kilometers. It's not far.

So when I was living at Tsukudu, I didn't have a problem there. I was all right. But I wasn't exactly staying at Tsukudu. Maybe I could go there for two or three weeks, and come back to Lomé for one week, and go back again. I was just going up and down like that. I still had my room in Lomé near the cemetery. I didn't want to leave that room. OK? Then when I met that man, he said that he wanted me to stay with him at Tsukudu. But at least every three weeks, I had to tell him that I was coming to Lomé to pay my rent. Then I would come and see Mama Amma and all the friends, and we would yab.[2] You know? So I wouldn't make one month there. Every three weeks, I said I was coming to pay my rent, that my landlord was a bad man, and you had to pay before the ending of the month, and if not so, he would put my things out. So this man at Tsukudu, he didn't mind. If I came to Lomé, I would make one week. In that one week, I would see all of the friends. We would yab good. Then I would go back for another three weeks' time.

1. small town northwest of Lomé

2. (Pidgin): to talk roughly (abusively or playfully), to run one's mouth, to mess with; in this context, hang out

I met this man at Pussycat. The girls in Lomé used to call him Django.[1] They said he resembled the man who used to act in Django cinema, so they called him Django. The first time I met him, he said he was at Kpalimé with his wife, but his wife would be going away in about three days, on Wednesday, and that when he took the wife to the airport, from there he would come to meet me at Pussycat. So that Wednesday night he came to Pussycat. We were at Pussycat dancing, and at about one-thirty he told me that he was going back to Tsukudu, because he had a young daughter about twelve years old. The wife had gone, but the daughter would go next week. Then he left us at Pussycat and he went. I was with one girl, Marie Zazu. She is a good girl, a nice tall girl. If you meet her, you will like her. Marie Zazu. So he left us and went back to Tsukudu, and he told me that the next week, when he took the daughter to the airport, he would come to town.

About three days later, he came to town in the daytime. He met one girl, Celia, and asked her did she know where Marie Zazu lived, because when he asked me where I was living, I said I was living with Marie Zazu. But I was not living there. So Celia also was a friend of Marie Zazu, and she knew her house, so she carried him to Marie Zazu's place, and Marie Zazu brought him to my place. He said, Oh, he had come to buy some food; they wanted to make a party, and because of that he was going back. He just came to get some things which they couldn't get there. He had passed to say hello to us, and this and that. So we had some talks, and he said we should drink, and he went and bought some beer. Me and him and Marie Zazu and Celia, we were drunk. Then he said he was going, so as we were three, he dashed all three of us money, five thousand, and he said we should share it, that as he was going back, it was for the three of us to go out in the evening time. Then he went his way.

And that week, when he dropped the daughter at the airport, he passed at Pussycat. At that time I was at the Hotel du Golfe. When I came back to Pussycat, Marie Zazu said, "Oh-h, where did you go? Your man has come here. Just now he has gone out, with some friends."

I said, "Oh, let him go." So I didn't see him. I think they went back to the village. That day was Friday. I didn't see him, up to Sunday. On Sunday we went to the beach, at Ramatou. You know, at Ramatou Beach they have a small restaurant. So we went to that place, and we saw these people

1. hero of Italian-made Western movies

from Tsukudu: my man and one of his friends and one of my girlfriends, too. She was called Tani; she is a Fulani.[1] So she said, "Oh, Hawa."

I said, "Hey, Tani, where are you from?"

She said, "I am from Tsukudu. That is my man, the one I said is in Tsukudu." Her man was a French man, but he could speak German more than a German man. He could speak *nice* German. He was called Henri.

So my man said, "Oh, I came to you that Friday at Pussycat, but I didn't meet you. But I had told you to wait for me there."

And I said, "Oh, that day I was sick, so I was sleeping." *Ha!*

So he said, did I want to eat with them at twelve o'clock? Then I said, Yes. You know, that is the day I ate some rice — that rice, every time I used to go to Lomé, I used to like it. They say it's Spanish cooking. They mix many, many, many, many, many things from the sea inside. That is the day I ate that rice first. After, we went to town. We drank, drank, drank, drank, up to the night. Then evening time, we went to dance. From dancing, then they said we should go to Tsukudu. I didn't know that it was *far* away, you know. I thought it was about three or four miles. Do you know that it's a hundred-and-something kilometers from Lomé? Tsukudu is a village, a small village near Kpalimé. These people were working at a company there: they are the people who are cutting timber. And we were going, going — hey, we didn't reach there.

Then I said, "Hey!" to Henri. Then I asked Tani, "Where are we going?"

Tani said, "Oh, but I am living there, so you shouldn't be afraid."

So we went to Tsukudu. I stayed three days, then I said, "No, I want to go back to Lomé." It was very *quiet! Ha!* That place was very quiet. Night time, sometimes, if the cinema was good, we would go to cinema. They had one restaurant. Now they have a big hotel there. I think they also have a nightclub. But before, there was only one restaurant. And a small bar — a small place, a dirty place: you won't suspect that they can sell beer inside. There's no chair, nothing. If you go, there is a bench outside. It's like a pito house.[2] You sit down and drink beer. The beer, too, it's not a cold one; it's a hot one. So I didn't feel much for the town. After that, too,

1. a large cultural group, known in French as Peul. They are spread across the West African savanna from Senegal into the Cameroons, with the largest concentration in northern Nigeria and Niger. Only a few Fulani groups remain nomadic herdsfolk; nonetheless, many retain their husbandry calling and make their living tending cows for other local peoples.

2. A pito house is a place where people gather, sitting on benches, to drink pito. In front of them are smaller benches with gouged out indentations to cradle a small half-calabash that holds a person's pito.

you know, we were only two African girls. All the rest, they were with their wives, white women, and some of them with their children. So that kind of place, you know, you can't be happy. *Ha-ha!*

Shit. Sometimes, if you go out, eh? They have a canteen. If you are living with somebody there, you just take the name of the man, and they supply you. You don't go with money. Anything you want, even food, they will give you everything and then keep the receipt for him. But every time, if you go there, you know, these fucking — these European children —*ha! Shit!*

You know, some of the children will come and look at you, and then they will ask the mother in German language, "Hey! Where's this girl from?" *Ha!* Yeah? I think as I lived with this man for some time, maybe I could hear their language a little bit.

And then maybe, some of the mothers, you know, when they see that maybe you are watching the baby, she will just make the baby like she's beating her, "*Sh-h!* Don't say anything!"

And some of them, they tried to scratch me. *Ha!* I am sure. *What?!* Look, one baby told the mother — the mother was a nice woman; she was called Ilsa. Every time she used to come to visit me. She would come with her small girl, about three years old. And this girl could talk. She said to her mother, "But it's not dirt that is making her like that?"

Then the mother said, "No."

Then this baby said, "No-o-o." She doesn't believe the mother. So she stopped and watched me and watched me. The next time, when she was coming, she was wearing a white cloth. She took a piece of the white cloth and started rubbing my arm. *Ha-ha!*

I asked her in French. I said, *"Mais, qu'est-ce qu'il y a?"*

"Mais non, mais je voulais voir. Je pense tu n'as pas prend ta douche. Tu pas prends la douche? C'est comme ça je —"[1]

I said, "Hey! What are you doing?"

She said, "No. I want to know. I think maybe you don't bathe, that's why you are like this." She couldn't speak French well, but she just said it plain-plain, eh?

Ah! I had nothing to say to her. Then the mother told me that, oh, I shouldn't mind, this baby is just somebody who is learning talking, so she doesn't know anything. Then later the mother told her that it was the sun that burned me, and then my body became like that. Sun burned me and my body came like that, because when I was a baby like her, I was always

1. (slightly broken French): But no, but I would like to see. I think you didn't take your bath. Don't you bathe? It's like that I—

in the sun. Suppose she would be staying here and growing up, before she would grow up, she would get my color. Then the baby said, Ah! Then she will go to the sun every day. *Ha! God!* Ah, *shit!* She wanted to get a black color, because now she saw that it's not dirt. You can go to the sun every time to get the color.

So, you know, I just didn't like the place. And I wondered. This kind of babies, they used to see many of the black people who work in the factory. But, you know, I think they didn't used to get close, to touch them. But I was free to her. She used to come to me, and do everything. So she thought it's the way to know these people, what kind of people they are. *Ha!*

Yeah. They were so much like that baby there, so I didn't enjoy the place. But if I went there, before I would come back to Lomé, if I needed anything, this man used to give me. Anyway, Django was not rich, but I thought he was somehow OK. So sometimes if I came to Lomé for about a week, and I saw that everything was hanging up,[1] then I would say, OK, let me be free. If I went back there, then maybe I would be getting fed up, and I would get something to come back to Lomé, to make my weekend. So every time I was going there. This man wanted me to stay there. Sometimes I could go there and stay three weeks, and nobody would see me outside. I wouldn't go out. Anything I wanted was in the house. I could cook inside, do everything. *Ha!* Any kind of food I wanted to eat, I would get it. You see, my girlfriend always used to go to town because her mother was living in Kpalimé. Or sometimes, if we needed something, we would give money to this girl's sisters if we went to the cinema in the evening time. Morning time they would bring it. So for me, every day: I could stay there three weeks; nobody would see me outside. Until night time, you will see me in cinema or in restaurant. Day time, you won't see me!

Ah-h, the place was just a fucking place, so if I went there, if I went out to see anything, there were some women, you know, these white women. Some of them are fucking. They used to come and just be teasing you. If they saw the man went to work and left you, then they would come to you and start asking you questions. *Ha-ha!* "Do you know this man has a wife? Do you think this man—he has told you that he going to marry you? Or he wants to keep you as a girlfriend?" You know, this kind of question, they have it.

So there was one fucking woman. Every time, she used to come and talk to me. Every time she came and told me, "Look, Max—" They called

1. going nowhere; nothing was happening; also, hassled

this man Max; I told you that in Lomé they called him Django, but his real name was Max. So this fucking woman had a very *sma-al-l-l* voice. She would say, “You see, you are nice girl. Max not good man. Max wife go—*one* week. Max take you, bring you here. Max should pick you a marriage?”

Then I would look at her, this woman, and say, “What do you want from me?”

“Why you come for Max?”

Then I said, “Why? Why do you ask me? Are you his mother?”

“Oh, no, you no *fâché*.” You see? She spoke English a little, and French a little: she could not speak French, and she could not speak English either, so she used to mix up. “You no *fâché*.” You see: “Don’t be annoyed.”

So then I said, “No, I don’t want this.”

Then she said, “OK, OK, OK. Finish, finish, finish—me no talk. Ah, Max make you marriage? Good!” She will say, “Me no talk.” But she will talk again! “Good, good, good. Max make you marriage. Good! Me no speak. Me speak—you fâché. No. Me no like. You fâché. Max, you, marriage.”

Then I’d be annoyed. I wouldn’t mind her. I would just get up and go to the bedroom and lock the door. Then she would be sitting down in the sitting room: “OK, OK, me go, eh? Me go. You come sit down. Me go.”

Ha-ha! She was a *fucking* woman! You know, they were next door to us. The village, they made it round, but the German people’s was in a line. How they built the houses, it was all one building, but everybody had his part. But their place was big; it was not small. Every place had a kitchen, and maybe two bedrooms. They made it something like quarters, and they built a wall around the compound. All the machines for the work were inside, too. And all the white men also lived inside the compound. All the white people who were working there, they were maybe fifty or forty. And all the compound—where they built the company—the people who were there were all white. The African people, the workers there, they lived in town, in Kpalimé.

So this fucking woman was next door to us, and she used to come to me. Because of her, if I went to Tsukudu, I used to get fed up. “You no go? You go for Lomé? You no stay? You come back.” *Ha-ha!* “Max—no good! Max, Madame, bébé, *two*.” The man had two children with the wife. “Max no good, no good, no good. No good. Max speak you, speak you, pa-pa-pa-pa. Nothing! Max marry for you? No. You stay Lomé, you get fine, fine man. You marry, OK?”

Ah! This woman! I told the man. I said, “Look, this woman is doing something with me. I don’t want it. Tell her that I also have my experience. I know what I'm doing. I don't say that you are going to marry me. I know that you won't marry me. But you should tell this woman not to disturb me."

So this man even had some talks with the woman's husband, and they had a problem, because I think he told the man to tell his wife not to say all these things, and the woman's husband was also annoyed. He said, "But why? Your wife has just gone, now, how many days?" *Ha!* So everybody hated my man in the place. All of them. Only Ilsa and her husband: they were good people. They were the people who used to make me happy a little bit. And then Tani, that African girl, her man, too—Henri—he was French man. He was a nice, good man.

So these people, if the time came when they were going on leave, one man would go maybe two or three weeks, then another one would go. They used to go and come like that. They were many there. It was a *big* compound. They had many African workers in Kpalimé. And when they would come from leave, they wouldn't go out: every time, one man will call a party in his house, another day another one will call his party. So the parties were going around like that, *every* day.

So these our men, as they knew the way, they also used to call their party. They would invite all the people from the compound. It was there: you see these fucking German women? Some of them were drunkards. Some of them, too, were very gentle. So Henri called a party. That day was the day for fighting there.

This fucking woman and the husband came and sat down. They had nothing to do. Only talk about me. And, you know, sometimes, if somebody is talking something about you, you are just there. I was sitting here, and she was sitting here, my man was here, and then her husband was there. So we two women, we were in a double chair. *Ha!* So *all* the ways I saw that this woman was talking about me, I couldn't keep it. I was drunk, too. As for me, if I am drunk, and somebody is talking fucking things, I don't have time. I used to give you cheek. But that time I didn't want to do that. As there were many people, I would disgrace myself. So I told this man, "I beg you:[1] you should give me the key to go and sleep, because I can't help it."

He said, "Why?"

I said, "I'm drunk."

Then this man gave me the key, you know. So this woman told my man, "Hey! You are giving your key to this girl? Your wife went and left all her things in the room, and you are giving your key to her? If your wife comes and something is lost from her things, I will tell her."

1. please

There, you know, that thing came to me like — I became like a fool. Then I told her, "*Prends!* Take the key." She wouldn't take it. I said, "Take."

Oh, there were many people. That day I did something there. But I had a *good* man. He was from Holland. He was also working there; he was the director. He didn't have a wife. This man just liked me like that.

So I said she should take the key. She should hold the key, because she is the sister of this man's wife. So if the man's wife is not there, she is holding the key. These German people, it's their business. So I just told her that and threw the key at her. Then her husband got up and held me: why should I throw the key at his wife?

Then I said, "Who are you? Who are you?" That time, I was drunk. Do you know Ricard, you know, that you put the water in? I had drunk that. And then wine. And I took Cointreau, too. You know, there is sugar in Cointreau. So my head was big. And I was going to do the big things, too. *Ha!* So this man held me. Then I said, "Hey! Don't hold me again! Who are you?"

Then when I pushed him and said that, then this Dutch man got up. He said, "Why? Why do you people want to beat this girl?" And he fucked my man. *Wow!* He said, "Max, God will punish you. You bring somebody's baby, and you give her to your people to be killing her. And you are sitting down there. For what? For what are you people talking? The girl heard it."

Then they said they were speaking German language. Did I speak German? Then the man said, yes, he speaks German. It is the same thing that I heard; it's the same thing that this woman was saying. I heard it. Even if it were that woman, she would be annoyed. So I was right to do it. It's not that I don't respect myself.

Pfft! That night, it was hot! I said that this man should take me to Lomé the *same* night. This man begged me. He did everything. I said, "No." Even to go inside the room and take my things, I said, "No! This door, I won't enter inside."

Drink can work, eh? If you get much drink — *ha!*

So I stood up there. I said, "Go inside and pack my everything from your room, and bring it to me. Because if I go into your room, your wife's things will get lost. In Lomé market, there are plenty of buroni-wawu; they are neater than your wife's things. What would I want hers for? Go and pack my things for me. Me, I dey.[1] Let me go my way."

This party was finished at one o'clock. We took the road. He brought me to Lomé. We were in Lomé at about two or half-past two. The car

1. (Pidgin): I'm here; I'm all right.

spoiled on the road, and we stopped a truck to take me to Lomé. I said he should take me home. He is the one who brought me: the same house where he packed my things, he should go and leave me there with my things. So he packed everything and came and left me.

The same day when he left me, he passed another house and took another girl! *Huh?* His other woman. Vera. Huh? All the girls in Lomé, there are only a few of them who don't know him. He knew every kind of girl. This girl, Marie Zazu, he knew her. She was the first girlfriend he took in Lomé when he came from his country. He said he stayed seven years in Togo. These seven years, the girls he took are more than millions. *Ha!* All the girls, everywhere you call his name, somebody will know him. So he took the girl and went back with the girl. He stayed four days with the girl, then he brought the girl back to Lomé. *Ha!* The girl's friends told me. They said, "Hey? Why? Where is Django?"

I said, "Why? I brought Django to Africa here? I don't like foolishness. He came for his work. Why should you people ask me about him? I'm not the one who brought him."

"Oh, no, it's not so. We saw him. He came and took that girl from our place. That girl, even she has conceived with some boy. She's working at Hotel de la Paix. So the boy said if she comes, he won't take the conceive."[1]

I said, "This is not my problem. You people leave me alone."

So then in four days' time, Django brought this girl and dropped her at her house. And then he came to me. But you know something which makes me laugh? He had promised me many things. Cloths, and then I had said I needed white cloth to make bed sheets. He promised me all this. He didn't give me. Then I was annoyed at him. That day when he was coming, he thought I am a fool. But that day he brought all these things — cloths and things — oh, many things — pieces of cloth — twelve-twelve yards — about six pieces. And different kinds of material which can make bed sheets. They make a special one for that: they were about seven — and pillow cases, curtains. *Heh-heh!*

When he brought these things, you know, he was very funny. The day when he had dropped me, I told him I didn't want to see him anymore. He shouldn't come to my place. The day when he was going to bring me these things, when he was coming, I was upstairs. I think when he was getting to the steps, it was left with about three steps, and he was standing there with the things.

1. He won't accept the baby.

I had a small maidservant, a small girl. Her real name was Yawa, but she was called Vodu. So I called her, "Vodu."

She said, "Auntie?"

I said, "You should go and make me some fire. I want to make tea."

Then she went out. Then: "Hey! Hey! Hey! Hey!" Every time when she saw this man, she used to make so.

Then I said, "Vodu, I said to make fire for me. What are you doing?"

She said, "Auntie? Come and see that white man."

I said, "Which white man?"

Then I went and looked there, and I saw him. I said, "Fuck off! You are coming here? Is it today you know here? Where is your girlfriend you went with last time? Where is she? You think you are a champion? Go and do your champion's work. You are bringing these things for what? I don't want these things. Go with them. Go with your fucking things."

Then my landlord was another drunkard. He also came outside. He was drunk. When he saw this man with the things, he went and got the things from the man, *ntɛm'tɛm'tɛm,*[1] and put them in my room. Then he brought the man. He said, "Sit down." Then he said, "Hey, Hawa, why are you treating people like that?"

Then I said, "Hey, it's not your lookout. I don't want that. Who am I treating?"

"But why is the man standing there, holding these things, and you are talking to him, and you wouldn't let him put them down before talking?"

And I said, "Is this your lookout?"

Then Django was just standing there. He was ashamed. He didn't know how I could know that he had taken a girl. So how I knew it, it was a very big shame to him. And so he was sitting there. He couldn't say anything.

Then I took my tea, finish. It was early in the morning. I finished my tea, then I said, "OK, I'm going to my friends."

He said, "Can I drop you?"

I said, "You can drop me, if you want to drop me."

He took me, and I dropped at Royal Hotel to go and drink. I didn't have any friend there. I just went to see the Guinness. At first I liked Guinness-o! *Tweaa!* Yeah.

That small girl I had, you know, I taught her to cook. She could cook *well.* I would go out, I didn't have any problem: before I would come back, there was food. So I didn't have anything to do in the house in Lomé. Sometimes I would come back and sleep, and she would wake me. It was

1. (Asante Twi): quickly, quick-quick-quick, from ntɛm ntɛm ntɛm

a funny thing: "Auntie, Auntie, wake up and eat small. You see? If you drink and you don't eat, it's not good." Sometimes I would be sitting there like that, and this girl would cut the banku,[1] and put the sauce on it and put it in my hand, and then take my hand like this and put it in my mouth! You know! I was drunk! Ah, you know, Lomé. I think that place just was not good for me. There was not good for me. I was becoming crazy there. *Ah!* I could drink from morning time to evening! Royal Hotel: even if I didn't have money, if I went to Royal Hotel, I could drink. They trusted me. I would pay. I could pay, too. So if I didn't have money, they used to give me drink there.

So this man dropped me at Royal Hotel, and I went there to have my drink. And he also went, and then later he came back to our place. He said that he was not going back to Tsukudu that evening. He would go back tomorrow, so we should meet. OK, then that time I also had another man. He was a stranger. He was not from Togo, but he had come from Nigeria to do some business there. He was in the Hôtel le Benin. I had a promise with that fellow, you know, so I didn't mind this Tsukudu man. I went out with that man, and then the next day I didn't see the Tsukudu man again. Maybe he came in the night and looked for me, and he couldn't see me.

But after that, he came back. The next Sunday again, they came back in a group. We went to the beach again. We went and ate that rice. And that girl Tani was also there with her boyfriend, so after we all went back to Tsukudu again. So I started again with him. OK. We were in Tsukudu three weeks. I came back to Lomé and stayed one week, and then went to Tsukudu, three weeks. Sometimes not quite three weeks, you know, and I would come to Lomé. If it was three weeks when I came to Lomé, then I knew that maybe the next week, maybe Sunday or Saturday, they would come and meet me in Lomé and then pick me back to Kpalimé.

And why I started with him again: he came and talked to me and he begged me and—*ha!* You know, I was annoyed. Actually I was annoyed, eh? But then I also thought, OK, if somebody does you bad, and then he says, "Forgive me," if you don't forgive the fellow, then you are walking in the wrong way. What do you think about that? It's better for you to know that if you are going the wrong way, it's better to forgive the person so that you will walk together again. So I thought of this and I said, "Oh. Shit! What this man has done, I have seen things more than this-o. We can still continue." Yeah. This was what I thought, eh? So I said, OK.

1. a pastelike food made from corn flour

You see? You will agree like that. And you know, maybe there is not anybody who will say that this way is good. Everybody knows that it is not good. But OK: if you think, this way is not good, and you don't know any way which is good for you, then you must follow the one you think is good for you. Maybe if you say it's not good, maybe you are going to stay and stay, and you can't do anything or you can't get any money. So you will *do* it, even if it's not good. You have to force to do it.

: LOMÉ :

Interlude: The Maidservant's Tale

OK? Vodu. She was about fifteen or sixteen. She was a nice girl. Oh, I enjoyed the girl. When I visited Lomé, I went and asked of her. They said she has given birth. She has a baby. *Ha-ha!* Since I left her, she went and married.

How I got her: one of our girlfriends, Patience, had a small girl staying with her. How she got that girl was because she knew the mother. The mother used to sell fufu in the market. We all, we used to go and eat there. When we were in Royal Hotel, we didn't have cooking pots and all these things, so we used to go and eat at the small market, where they sell buroni-wawu. This woman was there. She spoke Ashanti well, and she could make good food a little bit more than the others. So we used to like her fufu. We ate there every day. So Patience told the woman she wanted a maidservant, as a small girl. And the woman gave her her daughter. Her daughter was nice. Very slim. She was a beautiful girl. A black beauty—slim, portable. She must have been about eleven or twelve years. So I saw how she used to go to the market and do these things for my friend, so I also asked for one. We paid them one thousand five hundred for the month. Yeah, it was very cheap. So I looked for one, and I got my own. But my own was growing up. At first when I got her, I didn't like her at all. After about one month, I saw the girl was becoming smart. So I said, "Yeah, this girl, if I hold her, she will be smart." So I held her tight. I used to buy her plenty buroni-wawu. When people saw her in town: *hey!* It was not a joke. Vodu: Black Beauty.

She had a kind of Japanese eyes, so many people used to say she was my sister. I said, "Fuck off!" But many people used to believe that she was my younger sister. So she was with me, and she was a nice girl. It was nice. I paid her fifteen hundred a month. Her family told me to pay fifteen hundred, but I used to give her five hundred for *cadeau,*[1] because she was a nice girl. Ending of the month, I would give her two thousand. No balance.[2] I didn't want the balance. She kept the balance. And then I used to buy her clothes. She had big feet, too. *Ha!* My shoe could not go on her feet. She got big shoes! I bought this *Charlie-wɔti*, the big one, the guarantee Charlie-wɔti.[3] When she got it, she *liked* it. Oh, she was happy. And I bought her buroni-wawu. Different, different skirts; different kinds of dresses. Every time, every day, this girl could bathe about four times, and every time she bathed, she changed her dress. Even if she was in the house. She was funny, huh?

Sometimes, if I was sitting, you know, she used to come to me. I gave her a big valise, and I packed these buroni-wawu inside. Oh-h. Then she asked me, "Auntie, so even if you are going to your country, wouldn't you take me with you? Don't you have a brother?"

Then I said, "Yes, I have a brother."

"Wouldn't you go and give me to your brother to marry."

Then I said, "Why?"

She said, "No, Auntie, I don't want to leave you. I want you to—if I marry your brother, then I will be with you every time."

Then I said, "No. My brother has a wife."

She said, "In your country, they don't marry two times?"

I said, "No, we marry only once."

You know? She was funny. "So when you are going, you will give me all these my dresses?"

I said, "Yes, they are for you. Even if you like, today you can carry them to your place."

"Hey, Auntie! God will bless you. Hey, Auntie, you see, this time when I am going to the market, some people used to meet me and talk French. They think I am a student. I don't understand them. I used to laugh. I just smile, then they also think maybe I hear them." *Ha!*

So she was a funny girl, Vodu. When I was inside the room like that, alone, sometimes, you know—sometimes in Lomé I used to get some kind of—just fucking things. I used to come to the room like I was going to sleep, but I couldn't sleep. I used to turn in bed. This girl had studied

1. (French): gift, tip

2. She paid her with two 1,000 CFA notes and didn't ask for change.

3. flip-flops. The name refers to the easy way one slips into flip-flops; it is an allusion to someone getting up quickly to go out, saying in Ga, "Charlie, wɔti," meaning "Let's go, Charlie." "Charlie" is a generic "guy" name, like Mack or Buddy. Guarantee Charlie-wɔti, like guarantee shoes, are flip-flops with thick soles, i.e., that won't wear out quickly.

me well. As she stayed with me a long time, she knew my character a little bit. I would be so: when I was turning like that, then she would come, with a funny story. You see? She would come and sit down. And say, "Auntie, you see, I told you! You see? The drink is not good. Look how you are trying to balance and — it's not good to drink. You know? Even, if somebody wants to buy for you, if he doesn't give you money, leave your drink for him. Don't drink, huh? You see how you are tired?"

And I said, "Oh, it's not that I am tired. I just don't feel like sleeping."

She said, "Mm-m. Suppose you sit in the house, when you eat and finish, and we talk, talk, talk. You see? You could go to sleep. But this time you can't sleep now. You didn't drink anything, but you can't sleep now, you know?"

So I said, "Hey, Vodu. Go and sleep."

She said, "Uh-huh, Auntie. Tomorrow, what are we going to eat?" *Ha!* "I think the way, if you sleep, maybe I can't see you the time when we get the good market.[1] So you should tell me what we are going to eat."

But you know, there was something I used to do with this girl. I used to do something. I would just put about five thousand in some place. Then I would say, "OK, every time you should take some from inside and go to the market." Then I would see how long before it will finish. So I would give that money in her hand. But this girl, sometimes she could make economics to make one week, sometimes ten days, with this five thousand. But she was cooking well. Then I asked. I said, "Hey, Vodu, this meat: how much did you pay for it?"

She said, "I bought it for one hundred."

I said, "Oh, you lie. Do you know the person? The person has been with you?"

"Hee-hee-hee-hee, Auntie, no. Oh. No."

"But how can he give you —? This kind of meat which you used to buy for one hundred. Even me, I can't get it for three hundred."

You see? And every time, when I asked her if the money was finished, she would say, "No."

Ah! I used to wonder. So the last show, you know, was very funny before I left this girl. OK? My landlord was something like an inspector of police. He had three wives. The one, the child died and she traveled, so he was left with two. The two wives: when I would leave to go to Kpalimé, then this girl would go between these two women. When the small one said something to her, she would go and tell the senior one. When the

1. early

senior one said something to her, she would go and tell the young one. So there was a time when the senior one said that she had lost one pair of her earrings. It was gold. She said she lost it, and she talked this in front of my small girl. Then Vodu said, Ah, she saw that the younger wife of the landlord had brought some earrings to show her that, if I come, she would give it to me to buy. She didn't know whether it will be the same one. OK? So when they talked this thing, then the senior wife came and told the husband. Then the husband said, OK, if that will be the case, they should wait until I come. Nobody should say anything. When I come, maybe the junior wife will be first and see me and give the thing to me to buy. OK?

The day when I came, evening time about seven o'clock, the small wife brought the earrings, in some white material, that she wanted me to give her five hundred and hold this thing for her. She didn't say that she would sell it to me. So I should keep this thing and give her five hundred because she had a problem. The husband gave her chop money,[1] and every time when the husband gives her chop money, she has to give the balance. But she spent the five hundred. So if she doesn't have the five hundred, today the husband will beat her, or something like that, because this man used to beat his wives like horses. So she wouldn't want that.

Then I said, "OK, you know, as for me, I can't hold this thing." Nobody told me anything, but I just don't feel things like that. So I told her, "No. This kind of thing, I can't do it. You are my landlord's wife, huh? If there is something you need, if your husband knows something about it, I can give you. Not to say I will take it off from the rent, when I rent your husband's room. But I just don't want you as a married woman to be coming to me and asking for money. I'm not rich. If I were rich, I wouldn't do what you see me doing. So I can't give you anything. I haven't got money. And I can't keep this thing."

So this woman went away. Then the husband came home about ten o'clock in the night. This woman saw me about seven o'clock. When the husband came about ten o'clock, he sent the children to come and call me in my room. So I went there. Then he said, "Hawa, I want to ask you a question. But this question I'm going to ask you, you shouldn't get annoyed. Take patience and give me a good answer, because what I have seen, I think I have taken you to be just like my sister. So anything that will happen to me, it will happen to you, too. I want to ask you something. Tell me the truth. Did my small wife bring something for you?"

1. money for food

Then I said, "Like what?"

He said, "When you came, when you came from Kpalimé, did you see my small wife?"

Then I said, "Yes, I met her in the house."

Said, "What did she do?"

I said, "She helped me to put my things in the room, and after a few minutes, she came back with some — something. She said it was earrings. Because I didn't want it, I didn't open it. I didn't look at it. I don't know what was inside. It was in some white material. She said that I should hold these things and give her some money. But I thought, I cannot be here to be doing this work. I can take her as a sister. I can dash her five hundred. But married people, I don't go to dash them money, because they wanted to be married, to marry and take their blessing. That's why they have married. And I don't want the blessing, and I am going round and round. So I just took it like a joke."

Then the man laughed. He said, "Give me five! You are a woman." Then he said, "Yeah, you did well. Suppose you gave her this money, then this matter came outside, the way I would deal with you, you would run away from Togo."

Then I said, "Eh?

He said, "Yes, what you did is good."

So from there, he said, OK, I could go and sleep. So I went to my room. Then he called both the two wives upstairs. And this man, you know what he used to do with them when they had a problem like this? Sometimes if he was annoyed, he would *whip* both the two women. Look, the senior one is the one who lost her earrings. OK? The earrings are with the younger one, isn't it? Because the younger one has brought it for me. OK. Then the senior one hasn't got patience with the younger one. The husband was asking the younger one questions, and the younger one didn't say anything. The senior one said *all.* OK. Let the younger one also talk. But you know, some people, sometimes if you say something, they will say, "No, it's not true."

So when the small one wanted to talk, then the senior one said, "No, you lie, lie, lie!" Then they wanted to fight. So this man just got up and took a stick. He had a *big* stick for them —*cho cho cho!* Both of them, he was just beating them like that, and they were all running downstairs. *Ha!* Then I came up, and I wanted to hold him. Hey! He was about to beat me, too! Then I said, "Hey, hey, hey, *fo, fo.*" I said, "Brother, brother," in Togo language. You know, he used to call me his sister, so I thought maybe if I call him "brother," he will know that I am not one of them: "Hey, don't put the stick on me. Oh-h, why don't you take patience?"

He said, "No! But why? You have said your own. Let her say her own, too. Even if she is thief. You can catch a thief with your things in her hand. She can challenge you that it's not for you, because you are not the only person who has this thing. So let her say her own, too. She doesn't want her to open her mouth. What is all this?"

Then I said, "OK, take patience."

So by all means, they had it back from the younger one. And from there, after all this trouble, then I didn't feel happy with that girl, my maidservant. From that time, when she went between the wives and was doing this thing to involve me like that, from there I started not to feel the girl again as the first time when I was doing for her. And she also changed her mind, to do me bad.

You see? Vodu, that small girl who was living with me, every time she was going through all these talks. Look at the trouble: she brought it. She used to go between these women. She found out all these things. She was a friend to the senior wife and a friend to the younger wife. If the senior said something, she would come and tell the younger. If the younger said something, she would go and tell the senior. This is what Vodu started to do to me. So when all these talks were coming out, I was fed up with her, but I couldn't just tell her to go. I felt pity for her. But I was not doing like the first time when I was free with her. First time, we joked together. Then I started to change my life, and show her that, you know, I was older than her. And that time, too, she also was clever. She got to know my point, that I just wanted to see her at some point, so that I would just let her out. So she started to steal my things, one by one.

You know, this man in Tsukudu gave me many cloths. I don't know how many cloths I had. I just cut-cut them. My window curtains: I took cloth to make window curtains. If I wanted pieces, full pieces, maybe three or four, I would get.

So as this girl was living nicely with me, I didn't count my things. But then she started doing some things. If I went to Tsukudu, before I would come, she would open my portmanteau. I didn't lock my portmanteau. She could open my things and choose what she wanted inside. Then she would go and give to one of the wives of our houseowner, my landlord. When I came back, I didn't know that I had lost something because I didn't look at my things, and I trusted this girl. I had stayed with her a long time, so I didn't know that she also would change her mind as I had changed my mind. So she was doing this thing.

Then, I had a *nice* blouse. This man brought it from Germany: five different colors, the same style, but five colors. It had a belt. I liked this blouse, and I knew all the five colors. One day I took some trousers and looked for one of the colors. I didn't find it. *Wow!* I looked through all my things. I had lost two colors; it was left with three. And I said, What? Where's the other color of this blouse? I didn't look anywhere again. I called this girl and said, "Vodu."

She said, "Auntie."

I said, "Come here. Where is this blouse, the other color? You used to wash the things. You know it well. Where is it?"

"Ah, Auntie, look inside."

I said, "Look inside? Where? Go and look for me. Search it for me."

Then I went and sat down. She looked for it for me. She pulled *all* my things *down,* and packed them back. Then I was sitting down. And she said, "Auntie, I don't see it."

I said, "Hey! Don't talk this talk. Don't let me hear this. You don't see it? Who will see it? We are two here. Every time when I used to leave some dirty things, when I come back, you wash them, and you put them back. Now I'm back. So you have to find these things for me. If you don't find these things, get your things out. Right now. Get out."

Then she started crying. So our landlord's wife came up to ask me that, why is Vodu crying? I said, "No, Vodu wants to change her life. So she must go away. She's fed up with me. Maybe she will find another somebody she can stay with, who is better than me. I can't take Vodu today. What I asked Vodu to do, if she doesn't do it today and tomorrow, I can't take her if she doesn't bring that thing back."

Then the woman said, "What kind of thing?"

I brought out all the three blouses for her, that these five colors I had, I lost two of them. Then she said, "Oh. Then if because of that, I will let Vodu find it for you. So I beg you. You leave her."

So I said, "OK, if you are sure that you will let Vodu do it, then as for me, I will leave her. But from today to tomorrow, if I don't see it, I won't agree. She won't live with me again."

So from there, she lied something to Vodu, and then Vodu stopped crying and went inside and slept. Then I dressed up to go out, and I dropped down the stairs, and the woman called me. She said, "Hawa, come here." Then I went and she showed me the two blouses. She showed me three bed sheets, my bed sheets. Vodu had been taking my things, and she told the landlord's wife that I had given them to her. She gave all to the wife of landlord to keep for her, so that if the things were plenty, then she would carry them to her house. She had many of my things.

When the woman told me, then I said, "No. Should I go with this girl to the family house and take everything?" But something said no.

The time when the woman showed me this, it was about ten-thirty in the night. I swear, I was boiled up. I woke the girl the same ten-thirty and packed all her things and put her in taxi to go to her house. I paid the taxi.

You know, that month, when she worked for me, I didn't pay her. I said, "I won't pay you today. I won't pay you tomorrow. If you want, you should bring police."

Then the next day she came with the brother. Then the brother started to come and say something. I said, "If you people want, right now I will take police people to check your house, to see what your sister has been stealing. If she brings something to you people, if I have given it to her, then she should come and tell you as a brother. As we Africans are living, you know, if somebody has your daughter — Look. I came and found the girl. You said I should pay fifteen hundred. OK. I'm paying her two thousand. So it means that I have put something on top of her pay. And I used to buy her clothes. I used to give her some things, huh? Then you can't come to see me? If your sister brings something, 'Oh, it's my Auntie who gave me,' then the next day, you can come, 'Oh, Auntie, we thank you very much for what you have done for our younger sister. Yesterday, she brought things like this and that, that you have given her.' In our real African way, this is what we do. But not that your sister will bring something, to say, 'Auntie gave me,' and then she will keep it. You won't come to say, 'Thank-you, Auntie'? Hey! You are a thief too. Maybe your sister has come and told you that I have many things, so if she has taken some, I can't know."

And it was true. She took many things of mine. Before I got to know, it was too late. She had taken all my things to their place. So when the brother wanted to bluff. I said, "OK, if you people want, you should go and get my things for me."

So the case just finished like that. And you know, sometimes when she would see me in town, she used to bend down.[1] "Auntie, how are you?" And sometimes when she saw me and greeted me, I used to give her maybe a hundred francs or two hundred, if I had money. When I went to Lomé, I asked of her. I went to the woman who was making fufu. She was still in the market.

: KPALIMÉ :

Louky's Problem

So I was there with these German people. I didn't keep long there, anyway. I used to come and go. Maybe I was doing that for five months or some months like that.

1. lower herself in greeting, a gesture of respect

Then: there was one stupid old man. He was Swiss. They called him Louky. This Louky couldn't make love, because his thing didn't work, you know? So he couldn't make love. So every time, what he did, he went and picked up the small, small, small, small girls, the ones who are selling cola and groundnuts and things like that. He would fill up his car with these young girls. Then he would give them Coca-Cola, and he would put some small spirits inside the Coca, and they would drink. When they got drunk, then he would take off the dresses of all of them. Then he would tell them, "You have to finger your friend. And this one has to finger her friend." Then you are drunk, you know, then you people will start doing this, then he's holding your breasts, then he will feel you with the other one putting her hands in this thing, then he will take a photo of all of you. Then he'll wash[1] the photo.

When he took the pictures, he used to give it to the man I was living with, Django. That man was a good photographer; he could wash the pictures and all that. He had everything for developing film. Anyone who took pictures used to bring the film to him, and he will make your photo for you. And he also said, they were friends, you know, as a white life, you cannot charge your friend for small things like this. He said he was working at photography work for about three years before finding another work. So he was just keeping this place for film developing for his children, if he wanted to make a photo for them, or something like that. So if these people brought any photos for him, he wouldn't charge them. But he was buying the medicine, so what he also did, he did them plenty and kept some copies, and he would give you the others. You see his trouble? I don't know what he was keeping the copies for.

So when Louky took the photos, he would bring the film to this man. And this man would develop it. *Hee-hee!* Yeah! So: my man would wash this photo and print it, and then if he made the photos, if he made about six pictures, then three were for Louky, and three were for him, because Louky didn't pay him anything. My man had bought all this medicine for washing the photos with his money, and his profit was: when he washed the pictures, then he would share them fifty-fifty. And he had many, many friends. They used to bring him all kinds of pictures, and he was washing them. In some of the photos, you could even see Louky himself. The girls were holding him like this, and making him like this, in the pictures. And my man would wash all of them, and then they would share them together.

So one day, Louky went and picked two girls. These girls were not small. Even they were big girls. The one was fourteen and the other one

1. develop and print the photo

was eighteen. They were both Hausa girls, but they were born in Lomé. Louky took them, the two, with one of his friends. He was going to give the eighteen-year-old to the friend, and the fourteen-year-old was for him. So they went to Louky's house, in the night. They drank heavily, this Cointreau and all these drinks together. And these Hausa girls, you know, they don't drink. So how the first starting of drink is, when they started to drink, they couldn't know what they are doing again. They drank and finished, and then Louky told them to lie down and open — to be taking their hands to open their vaginas. And they lay down, they did that, and he took their picture. Then the one lay down; the other one made something like a dog. All these pictures — different, different ones, about ten.

And then the other old man said, "No. Louky." I think the old man told Louky it was too much. This old man took his hands to cover these two girls, to cover their vaginas like this. Then Louky cut that photo, too. But you could see the hands of the other old man. You could not see his face.

Then when these girls went home, the next morning when they went home, they were thinking, "Yea-a, yesterday I think we have done something bad." The eighteen-years girl, she didn't know anything; she was a fool. But the fourteen-years girl was very clever.

Then the fourteen-years girl said, "We did something bad yesterday, no?" Then she said, "Yes. It seems like a dream, but I think it was not a dream. We did something yesterday."

Then the other one said, "What did we do?"

"Didn't you see that Louky took us plenty of photos?"

Then the other one said, "Yea-ah, I remember. Why did we do so? What did we do before he took us these photos?"

Then they were asking each other. They didn't know what they did. The one will say, "I think we didn't wear a dress," and the other one will say, "I think I wore pants but I didn't wear a dress," and the other will say, "Yeah. Then me too, what did I do?" They didn't know what they did.

Then the small one said, "No! I will tell my sister." So the small one went to the big sister, and told her, "Yesterday Louky took us to Tsukudu. He made us drunk, and he took us some pictures. We don't like the pictures. So we are afraid. So we want you to go with us to Louky and get our pictures."

So the sister said, "What kind of pictures have you people taken?"

They said, "We don't know. We can't remember. But if somebody drinks, he can do something bad." So they didn't know the way they took the pictures, but they thought so.

So, there was one girl called Ladi. She was also living with these German people. She went to town for shopping. And this sister and the younger sister, they met Ladi. Then, they said, "Ey! Ladi. Louky, what he did he do to us yesterday? Did you—? Louky took us some pictures. Did you see it?"

Then Ladi said, "Yeah-h." Ladi didn't see anything, but Ladi already knew Louky, what he was doing and all that. She knew Louky well. Then she said, "*Ah-h-h!* I swear. They made the cinema[1] this morning. They used these photos to make the cinema. It's you people who made these photos? I didn't look well. Because I was annoyed. I will let people—They will arrest you people. What kind of bad photos did you make like this?"

Then these girls, the two of them, they started crying. "*Eh-h, yeh-h-h.* What shall we do to get these photos?" *Ha!*

And then the big sister said, "OK. If that will be the case, come with me. I will go and tell a big man. No? To go and catch Louky and take these photos from him."

So they went and saw one man. He had opened a bar there. I don't know what kind of man he was.[2] They told him because he was a friend to Louky. Every day Louky used to come to him to drink. So the big sister told this man. Two days: they didn't see his answer.

So there was one old army man, you know, he was in the old military, and now they pensioned him. They called him El Couté. That was his name. Everybody called him El Couté. They said he hadn't been to school, and when he was a soldier, when he was going to shout, *"Écoutes!"*[3] then he would say, *"El couté."* So they took it like his name, in that town. So they went and told El Couté. The fourteen-years girl was a friend to El Couté. Look at a funny thing: a fourteen-years girl was a friend to a person who was in the army and came to pension. An old, old grandfather, with the girlfriend, fourteen years old. *Hah!* So she thought because the boyfriend is one of the old soldiers, if she tells him, he can help to take these photos from Louky.

So when she went and told this man, and then this man said, "No-o. These people are spoiling this town. I must go and tell this case to—" *Ah!* What did they call him? Chef-Cir?[4] I don't know whether it's French or it's Togo language. I don't know. But it something's like—ah, what do you call it? You know, in Ghana they have something like District Officer

1. showed them to everybody
2. what was his cultural or national origin
3. (French): listen
4. Chef de Circonscription. An administrative district was called a *cercle* during the colonial period; after independence the term *circonscription* was used for some time; the recent term is *prefecture.*

or Regional Commissioner. *Mm-hmm.* It's like Regional Commissioner, because he is controlling the whole area. But these people called him Chef-Cir. In French countries, it's something like the chief of the area—*Ah!* So: "I'm going to tell this case to Chef-Cir."

So El Couté went and told this Chef-Cir, for the Chef-Cir to take police and soldiers around the place, to search everywhere, the whole place together with the factory. I told you these Germans had made a big compound like that where they were working, you know, with a wall, and then the factory and their houses were inside. But first, they didn't do that kind of search. First, the Chef-Cir and one friend just came to Louky as if they were coming as friends to take one Coca-Cola and one glass of beer. Before, the Chef-Cir used to come to Louky to drink. So the first time, they went there and talked to this man quietly, and they drank together. Then the Chef-Cir said, "Do you have some film in your camera?"

Then Louky said, "Yes."

"OK, I want to go and take my children. So I will take them. If you wash the film, then you can send my children's photo to me."

Then this Louky didn't have any idea, so he gave them the camera. The film which he took with these girls, the film didn't finish yet. It was remaining some of the film. So he thought this man was going to take the pictures, and then bring them to him, then when the film finished, he could get his chance to wash it. So they went straight and gave the camera to a photographer to take out the film and wash it, then they saw all those pictures. Then they came and arrested Louky. The soldiers came with police to go all around the place, and they entered the compound and made the special search.

When they arrested Louky, in two days, then they brought him to Lomé. Then when they joined the case,[1] they sent him home. They deported him. The day when they were going to deport Louky, he came home to pack his things. Then these people were fools, you know. When Louky got this trouble, they were a group. These our people we were living with, they were five. They were all in the same company. I was living with my man. And then there was Louky and the other old man. And then there were two French people, Alain and Henri. They were five who got this palaver in the compound. They sent them all away! Of these five, Alain had not got a wife; he just came about three months and he got this case.

The day when they were going to deport this Louky and the other old man, the one they saw his hand in the picture, they were the first people

1. hear a case, judge a case

they deported. So the day when they were going to deport them, they brought them back to pack their things. It was at that time, these three people who remained, they saw that this thing was very serious. So the rest of the photographs they had, they had to go and throw them away. And these police people were inside of Louky's room, and Louky's room was like: here is his door, and here is our door. So my man came and packed his own, all, and then Alain packed his own, all, and Henri packed his own, all. Then they put all the photos in an envelope and then put the envelope inside a plastic sack. Yeah, they said they are going to throw it in the bush. So Alain was working where they were getting the water, at a river where they got the water to work in the factory. He was the one who was looking at the machine which was pumping the water. He was an engineer, and he looked after all the machines. So he said they should give the plastic to him so that when he goes there, then he would dig up the sand and put all of the photos there. Then some people came and called him that one of the machines had stopped in the workshop. So he too, when he went to go out, he had this plastic bag. If he was not a fool—at that time they were not searching our rooms—he was afraid to leave the photos in his room, so he put this bag with the photos in his garden. He put it under the flowers. And you know, there were many garden boys there who were working in the garden. Then you go and hide things in your garden! French people, they are fools! *Hah!* So when he was hiding the thing, one of the watchmen saw him. So the watchman just removed the thing and took it to show to the laborer director. He was an African man; I think he was Togolese. He was the director for all the laborers. Then this man just took the pictures and went to give them to Chef-Cir.

When this watchman took the pictures, there was one Mossi man among them. This Mossi man came and knocked my door, and then he said, "Ah! I saw the friend of your husband. He took something to the garden, but I have seen that the watchman took it and ran with it." So that time, I didn't know what it was. So I asked the girlfriend of Alain to go to the workshop and ask Alain whether he had something in his garden. Then Alain came and said, yes, he had something.

And I said, "Oh, the watchman took it. So you too should go and tell my man."

So my man also left his work. They all went to see this African man. He controlled all the laborers, so if a laborer takes something, you must go to him. And this man said, "Oh-h-h, I will give you people. He brought it. It's a picture. I will give you people, but not now, because it's twelve o'clock. I'm tired. I'm going to eat. So if it's two o'clock or two-thirty, you people should come back. You can come and collect your photo." So this man went. Two o'clock, he didn't come back to work.

And then, evening time, these people rushed on our place—police, soldiers—searching everybody's room. They took the camera and all the things which my man used to work with the photos. They took all of it.

Then, we were three girls who were living with them. Henri's girlfriend was Tani, and Alain's was Arita. Arita was Anago[1] and Tani was a Fulani. They arrested *us!* All of us—all of us three! When they arrested me, I had just made ready to go to Lomé. But they just came and took the three of us girls. They didn't arrest the white people. They didn't do anything that day. They just took us girls along—the three of us. *Ah!*

Prisoners for the Lions

I think they took us to trick us. Yeah. They said that we were living with the white people, and then we used to tell them to go and bring the young girls who don't know how to drink. Then they took the pictures and went and sold them, and we shared. Look at the foolish case! *Ha!*

Then the Inspector said to me, "Where from you?"[2]

I said, "I am a Ghanaian."

He said, "*Aha-a!* You Ghanaians come and spoil our babies. We see."

And I said, "Hey, don't tell me this." You know, these white people were very funny, too. The year when they took a picture, they would write it on in the back of the picture. So some of the pictures made seven years. And I told the Inspector, "I'm in Togo here for how many years? And these photos, some of them are from seven years. I am the one who taught them?"

So they kept us for one good week. Oh, they kept us at a *nice* house. Ha! They didn't keep us in prison. They gave us the house where strangers used to sleep when they come to this Chef-Cir. It was a bungalow. There was a fridge; there was everything. We had a cook, every time. You know? The time when they took us, they took us in a way that if they make us good, you know, maybe we'll have some secret to tell them about. So the first time—oh! They kept us nicely. We had beer; we had everything; we would eat, with wine. Everything we wanted, we would get it. Cigarettes—they bought a carton for everyone—each person, a carton of

1. Yoruba
2. (Pidgin): Where are you from?

cigarettes. We didn't worry at all. And even this groove! When people came from town to greet us, they used to bring us groove. *Ha!* So we got it! And then we were enjoying inside!

So with me, there was Arita and Tani. And then Nana, the one girl who was in the picture, the eighteen-years old. The fourteen-years girl ran away to Cotonou. *Mm-hm.* So Arita, me, Tani, Nana, and then another girl again — I forgot her name — that girl, she also had a picture with these people — and the picture was seven years old! Even she left long ago from the time she made this fucking thing. She went and married some man, and she had conceived for three months. They went and arrested her from the husband's house. Togo is very funny, you know? They arrested her from Lomé, because one of the policemen knew her. But by then she had married some man and she had conceived for three months. They went and arrested her, too. She was among, too. That is five, eh?

And there was another one again. Another one with five or six months conceive, too. She had a baby with one man at Tsukudu, and her photo was there. It wasn't Louky who took her photo like the other girls, but the police people saw her picture among all the photos. She went to give birth to this baby in her village, and she didn't come back to Tsukudu again. She stayed in her village and married. The first baby had two years, and she conceived again. And then she was conceived again, five months. The man who had the half-caste baby with her was called Yves, and he had left the work about two years, I think. A long time ago, when Yves's girl left this ashawo work, and she went and married, she had made a report on this man, that he wasn't helping her with the baby, and that the police people should help to get something for her. She stayed quietly for about three or four years. Then the police people telephoned to that village, that they wanted to come and pick her, because they had arrested these people at Tsukudu. The police people said, "Ah, the case you reported to us — now, we understand. We know the fellow. He has done something. We want to send him home. So you must come and see — we want to send many of them away — you must come and see if your man is inside, then we'll let him pay an amount for you to look after your baby." When this girl came, then they locked her, too! *Ha!* And then they showed her her picture. Yeah, they also made their cinema. They said, "Do you see what you did? That's why we followed you. We didn't follow you to give you anything. Is this good?"

She said, "No."

Then, we three girls, me and Arita and Tani, we didn't know what we did to be in the police station. We had no pictures with Louky. Inside of all these pictures, we hadn't any picture. The two pictures we had, one was me and Tani, and we were wearing the same dress, with up-and-down. We were going to Kpalimé in the day time, and we stopped there on the road, so we held each other and kissed and took the picture with our dresses. Then, we also had one photo at some river near Kpalimé. We went there to swim, with our swimming pants. These were our pictures there. We hadn't got any other picture. But the police kept us with the other girls. They wouldn't tell us anything. The first time, they said that, eh, when we were together with these girls, we knew all their ways and so we must tell them.

Then Arita was annoyed. She said, "This is stupid. You can't put me in prison to be a—a spy to a prisoner. I'm a prisoner, too, no? Because you people are watching us. How can I be a spy to my friends? I can't do it."

Arita was a girl who was hot![1] When we went to Lomé, the man there asked her, "What kind of family are you from?" Then she called the family name: the father was a Yoruba man, but the mother was Togolese. Then they said, "Have you finished your school?"

Then she said, "Yes."

"But why don't you try to find some work to do?"

Then she said, "OK. I want work to do, but I didn't get. If you can give me something to do, I will do it." *Ha! Hee-hee.*

Yeah. So we were there for one week, and then after one week, this Arita, you know, she was senior to all of us, she said, "Hey, if we make ourselves cool here, we will remain here. So we mustn't make cool." So: everybody didn't eat that day. We drank all the drink from the fridge: it finished; the whiskey, everything was finished. Then we started to break the bottles in the house—*ch-ch, ta-kr, ta-kr.* The plates, with the food, all: we broke all. Then this police man who was guarding us, he tried to bring himself. Then Arita said, "If you don't know, you will open this room and enter here. I didn't kill anybody, I didn't do bad, and they put me by force in prison. I'll kill you, to get my first prison."

Then this man was afraid, so he didn't come in. Because we were drunk, and then we smoked groove, too, you know? *Ah!* That place was a *very nice* place. If we had to go to the toilet, we would go one by one; you can close yourself inside. You will booze fine with the groove, then you go out, then the next one comes. *Ha!* It was another good place, eh? Even, the day when they told me to go and leave the other people there, I was crying, "I don't want to leave! I want to stay!" *Ha! Ha!* Yeah. Then, every time, we used to get dash, too. If people came from town to greet us, they

1. She could become annoyed quickly or easily.

used to give us dash, so we had money all the time. We didn't buy anything, either! *Ha!*

So when we did all this, they went and telephoned the Chef-Cir. When he came, then Arita said, "*I swear,* any fucking man who enters, we will kill him."

So the Chef-Cir said, "Oh, Arita, it's me, it's me, Chef-Cir. Let me enter. I want to see you people. I know you people are suffering. Yes. I'm going to do something about it. Especially you three girls. You didn't do anything bad. I must leave you people free. But we want to understand these German people before." That time, they had made these people under house arrest in the compound. They were three. They couldn't go out. They could go to their work: police people were there with them. But they could not come to town. The police thought maybe they would run away.

So one Sunday, the Chef-Cir said, "OK, to finish everything, tomorrow is Monday. We are going to Lomé. Then we will finish everything. Then you people can go." *Ah!* We were happy, eh? Then the next morning, even it was before morning, we woke up early — about four o'clock in the morning. Then we left from Kpalimé, because from Kpalimé to Lomé, maybe it's one hour and some minutes when the car is going fast. So we took a car. The company of these German people, they gave them one of the busses with a driver, to take them. So we reached Lomé about five-thirty in the morning.

So, we had to go to the — ah, what do they call them? — they are army people — the big ones. I think it's like a *gendarmerie,* or something like that. It's the big place for all of them, where they are living and where they used to make their army training. They took us there. Then they said, "Everybody who wants to take tea can come and take." So we all refused: we don't want to take any tea; all of the girls, nobody took any tea. So they took us to the big man's office first, to make some papers with these white people. And about seven o'clock, we went to Eyadema's[1] office there. We stayed there up to eight or half-past eight. Then they called all of us. When we went first, everybody was standing, then one man brought out the photos. All the photos, oh, maybe they could pass three hundred or five hundred or one thousand. Different kinds of girls. They brought these photos, and they put all the photos on a table.

Then this man looked at these photos. He shook his head like that, then he asked these white people, "What did you people come here for? For this? Or what did you come here for?" Then they said they came to work. Then the man asked, "For what are you people doing all this?"

1. General Gnassingbe Eyadema, the Togolese head of state

Then they said, "Anyway, everybody used to do something bad, or make mistakes." So they made a mistake. They have nothing to say. They are guilty.

Then he said, "OK."

Then the man I was living with, you know, he said that all the photos, he was the one who had them, because he was the one who washed them. Louky and the other old man brought the film to him. You see? He wanted to save these other two people, you know, so that if he carries the trouble alone, then they will leave these people in the company to work. They were five, but the first two were deported fast, and now they were three remaining. The day when they arrested these three, they didn't send them. They kept them under house arrest, before they took them to join their case in Lomé. And we girls were also in that bungalow. So the day we came to Lomé, that was the day we all came together. Yeah?

So this man wanted to carry all the trouble for the other two. So he said, "All these photos are for me alone." But the mistake they did, everybody with his pictures, they wrote their names on back of the envelope.

Then they said, "But what are all these three envelopes for? So the three names are for you, too?"

Then he said, "No, the three names are not for me. What I said is that these photos are for me. It's me. I used to get the pictures, and then I used to give them some." He used to dash them, so he is the one who brought the whole trouble.

So they said, "OK, if that will be the case, then quickly, get lost from here. We don't want to see you anymore."

And they left these two people. So, my man, oh! It was very pitiful for him that day. The way they did this man to get him to the downstairs, pushing him, and some people slapping him. "Stupid idiot!"

And oh! It was very pitiful, eh? He poisoned himself. That man, they said he poisoned himself. The *same day!* Do you know, the day when they said they would bring them to police station, I think that in the morning time he took something. They put him on the plane, to go and drop him in his country. Everybody came down, and they saw him sitting like that. Then the women who are walking in the plane, one just turned to touch him, and then he fell down. And they took his body to the cemetery. The same day they put him on the plane, that day he was dead. Even he didn't go back to Tsukudu. The clothes he was wearing every day, and all his clothes, they said they would post it after. They didn't let him to go back to the village even to prepare something. From that place up to the airport with police people, then they were waiting for the plane. And they just put him inside. And then he too, before he dropped at his country, he was a dead body. How? I don't know, because the company wrote a letter, after this case, to the two boys remaining, Henri and Alain, to tell them all this. So I thought what made this man kill himself was shame. Yeah, it was shame, because he had two daughters. So maybe he felt that when he goes back, people will laugh at him. Maybe he thought the wife would be laughing at him.

You know, when Louky's palaver came, everybody was afraid. All of them in the compound, *all* of the German people, on that day they were shit. They were afraid. OK. So everybody—I think many of them had these pictures, and they threw their pictures away, so they were safe. There were many of them I knew who used to come to Lomé with the girls to the beach, and this and that. But they had wives: their wives were in Tsukudu, you see? So all of them threw away their things. It was only the five who were arrested.

Louky and the other one, they deported them first. Only this fucking Django, he didn't have luck, with Henri and Alain. But Django took three people's troubles. The one who was going to throw the photos away, at that moment they reported that the machine had spoiled, and he was the only engineer to repair the machine. So he only went and hid the photos in his garden behind his house.

And you know, the police still kept us girls. So Henri and Alain, these two people, every time they had to bring money for me, and they had to do everything for me. They said my man took all their trouble. So everything, even when I came back from that place, they were the ones who gave me money to make my transport. And all my things, my dresses with my suitcase, they kept it for me. When they wanted to make all the parcels of the man, then Alain and Henri said, no, they know my dresses and they know my things, so they chose my things out. The only thing I didn't get was my sewing machine. My man bought me a foot machine; that one, I didn't get it. I think they put it with his things.

Then this Henri and Alain were still in Togo. Then people started to watch them, too, small-small. Sometimes they would go out, and some small things, and then they would have problems at police station and all this, and so they also left. They went by themselves. They stayed for some time but they didn't keep long in Togo after this case.

But the police were still keeping us there! Yeah. The day they took us to Lomé, at Eyadema's place, when they finished sacking this man, it was now us girls they were asking questions. Yeah. This case, you know, they joined the case from the white people first, and they sacked this man. Then it was left with the girls. They called each of us, "Come here." Then we went. They showed you your picture. "What you did is good?" We said, "No. No, what I did, I—it is not good, but forgive me," you know, like that. All the girls who had photos, they asked them, and the girls said, "Forgive, forgive, forgive." Then it was finished. It was left with us three, you know. That time we were in Eyadema's office, the same day.

Then this Eyadema man[1] called Arita. Then Arita went. He said, "Look at all these things. Is it good?"

Then Arita said, "No, it is not good."

Then he said, "Go."

Then he called Tani, "Tani, you see what your sisters are doing? Is it good?"

And Tani said, "No."

Then they called me, "Eh, what you see your sisters do, is it good?"

Then I said, "No, it is not good."

Then he said, "OK. The best thing to do with these people: we must carry all of these girls who have the pictures, to go and put them on the road of Dapongo."[2]

Did you pass that road before? There is some place, a mountain place, with big, big stones, two of them: one is here, one is there, and a car passes in the middle. There are some holes, like a hill where you can pass inside. They said if it's day time, if we are coming from this place, we can go inside some hills, and it's like a house, down into the hole. So he said they should carry all these girls who have the photos, and go and throw them there, because there are many lions there. It's good for the lions to eat these girls. It's not good to let them live.

OK, when he said that, *Hey!* Come and see everybody: *"Wey, wey, wey, wey."* They were all crying.

Then, you know, I had grooved early in the morning—a thick one!—me and Tani. So it was making us laugh, me and Tani, every time. Any small time we looked at each other, then we would smile a little. We thought they were going to leave us, because the man said the people who have the pictures, but we didn't have pictures, so we knew that we were free. Then: they went and put us inside the car.

Then we asked, "Oh, Chef-Cir, but this man said you should leave us. So why?"

He said, "No, I didn't catch you people here in Lomé. I must go and leave you people in Kpalimé. It's Kpalimé that I have arrested you, so I must leave you people in Kpalimé." So then we knew that if we got to Kpalimé, he was going to drop us there. And he took us to Kpalimé. We

1. man from the party or employ of, representing Eyadema
2. town in the far north of Togo

passed straight, up to the place we were living. Then he said we have to wait there, and he is going to go someplace and come. For *three days,* we didn't see the Chef-Cir! Hey! After three days, he came there and said, eh — if he leaves us, the other girls — the girls who he is going to put in jail — they will say that and this — ah — so he cannot jail us — but we have to wait for some — for some time.

Look at the foolishness! So we were there. Every time, to see the Chef-Cir, the Chef-Cir said he has to go and see this man, and he said he's begging Eyadema, and he was saying, "Because Eyadema told me to give all of the girls to animals, because you don't have pictures, but you are following Europeans, you are also the same people." Look at the charge they put on us! Yeah. So we all must stay there until he begs Eyadema so that they will leave us.

If All the Prisons Were like This

So, you know, they have some kind of women there in Togo. They are like the time when Nkrumah was there, he had some people — the C.P.P. — on the women's part, like these market women from Makola market: when Nkrumah was going to some place, they used to beat gongongs[1] and dance and be putting their cloth down for him to touch. So in Togo they had something like this for Eyadema. He too had the same things. Yeah, he also got some people like that, and they called them R.P.T.[2] So this R.P.T., some of the big women inside, they came to see us. You know, this Tani had her mother at Kpalimé, and Arita's mother was at Atakpamé.[3] And this girl who conceived, all the family, and the mothers of Tani and Arita, they went to see these women. This Chef-Cir said that unless they go and beg Eyadema; if it not that, then he can't do anything about it. So they too, they went and saw these women, because they were big women, to go and beg Eyadema to leave their children, that they did bad but they won't do it again. Now, if the police people will leave their children, they will hold their children well.

So these women used to come there, and one woman said, "Yes! If this place was Zaire, it is good to put these girls in the grinding machines and mill them." *Ha!* Then, you know, Arita hasn't got patience. Arita said,

1. bells

2. Rassemblement du Peuple Togolais, the general assembly, like a parliament but basically a one-party movement under Eyadema

3. small town north of Lomé

"Hey! We all who are here, not all of us have pictures. So she is taking us to be the same thing." Arita just held this woman, and she said we should beat this woman, and we all beat this woman. So now we must be in jail! *Ha ha ha!* She was something like a big woman to Eyadema, something like the people who follow his back when he's going to some place; they are the people who dance and follow him and all this. Then, we caught this woman and we beat her.

So now, they had a chance. Already, they wouldn't leave us; already they didn't want to leave us. So then this case: they said that as for us, they begged and they said they should leave us, but how we beat this woman, they cannot leave us, so we must stay there. So we stayed there seven months. *Seven months!* In that house. When they left us, they were sending the other girls, the ones who had the pictures; they picked those girls with the car again. I don't know where they were going to put them, whether they were going to put them someplace, or they were going to put them in prison. I don't know. And so, with these girls, we made seven months there. All of us. When they left us three, then they took the other girls with the police car again. *M-hmm.* So I don't know where they put them. The girl who was conceived five months, she stayed there three months, and then they left her. The three-months girl, she was sick seriously when it was one month, so they took her to hospital. From there she was well, and she didn't come back; they left her to go away. So we were three from the company compound, and then the rest. We were nine girls, all of us; the time they arrested us, we were nine girls.

We had one girl: the father was Ivorien, from Côte d'Ivoire, but the mother was Togolese. This girl also had a picture there from a long time before, and then she went to Côte d'Ivoire. So by then, she wasn't doing any work, and she bought Ivorien cloth and brought it to Lomé to sell. She gave her things to the sister to sell, that she will come back for her money. And the sister was married to the Inspector of that area, so the sister took the money and gave it to the husband to hold. So when this girl came back, she went to the Inspector to collect the money, and then the Inspector carried her to the Chef-Cir, and they locked her.

So that seven months in the house, yeah! Food and drink, all, we had everything. Even sometimes we would go out. You know, we didn't feel the thing. When they did all this to us, we ourselves, we didn't understand. It was looking like they made us something;[1] we didn't feel like going away. We didn't feel anything like that. Look, you can come out to the

1. made juju on us

market to buy what you want, then you will walk back or you will take taxi back to the place. Look at the foolishness! Why? We didn't know!! We didn't know why! It was the day they left us before we said, "Ah! We were fools to stay here seven months." Look, the time you go to the market, you can take a car to Lomé. From Lomé, you can go to another place. But this type of mind didn't come to us when we were there. Because I thought we ate plenty, and we had groove, and every time we got drink. What we wanted, we got. Yeah, even we got grooving. We had drink, we had music, and all this. So: we forgot to go home!! *Hee! Ha!* Yeah, when I came back to Lomé, I was fine: red and fat, you know. Eating free, *ah!* We didn't cook. We didn't do anything.

And then too, the people in the town used to bring us food — plenty! — we couldn't eat all of it. The girls they arrested, their families used to cook food for them and bring it there from the house. Different, different, different foods. And they were cooking for us there, too. The place where we were living, we had a cook, and he was also cooking for us there. So the food was too much. When you come to the room, you will see different, different foods in a line. You open this, you don't like it, you close it, you go and open there. Yeah, if prison was like that, it would be good, not bad. I haven't seen any thing like this in Ghana or Upper Volta. I haven't seen this thing before. Only in Togo did I see this.

When I was there, nobody from Lomé came to visit me. Even Mama Amma knew the other girls. When I went back to Lomé, they said if they came there, the police would arrest them too, so they didn't come. That's what they told me when I went back. Even Jacqueline, Jacqueline came and stayed in my room in Lomé, about three months, I think. Then she told Mama Amma that she came there to Kpalimé, and they said they wouldn't let her see me. And I said it's a lie. Everybody who came to greet us, they would bring that person straight, anyone who wanted to see somebody. Even we ourselves, we were going to the market. We could go to Zongo[1] to get groove; if we didn't see somebody to send, we could go by ourselves to get the groove, and then go back there. The police people didn't know we were grooving, but sometimes, some of our friends from the town would bring it to us.

And what is funny, you know, the three of us, we said we didn't do anything bad, and so we don't have any bad name, and so we will stay up to the time they want. We used to go to town like that. Me and Arita and

1. (Hausa): a section of any town where people from other African cultures, generally savanna cultures, live

Tani, we could go to any place we wanted. Yeah. And sometimes, we used to do something funny. Sometimes we would go with a car to Tsukudu, to give a letter to the watchman at the gate to go and call these people for us, to talk to them, and we would use the car to go back to the place. *Ha!* Our minds didn't make us think of running away, because we thought we didn't do any bad. Maybe if we went away, they would say we ran away. But we didn't do any bad, so we wanted to understand the meaning of why they brought us here. But there was no meaning. Later they told us that because we beat that woman, we had to be in jail, so we had to stay there.

Ah! Togo! *Ha!* Yeah, one time when you came to Lomé, I was at Kpalimé in this case. When I came back, Mama told me, "John came here. He missed you. He was very sorry for you." Ah-h. But we had a nice prison in Togo. If all the prisons are like this, then every day I will cause trouble and go to prison. Oh, yeah! You can get drink, you can get groove, you can get anything. Even if we didn't have beer, or if the beer was getting short, if we didn't see the Chef-Cir, we would just boss the police people, "Good morning. Morning, morning," and they would send the houseboy, and he would go and buy us a case of beer. Even when we were there, we were having money, eh! We could buy everything. Even if somebody had about two thousand, she didn't have anything. People will come and greet you: "Oh, sorry! Take this, and you can buy something." And these people from Tsukudu, they always sent us money. With an envelope. They said if we are short of money, then we should write to them. Their driver used to bring food.

So this police case, our case, it was wonderful. Yeah, the first time I was in the jail, I was crying. "Yeah-h-h. Eh-h-h, so-o-o, if these people are going to kill me, how can my people hear of it? I don't have anybody here. Who will hear of my death, and then he will go and tell my family?" So in the night, it was only this that I was thinking. In the night, if I grooved heavily, I could not sleep. Every time, I would go to the toilet; I would come to the sitting room; I would go here, go there. Everybody was asleep, snoring, *"Houn, houn, houn."* Then I said, "Look at these animals." *Ha!* "They have nothing to think; their head is full up with yams." Yeah. Then every time I just used to go round, round, round.

And Tani too didn't sleep. Tani didn't sleep much, because she also was thinking about her mother. Every time, she said, "Yeah-h. If something happens to me now, what is my mother going to do with my young girls." Her father was dead, and the mother had small children. Tani was senior among them. And so she also used to think about her mother, the way her mother used to suffer. Every time, the mother would bring us food, too, and be walking up and down. From the town to where we were living, it was maybe one mile. This old lady would walk, and it was on top of a hill. They built this place on top of the hill. All these warders and then this Chef-Cir, they all had bungalows in back of there. So to go there, you will climb a hill, a big hill. So Tani used to say, "Eh! My Mama will climb this two times a day. Oh! My old lady will die for me."

And when they caught us, the girl who came from Côte d'Ivoire, you know, she was a friend to the Chef-Cir. She was called Rosalie. And when the Chef-Cir said he was taking this girl to lock her and all of this, this girl started fighting. She said, "Stupid idiot! Don't you know that you fucked me before? And you are going to put me in prison! I'm not going to enter!" So they were fighting, but the girl was strong. Eh? They were beating her—*pap, pap, pap*—and all this. She held one policeman on the ground. Ah-h! It was very nice. I saw that she held where she shouldn't hold, and this man was shouting, *"Make—her—leave—me!"* Then he just lay down quietly. And they were beating her, on top of this man. She didn't leave this man until they also left her, and then she let go of this man. So they put her in the cell. This cell was in the prison hall, the big hall. They had small cells in the middle. They said that if you kill somebody, they have to put you there.

So they kept this girl there about three weeks. She didn't eat. She pissed and slept with the piss. Morning time, they would bring her out to go and throw the piss away. And every day she abused these police people. She didn't care about anything. But she was not a smoker: she didn't know how to groove. Whenever we were grooving, she was just watching. After all this, after three weeks, they brought her to our place. Then she was very, very quiet. She said, "When I come out, I will show this man! If this man really fucked me as I said, this man will never be free. This Chef-Cir, I will show him." Ha! You know? So every time, when we were sitting together, she would become quiet.

Then I said, "Oh, sister Rosalie, why you are sitting quietly like this again?"

"I am praying to God. If I don't die here, then I will come out. This man! He won't leave his life, but it will be hard for him."

So, I don't know whether they left her. You know, the day when they were leaving us, I told her, "If I know where they are taking you, if I ask people, if they show me, I'll come and see you." But I was asking; they said they didn't know where they were taking her then. If they took these girls to Dapongo prison, I don't know. They have a prison in Dapongo. So maybe they carried them to that prison. Yeah. But as for us three girls from Tsukudu, we only stayed in the bungalow.

Fish from the Sea in Vaginas

And do you know something very funny? People were saying funny things in town. People used to come to us, plenty, to see us, and we thought, "Ah, why do these people come like that?" Do you know that these same people were talking? In town, in Kpalimé town, people said that they arrested some girls because when they went to the beach, they opened their vaginas and the fish were going in. And they said they had a picture. They said that if you see the picture, you will see that the fish is going inside, and then he makes so, and then he shakes, and then he turns and he goes out, and then he's going. *Ha! Ha! Ha! Hee-hee!*

So when we went to the town, and we heard this, we said, "Oh-h-h, *good God!* What kind of fish knows that this is a *toto*[1] so I must go and enter there, and then shake myself and go back again to the water? Did you hear this before? Which girl will open her vagina, and a fish is coming to go inside, and she doesn't fear and close it?" *Ha! Ha!* They are very funny, eh? So they were saying all this in the town.

So the day when they left us, when we came to the town, they said, "Is it true? Did you people see the photo films, of these girls — and the fish was going inside and coming out?"

Then we said, "Which kind of fish?"

And the people said, "But they said — the people who saw the photo — they said there was a fish — they said the girls opened this thing at the seaside, and a fish used to come inside, and then get in and shake, and then it would go back."

Then we said, "Ah, we didn't see that picture." Then I thought that maybe some people didn't look at it well, because maybe they saw that picture when that man was trying to cover the vagina with his hand, and when they saw his hand, they thought maybe it's a fish. This is what I think. Maybe they didn't look at it well, and then they thought, yeah, this is a fish. What kind of fish is that? What fish knows how to go inside and go back and get into the water?! How are you going to call the fish out of the water to come and see a vagina's inside and then go back to the beach? Ah! Togolese!

And some of them said, "Some of the girls, they put a candle to stand inside the vagina, and then they lit it, and they made a photo." Some of them said that. *Ha!* You know, if something happens, everybody just says what he likes. Even if he doesn't see anything, he can still have something

1. (Ga): vagina; vernacular: pussy

to say about it. And so this is what some of the people were saying in the town. You know, they didn't put anything about it in the newspapers for people to read, so the people were only talking about it. If they write it like that, it's their palaver; it's their disgrace in their country. So they didn't put it. They wouldn't do that. And so in the town, some of the people said that they put some eggs in some people's vaginas, and they took pictures. *Hey!* How can you do that? So when we went to town, they asked whether it is true and we saw these pictures.

We just said, "We didn't see that. We saw the vagina pictures, but we didn't see the fish one, and we didn't see the eggs one. If they have it — that one — they didn't show it to us." Yeah.

So this palavar, this trouble made plenty of Togolese girls run. Some of them went to Abidjan; some of them went to Ouagadougou. Because there were many of them who had photos inside. Even I had one friend called Maku — she is a Kotokoli — she had a picture, too. She went to her village, to hide herself for about six months before she came back to Lomé when the case passed. Many girls ran away from the town. *Mm-m.*

So after they left us, I went back to Lomé. But do you know? I went back to Kpalimé two times. Do you think I am afraid of things like this? *Ha-Ha!* You know, the day when they were leaving us, the Chef-Cir was giving us advice: "From this time, when you people go, you must sit quietly to find a husband to marry, eh? Don't follow these people again. We are just punishing you people so that you will stop following Europeans." Then, the very day when they left us, they got a car, and they said they would drop us where we wanted.

And Arita! Arita said, "As for me, you should drop me at Tsukudu."

"*Huh?* Tsukudu again?!"

She said, "Yes. But why? I didn't kill somebody. I must go there again, because my things are there, and my man is still there. When I was in prison, he used to bring me money to eat. He didn't leave me."

So this Chef-Cir said, "No, drop down and take a taxi. We are not taking you with this car to Tsukudu again." *Ha-ha!* So she didn't care; she didn't care at all.

Coda

After they left us, I was at Lomé for about two or three months. Then I got a man. He was doing some work at Parakou[1] in Dahomey, and I used

1. town in the middle of Benin

to go to Parakou with him. When we went, sometimes we used to pass Kpalimé for his work before we would go to the north of Togo and pass to Parakou. So when this man took me, we had to sleep at Kpalimé. We moved from Lomé at about seven o'clock in the night, and we reached Kpalimé around nine o'clock. So he said that we should rest, and then if we continue in morning time, it would be better. They have some hotel on top of a hill. So we went to that hotel.

When we were going to enter, I saw the Chef-Cir. I said, "*Eh! Hey!* Chef-Cir! How are you?"

He said, "I'm all right. And you?"

I said, "I'm all right." Then I said, "Here is my husband. Greet him."

Then he looked at me and said, "*Woa! Woa! Womule vɔn nu o.*[1] You! You! You don't fear anything."

And I said, "Why? Why? I want you to greet my husband. And you say I don't fear anything." You know, I wanted to show him that still I'm walking with a white man. Yeah?

Then he greeted this man, and this man asked what would he take? Then the Chef-Cir said he wanted beer, and they got him one bottle of beer. And the Chef-Cir wanted to return it again, and he asked us, what did we want to drink? Then I said I wouldn't drink again, and this man said it was OK, we didn't need anything. And then the Chef-Cir said, how can he see this man again.

Then this man said, "OK. Tomorrow, evening time, we should meet."

Then, when the Chef-Cir went away, I told this man all this story, you know, how they caught us, how they put me in that house, and all these things. And when I told this man, this man said that suppose he knew, he wouldn't buy the Chef-Cir a beer.

Then I said, "No, the way you bought him a beer, I like it. It's bluffing. *Ha-ha!* The next time when I meet him, I will say, 'You say I shouldn't follow white people. Suppose the day you met me in the hotel, if I didn't have a white man, who will buy you a beer?' *Ha-ha!* So it's nice when you buy him a beer. Yeah."

And the day when I passed Kpalimé again, I also saw the Chef-Cir, and I asked, "Where are the other girls?" He said he went and gave them to animals. I know he didn't give them to animals. He didn't want to show me where they were, because he knew I would go and greet them. He didn't want it. So that's why he didn't tell me where he put them.

1. Mina/Gen language

15 I REMEMBER MAMA

: *Drunkards*
: *The Trouble with Three Friends*
: *Quarreling in Secret*
: *Killer Girls from Ghana*

: LOMÉ :

Drunkards

So: Lomé. That was where I became friends with Mama Amma. When I came from Tsukudu, after that, I stayed with Mama Amma in Lomé before we left Lomé and went to Ouagadougou. And Mama and I stayed together in Ouagadougou up to the time Mama left from there back to Ghana.

I told you that I knew Mama in Accra, but the time we became good friends was the time I was sick. When I was staying in the hotel, when I was sick, I told her my problem, and she said I should go to see that musician, Brazil. But I didn't know this Brazil, and she led me to Brazil, and they took me to that Dahomey man. *Uh-huh!* When I was sick, this was the place when we were becoming tight friends.

So when I was better, then every time, we were together, me and Mama. When I left the hotel, I got a room by the small market, near the burial ground, the cemetery of Lomé. I was living there, near to that first house Jacqueline and I stayed, the house for Podo, where I said the man was a drunkard. Every time if he was drunk and he saw me, then *pa-pa-pa-pa-pa.* Then I told Mama that if I can get a room in their house, I want to move from my old house. Hey, my own house near the cemetery was nice; it had a chamber and hall,[1] and there was light and everything. But the man who had the house was not a nice man. Sometimes you will go out and come, and they will lock the outside gate; you can't enter. So then Mama said some people were going to go out from one room in their house, some Senegalese,[2] so if I wanted, I could come and stay with her

1. bedroom and sitting room. Generally in a compound house, the distinction among rental units is (1) a flat, which has a bathroom and usually a kitchen, (2) a single room off a courtyard, and (3) a chamber and hall, which has an entry hall or small sitting room between the outside door and the bedroom.

2. people from Senegal, Francophone country on the far western tip of Africa

up to the time these people would go out from the house, and then I would get the room. Then I left my place, and I came and stayed with Mama. In about two or three weeks, then these people moved, and I got the room at her house. And then we were together. Every time, Mama. And she came to be my friend, a tight one.

And you know, Mama is very, very funny. When she sleeps, nobody can wake her. You can knock her door; she won't mind you. But if you say, "Hey, Mama!" she will wake up. You have to call her. And so we two, we had a free way with each other. We used to laugh and joke all the time. Ha! Mama sometimes is very funny. When Mama laughs, she doesn't want to laugh and show her teeth much, you know, because one of her teeth is not there, and she is ashamed of it. Every time when she laughs, she makes *hmm-m.* Then I said, "Why don't you put in a new one? Every time when you laugh, you make '*Eh-hmm. Eh-hm.*'" *Ha! Ha! Hee-hee!* This is how I used to trouble her. Mama! I used to trouble her.

Yeah, in Lomé, I used to go to Pussycat with Mama, but you know, as for me and Mama Amma, when we were in Lomé, maybe we will go to Pussycat or we won't go to Pussycat, but as for Kakadou,[1] we must be there! Do you know that small bar? It's near Pergola Restaurant, opposite Pergola. They have tables inside and outside. If we didn't go to Kakadou, I don't think people there were enjoying themselves. And we, too, we wouldn't feel happy. So every night. There was not any night when we didn't go to Kakadou, me and Mama.

Yeah. We could stay at the Pussycat until Pussycat closed about four o'clock. And from Pussycat to Kakadou is not far, so we would go to Kakadou, and we would come from Kakadou at seven o'clock in the morning! Everybody would be going to work, passing and looking at us. We didn't care. We would be sitting at the outside table there, drinking!

And sometimes Mama used to drink, and we took her like a baby. We had another friend, Zenabu. So one time Zenabu said she wanted to make a party because she was going back to Ghana. So she invited *all* of us to go to Kakadou at three o'clock in the night. We started drinking—beer, beer, beer, beer, beer. And then Mama was sleeping on the chair, and I said, "Hey, Mama, what are you doing?"

Then she was crying, "*Oh-h-h, eh-h-h.* Why are you doing me like this? Won't you let me rest a little?"

Then I said, "Ah! Why is Mama doing that?"

Then Mama went to a corner. Then Zenabu said, "No!" And you know,

1. drinking bar in Lomé, open all night

Zenabu is a very strong guy! Zenabu just picked her up like a baby and went and put her on a chair inside. So she was on the chair, sleeping.

We were there up to seven o'clock — yeah — or a quarter to seven; then I said, "No. Zenabu, look. It's daylight. People are passing. It's not good. We must go and wake Mama to go home." So we said we should wake Mama with one beer, and we called for another beer again, and we cut it inside Kakadou. Then we went outside and we bought one more beer, too. Then Mama didn't want to drink, and we were forcing her and opening her mouth —*agh, gug-glugh, agh, agh-glugh. Ha!* That day! Then I thought the way Zenabu was holding Mama was not good, so I said, "Hey, Zenabu, don't kill her!"

She said, "No. I'm not going to kill her. If you take beer, then you go on top of it with another one, then her eyes will open." *Aghhh! Glugh!* So then she took the beer and by force, and she held Mama to open the mouth, and she put the beer by force. Then Mama made like this: *g-gug-gug-g-gug-g-g. Ha-ha!* Then I went and stopped a taxi. Zenabu just picked up Mama like a baby and then came and put her in the taxi. Then when we got home, Mama could not get down from the taxi. Zenabu had to carry her. Then we put her in the room.

Then, we were all drunk. As for me, if I am drunk, I don't feel to sleep: if I sleep, then my face is turning. So if I am drunk, I must bathe before I sleep. So I took a bucket of water — two buckets — to go and put in the bathroom, and I washed myself.[1] When I came, Mama was crying, *"Boo-hoo."*

"Mama, why?"

"*Waa-aa. Weh-h-h.* You people look at me like a baby. And you want to kill me." *Ha! Ha!* It was very funny, yeah?

"Mama! Oh, Mama, it's because of that you are crying?"

Then she said, "Why —*sniff-sniff*—Why should Zenabu —*sniff-sniff*— carry me like this?—*boo-hoo*—You see — everybody was looking at me." *Ha-ha!*

"But you couldn't walk! If we left you, you would sleep in the taxi."

Then she said, no, we should have held her hand, you know, to let her get down from the taxi; it's not good the way Zenabu carried her.

So I said, "OK. Zenabu, you have to come and beg her."

Then Zenabu came, "Mama, don't cry. I won't do that to you again. OK?"

Then Zenabu was putting her hand on Mama's head, and Mama said, "You see —*waa-a-ah*— you're doing me the same thing again —*sniff-*

1. Hawa is bathing with two buckets just because she wants to pour lots of water over her head.

sniff—you put your hand on my head like a—*sniff*—like a *bay-bee*." *Ha!* Mama is a very funny guy. She was talking slowly-slowly. She didn't open her eyes; if she opened her eyes, then she would just start crying again, "*Ehh-h-h, ehh-h-h.*"

So Zenabu had to beg Mama, and Mama didn't listen, and so Zenabu had to throw her away, "Go away from me! What? You think God will come down and beg you? I am the one who did it. I said, 'OK, you said you didn't like it,' and so I'm asking you, and I said, 'OK, I won't do it again.' So why?"

Then Mama was still crying, and so her voice was very small like this, and she said, "*Ehh-h-h, waa-ah*—I know everybody doesn't like me—*sniff-sniff*—Only Hawa likes me." *Ha!*

So: Zenabu went out and I closed the door. Then I said, "OK, Mama, let's sleep." We slept up to seven-thirty in the evening. We didn't wake up. They had to wake us to eat, by force. And everybody didn't feel like eating. Then when we woke up, we had a bath, and then we got some small grooving, and we were all right.

We didn't eat anything, and we went to Pussycat again. But before we got to Pussycat, you know, there was a small bar near our house. We had to pass there and take some Guinness before Pussycat.[1] Then at Pussycat, any time we can go out and groove. So when we finished from Pussycat again, then we went to Kakadou. Then Mama said, "No, today I won't drink. I will drink Fanta." *Ha!*

Then I said, "What about the Guinness you took before we came out? If you don't want to drink, why did you start with Guinness?"

Then she said, "But there no Guinness here."

Then I said, "OK, let's go, then we can find some Guinness." So we came from that bar and went to another bar. There is another bar inside Kakadou, and their drinks are also different, so we went there to get some Guinness. I said, "OK, they've got Guinness here, so we can drink. OK? Ah, we will drink only one, eh? Yes? Only one. I haven't got enough money." I had three hundred francs, yeah? Then we took a big Guinness.[2] It was 180 for a big bottle for the two of us. Before we finished, oh-oh, somebody bought me two more. *Ha!* So we had three.

Then Mama said, "No, let's keep this drink here with the barman.[3] Tomorrow if we come, we can drink it."

1. Drinks at the French discos are very expensive, so they would drink on the way or outside at a nearby bar, or go outside the disco to smoke marijuana, and then they would not have to buy the expensive drinks at the disco.

2. 66 cl. Beer and Guinness are generally sold in 66 cl bottles, and 33 cl bottles (about 11 ounces) are called "minis" or "small."

3. leave the unopened bottles to be held for them

I said, "No. You know, this Guinness, if we keep it here, this boy is not a good boy." I was lying: we used to keep drink with this boy, but I said, "I don't want that. I don't want to keep it, I want to drink it." So I told her, "You know, last time I kept some of my drink here, and when I came, this boy didn't give it to me. He told me some kind of ways.[1] So I will not keep it here. If you don't want to drink, you can wait for me to drink."

Then you know, she cannot wait on table[2] without drinking. The glass was in front of her, so I will serve her and serve myself. Then I said, "OK, Mama, drink quickly. Then we will go."

"But today I don't want to drink."

Then I said, "What should I do with it then? I have already served you." So she took it. *Ha!* Then when she took it, then when I wanted to serve her again, I served myself first. Then I said, "So you don't want more?"

And she said, "No."

Then I said, "Hey, what is wrong over there?" When she turned her face, before she came and looked front, then I filled her glass.

Then she said, "Oh, Hawa, you are troubling me."

"How am I troubling you? This is water. This is not trouble. You know, this kind of water, we drink and go and piss it off. It's nothing."

"Oh, but today I don't want to be drunk. You know, yesterday I was drunk. It was very bad. So I don't want to get drunk like that."

And I said, "You won't get drunk like that again. So if you like, let's drink APC."[3] APC: it's good! *Ha!* So we drank APC, and then we were there up to six o'clock in the morning. Mama didn't want to drink. But then, we sat there, talking, and we were getting more drink: after we finished these two bottles, then Mama also got somebody, and he brought another two bottles of Guinness—big ones, oh, not the small Guinness—the big ones. *Ha!* It was 180 in Togo—180 francs—in Kakadou. Then we got those two, so we had five bottles.

And then one woman—she was called Patience—when this woman came to Togo, she was a good friend to me. Patience's brother was a boyfriend of Jacqueline, so because of Jacqueline, we became good friends, and that woman too came there. She said she was staying with some old man in Tropicana Hotel,[4] and this man had gone today, so she wanted to get drunk. She had a little money, no? So she was just buying drinks like that. It was coming like water! *Ha!*

1. some kind of story
2. sit at the table
3. acetaminophen with caffeine. To drink APC is to take acetaminophen tablets.
4. large hotel in Lomé

Then I said, "Hey, Mama, you are leaving this thing![1] This drink, if you leave it, it is not good. The way this woman has been teaching us, every time she used to come to us and borrow our money. And she doesn't pay us. So let's drink all. Let's finish her money." *Ha-ha!* So we took more APC, and then we were drinking, drinking, drinking, drinking. Oh, if you take APC, you don't get drunk again. Yeah? So we drank well, up to six o'clock in the morning. Then from six o'clock, Mama said we should walk and go home because to find a taxi would be a problem; so we should walk. So: at this six o'clock in the morning, we were walking with our trousers, holding our bags. Oh! I think that day it was in the week. It was six o'clock in the morning: everybody was passing going to work; we didn't care, we just walked *chk, chk, chk,* like the army people, you know. *Ha!* The soldiers who go to training, how they walk, we were like that. We passed some corner ways and we went home and slept.

So one day Mama said, "Look—what we are doing? As for us, our eyes are not red at all."[2] You know, sometimes we used to get some people at the nightclub who will say, "Oh, I can wait for you after closing time and we will go home. Yes?" But when the nightclub closes, we won't go anywhere! Only Kakadou! If we don't see that area, we cannot sleep. So we were coming to look like big drunkards! All the people in Kakadou's area knew us.

So I also said, "Mama, no. This thing isn't good for us. We'd better stop." *Ha!* So we used to stop going to Kakadou for about one week. We wouldn't go there. When we went there, everybody would say, "We see you people, it kept long!"[3]

Then we would say, "Yeah, we have been to Ghana!" *Ha!* We were in Togo, but we told them we have been to Ghana! No? Then we stopped going there again. But before—*ahhh!* Especially the time when I was from that place—from my prison: when I came, we used to go to Kakadou. Oh-h, we used to drink! Every time I would say, "Hey Mama, let's go and drink."

"Oh, Hawa, don't you know that this time, when you have come back from this trouble, you must go home and look at your—your—your families—and that and this. You're going to spend money for drink?"

Then I would say, "Hey, my dear, if you are not going, I am going. To look at my family? They are the ones who should look at me. Ask them: when they arrested me, did I see one person from my family there? I'm

1. leaving it on the table; not drinking
2. We are not serious.
3. It's a long time since we've seen you!

going to Kakadou. Shit!" *Ha!* So if I had money, every day time, every night time, we got drunk. Day time, you know, near the latrine, there was a small store there, and they were selling drinks. And this man with the store had Guinness. So every time, if I didn't feel like going out, I would call these boys in the house and send them to buy Guinness. Then we would start drinking — drinking, drinking: before evening time — oh-oh. So evening time, if you go out and you're drunk, you won't drink again. It won't make you feel to drink much again because it all turns to water in your stomach, and you're full up! *Ha!* Yeah? So in Togo, oh, we did some kind of bad life. It was very bad, to be drinking, drinking, drinking. As a woman, if every time you have to be drunk, it's very bad.

The Trouble with Three Friends

And Zenabu: when Zenabu came, if she was drunk, you know, she is a giant, and every time, if she drinks, she has to cause trouble. Every time when Zenabu got drunk, she caused trouble. And she never caused trouble with a girl. Only with a boy. She was very funny: you can't see the girl who can stand her in a fight, so every time she caused trouble with boys. Sometimes she beat the fellow; sometimes the fellow beat her. Then she would say, "Yeah, if a boy beats you, it's better than a girl. They will say that he is a man, and he passed you; that's why he beat you." So Zenabu, every time when we would go out with her, sometimes Mama and I liked to dodge and leave her. If we were in Pussycat, we would say, "Oh, we are going to Le Rêve."[1] In Le Rêve, Zenabu had made trouble there, so they didn't allow her to enter there.

"You — you people are leaving me?"

Then we would say, "Oh, no. We have made a promise[2] for there. So we have to go." So we would go to Le Rêve. Then maybe if it was Pussycat and Zenabu was alone there, she wouldn't be happy; then she would also go to another place. And then we would come back to Pussycat. If we came back and she was not there, then we would stay. If we come back and we met her, we would say, "Oh-h, we are going to L'Abreuvoir."[3] At L'Abreuvoir too, she didn't go there, because they sacked her from that place. They sacked[4] her from three nightclubs in Togo. Le Rêve.

1. disco in Lomé
2. a date, appointment
3. disco in Lomé
4. in this context, threw her out and forbade her to enter again

L'Abreuvoir. And Disco Uno, they also sacked her from there. The time Antonio was *patron*[1] of Disco Uno, he took Zenabu home and gave her only 1,500 francs, and she said it was not enough, so she seized many materials from him to bring home. And Antonio had to borrow five thousand to come and give to Zenabu and take these things. So he didn't want Zenabu to come to Disco Uno. *Ha!*

So when we saw Zenabu, we would say, "Oh-h, today we have a promise at Disco Uno." Or Le Rêve. Or L'Abreuvoir. Then we would dodge and go somewhere. But at the last minute, when all the nightclubs had closed, we would see Zenabu in Kakadou. So if she would go there, sometimes if we saw her, we would make as if we didn't see her. Then we would go and take our table. She wouldn't talk to us. She was annoyed with us because we ran away and left her, and then later, when we came, we didn't come to her. And sometimes she would come and also see us when we were sitting there, and she wouldn't talk to us. We were doing like that for some time.

Then once, she got drunk and then she came and told Mama Amma, "*Maame Ama, woyɛ kɔnkɔnsani paa-a-a! Woyɛ kɔnkɔnsani paa!* Mama Amma, you are a big gossip!" Do you know kɔnkɔnsa? It's something like you hear something, and you want to say it, and then maybe the fellow doesn't want you to say it to somebody. If you say it, then it's kɔnkɔnsa, something like gossiping or telling someone's secret.

Then Mama Amma said, "Eh! Zenabu. *Na adɛn? Wobɛbo me?* Why? Are you going to beat me, Zenabu?"

Then Zenabu said, "Eh! Yes! If you play with me, I will beat you. You are kɔnkɔnsa. You are making Hawa not talk to me these days. When I came from Accra, it was because of Hawa I came. I stayed with Hawa in one room, but now we don't talk together. You are kɔnkɔnsa. What did you tell her that she hates me like that?"

Then I said, "Oh, Zenabu, who told you that I hate you?"

"Yes, but why don't you talk to me?"

And I said, "You rather don't talk to me! Because sometimes I used to ask you some questions, and you don't mind me. So I thought it's OK; we can still live together. If you don't want me — if you don't want to talk to me, I'm all right. Because if I ask you something, you don't mind me, so do you think tomorrow I will ask you again?"

Then she said, "Eh, it's not so. I know that all what is happening, it's Mama Amma who is doing me. Because Mama Amma is kɔnkɔnsa. Mama

1. (French): owner, manager, boss; also a form of address: sir, big man

Amma has talked something to you. That's why you don't want to talk to me."

Then I asked her, "Did you tell something bad about me to Mama Amma?"

She said, "No."

"Then how can Mama Amma tell me something?"

She said yeah, because one day she told Mama Amma she stayed with me before in Asylum Down and I'm not good.

But Mama Amma didn't tell me this! I didn't know that Zenabu talked something bad about me to Mama Amma! And Mama Amma didn't say it! And now Zenabu is rather proving the thing! So then I made as if I was annoyed, and I said to Mama, "*Aha!* So Mama: are you like that? So somebody can say something bad of me, and then you will keep it. You won't tell me. As for me, if I hear something bad of you, then I will tell you, 'Mama, this person, you must take your time with her.' Zenabu said that? But you didn't tell me. Oh-h, Mama, I thought you liked me. I didn't know that you just liked me in some way." *Ha-ha!* Yeah.

So then, Zenabu had to say what she said to Mama about me, and she thought because of that, Mama told me and now I don't talk to her. And I said, "No, Mama didn't tell me anything about that."

Then Zenabu said, "Even, that time, I only said that thing to see whether Mama is someone who can say something. I wanted to see if Mama likes you or Mama doesn't like you. That's why I said so. When I stayed with you in Asylum Down, you didn't do me anything bad. I was just playing a game to see Mama—how Mama is, or if Mama is bad, but Mama didn't say anything."

Look at things like this! How can you play games to see somebody? To see how it is between friends? Because we were all friends, I thought. She thought I liked Mama too much, and she didn't think Mama liked me the way I liked Mama, so she wanted to see if Mama liked me much. Suppose she said this and Mama also said something bad about me, then she would have come back and told me! But she told this thing to Mama, and Mama didn't say anything. And Mama also didn't tell me. Yeah. That is how we girls are living together.

So girls, we girls: for us to live together is hard. That's why I always don't want to be among three—three friends. When you are three and you are friends, it is not good at all. When you are two, it's OK. But three is not, because the three of you, your mouth cannot be one. But two of you, if you people like each other, and you understand each other, I think your mouth can become one. But three cannot be one. *Ha!*

Because maybe I am not here, OK? Then you are with the other friend, and I will come and meet you people. Then when I come, "Hello, hello." But after, I will think, "Hey, these two people? Maybe they were talking about me." This kind of sense, sometimes it will come. And sometimes, when you are two and you meet together, and the third one isn't there, if every time you two used to meet before the other one comes, by all means, you will have a chance to talk something about her. So three friends cannot be good.

When Zenabu was there, sometimes if I was fed up with cases like this, then I didn't talk to Mama and I didn't talk to Zenabu. I shit both of them. *Ha-ha!* Because Mama will bring a complaint about Zenabu. In two days Zenabu will bring her own. And Mama will say, "Yeah, I know. I am Ashanti. Zenabu is a Muslim like you. That's why." And this and that. What should I do myself? I cannot share myself, you know. *Ha!*

Yeah. Sometimes when Mama is sleeping, you know, to wake Mama is hard. If you wake her, unless you have time before you can wake Mama; if you haven't got time, you can't wake Mama. "Mama. Mama. *Hey, Mama!*"

"Hmm?"

"Wake up and take your bath. We will go."

"OK, OK." Then she will turn. She will turn; then she is opening her eyes, no?

"Oh, *Mama!*"

"Yeah, I'm coming, I'm coming." Then she will turn again.

So sometimes, if she was doing things like this, and I wanted to go to market or I wanted to get something, I used to leave her. Maybe I would be going to market, and somebody was going, then we would go together, or maybe I would go with Zenabu. Even maybe we had talked about the market in the night time. I would tell Mama, "Tomorrow morning you should wake up early. I am going to market to buy something. And the sun might be hot," or "Tomorrow I have a promise at this place, so we must be there by eleven or twelve." We could talk about this in the night. And morning time if I wake you and you don't wake up, then I will see that my time is going. So I must leave you. And sometimes I don't feel like going alone. So I can take Zenabu with me. Yeah. Yeah. Yeah. Yeah. In that case, after, Mama will say that she wouldn't like to see me. *Ha!* Then she will start to say, "Yeah, I know. I'm not from the North. You people are family. Me, I am Ashanti. So anything can happen." *Ha-ha!* And that and this.

And if I go to places with Mama for two days or three days, maybe I won't go out with Zenabu. *"Eh, eh, eh, eh!"* Zenabu also will bring herself.

"Yes. Hawa, I know. As for you, even in Accra, they say that as for you, you don't make friends with Pepe." *Pepe:* it means a Northerner. "Even you used to say this yourself. It's only Ashantis you like to be friends with. So anyway — that is — you don't — that's why you are not closer to me. And Mama Amma is your friend. Even I am the one who knew your family, and you don't care about me." And that and this. So if these things come on, then Zenabu will say this to me, and I used to be annoyed to Zenabu. So I will go back to Mama, you know. When I go to Mama, then me and Mama: *de-de-de-de-de.* Then sometimes if Mama sees that I start to be free a little bit with Zenabu, then she will also start again. Then if she does this thing, then I will be annoyed with both of them. I won't talk to Zenabu. I won't talk to Mama. Then Zenabu and Mama will become friends! *Ha-ha!* It's funny, no? So I think — to be three friends is not good.

And if — do you know that if these girls are happy, if they become friends, they will talk about me? They must talk about me. I know this. So any time when I saw them coming, then I used to close my eyes. *Ha-ha!* I don't want to see them, so I have to close my eyes. You know, I would make like somebody who is sometimes like this, thinking far, and then they will want to come and talk to me. If they do their everything and finish, they will come back to me. You know?

Then Zenabu will say, "No. Mama, I think you have some groove?" Zenabu didn't smoke, eh? She didn't smoke groove. Then Zenabu will say, "That thing, the one you brought from Aflao last time, it's a good one, eh?"

Then Mama will say, "Yes."

Then Zenabu will say, "No. As for you, you don't know it much. Let Hawa test it."

Then I will say, "I don't want to test anything from anybody. I also know Aflao."[1] *Ha!* Then I will say, "I don't want you people to talk to me."

Then Zenabu will say, "We said, 'Let Hawa test it.' Are you the only Hawa here?"

Then I will say, "Who is Hawa in this house?"

"But we have some friends called Hawa. Maybe we are talking about them. We aren't talking about you." *Ha!* Then: "If you don't want to talk to us, why did you reply us? You are not the only Hawa here in this place, in Togo here."

1. I also know how to go to Aflao to buy groove.

Then I will say, "OK, you people carry your trouble. I don't want to test anything." So Zenabu will look at Mama, and then they will make so, whispering together. Then I will say, "You can say anything you want. I see what you people are doing. I already know what is you people's mind. So I don't want to make this way. You can do whatever you like."

So that evening, Mama will come and boss me, "Hawa, won't you — do you think what we are doing is good?"

Then I will say, "What are we doing?"

"So: we can live together like this, and we don't talk together?"

Then I will say, "Why? I am not the one who brought you here. You are not the one who brought me here. I am not the one who pays your rent. You are not the one who pays my rent. You don't feel for me. I don't feel for you. So if we don't talk, then so what?"

Ha! So Mama has to say, "Oh-h-h, don't do that. You know, if we do that, people will laugh at us, because everybody knows that we are good friends here, and now we don't talk, and people are watching us. It's not good."

Then I will say, "No, as for me, I don't care. Somebody cannot laugh at me. Because I didn't shit on my dress. Yeah, I didn't shit on my dress. I didn't do anything bad. So if you laugh at me, you laugh at yourself. So as for me, I wouldn't like to talk to you people."

Then they will go and tell the old lady who was our houseowner. That old lady couldn't see. Then our houseowner will call me. She used to call me, "My daughter." So: "My daughter!"

Then I will say, "Mama."

"Va, va, va, va, vinye. Nye ɖeka fevi."[1] She said, "Come, you are the baby for me alone, you know. You are the only baby for me alone, not for anybody. *Oh-h-h*— come, come." This old lady too could *boss!* Then she will say, "You see, your friends came and gave me some complaint. It is not good, you know — you know, how your father used to pray '*Allahu Akubaru*'[2]— at home they used to tell you that if you get some argument, a small argument with your friends, if you don't talk to them, it's not good. Didn't your father tell you this before?"

"Yes, Mama. I heard of this before."

"But why? Your friends, if they talk something against you, and after they come and beg you, if they say you should talk together, then you should leave it. Just forget about what they said. They have come back. You are not the one who is begging them, no?"

1. (Ewe): Come, come, come, come, my baby. My baby alone, for me.
2. (Arabic): God is Great, i.e., as her father was a Muslim

"Yeah."

"OK, talk to them."

Then we would start again. And I would say, "You people are lucky! Like if this old lady didn't talk to me, I wouldn't talk to anybody!" *Ha!* So for that week, I will get a chance on them, and I will bluff on them. But getting to the next week, *unh-uhh.* They too will get over me and complain. This one will give complaint; that one will give complaint. And then, when — they are funny, too — if I don't talk to them, all what they will talk, the time will come when they will start to become annoyed with each other, too. Then this one will come and say, "The first time, when we didn't talk together, when we went to this place, that one was saying this and that and this." *Ha!*

Yeah, one time Zenabu went and told Mama that the time when she knew me from Accra, she was a little girl, and so I'm a kind of "old lady" to Zenabu. Then, they talked this thing for about two weeks. I didn't hear anything. So then Zenabu and Mama Amma were coming to make a palaver, and then Zenabu told Mama that, "Eh, as for me, nobody can tell me anything to do here, and nobody can talk to me to listen, apart from Hawa, because the time I knew her it was a long time ago." And she said that before, when she knew me, too, I was living with her sister, and we were not living the same room, but we were living the same house. At that time, Zenabu had a baby — about two or three months' baby. I thought she had just run from the husband — with the baby — and come to Accra. So she told Mama that the time when she knew me, she had just brought her baby from the village to live with her sister, and we were all in the same house.

Then Mama Amma said, "Oh, *kohwini!*"[1] Do you know *kohwini?* Something like a big liar. *Ha!* So Mama said, "A big liar like you! But last time you told me that when you knew Hawa, you had no breasts. Isn't it the way you told me?"

Then, you know, as Zenabu was strong, so she went and hooked[2] Mama Amma, and she wanted to beat her. "Me? I said that?"

And Mama just said, "Yes, you said that. When we went to Hotel de la Plage, the time when Hawa didn't talk to us, you told me that if Hawa doesn't talk to us, we should go away from her. Isn't that what you said? And even, that she is not our size, that she is a kind of old lady."

Hotel de la Plage, yeah, you know, where they used to swim. They used to go to that beach. If we didn't talk, they didn't sit down. They would

1. (Asante Twi): a habitual liar
2. grabbed hold of

just go out together every time, just so it would pain me. And me, something like that cannot pain me. It cannot pain me because I used to like sleeping, so if I got a heavy grooving, I would sleep. Or sometimes I would get some appointment, and when I would go there, maybe I wouldn't come home, because I know I don't talk to these people, so I don't need to come home and sit alone.

So they started to talk. So I said, "*Ahaa!* So, if we don't talk together, then you people have to talk about me."

Then Zenabu said to Mama, "But you said, even, when Hawa came back from the prison, she borrowed your money. She took two months before she paid you."

Then I said, "Oh, but I have paid it. Did she tell you that I have paid it?"

Then Zenabu said, "Yes."

Then I said, "Is that it? She has to say that because it is true. When I came, I borrowed money. I didn't have money, and I borrowed from her, and then I paid her after two weeks; it wasn't two months." So: what Mama Amma told Zenabu, Zenabu had to say it. And what Zenabu also told Mama about me, if they make trouble, then everybody will sit and make so, "*Ah-hah!* It's true!"

So every time, when I am with three friends, you know, when we are three girls walking together, I don't want to tell the other one, "This one is like that; she is like this." No. I don't want it, because I know that one day she will come and make trouble, and then she will tell me that the other one said this, or that I said that the other one did that and this.

So every time, when we are three friends and we walk together, I'm not happy. I'm not happy as three friends. I will be among, you know, but I won't be happy. Yeah. That's why, if I have one friend, and I see, "Ah, maybe she understands me," then I don't want another friend again. Every time I want to be with her, together, as two. Yeah?

: OUAGADOUGOU :

Quarreling in Secret

You know, some people don't like friends at all. There are some people like that. Yeah. Even for me, if I have traveled to some country, and I don't know many people, I will think, "I don't know these people." Even if I meet somebody I know from someplace, sometimes she was not anything to me before. So I don't want to have a friend; I want to be alone.

Yeah, sometimes it's good, in some places, to live alone, without any friend.

You see, in Ouagadougou, since Mama left Ouagadougou, I have friends but I haven't got friends. You know, Limata is now my friend, but Limata — oh — I have no time for her, and she has no time for me: we are friends when we meet. But in Togo, with Mama, everywhere, if I was going to some place — even to market, I didn't want to go and leave Mama. I would want us to go together. Yeah. Mama was my best friend.

I like Mama because I think she's somebody who understands, and she doesn't want palaver. She doesn't want too much talking like — you know — some girls, every time they want quarreling and making trouble. But Mama is very quiet. She's very quiet. And she has understanding. If you tell Mama something, she has understanding. If she does something, and you see that this thing is not good, "Hey, Mama, what are you doing? Do you know that it is not good?"

Then she will say, "Oh, but I didn't know. You know that if I knew it is bad, I wouldn't do it." Then it's finished. But some people don't understand: "Why did you tell me that? Why did you tell me that?" And then people will hear of you.

Sometimes Mama and I used to quarrel when we were together, in Ouagadougou, and nobody would hear of us. The time we went to Ouagadougou, we could stay in the room for about one week, and we wouldn't talk together. But —*ha!*— these people in the house won't know that we don't talk together, because the time when we are going to eat, we are eating together. We don't talk to each other, but we eat together. When I cook, I will finish cooking the food, and then I put all on the plate, because we all, we eat together in the house. Oh, we were many girls in that house. Then everybody will come. Then Mama also will wash her hand[1] and come and sit down to eat. You wouldn't know that there's something between me and her, or whether we are talking or we don't talk. And sometimes when I'm going to market, or Mama is going to market, maybe we will go out together, but maybe she will go to market and I go to another place. Maybe I will come before her, or she will come before me. And we will start cooking, and she will just call, "Hey, everybody must come out![2] We are going to eat. So you should get up and wash your hands. Come and sit down." *Ha!* After we eat, the one who cooked, she has to wash all the plates. Before Mama washes the plates and finishes,

1. wash the right hand, which alone is used in eating from a communal bowl. A bowl of clean water is passed around to those who will eat.

2. from the rooms to the courtyard of the compound, where they will eat

and she will come back to the room, maybe I will pretend as if I am sleeping. I don't sleep, but I will pretend as if I am asleep. If she comes, she will also sleep. Evening time, everybody will take the bucket to bathe. I will go and bathe, and when I come and put it down, she will take the bucket and bathe too. And then, I know Mama: for Mama to prepare to go out is hard. And I used to dress up quickly. So every time I have to wait for her. When she finishes, then we will go out together. We will take the same taxi. When I stop the taxi, and I am going to enter, she will enter, too. Or when she stops a taxi, she will enter, and I enter, too. That time we were working at one nightclub, La Tringle; the taxi charge was fifty francs each. Maybe I will have one hundred francs, and I will give it to the driver that it's for the two of us. Or she will have to give to the driver for the two of us. And then we will go to the work. And *all* this time, we won't talk. No! *Ha-ha!*

One funny day, we weren't talking. And Mama didn't have money. She couldn't ask me, either. So she was telling one girl that today she is going to work, but she hasn't even got money to buy cigarettes, so if this girl has two hundred francs, she should give her. Then this girl said, "But Hawa has changed five thousand francs[1] just now. Why don't you ask her?"

Then Mama said, "No, I don't want to. I don't want to ask her. You know, she has been giving me much. She gives me everyday, so I don't want to ask her again." Then I heard this; I was in the room. She didn't want to tell this girl that we weren't talking, you see. We don't talk to each other, so she didn't want to ask me for the money, and the excuse she was giving out was that it was because I've been giving her money all the time, so now when she wanted to ask me for something, she used to shame. That's why she didn't want to ask me. Mama is good, eh?

And this girl said, "Oh-h. I don't have money today. But I will borrow five hundred from Hawa."

So I didn't say anything. Then when we went to La Tringle, I paid the taxi fare. Then I gave money to the man who was selling the cigarettes, and I said, "Can you give me two packets of King-Size?" So he gave me two packets of King-Size, and then I took one packet and I said, "Call that girl, and give her one."

Then he called Mama. *Ha! Ha!* He called her, and he gave the packet of King-Size to Mama. Then I told this boy, "OK, the balance, you keep it. I am coming." So we went inside to La Tringle. We were sitting down, you know. We didn't talk to each other there. Mama was there; I was just here beside her. Then I said, "Oh, as for me, I'm going to Caban Bamboo to

1. bought something with a 5,000-franc note and got change

take one bottle of beer."[1] Then Mama got up and went to the toilet. Before she came, I had gone to Caban Bamboo.

I was in Caban Bamboo when Mama came. Then I told the barman to give her one beer. So Mama drank this beer, then she said, "No, I will ask this girl a question." Then she said, "Hawa?"

Then I said, "*Tsk!* Don't talk to me." *Ha-ha!*

Then she said, "I shouldn't talk to you? But why did you buy me the beer? Why did you buy me the cigarettes? Why did you pay my transport if you don't want me to talk to you?"

Then I said, "Yes, I did that because I am the one who brought you here. Maybe you will go and spoil my name in Ghana that I brought you to Ouagadougou and then you have been suffering. That's why I did it for you. I don't want to talk to you." *Ha!*

Then she said, "You can beat me! As for me, I will talk to you!" *Ha!*

So: we don't talk, but we are making something like fighting, too! You know, so one man there was speaking Ashanti and he was listening to us. Then he said, "Ah, you two girls, you are very, very funny." Then he called me and said, "Come here." He was an old man. He was making kebabs at that place. They say that man has now died. They called him Faoto. Faoto called me, "The two of you, come here!" Then we went. Then he said, "So, you people don't talk to each other?"

And I said, "Yes."

"For what?"

I said, "Because she's not a good girl, and I don't want to talk to her."

And he asked Mama, "For what don't you talk to her?"

She said, "Ah! I didn't do anything. She says she won't talk to me." *Ha!*

Then he said, "*No, no, no, no!* You are good friends. You should talk together, eh?"

Then I told Mama, "OK. You are lucky this man said something. Otherwise I won't talk to you." *Ha-ha!* So we started to talk together again, you know.

So, after about three weeks—yeah, about three weeks, then Mama: every time she used to let us be late for the work. And I said, "Oh, Mama, what kind of dress—? If you are dressing, you are dressing to go where? Here is Ouagadougou. You dress and dress: I don't know what kind of dress you are dressing. If you come out too, I don't see what you changed. You have to let us waste all this time, and when we go there late, that

1. Caban Bamboo is a drinking bar in Ouagadougou, like Kakadou in Lomé. Beer in the French nightclubs of Ouagadougou is very expensive, as in Lomé, so she is going to a nearby bar to buy beer at the normal price.

fucking boy at the nightclub will be abusing us like some type of children. I don't want this."

Then she said, "OK. You can go. If I come alone, if they abuse me, it's me alone they will abuse. You can go. I am not holding your legs."

And I said, "OK." Then I went. So she came about nine-thirty. And we started fine. So the boy at the nightclub started: *ta-ba-ba-baba-ba.*

Then she said, "Yes, I know. Because you come from here, you can tell them to abuse me."

"Huh?!"

Then she said, "Yes, because if you didn't tell the boy anything about me, why, every time when we come, does this boy abuse us? But first time he didn't abuse us like this, like how he's abusing me."

So I went and told that boy, "You know, this Ouagadougou is my country, so even if I want to let you sack this woman from the work, she's not worried about this. She can go away and leave me in my place, to work alone. So why?" Then he started against me.

Then I left him, and I went back to Mama and said, "Oh, Mama, why? Are you crazy or did you drink some water of piss?"

Then she said, "Yes, the water of piss which you boiled for me is the one I drank."

Then I said, "Is this your way? I don't want to talk to you. It's that old man—you were lucky that that old man was talking to me that day, and then I talked to you. From today going, if that will be the case, don't talk to me. Don't come where I am. Don't touch any thing of mine." *Ha-ha!*

Then we are fighting again. It's our fighting. No one is going to know that we are fighting. We are in the same house, but nobody knows. So when I told Mama this, Mama doesn't want to take my bucket, Mama doesn't want to take my cooking pan. When we came to Ouagadougou, I bought all these things that were in the house. She didn't buy anything. Then she didn't want to touch anything from me. So if she wanted to bathe, she had to go to some old woman, Fulera, to ask for her bucket to bathe. She was a Ghanaian woman. Then Fulera said to her, "But why? Your sister has finished her bath. Why don't you take her bucket?"

And Mama said, "No, her bucket is too big. It's heavy for me. This time I don't know why I don't feel strong to carry a big bucket." So every time she would go and take the little bucket from this woman.

And this thing was paining me, too! How can we come together, and then you are going to ask somebody for a bucket to bathe? So I went and told that woman, "If you are giving your bucket to my sister to bathe, then you will take care of her. You don't know the way I brought her.

Who told you to give your bucket to her?" *Ha-ha!* "Who told you to give your bucket to her to bathe?"

Then that woman said, "Ah, but your sister says your bucket is too big."

Then I said, "Before—before, this bucket, was it too big? It's not the same bucket? Or the water is growing? I don't want this kɔnkɔnsa. You don't know the way we came here. You don't know the way we are living together. You cannot take your bucket and come between us and make kɔnkɔnsa. I don't want that."

Then she asked me, "Are you two making palaver?"

Then I said, "Yeah, because since you've been giving your bucket to her, she doesn't talk to me. Every time. If she wants to eat, she goes and takes your cooking pan and goes out and buys food. I don't want this kind of way. This you Ghana people's kɔnkɔnsa life, why you do carry it everywhere? Here is my country; don't carry it and follow me here. I don't want these things." *Ha!*

So when Mama was going to take the bucket, this woman said, "Eh, no-o-o. I can't give my bucket to you. Your sister has come here this morning to beat me that I'm giving you my bucket to bathe."

Then Mama came to me: "You say I shouldn't touch your anything. And if I ask somebody—"

"Yeah! You must buy one by yourself!" *Ha-ha!* "If I tell you to don't touch mine, then I mean that don't touch one from somebody too. If—if—if I am the one—if I am you, the way I will be annoyed, I won't want to touch your thing. The next day, you will find that—the same thing, what you have—I will go and buy it too."

Then she said, "Yeah, I don't feel to buy this thing because I'm going back to Ghana. I have no one from my family here. You have family. When you are going, you can give them these things. I can't carry all these things to Ghana. So I won't buy anything." *Ha!*

Then I say, "OK, then you will bathe outside the house, or you will go to the pipe[1]—under the pipe, and bathe!"

So Mama, for one or about two days, she just took my bucket and bathed. I didn't say anything again. We talked this and it was finished, and evening time she took the bucket, she went to bathe. I didn't say anything. Then morning time, she went to market, came and cooked. We ate together. The next morning I went to market, I cooked, we ate together. Every time. How we eat together, it's Mama who will cook today, and to-

1. household or public water tap, where people can fill buckets of water for household use

morrow I will cook. If I cook today, then the next day Mama will cook. It's the way we used to do. Or sometimes, she can take me for about two or three days if I haven't got money. If Mama has money, she has to cook. Sometimes I can make Mama the same thing; if I have money, I have to cook, every time. This is the way we made it, you know.

So, sometimes, if we make trouble — our heavy trouble we had is that one, when I said she shouldn't touch anything of mine, and this and this, and she started to eat food from outside. But apart from that trouble, every time we can make trouble, but we will eat together, we will cook, we will make everything together. But only we don't — only to talk to each other, we won't. *Ha!* So Mama and I are like this.

Yeah. So for about two days, Mama was taking the bucket like that, and then Mama said she wouldn't work again at La Tringle. She would leave La Tringle. She went to live with some man at Kaya. Every two weeks, or three weeks, she would come to see me in Ouagadougou. After maybe one week, she would go back to Kaya.

Yeah, so Mama and I, we can be two like that, and inside that one too, we can get problems, because sometimes — you know, something like this, I think it's for everybody. There are sometimes when you don't feel like talking to somebody. Some days, you can wake up in the morning time, and then you will feel this way. You don't want to talk to somebody. You don't want even to talk to anybody. For me, sometimes I have to do this thing, to be quiet and not to talk to anybody. *Mmmm?* Then, if this thing happens, and maybe you have two people living together, if the other one wants to worry you about a long talk, you can just say some words like this: "Foolish words — that will make me annoyed." Then she will also just be annoyed. *Ha!*

So sometimes I just won't feel to talk to Mama. And this way, Mama also used to do this thing: sometimes, maybe for some days she doesn't want too much talking, or to be hearing some talks like this. But if she is like that, then I will try to worry her. I will think that if she's quiet, it's not good. I must force her to be happy. And that one, maybe she will talk something, and when she says that thing, then I will become annoyed. Then I will think, "Ah! I thought you are not happy. I want to make you happy, and you are telling this foolish shit! Don't talk to me!" This is the way we used not to talk with one another.

And you know, every time, our best time when we will make our palaver: early in the morning! Sometimes we will wake up, *tsk,* and we don't feel happy. And every time, we used to wake each other. If Mama wakes up first, she must wake me. And this is the thing bringing us trouble every time. *Ha!* Or if I am first, I must wake Mama, and maybe that time, she doesn't want to wake up. I told you that to wake Mama is hard, no? Then I will try to force her, because every time we are so foolish: when we are going to sleep in the night, this one will say, "OK, if you wake up first, try to wake me even if I don't want to wake up. Force to wake me." And it's not every day you will like forcing. So the day when it's bad for you, and you don't want force, then that day we have to be in our palaver. *Ha!* We are so foolish. Yeah, because I will say, "Hey, Mama, if you wake up at any time, try to force me, eh? I want to do something." And sometimes Mama will also tell me this. So the first one must force the other. Yeah. And every time, we used to get our palaver from that thing, you know.

"Why? I'm the one who said that you should wake me — to force me and wake me — but I don't need it again. I won't wake up! I won't do what I wanted to do. Oh! I'm telling you again!"

Then the other one will say, "Oh, but you are trying to fool me — you — you want to fool me. You will wake up. Last time you also forced me, you know."

Then all this is trouble. *Ha!* You are feeling sleeping, so you will find some words to use on her so that she will be annoyed and leave you. Or sometimes, if she's forcing like that, then maybe she tries to wake you and then you will talk this, and maybe she's annoyed and she will let you sleep. Then the time you wake up: "But why didn't you wake me up? Didn't I tell you to force me and wake me?" Then this one too brings trouble. *Ha-ha!*

So every time, for us, we used to get our trouble in the morning. The morning time, when we get our trouble — the two of us in one room and one bed, you know — then this one will draw herself — sometimes, if we are in bed, maybe I will pull the covers, or Mama, if she is near to me, I will take my cloth and put it over there, and take one pillow and leave her in the bed. Or sometimes, she will do that and go to sleep there and leave me in the bed. *Ha!* So we are starting. When we say we won't talk to each other, then we don't sleep together, too, you know. *Ha!*

One day we didn't talk to each other. That time, I think we were drunk, so when we came in the night, we didn't close our door. Then we slept. So Mama was sleeping, then Mama slept on my hand like this, and then she held me like this. Then we were sleeping. So it was the ending of the month, and this man was coming to take his rent money. We slept up to nine or ten o'clock in the morning; we didn't wake up. Then this man came to all the girls to collect his money, and he asked whether we were inside. Then these people said that since morning time they didn't hear us, so maybe we are in or we are sleeping or we went out. Then one girl said, no, since morning she saw that the door was open. So this man came. The way we held each other and slept, he called all these girls in the house to ask whether we are two boys or we are two girls? He doesn't understand. Or is it a girl and a boy? So these people should come and see the way we sleep! *Ha-ha!* You know, that time too, it was very hot, so every time we slept with only our underpants; we don't put on any cloth.

So these people were laughing. Then that time, I tried to wake up. So it was a long way; it was making me like dreaming. Then I forced myself to open my eyes. I saw about five girls in our room. Then I said, "What do you people want here? What do you people—?" I started shouting on them. "Mama, wake up and see!" Then Mama woke up, then we started to talk. Before, we weren't talking. But that day, when we saw the people come to look at how we were sleeping, then we didn't talk about our case again: we just started to talk. So we fucked them, and when we fucked the girls and finished, then we forgot that we weren't talking together. So we started. *Ha!* Oh, yeah, we started to talk. Oh, Mama! Me and Mama, we are so funny, you know.

Uh-huh. Sometimes, with me and Mama, when we don't talk, then, in about two days, we will talk again. We don't keep long! Two days, then we will start to talk, and then Mama will say, "Um-hm. Do you know how I made my mind?"

Then I will say, "No."

"Yeah, suppose we made about three or four days and we don't talk, then I was going to go to Ghana. I wouldn't tell you. I would tell you I am going to Kaya. Then I would go to Ghana. All this is the way I made up my mind."

Then I will say, "Oh, then you wanted to go without telling me?"

Then she will say, "Yeah, because every time you don't talk to me. What should I do?" *Ha!* "Then I was thinking that if it's three or four days more, then one day I will just take my bag, my things, and I will say I am going to Kaya and then I will go to Ghana. And I will write you that I have gone away."

Then I will say, "Then I'm lucky, then. How we are talking together now."

"Yes, you are lucky."

"You are also lucky."

Then she will say, "Yes, I am also lucky."

So, me and Mama, our traveling together was nice. When we travel, we see ourselves like sisters. We can live together, and we can make trouble, and nobody will hear of it. It's between me and her, and no one will know that we have trouble, or that we don't talk to each other.

So me and Mama—*ah!* You know, I have been meeting many friends, and for me, every time I used to make friends. But of all my friends, when I used to take them like a best, best friend, then the last one: they will show me and then we will come and just finish like that. But as for Mama, no. We don't have anything like that. Every time I used to have a feeling for her, when I don't see her. Yeah. Sometimes when I am in Ouagadougou, I will say, "Oh, maybe if suppose Mama was here, we could do this, or we could do that."

Yeah. I have other friends, but I don't think of them. I will leave them and go away, and I won't think of them, even one day. Somebody like Jacqueline, I don't think of her on any day. But before, I thought she was also a good friend for me. Mama didn't want talk, but as for Jacqueline, she leaves her mouth free. *Shit!* When we make trouble, you know, Mama and I can abuse each other seriously, and somebody wouldn't hear it outside. But as for Jacqueline, everybody will come and see that we are making trouble. And it's funny, too. If we are fighting like that, they will come to separate us. Then Jacqueline will say, "Leave us! You don't know the way we are. Even if she does me something bad, you are not a judge here. We didn't ask you to judge our case." Then the two of us will leave our own fighting and start abusing you. "Eh-h, *kɔnkɔnsa w'ani abre.*[1] Your eyes are red because we are friends. Oh, *kɔnkɔnsa.*" *Ha-ha!* So from there, then Jacqueline will say, *"Koo!"* You know, me and Jacqueline, we used to call each other: *"Koo."*[2] Have you heard this? They used to say this thing in concerts[3] in Ghana. *Koo! Me ne wo mmienu,* like me and you, two. *"Me ne wo":* me and you. So this is like "me and you, we two." You know, it's like friends. Jacqueline and I used to call each other like that. So when we finish, and we get somebody to fuck, then we too are happy, then we forget our problem. We say, "Hey, Koo! Hey, Koo! *Kɔnkɔnsafoɔ bɛbrɛ.*[4] The kɔnkɔnsa people, the liars, are going to tire. Me and you, two. *Koo!*" Then we will shake our hands: *kpa!* Then we will forget our palaver. So me and Jacqueline, we used to get some funny stories like that.

So, we have funny, funny quarrels. But it's nice, you know. I think it's nice. Like some people, if they are friends, they can make a palaver, and then many people have to call them to judge this case. To judge it, what

1. (Asante Twi): Your eyes are red; you are jealous or hatefully envious.

2. (Asante Twi): a nickname for a "guy," from Kofi

3. popular comedy plays with Highlife music, performed throughout Ghana by touring bands

4. (Asante Twi): Gossipers will be tired (will suffer). The expression is proverbial and is also said in the singular form, Kɔnkɔnsani bɛbrɛ.

you do: "You are not doing well, so you must beg your friend with this or that." In our African cases, many of them are like that. Then you have to beg your friend with something, and you have to buy him some drink to say, "OK, let's forget about this and that." But we girls, how we judge our cases, we have no problems. We only judge our cases with drinks, because we know we are all poor. When we get it, we drink together. And the day when we don't get something to judge our case, we have nothing to charge the other to show that the fellow did what is not good. We will just say, "OK, last time, we have done some foolishness. Let's just forget about that." We won't get someone to judge our case; we will judge our case by ourselves. It's better. Yeah, to have a case and to let other people judge the case every time, you know, it doesn't give a good idea at all.[1] If we are judging this case by ourselves: you wouldn't say I am bad, and then I won't say that what you did is bad. We just say, "Let's forget about it," and then it's finished. But if people are judging the case, they will look, and then they will see the way you talked to the other one, it was not good words, and you shouldn't do that next time, and then that fellow will always have power on you. But as for us, we will forget how we started the quarrel. We just forget it. It's better the two of you people judge it yourselves, and you won't bring all these topics, so you will never feel shy of what you did after. So we used to get our cases, and we judge them ourselves. *Ha!*

: LOMÉ :

Killer Girls from Ghana

Yeah. You know, in Lomé, I used to go to court to see cases. They had court in the night. In Upper Volta, since I came to Ouagadougou, I haven't got time to go to the court. In Ouagadougou, our house is far from the court. And I work in the night. I cannot get up in daytime and waste my sleeping to go to the court and listen to the cases. But in Lomé, I used to go with one boy in our house, Vélé. Every night, when Vélé came from work, he would say, "Sister Hawa, let's go to the court, and listen."

Sometimes, if you went to hear some talks from the people in the courts, the people didn't hear French. If you can't talk French, they have an interpreter who can talk Ewe to you. In the court, they speak any kind

1. It doesn't leave you feeling happy with the result (because someone will have the blame).

of language. When they have a case, and there are lawyers inside, the lawyers speak French, and the people who have their case speak Ewe.

There was one case, and that case was a *hot* case. This case: there was a girl from Ghana, from Hohoe,[1] and a boy from Cotonou. And this boy had a gang. Yeah, they were a group. He had some friends who were doing this with him. And how they did their work: when this girl would go out with somebody who was rich, then she would come and show this boy all the ways he should pass to enter into the room. Sometimes this girl will go with somebody, and then they will be inside the bedroom: she will tell the man she is going to toilet, and then she will come and open the door to outside for the boys to enter and pack everything away. They were doing this thing in Lomé. So they did this about four times, and the fifth one, they killed one man, an Italian man.

Oh! You know, it's very interesting when you go to these courts. They will be judging the case from morning time to the night, twelve o'clock midnight. They won't finish the case. They will go home, and the next morning, they will start it again. This case, they judged it for four days.

Yeah, I didn't want to be in the court myself, but if it's something like this kind of case, I used to go. I wanted to hear the cases. That case, the one with the Italian man, many people were going to the court. You will see many people, hanging over. Everybody wanted to hear this, whites and blacks. Many people in Lomé were trying to go and hear that case, because it was wonderful. Some people went to the court from their work; they didn't even pass home.

And the time of this case, it was *hot* for the Ghanaian girls. They used to arrest them to the police station just like that. Once, we came out from the court, and we passed to L'Abreuvoir because they used to sell rice there. We went to buy this rice to take to the house, me and Vélé. Then I saw one girl I knew from Tema. The people were eating rice outside the nightclub, and I saw her, "Hey! Helen!"

"Hey! Hawa! You've come here?"

"Yeah. And you?"

Then she said, "I also came about three days ago today." So we were talking, and then two police people were eating rice there, too, and they just got up and carried all of us. We were six. Six girls.

Then Vélé said he didn't understand. And the police said if he doesn't understand, then he also has to come to police station. Then Vélé said, "Why? I'm walking with her. She has not come here alone."

1. small town north of Ho

Then they said, "*Aha!!* You are the bad boys here who are stealing. You get these Ghana girls, and then you rob from men. We've got all you people. You, too, go inside!"

So they got us, with Vélé, and they took us to police station. Then they asked for my passport. I didn't have a passport, so I showed my identity card, and it said "Voltaique." So then they said I have to go out, me and Vélé, we should go away. So we left. The next day, the girl from Tema said the other girls had to pay three thousand each before they left them from the police station.

So that time, if you were a Ghanaian girl who went to the nightclub, and a white man wanted to dance with you, if you said, "Hey, I don't speak French," then: *Hey!! The killers!* The killer girls! The Ghanaians! *Ha-ha.* So at that time, many Ghanaians went to Cotonou. Some of them went to Lagos, and all these places. They weren't happy in the town again, Lomé.

So in Lomé, they used to have this kind of case. You know, this case of the Italian man, when they were talking at the court, they showed all the people they robbed before, and all these people they robbed, it was the girl who knew these people first and she was taking the boys there. And so you know, people used to say that the Ghanaian girls were doing this. People used to say they were afraid of Ghanaians, because this thing happened two times in Togo, and both times the girls were Ghanaians.

The first case: the time when Mama Amma went to Lomé first, I don't know if she told you or not, they took her to police station for some days, too. She was staying with a Fanti woman; they called that woman Vanessa. She also had stayed in Togo a long time. And one night she was with one of those people who are bringing the cows and sheep to Togo to sell. I think he was from Niger. She saw the man one night in a bar. He was buying a lot of drinks. If you bought a drink, before you could pay, he would just pull big money from his pocket. So he went with this girl to the house. She was living with Mama Amma and another girl called Nana Mawu. All the Ghanaian girls stayed in the same house, and they were working for some man who had a nightclub.

So this girl went with that Niger man to the house. And the next morning, ah! The girl ran to the police. The people in the house also got up in the morning. They didn't know what was happening. They were going to take water from the well. That house had a well, like the well in our house in Togo. So one woman put her bucket inside. At that time it was dark a little bit, so she couldn't see inside the water. So something caught the bucket, and she said, "Ah! These children! They put their shoes inside of the water. And you people know this is the water we have been drinking, and doing all these things with it." Then that woman took her water and went to bathe.

She was in the bathroom when another woman came to take water. Then that women saw this thing again: it was a shoe. I think maybe the man's head was inside, and his foot was out. And when she saw, then she said, "Ah, ah ah! Come and see! The people—they put a shoe—the children are spoiling the water, so anyone shouldn't take it to cook, because there are some shoes inside."

Then one man in the house came and took the bucket, and he looked. "What kind of shoes?"

"We have been trying to get the shoe with the bucket, but it does not come out."

Then the man said, "No. I'm not sure that this is a shoe."

Then the housepeople were very afraid. And the other woman who was in the bathroom told her sister, "I am coming; then we will go to get the police to come and see the water."

Before they got out of the gate, this girl also came with the police people. There was a dead body in the water. The girl said she came home with the man, and she told the man to sit down, that she was going to get the key to open the door. When she came, she didn't find the man. Then she heard the water going *plo-plo-plo.*

So you know, this stick they use to pound fufu with, it was just behind the well, and when the police people came and saw it, they took the girl and went with her. The girl said she just told the man to sit down, and she didn't know the man sat on top of the well. And the police people said, how they saw this pestle just behind the well, maybe the girl took the man's money because the man was drunk, and then she took that thing and beat him and threw him in the water. They took the dead body and took the girl and caught all the people in the house. Mama Amma was not in the house; she had slept at someplace. The next day, she didn't know the problem when she came to the house. They got all of them to the police station.

So this girl Vanessa kept about six months in prison in Lomé, and every time she would come to court. Then she was free. And she went straight out of the country.

And this case with the Italian man was the second one. And from that time, then the people were taking it to be true, saying that Ghanaian girls, they are killers in Lomé.

Oh! Lomé! I think that Lomé is good to go there to say, "Hello, hello."

Or if you want to buy something, they have many things. But it's not a good country to go and stay. *Shit!* Just going to get rice from the court, and then they took me to police again!

I was in Togo for about two years and some months, maybe getting to three years. I was in Kpalimé for about seven months. When I got out from that place, I didn't stay all that long in Togo. Anyway, it was a bit long. I was there for some months, and then I left with Mama to go to Ouagadougou. That was when we saw you in Accra, me and Mama and Jacqueline.

EPILOGUE

Hawa's stories continue in a second volume, *Exchange Is Not Robbery.* Fed up with Togo, and with Ghana still suffering under the Acheampong regime, Hawa and Mama travel to Burkina Faso. The second volume takes place mainly in Ouagadougou and in Hawa's village in Burkina Faso. Several stories occur in Korhogo in Côte d'Ivoire; in Banfora, Bobo-Dioulasso, and Koudougou in Burkina Faso; and in flashbacks to Kumasi in Ghana and to Lomé, Togo.

Hustling Is Not Stealing and *Exchange Is Not Robbery* were originally written o be read as one book. Together the two books provide a more comprehensive portrait of Hawa's world. I stated in the Introduction that it was not until I finished assembling everything that I was able to perceive the full range of her chronicle and acknowledge the deliberateness and scope of her conception. The decision to split this work into two parts was based on an editorial sense of the ungainly weight that a single volume would present a reader. The split was made feasible by a natural division in the story with the change of location when Hawa returns to her native Burkina Faso and also by the subtle differences in her own experience between the two periods of our intensive work together.

The Hawa we meet in Ouagadougou is the same playful and intelligent warrior as the Hawa we met in Ghana and Togo, but in Ouagadougou, she seems to grow more into her trickster identity as a solution. In *Hustling Is Not Stealing,* despite her successes, she struggles with luck and circumstances, and she gets pushed around a lot. In *Exchange Is Not Robbery,* Hawa maneuvers to gain greater control of her life. Her ethnographic motive becomes more self-consciously apparent. She becomes more active in collecting stories among her associates in town and her family in her village. Through these stories, along with recollections from her youth and some analytical reflections, she puts her life into perspective. Whether the stories are hilarious, shocking, or touching, she remains a brilliant social observer and verbal artist and a satirical cultural critic. In *Exchange Is Not Robbery,* consistent with her continuing development, she comes to terms with her destiny and completes her narrative vision.

Exchange Is Not Robbery

MORE STORIES OF AN AFRICAN BAR GIRL

PART THREE *Hawa Contextualizes Her Life*

PART FOUR *African Independence*

GLOSSARY

abi (Yoruba, also Pidgin). or. The word is used for emphasis, like saying, "Or what?!" or "Isn't it?"

akpeteshie (Ga). Akpeteshie *(akpɛtɛshi)* is locally distilled spirits, usually made from sugar cane or palm wine. Akpeteshie was illegal during colonial times, and the name has two applicable Ga meanings, one from "hide-out" and the other from "lean over or against."

all. at all not at all (from Asante Twi: *koraa*); *all the house:* the whole house

Amariya (Hausa). title of the most recently married wife in a Muslim household; a woman without cowives who was married in a Muslim ceremony; also, the marriage ceremony itself

area. neighborhood or section of a town

Asante Twi. the Ashanti dialect of the Akan language

Ashanti. large cultural group in central Ghana, centered in Kumasi. "Ashanti" is the English form of "Asante."

ashawo (Yoruba). a "loose" or "free" woman; literally, money changer

ask. *ask for myself:* to speak on my own behalf

back. descendants, followers, dependents; people coming in the family; *at the back of:* behind

balance. *n.:* change

beg. to apologize; to ask forgiveness, often with a sacrifice or gift. *I beg:* Please.

Biafran. Ibo; large cultural group in southeastern Nigeria

blow. *v.:* to give a blow; to hit; *n.:* a punch

bluff. to take oneself high, to boast, to present oneself as better than others

Bob Marley. hair style with dreadlocks, taken from the name of the Jamaican musician

boil. to give medicine or juju to; *boil up:* to become furious, to become very angry

borne. to have given birth to. The idiom is used for both men and women, and it is normal for a man to say he has borne his children.

boss. to persuade or convince; to talk nicely or gently to, sometimes but not necessarily with a connotation of insincerity; to trick; to cool someone out, to calm someone

bottom. buttocks; underside

buroni-wawu (Asante Twi). second-hand clothing from overseas. *See* Oburoni w'awu. The pronunciation is "broni-wawu."

bush. any wild or uncivilized area; *from bush:* an abuse, that a person has no sense or manners

car. a taxi or minibus; any transport

cedi. unit of currency in Ghana. One New Cedi is one hundred *pesewas* or ten shillings. Decimal currency was introduced in Ghana in 1965, replacing and phasing out the Ghanaian pound that had replaced British West African currency in 1958. The old or Nkrumah cedis were originally valued at eight shillings and fourpence; for ease of calculation, the New Cedi was introduced in 1966, valued at ten shillings, with two New Cedis being a pound. The New Cedi was aligned with the U.S. dollar but was progressively devalued, slowly in official trading, radically in black market trading.

The actual value of the cedi, and by extension the actual cost of goods in hard currency, could only be known via the black market rate. In 1970, the cedi was trading at 1.15 to the dollar officially and 1.50 unofficially. In 1977, when most of the interviews for this book took place, a dollar bought 4.00 to 4.50 black-market cedis; in 1979, when additional interviews were conducted, the figure was 12–14 cedis. Eventually, the currency was floated under a "structural adjustment" program of the World Bank, and in early 2001, a dollar was about 7,500 cedis.

For a rough calculation of cedi values, one can divide the black-market value of a dollar in cedis into the inflation factor for a given year. For example, in 1974, a dollar bought 1.80 cedis, and a 1974 dollar is worth about $3.60 in 2001, so in 1974 a cedi was worth about two 2001 dollars. Generally for this book, from the late 1960s to the early 1970s, when Hawa was in Accra and Tamale, one cedi would be equivalent to between two and four dollars after adjusting for inflation. In 1971, when I knew Hawa in Accra, a bottle of beer was fifty-five pesewas; an orange was threepence; a trotro ride across town might have been sixpence; a short taxi ride from one area to another cost two shillings. By 1977, in 2001 terms, a cedi was worth about seventy-five cents.

CFA. francs. Francophone African currency indexed to French francs. CFA stands for la Communauté Financière Africaine. 50 CFA were previously equal to one French franc; in 1994, the currency was devalued to 100 francs CFA to 1 French franc, or 1 centime. In 1999, CFA francs were pegged to the euro at just under 656 francs per euro. In this book, U.S. dollar prices for CFA therefore directly reflect the prices for French francs. In the 1970s, with the dollar generally between 4 and 5 French francs, CFA varied between 200 and 250 to the dollar, only occasionally pushing 300 or above. Generally in this book, one can use 250 CFA per dollar to calculate amounts.

cheap. easy; easy to get, easy to learn

chook (Pidgin). to stick, prick, stab

chop (Pidgin). to eat, consume, use, spend; also, to have sex with; also, to kill; *chop money, n.:* money for cooking or food

Christmas. any festival

cinema. movie, movie theater

cloth. normally refers to wax-print cotton cloth. Wax-print cloth made in local factories in West Africa is regarded as lower quality than cloth from overseas. Quality is judged by how fast the colors are and by whether the printing is done on both sides. Particular print designs from various manufacturers can become fads, but in general wax-print cloth from different countries is ranked and priced accordingly, with "Hollandais" at the top, followed by English and then specific African countries, headed by Côte d'Ivoire and Senegal; local factories also produce different "qualities" or grades. "Different kinds" of cloth generally refers to different patterns.

cola. a type of bitter seed about the size of a chestnut. Used for soft drinks in the West, in Africa cola is chewed as a mild stimulant.

comedies. short subjects or ads or diversions before the main film at a movie theater

coming. coming back. *I'm coming:* I'll be right back.

conceive. *v.:* to become pregnant, to make someone pregnant; *n.:* pregnancy; also, the fetus; *conceived, adj.:* pregnant

corner. *corner-corner, adj.:* dodging; moving in a hidden or secret way; *corner ways:* shortcuts or indirect ways; back ways, as behind or between the houses

cut. to take; to pull away a bit of something; to drink

Dagbamba. large cultural group in northern Ghana, around Tamale and Yendi

dash. *n.:* gift, tip; *v.:* to give, to tip

do. *do someone something:* to do something to someone; to make medicine against someone

dodge. to elude, avoid

dress, dresses. clothes, any outer garment; applies to both men's and women's clothing

drink. *n.:* hard liquor

eat. *See* chop.

estate. a residential or suburban area, normally of one-family bungalows

European. any white person

every. *every time, every day:* all the time; always

Ewe (*pr.* eh-veh). cultural group in southeastern Ghana and southern Togo

experience. intelligence; also, ideas, sense, wisdom

eyes. *whose eyes are red:* who is serious, who is angry; *whose eyes are strong:* who is proud, connoting stubborn pride

face. *give face:* to respond to; to relate to; to give respect to; *squeeze (one's) face:* to frown; to tighten (one's) face

Fanti. cultural group in south central Ghana, around Cape Coast and Takoradi

feel. to have a feeling for; to like; to want; to enjoy

find. to look for; to get

finish. and finished; *die finish:* be dead

first-time. at first

fix. to get; also, to know or recognize

force. to make a hard effort

Frafra. cultural group in northern Ghana, around Bolgatanga

franc. *See* CFA.

fuck. to abuse verbally

fuck off. *exclam.:* Get away! *v.:* blow off, dismiss; verbally abuse

fufu. a pounded, starchy food, eaten with soup. Fufu is a staple food of Akan people. It is pounded with a heavy pestle in a large mortar. The ingredients are generally boiled cassava blended with plantain, but fufu can be made with cassava alone, or occasionally cocoyam can be substituted for plantain. Fufu can also be made from yam, and yam fufu is more common (and is preferred) in savanna regions where cassava and plantain are not grown. Generally two people prepare fufu, one pounding and the other turning the fufu in the mortar.

Fulani. large cultural group, widely dispersed across the savanna region from Senegal to the Cameroons, with concentrations in northern Nigeria and Niger; known in French as Peul

full. *are full up in:* to be filled up

Ga. cultural group in Accra area. The pronunciation is nasalized as "Gã."

groove. *v.:* to smoke marijuana; *n.:* marijuana; also, Indian hemp, wee; *groover, groovier:* marijuana smoker

groundnuts. peanuts

guy. a term that can apply to men or women; a person who is modern in every way, but is unpretentious and easygoing; someone who fits in with the other young people in a place

habit. way of living, character; also, culture

half-caste. a person of mixed race, generally African and European

Hausa. large cultural group in northern Nigeria

hear. *hear a language:* to understand a language, to speak a language

heart. *by heart:* senselessly, roughly, without sense of purpose, carelessly; also, *adj.:* careless

hot. easily annoyed, angry; worried; broke; *to heat:* to become annoyed or angry

inside. among

join. *join a car:* to board a passenger vehicle; *join a case:* to judge a case, to hear a case

juju. The word "juju" is no longer generally used by anthropologists because it has derogatory connotations, but the word is still used in common parlance to refer to animist (or pagan) religious activities, to medicine for herbal or sympathetic treatment of sickness if administered in an animist context, to animist religious or superstitious practices, to the animist deity or spirit itself, or to the shrine of that spirit. *Make juju:* to make a sacrifice for medicine; *make the juju:* to do a sacrifice to the spirit; *beg the juju:* to do a sacrifice; *show the juju:* to make the juju manifest; to become possessed

Kaɛ (Asante Twi). an exclamation of objection, rejecting a situation or statement as useless. It can also be used as an affirmation, like saying "No!" or "No way!"

Kanjaga. town in northern Ghana; also, Builsa cultural group

keep. to manage; to hold; to stay, take (time); *keep long:* to take a long time

Koo *or* Ko. nickname for any "guy," short for Kofi; also used as an exclamation, like "Hey, man!"

kɔnkɔnsa. *Kɔnkɔnsa* (Asante Twi) refers to talking about people, often in a manipulative or distorting way, to meddling, or to gossip that causes trouble between people. Gossiper: *kɔnkɔnsani* (s.); *kɔnkɔnsafoɔ* (pl.). *Make kɔnkɔnsa:* to talk about people, to gossip, to cause trouble between people; *make kɔnkɔnsa on:* to tell on; *adj.:* fake, bullshit, lying, indirect, hypocritical

Krobo. cultural group in southeastern Ghana

lead. to accompany someone part of the way when that person leaves your place, a custom in many African societies; occasionally, to drop off

leave. to let something be, to let something go, to stop doing something; to let someone be free. *Leave me:* Let me go.

light. electricity; any light

life. *for life:* for enjoyment; for experience

mean. *to mean somebody:* to intend something toward somebody

Mina. alternate name for Gen, a cultural group in southern Togo

Mossi. large cultural group in Burkina Faso, centered in Ouagadougou

mouth. *one mouth:* agreement; *make one mouth:* to agree, to say the same thing

Nkwadaabɔne (Asante Twi). Reform School; literally, Nkwadaa (children) bɔne (bad)

North. *the North:* northern Ghana, former colonial Northern Territories; *Northerners:* people from the North, the savanna area north of the coastal forest, about 150–200 miles inland, i.e., northern Ghana; people to the north of the Akan traditional area; also sometimes used to refer to Muslims; also sometimes applied to people from Muslim cultures in northern Togo, Burkina Faso, northern Nigeria, Mali, etc.

now-now. just now; at this very moment

nyama-nyama (Hausa). general word for anything of low quality or messed up; pathetic, lousy, cheap, poor, dirty, messy, run-down, worn-out, torn, nasty; literally, a pile or assortment of "stuff"

-o. *suffix:* adds emphasis to a word

Oburoni w'awu (Asante Twi). second-hand clothing from overseas; literally, "White man, you died." The noun form is shortened to *buroni-wawu.*

pack. to gather; to take and set down

palaver. problem, case, argument, matter, worrisome or troubling talk, quarrel, dispute

palm wine. the sap of a type of palm tree, which rapidly ferments into a slightly sweet drink

pants. underpants

pass. to be more than; also, to go, go by or through; *pass menstruation:* to menstruate

Pepe (Asante Twi). name used to refer to Northerners, people north of the Akan cultural area; *Pepeni* (s.); *Mpepefoɔ* (pl.). *See* North.

pesewa. unit of Ghanaian currency like a penny, one hundred pesewas to a cedi

piece. A *piece* of cloth is twelve yards. A half-piece (six yards) is used for women's traditional dresses with skirt, blouse, scarf or head-tie, and waist-wrap; two yards (one *pan* in Francophone countries) is used by men for shirts.

pick. to take; to carry

pito. a fermented drink generally brewed over three days from malted sorghum or sometimes from millet, reddish-brown in color with a somewhat sour taste; *pito house:* normally a brewing house, with an area or a room with benches where people come to buy and drink pito

play. *play with:* to joke with; to be free with; also, to mess with, bother; to do (something) to

portable. small, easy to carry, manageable, i.e., not expensive

proper. *adv.:* really, well; generally used simply to emphasize a verb

quarters. the rooms for cooks or stewards or other servants, generally a separate small building behind a house

quick. *make quick:* to hurry

report. to take into custody; *report oneself:* to go to a police station

right. good, correct
road. the way, the manner or means
rough. *make rough:* to quarrel; *do rough:* to be careless
sack. to drive away, make someone go away; also, to fire (from a job)
seize. to take possession of
shame. to be ashamed
shit. to get rid of, ignore; to dismiss, snub
show. to teach; also, to take advantage of, cheat; *show oneself:* to bluff; *show to:* to introduce; to let someone be known to
size. age; also, in some contexts, standard, status
small. *adj.:* little; also, "some small"; *adv.:* a little; *small-small, adj.:* doubled for emphasis, i.e., very small; *adv.:* little by little, bit by bit
smart. fast, quick; fast-moving, on top of things, hip
spoil. *spoil a baby:* to have an abortion
stranger. visitor, guest. In many African languages, the same word refers to stranger or guest; you would call your visitor a "stranger" even if you knew him or her very well, and you would introduce the person to your friends as "This is my stranger I have brought to greet you."
suck. to get much; to consume all, as in sucking the marrow from a bone
sweet. *v.:* to be sweet or good to; to please; *adj.:* tasty, delicious (not necessarily sweet)
tam-tam (from French). drum; drumming
teach. to cheat; to show someone about life or give someone experience, with the implication of taking advantage of the person. The idea is of somebody opening one's eyes to something one didn't think or know about.
tie. *tie cloth:* to dress in African (wax-print) style. The verb refers to the final piece of cloth that is wrapped around the waist. Also, *tie hair:* to wrap with thread, or braid; *tie with witchcraft:* to make witchcraft against
tigernut. a kind of dried berry, slightly sweet. One chews it for the juices and then spits out the roughage. Tigernuts have the reputation of being an aphrodisiac, and sometimes people refer to them as "charge-your-battery," as in "I want to buy some charge-your-battery."
tin. a can
too. very. "Too" as a modifier normally means "very," without implying comparison or excess.
tot. a shot of liquor
tough. heavily built, heavy-set, thick and large-framed; strong
trotro. a privately owned, inexpensive bus. The name derives from *tro,* meaning threepence, which was once the fare. The boy who collected money from the passengers would call *"Tro, tro!"*

tuwo (Hausa). food; staple hot food of the savanna region, made from boiled flour of sorghum or occasionally other grain, eaten with sauce or soup. *See* T-Zed.

Tweaa (Asante Twi). an exclamation of disgust

type. age, standard, size

T-Zed. staple hot food of the savanna region, made from boiled flour of sorghum or occasionally other grain, eaten with sauce or soup. T-Zed is a conversational acronym for T-Z, which is Hausa for *tuwon zafi,* literally, a linked form of "hot *(zafi)* food *(tuwo).*" *See* tuwo.

up. *up and down, adv.:* around; *up-and-down, n.:* an outfit that uses the same material or cloth for blouse and skirt, or shirt and trousers; *upstairs:* upper story; *upstairs building:* a building with more than one story

vex. become annoyed

waist. lower back

waka-waka (Pidgin). to walk and walk, i.e., to be going around or carrying on with a job

wake up. to get up; to stand up

way. *which kind way, what kind way:* which kind of way, what kind of way; also, *some kind way.* The phrase usually is meant to question an unacceptable or unknown alternative.

wonder. to be surprised

Yoruba. large cultural group in southwestern Nigeria and southern Benin